Elementary Linear Algebra

C.H. Edwards, Jr.
David E. Penney

Custom Edition for Arizona State University

Taken from:

Elementary Linear Algebra
by C.H. Edwards, Jr. and David E. Penney

Custom Publishing

New York Boston San Francisco
London Toronto Sydney Tokyo Singapore Madrid
Mexico City Munich Paris Cape Town Hong Kong Montreal

Cover photograph courtesy of David Morgan/istockphoto.com

Taken from:

Elementary Linear Algebra
by C.H. Edwards, Jr. and David E. Penney

A Pearson Education Company
Upper Saddle River, New Jersey 07458

This special edition published in cooperation with Pearson Custom Publishing.

Printed in the United States of America

V036 10 9 8 7 6 5 4 3 2

2009361128

LR/KL

Pearson
Custom Publishing
is a division of

PEARSON

www.pearsonhighered.com

ISBN 10: 0-558-37145-0
ISBN 13: 978-0-558-37145-6

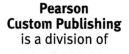

Contents

3

Vectors in the Plane and in Space 116

4

Vector Spaces 162

5

Orthogonality and Least Squares 210

6

Eigenvalues and Eigenvectors 259

Preface

This is a text for the first course in linear algebra that is now taken during the freshman or sophomore year by a wide range of students majoring in computer science, business and economics, the natural and social sciences, engineering, or mathematics. These diverse students have a common need to understand the solution of linear systems of equations, and this concrete goal is the basis for our approach to the subject; it is most apparent in the first five chapters of the book.

We do *not* assume calculus as a prerequisite. We do, however, offer some interesting applications involving elementary calculus in the optional final sections of several chapters. These sections are footnoted as being "for those students who have studied elementary calculus," and all the book's optional sections are marked with asterisks (both in the table of contents and in the text itself); each can be omitted with no loss of continuity.

CONCRETENESS We hope the distinguishing feature of our exposition is a concrete and tangible flavor that will engage the active interest of students. We illustrate all the basic ideas of linear algebra by means of computational examples and geometric interpretations. Computational questions that arise naturally in the solution of linear systems are employed to motivate the more theoretical concepts of linear algebra. In this way the study of elementary linear algebra affords an excellent opportunity for students to begin to appreciate the need for precise thought and clear understanding as well as computational facility in mathematics.

APPLICATIONS Many disciplines now routinely use discrete models whose analysis involves linear algebra, and most of the students in an elementary linear algebra course are there because of the wide-ranging applications of the subject. We have therefore included in this text several self-contained applications that illustrate the active role of linear algebra in the real world. These applications are, however, restricted to optional sections that usually appear at the ends of chapters. The initial sections and the central core of each chapter present those fundamental concepts of the chapter that every course is likely to cover. This leaves the instructor free, as time permits, to pick and choose which (if any) of the ensuing applications to include.

CHAPTER 1 Chapter 1 introduces the problem of solving a system of linear equations, the fundamental method of Gaussian elimination, and the use of matrix algebra and its notation to simplify the required computations. The final three optional sections include brief applications to curve fitting, population models, and cryptography.

CHAPTER 2 The subject is determinants. For the sake of concreteness and a quick start, we employ an inductive definition of determinants based on row and column expansions. The more abstract definition based on permutations is then described briefly as an alternative approach.

CHAPTER 3 Chapter 3 introduces vectors and the geometry of lines and planes in 2- and 3-dimensional space. In the case of students who have studied vectors and analytic geometry in a standard calculus course, this material can either be omitted or covered rapidly for the purpose of review. Although the concepts of vector spaces, linear independence, and orthogonality are discussed briefly in Chapter 3 for the benefit of students who have no prior experience with the geometry of space, Chapter 4 is self-contained with respect to these concepts. Therefore no loss of continuity will result in a course where it is appropriate to omit Chapter 3.

CHAPTER 4 This chapter presents the basic theory of vector spaces, which comprises the heart of elementary linear algebra. In the first four sections we concentrate on finite-dimensional real vector spaces, and emphasize throughout the applications to the problem of solving a linear system of equations. In the final section of Chapter 4 we treat abstract vector spaces and more general problems.

CHAPTER 5 This chapter treats inner products and orthogonality in vector spaces. We devote slightly more space than usual to least squares solutions and least squares curve fitting (optional Section 5.3) because least squares methods are among the most prominent of all the practical applications of linear algebra.

CHAPTER 6 Chapter 6 takes up eigenvalues and eigenvectors. Section 6.3 (optional) presents what we think are some especially concrete applications of diagonalization of matrices.

CHAPTER 7 Chapter 7 treats the elementary theory of linear transformations, and concludes in (optional) Section 7.4 with applications of orthogonal transformations to computer graphics.

CHAPTER 8 This chapter presents further applications of diagonalization to problems involving classification of conic sections, quadratic forms and maximum-minimum values, and elementary differential equations.

CHAPTER 9 This chapter gives a very brief introduction to numerical methods in linear algebra, with an emphasis on some of the practical difficulties that can arise in the numerical solution of linear systems.

Several different permutations in the order of presentation of these topics are possible. The table that follows this preface exhibits the essential logical dependence between the chapters.

COMPUTING Much of the discussion throughout this book—ranging from material on operation counts to the codification of linear algebra procedures in the form of algorithms—reflects the prevalence of automatic computing in current applications of linear algebra. Many of the students in a typical course will go on to use linear algebra principally in conjunction with computing. We conclude with Section 9.3, which is an appendix on automated Gaussian elimination. It contains both a BASIC program for the automatic reduction of matrices to echelon form and an interactive program that students can use to practice reduction of matrices to echelon form. After entering an arbitrary matrix (of size up to 10×10), the student is presented at each step with a menu listing the available row operations. The student selects one, and with the press of a key it is done and the new matrix is displayed. The use of such programs can enable students to develop effective elimination tactics without getting bogged down in tedious arithmetic.

PROBLEMS The problem sets are as crucial to student learning in linear algebra as in other elementary mathematics courses. The problem set at the end of each section in this book begins with routine computational exercises that illustrate the techniques discussed in the section, then progresses to a selection of more conceptual problems. Indeed, we have included a somewhat larger number of routine computational exercises than is typical in other linear algebra texts; our experience is that students in this course need to develop confidence by means of systematic computations before going on to more theoretical problems.

SUPPLEMENTARY MATERIAL The answer section includes the answers to the odd-numbered problems. The *Student Solutions Manual* that accompanies this text includes either an answer or an outline of a solution to essentially every problem in the book. The BASIC programs that appear in the text are simplified versions of programs that are included on the LINPRAC diskette (with instruction booklet) available to instructors and students who use this book. These programs provide a simple system that students can use in a computer laboratory setting to practice the standard computational techniques of elementary linear algebra, including

- routine matrix operations,
- Gaussian elimination and its applications,
- least squares curve fitting,
- calculation of eigenvalues and eigenvectors,
- iterative solutions of systems, and
- linear transformations and simple computer graphics.

ACKNOWLEDGMENTS In writing this book we profited greatly from the advice of the following very able reviewers.

- Carl C. Cowen, Purdue University
- James Dowdy, West Virginia University
- George Graham, Indiana State University
- Irvin Hentzel, Iowa State University
- Kenneth Kalmanson, Montclair State College
- Gloria Langer, University of Colorado, Boulder
- Robert Lohman, Kent State University
- Stephen D. Smith, The University of Illinois

We also want to thank the excellent staff at Prentice Hall for their skill, diligence, and professionalism, with special appreciation to David Ostrow, mathematics editor; Zita de Schauensee, production editor; and Maureen Eide, designer. Other professionals whose talents have improved and enhanced our work include Linda L. Thompson, copyeditor; Muriel L. Smith, editor-proofreader; and Eric G. Hieber, illustrator. Finally, we again cannot adequately thank Alice F. Edwards and Carol W. Penney for their continued assistance, encouragement, support, and patience.

Athens, Georgia

C. H. E., Jr.
D. E. P

Dependence of Chapters

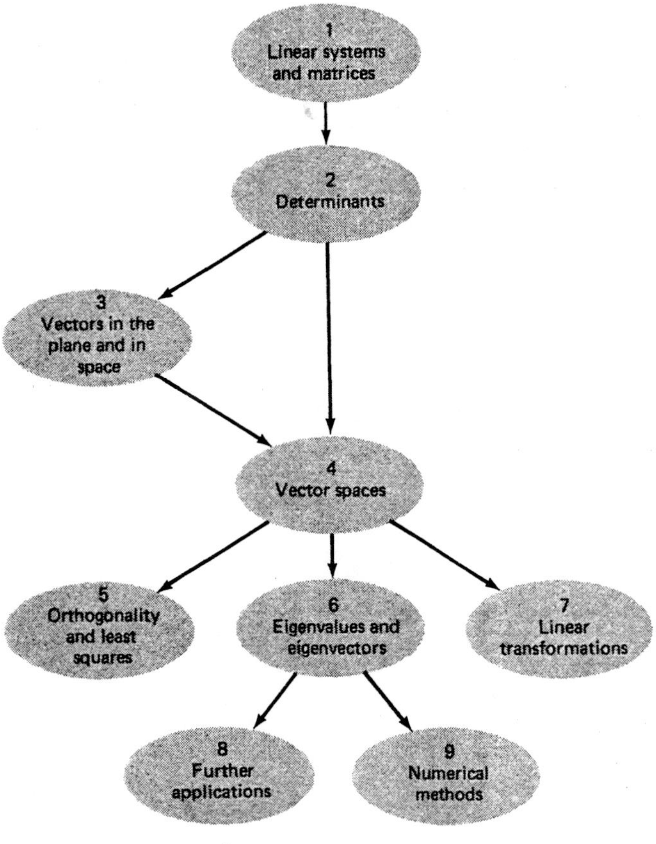

1

Linear Systems and Matrices

1.1

Introduction to Linear Systems

The subject of **linear algebra** centers around the problem of solving systems of *linear equations.* In this section we introduce some of the basic terminology of the subject by reviewing the *method of elimination* used in high-school algebra to solve systems of two and three (simultaneous) linear equations. This is a simple technique, but its applications are diverse and important because so many different mathematical problems involve the solution of systems of linear equations.

Recall that if a, b, and c are constants with a and b not both zero, then the graph of the equation

$$ax + by = c \tag{1}$$

is a (straight) *line* in the xy-plane. For this reason an equation of the form in (1) is called a **linear equation** in the **variables** x and y. Similarly, an equation that can be written in the form

$$ax + by + cz = d \tag{2}$$

is called **linear** in the three variables x, y, and z (even though its graph in xyz-space is a plane rather than a line). Thus the equations

$$3x - 2y = 5 \quad \text{and} \quad x - 7y + 5z = -11$$

are linear, because they involve only the first powers of the variables. By contrast, the equations

$$x + y + xy = 5 \quad \text{and} \quad x^2 + y^3 + \sqrt{z} = 1$$

are *not* linear, because they cannot be rewritten to eliminate the higher powers, roots, and products of the variables.

TWO EQUATIONS IN TWO UNKNOWNS

A **system** of linear equations (also called a **linear system**) is simply a finite collection of linear equations involving certain variables. Sometimes we refer to the variables as the "unknowns" in the system. Thus a system of two linear equations in two unknowns may be written in the form

$$\begin{aligned} a_1x + b_1y &= c_1 \\ a_2x + b_2y &= c_2. \end{aligned} \tag{3}$$

By a **solution** of the system in (3) is meant a pair (x, y) of values—normally real numbers—that satisfy *both* equations *simultaneously*.

EXAMPLE 1 The values $x = 2$, $y = -1$ constitute a solution of the system

$$\begin{aligned} 2x - y &= 5 \\ x + 2y &= 0 \end{aligned} \tag{4}$$

because both

$$2(2) - (-1) = 5 \quad \text{and} \quad (2) + 2(-1) = 0.$$

The values $x = 3$, $y = 1$ satisfy the first equation in (4) but do not satisfy the second. Hence $(3, 1)$ is not a solution of the system in (4).

EXAMPLE 2 The linear system

$$\begin{aligned} x + y &= 1 \\ 2x + 2y &= 3 \end{aligned} \tag{5}$$

has no solution at all, because if $x + y = 1$, then $2x + 2y = 2$, and so $2x + 2y \neq 3$. Thus two numbers that satisfy the first equation in (5) cannot simultaneously satisfy the second.

A linear system is said to be **consistent** if it has at least one solution and **inconsistent** if it has none. Thus the system in Example 1 is consistent, whereas the system in Example 2 is inconsistent.

Given a system of linear equations, we ask what is the set of all solutions of the system. In brief, what is the **solution set** of the system?

In the case of a linear system

$$\begin{aligned} a_1x + b_1y &= c_1 \\ a_2x + b_2y &= c_2 \end{aligned} \tag{6}$$

of two equations in two unknowns, we can use our knowledge of elementary geometry to sort out the possibilities for its solution set. Let L_1 and L_2 denote the straight line graphs of the two equations in (6). Then exactly one of the following situations must hold.

- The lines L_1 and L_2 intersect at a single point (as in Figure 1.1).
- The lines L_1 and L_2 are parallel nonintersecting lines (as in Figure 1.2).
- The lines L_1 and L_2 coincide—they actually are the same line (see Figure 1.3).

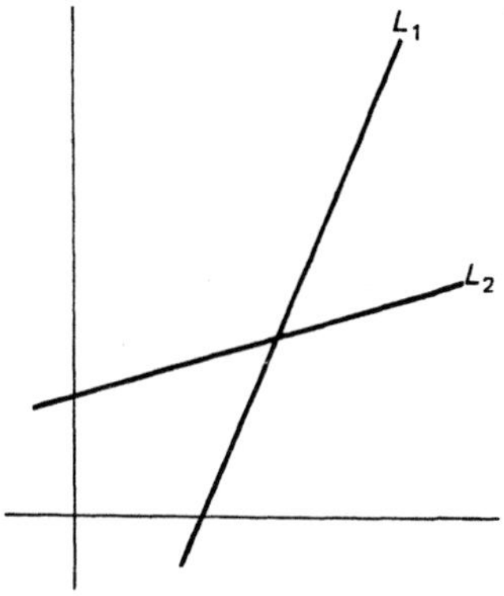

1.1 Two intersecting lines: a unique solution.

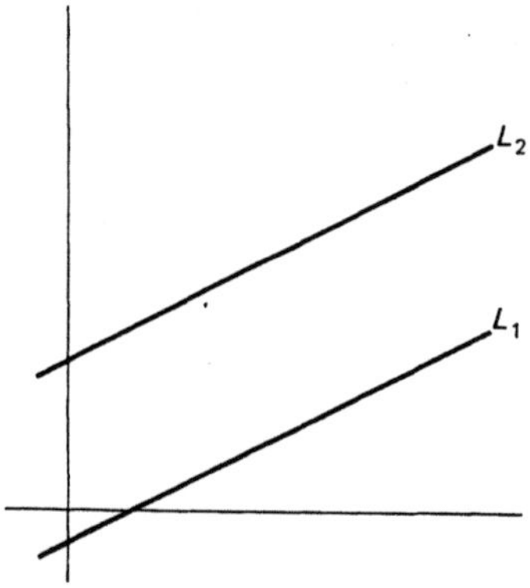

1.2 Two parallel lines: no solutions.

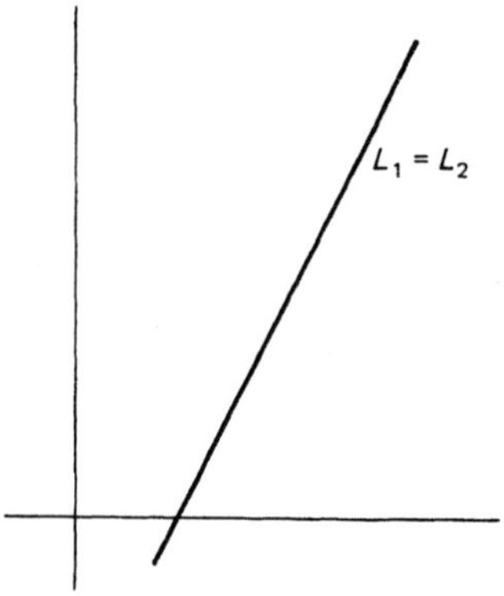

1.3 Two coincident lines: infinitely many solutions.

A pair (x, y) of real numbers constitutes a solution of the system in (6) if and only if the point (x, y) in the coordinate plane lies on *both* the two lines L_1 and L_2. In the case shown in Figure 1.1, there is exactly one such point. In the case shown in Figure 1.2, there is no such point, and in the case in Figure 1.3, there are infinitely many such points—every point on the line $L_1 = L_2$ is such a point. We therefore see that there are just *three possibilities* for a linear system of two equations in two unknowns: It has either

- Exactly one solution;
- No solution; or
- Infinitely many solutions.

It is a fundamental fact of linear algebra (which we will establish in Section 1.3) that, however many equations and variables may appear in a linear system, precisely these same three possibilities occur: A system of m linear equations in n variables either has a **unique** solution (that is, exactly one solution), or it has no solution, or it has infinitely many solutions. Thus it is impossible, for instance, for a linear system to have exactly 2 solutions or to have exactly 17 solutions.

THE METHOD OF ELIMINATION

The next three examples illustrate how we can use the elementary method of elimination to solve a system of two equations in two unknowns. To **solve** a system means to determine what its solution set is. The basic idea of the method is this: First we add an appropriate constant multiple of the first equation to the second equation. The idea is to choose the constant in such a way to eliminate the variable x from the second equation. Next, the new second equation contains only the variable y, so we readily solve it for the value of y. Finally we determine the value of x by substitution of this value of y in the first equation.

EXAMPLE 3 In order to solve the system

$$\begin{aligned} 5x + 3y &= 1 \\ x - 2y &= 8, \end{aligned} \tag{7}$$

we first interchange the two equations:

$$\begin{aligned} x - 2y &= 8 \\ 5x + 3y &= 1. \end{aligned}$$

Then we multiply the first equation by -5 and add the resulting terms to the second (without changing the first equation). The result is

$$\begin{aligned} x - 2y &= 8 \\ 13y &= -39. \end{aligned} \tag{8}$$

Now the second equation immediately yields the value $y = -3$, and *back substitution* of this value in the first equation yields

$$x = 2y + 8 = 2(-3) + 8 = 2.$$

Taking it as obvious (for the moment) that the systems in (7) and (8) have the same solution set, we conclude that the original system in (7) has the *unique solution* $x = 2$, $y = -3$.

EXAMPLE 4 To solve the system

$$\begin{aligned} 2x + 6y &= 4 \\ 3x + 9y &= 11, \end{aligned} \tag{9}$$

we first multiply the first equation by $\frac{1}{2}$ and get

$$\begin{aligned} x + 3y &= 2 \\ 3x + 9y &= 11. \end{aligned}$$

We next multiply the first equation by -3 and add each term to the corresponding term in the second equation. The result is

$$\begin{aligned} x + 3y &= 2 \\ 0 &= 5. \end{aligned} \tag{10}$$

But what are we to make of the new second equation, $0 = 5$? The system in (10) actually is

$$\begin{aligned} x + 3y &= 2 \\ 0x + 0y &= 5. \end{aligned}$$

Because 0 is simply not equal to 5, there are *no* values of x and y that satisfy the second equation. Hence there certainly can be no values that satisfy both simultaneously. We conclude that the original system in (9) has *no solution*.

EXAMPLE 5 If instead of the system in (9) we had begun in Example 4 with the system

$$\begin{aligned} 2x + 6y &= 4 \\ 3x + 9y &= 6 \end{aligned} \tag{11}$$

and performed the same operations, we would have obtained, instead of (10), the system

$$\begin{aligned} x + 3y &= 2 \\ 0 &= 0. \end{aligned} \tag{12}$$

Here, $0 = 0$ is shorthand for the equation

$$0x + 0y = 0,$$

which is satisfied by *all* values of x and y. In terms of restrictions or conditions on x and y, one of our original two equations has in effect disappeared, leaving us with the single equation

$$x + 3y = 2. \tag{13}$$

Of course this is hardly surprising, because each equation in (11) is a multiple of the one in (13); in some sense we really had only one equation to begin with. At any rate, we can substitute any value of y we please in (13) and then solve for x. Thus our system in (11) has *infinitely many solutions.* To describe them explicitly, let us write $y = t$, where the **parameter** t is a new independent variable that we will use to generate solution pairs (x, y). Then Equation (13) yields $x = 2 - 3t$, so our infinite solution set of the system in (11) may be described as follows:

$$x = 2 - 3t, \qquad y = t$$

as the arbitrary parameter t ranges over the set of all real numbers. For instance, $t = 2$ yields the solution $(-4, 2)$, and $t = -3$ yields the solution $(11, -3)$.

COMMENT These three examples illustrate the basic features of the method of elimination, which involves "transforming" a given linear system by means of a sequence of successive steps. Each of these steps consists of performing one of the following three **elementary operations**:

1. Multiply one equation by a nonzero constant.
2. Interchange two equations.
3. Add a constant multiple of (the terms of) one equation to (corresponding terms of) another equation.

In subsequent sections of this chapter we discuss the systematic use of these elementary operations to eliminate variables successively in any linear system, whatever the number of equations and variables. In this way we will see that every linear system corresponds to precisely one of the three situations illustrated in Examples 3–5. That is, either

- We discover (as in Example 3) a unique solution of the system; or
- We eventually arrive at an inconsistent equation (as in Example 4), so that the system has no solution; or
- We find that the original system has infinitely many solutions.

In the case of a system of three linear equations in three variables x, y, and z, we may proceed as follows: Assuming that the first equation involves x, use the first equation to eliminate x from the second and third equations by adding appropriate multiples of the first equation. Then, assuming that the new second equation involves y, use the new second equation to eliminate y from the new third equation. Solve the new third equation for z, back substitute in the second equation to determine y, and finally back substitute y and z in the first equation to find x. The following two examples illustrate this procedure.

EXAMPLE 6 Solve the linear system

$$\begin{aligned} x + 2y + z &= 4 \\ 3x + 8y + 7z &= 20 \\ 2x + 7y + 9z &= 23. \end{aligned} \tag{14}$$

Solution First we add -3 times the first equation to the second equation; the result is

$$\begin{aligned} x + 2y + z &= 4 \\ 2y + 4z &= 8 \\ 2x + 7y + 9z &= 23. \end{aligned}$$

Then addition of -2 times the first equation to the third equation yields

$$\begin{aligned} x + 2y + z &= 4 \\ 2y + 4z &= 8 \\ 3y + 7z &= 15. \end{aligned}$$

We have now eliminated x from the second and third equations. To simplify the process of eliminating y from the third equation, we multiply the second equation by $\frac{1}{2}$ to obtain

$$\begin{aligned} x + 2y + z &= 4 \\ y + 2z &= 4 \\ 3y + 7z &= 15. \end{aligned}$$

Finally, addition of -3 times the second equation to the third equation gives

$$\begin{aligned} x + 2y + z &= 4 \\ y + 2z &= 4 \\ z &= 3. \end{aligned} \tag{15}$$

This system has a *triangular* form that makes its solution easy. By back substitution of $z = 3$ in the second equation in (15), we find that

$$y = 4 - 2z = 4 - 2(3) = -2;$$

then the first equation yields

$$\begin{aligned} x &= 4 - 2y - z \\ &= 4 - 2(-2) - (3) = 5. \end{aligned}$$

Thus our original system in (14) has the unique solution $x = 5$, $y = -2$, $z = 3$.

COMMENT The steps by which we transformed (14) into (15) show that every solution of the system in (14) is a solution of the system in (15). But these steps can be reversed to show similarly that every solution of the system in (15) is also a solution of the system in (14). Thus the two systems are equivalent in the sense that they have the same solution set. The computation at the end of Example 6 shows that (15) has the unique solution $(x, y, z) = (5, -2, 3)$, and it follows that this also is the unique solution of the original system in (14).

EXAMPLE 7 Solve the system

$$\begin{aligned} 3x - 8y + 10z &= 22 \\ x - 3y + 2z &= 5 \\ 2x - 9y - 8z &= -11. \end{aligned} \tag{16}$$

Solution In order to avoid fractions in the elimination of x, we first interchange the first two equations to get

$$\begin{aligned} x - 3y + 2z &= 5 \\ 3x - 8y + 10z &= 22 \\ 2x - 9y - 8z &= -11. \end{aligned}$$

Addition of -3 times the first equation to the second gives

$$\begin{aligned} x - 3y + 2z &= 5 \\ y + 4z &= 7 \\ 2x - 9y - 8z &= -11, \end{aligned}$$

and then addition of -2 times the first equation to the third equation gives

$$\begin{aligned} x - 3y + 2z &= 5 \\ y + 4z &= 7 \\ -3y - 12z &= -21. \end{aligned}$$

Finally, addition of 3 times the second equation to the third equation yields

$$\begin{aligned} x - 3y + 2z &= 5 \\ y + 4z &= 7 \\ 0 &= 0. \end{aligned} \tag{17}$$

Because the third equation has disappeared, we can choose $z = t$ arbitrarily and then solve for x and y:

$$\begin{aligned} y &= 7 - 4z = 7 - 4t, \\ x &= 5 + 3y - 2z \\ &= 5 + 3(7 - 4t) - 2t = 26 - 14t. \end{aligned}$$

Thus our original system in (16) has infinitely many solutions. Moreover, one convenient way of describing them is this:

$$x = 26 - 14t, \qquad y = 7 - 4t, \qquad z = t. \tag{18}$$

The arbitrary parameter t may take on all real number values, and in so doing generates all the solutions of the original system.

1.1 PROBLEMS

In each of Problems 1-22, use the method of elimination to determine whether the given linear system is consistent or inconsistent. For each consistent system, find the solution if it is unique; otherwise, describe the infinite solution set in terms of an arbitrary parameter t (as in Examples 5 and 7).

1. $\begin{aligned} x + 3y &= 9 \\ 2x + y &= 8 \end{aligned}$

2. $\begin{aligned} 3x + 2y &= 9 \\ x - y &= 8 \end{aligned}$

3. $\begin{aligned} 2x + 3y &= 1 \\ 3x + 5y &= 3 \end{aligned}$

4. $\begin{aligned} 5x - 6y &= 1 \\ 6x - 5y &= 10 \end{aligned}$

5. $\begin{aligned} x + 2y &= 4 \\ 2x + 4y &= 9 \end{aligned}$

6. $\begin{aligned} 4x - 2y &= 4 \\ 6x - 3y &= 7 \end{aligned}$

7. $\begin{aligned} x - 4y &= -10 \\ -2x + 8y &= 20 \end{aligned}$

8. $\begin{aligned} 3x - 6y &= 12 \\ 2x - 4y &= 8 \end{aligned}$

9. $\begin{aligned} x + 5y + z &= 2 \\ 2x + y - 2z &= 1 \\ x + 7y + 2z &= 3 \end{aligned}$

10. $\begin{aligned} x + 3y + 2z &= 2 \\ 2x + 7y + 7z &= -1 \\ 2x + 5y + 2z &= 7 \end{aligned}$

11. $\begin{aligned} 2x + 7y + 3z &= 11 \\ x + 3y + 2z &= 2 \\ 3x + 7y + 9z &= -12 \end{aligned}$

12. $\begin{aligned} 3x + 5y - z &= 13 \\ 2x + 7y + z &= 28 \\ x + 7y + 2z &= 32 \end{aligned}$

13. $\begin{aligned} 3x + 9y + 7z &= 0 \\ 2x + 7y + 4z &= 0 \\ 2x + 6y + 5z &= 0 \end{aligned}$

14. $\begin{aligned} 4x + 9y + 12z &= -1 \\ 3x + y + 16z &= -46 \\ 2x + 7y + 3z &= 19 \end{aligned}$

15. $\begin{aligned} x + 3y + 2z &= 5 \\ x - y + 3z &= 3 \\ 3x + y + 8z &= 10 \end{aligned}$

16. $\begin{aligned} x - 3y + 2z &= 6 \\ x + 4y - z &= 4 \\ 5x + 6y + z &= 20 \end{aligned}$

17. $\begin{aligned} 2x - y + 4z &= 7 \\ 3x + 2y - 2z &= 3 \\ 5x + y + 2z &= 15 \end{aligned}$

18. $\begin{aligned} x + 5y + 6z &= 3 \\ 5x + 2y - 10z &= 1 \\ 8x + 17y + 8z &= 5 \end{aligned}$

19. $\begin{aligned} x - 2y + z &= 2 \\ 2x - y - 4z &= 13 \\ x - y - z &= 5 \end{aligned}$

20. $\begin{aligned} 2x + 3y + 7z &= 15 \\ x + 4y + z &= 20 \\ x + 2y + 3z &= 10 \end{aligned}$

21. $\begin{aligned} x + y - z &= 5 \\ 3x + y + 3z &= 11 \\ 4x + y + 5z &= 14 \end{aligned}$

22. $\begin{aligned} 4x - 2y + 6z &= 0 \\ x - y - z &= 0 \\ 2x - y + 3z &= 0 \end{aligned}$

23. A system of the form

$$a_1x + b_1y = 0$$
$$a_2x + b_2y = 0,$$

in which the constants on the right-hand side are all zero, is said to be **homogeneous**. Explain by geometric reasoning why such a system has either a unique solution or infinitely many solutions.

24. Consider the system

$$a_1x + b_1y + c_1z = d_1$$
$$a_2x + b_2y + c_2z = d_2$$

of two equations in three unknowns.

(a) Use the fact that the graph of each such equation is a plane in xyz-space to explain why such a system always has either no solution or infinitely many solutions.

(b) Explain why the system must have infinitely many solutions if $d_1 = 0 = d_2$.

25. The linear system

$$a_1x + b_1y = c_1$$
$$a_2x + b_2y = c_2$$
$$a_3x + b_3y = c_3$$

of three equations in two unknowns represents three lines L_1, L_2, and L_3 in the xy-plane. Figure 1.4 shows six possible configurations of these three lines. In each case describe the solution set of the system.

26. Consider the linear system

$$a_1x + b_1y + c_1z = d_1$$
$$a_2x + b_2y + c_2z = d_2$$
$$a_3x + b_3y + c_3z = d_3$$

of three equations in three unknowns to represent three planes P_1, P_2, and P_3 in xyz-space. Describe the solution set of the system in each case.

(a) The three planes are parallel and distinct.
(b) The three planes coincide—$P_1 = P_2 = P_3$.
(c) P_1 and P_2 coincide and are parallel to P_3.
(d) P_1 and P_2 intersect in a line L that is parallel to P_3.
(e) P_1 and P_2 intersect in a line L that lies in P_3.
(f) P_1 and P_2 intersect in a line L that intersects P_3 in a single point.

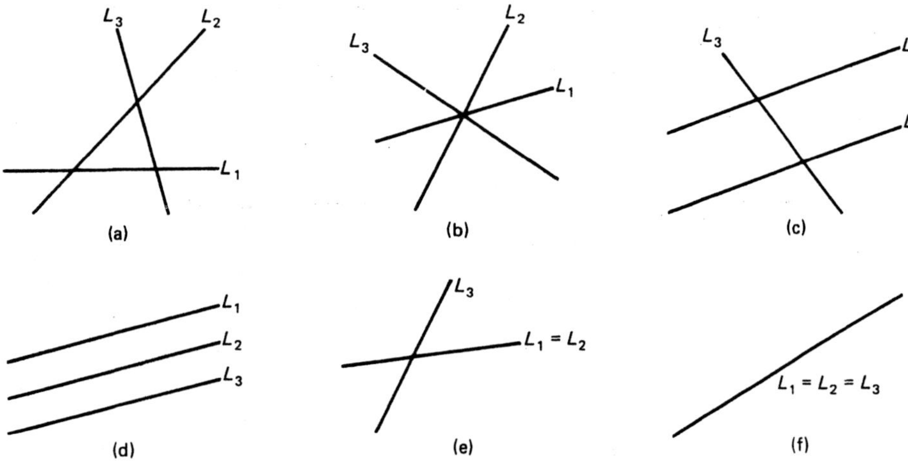

1.4 Three lines in the plane.

1.2

Matrices and Gaussian Elimination

In Example 6 of Section 1.1 we applied the method of elimination to solve the linear system

$$\begin{aligned} 1x + 2y + 1z &= \ 4 \\ 3x + 8y + 7z &= 20 \\ 2x + 7y + 9z &= 23. \end{aligned} \tag{1}$$

There we employed elementary operations to transform this system into the equivalent system

$$\begin{aligned} 1x + 2y + 1z &= 4 \\ 0x + 1y + 2z &= 4 \\ 0x + 0y + 1z &= 3, \end{aligned} \tag{2}$$

which we found easy to solve by back substitution. Here we have printed in color the coefficients and constants (including the 0s and 1s that would normally be omitted) because everything else—the symbols x, y, and z for the variables and the $+$ and $=$ signs—is excess baggage that means only extra writing, for we can keep track of these symbols mentally. In effect, in Example 6 we used an appropriate sequence of operations to transform the array

$$\begin{bmatrix} 1 & 2 & 1 & 4 \\ 3 & 8 & 7 & 20 \\ 2 & 7 & 9 & 23 \end{bmatrix} \tag{3}$$

of coefficients and constants in (1) into the array

$$\begin{bmatrix} 1 & 2 & 1 & 4 \\ 0 & 1 & 2 & 4 \\ 0 & 0 & 1 & 3 \end{bmatrix} \tag{4}$$

of constants and coefficients in (2).

Rectangular arrays of numbers like those in (3) and (4) are called *matrices*. Thus a **matrix** is simply a rectangular array of numbers, which are called the **entries** or **elements** of the matrix. The **size**, or **shape**, of a matrix is specified by telling how many horizontal **rows** and vertical **columns** it has. Each matrix in (3) and (4) has three rows and four columns; therefore, each is a 3×4 (read "three by four") matrix. We *always* specify the number of rows *first* and *then* specify the number of columns.

EXAMPLE 1 The matrices

$$\begin{bmatrix} 3 & -7 \\ -2 & 5 \end{bmatrix} \qquad \begin{bmatrix} 3 & 0 & -1 & 5 \end{bmatrix} \qquad \begin{bmatrix} 2 \\ 0 \\ -3 \end{bmatrix}$$

have sizes 2×2, 1×4, and 3×1, respectively.

A general system of m linear equations in the n variables $x_1, x_2, \ldots, x_n$ may be written in the form

$$\begin{aligned} a_{11}x_1 + a_{21}x_2 + a_{13}x_3 + \cdots + a_{1n}x_n &= b_1 \\ a_{21}x_1 + a_{22}x_2 + a_{23}x_3 + \cdots + a_{2n}x_n &= b_2 \\ &\vdots \\ a_{m1}x_1 + a_{m2}x_2 + a_{m3}x_3 + \cdots + a_{mn}x_n &= b_m. \end{aligned} \tag{5}$$

Observe that a_{ij} denotes the (constant) coefficient in the ith equation of the jth variable x_j and that b_i denotes the constant on the right-hand side in the ith equation. Thus the first subscript i refers to the equation and the second subscript j to the variable. For instance, a_{32} denotes the coefficient of x_2 in the 3rd equation. This scheme of systematic double subscripts enables us to specify readily the location of each coefficient in a system with many equations and variables. It also helps us get rid of the excess baggage in (5) by focusing our attention on the coefficients.

The **coefficient matrix** of the linear system in (5) is the $m \times n$ matrix

$$A = \begin{bmatrix} a_{11} & a_{12} & a_{13} & \cdots & a_{1n} \\ a_{21} & a_{22} & a_{23} & \cdots & a_{2n} \\ \vdots & \vdots & \vdots & \ddots & \vdots \\ a_{m1} & a_{m2} & a_{m3} & \cdots & a_{mn} \end{bmatrix}. \tag{6}$$

We will use capital letters to denote matrices and lowercase letters to denote numbers. When we want to refer more briefly to the matrix A and its entries, we can write

$$A = [a_{ij}]. \tag{7}$$

The first subscript i specifies the row and the second subscript j the column of A in which the element a_{ij} appears:

First subscript	Second subscript
Row	Column

Although double subscripts may seem tedious when first encountered, their usefulness should not be underestimated. For instance, they are consistent with the notation used in most programming languages. Many practical applications lead to linear systems with hundreds or even thousands of variables and equations. In BASIC, for example, the coefficient matrix A of such a system would be represented by a two-dimensional array in which $A(I, J)$ denotes a_{ij}. With this approach the computer can store a 100×100 matrix in the same way as it stores a 3×3 matrix.

The matrices in (3) and (4) include not only the coefficients but also the constants on the right-hand sides in the corresponding linear systems in (1) and (2). Let us write

$$\mathbf{b} = \begin{bmatrix} b_1 \\ b_2 \\ \vdots \\ b_m \end{bmatrix} \tag{8}$$

for the column of constants in the general system in (5). An $m \times 1$ matrix—that is, one with a single column—is often called a **(column) vector** and is denoted by a boldface letter. When we adjoin the constant vector **b** to the coefficient matrix A (as a final column), we get the matrix

$$[A \;\; \mathbf{b}] = \begin{bmatrix} a_{11} & a_{12} & \cdots & a_{1n} & b_1 \\ a_{21} & a_{22} & \cdots & a_{2n} & b_2 \\ \vdots & \vdots & \ddots & \vdots & \vdots \\ a_{m1} & a_{m2} & \cdots & a_{mn} & b_m \end{bmatrix}. \tag{9}$$

This $m \times (n + 1)$ matrix is called the **augmented coefficient matrix**, or simply the augmented matrix, of the $m \times n$ system in (5).

Although it takes a good deal of notation to describe the augmented matrix of a *general* linear system, it is a very simple matter to write the augmented matrix of a *particular* system. If the system is written in chalk on a blackboard with the variables in the same order in each equation, we merely erase all the x_j's and the plus and equal signs (retaining a minus sign for each negative coefficient) and insert a zero in each spot where a variable is missing in an equation.

EXAMPLE 2 The augmented matrix of the system

$$\begin{aligned} 2x_1 + 3x_2 - 7x_3 + 4x_4 &= 6 \\ x_2 + 3x_3 - 5x_4 &= 0 \\ -x_1 + 2x_2 \qquad\quad - 9x_4 &= 17 \end{aligned}$$

of three equations in four variables is the 3×5 matrix

$$\begin{bmatrix} 2 & 3 & -7 & 4 & 6 \\ 0 & 1 & 3 & -5 & 0 \\ -1 & 2 & 0 & -9 & 17 \end{bmatrix}.$$

ELEMENTARY ROW OPERATIONS

In Section 1.1 we described the three elementary operations that are used in the method of elimination. To each of these corresponds an *elementary row operation* on the augmented matrix of the system. For instance, when we interchange two equations in the system, we interchange the corresponding two rows of its augmented matrix.

Definition: *Elementary Row Operations*

The following are the three types of **elementary row operations** on the matrix A:

1. Multiply any (single) row of A by a nonzero constant.
2. Interchange two rows of A.
3. Add a constant multiple of one row of A to another row.

Figure 1.5 shows notation that we can use to describe elementary row operations briefly. For instance,

$$\begin{bmatrix} 1 & 2 \\ 3 & 4 \end{bmatrix} \xrightarrow{(3)R_1 + R_2} \begin{bmatrix} 1 & 2 \\ 6 & 10 \end{bmatrix} \tag{10}$$

shows the result of adding 3 times row 1 to row 2. Note that when we perform the operation $(c)R_p + R_q$ on a matrix, adding c times row p to row q, row p itself remains unchanged.

Type	Row Operation	Notation
1	Multiply row p by c	cR_p
2	Interchange row p and row q	SWAP(R_p, R_q)
3	Add c times row p to row q	$(c)R_p + R_q$

1.5 Notation for elementary row operations.

If the $m \times n$ matrix A is stored as a two-dimensional array in a computer, then in BASIC this operation could be described by the following program lines.

```
FOR J = 1 TO N
     LET A(Q, J) = A(Q, J) + C*A(P, J)
NEXT J
```

EXAMPLE 3 To solve the system

$$\begin{aligned} x_1 + 2x_2 + x_3 &= 4 \\ 3x_1 + 8x_2 + 7x_3 &= 20 \\ 2x_1 + 7x_2 + 9x_3 &= 23, \end{aligned} \tag{11}$$

whose augmented coefficient matrix is exhibited in (3), we carry out the following sequence of elementary row operations, corresponding to the steps in the solution of Example 6 in Section 1.1:

$$\begin{bmatrix} 1 & 2 & 1 & 4 \\ 3 & 8 & 7 & 20 \\ 2 & 7 & 9 & 23 \end{bmatrix} \tag{12}$$

$$\xrightarrow{(-3)R_1 + R_2} \begin{bmatrix} 1 & 2 & 1 & 4 \\ 0 & 2 & 4 & 8 \\ 2 & 7 & 9 & 23 \end{bmatrix}$$

$$\xrightarrow{(-2)R_1 + R_3} \begin{bmatrix} 1 & 2 & 1 & 4 \\ 0 & 2 & 4 & 8 \\ 0 & 3 & 7 & 15 \end{bmatrix}$$

$$\xrightarrow{(\frac{1}{2})R_2} \begin{bmatrix} 1 & 2 & 1 & 4 \\ 0 & 1 & 2 & 4 \\ 0 & 3 & 7 & 15 \end{bmatrix}$$

$$\xrightarrow{(-3)R_2 + R_3} \begin{bmatrix} 1 & 2 & 1 & 4 \\ 0 & 1 & 2 & 4 \\ 0 & 0 & 1 & 3 \end{bmatrix}. \tag{13}$$

The final matrix here is the augmented matrix of the system

$$\begin{aligned} x_1 + 2x_2 + x_3 &= 4 \\ x_2 + 2x_3 &= 4 \\ x_3 &= 3 \end{aligned} \tag{14}$$

whose unique solution (readily found by back substitution) is $x_1 = 5$, $x_2 = -2$, $x_3 = 3$.

It is not quite self-evident that a sequence of elementary row operations produces a linear system having the same solution set as the original system. To state the pertinent result concisely, we need the following definition.

> ***Definition***: *Row-Equivalent Matrices*
>
> Two matrices are called **row-equivalent** if one can be obtained from the other by a (finite) sequence of elementary row operations.

Thus the two matrices in (10) are row-equivalent, as are the two matrices in (12) and (13). In Problem 29 we ask you to show that if B can be obtained from A by elementary row operations, then A can be obtained from B by elementary row operations. This follows from the observation that row operations are "reversible." In Problem 30 we suggest a proof of the following theorem.

> ***Theorem***: *Equivalent Systems and Equivalent Matrices*
>
> If the augmented coefficient matrices of two linear systems are row-equivalent, then the two systems have the same solution set.

Thus the linear systems in (11) and (14) have the same solution set, because their augmented matrices in (12) and (13) are row-equivalent.

Up to this point we have been somewhat informal in our description of the method of elimination. Its objective is to transform, by elementary row operations, a given linear system into one for which back substitution leads easily and routinely to a solution. The following definition tells what should be the appearance of the augmented matrix of the transformed system.

> ***Definition***: *Echelon Matrix*
>
> The matrix E is called an **echelon matrix** provided it has the following two properties:
>
> **1.** Every row of E that consists entirely of zeros (if any) lies *beneath* every row that contains a nonzero element.
>
> **2.** In each row of E that contains a nonzero element, the *first* nonzero element lies strictly to the *right* of the first nonzero element in the preceding row (if there is a preceding row).

Echelon matrices are sometimes called *row-echelon matrices.* Property 1 says that if E has any all-zero rows, then they are grouped together at the bottom of the matrix. The first (from the left) *nonzero* element in each of the other rows is called its **leading entry**. Property 2 says that the leading entries form a "descending staircase" pattern from upper left to lower right, as in the following echelon matrix.

$$E = \begin{bmatrix} 2 & -1 & 0 & 4 & 7 \\ 0 & 1 & 2 & 0 & -5 \\ 0 & 0 & 0 & 3 & 0 \\ 0 & 0 & 0 & 0 & 0 \end{bmatrix}$$

Here we have highlighted the leading entries and indicated the descending staircase pattern.

The following list exhibits *all* possibilities for the form of a 3 × 3 echelon matrix, with red asterisks denoting the leading entries; an x denotes an element that may be either zero or nonzero.

$$\begin{bmatrix} * & x & x \\ 0 & * & x \\ 0 & 0 & * \end{bmatrix} \quad \begin{bmatrix} 0 & 0 & 0 \\ 0 & 0 & 0 \\ 0 & 0 & 0 \end{bmatrix}$$

$$\begin{bmatrix} * & x & x \\ 0 & * & x \\ 0 & 0 & 0 \end{bmatrix} \quad \begin{bmatrix} * & x & x \\ 0 & 0 & * \\ 0 & 0 & 0 \end{bmatrix} \quad \begin{bmatrix} 0 & * & x \\ 0 & 0 & * \\ 0 & 0 & 0 \end{bmatrix}$$

$$\begin{bmatrix} * & x & x \\ 0 & 0 & 0 \\ 0 & 0 & 0 \end{bmatrix} \quad \begin{bmatrix} 0 & * & x \\ 0 & 0 & 0 \\ 0 & 0 & 0 \end{bmatrix} \quad \begin{bmatrix} 0 & 0 & * \\ 0 & 0 & 0 \\ 0 & 0 & 0 \end{bmatrix}$$

It follows from Properties 1 and 2 that the elements *beneath* any leading entry in the same column are all zero. The matrices

$$A = \begin{bmatrix} 1 & 3 & -2 \\ 0 & 0 & 0 \\ 0 & 1 & 5 \end{bmatrix} \quad \text{and} \quad B = \begin{bmatrix} 0 & 1 & 5 \\ 1 & 3 & -2 \\ 0 & 0 & 0 \end{bmatrix}$$

are not echelon matrices because A does not have Property 1 and B does not have Property 2.

Suppose that a linear system is in **echelon form**—its augmented matrix is an echelon matrix. Then those variables that correspond to *columns* containing leading entries are called **leading variables**; all the other variables are called **free variables**. The following algorithm describes the process of **back substitution** to solve such a system.

Algorithm: *Back Substitution*

To solve a consistent linear system in echelon form by back substitution, carry out the following steps.

1. Set each free variable equal to an arbitrary parameter (a different parameter for each free variable).

2. Solve the *final* (nonzero) equation for its leading variable.
3. Substitute the result in the next-to-last equation and then solve for its leading variable.
4. Continuing in this fashion, work upward through the system of equations until all variables have been determined.

EXAMPLE 4 The augmented matrix of the system

$$\begin{aligned} x_1 - 2x_2 + 3x_3 + 2x_4 + x_5 &= 10 \\ x_3 + 2x_5 &= -3 \\ x_4 - 4x_5 &= 7 \end{aligned} \tag{15}$$

is the echelon matrix

$$\begin{bmatrix} 1 & -2 & 3 & 2 & 1 & 10 \\ 0 & 0 & 1 & 0 & 2 & -3 \\ 0 & 0 & 0 & 1 & -4 & 7 \end{bmatrix}. \tag{16}$$

The leading entries are in the first, third, and fourth columns. Hence x_1, x_3, and x_4 are the leading variables and x_2 and x_5 are the free variables. To solve the system by back substitution, we first write

$$x_2 = s, \qquad x_5 = t \tag{17a}$$

where s and t are arbitrary parameters. Then the third equation in (15) gives

$$x_4 = 7 + 4x_5 = 7 + 4t; \tag{17b}$$

the second equation gives

$$x_3 = -3 - 2x_5 = -3 - 2t; \tag{17c}$$

finally, the first equation in (15) yields

$$\begin{aligned} x_1 &= 10 + 2x_2 - 3x_3 - 2x_4 - x_5 \\ &= 10 + 2s - 3(-3 - 2t) - 2(7 + 4t) - t. \end{aligned}$$

Therefore

$$x_1 = 5 + 2s - 3t. \tag{17d}$$

Thus the system in (15) has an infinite solution set consisting of all $(x_1, x_2, x_3, x_4, x_5)$ given in terms of the two parameters s and t as follows:

$$\begin{aligned} x_1 &= 5 + 2s - 3t \\ x_2 &= s \\ x_3 &= -3 - 2t \\ x_4 &= 7 + 4t \\ x_5 &= t. \end{aligned}$$

For instance, with $s = 2$ and $t = 1$ we get the solution $x_1 = 6$, $x_2 = 2$, $x_3 = -5$, $x_4 = 11$, and $x_5 = 1$.

GAUSSIAN ELIMINATION

Because we can use back substitution to solve any linear system already in echelon form, it remains only to establish that we can transform any matrix (using elementary row operations) into an echelon matrix. The procedure that we have already illustrated in several examples is known as **Gaussian elimination.** The following systematic description of the procedure makes it clear that it succeeds with *any* given matrix A.

Algorithm: *Gaussian Elimination*

1. Locate the first column of A that contains a nonzero element.
2. If the first (top) entry in this column is zero, interchange the first row of A with a row in which the corresponding entry is nonzero.
3. Now the first entry in our column is nonzero. Replace the entries below it in the same column with zeros by adding appropriate multiples of the first row of A to lower rows.
4. After Steps 1–3 the matrix looks like the matrix below, although there may be several initial columns of zeros or even none at all. Perform Steps 1–3 on the indicated lower right matrix A_1.
5. Repeat this cycle of steps until an echelon matrix is obtained.

$$A = \left[\begin{array}{cc:cccc} 0 & * & x & x & \cdots & x \\ \hdashline 0 & 0 & & & & \\ 0 & 0 & & A_1 & & \\ \vdots & \vdots & & & & \\ 0 & 0 & & & & \end{array}\right].$$

In brief, we work on the matrix A one column at a time, from left to right. In each column containing a leading entry (perhaps after a row interchange) we "clear out" the nonzero elements below it and then move on to the next column.

EXAMPLE 5 To solve the system

$$\begin{aligned} x_1 - 2x_2 + 3x_3 + 2x_4 + x_5 &= 10 \\ 2x_1 - 4x_2 + 8x_3 + 3x_4 + 10x_5 &= 7 \\ 3x_1 - 6x_2 + 10x_3 + 6x_4 + 5x_5 &= 27, \end{aligned} \tag{18}$$

we reduce its augmented coefficient matrix to echelon form as follows.

$$\begin{bmatrix} 1 & -2 & 3 & 2 & 1 & 10 \\ 2 & -4 & 8 & 3 & 10 & 7 \\ 3 & -6 & 10 & 6 & 5 & 27 \end{bmatrix}$$

$$\xrightarrow{(-2)R_1+R_2} \begin{bmatrix} 1 & -2 & 3 & 2 & 1 & 10 \\ 0 & 0 & 2 & -1 & 8 & -13 \\ 3 & -6 & 10 & 6 & 5 & 27 \end{bmatrix}$$

$$\xrightarrow{(-3)R_1+R_3} \begin{bmatrix} 1 & -2 & 3 & 2 & 1 & 10 \\ 0 & 0 & 2 & -1 & 8 & -13 \\ 0 & 0 & 1 & 0 & 2 & -3 \end{bmatrix}$$

$$\xrightarrow{\text{SWAP}(R_2,R_3)} \begin{bmatrix} 1 & -2 & 3 & 2 & 1 & 10 \\ 0 & 0 & 1 & 0 & 2 & -3 \\ 0 & 0 & 2 & -1 & 8 & -13 \end{bmatrix}$$

$$\xrightarrow{(-2)R_2+R_3} \begin{bmatrix} 1 & -2 & 3 & 2 & 1 & 10 \\ 0 & 0 & 1 & 0 & 2 & -3 \\ 0 & 0 & 0 & -1 & 4 & -7 \end{bmatrix}$$

$$\xrightarrow{(-1)R_3} \begin{bmatrix} 1 & -2 & 3 & 2 & 1 & 10 \\ 0 & 0 & 1 & 0 & 2 & -3 \\ 0 & 0 & 0 & 1 & -4 & 7 \end{bmatrix}$$

Our final result is the echelon matrix in (16), so by Equations (17a)–(17d) in Example 4 the infinite solution set of the system in (18) is described in terms of arbitrary parameters s and t as follows:

$$\begin{aligned} x_1 &= 5 + 2s - 3t \\ x_2 &= s \\ x_3 &= -3 - 2t \\ x_4 &= 7 + 4t \\ x_5 &= t. \end{aligned} \tag{19}$$

Thus the substitution of any two specific values for s and t in (19) yields a particular solution $(x_1, x_2, x_3, x_4, x_5)$ of the system, and each of the system's infinitely many different solutions is the result of some such substitution.

Examples 3 and 5 illustrate the ways in which Gaussian elimination can result in either a unique solution or infinitely many solutions. If the reduction of the augmented matrix to echelon form leads to a row of the form

$$0 \quad 0 \quad \cdots \quad 0 \quad 0 \quad *$$

where the asterisk denotes a nonzero entry in the last column, then we have an inconsistent equation,

$$0x_1 + 0x_2 + \cdots + 0x_n = *,$$

and therefore the system has no solution.

REMARK We use algorithms such as the back substitution and Gaussian elimination algorithms of this section to outline the basic computational procedures of linear algebra. In modern numerical work these procedures often are implemented on a computer. For instance, linear systems of more than four equations are usually solved in practice by using a computer to carry out the process of Gaussian elimination. Computer programs for this purpose are discussed in Section 9.3.

1.2 PROBLEMS

The linear systems in problems 1–10 are in echelon form. Solve each by back substitution.

1. $\begin{aligned} x_1 + x_2 + 2x_3 &= 5 \\ x_2 + 3x_3 &= 6 \\ x_3 &= 2 \end{aligned}$

2. $\begin{aligned} 2x_1 - 5x_2 + x_3 &= 2 \\ 3x_2 - 2x_3 &= 9 \\ x_3 &= -3 \end{aligned}$

3. $\begin{aligned} x_1 - 3x_2 + 4x_3 &= 7 \\ x_2 - 5x_3 &= 2 \end{aligned}$

4. $\begin{aligned} x_1 - 5x_2 + 2x_3 &= 10 \\ x_2 - 7x_3 &= 5 \end{aligned}$

5. $\begin{aligned} x_1 + x_2 - 2x_3 + x_4 &= 9 \\ x_2 - x_3 + 2x_4 &= 1 \\ x_3 - 3x_4 &= 5 \end{aligned}$

6. $\begin{aligned} x_1 - 2x_2 + 5x_3 - 3x_4 &= 7 \\ x_2 - 3x_3 + 2x_4 &= 3 \\ x_4 &= -4 \end{aligned}$

7. $\begin{aligned} x_1 + 2x_2 + 4x_3 - 5x_4 &= 17 \\ x_2 - 2x_3 + 7x_4 &= 7 \end{aligned}$

8. $\begin{aligned} x_1 - 10x_2 + 3x_3 - 13x_4 &= 5 \\ x_3 + 3x_4 &= 10 \end{aligned}$

9. $\begin{aligned} 2x_1 + x_2 + x_3 + x_4 &= 6 \\ 3x_2 - x_3 - 2x_4 &= 2 \\ 3x_3 + 4x_4 &= 9 \\ x_4 &= 6 \end{aligned}$

10. $\begin{aligned} x_1 - 5x_2 + 2x_3 - 7x_4 + 11x_5 &= 0 \\ x_2 - 13x_3 + 3x_4 - 7x_5 &= 0 \\ x_4 - 5x_5 &= 0 \end{aligned}$

In Problems 11–22, use elementary row operations to transform each augmented coefficient matrix to echelon form. Then solve the system by back substitution.

11. $\begin{aligned} 2x_1 + 8x_2 + 3x_3 &= 2 \\ x_1 + 3x_2 + 2x_3 &= 5 \\ 2x_1 + 7x_2 + 4x_3 &= 8 \end{aligned}$

12. $\begin{aligned} 3x_1 + x_2 - 3x_3 &= 6 \\ 2x_1 + 7x_2 + x_3 &= -9 \\ 2x_1 + 5x_2 &= -5 \end{aligned}$

13. $\begin{aligned} x_1 + 3x_2 + 3x_3 &= 13 \\ 2x_1 + 5x_2 + 4x_3 &= 23 \\ 2x_1 + 7x_2 + 8x_3 &= 29 \end{aligned}$

14. $\begin{aligned} 3x_1 - 6x_2 - 2x_3 &= 1 \\ 2x_1 - 4x_2 + x_3 &= 17 \\ x_1 - 2x_2 - 2x_3 &= -9 \end{aligned}$

15. $\begin{aligned} 3x_1 + x_2 - 3x_3 &= -4 \\ x_1 + x_2 + x_3 &= 1 \\ 5x_1 + 6x_2 + 8x_3 &= 8 \end{aligned}$

16. $\begin{aligned} 2x_1 + 5x_2 + 12x_3 &= 6 \\ 3x_1 + x_2 + 5x_3 &= 12 \\ 5x_1 + 8x_2 + 21x_3 &= 17 \end{aligned}$

17. $\begin{aligned} x_1 - 4x_2 - 3x_3 - 3x_4 &= 4 \\ 2x_1 - 6x_2 - 5x_3 - 5x_4 &= 5 \\ 3x_1 - x_2 - 4x_3 - 5x_4 &= -7 \end{aligned}$

18. $\begin{aligned} 3x_1 - 6x_2 + x_3 + 13x_4 &= 15 \\ 3x_1 - 6x_2 + 3x_3 + 21x_4 &= 21 \\ 2x_1 - 4x_2 + 5x_3 + 26x_4 &= 23 \end{aligned}$

19. $$\begin{aligned} 3x_1 + x_2 + x_3 + 6x_4 &= 14 \\ x_1 - 2x_2 + 5x_3 - 5x_4 &= -7 \\ 4x_1 + x_2 + 2x_3 + 7x_4 &= 17 \end{aligned}$$

20. $$\begin{aligned} 2x_1 + 4x_2 - x_3 - 2x_4 + 2x_5 &= 6 \\ x_1 + 3x_2 + 2x_3 - 7x_4 + 3x_5 &= 9 \\ 5x_1 + 8x_2 - 7x_3 + 6x_4 + x_5 &= 4 \end{aligned}$$

21. $$\begin{aligned} x_1 + x_2 + x_3 \qquad &= 6 \\ 2x_1 - 2x_2 - 5x_3 \qquad &= -13 \\ 3x_1 \qquad + x_3 + x_4 &= 13 \\ 4x_1 - 2x_2 - 3x_3 + x_4 &= 1 \end{aligned}$$

22. $$\begin{aligned} 4x_1 - 2x_2 - 3x_3 + x_4 &= 3 \\ 2x_1 - 2x_2 - 5x_3 \qquad &= -10 \\ 4x_1 + x_2 + 2x_3 + x_4 &= 17 \\ 3x_1 \qquad + x_3 + x_4 &= 12 \end{aligned}$$

In Problems 23–27, determine for what values of k each system has (a) a unique solution; (b) no solution; (c) infinitely many solutions.

23. $$\begin{aligned} 3x + 2y &= 1 \\ 6x + 4y &= k \end{aligned}$$

24. $$\begin{aligned} 3x + 2y &= 0 \\ 6x + ky &= 0 \end{aligned}$$

25. $$\begin{aligned} 3x + 2y &= 11 \\ 6x + ky &= 21 \end{aligned}$$

26. $$\begin{aligned} 3x + 2y &= 1 \\ 7x + 5y &= k \end{aligned}$$

27. $$\begin{aligned} x + 2y + z &= 3 \\ 2x - y - 3z &= 5 \\ 4x + 3y - z &= k \end{aligned}$$

28. Under what condition on the constants a, b, and c does the system

$$\begin{aligned} 2x - y + 3z &= a \\ x + 2y + z &= b \\ 7x + 4y + 9z &= c \end{aligned}$$

have a unique solution? No solution? Infinitely many solutions?

29. This problem deals with the reversibility of elementary row operations.
(a) If the elementary row operation cR_p changes the matrix A to the matrix B, show that $(1/c)R_p$ changes B to A.
(b) If SWAP(R_p, R_q) changes A to B, show that SWAP(R_p, R_q) also changes B to A.
(c) If $cR_p + R_q$ changes A to B, show that $(-c)R_p + R_q$ changes B to A.
(d) Conclude that if A can be transformed into B by a finite sequence of elementary row operations, then B can similarly be transformed into A.

30. This problem outlines a proof that two linear systems LS_1 and LS_2 are equivalent (that is, have the same solution set) if their augmented coefficient matrices A_1 and A_2 are row equivalent.
(a) If a *single* elementary row operation transforms A_1 to A_2, show directly—considering separately the three cases—that every solution of LS_1 is also a solution of LS_2.
(b) Explain why it now follows from Problem 29 that every solution of either system is also a solution of the other system; thus the two systems have the same solution set.

1.3 Gauss–Jordan Elimination

The result of the process of Gaussian elimination described in Section 1.2 is not uniquely determined. That is, two different sequences of elementary row operations, both starting with the same matrix A, may yield two different echelon matrices, each of course still row-equivalent to A. For instance, the two echelon matrices

$$\begin{bmatrix} 1 & 2 & 3 \\ 0 & 4 & 5 \\ 0 & 0 & 6 \end{bmatrix} \quad \text{and} \quad \begin{bmatrix} 1 & 1 & 1 \\ 0 & 2 & 2 \\ 0 & 0 & 3 \end{bmatrix} \tag{1}$$

are readily seen (see Problem 31) to be row-equivalent. Hence it is possible to begin with an appropriate 3×3 matrix and derive by Gaussian elimination either of the two different echelon matrices in (1).

A full understanding of the structure of systems of linear equations depends upon the definition of a special class of echelon matrices, a class such that every matrix is row-equivalent to one and only one of these special echelon matrices. Recall that an echelon matrix E is one that has the following two properties:

1. Every all-zero row of E lies beneath every row that contains a nonzero element.
2. The leading nonzero entry in each row lies to the right of the leading nonzero entry in the preceding row.

A *reduced* echelon matrix (sometimes called a reduced row-echelon matrix) has two additional properties.

Definition: *Reduced Echelon Matrix*

A **reduced echelon matrix** E is an echelon matrix that—in addition to Properties 1 and 2—has the following properties:

3. Every leading entry of E is 1.
4. Each leading entry of E is the only nonzero element in its column.

A matrix is said to be in **reduced echelon form** if it is a reduced echelon matrix. Similarly, a linear system is in **reduced echelon form** if its augmented coefficient matrix is a reduced echelon matrix.

EXAMPLE 1 The following matrices are reduced echelon matrices.

$$\begin{bmatrix} 1 & 0 \\ 0 & 1 \end{bmatrix} \qquad \begin{bmatrix} 1 & 0 & -3 & 0 \\ 0 & 1 & 4 & 0 \\ 0 & 0 & 0 & 1 \end{bmatrix}$$

$$\begin{bmatrix} 1 & -2 & 0 \\ 0 & 0 & 1 \\ 0 & 0 & 0 \end{bmatrix} \qquad \begin{bmatrix} 1 & 0 & -7 \\ 0 & 1 & 5 \\ 0 & 0 & 0 \end{bmatrix}$$

The echelon matrices

$$A = \begin{bmatrix} 1 & 0 & 0 \\ 0 & 2 & 1 \\ 0 & 0 & 0 \end{bmatrix} \quad \text{and} \quad B = \begin{bmatrix} 1 & 0 & 2 \\ 0 & 1 & 0 \\ 0 & 0 & 1 \end{bmatrix}$$

are not in *reduced* echelon form because A does not have Property 3 and B does not have Property 4.

The process of transforming a matrix A into reduced echelon form is called **Gauss-Jordan elimination**.

Algorithm: *Gauss-Jordan Elimination*

1. First transform A into echelon form by Gaussian elimination.
2. Then divide each element of each nonzero *row* by its leading entry (to satisfy Property 3).
3. Finally use each leading 1 to "clear out" any remaining nonzero elements in its *column* (to satisfy Property 4).

The reduced echelon form of a matrix *is* unique. The special class of matrices that we mentioned at the beginning of this discussion is simply the class of all reduced echelon matrices. A proof of the following theorem may be found in Section 3.5 of B. Noble and J. W. Daniel, *Applied Linear Algebra*, 2nd ed. (Englewood Cliffs, N.J.: Prentice-Hall, 1977).

> ***Theorem 1***: *Unique Reduced Echelon Form*
> Every matrix is row-equivalent to one and only one reduced echelon matrix.

EXAMPLE 2 Find the reduced echelon form of the matrix

$$\begin{bmatrix} 1 & 2 & 1 & 4 \\ 3 & 8 & 7 & 20 \\ 2 & 7 & 9 & 23 \end{bmatrix}.$$

Solution In Example 3 of Section 1.2 we found the echelon form

$$\begin{bmatrix} 1 & 2 & 1 & 4 \\ 0 & 1 & 2 & 4 \\ 0 & 0 & 1 & 3 \end{bmatrix},$$

which already satisfies Property 3. To clear out columns 2 and 3 (in order to satisfy Property 4), we continue the reduction as follows.

$$\begin{bmatrix} 1 & 2 & 1 & 4 \\ 0 & 1 & 2 & 4 \\ 0 & 0 & 1 & 3 \end{bmatrix} \xrightarrow{(-2)R_2+R_1} \begin{bmatrix} 1 & 0 & -3 & -4 \\ 0 & 1 & 2 & 4 \\ 0 & 0 & 1 & 3 \end{bmatrix}$$

$$\xrightarrow{(-2)R_3+R_2} \begin{bmatrix} 1 & 0 & -3 & -4 \\ 0 & 1 & 0 & -2 \\ 0 & 0 & 1 & 3 \end{bmatrix}$$

$$\xrightarrow{(3)R_3+R_1} \begin{bmatrix} 1 & 0 & 0 & 5 \\ 0 & 1 & 0 & -2 \\ 0 & 0 & 1 & 3 \end{bmatrix}.$$

EXAMPLE 3 To use Gauss-Jordan elimination to solve the linear system

$$\begin{aligned} x_1 + x_2 + x_3 + x_4 &= 12 \\ x_1 + 2x_2 \qquad + 5x_4 &= 17 \\ 3x_1 + 2x_2 + 4x_3 - x_4 &= 31, \end{aligned} \tag{2}$$

we transform its augmented coefficient matrix into *reduced* echelon form, as follows:

$$\begin{bmatrix} 1 & 1 & 1 & 1 & 12 \\ 1 & 2 & 0 & 5 & 17 \\ 3 & 2 & 4 & -1 & 31 \end{bmatrix} \xrightarrow{(-1)R_1+R_2} \begin{bmatrix} 1 & 1 & 1 & 1 & 12 \\ 0 & 1 & -1 & 4 & 5 \\ 3 & 2 & 4 & -1 & 31 \end{bmatrix}$$

$$\xrightarrow{(-3)R_1+R_3} \begin{bmatrix} 1 & 1 & 1 & 1 & 12 \\ 0 & 1 & -1 & 4 & 5 \\ 0 & -1 & 1 & -4 & -5 \end{bmatrix}$$

$$\xrightarrow{(1)R_2+R_3} \begin{bmatrix} 1 & 1 & 1 & 1 & 12 \\ 0 & 1 & -1 & 4 & 5 \\ 0 & 0 & 0 & 0 & 0 \end{bmatrix}$$

$$\xrightarrow{(-1)R_2+R_1} \begin{bmatrix} 1 & 0 & 2 & -3 & 7 \\ 0 & 1 & -1 & 4 & 5 \\ 0 & 0 & 0 & 0 & 0 \end{bmatrix}$$

Thus the reduced echelon form of the system in (2) is

$$\begin{aligned} x_1 \qquad + 2x_3 - 3x_4 &= 7 \\ x_2 - x_3 + 4x_4 &= 5 \\ 0 &= 0. \end{aligned} \tag{3}$$

The leading variables are x_1 and x_2; the free variables are x_3 and x_4. If we set

$$x_3 = s \quad \text{and} \quad x_4 = t,$$

then (3) immediately yields

$$\begin{aligned} x_1 &= 7 - 2s + 3t, \\ x_2 &= 5 + s - 4t. \end{aligned}$$

As a practical matter, Gauss-Jordan elimination generally offers no significant computational advantage over Gaussian elimination (transformation to nonreduced echelon form) followed by back substitution. Therefore, Gaussian elimination is commonly employed in practical procedures and computer programs used to solve linear systems numerically.

The chief importance of Gauss-Jordan elimination stems from the fact that the reduced echelon form of a general linear system

$$\begin{aligned} a_{11}x_1 + a_{12}x_2 + a_{13}x_3 + \cdots + a_{1n}x_n &= b_1 \\ a_{21}x_1 + a_{22}x_2 + a_{23}x_3 + \cdots + a_{2n}x_n &= b_2 \\ &\vdots \\ a_{m1}x_1 + a_{m2}x_2 + a_{m3}x_3 + \cdots + a_{mn}x_n &= b_m \end{aligned} \tag{4}$$

most clearly exhibits its underlying structure and enables us most readily to answer questions about the number and type of its solutions. If the leading variables are x_{j_1}, $x_{j_2}, \ldots, x_{j_r}$, then the reduced echelon form of the system in (4) looks like

$$\begin{aligned} x_{j_1} \qquad\qquad\qquad + \textstyle\sum c_{1j}x_j &= d_1 \\ x_{j_2} \qquad\quad + \textstyle\sum c_{2j}x_j &= d_2 \\ \ddots \qquad\qquad\qquad &\vdots \\ x_{j_r} + \textstyle\sum c_{rj}x_j &= d_r \\ 0 &= d_{r+1} \\ &\vdots \\ 0 &= d_m, \end{aligned} \tag{5}$$

where the summations involve only the free variables.

The system is consistent if and only if the constants $d_{r+1}, d_{r+2}, \ldots, d_m$ in (5) are all zero. If this is so and $r < n$, then there are free variables that we can set equal to arbitrary parameters. If the system is consistent and $r = n$, then the summations in (5) disappear and we have the unique solution $x_1 = d_1$, $x_2 = d_2, \ldots, x_n = d_n$. These observations establish the following result, to which we have already alluded.

> ***Theorem 2:*** *The Three Possibilities*
>
> A linear system of equations either has a unique solution, has no solution, or has infinitely many solutions.

HOMOGENEOUS SYSTEMS

The linear system in (4) is called **homogeneous** provided that the constants b_1, $b_2, \ldots, b_m$ on the right-hand side are all zero. Thus a homogeneous system of m equations in n variables has the form

$$\begin{aligned} a_{11}x_1 + a_{12}x_2 + a_{13}x_3 + \cdots + a_{1n}x_n &= 0 \\ a_{21}x_1 + a_{22}x_2 + a_{23}x_3 + \cdots + a_{2n}x_n &= 0 \\ &\vdots \\ a_{m1}x_1 + a_{m2}x_2 + a_{m3}x_3 + \cdots + a_{mn}x_n &= 0 \end{aligned} \tag{6}$$

Any homogeneous system obviously has at least the **trivial solution**

$$x_1 = 0, \qquad x_2 = 0, \ldots, x_n = 0. \tag{7}$$

Thus we know from the outset that *every homogeneous linear system either has only the trivial solution or has infinitely many solutions.* If it has a *nontrivial* solution—one with not every x_i equal to zero—then it must have infinitely many solutions.

An important special case, in which a nontrivial solution is guaranteed, is that of a homogeneous system with *more variables than equations*: $m < n$. To see why there must be a solution, consider the reduced echelon system in (5) with the constants on the right-hand side all zero (because the original system is homogeneous). The number r of leading variables is at most the number m of equations (because there is at most one leading variable per equation). If $m < n$, it then follows that $r < n$, so there is at least one free variable that can be set equal to an arbitrary parameter, thereby yielding infinitely many solutions. This argument establishes the following key result.

***Theorem 3*:** *Homogeneous Systems with More Variables than Equations*
Every homogeneous linear system with more variables than equations has infinitely many solutions.

EXAMPLE 4 The homogeneous linear system

$$\begin{aligned} 47x_1 - 73x_2 + 56x_3 + 21x_4 &= 0 \\ 19x_1 + 81x_2 - 17x_3 - 99x_4 &= 0 \\ 53x_1 + 62x_2 + 39x_3 + 25x_4 &= 0 \end{aligned}$$

of three equations in four unknowns necessarily has infinitely many solutions. The only question (which we could answer by reducing the system to echelon form) is whether the system has one, two, or three free variables.

The situation is different for a *nonhomogeneous* system with more variables than equations. The simple example

$$\begin{aligned} x_1 + x_2 + x_3 &= 0 \\ x_1 + x_2 + x_3 &= 1 \end{aligned}$$

shows that such a system may be inconsistent. But if it is consistent—meaning that $d_{r+1} = \cdots = d_m = 0$ in the reduced echelon form in (5)—then the fact that $m < n$ implies (just as in the proof of Theorem 3) that there is at least one free variable, and therefore the system has infinitely many solutions. Hence *every nonhomogeneous system with more variables than equations either has no solution or has infinitely many solutions.*

An especially important case in the theory of linear systems is that of a homogeneous system

$$\begin{aligned} a_{11}x_1 + a_{12}x_2 + a_{13}x_3 + \cdots + a_{1n}x_n &= 0 \\ a_{21}x_1 + a_{22}x_2 + a_{23}x_3 + \cdots + a_{2n}x_n &= 0 \\ &\vdots \\ a_{n1}x_1 + a_{n2}x_2 + a_{n3}x_3 + \cdots + a_{nn}x_n &= 0 \end{aligned} \tag{8}$$

with the *same* number n of variables and equations. The coefficient matrix $A = [a_{ij}]$ then has the same number of rows and columns and thus is an $n \times n$ **square matrix.**

Here we are most interested in the situation when (8) has *only* the trivial solution $x_1 = x_2 = \cdots = x_n = 0$. This can occur if and only if the reduced echelon system contains *no* free variables. That is, all n of the variables $x_1, x_2, \ldots, x_n$ must be leading variables. Because the system consists of exactly n equations, we conclude that the reduced echelon system is simply

$$\begin{array}{lllll} x_1 & & & & = 0 \\ & x_2 & & & = 0 \\ & & x_3 & & = 0 \\ & & & \ddots & \vdots \\ & & & & x_n = 0, \end{array}$$

and therefore the reduced echelon form of the coefficient matrix A is the matrix

$$\begin{bmatrix} 1 & 0 & 0 & \cdots & 0 \\ 0 & 1 & 0 & \cdots & 0 \\ 0 & 0 & 1 & \cdots & 0 \\ \vdots & \vdots & \vdots & \ddots & \vdots \\ 0 & 0 & 0 & \cdots & 1 \end{bmatrix}. \tag{9}$$

Such a (square) matrix, with 1s on its **principal diagonal** (the one from upper left to lower right) and zeros elsewhere, is called an **identity matrix** (for reasons given in Section 1.5). For instance, the 2×2 and 3×3 identity matrices are

$$\begin{bmatrix} 1 & 0 \\ 0 & 1 \end{bmatrix} \quad \text{and} \quad \begin{bmatrix} 1 & 0 & 0 \\ 0 & 1 & 0 \\ 0 & 0 & 1 \end{bmatrix}.$$

The matrix in (9) is the $n \times n$ identity matrix. With this terminology, the preceding argument establishes the following theorem.

> ***Theorem 4:*** *Homogeneous Systems with Unique Solutions*
>
> Let A be an $n \times n$ matrix. Then the homogeneous system with coefficient matrix A has only the trivial solution if and only if A is row-equivalent to the $n \times n$ identity matrix.

EXAMPLE 5 The computation in Example 2 (disregarding the fourth column in each matrix there) shows that the matrix

$$A = \begin{bmatrix} 1 & 2 & 1 \\ 3 & 8 & 7 \\ 2 & 7 & 9 \end{bmatrix}$$

is row-equivalent to the 3×3 identity matrix. Hence Theorem 4 implies that the homogeneous system

$$\begin{aligned} x_1 + 2x_2 + x_3 &= 0 \\ 3x_1 + 8x_2 + 7x_3 &= 0 \\ 2x_1 + 7x_2 + 9x_3 &= 0 \end{aligned}$$

with coefficient matrix A has only the trivial solution $x_1 = x_2 = x_3 = 0$.

1.3 PROBLEMS

Find the reduced echelon form of each of the matrices given in Problems 1–20.

1. $\begin{bmatrix} 1 & 2 \\ 3 & 7 \end{bmatrix}$

2. $\begin{bmatrix} 3 & 7 \\ 2 & 5 \end{bmatrix}$

3. $\begin{bmatrix} 3 & 7 & 15 \\ 2 & 5 & 11 \end{bmatrix}$

4. $\begin{bmatrix} 3 & 7 & -1 \\ 5 & 2 & 8 \end{bmatrix}$

5. $\begin{bmatrix} 1 & 2 & -11 \\ 2 & 3 & -19 \end{bmatrix}$

6. $\begin{bmatrix} 1 & -2 & 19 \\ 4 & -7 & 70 \end{bmatrix}$

7. $\begin{bmatrix} 1 & 2 & 3 \\ 1 & 4 & 1 \\ 2 & 1 & 9 \end{bmatrix}$

8. $\begin{bmatrix} 1 & -4 & -5 \\ 3 & -9 & 3 \\ 1 & -2 & 3 \end{bmatrix}$

9. $\begin{bmatrix} 5 & 2 & 18 \\ 0 & 1 & 4 \\ 4 & 1 & 12 \end{bmatrix}$

10. $\begin{bmatrix} 5 & 2 & -5 \\ 9 & 4 & -7 \\ 4 & 1 & -7 \end{bmatrix}$

11. $\begin{bmatrix} 3 & 9 & 1 \\ 2 & 6 & 7 \\ 1 & 3 & -6 \end{bmatrix}$

12. $\begin{bmatrix} 1 & -4 & -2 \\ 3 & -12 & 1 \\ 2 & -8 & 5 \end{bmatrix}$

13. $\begin{bmatrix} 2 & 7 & 4 & 0 \\ 1 & 3 & 2 & 1 \\ 2 & 6 & 5 & 4 \end{bmatrix}$

14. $\begin{bmatrix} 1 & 3 & 2 & 5 \\ 2 & 5 & 2 & 3 \\ 2 & 7 & 7 & 22 \end{bmatrix}$

15. $\begin{bmatrix} 2 & 2 & 4 & 2 \\ 1 & -1 & -4 & 3 \\ 2 & 7 & 19 & -3 \end{bmatrix}$

16. $\begin{bmatrix} 1 & 3 & 15 & 7 \\ 2 & 4 & 22 & 8 \\ 2 & 7 & 34 & 17 \end{bmatrix}$

17. $\begin{bmatrix} 1 & 1 & 1 & -1 & -4 \\ 1 & -2 & -2 & 8 & -1 \\ 2 & 3 & -1 & 3 & 11 \end{bmatrix}$

18. $\begin{bmatrix} 1 & -2 & -5 & -12 & 1 \\ 2 & 3 & 18 & 11 & 9 \\ 2 & 5 & 26 & 21 & 11 \end{bmatrix}$

19. $\begin{bmatrix} 2 & 7 & -10 & -19 & 13 \\ 1 & 3 & -4 & -8 & 6 \\ 1 & 0 & 2 & 1 & 3 \end{bmatrix}$

20. $\begin{bmatrix} 3 & 6 & 1 & 7 & 13 \\ 5 & 10 & 8 & 18 & 47 \\ 2 & 4 & 5 & 9 & 26 \end{bmatrix}$

21–30. Use the method of Gauss-Jordan elimination (transforming the augmented matrix into reduced echelon form) to solve Problems 11–20 in Section 1.2.

31. Show that the two matrices in (1) are both row-equivalent to the 3×3 identity matrix.

32. Show that the 2×2 matrix

$$A = \begin{bmatrix} a & b \\ c & d \end{bmatrix}$$

is row-equivalent to the 2×2 identity matrix provided that $ad - bc \neq 0$.

33. List all possible reduced row-echelon forms of a 2×2 matrix, using asterisks to indicate elements that may be either zero or nonzero.

34. List all possible reduced row-echelon forms of a 3×3 matrix, using asterisks to indicate elements that may be either zero or nonzero.

35. Consider the homogeneous system

$$ax + by = 0$$
$$cx + dy = 0.$$

(a) If $x = x_0$ and $y = y_0$ is a solution and k is a real number, then show that $x = kx_0$ and $y = ky_0$ is also a solution.

(b) If $x = x_1$, $y = y_1$ and $x = x_2$, $y = y_2$ are both solutions, then show that $x = x_1 + x_2$, $y = y_1 + y_2$ is a solution.

36. Suppose that $ad - bc \neq 0$ in the homogeneous system in Problem 35. Use Problem 32 to show that its only solution is the trivial solution.

37. Show that the homogeneous system in Problem 35 has a nontrivial solution if and only if $ad - bc = 0$.

38. Use the result of Problem 37 to find all values of c for which the homogeneous system

$$(c + 2)x \qquad + 3y = 0$$
$$2x + (c - 3)y = 0$$

has a nontrivial solution.

39. Consider a *homogeneous* system of three equations in three unknowns. Suppose that the third equation is the sum of some multiple of the first equation and some multiple of the second equation. Show that the system has a nontrivial solution.

40. Let E be an echelon matrix that is row-equivalent to the matrix A. Show that E has the same number of nonzero rows as does the reduced echelon form E^* of A. Thus the number of nonzero rows in an echelon form of A is an "invariant" of the matrix A. *Suggestion*: Consider reducing E to E^*.

1.4
Matrix Operations

As yet we have used matrices only to simplify our record keeping in the solution of linear systems. But it turns out that matrices can be added and multiplied in ways similar to the ways in which numbers are added and multiplied and that these operations with matrices have far-reaching applications.

At the level of this text everyone "knows" that $2 + 3 = 5$, and we do not dwell on the underlying meaning of this equation. But in the case of matrices we must begin with precise definitions of what the familiar language of algebra is to mean when it is applied to matrices rather than to numbers.

Two matrices A and B *of the same size* are called **equal**, and we write $A = B$, provided that each element of A is equal to the corresponding element of B. Thus two matrices of the same size (the same number of rows and the same number of columns) are equal if they are *elementwise equal.*

EXAMPLE 1 If

$$A = \begin{bmatrix} 3 & 4 \\ 5 & 6 \end{bmatrix}, \quad B = \begin{bmatrix} 3 & 4 \\ 5 & 7 \end{bmatrix}, \quad \text{and} \quad C = \begin{bmatrix} 3 & 4 & 7 \\ 5 & 6 & 8 \end{bmatrix},$$

then $A \neq B$ because $a_{22} = 6$, whereas $b_{22} = 7$, and $A \neq C$ because the matrices A and C are not of the same size.

The next two definitions are further examples of "doing it elementwise."

> ***Definition***: *Addition of Matrices*
> If $A = [a_{ij}]$ and $B = [b_{ij}]$ are matrices *of the same size*, then their **sum** $A + B$ is the matrix obtained by adding corresponding elements of the matrices A and B. That is,
>
> $$A + B = [a_{ij} + b_{ij}], \tag{1}$$
>
> where the notation on the right signifies that the element in the ith row and jth column of the matrix $A + B$ is $a_{ij} + b_{ij}$.

EXAMPLE 2 If

$$A = \begin{bmatrix} 3 & 0 & -1 \\ 2 & -7 & 5 \end{bmatrix}, \quad B = \begin{bmatrix} 4 & -3 & 6 \\ 9 & 0 & -2 \end{bmatrix}, \quad \text{and} \quad C = \begin{bmatrix} 3 & -2 \\ -1 & 6 \end{bmatrix},$$

then

$$A + B = \begin{bmatrix} 7 & -3 & 5 \\ 11 & -7 & 3 \end{bmatrix}.$$

But the sum $A + C$ is not defined because the matrices A and C are not of the same size.

> ***Definition***: *Multiplication of a Matrix by a Number*
> If $A = [a_{ij}]$ is a matrix and c is a number, then cA is the matrix obtained by multiplying each element of A by c. That is,
>
> $$cA = [ca_{ij}]. \tag{2}$$
>
> We also write
>
> $$-A = (-1)A \quad \text{and} \quad A - B = A + (-B).$$

EXAMPLE 3 If A and B are the 2×3 matrices of Example 2, then

$$3A = \begin{bmatrix} 9 & 0 & -3 \\ 6 & -21 & 15 \end{bmatrix}, \qquad -B = \begin{bmatrix} -4 & 3 & -6 \\ -9 & 0 & 2 \end{bmatrix},$$

and

$$3A - B = \begin{bmatrix} 5 & 3 & -9 \\ -3 & -21 & 17 \end{bmatrix}.$$

VECTORS

Our first application of these matrix operations is to vectors. As mentioned in Section 1.2, a **column vector** (or simply **vector**) is merely an $n \times 1$ matrix, one having a single column. We normally use boldface lowercase letters, rather than lightface uppercase letters, to denote vectors. If

$$\mathbf{a} = \begin{bmatrix} 6 \\ -2 \\ 5 \end{bmatrix} \quad \text{and} \quad \mathbf{b} = \begin{bmatrix} -2 \\ 3 \\ -4 \end{bmatrix},$$

we can form such combinations as

$$3\mathbf{a} + 2\mathbf{b} = \begin{bmatrix} 18 \\ -6 \\ 15 \end{bmatrix} + \begin{bmatrix} -4 \\ 6 \\ -8 \end{bmatrix} = \begin{bmatrix} 14 \\ 0 \\ 7 \end{bmatrix}.$$

Largely for typographical reasons, we sometimes write

$$\mathbf{a} = \begin{bmatrix} a_1 \\ a_2 \\ \vdots \\ a_n \end{bmatrix} = (a_1, a_2, \ldots, a_n). \tag{3}$$

That is, $(a_1, a_2, \ldots, a_n)$ is simply another notation for the *column* vector with elements $a_1, a_2, \ldots, a_n$. It should not be confused with the *row vector*

$$[a_1 \quad a_2 \quad \ldots \quad a_n]. \tag{4}$$

A **row vector** is a $1 \times n$ (rather than $n \times 1$) matrix having a single row, and

$$(3, 2, 1) = \begin{bmatrix} 3 \\ 2 \\ 1 \end{bmatrix} \neq [3 \quad 2 \quad 1]$$

because the two matrices here have different sizes (even though they have the same elements).

Now consider the linear system

$$
\begin{aligned}
a_{11}x_1 + a_{12}x_2 + a_{13}x_3 + \cdots + a_{1n}x_n &= b_1 \\
a_{21}x_1 + a_{22}x_2 + a_{23}x_3 + \cdots + a_{2n}x_n &= b_2 \\
&\vdots \\
a_{m1}x_1 + a_{m2}x_2 + a_{m3}x_3 + \cdots + a_{mn}x_n &= b_m.
\end{aligned}
\tag{5}
$$

of m equations in n variables. We may regard a solution of this system as a *vector*

$$
\mathbf{x} = \begin{bmatrix} x_1 \\ x_2 \\ x_3 \\ \vdots \\ x_n \end{bmatrix} = (x_1, x_2, x_3, \ldots, x_n) \tag{6}
$$

whose elements satisfy each of the equations in (5). If we want to refer explicitly to the number of elements, we may call $\mathbf{x}$ an ***n*-vector**.

EXAMPLE 4 Consider the homogeneous system

$$
\begin{aligned}
x_1 + 3x_2 - 15x_3 + 7x_4 &= 0 \\
x_1 + 4x_2 - 19x_3 + 10x_4 &= 0 \\
2x_1 + 5x_2 - 26x_3 + 11x_4 &= 0.
\end{aligned}
\tag{7}
$$

We find readily that the reduced echelon form of the augmented coefficient matrix of this system is

$$
\begin{bmatrix} 1 & 0 & -3 & -2 & 0 \\ 0 & 1 & -4 & 3 & 0 \\ 0 & 0 & 0 & 0 & 0 \end{bmatrix}.
$$

Hence x_1 and x_2 are leading variables and x_3 and x_4 are free variables. In the manner of Sections 1.2 and 1.3, we therefore see that the infinite solution set of the system in (7) is described by the equations

$$
\begin{aligned}
x_4 &= t, \\
x_3 &= s, \\
x_2 &= 4s - 3t, \\
x_1 &= 3s + 2t
\end{aligned}
\tag{8}
$$

in terms of the arbitrary parameters s and t.

Now let us write the solution $\mathbf{x} = (x_1, x_2, x_3, x_4)$ in vector notation. The equations in (8) yield

$$
\mathbf{x} = \begin{bmatrix} x_1 \\ x_2 \\ x_3 \\ x_4 \end{bmatrix} = \begin{bmatrix} 3s + 2t \\ 4s - 3t \\ s \\ t \end{bmatrix},
$$

and "separating" the s and t parts gives

$$\mathbf{x} = \begin{bmatrix} 3s \\ 4s \\ s \\ 0 \end{bmatrix} + \begin{bmatrix} 2t \\ -3t \\ 0 \\ t \end{bmatrix} = s\begin{bmatrix} 3 \\ 4 \\ 1 \\ 0 \end{bmatrix} + t\begin{bmatrix} 2 \\ -3 \\ 0 \\ 1 \end{bmatrix}$$

—that is,

$$\mathbf{x} = s(3, 4, 1, 0) + t(2, -3, 0, 1). \tag{9}$$

Equation (9) expresses in **vector form** the general solution of the linear system in (7). It says that the vector $\mathbf{x}$ is a solution if and only if $\mathbf{x}$ is a *linear combination*—a sum of multiples—of the particular solutions (3, 4, 1, 0) and (2, −3, 0, 1). The parameters s and t are simply the coefficients in this "sum of multiples."

In the same manner as we derived Equation (9) from the equations in (8), the general solution of every homogeneous linear system can be expressed as a linear combination of particular solution vectors. For this reason (as well as others) linear combinations of vectors will play a central role in succeeding chapters.

MATRIX MULTIPLICATION

The first surprise is that matrices are *not* simply multiplied elementwise. The initial purpose of matrix multiplication is to simplify the notation for systems of linear equations. If we write

$$A = [a_{ij}], \qquad \mathbf{x} = \begin{bmatrix} x_1 \\ x_2 \\ \vdots \\ x_n \end{bmatrix}, \qquad \text{and} \qquad \mathbf{b} = \begin{bmatrix} b_1 \\ b_2 \\ \vdots \\ b_n \end{bmatrix}, \tag{10}$$

then A, $\mathbf{x}$, and $\mathbf{b}$ are, respectively, the coefficient matrix, the unknown vector, and the constant vector for the linear system in (5). We want to define the matrix product $A\mathbf{x}$ in such a way that the entire system of linear equations reduces to the single matrix equation

$$A\mathbf{x} = \mathbf{b}. \tag{11}$$

The first step is to define the product of a *row* vector $\mathbf{a}$ and a *column* vector $\mathbf{b}$,

$$\mathbf{a} = [a_1 \quad a_2 \quad \dots \quad a_n] \qquad \text{and} \qquad \mathbf{b} = \begin{bmatrix} b_1 \\ b_2 \\ \vdots \\ b_n \end{bmatrix}.$$

In this case the product $\mathbf{ab}$ is *defined* to be

$$\mathbf{ab} = a_1b_1 + a_2b_2 + \cdots + a_nb_n. \tag{12}$$

Thus **ab** is the *sum of products* of corresponding elements of **a** and **b**. For instance,

$$[2 \quad -3]\begin{bmatrix}3\\5\end{bmatrix} = (2)(3) + (-3)(5) = -9$$

and

$$[3 \quad 0 \quad -1 \quad 7]\begin{bmatrix}5\\2\\-3\\4\end{bmatrix} = 3\cdot 5 + 0\cdot 2 + (-1)(-3) + 7\cdot 4 = 46.$$

Note that if

$$\mathbf{a} = [a_1 \quad a_2 \quad \cdots \quad a_n] \qquad \text{and} \qquad \mathbf{x} = \begin{bmatrix}x_1\\x_2\\\vdots\\x_n\end{bmatrix}$$

then

$$\mathbf{ax} = a_1x_1 + a_2x_2 + \cdots + a_nx_n.$$

Hence the single equation

$$a_1x_1 + a_2x_2 + \cdots + a_nx_n = b \tag{13}$$

reduces to the equation

$$\mathbf{ax} = b, \tag{14}$$

which is a step toward the objective expressed in Equation (11). This observation is the underlying motivation for the following definition.

> ***Definition*: *Matrix Multiplication***
> Suppose that A is an $m \times p$ matrix and B is a $p \times n$ matrix. Then the **product** AB is the $m \times n$ matrix defined as follows: The element of AB in its ith row and jth column is the *sum of products* of corresponding elements in the ith row of A and the jth column of B.

That is, if the ith row of A is

$$[a_{i1} \quad a_{i2} \quad a_{i3} \cdots a_{ip}]$$

and the jth column of B is

$$\begin{bmatrix}b_{1j}\\b_{2j}\\b_{3j}\\\vdots\\b_{pj}\end{bmatrix},$$

then the element in the ith row and jth column of the product AB is

$$a_{i1}b_{1j} + a_{i2}b_{2j} + a_{i3}b_{3j} + \cdots + a_{ip}b_{pj}.$$

EXAMPLE 5 If

$$A = \begin{bmatrix} 2 & -1 \\ -4 & 3 \end{bmatrix} \quad \text{and} \quad B = \begin{bmatrix} 1 & 5 \\ 3 & 7 \end{bmatrix}$$

then $m = p = n = 2$, so AB will also be a 2×2 matrix. To find AB we calculate sums of products as follows:

$$\begin{aligned} AB, \text{ row 1, column 1:} &\quad (2)(1) + (-1)(3) = -1 \\ AB, \text{ row 1, column 2:} &\quad (2)(5) + (-1)(7) = 3 \\ AB, \text{ row 2, column 1:} &\quad (-4)(1) + (3)(3) = 5 \\ AB, \text{ row 2, column 2:} &\quad (-4)(5) + (3)(7) = 1 \end{aligned}$$

Thus

$$AB = \begin{bmatrix} -1 & 3 \\ 5 & 1 \end{bmatrix}.$$

For your first practice with matrix multiplication you should compute

$$BA = \begin{bmatrix} 1 & 5 \\ 3 & 7 \end{bmatrix}\begin{bmatrix} 2 & -1 \\ -4 & 3 \end{bmatrix} = \begin{bmatrix} -18 & 14 \\ -22 & 18 \end{bmatrix}.$$

Note that $AB \neq BA$. This shows that multiplication of matrices is *not* commutative! We must therefore be careful about the order in which we write the matrices in a matrix product.

The definition of the matrix product bears careful examination to see how it fits together. First, the fact that A is $m \times p$ and B is $p \times n$ implies that the number of *columns* of A is equal to the number of *rows* of B. If so, then the size of the product AB is obtained by a sort of cancellation of the "inside" dimensions:

$$\begin{array}{cccc} A & \text{times} & B & = \; AB \\ m \times p & & p \times n & m \times n. \end{array}$$

These "cancel."

If the inside dimensions are not equal, then the product AB is *not defined.*

EXAMPLE 6 If A is a 3×2 matrix and B is a 2×3 matrix, then AB will be a 3×3 matrix, whereas BA will be a 2×2 matrix. If C is a 3×5 matrix and D is a 5×7 matrix, then CD will be a 3×7 matrix, but DC is undefined.

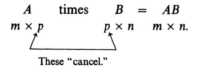

To emphasize the fact that the ijth element of AB is the product of the ith row of A and the jth column of B, we may write

$$AB = \begin{bmatrix} \text{———} \mathbf{a}_1 \text{———} \\ \text{———} \mathbf{a}_2 \text{———} \\ \vdots \\ \text{———} \mathbf{a}_i \text{———} \\ \vdots \\ \text{———} \mathbf{a}_m \text{———} \end{bmatrix} \begin{bmatrix} | & | & & | & & | \\ \mathbf{b}_1 & \mathbf{b}_2 & \cdots & \mathbf{b}_j & \cdots & \mathbf{b}_n \\ | & | & & | & & | \end{bmatrix}$$

where $\mathbf{a}_1, \mathbf{a}_2, \ldots, \mathbf{a}_m$ denote the m **row vectors** of A and $\mathbf{b}_1, \mathbf{b}_2, \ldots, \mathbf{b}_n$ denote the n **column vectors** of B. More briefly, if

$$A = \begin{bmatrix} \mathbf{a}_1 \\ \mathbf{a}_2 \\ \vdots \\ \mathbf{a}_m \end{bmatrix} \quad \text{and} \quad B = [\mathbf{b}_1 \quad \mathbf{b}_2 \quad \cdots \quad \mathbf{b}_n]$$

in terms of the rows of A and the columns of B, then

$$AB = [\mathbf{a}_i \mathbf{b}_j]. \tag{15}$$

Therefore, as mentioned earlier, the ijth element $\mathbf{a}_i \mathbf{b}_j$ of AB is given in terms of elements of A and B by

$$\mathbf{a}_i \mathbf{b}_j = [a_{i1} \quad a_{i2} \quad \cdots \quad a_{ip}] \begin{bmatrix} b_{1j} \\ b_{2j} \\ \vdots \\ b_{pj} \end{bmatrix} = a_{i1}b_{1j} + a_{i2}b_{2j} + \cdots + a_{ip}b_{pj}.$$

That is,

$$\mathbf{a}_i \mathbf{b}_j = \sum_{k=1}^{p} a_{ik} b_{kj}. \tag{16}$$

One can visualize "pouring the ith row of A down the jth column of B" until elements match in pairs, then forming the sum of the products of these pairs, to obtain the element c_{ij} of the matrix $C = AB$. Those who are familiar with BASIC programming may find it useful to see how this computation is carried out in the program shown in Figure 1.6.

SUGGESTION The key to accuracy and confidence in computing matrix products lies in doing it systematically. Always perform your computations in the same order. *First* calculate the elements of the *first* row of AB by multiplying the *first* row of A by the successive columns of B. *Second*, calculate the elements of the *second* row of AB by multiplying the *second* row of A by the successive columns of B. And so forth.

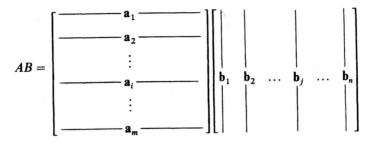

```
100 REM      A IS M BY P, B IS P BY N
110          INPUT M, P, N
120          DIM A(M,P), B(P,N), C(M,N)
130          DATA [elements of A go here]
140          DATA [elements of B go here]
150 REM          LOAD MATRI X A
160          FOR I = 1 TO M : FOR J = 1 TO P
170          READ A(I,J)
180          NEXT J : NEXT I
190 REM          LOAD MATRIX B
200          FOR I = 1 TO P : FOR J = 1 TO N
210          READ B(I,J)
220          NEXT J : NEXT I
230 REM          CALCULATE MATRIX C = AB
240          FOR I = 1 TO M : FOR J = 1 TO N
250          X = 0
260              FOR K = 1 TO P
270              X = X + A(I,K)*B(K,J)
280              NEXT K
290          C(I,J) = X
300          NEXT J : NEXT I
310 REM          PRINT MATRIX C
320          FOR I = 1 TO M : FOR J = 1 TO N
330          PRINT C(I,J)
340          NEXT J : PRINT : NEXT I
350          END
```

1.6 BASIC program for finding the product of two matrices *A* and *B*.

EXAMPLE 7 If $A = [a_{ij}]$ is an $m \times n$ coefficient matrix and $\mathbf{x} = (x_1, x_2, \ldots, x_n)$ is an $n \times 1$ variable (column) matrix, then the product $A\mathbf{x}$ is the $m \times 1$ matrix

$$A\mathbf{x} = \begin{bmatrix} a_{11} & a_{12} & \cdots & a_{1n} \\ a_{21} & a_{22} & \cdots & a_{2n} \\ \vdots & \vdots & \ddots & \vdots \\ a_{m1} & a_{m2} & \cdots & a_{mn} \end{bmatrix} \begin{bmatrix} x_1 \\ x_2 \\ \vdots \\ x_n \end{bmatrix}$$

$$= \begin{bmatrix} a_{11}x_1 + a_{12}x_2 + \cdots + a_{1n}x_n \\ a_{21}x_1 + a_{22}x_2 + \cdots + a_{2n}x_n \\ \vdots \\ a_{m1}x_1 + a_{m2}x_2 + \cdots + a_{mn}x_n \end{bmatrix} \overset{(?)}{=} \begin{bmatrix} b_1 \\ b_2 \\ \vdots \\ b_m \end{bmatrix} = \mathbf{b}.$$

We therefore see that

$$A\mathbf{x} = \mathbf{b} \tag{17}$$

if and only if $\mathbf{x} = (x_1, x_2, \ldots, x_n)$ is a solution of the linear system in (5). Thus matrix multiplication enables us to "boil down" a system of m scalar equations in n unknowns to the single matrix equation in (17), which is analogous in notation to the single scalar equation $ax = b$ in a single variable x.

EXAMPLE 8 The system

$$\begin{aligned} 3x_1 - 4x_2 + x_3 + 7x_4 &= 10 \\ 4x_1 - 5x_3 + 2x_4 &= 0 \\ x_1 + 9x_2 + 2x_3 - 6x_4 &= 5 \end{aligned}$$

of three equations in four unknowns is equivalent to the single matrix equation

$$\begin{bmatrix} 3 & -4 & 1 & 7 \\ 4 & 0 & -5 & 2 \\ 1 & 9 & 2 & -6 \end{bmatrix} \begin{bmatrix} x_1 \\ x_2 \\ x_3 \\ x_4 \end{bmatrix} = \begin{bmatrix} 10 \\ 0 \\ 5 \end{bmatrix}.$$

The definitions of matrix addition and multiplication can be used to establish the rules of matrix arithmetic listed in the following theorem.

Theorem: *Rules of Matrix Arithmetic*

If A, B, and C are matrices of appropriate sizes to make the indicated operations possible, then the following identities hold.

Commutative law of addition: $A + B = B + A$

Associative law of addition: $A + (B + C) = (A + B) + C$

Associative law of multiplication: $A(BC) = (AB)C$

Distributive laws: $A(B + C) = AB + AC$ and $(A + B)C = AC + BC$

The only verification that is not entirely routine is that of the associative law of multiplication; see Problem 44 for an outline. Each of the others follows quickly from the corresponding law for the ordinary arithmetic of real numbers. As an illustration, we prove the first distributive law. Suppose that $A = [a_{ij}]$ is an $m \times p$ matrix and that $B = [b_{ij}]$ and $C = [c_{ij}]$ are $p \times n$ matrices. Then

$$B + C = [b_{ij} + c_{ij}],$$

so by (16) the ijth element of the $m \times n$ matrix $A(B + C)$ is

$$\sum_{k=1}^{p} a_{ik}(b_{kj} + c_{kj}). \tag{18}$$

The ijth element of the $m \times n$ matrix $AB + AC$ is

$$\sum_{k=1}^{p} a_{ik}b_{kj} + \sum_{k=1}^{p} a_{ik}c_{kj} = \sum_{k=1}^{p} (a_{ik}b_{kj} + a_{ik}c_{kj}). \tag{19}$$

But the distributive law for real numbers, $a(b + c) = ab + ac$, tells us that corresponding terms of the sums in (18) and (19) are equal. Hence the ijth terms of the two $m \times n$ matrices $A(B + C)$ and $AB + AC$ are equal, and so these matrices are equal: $A(B + C) = AB + AC$.

If a and b are real numbers, then rules such as

$$(a + b)C = aC + bC, \qquad (ab)C = a(bC), \qquad a(BC) = (aB)C$$

are even easier to verify. What all these rules amount to is this: *In matrix manipulations, pairs of parentheses can be inserted or deleted in the same ways as in the ordinary algebra of real numbers.*

But not all of the rules of "ordinary" algebra carry over to matrix algebra. In Example 5 we saw that multiplication of matrices is *not* commutative—in general, $AB \neq BA$. Other exceptions are associated with zero matrices. A **zero matrix** is one whose elements are *all* zero, such as

$$\begin{bmatrix} 0 & 0 \\ 0 & 0 \end{bmatrix}, \quad \begin{bmatrix} 0 & 0 & 0 & 0 \\ 0 & 0 & 0 & 0 \end{bmatrix}, \quad \begin{bmatrix} 0 & 0 \\ 0 & 0 \\ 0 & 0 \end{bmatrix}, \quad \begin{bmatrix} 0 \\ 0 \end{bmatrix}.$$

We ordinarily denote a zero matrix (whatever its size) by $\mathit{0}$. It should be clear that for any matrix A,

$$\mathit{0} + A = A = A + \mathit{0}, \qquad A\mathit{0} = \mathit{0}, \qquad \text{and} \qquad \mathit{0}A = \mathit{0},$$

where in each case $\mathit{0}$ is a zero matrix of appropriate size. Thus zero matrices appear to play a role in the arithmetic of matrices similar to the role of the real number 0 in ordinary arithmetic.

For real numbers the following two rules are familiar:

- If $ab = ac$ and $a \neq 0$, then $b = c$
  (the "cancellation law").
- If $ad = 0$, then either $a = 0$ or $d = 0$.

The following example shows that matrices do *not* obey either of these rules.

EXAMPLE 9 If

$$A = \begin{bmatrix} 4 & 1 & -2 & 7 \\ 3 & 1 & -1 & 5 \end{bmatrix}, \quad B = \begin{bmatrix} 1 & 5 \\ 3 & -1 \\ -2 & 4 \\ 2 & -3 \end{bmatrix}, \quad \text{and} \quad C = \begin{bmatrix} 3 & 4 \\ 2 & 1 \\ -2 & 3 \\ 1 & -3 \end{bmatrix},$$

then $B \neq C$, but

$$AB = \begin{bmatrix} 25 & -10 \\ 18 & -5 \end{bmatrix} = AC \qquad \text{(Check this!)}$$

Thus the cancellation law does not generally hold for matrices. If

$$D = B - C = \begin{bmatrix} -2 & 1 \\ 1 & -2 \\ 0 & 1 \\ 1 & 0 \end{bmatrix},$$

then

$$AD = \begin{bmatrix} 0 & 0 \\ 0 & 0 \end{bmatrix} = 0,$$

despite the fact that neither A nor D is a zero matrix. See Problems 31–38 for additional ways in which the algebra of matrices differs significantly from the familiar algebra of real numbers.

The identity matrices play a role in matrix arithmetic strongly analogous to that of the real number 1, for which $a \cdot 1 = 1 \cdot a = a$ for all values of the real number a. For instance,

$$\begin{bmatrix} a & b \\ c & d \end{bmatrix}\begin{bmatrix} 1 & 0 \\ 0 & 1 \end{bmatrix} = \begin{bmatrix} 1 & 0 \\ 0 & 1 \end{bmatrix}\begin{bmatrix} a & b \\ c & d \end{bmatrix} = \begin{bmatrix} a & b \\ c & d \end{bmatrix}.$$

Similarly, if

$$A = \begin{bmatrix} a_{11} & a_{12} & a_{13} \\ a_{21} & a_{22} & a_{23} \\ a_{31} & a_{32} & a_{33} \end{bmatrix} \quad \text{and} \quad I = \begin{bmatrix} 1 & 0 & 0 \\ 0 & 1 & 0 \\ 0 & 0 & 1 \end{bmatrix},$$

then $AI = IA = A$. For instance, the element in the second row and third column of AI is

$$(a_{21})(0) + (a_{22})(0) + (a_{23})(1) = a_{23}.$$

If a is a nonzero real number and $b = a^{-1}$, then $ab = ba = 1$. Given a nonzero square matrix A, the question as to whether there exists an *inverse matrix* B, one such that $AB = BA = I$, is more complicated and is investigated in Section 1.5.

1.4 PROBLEMS

In Problems 1–4, two matrices A and B and two numbers c and d are given. Compute the matrix $cA + dB$.

1. $A = \begin{bmatrix} 3 & -5 \\ 2 & 7 \end{bmatrix}$, $B = \begin{bmatrix} -1 & 0 \\ 3 & -4 \end{bmatrix}$, $c = 3, d = 4$

2. $A = \begin{bmatrix} 2 & 0 & -3 \\ -1 & 5 & 6 \end{bmatrix}$, $B = \begin{bmatrix} -2 & 3 & 1 \\ 7 & 1 & 5 \end{bmatrix}$, $c = 5, d = -3$

3. $A = \begin{bmatrix} 5 & 0 \\ 0 & 7 \\ 3 & -1 \end{bmatrix}$, $B = \begin{bmatrix} -4 & 5 \\ 3 & 2 \\ 7 & 4 \end{bmatrix}$, $c = -2$, $d = 4$

4. $A = \begin{bmatrix} 2 & -1 & 0 \\ 4 & 0 & -3 \\ 5 & -2 & 7 \end{bmatrix}$, $B = \begin{bmatrix} 6 & -3 & -4 \\ 5 & 2 & -1 \\ 0 & 7 & 9 \end{bmatrix}$, $c = 7, d = 5$

In Problems 5–12, two matrices A and B are given. Calculate whichever of the matrices AB and BA is defined.

5. $A = \begin{bmatrix} 2 & -1 \\ 3 & 2 \end{bmatrix}, B = \begin{bmatrix} -4 & 2 \\ 1 & 3 \end{bmatrix}$

6. $A = \begin{bmatrix} 1 & 0 & -3 \\ 3 & 2 & 4 \\ 2 & -3 & 5 \end{bmatrix}, B = \begin{bmatrix} 7 & -4 & 3 \\ 1 & 5 & -2 \\ 0 & 3 & 9 \end{bmatrix}$

7. $A = [1 \quad 2 \quad 3], B = \begin{bmatrix} 3 \\ 4 \\ 5 \end{bmatrix}$

8. $A = \begin{bmatrix} 1 & 0 & 3 \\ 2 & -5 & 4 \end{bmatrix}, B = \begin{bmatrix} 3 & 0 \\ -1 & 4 \\ 6 & 5 \end{bmatrix}$

9. $A = \begin{bmatrix} 3 \\ -2 \end{bmatrix}, B = \begin{bmatrix} 0 & -2 \\ 3 & 1 \\ -4 & 5 \end{bmatrix}$

10. $A = \begin{bmatrix} 2 & 1 \\ 4 & 3 \end{bmatrix}, B = \begin{bmatrix} -1 & 0 & 4 \\ 3 & -2 & 5 \end{bmatrix}$

11. $A = [3 \quad -5], B = \begin{bmatrix} 2 & 7 & 5 & 6 \\ -1 & 4 & 2 & 3 \end{bmatrix}$

12. $A = [1 \quad 0 \quad 3 \quad -2]$,
$B = \begin{bmatrix} 2 & -7 & 5 \\ 3 & 9 & 10 \end{bmatrix}$

In Problems 13–16, three matrices A, B, and C are given. Verify by computation of both sides the associative law $A(BC) = (AB)C$.

13. $A = \begin{bmatrix} 3 & 1 \\ -1 & 4 \end{bmatrix}, B = \begin{bmatrix} 2 & 5 \\ -3 & 1 \end{bmatrix}, C = \begin{bmatrix} 0 & 1 \\ 2 & 3 \end{bmatrix}$

14. $A = [2 \quad -1], B = \begin{bmatrix} 2 & 5 \\ -3 & 1 \end{bmatrix}, C = \begin{bmatrix} 6 \\ -5 \end{bmatrix}$

15. $A = \begin{bmatrix} 3 \\ 2 \end{bmatrix}, B = [1 \quad -1 \quad 2], C = \begin{bmatrix} 2 & 0 \\ 0 & 3 \\ 1 & 4 \end{bmatrix}$

16. $A = \begin{bmatrix} 2 & 0 \\ 0 & 3 \\ 1 & 4 \end{bmatrix}, B = \begin{bmatrix} 1 & -1 \\ 3 & -2 \end{bmatrix}$,
$C = \begin{bmatrix} 1 & 0 & -1 & 2 \\ 3 & 2 & 0 & 1 \end{bmatrix}$

In Problems 17–22 first write each given homogeneous system in the matrix form $A\mathbf{x} = \mathbf{0}$. Then find the solution in vector form, as in Equation (9).

17.
$$\begin{aligned} x_1 \qquad - 5x_3 + 4x_4 &= 0 \\ x_2 + 2x_3 - 7x_4 &= 0 \end{aligned}$$

18.
$$\begin{aligned} x_1 - 3x_2 \qquad + 6x_4 &= 0 \\ x_3 + 9x_4 &= 0 \end{aligned}$$

19.
$$\begin{aligned} x_1 \qquad + 3x_4 - x_5 &= 0 \\ x_2 \qquad - 2x_4 + 6x_5 &= 0 \\ x_3 + x_4 - 8x_5 &= 0 \end{aligned}$$

20.
$$\begin{aligned} x_1 - 3x_2 \qquad + 7x_5 &= 0 \\ x_3 \qquad - 2x_5 &= 0 \\ x_4 - 10x_5 &= 0 \end{aligned}$$

21.
$$\begin{aligned} x_1 \qquad - x_3 + 2x_4 + 7x_5 &= 0 \\ x_2 + 2x_3 - 3x_4 + 4x_5 &= 0 \end{aligned}$$

22.
$$\begin{aligned} x_1 - x_2 \qquad + 7x_4 + 3x_5 &= 0 \\ x_3 - x_4 - 2x_5 &= 0 \end{aligned}$$

23. Let

$$A = \begin{bmatrix} 2 & 1 \\ 3 & 2 \end{bmatrix}, \quad B = \begin{bmatrix} a & b \\ c & d \end{bmatrix},$$

and

$$I = \begin{bmatrix} 1 & 0 \\ 0 & 1 \end{bmatrix}.$$

Find B so that $AB = I = BA$ as follows: First equate entries on the two sides of the equation $AB = I$. Then solve the resulting four equations for a, b, c, and d. Finally verify that $BA = I$ as well.

24. Repeat Problem 23, but with A replaced by the matrix

$$A = \begin{bmatrix} 3 & 4 \\ 5 & 7 \end{bmatrix}.$$

25. Repeat Problem 23, but with A replaced by the matrix

$$A = \begin{bmatrix} 5 & 7 \\ 2 & 3 \end{bmatrix}.$$

26. Use the technique of Problem 23 to show that if

$$A = \begin{bmatrix} 1 & -2 \\ -2 & 4 \end{bmatrix}$$

then there does not exist a matrix B such that $AB = I$. *Suggestion*: Show that the system of four equations in a, b, c, and d is inconsistent.

27. A **diagonal matrix** is a square matrix of the form

$$\begin{bmatrix} a_1 & 0 & 0 & \cdots & 0 \\ 0 & a_2 & 0 & \cdots & 0 \\ 0 & 0 & a_3 & \cdots & 0 \\ \vdots & \vdots & \vdots & \ddots & \vdots \\ 0 & 0 & 0 & \cdots & a_n \end{bmatrix},$$

in which every element off the main diagonal is zero. Show that the product AB of two $n \times n$ diagonal matrices A and B is again a diagonal matrix. State a concise rule for quickly computing AB. Is it clear that $AB = BA$? Explain.

28. The positive integral powers of a square matrix A are defined as follows:

$$A^1 = A, \quad A^2 = AA, \quad A^3 = AA^2,$$
$$A^4 = AA^3, \ldots, \quad A^{n+1} = AA^n, \ldots.$$

Suppose that r and s are positive integers. Prove that $A^rA^s = A^{r+s}$ and that $(A^r)^s = A^{rs}$ (in close analogy with the laws of exponents for real numbers).

29. If $A = \begin{bmatrix} a & b \\ c & d \end{bmatrix}$ then show that

$$A^2 = (a + d)A - (ad - bc)I$$

where I denotes the 2×2 identity matrix.

30. The formula in Problem 29 can be used to compute A^2 without an explicit matrix multiplication. It follows that

$$A^3 = (a + d)A^2 - (ad - bc)A$$

without an explicit matrix multiplication,

$$A^4 = (a + d)A^3 - (ad - bc)A^2,$$

and so on. Use this method to compute A^2, A^3, A^4, and A^5 given

$$A = \begin{bmatrix} 2 & 1 \\ 1 & 2 \end{bmatrix}.$$

Problems 31–38 illustrate ways in which the algebra of matrices is *not* analogous to the algebra of real numbers.

31. (a) Suppose that A and B are the matrices of Example 5. Show that $(A + B)(A - B) \neq A^2 - B^2$.
(b) Suppose that A and B are square matrices with the property that $AB = BA$. Show that $(A + B)(A - B) = A^2 - B^2$.

32. (a) Suppose that A and B are the matrices of Example 5. Show that $(A + B)^2 \neq A^2 + 2AB + B^2$.
(b) Suppose that A and B are square matrices such that $AB = BA$. Show that $(A + B)^2 = A^2 + 2AB + B^2$.

33. Find four different 2×2 matrices A, with each main diagonal element either $+1$ or -1, such that $A^2 = I$.

34. Find a 2×2 matrix A with each element $+1$ or -1 such that $A^2 = 0$. The formula of Problem 29 may be helpful.

35. Use the formula of Problem 29 to find a 2×2 matrix A such that $A \neq 0$ and $A \neq I$ but such that $A^2 = A$.

36. Find a 2×2 matrix A with each main diagonal element zero such that $A^2 = I$.

37. Find a 2×2 matrix A with each main diagonal element zero such that $A^2 = -I$.

38. This is a continuation of the previous two problems. Find two nonzero 2×2 matrices A and B such that $A^2 + B^2 = 0$.

39. Use matrix multiplication to show that if $\mathbf{x}_1$ and $\mathbf{x}_2$ are two solutions of the homogeneous system $A\mathbf{x} = \mathbf{0}$ and c_1 and c_2 are real numbers, then $c_1\mathbf{x}_1 + c_2\mathbf{x}_2$ is also a solution.

40. (a) Use matrix multiplication to show that if $\mathbf{x}_0$ is a solution of the homogeneous system $A\mathbf{x} = \mathbf{0}$ and $\mathbf{x}_1$ is a solution of the nonhomogeneous system $A\mathbf{x} = \mathbf{b}$, then $\mathbf{x}_0 + \mathbf{x}_1$ is also a solution of the nonhomogeneous system.
(b) Suppose that $\mathbf{x}_1$ and $\mathbf{x}_2$ are solutions of the nonhomogeneous system of part (a). Show that $\mathbf{x}_1 - \mathbf{x}_2$ is a solution of the homogeneous system $A\mathbf{x} = \mathbf{0}$.

41. This is a continuation of Problem 32. Show that if A and B are square matrices such that $AB = BA$, then

$$(A + B)^3 = A^3 + 3A^2B + 3AB^2 + B^3$$

and

$$(A + B)^4 = A^4 + 4A^3B + 6A^2B^2 + 4AB^3 + B^4.$$

42. Let

$$A = \begin{bmatrix} 1 & 2 & 0 \\ 0 & 1 & 2 \\ 0 & 0 & 1 \end{bmatrix}$$

$$= \begin{bmatrix} 1 & 0 & 0 \\ 0 & 1 & 0 \\ 0 & 0 & 1 \end{bmatrix} + \begin{bmatrix} 0 & 2 & 0 \\ 0 & 0 & 2 \\ 0 & 0 & 0 \end{bmatrix} = I + N.$$

(a) Show that $N^2 \neq 0$ but that $N^3 = 0$.
(b) Use the binomial formulas of Problem 41 to compute

$$A^2 = (I + N)^2 = I + 2N + N^2,$$

$$A^3 = (I + N)^3 = I + 3N + 3N^2,$$

and

$$A^4 = (I + N)^4 = I + 4N + 6N^2.$$

43. Consider the 3×3 matrix

$$A = \begin{bmatrix} 2 & -1 & -1 \\ -1 & 2 & -1 \\ -1 & -1 & 2 \end{bmatrix}.$$

First verify by direct computation that $A^2 = 3A$. Then conclude that $A^{n+1} = 3^n A$ for every positive integer n.

44. Let $A = [a_{hi}]$, $B = [b_{ij}]$, and $C = [c_{jk}]$ be matrices of sizes $m \times n$, $n \times p$, and $p \times q$, respectively. To establish the associative law $A(BC) = (AB)C$, proceed as follows. By Equation (16) the hjth element of AB is

$$\sum_{i=1}^{n} a_{hi} b_{ij}.$$

By another application of Equation (16), the hkth element of $(AB)C$ is

$$\sum_{j=1}^{p} \left(\sum_{i=1}^{n} a_{hi} b_{ij} \right) c_{jk} = \sum_{i=1}^{n} \sum_{j=1}^{p} a_{hi} b_{ij} c_{jk}.$$

Show similarly that the double sum on the right is also equal to the hkth element of $A(BC)$. Hence the $m \times q$ matrices $(AB)C$ and $A(BC)$ are equal.

1.5 Inverses of Matrices

Recall that the $n \times n$ **identity matrix** is the diagonal matrix

$$I = \begin{bmatrix} 1 & 0 & 0 & \cdots & 0 \\ 0 & 1 & 0 & \cdots & 0 \\ 0 & 0 & 1 & \cdots & 0 \\ \vdots & \vdots & \vdots & \ddots & \vdots \\ 0 & 0 & 0 & \cdots & 1 \end{bmatrix} \tag{1}$$

having 1s on its main diagonal and 0s elsewhere. It is not difficult to deduce directly from the definition of the matrix product that I acts like an identity for matrix multiplication:

$$AI = A \quad \text{and} \quad IB = B \tag{2}$$

if the sizes of A and B are such that the products AI and IB are defined. It is nevertheless instructive to derive the identities in (2) formally from the two basic facts about matrix multiplication that we state below. First, recall that the notation

$$A = [\mathbf{a}_1 \quad \mathbf{a}_2 \quad \mathbf{a}_3 \quad \cdots \quad \mathbf{a}_n] \tag{3}$$

expresses the $m \times n$ matrix A in terms of its column vectors $\mathbf{a}_1, \mathbf{a}_2, \mathbf{a}_3, \ldots,$ and $\mathbf{a}_n$.

Fact 1 *$A\mathbf{x}$ in terms of columns of A*

If $A = [\mathbf{a}_1 \quad \mathbf{a}_2 \quad \cdots \quad \mathbf{a}_n]$ and $\mathbf{x} = (x_1, x_2, \ldots, x_n)$ is an n-vector, then

$$A\mathbf{x} = x_1\mathbf{a}_1 + x_2\mathbf{a}_2 + \cdots + x_n\mathbf{a}_n. \tag{4}$$

The reason is that when each row vector of A is multiplied by the column vector $\mathbf{x}$, its jth element is multiplied by x_j.

Fact 2 *AB in terms of columns of B*

If A is an $m \times n$ matrix and $B = [\mathbf{b}_1 \quad \mathbf{b}_2 \quad \cdots \quad \mathbf{b}_p]$ is an $n \times p$ matrix, then

$$AB = [A\mathbf{b}_1 \quad A\mathbf{b}_2 \quad \cdots \quad A\mathbf{b}_p]. \tag{5}$$

That is, *the jth column of AB is the product of A and the jth column of B.* The reason is that the elements of the jth column of AB are obtained by multiplying the individual rows of A by the individual columns of B.

EXAMPLE 1 The third column of the product AB of the matrices

$$A = \begin{bmatrix} 2 & -1 & 0 \\ 4 & 0 & 3 \end{bmatrix} \quad \text{and} \quad B = \begin{bmatrix} 3 & 7 & 5 & -4 \\ -2 & 6 & 3 & 6 \\ 5 & 1 & -2 & -1 \end{bmatrix}$$

is

$$A\mathbf{b}_3 = \begin{bmatrix} 2 & -1 & 0 \\ 4 & 0 & 3 \end{bmatrix} \begin{bmatrix} 5 \\ 3 \\ -2 \end{bmatrix} = \begin{bmatrix} 7 \\ 14 \end{bmatrix}.$$

To prove that $AI = A$, note first that

$$I = [\mathbf{e}_1 \quad \mathbf{e}_2 \quad \cdots \quad \mathbf{e}_n] \tag{6}$$

where the jth column vector of I is the jth **basic unit vector**

$$\mathbf{e}_j = \begin{bmatrix} 0 \\ \vdots \\ 1 \\ \vdots \\ 0 \end{bmatrix} \leftarrow j\text{th entry.} \tag{7}$$

If $A = [\mathbf{a}_1 \quad \mathbf{a}_2 \quad \cdots \quad \mathbf{a}_n]$, then Fact 1 yields

$$A\mathbf{e}_j = 0 \cdot \mathbf{a}_1 + \cdots + 1 \cdot \mathbf{a}_j + \cdots + 0 \cdot \mathbf{a}_n = \mathbf{a}_j. \tag{8}$$

Hence Fact 2 gives

$$\begin{aligned} AI &= A[\mathbf{e}_1 \quad \mathbf{e}_2 \quad \ldots \quad \mathbf{e}_n] \\ &= [A\mathbf{e}_1 \quad A\mathbf{e}_2 \quad \ldots \quad A\mathbf{e}_n] = [\mathbf{a}_1 \quad \mathbf{a}_2 \quad \ldots \quad \mathbf{a}_n]; \end{aligned}$$

that is, $AI = A$. The proof that $IB = B$ is similar (see Problems 41 and 42).

THE INVERSE MATRIX A^{-1}

If $a \neq 0$ then there is a number $b = a^{-1} = 1/a$ such that $ab = ba = 1$. Given a nonzero matrix A, we therefore wonder whether there is a matrix B such that $AB = BA = I$. The following two examples show that the answer to this question depends upon the particular matrix A.

EXAMPLE 2 If

$$A = \begin{bmatrix} 4 & 9 \\ 3 & 7 \end{bmatrix} \quad \text{and} \quad B = \begin{bmatrix} 7 & -9 \\ -3 & 4 \end{bmatrix},$$

then

$$AB = \begin{bmatrix} 4 & 9 \\ 3 & 7 \end{bmatrix}\begin{bmatrix} 7 & -9 \\ -3 & 4 \end{bmatrix} = \begin{bmatrix} 1 & 0 \\ 0 & 1 \end{bmatrix} = I;$$

$BA = I$ by a similar computation.

EXAMPLE 3 Let

$$A = \begin{bmatrix} 1 & -3 \\ -2 & 6 \end{bmatrix} \quad \text{and} \quad B = \begin{bmatrix} a & b \\ c & d \end{bmatrix}.$$

If the matrix B had the property that $AB = BA = I$, then

$$\begin{aligned} AB &= \begin{bmatrix} 1 & -3 \\ -2 & 6 \end{bmatrix}\begin{bmatrix} a & b \\ c & d \end{bmatrix} \\ &= \begin{bmatrix} a - 3c & b - 3d \\ -2a + 6c & -2b + 6d \end{bmatrix} = \begin{bmatrix} 1 & 0 \\ 0 & 1 \end{bmatrix}. \end{aligned}$$

But upon equating corresponding elements of AB and the 2×2 identity matrix in the last line, we find that

$$\begin{aligned} a - 3c &= 1 \\ -2a + 6c &= 0 \end{aligned} \quad \text{and} \quad \begin{aligned} b - 3d &= 0 \\ -2b + 6d &= 1. \end{aligned}$$

It is clear that these equations are inconsistent. Thus there can exist *no* 2×2 matrix B such that $AB = I$.

Definition: *Invertible Matrix*

The square matrix A is called **invertible** if there exists a matrix B such that

$$AB = BA = I.$$

Thus the matrix A of Example 2 is invertible, whereas the matrix A of Example 3 is not invertible.

A matrix B such that $AB = BA = I$ is called an **inverse matrix** of the matrix A. The following theorem says that no matrix can have two different inverse matrices.

> ***Theorem 1:*** *Uniqueness of Inverse Matrices*
> If the matrix A is invertible then there exists precisely one matrix B such that $AB = BA = I$.

PROOF If C is a (possibly different) matrix such that $AC = CA = I$ as well, then

$$C = CI = C(AB) = (CA)B = IB = B.$$

Thus C is in fact the same matrix as B. ■

The unique inverse of an invertible matrix A is denoted by A^{-1}. Thus we say in Example 2 that

$$\text{If} \quad A = \begin{bmatrix} 4 & 9 \\ 3 & 7 \end{bmatrix} \quad \text{then} \quad A^{-1} = \begin{bmatrix} 7 & -9 \\ -3 & 4 \end{bmatrix}.$$

In the case of a 2×2 matrix A, it is easy to determine whether or not A is invertible, and to find A^{-1} if it exists. In Problems 36 and 37 we ask you to verify the following result.

> ***Theorem 2:*** *Inverses of* 2×2 *Matrices*
> The 2×2 matrix
>
> $$A = \begin{bmatrix} a & b \\ c & d \end{bmatrix}$$
>
> is invertible if and only if $ad - bc \neq 0$, in which case
>
> $$A^{-1} = \frac{1}{ad - bc} \begin{bmatrix} d & -b \\ -c & a \end{bmatrix}. \tag{9}$$

Equation (9) gives us the following prescription for writing the inverse of an invertible 2×2 matrix:

- First interchange the two main diagonal entries.
- Then change the signs of the two off-diagonal elements.
- Finally, divide each element of the resulting matrix by $ad - bc$.

You might check that this is how $B = A^{-1}$ is obtained from A in Example 2 (in which $ad - bc = 1$).

EXAMPLE 4 If

$$A = \begin{bmatrix} 4 & 6 \\ 5 & 9 \end{bmatrix},$$

then $ad - bc = 36 - 30 = 6 \neq 0$, so

$$A^{-1} = \frac{1}{6}\begin{bmatrix} 9 & -6 \\ -5 & 4 \end{bmatrix} = \begin{bmatrix} \frac{3}{2} & -1 \\ -\frac{5}{6} & \frac{2}{3} \end{bmatrix}.$$

Arbitrary integral powers of a square matrix A are defined as follows, though in the case of a negative exponent we must assume that A is also invertible. If n is a positive integer, we define

$$A^0 = I \qquad \text{and} \qquad A^1 = A;$$
$$A^{n+1} = A^n A \qquad \text{for } n \geq 1;$$
$$A^{-n} = (A^{-1})^n.$$

In Problem 28 of Section 1.4 we asked you to verify the laws of exponents

$$A^r A^s = A^{r+s}, \qquad (A^r)^s = A^{rs} \tag{10}$$

in the case of positive integral exponents, and Problem 31 of this section deals with the case of negative integral exponents. In Problem 29 we ask you to establish parts (a) and (b) of the following theorem.

Theorem 3: *Algebra of Inverse Matrices*

If the matrices A and B of the same size are invertible, then

(a) A^{-1} is invertible and $(A^{-1})^{-1} = A$;

(b) If n is a nonnegative integer, then A^n is invertible and $(A^n)^{-1} = (A^{-1})^n$;

(c) The product AB is invertible and

$$(AB)^{-1} = B^{-1}A^{-1}. \tag{11}$$

PROOF OF (c)

$$(AB)(B^{-1}A^{-1}) = A(BB^{-1})A^{-1} = AIA^{-1} = AA^{-1} = I;$$
$$(B^{-1}A^{-1})(AB) = B^{-1}(A^{-1}A)B = B^{-1}IB = B^{-1}B = I.$$

Thus we get I when we multiply AB *on either side* by $B^{-1}A^{-1}$. Because the inverse of the matrix AB is unique, this proves that AB is invertible and that its inverse matrix is $B^{-1}A^{-1}$. ■

In mathematics it is frequently important to note the surprises. The surprise in Equation (11) is the reversal of the natural order of the factors in the right-hand side. You should now be able to show that

$$(ABC)^{-1} = C^{-1}B^{-1}A^{-1}.$$

In general, any product of invertible matrices of the same size is again invertible, and the inverse of a product of invertible matrices is the product *in reverse order* of their inverses.

Theorem 4: *Inverse Matrix Solution of* $A\mathbf{x} = \mathbf{b}$

If the $n \times n$ matrix A is invertible, then for any n-vector $\mathbf{b}$ the system

$$A\mathbf{x} = \mathbf{b} \tag{12}$$

has the unique solution

$$\mathbf{x} = A^{-1}\mathbf{b} \tag{13}$$

that is obtained by multiplying both sides in (12) on the left by the matrix A^{-1}.

Proof We must show both that $\mathbf{x} = A^{-1}\mathbf{b}$ is a solution, and that it is the only solution of Equation (12). First, the computation

$$A(A^{-1}\mathbf{b}) = (AA^{-1})\mathbf{b} = I\mathbf{b} = \mathbf{b}$$

shows that $\mathbf{x} = A^{-1}\mathbf{b}$ *is* a solution. Second, if $\mathbf{x}_1$ is any (possibly different) solution, we observe that multiplication of each side of the equation $A\mathbf{x}_1 = \mathbf{b}$ on the left by A^{-1} yields $\mathbf{x}_1 = A^{-1}\mathbf{b}$, and hence $\mathbf{x}_1$ is the same solution as $\mathbf{x}$ after all. ■

EXAMPLE 5 To solve the system

$$\begin{aligned} 4x_1 + 6x_2 &= 6 \\ 5x_1 + 9x_2 &= 18, \end{aligned}$$

we use the inverse of the coefficient matrix

$$A = \begin{bmatrix} 4 & 6 \\ 5 & 9 \end{bmatrix}$$

that we found in Example 4. Then Equation (13) yields

$$\begin{aligned} \mathbf{x} = A^{-1}\mathbf{b} &= \begin{bmatrix} 4 & 6 \\ 5 & 9 \end{bmatrix}^{-1} \begin{bmatrix} 6 \\ 18 \end{bmatrix} \\ &= \begin{bmatrix} \frac{3}{2} & -1 \\ -\frac{5}{6} & \frac{2}{3} \end{bmatrix} \begin{bmatrix} 6 \\ 18 \end{bmatrix} = \begin{bmatrix} -9 \\ 7 \end{bmatrix}. \end{aligned}$$

Thus $x_1 = -9$, $x_2 = 7$ is the unique solution.

HOW TO FIND A^{-1}

Theorem 2 tells us only how to invert 2×2 matrices. The development of a method for inverting larger matrices involves a special class of matrices, which we define next.

> ***Definition:*** *Elementary Matrix*
> The $n \times n$ matrix E is called an **elementary matrix** if it can be obtained by performing a *single* elementary row operation on the $n \times n$ identity matrix I.

EXAMPLE 6 We obtain some typical elementary matrices as follows.

$$\begin{bmatrix} 1 & 0 \\ 0 & 1 \end{bmatrix} \xrightarrow{(3)R_1} \begin{bmatrix} 3 & 0 \\ 0 & 1 \end{bmatrix} = E_1$$

$$\begin{bmatrix} 1 & 0 & 0 \\ 0 & 1 & 0 \\ 0 & 0 & 1 \end{bmatrix} \xrightarrow{(2)R_1 + R_3} \begin{bmatrix} 1 & 0 & 0 \\ 0 & 1 & 0 \\ 2 & 0 & 1 \end{bmatrix} = E_2$$

$$\begin{bmatrix} 1 & 0 & 0 \\ 0 & 1 & 0 \\ 0 & 0 & 1 \end{bmatrix} \xrightarrow{\text{SWAP}(R_1, R_2)} \begin{bmatrix} 0 & 1 & 0 \\ 1 & 0 & 0 \\ 0 & 0 & 1 \end{bmatrix} = E_3$$

The three elementary matrices E_1, E_2, and E_3 correspond to three typical elementary row operations.

Now suppose that the $m \times m$ elementary matrix E corresponds to a certain elementary row operation. It turns out that if we perform this same operation on an arbitrary $m \times n$ matrix A, we get the product matrix EA that results upon multiplying A on the *left* by the matrix E. Thus we can carry out an elementary row operation by means of left multiplication by the corresponding elementary matrix. Problems 38–40 illustrate typical cases in the proof of the following theorem.

> ***Theorem 5:*** *Elementary Matrices and Row Operations*
> If an elementary row operation is performed on the $m \times n$ matrix A, then the result is the product matrix EA, where E is the elementary matrix obtained by performing the same row operation on the $m \times m$ identity matrix.

Elementary row operations are reversible. That is, to every elementary row operation there corresponds an *inverse* elementary row operation that cancels its effects (see Figure 1.7). It follows that *every elementary matrix is invertible.* To see why, let E be a given elementary matrix and let E_1 be the elementary matrix corresponding

Elementary Row Operation	Inverse Operation
$(c)R_i$	$\frac{1}{c}R_i$
SWAP(R_i, R_j)	SWAP(R_i, R_j)
$(c)R_i + R_j$	$(-c)R_i + R_j$

1.7 Inverse elementary row operations.

to the inverse of the row operation that transforms I into E. Then the inverse operation transforms E to I, so Theorem 5 implies that $E_1E = I$. We see similarly that $EE_1 = I$. Hence the elementary matrix E is invertible with $E^{-1} = E_1$.

Elementary matrices are not ordinarily used for computational purposes; it is simpler to carry out row operations directly than to multiply by elementary matrices. Instead, their principal role is in the proof of the following theorem, which leads in turn to a practical method for inverting matrices.

Theorem 6: *Invertible Matrices and Row Operations*

The $n \times n$ matrix A is invertible if and only if it is row-equivalent to the $n \times n$ identity matrix I.

Proof Assume first that A is invertible. Then by Theorem 4 (with $\mathbf{b} = \mathbf{0}$) it follows that $A\mathbf{x} = \mathbf{0}$ has only the trivial solution $\mathbf{x} = \mathbf{0}$. But Theorem 4 in Section 1.3 implies that this is so (if and) only if A is row-equivalent to I.

Now assume, conversely, that A is row-equivalent to I. That is, there is a finite sequence of elementary row operations that transforms A into I. According to Theorem 5, each of these operations can be performed by multiplying on the left by the corresponding elementary matrix. If $E_1, E_2, \ldots, E_k$ are the elementary matrices corresponding to these row operations, it follows that

$$E_kE_{k-1}\ldots E_2E_1A = I. \tag{14}$$

If we now multiply each side in Equation (14) by the inverse matrices $(E_k)^{-1}$, $(E_{k-1})^{-1}, \ldots, (E_2)^{-1}, (E_1)^{-1}$ in turn, we find that

$$A = (E_1)^{-1}(E_2)^{-1}\ldots(E_{k-1})^{-1}(E_k)^{-1}. \tag{15}$$

Thus A is a product of invertible elementary matrices, and it follows from part (c) of Theorem 3 that A is invertible. ■

The proof of Theorem 6 actually tells us *how to find* the inverse matrix of A. If we invert each side in Equation (15) (remembering to reverse the order on the right), we get

$$A^{-1} = E_kE_{k-1}\ldots E_2E_1I. \tag{16}$$

Because each left multiplication by an elementary matrix is equivalent to performing the corresponding row operation, we see by comparison of Equations (14) and (16) that *the same sequence of elementary row operations that transforms* A *into* I *also transforms* I *into* A^{-1}.

Algorithm: *Finding* A^{-1}

To find the inverse A^{-1} of the invertible $n \times n$ matrix A, find a sequence of elementary row operations that reduces A to the $n \times n$ identity matrix I. Then apply the same sequence of operations in the same order to I to transform it into A^{-1}.

As a practical matter, it generally is more convenient to carry out the two reductions—from A to I and from I to A^{-1}— in parallel, as illustrated in our next example.

EXAMPLE 7 Find the inverse of the 3×3 matrix

$$A = \begin{bmatrix} 4 & 3 & 2 \\ 5 & 6 & 3 \\ 3 & 5 & 2 \end{bmatrix}.$$

Solution We want to reduce A to the 3×3 identity matrix I while simultaneously performing the same sequence of row operations on I to obtain A^{-1}. In order to carry out this process efficiently, we adjoin I on the right of A to form the 3×6 matrix

$$\left[\begin{array}{ccc|ccc} 4 & 3 & 2 & 1 & 0 & 0 \\ 5 & 6 & 3 & 0 & 1 & 0 \\ 3 & 5 & 2 & 0 & 0 & 1 \end{array}\right].$$

We now apply the following sequence of elementary row operations to this 3×6 matrix (designed to transform its left half into the 3×3 identity matrix).

$$\xrightarrow{(-1)R_3 + R_1} \left[\begin{array}{ccc|ccc} 1 & -2 & 0 & 1 & 0 & -1 \\ 5 & 6 & 3 & 0 & 1 & 0 \\ 3 & 5 & 2 & 0 & 0 & 1 \end{array}\right]$$

$$\xrightarrow{(-1)R_3 + R_2} \left[\begin{array}{ccc|ccc} 1 & -2 & 0 & 1 & 0 & -1 \\ 2 & 1 & 1 & 0 & 1 & -1 \\ 3 & 5 & 2 & 0 & 0 & 1 \end{array}\right]$$

$$\xrightarrow{(-2)R_1 + R_2} \left[\begin{array}{ccc|ccc} 1 & -2 & 0 & 1 & 0 & -1 \\ 0 & 5 & 1 & -2 & 1 & 1 \\ 3 & 5 & 2 & 0 & 0 & 1 \end{array}\right]$$

$$\xrightarrow{(-3)R_1 + R_3} \left[\begin{array}{ccc|ccc} 1 & -2 & 0 & 1 & 0 & -1 \\ 0 & 5 & 1 & -2 & 1 & 1 \\ 0 & 11 & 2 & -3 & 0 & 4 \end{array}\right]$$

$$\xrightarrow{(-2)R_2+R_3} \left[\begin{array}{rrr|rrr} 1 & -2 & 0 & 1 & 0 & -1 \\ 0 & 5 & 1 & -2 & 1 & 1 \\ 0 & 1 & 0 & 1 & -2 & 2 \end{array}\right]$$

$$\xrightarrow{\text{SWAP}(R_2, R_3)} \left[\begin{array}{rrr|rrr} 1 & -2 & 0 & 1 & 0 & -1 \\ 0 & 1 & 0 & 1 & -2 & 2 \\ 0 & 5 & 1 & -2 & 1 & 1 \end{array}\right]$$

$$\xrightarrow{(2)R_2+R_1} \left[\begin{array}{rrr|rrr} 1 & 0 & 0 & 3 & -4 & 3 \\ 0 & 1 & 0 & 1 & -2 & 2 \\ 0 & 5 & 1 & -2 & 1 & 1 \end{array}\right]$$

$$\xrightarrow{(-5)R_2+R_3} \left[\begin{array}{rrr|rrr} 1 & 0 & 0 & 3 & -4 & 3 \\ 0 & 1 & 0 & 1 & -2 & 2 \\ 0 & 0 & 1 & -7 & 11 & -9 \end{array}\right].$$

Now that we have reduced the left half of the 3×6 matrix to I, we simply examine its right half to see that the inverse of A is

$$A^{-1} = \begin{bmatrix} 3 & -4 & 3 \\ 1 & -2 & 2 \\ -7 & 11 & -9 \end{bmatrix}.$$

REMARK Ordinarily we do not know in advance whether a given square matrix is invertible or not. To find out, we attempt to carry out the reduction process illustrated in Example 7. If we succeed in reducing A to I, then A is invertible and thereby we find A^{-1}. Otherwise—if somewhere along the way an all-zero row appears in the left half—we conclude that A is not row-equivalent to I, and therefore (by Theorem 6) A is not invertible.

In certain applications one needs to solve a system $A\mathbf{x} = \mathbf{b}$ of n equations in n unknowns several times in succession—with the same $n \times n$ coefficient matrix A each time, but with different constant vectors $\mathbf{b}_1, \mathbf{b}_2, \ldots, \mathbf{b}_k$ on the right. Thus we want to find solution vectors $\mathbf{x}_1, \mathbf{x}_2, \ldots, \mathbf{x}_k$ such that

$$A\mathbf{x}_1 = \mathbf{b}_1, \qquad A\mathbf{x}_2 = \mathbf{b}_2, \quad \ldots, \quad A\mathbf{x}_k = \mathbf{b}_k. \tag{17}$$

By Fact 2 at the beginning of this section,

$$[A\mathbf{x}_1 \quad A\mathbf{x}_2 \quad \cdots \quad A\mathbf{x}_n] = A[\mathbf{x}_1 \quad \mathbf{x}_2 \quad \cdots \quad \mathbf{x}_k].$$

So the k equations in (17) are equivalent to the single matrix equation

$$AX = B, \tag{18}$$

where

$$X = [\mathbf{x}_1 \quad \mathbf{x}_2 \quad \cdots \quad \mathbf{x}_k] \qquad \text{and} \qquad B = [\mathbf{b}_1 \quad \mathbf{b}_2 \quad \cdots \quad \mathbf{b}_k].$$

If A is invertible and we know A^{-1}, we can find the $n \times k$ matrix of "unknowns" by multiplying each term in Equation (18) on the left by A^{-1}:

$$X = A^{-1}B. \tag{19}$$

Note that this equation is a generalization of Equation (13) in Theorem 4. If $k = 1$, it usually is simplest to solve the system by Gaussian elimination. But when several different solutions are sought, it may be simpler to find A^{-1} first and then to apply (19).

EXAMPLE 8 Find a 3×4 matrix X such that

$$\begin{bmatrix} 4 & 3 & 2 \\ 5 & 6 & 3 \\ 3 & 5 & 2 \end{bmatrix} X = \begin{bmatrix} 3 & -1 & 2 & 6 \\ 7 & 4 & 1 & 5 \\ 5 & 2 & 4 & 1 \end{bmatrix}.$$

Solution The coefficient matrix is the matrix A whose inverse we found in Example 7, so Equation (19) yields

$$X = A^{-1}B = \begin{bmatrix} 3 & -4 & 3 \\ 1 & -2 & 2 \\ -7 & 11 & -9 \end{bmatrix} \begin{bmatrix} 3 & -1 & 2 & 6 \\ 7 & 4 & 1 & 5 \\ 5 & 2 & 4 & 1 \end{bmatrix},$$

and hence

$$X = \begin{bmatrix} -4 & -13 & 14 & 1 \\ -1 & -5 & 8 & -2 \\ 11 & 33 & -39 & 4 \end{bmatrix}.$$

Looking at the third columns of B and X, for instance, we see that the solution of

$$4x_1 + 3x_2 + 2x_3 = 2$$
$$5x_1 + 6x_2 + 3x_3 = 1$$
$$3x_1 + 5x_2 + 2x_3 = 4$$

is $x_1 = 14$, $x_2 = 8$, $x_3 = -39$.

NONSINGULAR MATRICES

Theorem 6 tells us that the square matrix A is invertible if and only if it is row-equivalent to the identity matrix I, and Theorem 4 in Section 1.3 implies that the latter is true if and only if the system $A\mathbf{x} = \mathbf{0}$ has only the trivial solution $\mathbf{x} = \mathbf{0}$. A square matrix having these equivalent properties is sometimes called a **nonsingular matrix.**

Theorem 7: *Properties of Nonsingular Matrices*

The following properties of an $n \times n$ matrix A are equivalent.

(a) A is invertible.

(b) A is row-equivalent to the $n \times n$ identity matrix I.

(c) $A\mathbf{x} = \mathbf{0}$ has only the trivial solution.

(d) For every n-vector $\mathbf{b}$, the system $A\mathbf{x} = \mathbf{b}$ has a unique solution.

(e) For every n-vector $\mathbf{b}$, the system $A\mathbf{x} = \mathbf{b}$ is consistent.

Proof By the remarks preceding the statement of Theorem 7, we already know that properties (a), (b), and (c) are equivalent—if A has any one of these properties, then it also has the other two. We can therefore complete the proof by establishing the chain of logical implications

$$(c) \Rightarrow (d) \Rightarrow (e) \Rightarrow (a).$$

That is, we need to show that if A has property (c) then it has property (d) and, similarly, that (d) implies (e) and that (e) implies (a).

(c) $\Rightarrow$ (d): We already know that (c) implies (a), and Theorem 4 says that (a) implies (d). Therefore (c) implies (d).

(d) $\Rightarrow$ (e): This is obvious, because if the system $A\mathbf{x} = \mathbf{b}$ has a unique solution, then it certainly has a solution, and thus is consistent.

(e) $\Rightarrow$ (a): Given the hypothesis that $A\mathbf{x} = \mathbf{b}$ is consistent for every $\mathbf{b}$, we must prove that A is invertible. Let $\mathbf{b} = \mathbf{e}_j$, the jth column vector of the identity matrix I. Then the consistency of $A\mathbf{x} = \mathbf{e}_j$ yields an n-vector $\mathbf{x}_j$ such that

$$A\mathbf{x}_j = \mathbf{e}_j. \tag{20}$$

Let the vectors $\mathbf{x}_1, \mathbf{x}_2, \ldots, \mathbf{x}_n$ be obtained in this way for $j = 1, 2, \ldots, n$, and let B be the $n \times n$ matrix with these vectors as its columns:

$$B = [\mathbf{x}_1 \quad \mathbf{x}_2 \quad \cdots \quad \mathbf{x}_n].$$

Then

$$\begin{aligned} AB &= A[\mathbf{x}_1 \quad \mathbf{x}_2 \quad \cdots \quad \mathbf{x}_n] \\ &= [A\mathbf{x}_1 \quad A\mathbf{x}_2 \quad \cdots \quad A\mathbf{x}_n] \\ &= [\mathbf{e}_1 \quad \mathbf{e}_2 \quad \cdots \quad \mathbf{e}_n] \qquad \text{(by (20))}. \end{aligned}$$

Therefore $AB = I$, and thus we have found a matrix B such that $AB = I$.

We next show that B is invertible by showing that $B\mathbf{x} = \mathbf{0}$ has only the trivial solution (and by using the fact that property (c) implies property (a)). But if $B\mathbf{x} = \mathbf{0}$, then

$$A(B\mathbf{x}) = A\mathbf{0} = \mathbf{0},$$

which implies that $I\mathbf{x} = \mathbf{0}$ and thus that $\mathbf{x} = \mathbf{0}$. So B is indeed invertible. We can therefore multiply each term in the equation $AB = I$ on the right by B^{-1} to get

$$ABB^{-1} = IB^{-1},$$

so that $A = B^{-1}$. Thus A is the inverse of an invertible matrix, and so is itself invertible. This establishes that property (e) implies property (a), and therefore we have completed the proof. ■

The proof of Theorem 7 is a bit long, but it summarizes most of the basic theory of Chapter 1 and is therefore well worth the effort. Indeed, this theorem is one of the central theorems of elementary linear algebra, and we will need to refer to it repeatedly in subsequent chapters.

1.5 PROBLEMS

In Problems 1–8, first apply the formula in (9) to find A^{-1}. Then use A^{-1} (as in Example 5) to solve the system $A\mathbf{x} = \mathbf{b}$.

1. $A = \begin{bmatrix} 3 & 2 \\ 4 & 3 \end{bmatrix}, \mathbf{b} = \begin{bmatrix} 5 \\ 6 \end{bmatrix}$

2. $A = \begin{bmatrix} 3 & 7 \\ 2 & 5 \end{bmatrix}, \mathbf{b} = \begin{bmatrix} -1 \\ 3 \end{bmatrix}$

3. $A = \begin{bmatrix} 6 & 7 \\ 5 & 6 \end{bmatrix}, \mathbf{b} = \begin{bmatrix} 2 \\ -3 \end{bmatrix}$

4. $A = \begin{bmatrix} 5 & 12 \\ 7 & 17 \end{bmatrix}, \mathbf{b} = \begin{bmatrix} 5 \\ 5 \end{bmatrix}$

5. $A = \begin{bmatrix} 3 & 2 \\ 5 & 4 \end{bmatrix}, \mathbf{b} = \begin{bmatrix} 5 \\ 6 \end{bmatrix}$

6. $A = \begin{bmatrix} 4 & 7 \\ 3 & 6 \end{bmatrix}, \mathbf{b} = \begin{bmatrix} 10 \\ 5 \end{bmatrix}$

7. $A = \begin{bmatrix} 7 & 9 \\ 5 & 7 \end{bmatrix}, \mathbf{b} = \begin{bmatrix} 3 \\ 2 \end{bmatrix}$

8. $A = \begin{bmatrix} 8 & 15 \\ 5 & 10 \end{bmatrix}, \mathbf{b} = \begin{bmatrix} 7 \\ 3 \end{bmatrix}$

In Problems 9–22, use the method of Example 7 to find the inverse A^{-1} of each given matrix A.

9. $\begin{bmatrix} 5 & 6 \\ 4 & 5 \end{bmatrix}$

10. $\begin{bmatrix} 5 & 7 \\ 4 & 6 \end{bmatrix}$

11. $\begin{bmatrix} 1 & 5 & 1 \\ 2 & 5 & 0 \\ 2 & 7 & 1 \end{bmatrix}$

12. $\begin{bmatrix} 1 & 3 & 2 \\ 2 & 8 & 3 \\ 3 & 10 & 6 \end{bmatrix}$

13. $\begin{bmatrix} 2 & 7 & 3 \\ 1 & 3 & 2 \\ 3 & 7 & 9 \end{bmatrix}$

14. $\begin{bmatrix} 3 & 5 & 6 \\ 2 & 4 & 3 \\ 2 & 3 & 5 \end{bmatrix}$

15. $\begin{bmatrix} 1 & 1 & 5 \\ 1 & 4 & 13 \\ 3 & 2 & 12 \end{bmatrix}$

16. $\begin{bmatrix} 1 & -3 & -3 \\ -1 & 1 & 2 \\ 2 & -3 & -3 \end{bmatrix}$

17. $\begin{bmatrix} 1 & -3 & 0 \\ -1 & 2 & -1 \\ 0 & -2 & 2 \end{bmatrix}$

18. $\begin{bmatrix} 1 & -2 & 2 \\ 3 & 0 & 1 \\ 1 & -1 & 2 \end{bmatrix}$

19. $\begin{bmatrix} 1 & 4 & 3 \\ 1 & 4 & 5 \\ 2 & 5 & 1 \end{bmatrix}$

20. $\begin{bmatrix} 2 & 0 & -1 \\ 1 & 0 & 3 \\ 1 & 1 & 1 \end{bmatrix}$

21. $\begin{bmatrix} 0 & 0 & 1 & 0 \\ 1 & 0 & 0 & 0 \\ 0 & 1 & 2 & 0 \\ 3 & 0 & 0 & 1 \end{bmatrix}$

22. $\begin{bmatrix} 4 & 0 & 1 & 1 \\ 3 & 1 & 3 & 1 \\ 0 & 1 & 2 & 0 \\ 3 & 2 & 4 & 1 \end{bmatrix}$

In Problems 23–28 use the method of Example 8 to find a matrix X such that $AX = B$.

23. $A = \begin{bmatrix} 4 & 3 \\ 5 & 4 \end{bmatrix}, B = \begin{bmatrix} 1 & 3 & -5 \\ -1 & -2 & 5 \end{bmatrix}$

24. $A = \begin{bmatrix} 7 & 6 \\ 8 & 7 \end{bmatrix}, B = \begin{bmatrix} 2 & 0 & 4 \\ 0 & 5 & -3 \end{bmatrix}$

25. $A = \begin{bmatrix} 1 & 4 & 1 \\ 2 & 8 & 3 \\ 2 & 7 & 4 \end{bmatrix}, B = \begin{bmatrix} 1 & 0 & 3 \\ 0 & 2 & 2 \\ -1 & 1 & 0 \end{bmatrix}$

26. $A = \begin{bmatrix} 1 & 5 & 1 \\ 2 & 1 & -2 \\ 1 & 7 & 2 \end{bmatrix}, B = \begin{bmatrix} 2 & 0 & 1 \\ 0 & 3 & 0 \\ 1 & 0 & 2 \end{bmatrix}$

27. $A = \begin{bmatrix} 1 & -2 & 3 \\ 2 & 1 & 7 \\ 2 & 2 & 7 \end{bmatrix}, B = \begin{bmatrix} 0 & 0 & 1 & 1 \\ 0 & 1 & 0 & 1 \\ 1 & 0 & 1 & 0 \end{bmatrix}$

28. $A = \begin{bmatrix} 6 & 5 & 3 \\ 5 & 3 & 2 \\ 3 & 4 & 2 \end{bmatrix}, B = \begin{bmatrix} 2 & 1 & 0 & 2 \\ -1 & 3 & 5 & 0 \\ 1 & 1 & 0 & 5 \end{bmatrix}$

29. Verify parts (a) and (b) of Theorem 3.

30. Suppose that A, B, and C are invertible matrices of the same size. Show that the product ABC is invertible and that $(ABC)^{-1} = C^{-1}B^{-1}A^{-1}$.

31. Suppose that A is an invertible matrix and that r and s are negative integers. Verify that $A^rA^s = A^{r+s}$ and that $(A^r)^s = A^{rs}$.

32. Prove that if A is an invertible matrix and $AB = AC$, then $B = C$. Thus *invertible* matrices can be canceled.

33. Let A be an $n \times n$ matrix such that $A\mathbf{x} = \mathbf{x}$ for every n-vector $\mathbf{x}$. Show that $A = I$.

34. Show that a diagonal matrix is invertible if and only if each diagonal element is nonzero. In this case, state concisely how the inverse matrix is obtained.

35. Let A be an $n \times n$ matrix with either a row or a column consisting only of zeros. Show that A is not invertible.

36. Show that $A = \begin{bmatrix} a & b \\ c & d \end{bmatrix}$ is not invertible if $ad - bc = 0$.

37. Suppose that $ad - bc \neq 0$ and A^{-1} is defined as in Equation (9). Verify directly that $AA^{-1} = A^{-1}A = I$.

38. Let E be the elementary matrix E_1 of Example 6. If A is a 2×2 matrix, show that EA is the result of multiplying the first row of A by 3.

39. Let E be the elementary matrix E_2 of Example 6 and suppose that A is a 3×3 matrix. Show that EA is the result upon adding twice the first row of A to its third row.

40. Let E be the elementary matrix E_3 of Example 6. Show that EA is the result of interchanging the first two rows of the matrix A.

41. Show that the ith row of the product AB is A_iB, where A_i is the ith row of the matrix A.

42. Apply the result of Problem 41 to show that if B is an $m \times n$ matrix and I is the $m \times m$ identity matrix, then $IB = B$.

43. Suppose that the matrices A and B are row-equivalent. Use Theorem 5 to prove that $B = GA$ where G is a product of elementary matrices.

44. Show that every invertible matrix is a product of elementary matrices.

45. Extract from the proof of Theorem 7 a self-contained proof of the following fact: If A and B are square matrices such that $AB = I$, then A and B are invertible.

46. Deduce from the result of Problem 45 that if A and B are square matrices whose product AB is invertible, then A and B are themselves invertible.

*1.6
Linear Equations and Curve Fitting

Linear algebra has important applications to the common scientific problem of representing empirical data by means of equations or functions of specified types. We give here a brief introduction to this subject, and discuss it in more detail in Chapter 5.

Typically we begin with a collection of given *data points* (x_0, y_0), $(x_1, y_1), \ldots, (x_n, y_n)$ that are to be represented by a specific type of function $y = f(x)$. For instance, y might be the number of units of a product that are sold when the price is x, or y might be the volume of a sample of gas when its temperature is x. The given data points are the results of experiment or measurement, and we want to determine

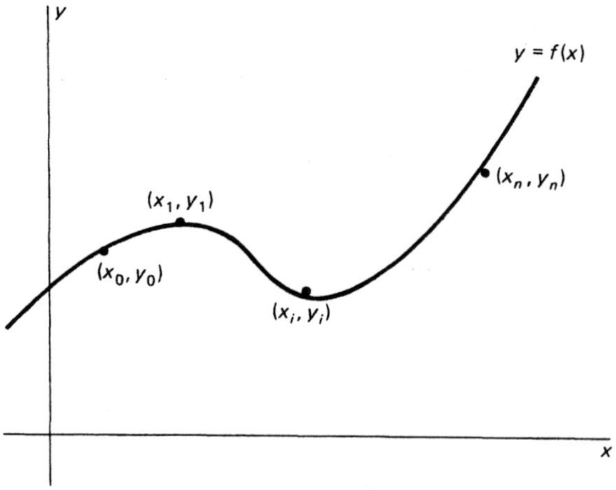

1.8 A curve $y = f(x)$ fitting given data points.

the curve $y = f(x)$ in the xy-plane so that it passes through each of these points; see Figure 1.8. Thus we speak of "fitting" the curve to the data points.

We will confine our attention largely to polynomial curves. A **polynomial of degree** n is a function of the form

$$f(x) = a_0 + a_1x + a_2x^2 + \cdots + a_nx^n \tag{1}$$

where the coefficients $a_0, a_1, a_2, \ldots a_n$ are constants. The data point (x_i, y_i) lies on the curve $y = f(x)$ provided that $f(x_i) = y_i$. The condition that this be so for each $i = 0, 1, 2, \ldots, n$ yields the $n + 1$ equations

$$\begin{aligned} a_0 + a_1x_0 + a_2(x_0)^2 + \cdots + a_n(x_0)^n &= y_0 \\ a_0 + a_1x_1 + a_2(x_1)^2 + \cdots + a_n(x_1)^n &= y_1 \\ a_0 + a_1x_2 + a_2(x_2)^2 + \cdots + a_n(x_2)^n &= y_2 \\ &\vdots \\ a_0 + a_1x_n + a_2(x_n)^2 + \cdots + a_n(x_n)^n &= y_n. \end{aligned} \tag{2}$$

Because the numbers x_i and y_i are given, this is a system of $n + 1$ *linear* equations in the $n + 1$ unknowns $a_0, a_1, a_2, \ldots, a_n$ (the coefficients that determine the polynomial in (1)).

In Chapter 2 we will show that if the numbers $x_0, x_1, x_2, \ldots, x_n$ are distinct, then the $(n + 1) \times (n + 1)$ coefficient matrix

$$A = \begin{bmatrix} 1 & x_0 & (x_0)^2 & \cdots & (x_0)^n \\ 1 & x_1 & (x_1)^2 & \cdots & (x_1)^n \\ 1 & x_2 & (x_2)^2 & \cdots & (x_2)^n \\ \vdots & \vdots & \vdots & \ddots & \vdots \\ 1 & x_n & (x_n)^2 & \cdots & (x_n)^n \end{bmatrix} \tag{3}$$

is nonsingular (see Problems 35–37 in Section 2.2). Hence Theorem 7 in Section 1.5 implies that the system in (2) has a unique solution for the coefficients a_0, a_1,

$a_2, \ldots, a_n$. Thus there is a unique polynomial of degree n that fits the $n + 1$ given data points.

EXAMPLE 1 Find a cubic polynomial of the form

$$y = A + Bx + Cx^2 + Dx^3$$

that fits the data points $(-1, 4)$, $(1, 2)$, $(2, 1)$, and $(3, 16)$.

Solution In a particular problem it generally is simpler to use distinct capital letters rather than subscripted symbols to denote the coefficients. Here we want to find the values of A, B, C, and D so that $y(-1) = 4$, $y(1) = 2$, $y(2) = 1$, and $y(3) = 16$. These conditions yield the four linear equations

$$\begin{aligned} A - B + C - D &= 4 \\ A + B + C + D &= 2 \\ A + 2B + 4C + 8D &= 1 \\ A + 3B + 9C + 27D &= 16. \end{aligned}$$

We readily reduce this system to the echelon form

$$\begin{aligned} A - B + C - D &= 4 \\ B + D &= -1 \\ C + 2D &= 0 \\ D &= 2, \end{aligned}$$

and then back substitution yields $A = 7$, $B = -3$, $C = -4$, and $D = 2$. Thus the desired cubic polynomial is

$$y = 7 - 3x - 4x^2 + 2x^3.$$

It is a geometric fact that if (x_1, y_1), (x_2, y_2), and (x_3, y_3) are three points in the xy-plane that do not lie on a straight line, then there is a unique circle that contains these three points. Thus three points determine a circle, just as two points determine a line. If the circle has center (h, k) and radius r, then by calculating the *square* of the distance between the points (h, k) and (x, y) in Figure 1.9 we obtain the equation

$$(x - h)^2 + (y - k)^2 = r^2 \tag{4}$$

of the circle. Simplification yields

$$x^2 - 2xh + h^2 + y^2 - 2ky + k^2 = r^2;$$

that is,

$$x^2 + y^2 + Ax + By + C = 0 \tag{5}$$

(where $A = -2h$, $B = -2k$, and $C = h^2 + k^2 - r^2$) as the *general equation* of a circle in the plane.

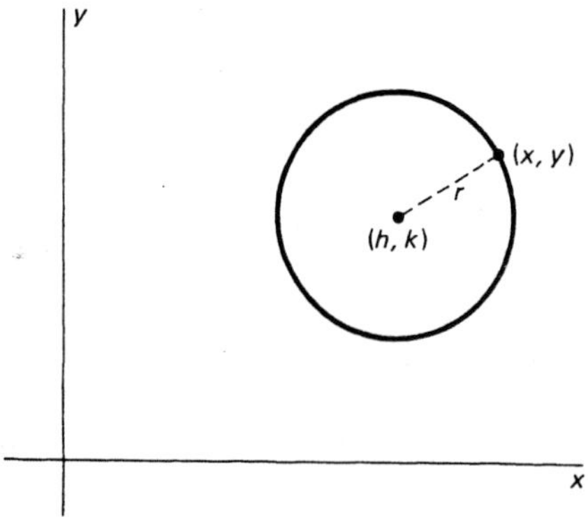

1.9 The circle with center (h, k) and radius r.

Given the three points (x_1, y_1), (x_2, y_2), and (x_3, y_3), we can substitute these three points in Equation (5) to get three equations in the unknowns A, B, and C. We solve these equations and then reverse the steps from (5) to (4) to find the center and radius of the circle determined by these three points.

EXAMPLE 2 Find the center and radius of the circle that contains the points $(-1, 5)$, $(5, -3)$, and $(6, 4)$.

Solution When we substitute the three given points (x_i, y_i) in turn in Equation (5) and simplify slightly, we get the three equations

$$\begin{aligned} -A + 5B + C &= -26 \\ 5A - 3B + C &= -34 \\ 6A + 4B + C &= -52. \end{aligned}$$

By reduction of this system to echelon form, followed by back substitution, we readily solve for $A = -4$, $B = -2$, and $C = -20$. Thus the equation of the circle is

$$x^2 + y^2 - 4x - 2y - 20 = 0.$$

To find its center and radius, we complete the square in the variables x and y:

$$\begin{aligned} (x^2 - 4x + 4) + (y^2 - 2y + 1) &= 20 + 4 + 1; \\ (x - 2)^2 + (y - 1)^2 &= 25. \end{aligned}$$

Upon comparison of the last equation with Equation (4), we see that the circle has center $(2, 1)$ and radius 5.

The orbit of a comet is generally an ellipse with the sun at one focus. Figure 1.10 shows a (rotated) ellipse placed in an xy-coordinate system with its center located at the origin. We call such an ellipse a *central ellipse*. It is shown in Section 10.7 of Edwards and Penney, *Calculus and Analytic Geometry*, 2nd ed. (Englewood Cliffs,

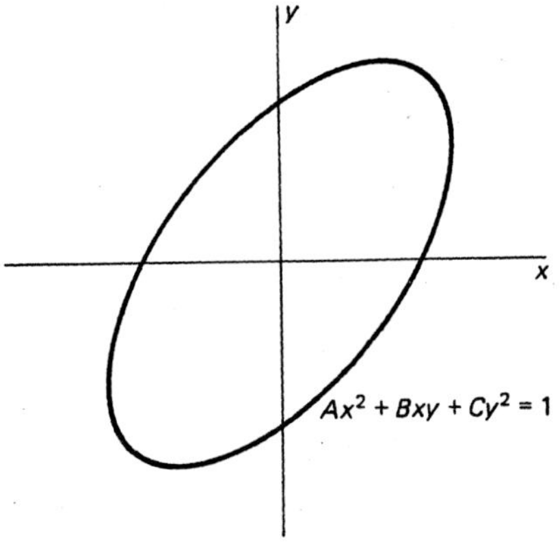

1.10 A rotated central ellipse.

N.J.: Prentice Hall, 1986) that the general equation of a (rotated) central ellipse has the form

$$Ax^2 + Bxy + Cy^2 = 1 \tag{6}$$

(though the graph of such an equation can also be a parabola or a hyperbola rather than an ellipse).

Suppose now—perhaps as a result of observation of our comet—that we know three points (x_1, y_1), (x_2, y_2), and (x_3, y_3) that lie on its orbit, a central ellipse. Then upon substitution of the coordinates of these three points in Equation (6), we obtain three linear equations that we can solve for the coefficients A, B, and C, and thereby find the equation of the ellipse.

EXAMPLE 3 Find the equation of the central ellipse that passes through the three points (1.378, 4.070), (2.769, 2.986), and (3.217, 2.602).

Solution *Real* problems usually involve *real* numbers—that is, "messy" data. When we substitute the coordinates (x_i, y_i) of the three given points in (6) (retaining three decimal places throughout), we get the three equations

$$\begin{aligned}(1.899)A + (5.608)B + (16.565)C &= 1\\(7.667)A + (8.268)B + \;\;(8.916)C &= 1\\(10.349)A + (8.371)B + \;\;(6.770)C &= 1\end{aligned}$$

A calculator eliminates some of the tedium involved in reducing this system to the echelon form

$$\begin{aligned}A + (2.953)B + (8.723)C &= 0.527\\B + (4.033)C &= 0.211\\C &= 0.040.\end{aligned}$$

Back substitution yields $A = 0.030$, $B = 0.050$, and $C = 0.040$. These values for the coefficients in (6) yield the equation

$$(0.030)x^2 + (0.050)xy + (0.040)y^2 = 1,$$

and, finally, multiplication by 100 gives

$$3x^2 + 5xy + 4y^2 = 100.$$

(For illustrative purposes, the original data points in Example 3 were chosen in advance to lie on this ellipse. In a real-world problem the final equation would not likely be so simple.)

1.6 PROBLEMS

In each of Problems 1–10, $n + 1$ data points are given. Find the nth degree polynomial $y = f(x)$ that fits these points.

1. (1, 1) and (3, 7)

2. (−1, 11) and (2, −10)

3. (0, 3), (1, 1), and (2, −5)

4. (−1, 1), (1, 5), and (2, 16)

5. (1, 3), (2, 3), and (3, 5)

6. (−1, −1), (3, −13), and (5, 5)

7. (−1, 1), (0, 0), (1, 1), and (2, −4)

8. (−1, 3), (0, 5), (1, 7), and (2, 3)

9. (−2, −2), (−1, 2), (1, 10), and (2, 26)

10. (−1, 27), (1, 13), (2, 3), and (3, −25)

Three points are given in each of Problems 11–14. Find the equation of the circle determined by these points, as well as its center and radius.

11. (−1, −1), (6, 6), and (7, 5)

12. (3, −4), (5, 10), and (−9, 12)

13. (1, 0), (0, −5), and (−5, −4)

14. (0, 0), (10, 0), and (−7, 7)

Three points are given in each of Problems 15 and 16. Find (as in Example 3) the equation of the central ellipse passing through these points.

15. (0.534, 2.815), (1.319, 1.978), and (2.076, 0.530)

16. (1.567, 5.239), (2.731, 3.499), and (3.815, 1.492)

17. Find a curve of the form $y = A + (B/x)$ that passes through the points (1, 5) and (2, 4).

18. Find a curve of the form $y = Ax + (B/x) + (C/x^2)$ that passes through the points (1, 2), (2, 20), and (4, 41).

*1.7 Matrices and Population Models

Linear algebra is an important tool for the analysis of population growth. A given population of individuals may be subdivided into different age groups or species, and we seek to determine how the population changes from year to year.

The simplest case is that of a single homogeneous population, beginning at time $t = 0$ with P_0 individuals and thereafter growing at a constant annual rate. That is, there is a number a such that the population after 1 year is $P_1 = aP_0$, the population after 2 years is $P_2 = aP_1 = a^2 P_0$, and so forth. Each year's population is simply multiplied by a to get the next year's population. After n years the initial population P_0 has been multiplied n times by a, so the population then is

$$P_n = a^n P_0. \tag{1}$$

In the case of a population that is subdivided into groups, the (scalar) population P_n is replaced by a vector $\mathbf{p}_n$ whose different entries specify the numbers of individuals in the different groups. As the two examples of this section illustrate, the "transition number" a in (1) is then replaced by a *transition matrix* A such that each year's population vector is multiplied by the matrix A to obtain the following year's population vector.

EXAMPLE 1 Consider a metropolitan area with a *constant* population of 1 million individuals. This area consists of a city and its suburbs, and we want to analyze the changing urban and suburban populations. Let C_n denote the population of the city and S_n the population of its suburbs after n years. The distribution of population between city and suburbs after n years is described by the *population vector*

$$\mathbf{p}_n = \begin{bmatrix} C_n \\ S_n \end{bmatrix}. \tag{2}$$

Suppose that each year 15% of the people in the city move to the suburbs and that 10% of the people in the suburbs move into the city. Hence next year's city population C_{n+1} will equal 85% of this year's city population C_n plus 10% of this year's suburban population S_n, so that

$$C_{n+1} = (0.85)C_n + (0.10)S_n \tag{3}$$

for each $n \geq 0$. Similarly,

$$S_{n+1} = (0.15)C_n + (0.90)S_n. \tag{4}$$

When we write Equations (3) and (4) in matrix form we get

$$\begin{bmatrix} C_{n+1} \\ S_{n+1} \end{bmatrix} = \begin{bmatrix} 0.85 & 0.10 \\ 0.15 & 0.90 \end{bmatrix} \begin{bmatrix} C_n \\ S_n \end{bmatrix}. \tag{5}$$

The *transition matrix* for this example is

$$A = \begin{bmatrix} 0.85 & 0.10 \\ 0.15 & 0.90 \end{bmatrix}, \tag{6}$$

and Equation (5) takes the form

$$\mathbf{p}_{n+1} = A\mathbf{p}_n. \tag{7}$$

It follows that

$$\mathbf{p}_1 = A\mathbf{p}_0, \qquad \mathbf{p}_2 = A\mathbf{p}_1 = A^2\mathbf{p}_0, \qquad \mathbf{p}_3 = A\mathbf{p}_2 = A^3\mathbf{p}_0,$$

and in general that

$$\mathbf{p}_n = A^n\mathbf{p}_0 \tag{8}$$

for $n = 1, 2, 3, \ldots$. Note that Equation (8) is a matrix analogue of Equation (1).

Now suppose that the initial urban and suburban populations are (in thousands) $C_0 = 700$ and $S_0 = 300$. Our goal is to determine the "long-term" distribution of city and suburban populations that results from the given urban-suburban migration rates. For the first two years we find that

$$\begin{bmatrix} C_1 \\ S_1 \end{bmatrix} = \begin{bmatrix} 0.85 & 0.10 \\ 0.15 & 0.90 \end{bmatrix} \begin{bmatrix} 700 \\ 300 \end{bmatrix} = \begin{bmatrix} 625 \\ 375 \end{bmatrix}$$

and

$$\begin{bmatrix} C_2 \\ S_2 \end{bmatrix} = \begin{bmatrix} 0.85 & 0.10 \\ 0.15 & 0.90 \end{bmatrix} \begin{bmatrix} 625 \\ 375 \end{bmatrix} = \begin{bmatrix} 568.75 \\ 431.25 \end{bmatrix}.$$

So the population of the city is decreasing and that of the suburbs is increasing over this time interval.

To investigate the long-term situation, we see from Equation (8) that we need to determine how the *matrix power* A^n changes as n increases. A brute-force way to explore this question is to compute in turn the powers

$$\begin{aligned} A^2 &= AA, & A^{20} &= A^{10}A^{10}, \\ A^4 &= A^2A^2, & A^{30} &= A^{10}A^{20}, \\ A^8 &= A^4A^4, & A^{40} &= A^{10}A^{30}, \\ A^{10} &= A^2A^8, & A^{50} &= A^{10}A^{40}. \end{aligned} \tag{9}$$

Thus with eight 2×2 times 2×2 matrix multiplications, we can check our urban and suburban populations for 50 years at 10-year intervals. When we carry out the matrix multiplications in (9), retaining three decimal places in the results, we find that

$$A^{10} = \begin{bmatrix} 0.434 & 0.377 \\ 0.566 & 0.623 \end{bmatrix}, \qquad A^{20} = \begin{bmatrix} 0.402 & 0.399 \\ 0.598 & 0.601 \end{bmatrix},$$

and

$$A^{30} = A^{40} = A^{50} = \begin{bmatrix} 0.400 & 0.400 \\ 0.600 & 0.600 \end{bmatrix}.$$

Thus something quite remarkable happens: The matrix powers of A "stabilize" to the *constant* matrix

$$A^n = \begin{bmatrix} 0.400 & 0.400 \\ 0.600 & 0.600 \end{bmatrix} \tag{10}$$

when n is large. To verify that (10) holds for *all* $n \geq 30$ (and not only at 10-year intervals), we need only the observation that the constant matrix in (10) is not altered when it is multiplied by A. For instance,

$$\begin{aligned} A^{51} = AA^{50} &= \begin{bmatrix} 0.85 & 0.10 \\ 0.15 & 0.90 \end{bmatrix} \begin{bmatrix} 0.400 & 0.400 \\ 0.600 & 0.600 \end{bmatrix} \\ &= \begin{bmatrix} 0.400 & 0.400 \\ 0.600 & 0.600 \end{bmatrix}. \end{aligned}$$

Finally, when we substitute (10) in (8) we find that

$$\begin{bmatrix} C_n \\ S_n \end{bmatrix} = \begin{bmatrix} 0.400 & 0.400 \\ 0.600 & 0.600 \end{bmatrix} \begin{bmatrix} 700 \\ 300 \end{bmatrix} = \begin{bmatrix} 400 \\ 600 \end{bmatrix}$$

for $n \geq 30$. Thus in thirty years the urban and suburban populations reach a steady-state situation, with 40% of the metropolitan population in the city and 60% in the suburbs.

EXAMPLE 2 Now our total population consists of the foxes and rabbits in a forest. Initially there are $F_0 = 100$ foxes and $R_0 = 100$ rabbits. After n months there are F_n foxes and R_n rabbits, so the population vector is

$$\mathbf{p}_n = \begin{bmatrix} F_n \\ R_n \end{bmatrix}. \tag{11}$$

The rabbits eat plants in the forest and the foxes eat the rabbits. We assume that the transition from one month to the next is described by the equations

$$F_{n+1} = \quad (0.4)F_n + (0.3)R_n, \tag{12}$$

$$R_{n+1} = (-0.4)F_n + (1.2)R_n. \tag{13}$$

Equations (12) and (13) constitute a mathematical model of the fox-rabbit population. Such a model is difficult to come by (especially if it is to be realistic) but is not hard to interpret. The term $(0.4)F_n$ in (12) indicates that without rabbits to eat, only 40% of the foxes would survive each month; the term $(0.3)R_n$ represents the growth in the fox population due to the available food supply of rabbits. The term $(1.2)R_n$ in (13) indicates that in the absence of any foxes, the rabbit population would increase by 20% each month; the term $(-0.4)F_n$ represents the decline in the rabbit population because of predation by foxes. In setting up a mathematical model of a complicated situation, one always faces a trade-off between realism and mathematical tractability, and the model in (12) and (13) may be weighted on the side of tractability.

When we write Equations (12) and (13) in the matrix form

$$\begin{bmatrix} F_{n+1} \\ R_{n+1} \end{bmatrix} = \begin{bmatrix} 0.4 & 0.3 \\ -0.4 & 1.2 \end{bmatrix} \begin{bmatrix} F_n \\ R_n \end{bmatrix}, \tag{14}$$

we see that the transition matrix is

$$A = \begin{bmatrix} 0.4 & 0.3 \\ -0.4 & 1.2 \end{bmatrix}. \tag{15}$$

To investigate the long-term situation, we compute powers of this matrix A as in the equations in (9) of Example 1. Retaining three decimal places of accuracy, we find that

$$A^{10} = \begin{bmatrix} -0.491 & 0.745 \\ -0.994 & 1.497 \end{bmatrix}$$

and

$$A^{20} = A^{30} = \begin{bmatrix} -0.500 & 0.750 \\ -1.000 & 1.500 \end{bmatrix} \tag{16}$$

It follows that when $n \geq 20$, the fox and rabbit populations are given by

$$\mathbf{p}_n = A^n \mathbf{p}_0;$$

that is,

$$\begin{bmatrix} F_n \\ R_n \end{bmatrix} = \begin{bmatrix} -0.500 & 0.750 \\ -1.000 & 1.500 \end{bmatrix} \begin{bmatrix} 100 \\ 100 \end{bmatrix} = \begin{bmatrix} 25 \\ 50 \end{bmatrix}.$$

Thus in 20 months the fox and rabbit populations reach a steady-state situation with 25 foxes and 50 rabbits.

Both Example 1 and Example 2 involve a matrix A such that A^n approaches a constant nonzero matrix as n increases. This is the exception rather than the rule. In some of the problems that follow, A^n approaches the zero matrix, meaning that both populations become extinct. In others, both populations increase without bound.

Given an arbitrary square matrix A, the question of how the matrix power A^n behaves with increasing n is a deep and important one, and we pursue it further in Chapter 6. The purpose of the examples in this section is to raise the question and to show that its answer can have very interesting consequences.

1.7 PROBLEMS

Each problem in this section calls for you to rework either Example 1 or Example 2 with a different transition matrix A. You will certainly need a calculator, and a calculator or a computer that you can program to compute matrix products will save you much time.

In Problems 1–6, rework Example 1 with the given transition matrix A in place of the one in Equation (6) but with the same initial populations $C_0 = 700$ and $S_0 = 300$. In each case first calculate the matrix powers in (9). Then find the steady-state urban and suburban populations.

1. $A = \begin{bmatrix} 0.9 & 0.1 \\ 0.1 & 0.9 \end{bmatrix}$

2. $A = \begin{bmatrix} 0.85 & 0.05 \\ 0.15 & 0.95 \end{bmatrix}$

3. $A = \begin{bmatrix} 0.75 & 0.15 \\ 0.25 & 0.85 \end{bmatrix}$

4. $A = \begin{bmatrix} 0.8 & 0.1 \\ 0.2 & 0.9 \end{bmatrix}$

5. $A = \begin{bmatrix} 0.9 & 0.05 \\ 0.1 & 0.95 \end{bmatrix}$

6. $A = \begin{bmatrix} 0.8 & 0.15 \\ 0.2 & 0.85 \end{bmatrix}$

In Problems 7 and 8, rework Example 2 with the given transition matrix A in place of the one in Equation (15) but with the same initial populations ($F_0 = R_0 = 100$). In Problem 7 you should find that both populations die out, and in Problem 8 you should find that each increases without bound.

7. $A = \begin{bmatrix} 0.4 & 0.3 \\ -0.5 & 1.2 \end{bmatrix}$

8. $A = \begin{bmatrix} 0.4 & 0.3 \\ -0.2 & 1.2 \end{bmatrix}$

In Problems 9 and 10, rework Example 2 with the given transition matrix A and initial populations $F_0 = 25$, $R_0 = 30$. In Problem 9 find the steady-state populations and in Problem 10 show that both populations die out.

9. $A = \begin{bmatrix} 0.60 & 0.5 \\ -0.16 & 1.2 \end{bmatrix}$

10. $A = \begin{bmatrix} 0.60 & 0.5 \\ -0.18 & 1.2 \end{bmatrix}$

*1.8 Matrices and Cryptography

Many techniques for encoding and decoding secret messages make extensive use of linear algebra. Here we describe a rather simple method that involves only a pair of inverse matrices, A and $B = A^{-1}$, whose entries are all *integers.* We first illustrate this method using the pair

$$A = \begin{bmatrix} 3 & 1 \\ 2 & 1 \end{bmatrix} \quad \text{and} \quad B = \begin{bmatrix} 1 & -1 \\ -2 & 3 \end{bmatrix}, \tag{1}$$

for which you can readily verify that $AB = BA = I$. The sender will use the matrix A to *encode* the message, and the receiver will use the matrix B to *decode* the message. The point of this method is that the message is encoded using *pairs* of characters, so that tables of letter frequencies and the like are of less help than usual to an unfriendly decoder: We describe here a **code** rather than a **cryptogram.**

Given a message to be encoded, the first step is to convert it from alphabetical to numerical form. For this purpose we use the following correspondence between letters and numbers.

A	B	C	D	E	F	G	H	I	J
1	2	3	4	5	6	7	8	9	10
K	L	M	N	O	P	Q	R	S	T
11	12	13	14	15	16	17	18	19	20
U	V	W	X	Y	Z	.	,	#	
21	22	23	24	25	26	27	28	29	

Any other numbering of the 29 typographical symbols would do as well, but the sender and receiver must agree on a specific one. For clarity we use the symbol # to indicate a *space* between words (or elsewhere).

Suppose that

THE GAME IS AFOOT

is the message to be encoded and transmitted. To convert it to numerical form, we use the pairing shown above: We write

T	H	E	#	G	A	M	E	#	I	S	#	A	F	O	O	T
20	8	5	29	7	1	13	5	29	9	19	29	1	6	15	15	20.

Because the *encoding matrix* A is a 2×2 matrix, we arrange our sequence of numbers as the elements of a matrix with two rows:

$$M = \begin{bmatrix} 20 & 8 & 5 & 29 & 7 & 1 & 13 & 5 & 29 \\ 9 & 19 & 29 & 1 & 6 & 15 & 15 & 20 & 29 \end{bmatrix}.$$

Because the message has an odd number of letters, we have padded the second row with a final 29, which represents a harmless final space (a "null") added to the message.

To encode the message, we multiply the matrix M on the left by the encoding matrix A:

$$\begin{aligned} N &= AM \\ &= \begin{bmatrix} 3 & 1 \\ 2 & 1 \end{bmatrix} \begin{bmatrix} 20 & 8 & 5 & 29 & 7 & 1 & 13 & 5 & 29 \\ 9 & 19 & 29 & 1 & 6 & 15 & 15 & 20 & 29 \end{bmatrix}, \end{aligned}$$

so that

$$N = \begin{bmatrix} 69 & 43 & 44 & 88 & 27 & 18 & 54 & 35 & 116 \\ 49 & 35 & 39 & 59 & 20 & 17 & 41 & 30 & 87 \end{bmatrix}.$$

The entries of $N = AM$ constitute the coded message

69, 43, 44, 88, 27, 18, 54, 35, 116, 49, 35, 39, 59, 20, 17, 41, 30, 87

with commas inserted for clarity. Note that whereas there were repetitions representing repeated letters in the original message, there are none in the coded message, so the more simple-minded codebreakers will have no place to begin.

When this coded message arrives, the receiver uses the *decoding matrix* B to reverse the steps above, knowing that

$$BN = BAM = IM = M. \tag{2}$$

Thus if the decoder uses the coded message to construct a matrix with two rows and then multiplies this matrix on the left by B, he or she will obtain the sender's matrix M. This multiplication is

$$\begin{aligned} BN &= \begin{bmatrix} 1 & -1 \\ -2 & 3 \end{bmatrix} \begin{bmatrix} 69 & 43 & 44 & 88 & 27 & 18 & 54 & 35 & 116 \\ 49 & 35 & 39 & 59 & 20 & 17 & 41 & 30 & 87 \end{bmatrix} \\ &= \begin{bmatrix} 20 & 8 & 5 & 29 & 7 & 1 & 13 & 5 & 29 \\ 9 & 19 & 29 & 1 & 6 & 15 & 15 & 20 & 29 \end{bmatrix}. \end{aligned}$$

Note that the product is indeed the sender's matrix M. The final decoding step is

20	8	5	29	7	1	13	5	29	9	19	29	1	6	15	15	20	29
T	H	E	#	G	A	M	E	#	I	S	#	A	F	O	O	T	#

Equation (2) is the heart of the matter. In brief, the sender multiplies the original message (in numerical matrix form M) by A to get the encoded message. The receiver multiplies the encoded message (in matrix form N) by B to reconstruct the original message. Because A and B are inverse matrices, the receiver's multiplication by B undoes the effect of the sender's multiplication by A.

Note that the process can be carried out quickly and automatically by computer (thus adding to its security), but in a pinch, it can be done with pencil and paper alone (thus enhancing its usefulness). All that need be kept secret are the encoding and decoding matrices, a much simpler task than keeping a bulky codebook from an unfriendly codebreaker.

For a second example, we use the 3×3 inverse matrices

$$A = \begin{bmatrix} 3 & 1 & 2 \\ 2 & 1 & -1 \\ 3 & 1 & 3 \end{bmatrix} \quad \text{and} \quad B = \begin{bmatrix} 4 & -1 & -3 \\ -9 & 3 & 7 \\ -1 & 0 & 1 \end{bmatrix} \tag{3}$$

and suppose that

THE PLOT THICKENS

is the message to be encoded. First we convert the letters to numbers (using the same scheme as before) and then arrange these numbers into a matrix with *three* rows:

$$M = \begin{bmatrix} 20 & 8 & 5 & 29 & 16 & 12 \\ 15 & 20 & 29 & 20 & 8 & 9 \\ 3 & 11 & 5 & 14 & 19 & 29 \end{bmatrix}.$$

To encode the message, we multiply M on the left by A to obtain

$$\begin{aligned} N &= AM \\ &= \begin{bmatrix} 3 & 1 & 2 \\ 2 & 1 & -1 \\ 3 & 1 & 3 \end{bmatrix} \begin{bmatrix} 20 & 8 & 5 & 29 & 16 & 12 \\ 15 & 20 & 29 & 20 & 8 & 9 \\ 3 & 11 & 5 & 14 & 19 & 29 \end{bmatrix} \\ &= \begin{bmatrix} 81 & 66 & 54 & 135 & 94 & 103 \\ 52 & 25 & 34 & 64 & 21 & 4 \\ 84 & 77 & 59 & 149 & 113 & 132 \end{bmatrix}. \end{aligned}$$

Thus the encoded message is

81, 66, 54, 135, 94, 103, 52, 25, 34, 64, 21, 4, 84, 77, 59, 149, 113, 132.

We leave it as an exercise for you to calculate BN and thereby to recover the original message.

1.8 PROBLEMS

The following problems make use of these six pairs of inverse matrices.

(a) $A = \begin{bmatrix} 2 & 1 \\ 1 & 1 \end{bmatrix}$, $B = \begin{bmatrix} 1 & -1 \\ -1 & 2 \end{bmatrix}$

(b) $A = \begin{bmatrix} 3 & 2 \\ 1 & 1 \end{bmatrix}$, $B = \begin{bmatrix} 1 & -2 \\ -1 & 3 \end{bmatrix}$

(c) $A = \begin{bmatrix} 2 & 3 \\ 1 & 2 \end{bmatrix}$, $B = \begin{bmatrix} 2 & -3 \\ -1 & 2 \end{bmatrix}$

(d) $A = \begin{bmatrix} 3 & 1 \\ 5 & 2 \end{bmatrix}$, $B = \begin{bmatrix} 2 & -1 \\ -5 & 3 \end{bmatrix}$

(e) $A = \begin{bmatrix} 3 & 4 \\ 2 & 3 \end{bmatrix}$, $B = \begin{bmatrix} 3 & -4 \\ -2 & 3 \end{bmatrix}$

(f) $A = \begin{bmatrix} 5 & 3 \\ 3 & 2 \end{bmatrix}$, $B = \begin{bmatrix} 2 & -3 \\ -3 & 5 \end{bmatrix}$

In Problems 1–6, use the matrix A in (a)–(f), respectively, to encode the given message.

1. SHERLOCK
2. WATSON
3. MORIARTY
4. LESTRADE
5. MYCROFT
6. BASKERVILLE

In Problems 7–12, use the matrix B in (a)–(f), respectively, to decode the given message.

7. 56, 27, 44, 34, 18, 29
8. 69, 78, 56, 51, 59, 30, 30, 19, 23, 26
9. 52, 84, 13, 80, 85, 33, 52, 7, 49, 55
10. 28, 58, 27, 47, 33, 116, 47, 98, 49, 80, 61, 203
11. 25, 105, 142, 51, 62, 203, 18, 75, 103, 38, 43, 145
12. 67, 65, 109, 40, 105, 205, 44, 43, 69, 25, 64, 127

CHAPTER REVIEW QUESTIONS

1. What does it mean to say that an equation is linear in the variables x, y, and z? Write an example of a single equation in the six variables a, b, c, x, y, and z that is linear in the variables a, b, and c but is not linear in the variables x, y, and z.

2. Two linear equations in x and y correspond to two straight lines in the xy-plane. Describe the possible geometric configurations of these two lines, and in each case tell how many solutions the system of two equations has.

3. What is the augmented coefficient matrix of a linear system?

4. Describe the three elementary row operations on matrices.

5. When are two matrices said to be row-equivalent?

6. What can be said about the solution sets of two linear systems whose augmented coefficient matrices are row-equivalent?

7. What is the difference between an echelon matrix and a reduced echelon matrix?

8. What is the difference between Gaussian elimination and Gauss–Jordan elimination?

9. Let E be an echelon form of the augmented coefficient matrix of a linear system and let F be the matrix obtained by deleting the rightmost column of E. Tell how many solutions the linear system has in each of the following cases.
(a) E has an all-zero row.
(b) F has an all-zero row but E does not.
(c) F has no all-zero row.

10. What are the possibilities for the number of solutions of a homogeneous linear system with more variables than equations? With more equations than variables?

11. What are the possibilities for the number of solutions of a nonhomogeneous linear system with more variables than equations?

12. Given three matrices A, B, and C such that the product ABC is defined, does it follow that the product CBA is defined?

13. Do there exist 2×2 matrices A and B such that $AB = 0$ but $BA \neq 0$? Such that $AB = I$ but $BA \neq I$?

14. Can you find a 2×3 matrix A and a 3×2 matrix B such that $AB = I$ but $BA \neq I$?

15. Let A, B, and C be square matrices such that

$$AB = I = CA.$$

Does it follow that $B = C$?

16. Does there exist an invertible $n \times n$ matrix A and an n-vector $\mathbf{b}$ such that the system $A\mathbf{x} = \mathbf{b}$ has no solution?

17. If two square matrices are row-equivalent, why does it follow that either both are invertible or neither is invertible?

18. Under what conditions on the matrix A are the following two statements equivalent?
(a) For every $\mathbf{b}$ the system $A\mathbf{x} = \mathbf{b}$ has at most one solution.
(b) For every $\mathbf{b}$ the system $A\mathbf{x} = \mathbf{b}$ has at least one solution.

19. Given a square matrix A that is a product of elementary matrices, list as many additional properties of A as you can.

20. Given a square matrix A whose reduced echelon form has an all-zero row, list as many additional properties of A as you can. *Suggestion*: Consider the implications of Theorem 7 in Section 1.5.

2

Determinants

2.1
2×2 Determinants

In Theorem 2 of Section 1.5 we saw that the 2×2 matrix

$$A = \begin{bmatrix} a & b \\ c & d \end{bmatrix}$$

is invertible if and only if $ad - bc \neq 0$. The number $ad - bc$ is called the **determinant** of the 2×2 matrix A. There are several common notations for determinants:

$$\det A = \det\begin{bmatrix} a & b \\ c & d \end{bmatrix} = \begin{vmatrix} a & b \\ c & d \end{vmatrix} = ad - bc. \tag{1}$$

In particular, note the vertical bars that distinguish a determinant from a matrix.

EXAMPLE 1

$$\begin{vmatrix} 3 & 7 \\ 4 & -6 \end{vmatrix} = (3)(-6) - (4)(7) = -46.$$

The determinant actually is a *function* that associates with each 2×2 matrix A the number $\det A$. In this section we list a number of properties of this determinant function that follow readily from the definition $\det A = ad - bc$. In succeeding sections we will see that analogous properties play an important role in the computation and application of determinants of higher order.

PROPERTY 1: If the 2×2 matrix B is obtained from A by multiplying one row of A by the constant k, then $\det B = k \det A$.

Thus when a row of a 2×2 matrix is multiplied by k, its determinant is also multiplied by k. For instance,

$$\begin{vmatrix} ka & kb \\ c & d \end{vmatrix} = (ka)(d) - (kb)(c) = k(ad - bc) = k\begin{vmatrix} a & b \\ c & d \end{vmatrix}.$$

Note the contrast between the formulas

$$\begin{vmatrix} ka & kb \\ c & d \end{vmatrix} = k\begin{vmatrix} a & b \\ c & d \end{vmatrix} \quad \text{and} \quad \begin{bmatrix} ka & kb \\ kc & kd \end{bmatrix} = k\begin{bmatrix} a & b \\ c & d \end{bmatrix}$$

for determinants and matrices, respectively.

PROPERTY 2: If the 2×2 matrix B is obtained by interchanging the two rows of A, then $\det B = -\det A$.

The reason that interchanging the rows of a 2×2 matrix changes the *sign* of its determinant is that

$$\begin{vmatrix} c & d \\ a & b \end{vmatrix} = bc - ad = -(ad - bc) = -\begin{vmatrix} a & b \\ c & d \end{vmatrix}.$$

PROPERTY 3: If the two rows of the 2×2 matrix A are identical, then $\det A = 0$.

This is obvious because

$$\begin{vmatrix} a & b \\ a & b \end{vmatrix} = ab - ab = 0.$$

PROPERTY 4: Suppose that the 2×2 matrices A_1, A_2, and B have the same second (or first) row, but that the first (or second) row of B is the sum of the corresponding rows of A_1 and A_2. Then $\det B = \det A_1 + \det A_2$.

For instance, if

$$A_1 = \begin{bmatrix} a_1 & b_1 \\ c & d \end{bmatrix}, \quad A_2 = \begin{bmatrix} a_2 & b_2 \\ c & d \end{bmatrix},$$

and

$$B = \begin{bmatrix} a_1 + a_2 & b_1 + b_2 \\ c & d \end{bmatrix},$$

then

$$\begin{aligned} \det B &= \begin{vmatrix} a_1 + a_2 & b_1 + b_2 \\ c & d \end{vmatrix} \\ &= (a_1 + a_2)d - (b_1 + b_2)c = (a_1 d - b_1 c) + (a_2 d - b_2 c) \\ &= \begin{vmatrix} a_1 & b_1 \\ c & d \end{vmatrix} + \begin{vmatrix} a_2 & b_2 \\ c & d \end{vmatrix} \end{aligned}$$

—that is, $\det B = \det A_1 + \det A_2$.

Properties 1 and 4 together are sometimes summarized by saying that the determinant of a 2×2 matrix is a linear function of each row.

PROPERTY 5: If the 2×2 matrix B is obtained by adding a constant multiple of one row of A to the other row, then $\det B = \det A$.

For instance, if the first row is multiplied by k and the result added to the second row, then

$$\begin{aligned}
\det B &= \begin{vmatrix} a & b \\ c + ka & d + kb \end{vmatrix} \\
&= \begin{vmatrix} a & b \\ c & d \end{vmatrix} + \begin{vmatrix} a & b \\ ka & kb \end{vmatrix} && \text{(by Property 4)} \\
&= \begin{vmatrix} a & b \\ c & d \end{vmatrix} + k\begin{vmatrix} a & b \\ a & b \end{vmatrix} && \text{(by Property 1)} \\
&= \det A + k \cdot 0 && \text{(by Property 3)},
\end{aligned}$$

and therefore $\det B = \det A$.

Note that Properties 1, 2, and 5 pertain to the effect on $\det A$ when an elementary row operation is performed on the 2×2 matrix A. The following property follows immediately from the definition in (1).

PROPERTY 6: The determinant of the 2×2 identity matrix I is $\det I = 1$.

The **transpose** of the 2×2 matrix A is the matrix A^T obtained by interchanging the off-diagonal elements of A. That is,

$$\text{if} \quad A = \begin{bmatrix} a & b \\ c & d \end{bmatrix} \quad \text{then} \quad A^T = \begin{bmatrix} a & c \\ b & d \end{bmatrix}.$$

For instance,

$$\begin{bmatrix} 3 & -4 \\ 5 & 6 \end{bmatrix}^T = \begin{bmatrix} 3 & 5 \\ -4 & 6 \end{bmatrix}.$$

It follows immediately from (1) that taking the transpose of the matrix A does not change its determinant.

PROPERTY 7: If A is a 2×2 matrix, then $\det A = \det A^T$.

Although Property 7 is obvious for 2×2 determinants, it has a big payoff: In each of Properties 1 through 5, the word *row* may be replaced throughout by the word *column*. In particular,

- If a single column of A is multiplied by k, then the determinant of A is multiplied by k (Property 1).
- If the two columns of A are interchanged, then the sign of $\det A$ is changed (Property 2).
- The determinant of A is not changed when a constant multiple of one column is added to the other column of A (Property 5).

The reason that these properties regarding columns follow from the corresponding properties regarding rows is that each *column* of A^T has the same elements as the corresponding *row* of A. In short, taking the transpose of A changes rows to columns (and columns to rows).

For instance, to derive Property 1 for columns from Property 1 for rows, we observe that

$$\begin{aligned}\begin{vmatrix} ka & b \\ kc & d \end{vmatrix} &= \begin{vmatrix} ka & kc \\ b & d \end{vmatrix} && \text{(by Property 7)} \\ &= k\begin{vmatrix} a & c \\ b & d \end{vmatrix} && \text{(by Property 1 for rows)}\end{aligned}$$

and therefore

$$\begin{vmatrix} ka & b \\ kc & d \end{vmatrix} = k\begin{vmatrix} a & b \\ c & d \end{vmatrix} \qquad \text{(by Property 7 again).}$$

In Problems 21–25 we ask you to deduce Properties 1–5 for columns directly from the definition of the determinant of a 2×2 matrix.

CRAMER'S RULE

As a first application of the properties of determinants listed previously, we show how to use determinants to solve a system

$$\begin{aligned} a_{11}x + a_{12}y &= b_1 \\ a_{21}x + a_{22}y &= b_2 \end{aligned} \tag{2}$$

of two linear equations in two unknowns. It follows from Theorems 2 and 7 in Section 1.5 that this system has a unique solution if and only if its coefficient determinant is nonzero:

$$\det A = \begin{vmatrix} a_{11} & a_{12} \\ a_{21} & a_{22} \end{vmatrix} \neq 0. \tag{3}$$

What we seek now are explicit formulas for the solution (x, y).

If the numbers x and y satisfy the equations in (2), then

$$\begin{aligned}\begin{vmatrix} b_1 & a_{12} \\ b_2 & a_{22} \end{vmatrix} &= \begin{vmatrix} a_{11}x + a_{12}y & a_{12} \\ a_{21}x + a_{22}y & a_{22} \end{vmatrix} \\ &= \begin{vmatrix} a_{11}x & a_{12} \\ a_{21}x & a_{22} \end{vmatrix} + \begin{vmatrix} a_{12}y & a_{12} \\ a_{22}y & a_{22} \end{vmatrix} && \text{(by Property 4)} \\ &= x\begin{vmatrix} a_{11} & a_{12} \\ a_{21} & a_{22} \end{vmatrix} + y\begin{vmatrix} a_{12} & a_{12} \\ a_{22} & a_{22} \end{vmatrix} && \text{(by Property 1)} \\ &= x \cdot \det A + y \cdot 0 && \text{(by Property 3);}\end{aligned}$$

thus

$$\begin{vmatrix} b_1 & a_{12} \\ b_2 & a_{22} \end{vmatrix} = x \cdot \det A. \tag{4}$$

Therefore division of each side in (4) by $\det A \neq 0$ yields the formula for x in the next theorem, and the formula for y can be derived similarly (Problem 26).

> ***Theorem*: *Cramer's Rule***
> The unique solution of the system
>
> $$\begin{aligned} a_{11}x + a_{12}y &= b_1 \\ a_{21}x + a_{22}y &= b_2 \end{aligned} \tag{2}$$
>
> with nonzero coefficient determinant is given by
>
> $$x = \frac{\begin{vmatrix} b_1 & a_{12} \\ b_2 & a_{22} \end{vmatrix}}{\begin{vmatrix} a_{11} & a_{12} \\ a_{21} & a_{22} \end{vmatrix}}, \qquad y = \frac{\begin{vmatrix} a_{11} & b_1 \\ a_{21} & b_2 \end{vmatrix}}{\begin{vmatrix} a_{11} & a_{12} \\ a_{21} & a_{22} \end{vmatrix}}. \tag{5}$$

Thus Cramer's rule gives each of x and y as a quotient of two determinants, the denominator in each case being the determinant of the coefficient matrix. In the numerator for x the coefficients a_{11} and a_{21} of x are replaced with the right-side coefficients b_1 and b_2, whereas in the numerator for y the coefficients of y are replaced with b_1 and b_2.

EXAMPLE 2 To apply Cramer's rule to solve the system

$$\begin{aligned} 7x + 8y &= 5 \\ 6x + 9y &= 4 \end{aligned}$$

with coefficient determinant

$$\begin{vmatrix} 7 & 8 \\ 6 & 9 \end{vmatrix} = 15,$$

we simply substitute in the equations in (5) to get

$$x = \frac{\begin{vmatrix} 5 & 8 \\ 4 & 9 \end{vmatrix}}{15} = \frac{13}{15}, \qquad y = \frac{\begin{vmatrix} 7 & 5 \\ 6 & 4 \end{vmatrix}}{15} = -\frac{2}{15}.$$

The remainder of Chapter 2 consists largely of defining $n \times n$ determinants and carrying out for higher order determinants what this section carries out for 2×2 determinants.

2.1 PROBLEMS

Evaluate the determinants in Problems 1–10.

1. $\begin{vmatrix} 17 & 17 \\ 29 & 29 \end{vmatrix}$

2. $\begin{vmatrix} 5 & 8 \\ 8 & 13 \end{vmatrix}$

3. $\begin{vmatrix} 4 & -8 \\ 8 & 9 \end{vmatrix}$

4. $\begin{vmatrix} 7 & 9 \\ 0 & -11 \end{vmatrix}$

5. $\begin{vmatrix} 7 & 11 \\ 4 & -8 \end{vmatrix}$

6. $\begin{vmatrix} 100 & 101 \\ 102 & 103 \end{vmatrix}$

7. $\begin{vmatrix} x-2 & -2 \\ 3 & x+3 \end{vmatrix}$

8. $\begin{vmatrix} x-y & x \\ x & x+y \end{vmatrix}$

9. $\begin{vmatrix} x+y & 2y \\ 2x & x+y \end{vmatrix}$

10. $\begin{vmatrix} x & x+1 \\ x+2 & x+3 \end{vmatrix}$

Use Cramer's rule to solve the systems in Problems 11–20.

11. $3x + 4y = 2$
$5x + 7y = 1$

12. $5x + 8y = 3$
$8x + 13y = 5$

13. $17x + 7y = 6$
$12x + 5y = 4$

14. $11x + 15y = 10$
$8x + 11y = 7$

15. $5x + 6y = 12$
$3x + 4y = 6$

16. $6x + 7y = 3$
$8x + 9y = 4$

17. $7x + 4y = 2$
$8x + 5y = 1$

18. $3x - 2y = 5$
$2x + 3y = 4$

19. $3x - 5y = 4$
$x + 4y = -3$

20. $5x - 2y = 25$
$2x + 5y = 10$

21–25. Deduce Properties 1–5 (respectively) for columns (rather than for rows) directly from the definition of a 2×2 matrix.

26. Derive the formula for y in Cramer's rule (Equation (5)) by evaluating the determinant

$$\begin{vmatrix} a_{11} & b_1 \\ a_{21} & b_2 \end{vmatrix}.$$

27. Use Cramer's rule to solve for x and y in terms of u and v:

$$u = 5x + 8y$$
$$v = 3x + 5y.$$

28. Use Cramer's rule to solve for x and y in terms of u and v (where θ is a constant):

$$u = x\cos\theta - y\sin\theta$$
$$v = x\sin\theta + y\cos\theta.$$

Recall that $\cos^2\theta + \sin^2\theta = 1$.

29. Use Cramer's rule to show that for each real value of λ the only solution of

$$2x - 3y = \lambda x$$
$$3x - 2y = \lambda y$$

is the trivial solution $x = 0$, $y = 0$.

30. If $\mathbf{x}$ and $\mathbf{y}$ are 2-vectors, then $[\mathbf{x}\ \ \mathbf{y}]$ is the 2×2 matrix with column vectors $\mathbf{x}$ and $\mathbf{y}$. Suppose that $\mathbf{x}_1$, $\mathbf{x}_2$, and $\mathbf{y}$ are 2-vectors and a_1 and a_2 are numbers. Show that

$$\det[a_1\mathbf{x}_1 + a_2\mathbf{x}_2\ \ \mathbf{y}] = a_1 \cdot \det[\mathbf{x}_1\ \ \mathbf{y}] + a_2 \cdot \det[\mathbf{x}_2\ \ \mathbf{y}].$$

31. Show that $(AB)^T = B^T A^T$ if A and B are arbitrary 2×2 matrices.

32. Consider the 2×2 matrices

$$A = \begin{bmatrix} a & b \\ c & d \end{bmatrix} \quad \text{and} \quad B = \begin{bmatrix} \mathbf{x} \\ \mathbf{y} \end{bmatrix}$$

where $\mathbf{x}$ and $\mathbf{y}$ denote the row vectors of B. Then the product AB can be written in the form

$$AB = \begin{bmatrix} a\mathbf{x} + b\mathbf{y} \\ c\mathbf{x} + d\mathbf{y} \end{bmatrix}.$$

Use this expression and the properties of determinants to show that

$$\det AB = (ad - bc)\begin{vmatrix} \mathbf{x} \\ \mathbf{y} \end{vmatrix} = (\det A)(\det B).$$

Thus the determinant of the product of matrices is equal to the product of their determinants.

2.2 Higher-Order Determinants

In this section we define 3×3 determinants in terms of 2×2 determinants, 4×4 determinants in terms of 3×3 determinants, and so on. This type of definition—one dimension at a time, with the definition in each dimension depending on its meaning in lower dimensions—is called an *inductive definition.*

The determinant $\det A = |a_{ij}|$ of a 3×3 matrix $A = [a_{ij}]$ is defined as follows:

$$\begin{vmatrix} a_{11} & a_{12} & a_{13} \\ a_{21} & a_{22} & a_{23} \\ a_{31} & a_{32} & a_{33} \end{vmatrix} = a_{11}\begin{vmatrix} a_{22} & a_{23} \\ a_{32} & a_{33} \end{vmatrix} - a_{12}\begin{vmatrix} a_{21} & a_{23} \\ a_{31} & a_{33} \end{vmatrix} + a_{13}\begin{vmatrix} a_{21} & a_{22} \\ a_{31} & a_{32} \end{vmatrix}. \tag{1}$$

Note the single minus sign on the right-hand side. The three 2×2 determinants in (1) are multiplied by the elements a_{11}, a_{12}, and a_{13} along the *first row* of the matrix A. Each of these elements a_{1j} is multiplied by the determinant of the 2×2 submatrix of A that remains after the row and column containing a_{1j} are deleted.

EXAMPLE 1

$$\begin{vmatrix} 5 & -2 & -3 \\ 4 & 0 & 1 \\ 3 & -1 & 2 \end{vmatrix} = (5)\begin{vmatrix} 0 & 1 \\ -1 & 2 \end{vmatrix} - (-2)\begin{vmatrix} 4 & 1 \\ 3 & 2 \end{vmatrix} + (-3)\begin{vmatrix} 4 & 0 \\ 3 & -1 \end{vmatrix}$$

$$= (5)(1) + (2)(5) - (3)(-4) = 27.$$

The definition of higher-order determinants is simplified by the following notation and terminology.

Definition: *Minors and Cofactors*

Let $A = [a_{ij}]$ be an $n \times n$ matrix. The ijth **minor** of A (also called the **minor** of a_{ij}) is the determinant M_{ij} of the $(n-1) \times (n-1)$ submatrix that remains after deleting the ith row and the jth column of A. The ijth **cofactor** A_{ij} of A (or the **cofactor** of a_{ij}) is defined to be

$$A_{ij} = (-1)^{i+j}M_{ij}. \tag{2}$$

For example, the minor of a_{12} in a 3×3 matrix is

$$M_{12} = \begin{vmatrix} \not{a}_{11} & \not{a}_{12} & \not{a}_{13} \\ a_{21} & a_{22} & a_{23} \\ a_{31} & a_{32} & a_{33} \end{vmatrix} = \begin{vmatrix} a_{21} & a_{23} \\ a_{31} & a_{33} \end{vmatrix}.$$

The minor of a_{32} in a 4×4 matrix is

$$M_{32} = \begin{vmatrix} a_{11} & a_{12} & a_{13} & a_{14} \\ a_{21} & a_{22} & a_{23} & a_{24} \\ \not{a}_{31} & \not{a}_{32} & \not{a}_{33} & \not{a}_{34} \\ a_{41} & a_{42} & a_{43} & a_{44} \end{vmatrix} = \begin{vmatrix} a_{11} & a_{13} & a_{14} \\ a_{21} & a_{23} & a_{24} \\ a_{41} & a_{43} & a_{44} \end{vmatrix}.$$

According to Equation (2), the cofactor A_{ij} is obtained by attaching the sign $(-1)^{i+j}$ to the minor M_{ij}. This sign is most easily remembered as the one that appears in the ijth position in checkerboard arrays such as

$$\begin{bmatrix} + & - & + \\ - & + & - \\ + & - & + \end{bmatrix} \quad \text{and} \quad \begin{bmatrix} + & - & + & - \\ - & + & - & + \\ + & - & + & - \\ - & + & - & + \end{bmatrix}.$$

Note that a plus sign always appears in the upper left corner and that the signs alternate both horizontally and vertically. In the 4×4 case, for instance,

$$\begin{array}{llll} A_{11} = +M_{11}, & A_{12} = -M_{12}, & A_{13} = +M_{13}, & A_{14} = -M_{14}, \\ A_{21} = -M_{21}, & A_{22} = +M_{22}, & A_{23} = -M_{23}, & A_{24} = +M_{24}, \end{array}$$

and so forth.

With this notation the definition of 3×3 determinants in (1) can be rewritten as

$$\begin{aligned} \det A &= a_{11}M_{11} - a_{12}M_{12} + a_{13}M_{13} \\ &= a_{11}A_{11} + a_{12}A_{12} + a_{13}A_{13}. \end{aligned} \tag{3}$$

The last formula is the **cofactor expansion** of det A along the *first row* of A. Its natural generalization yields the definition of the determinant of an $n \times n$ matrix, under the inductive assumption that $(n-1) \times (n-1)$ determinants have already been defined.

Definition: *$n \times n$ Determinants*

The **determinant** $\det A = |a_{ij}|$ of an $n \times n$ matrix $A = [a_{ij}]$ is defined to be

$$\det A = a_{11}A_{11} + a_{12}A_{12} + \cdots + a_{1n}A_{1n}. \tag{4}$$

Thus we multiply each element of the first row of A by its cofactor and then add these n products to get det A.

In numerical computations it frequently is more convenient to work first with minors rather than with cofactors and then attach signs in accord with the checkerboard pattern illustrated previously. Note that only determinants of *square* matrices are defined.

EXAMPLE 2 To evaluate the determinant of

$$A = \begin{bmatrix} 2 & 0 & 0 & -3 \\ 0 & -1 & 0 & 0 \\ 7 & 4 & 3 & 5 \\ -6 & 2 & 2 & 4 \end{bmatrix},$$

we observe that there are only two nonzero terms in the cofactor expansion along the first row. We need not compute the cofactors of zeros because they will be multiplied by zero in computing the determinant, and hence

$$\det A = +(2)\begin{vmatrix} -1 & 0 & 0 \\ 4 & 3 & 5 \\ 2 & 2 & 4 \end{vmatrix} - (-3)\begin{vmatrix} 0 & -1 & 0 \\ 7 & 4 & 3 \\ -6 & 2 & 2 \end{vmatrix}.$$

Each of the 3 × 3 determinants on the right-hand side has only a single nonzero term in its cofactor expansion along the first row, so

$$\det A = (2)(-1)\begin{vmatrix} 3 & 5 \\ 2 & 4 \end{vmatrix} + (3)(+1)\begin{vmatrix} 7 & 3 \\ -6 & 2 \end{vmatrix}$$

$$= (-2)(12 - 10) + (3)(14 + 18) = 92.$$

Note that if we could expand along the second row in Example 2, there would be only a single 3 × 3 determinant to evaluate. It is in fact true that a determinant can be evaluated by expansion along *any* row *or* column. The proof of the following theorem is discussed at the end of this section.

Theorem: *Cofactor Expansions of Determinants*
The determinant of an $n \times n$ matrix $A = [a_{ij}]$ can be obtained by expansion along any row or column. The cofactor expansion along the ith row is

$$\det A = a_{i1}A_{i1} + a_{i2}A_{i2} + \cdots + a_{in}A_{in}. \tag{5}$$

The cofactor expansion along the jth column is

$$\det A = a_{1j}A_{1j} + a_{2j}A_{2j} + \cdots + a_{nj}A_{nj}. \tag{6}$$

The formulas in (5) and (6) provide $2n$ different cofactor expansions of an $n \times n$ determinant. For $n = 3$, for instance, we have

$$\begin{aligned}\det A &= a_{11}A_{11} + a_{12}A_{12} + a_{13}A_{13} \\ &= a_{21}A_{21} + a_{22}A_{22} + a_{23}A_{23} \\ &= a_{31}A_{31} + a_{32}A_{32} + a_{33}A_{33} \\ &= a_{11}A_{11} + a_{21}A_{21} + a_{31}A_{31} \\ &= a_{12}A_{12} + a_{22}A_{22} + a_{32}A_{32} \\ &= a_{13}A_{13} + a_{23}A_{23} + a_{33}A_{33}\end{aligned}$$

In a specific example we naturally attempt to choose the expansion that requires the least computational labor.

EXAMPLE 3 To evaluate the determinant of

$$A = \begin{bmatrix} 7 & 6 & 0 \\ 9 & -3 & 2 \\ 4 & 5 & 0 \end{bmatrix}$$

we expand along the third column because it has only a single nonzero entry. Thus

$$\det A = -(2)\begin{vmatrix} 7 & 6 \\ 4 & 5 \end{vmatrix} = (-2)(35 - 24) = -22.$$

In addition to providing ways of evaluating determinants, the theorem on cofactor expansions is a valuable tool for investigating the general properties of determinants. For instance, it follows immediately from the formulas in (5) and (6) that *if the square matrix A has either an all-zero row or an all-zero column, then* $\det A = 0$. For example, by expanding along the second row we see immediately that

$$\begin{vmatrix} 17 & 33 & -24 \\ 0 & 0 & 0 \\ 80 & -62 & 41 \end{vmatrix} = 0.$$

We now list the seven properties of $n \times n$ determinants that are generalizations of Properties 1–7 in Section 2.1. Just as our definition of $n \times n$ determinants was inductive, the following discussion of their properties is inductive: We suppose that $n \geq 3$ and assume that Properties 1–7 have already been verified for $(n-1) \times (n-1)$ determinants.

PROPERTY 1: If the $n \times n$ matrix B is obtained from A by multiplying a single row (or column) of A by the constant k, then $\det B = k \det A$.

For instance, if the ith row of A is multiplied by k, then the elements *off* the ith row of A are unchanged. Hence for each $j = 1, 2, \ldots, n$, the ijth cofactors of A and B are equal: $A_{ij} = B_{ij}$. Therefore, expansion of B along the ith row gives

$$\begin{aligned} \det B &= (ka_{i1})B_{i1} + (ka_{i2})B_{i2} + \cdots + (ka_{in})B_{in} \\ &= k(a_{i1}A_{i1} + a_{i2}A_{i2} + \cdots + a_{in}A_{in}), \end{aligned}$$

and thus $\det B = k \det A$.

Property 1 implies simply that a constant can be factored out of a single row or column of a determinant. Thus we see that

$$\begin{vmatrix} 7 & 15 & -17 \\ -2 & 9 & 6 \\ 5 & -12 & 10 \end{vmatrix} = (3) \begin{vmatrix} 7 & 5 & -17 \\ -2 & 3 & 6 \\ 5 & -4 & 10 \end{vmatrix}$$

by factoring 3 out of the second column.

PROPERTY 2: If the $n \times n$ matrix B is obtained from A by interchanging two rows (or two columns), then $\det B = -\det A$.

To see why this is so, suppose (for instance) that the first row is *not* one of the two that are interchanged (recall that $n \geq 3$). Then for each $j = 1, 2, \ldots, n$, the cofactor B_{1j} is obtained by interchanging two rows of the cofactor A_{1j}. Therefore, $B_{1j} = -A_{1j}$ by Property 2 for $(n-1) \times (n-1)$ determinants. Because $b_{1j} = a_{1j}$ for each j, it follows by expanding along the first row that

$$\begin{aligned} \det B &= b_{11}B_{11} + b_{12}B_{12} + \cdots + b_{1n}B_{1n} \\ &= a_{11}(-A_{11}) + a_{12}(-A_{12}) + \cdots + a_{1n}(-A_{1n}) \\ &= -(a_{11}A_{11} + a_{12}A_{12} + \cdots + a_{1n}A_{1n}), \end{aligned}$$

and thus $\det B = -\det A$.

PROPERTY 3: If two rows (or two columns) of the $n \times n$ matrix A are identical, then $\det A = 0$.

To see why, let B denote the matrix obtained by interchanging the two identical rows of A. Then $B = A$, so $\det B = \det A$. But Property 2 implies that $\det B = -\det A$. Thus $\det A = -\det A$, and it follows immediately that $\det A = 0$.

PROPERTY 4: Suppose that the $n \times n$ matrices A_1, A_2, and B are identical except for their ith rows—that is, the other $n - 1$ rows of the three matrices are identical—and that the ith row of B is the sum of the ith rows of A_1 and A_2. Then

$$\det B = \det A_1 + \det A_2.$$

This result also holds if columns are involved instead of rows.

Property 4 is readily established by expanding B along its ith row. In Problem 29 we ask you to supply the details for a typical case. The main importance (at this point) of Property 4 is that it implies the following property relating determinants and elementary row operations.

PROPERTY 5: If the $n \times n$ matrix B is obtained by adding a constant multiple of one row (or column) of A to another row (or column) of A, then $\det B = \det A$.

Thus the value of a determinant is *not* changed either by the type of elementary row operation described or by the corresponding type of elementary column operation. The following computation with 3×3 matrices illustrates the general proof of Property 5. Let

$$A = \begin{bmatrix} a_{11} & a_{12} & a_{13} \\ a_{21} & a_{22} & a_{23} \\ a_{31} & a_{32} & a_{33} \end{bmatrix} \quad \text{and} \quad B = \begin{bmatrix} a_{11} & a_{12} & a_{13} + ka_{11} \\ a_{21} & a_{22} & a_{23} + ka_{21} \\ a_{31} & a_{32} & a_{33} + ka_{31} \end{bmatrix}.$$

So B is the result of adding k times the first column of A to its third column. Then

$$\det B = \begin{vmatrix} a_{11} & a_{12} & a_{13} + ka_{11} \\ a_{21} & a_{22} & a_{23} + ka_{21} \\ a_{31} & a_{32} & a_{33} + ka_{31} \end{vmatrix}$$

$$= \begin{vmatrix} a_{11} & a_{12} & a_{13} \\ a_{21} & a_{22} & a_{23} \\ a_{31} & a_{32} & a_{33} \end{vmatrix} + k \begin{vmatrix} a_{11} & a_{12} & a_{11} \\ a_{21} & a_{22} & a_{21} \\ a_{31} & a_{32} & a_{31} \end{vmatrix}. \tag{7}$$

Here we first applied Property 4 and then factored k out of the second summand with the aid of Property 1. Now the first determinant on the right-hand side in (7) is simply $\det A$, whereas the second determinant is zero by Property 3 (its first and third columns are identical). We therefore have shown that $\det B = \det A$, as desired.

Although we use only elementary row operations in reducing a matrix to echelon form, Properties 1, 2, and 5 imply that we may use both elementary row operations and the analogous elementary column operations in simplifying the evaluation of determinants.

EXAMPLE 4 The matrix

$$A = \begin{bmatrix} 2 & -3 & -4 \\ -1 & 4 & 2 \\ 3 & 10 & 1 \end{bmatrix}$$

has no zero elements to simplify the computation of its determinant *as it stands*, but we notice that we can "knock out" the first two elements of its third column by adding twice the first column to the third column. This gives

$$\det A = \begin{vmatrix} 2 & -3 & -4 \\ -1 & 4 & 2 \\ 3 & 10 & 1 \end{vmatrix} = \begin{vmatrix} 2 & -3 & 0 \\ -1 & 4 & 0 \\ 3 & 10 & 7 \end{vmatrix}$$

$$= (+7)\begin{vmatrix} 2 & -3 \\ -1 & 4 \end{vmatrix} = 35.$$

The moral of the example is this: Evaluate determinants with your eyes open.

An **upper triangular matrix** is a square matrix having only zeros *below* its main diagonal. A **lower triangular matrix** is a square matrix having only zeros *above* its main diagonal. A **triangular matrix** is one like

$$\begin{bmatrix} 3 & 6 & 10 \\ 0 & 5 & 8 \\ 0 & 0 & 7 \end{bmatrix} \quad \text{or} \quad \begin{bmatrix} 1 & 0 & 0 \\ 3 & 7 & 0 \\ 4 & 6 & 5 \end{bmatrix};$$

thus a triangular matrix is one that is either upper triangular or lower triangular. The next property tells us that determinants of triangular matrices are especially easy to evaluate.

PROPERTY 6: The determinant of a triangular matrix is equal to the product of its diagonal elements.

The reason is that the determinant of any triangular matrix can be evaluated as in the following computation:

$$\begin{vmatrix} 3 & 11 & 9 & 2 \\ 0 & -2 & 8 & -6 \\ 0 & 0 & 5 & 17 \\ 0 & 0 & 0 & -4 \end{vmatrix} = (3)\begin{vmatrix} -2 & 8 & -6 \\ 0 & 5 & 17 \\ 0 & 0 & -4 \end{vmatrix}$$

$$= (3)(-2)\begin{vmatrix} 5 & 17 \\ 0 & -4 \end{vmatrix} = (3)(-2)(5)(-4) = 120.$$

At each step we expand along the first column and pick up another diagonal element as a factor of the determinant.

EXAMPLE 5 To evaluate

$$\begin{vmatrix} 2 & -1 & 3 \\ -2 & 1 & 5 \\ 4 & -2 & 10 \end{vmatrix},$$

we first add the first row to the second and then subtract twice the first row from the third. This yields

$$\begin{vmatrix} 2 & -1 & 3 \\ -2 & 1 & 5 \\ 4 & -2 & 10 \end{vmatrix} = \begin{vmatrix} 2 & -1 & 3 \\ 0 & 0 & 8 \\ 0 & 0 & 4 \end{vmatrix} = 0,$$

because we produced a triangular matrix having a zero on its main diagonal. (Can you see an even quicker way to do it by keeping your eyes open?)

In Section 2.1 we defined the transpose of a 2×2 matrix. More generally, the **transpose** of the $m \times n$ matrix $A = [a_{ij}]$ is the $n \times m$ matrix A^T defined as follows:

$$A^T = [a_{ji}]. \tag{8}$$

Note the reversal of subscripts; this means that the element of A^T in its jth row and ith column is the element of A in the ith row and the jth column of A. Hence the rows of the transpose A^T are (in order) the columns of A, and the columns of A^T are the rows of A. Thus we obtain A^T by changing the rows of A into columns. For instance,

$$\begin{bmatrix} 2 & 0 & 5 \\ 4 & -1 & 7 \end{bmatrix}^T = \begin{bmatrix} 2 & 4 \\ 0 & -1 \\ 5 & 7 \end{bmatrix}$$

and

$$\begin{bmatrix} 7 & -2 & 6 \\ 1 & 2 & 3 \\ 5 & 0 & 4 \end{bmatrix}^T = \begin{bmatrix} 7 & 1 & 5 \\ -2 & 2 & 0 \\ 6 & 3 & 4 \end{bmatrix}.$$

If the matrix A is square then we get A^T by interchanging elements of A that are located symmetrically with respect to its main diagonal. Thus A^T is the mirror reflection of A through its main diagonal.

In Problems 31 and 32 we ask you to verify the following properties of the transpose operation (under the assumption that A and B are matrices of appropriate sizes and c is a number):

(i) $(A^T)^T = A$;
(ii) $(A + B)^T = A^T + B^T$;
(iii) $(cA)^T = cA^T$;
(iv) $(AB)^T = B^T A^T$.

PROPERTY 7: If A is a square matrix then $\det(A^T) = \det A$.

This property of determinants can be verified by writing the cofactor expansion of det A along its first *row* and the cofactor expansion of $\det(A^T)$ along its first *column.* When this is done we see that the two expansions are identical because the rows of A are the columns of A^T (see Problem 33).

*DETERMINANTS AND PERMUTATIONS

The proof of the theorem on row and column cofactor expansions involves an alternative interpretation of determinants that in more advanced treatments is usually taken as the original definition. Consider the following elementary scheme for evaluating a 3×3 determinant:

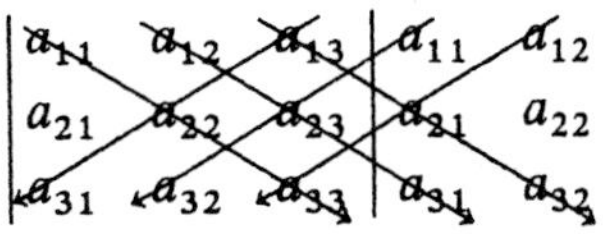

The first two columns of $A = [a_{ij}]$ are duplicated to its right. It is readily verified (see Problem 34) that det A is equal to the sum of the three products along the indicated diagonals that point down and to the *right,* minus the sum of the products along the three diagonals that point down and to the *left*:

$$\begin{aligned} \det A = &+a_{11}a_{22}a_{33} + a_{12}a_{23}a_{31} + a_{13}a_{21}a_{32} \\ &- a_{13}a_{22}a_{31} - a_{11}a_{23}a_{32} - a_{12}a_{21}a_{33}. \end{aligned} \tag{9}$$

REMARK This scheme works **only** in dimensions 2 and 3. Neither the analogous scheme nor anything resembling it gives the correct value of an $n \times n$ determinant with $n \geq 4$.

Note that each of the six terms on the right in (9) is of the form $\pm a_{1i}a_{2j}a_{3k}$, where $(i \quad j \quad k)$ is a **permutation** of $(1 \quad 2 \quad 3)$. That is, the triple $(i \quad j \quad k)$ consists of the three distinct numbers 1, 2, and 3 written in some specific order. The six terms in (9) correspond to the six possible permutations of $(1 \quad 2 \quad 3)$:

$$\begin{matrix} (1 \quad 2 \quad 3) & (2 \quad 1 \quad 3) & (3 \quad 1 \quad 2) \\ (1 \quad 3 \quad 2) & (2 \quad 3 \quad 1) & (3 \quad 2 \quad 1) \end{matrix} \tag{10}$$

The + and − signs in (9) can also be explained in terms of these permutations. A **transposition** of an ordered sequence of objects (such as the numbers 1, 2, 3) is the operation of *interchanging* some single pair of them. For instance, the operation $(1 \quad 2 \quad 3) \to (1 \quad 3 \quad 2)$ is a transposition that consists of interchanging 2 and 3. But it requires two transpositions to change $(1 \quad 2 \quad 3)$ into the permutation $(3 \quad 1 \quad 2)$:

$$(1 \quad 2 \quad 3) \to (3 \quad 2 \quad 1) \to (3 \quad 1 \quad 2).$$

Given a permutation $P = (i \quad j \quad k)$ of $(1 \quad 2 \quad 3)$, we denote by $s(P)$ the *minimum* number of transpositions required to change $(1 \quad 2 \quad 3)$ into $(i \quad j \quad k)$. For the six permutations in (10) it is easy to verify that

$$\begin{array}{lll} s(1 \quad 2 \quad 3) = 0, & s(2 \quad 1 \quad 3) = 1, & s(3 \quad 1 \quad 2) = 2, \\ s(1 \quad 3 \quad 2) = 1, & s(2 \quad 3 \quad 1) = 2, & s(3 \quad 2 \quad 1) = 1. \end{array} \tag{11}$$

Now for the point to all this: If you check each of the six terms in (9) you will find that the *sign* of the term $a_{1i}a_{2j}a_{3k}$ is $(-1)^{s(P)}$, where $P = (i \quad j \quad k)$. Therefore, we can rewrite (9) more concisely as

$$\det A = \sum_P (-1)^{s(P)} a_{1i}a_{2j}a_{3k}, \tag{12}$$

where there is one term on the right for each possible permutation $P = (i \quad j \quad k)$ of $(1 \quad 2 \quad 3)$.

The formula in (12) generalizes to determinants of higher order. If A is an $n \times n$ matrix, then

$$\det A = \sum_P (-1)^{s(P)} a_{1i_1}a_{2i_2} \cdots a_{ni_n}, \tag{13}$$

where there is one term on the right for each possible permutation $P = (i_1 \quad i_2 \quad \ldots \quad i_n)$ of $(1 \quad 2 \quad \ldots \quad n)$, and $s(P)$ denotes the minimum number of transpositions required to change $(1 \quad 2 \quad \ldots \quad n)$ into $(i_1 \quad i_2 \quad \ldots \quad i_n)$. The formula in (13) can be established by induction on n. Assuming its validity for $(n-1) \times (n-1)$ determinants, the formula can be verified for an $n \times n$ matrix A by expanding along its first row. It is fairly easy to see that this gives terms of the form $\pm a_{1i_1}a_{2i_2} \ldots a_{ni_n}$, but somewhat more difficult to check the signs.

Finally, the proof of the cofactor expansion theorem consists of verifying similarly that the cofactor expansion of det A along *any* row *or* column of A agrees with the formula in (13). The details are more lengthy than instructive, and therefore we omit them.

2.2 PROBLEMS

Evaluate each of the determinants in Problems 1–6 by inspection—that is, by applying one of the seven properties of determinants stated in this section.

1. $\begin{vmatrix} 1 & 1 & 1 \\ 1 & 1 & 1 \\ 1 & 1 & 1 \end{vmatrix}$

2. $\begin{vmatrix} 1 & 0 & 4 \\ 2 & 0 & 5 \\ 3 & 0 & 6 \end{vmatrix}$

3. $\begin{vmatrix} 0 & 1 & 0 \\ 1 & 0 & 0 \\ 0 & 0 & 1 \end{vmatrix}$

4. $\begin{vmatrix} 0 & 0 & 1 \\ 0 & 1 & 0 \\ 1 & 0 & 0 \end{vmatrix}$

5. $\begin{vmatrix} 1 & 2 & 3 \\ 0 & 4 & 5 \\ 0 & 0 & 6 \end{vmatrix}$

6. $\begin{vmatrix} 1 & 0 & 0 & 0 \\ 2 & 1 & 0 & 0 \\ 4 & 2 & 1 & 0 \\ 8 & 4 & 2 & 1 \end{vmatrix}$

Use cofactor expansions to evaluate the determinants in Problems 7–18. Expand along the row or column that minimizes the amount of computation that is required.

7. $\begin{vmatrix} 0 & -3 & 0 \\ 7 & 11 & 4 \\ 5 & -2 & 3 \end{vmatrix}$

8. $\begin{vmatrix} 5 & 0 & 6 \\ 9 & -3 & -1 \\ 4 & 0 & 5 \end{vmatrix}$

9. $\begin{vmatrix} 4 & 0 & 6 \\ 5 & 0 & 8 \\ 7 & -4 & -9 \end{vmatrix}$

10. $\begin{vmatrix} 2 & 4 & 5 \\ -1 & 3 & 6 \\ 0 & 0 & 7 \end{vmatrix}$

11. $\begin{vmatrix} 0 & 2 & -3 \\ 1 & 4 & -2 \\ 3 & 5 & 2 \end{vmatrix}$

12. $\begin{vmatrix} 2 & -1 & 3 \\ 3 & -4 & 0 \\ -1 & 2 & 1 \end{vmatrix}$

13. $\begin{vmatrix} 0 & 0 & 3 \\ 4 & 0 & 0 \\ 0 & 5 & 0 \end{vmatrix}$

14. $\begin{vmatrix} 2 & 1 & 0 \\ 1 & 2 & 1 \\ 0 & 1 & 2 \end{vmatrix}$

15. $\begin{vmatrix} 1 & 0 & 0 & 0 \\ 2 & 0 & 5 & 0 \\ 3 & 6 & 9 & 8 \\ 4 & 0 & 10 & 7 \end{vmatrix}$

16. $\begin{vmatrix} 5 & 11 & 8 & 7 \\ 3 & -2 & 6 & 23 \\ 0 & 0 & 0 & -3 \\ 0 & 4 & 0 & 17 \end{vmatrix}$

17. $\begin{vmatrix} 0 & 0 & 1 & 0 & 0 \\ 2 & 0 & 0 & 0 & 0 \\ 0 & 0 & 0 & 3 & 0 \\ 0 & 0 & 0 & 0 & 4 \\ 0 & 5 & 0 & 0 & 0 \end{vmatrix}$

18. $\begin{vmatrix} 3 & 0 & 11 & -5 & 0 \\ -2 & 4 & 13 & 6 & 5 \\ 0 & 0 & 5 & 0 & 0 \\ 7 & 6 & -9 & 17 & 7 \\ 0 & 0 & 8 & 2 & 0 \end{vmatrix}$

In Problems 19–24, evaluate each given determinant after first simplifying the computation (as in Example 4) by adding an appropriate multiple of some row or column to another.

19. $\begin{vmatrix} 1 & 1 & 1 \\ 2 & 2 & 2 \\ 3 & 3 & 3 \end{vmatrix}$

20. $\begin{vmatrix} 2 & 3 & 4 \\ -2 & -3 & 1 \\ 3 & 2 & 7 \end{vmatrix}$

21. $\begin{vmatrix} 3 & -2 & 5 \\ 0 & 5 & 17 \\ 6 & -4 & 12 \end{vmatrix}$

22. $\begin{vmatrix} -3 & 6 & 5 \\ 1 & -2 & -4 \\ 2 & -5 & 12 \end{vmatrix}$

23. $\begin{vmatrix} 1 & 2 & 3 & 4 \\ 0 & 5 & 6 & 7 \\ 0 & 0 & 8 & 9 \\ 2 & 4 & 6 & 9 \end{vmatrix}$

24. $\begin{vmatrix} 2 & 0 & 0 & -3 \\ 0 & 1 & 11 & 12 \\ 0 & 0 & 5 & 13 \\ -4 & 0 & 0 & 7 \end{vmatrix}$

In Problems 25 and 26, show that $\det A = 0$ without direct evaluation of the determinant.

25. $A = \begin{bmatrix} 1 & 1 & 1 \\ \frac{1}{a} & \frac{1}{b} & \frac{1}{c} \\ bc & ac & ab \end{bmatrix}$

26. $A = \begin{bmatrix} 1 & 1 & 1 \\ a & b & c \\ b+c & a+c & a+b \end{bmatrix}$

Each of Problems 27–30 lists a special case of one of Property 1 through Property 5. Verify it by expanding the determinant on the left-hand side along an appropriate row or column.

27. $\begin{vmatrix} ka_{11} & a_{12} & a_{13} \\ ka_{21} & a_{22} & a_{23} \\ ka_{31} & a_{32} & a_{33} \end{vmatrix} = k \begin{vmatrix} a_{11} & a_{12} & a_{13} \\ a_{21} & a_{22} & a_{23} \\ a_{31} & a_{32} & a_{33} \end{vmatrix}$

28. $\begin{vmatrix} a_{21} & a_{22} & a_{23} \\ a_{11} & a_{12} & a_{13} \\ a_{31} & a_{32} & a_{33} \end{vmatrix} = - \begin{vmatrix} a_{11} & a_{12} & a_{13} \\ a_{21} & a_{22} & a_{23} \\ a_{31} & a_{32} & a_{33} \end{vmatrix}$

29. $\begin{vmatrix} a_1 & b_1 & c_1 + d_1 \\ a_2 & b_2 & c_2 + d_2 \\ a_3 & b_3 & c_3 + d_3 \end{vmatrix}$

$$= \begin{vmatrix} a_1 & b_1 & c_1 \\ a_2 & b_2 & c_2 \\ a_3 & b_3 & c_3 \end{vmatrix} + \begin{vmatrix} a_1 & b_1 & d_1 \\ a_2 & b_2 & d_2 \\ a_3 & b_3 & d_3 \end{vmatrix}$$

30. $\begin{vmatrix} a_{11} + ka_{12} & a_{12} & a_{13} \\ a_{21} + ka_{22} & a_{22} & a_{23} \\ a_{31} + ka_{32} & a_{32} & a_{33} \end{vmatrix} = \begin{vmatrix} a_{11} & a_{12} & a_{13} \\ a_{21} & a_{22} & a_{23} \\ a_{31} & a_{32} & a_{33} \end{vmatrix}$

31. Suppose that A and B are matrices of the same size. Show that: (a) $(A^T)^T = A$; (b) $(cA)^T = cA^T$; and (c) $(A + B)^T = A^T + B^T$.

32. Let A and B be matrices such that AB is defined. Show that $(AB)^T = B^T A^T$. Begin by recalling that the ijth element of AB is obtained by multiplying elements in the ith row of A with those in the jth column of B. What is the ijth element of $B^T A^T$?

33. Let $A = [a_{ij}]$ be a 3×3 matrix. Show that $\det(A^T) = \det A$ by expanding $\det A$ along its first row and $\det(A^T)$ along its first column.

34. Verify the formula in (9) for the determinant of a 3×3 matrix.

Problems 35–38 deal with the **Vandermonde determinant**

$$V(x_1, x_2, \ldots, x_n) = \begin{vmatrix} 1 & x_1 & x_1^2 & \cdots & x_1^{n-1} \\ 1 & x_2 & x_2^2 & \cdots & x_2^{n-1} \\ \vdots & \vdots & \vdots & \ddots & \vdots \\ 1 & x_n & x_n^2 & \cdots & x_n^{n-1} \end{vmatrix}.$$

35. Show by direct computation that $V(a, b) = b - a$ and that

$$V(a, b, c) = \begin{vmatrix} 1 & a & a^2 \\ 1 & b & b^2 \\ 1 & c & c^2 \end{vmatrix} = (b - a)(c - a)(c - b).$$

36. The formulas in Problem 35 are the cases $n = 2$ and $n = 3$ of the general formula

$$V(x_1, x_2, \ldots, x_n) = \prod_{\substack{i,j=1 \\ i>j}}^{n} (x_i - x_j). \tag{14}$$

The case $n = 4$ is

$$V(x_1, x_2, x_3, x_4)$$
$$= (x_2 - x_1)(x_3 - x_1)(x_3 - x_2) \times (x_4 - x_1)(x_4 - x_2)(x_4 - x_3).$$

Prove this as follows. Given x_1, x_2, and x_3, define the cubic polynomial $P(y)$ to be

$$P(y) = \begin{vmatrix} 1 & x_1 & x_1^2 & x_1^3 \\ 1 & x_2 & x_2^2 & x_2^3 \\ 1 & x_3 & x_3^2 & x_3^3 \\ 1 & y & y^2 & y^3 \end{vmatrix}. \tag{15}$$

Because $P(x_1) = P(x_2) = P(x_3) = 0$ (why?), the roots of $P(y)$ are x_1, x_2, and x_3. It follows that

$$P(y) = k(y - x_1)(y - x_2)(y - x_3),$$

where k is the coefficient of y^3 in $P(y)$. Finally observe that expansion of the 4×4 determinant in (15) along its last row gives $k = V(x_1, x_2, x_3)$ and that $V(x_1, x_2, x_3, x_4) = P(x_4)$.

37. Generalize the argument in Problem 36 to prove the formula in (14) by induction on n. Begin

with the $(n-1)$st degree polynomial

$$P(y) = \begin{vmatrix} 1 & x_1 & x_1^2 & \cdots & x_1^{n-1} \\ 1 & x_2 & x_2^2 & \cdots & x_2^{n-1} \\ \vdots & \vdots & \vdots & \ddots & \vdots \\ 1 & x_{n-1} & x_{n-1}^2 & \cdots & x_{n-1}^{n-1} \\ 1 & y & y^2 & \cdots & y^{n-1} \end{vmatrix}.$$

38. Use the formula in (14) to evaluate the two determinants given next.

(a) $\begin{vmatrix} 1 & 1 & 1 & 1 \\ 1 & 2 & 4 & 8 \\ 1 & 3 & 9 & 27 \\ 1 & 4 & 16 & 64 \end{vmatrix}$ (b) $\begin{vmatrix} 1 & -1 & 1 & -1 \\ 1 & 2 & 4 & 8 \\ 1 & -2 & 4 & -8 \\ 1 & 3 & 9 & 27 \end{vmatrix}$

2.3

Determinants and Elementary Row Operations

As we described in Section 2.2, the determinant of any square matrix A can be evaluated directly by carrying out a cofactor expansion of $\det A$ along any row or column of A. Because this approach involves so much computational labor, it is more efficient instead to reduce A to an echelon matrix R. Because any square echelon matrix is (upper) triangular, the determinant of the echelon matrix R is simply the product of its diagonal elements. But because we have altered the matrix A by transforming it into R, the question is this: What effects do elementary row operations have on the determinant of A?

The following theorem summarizes Properties 1, 2, and 5 of Section 2.2 and tells how to keep track of the effect each elementary row operation will have on $\det A$ as we reduce A to echelon form. We use here the concise notation

$$|A| = \det A$$

for the determinant of the matrix A.

***Theorem 1**: Effect of Elementary Row Operations*

Let A be a square matrix and let B be the matrix obtained by performing one of the three types of elementary row operations on A.

(a) Type 1: If B is obtained by *dividing* some row of A by k, then

$$|A| = k|B|. \tag{1}$$

(b) Type 2: If B is obtained by interchanging two rows of A, then

$$|A| = -|B|. \tag{2}$$

(c) Type 3: If B is obtained by adding a multiple of some row of A to another row, then

$$|A| = |B|. \tag{3}$$

The following example shows how to lay out the computation of det A by using row operations to reduce A to echelon form.

EXAMPLE 1

$$\begin{vmatrix} 2 & 2 & -2 & 0 \\ -4 & 2 & 3 & 1 \\ 0 & 4 & -1 & -4 \\ 3 & 1 & 3 & -1 \end{vmatrix} = 2\begin{vmatrix} 1 & 1 & -1 & 0 \\ -4 & 2 & 3 & 1 \\ 0 & 4 & -1 & -4 \\ 3 & 1 & 3 & -1 \end{vmatrix}$$

We have divided row 1 by 2.

$$= 2\begin{vmatrix} 1 & 1 & -1 & 0 \\ 0 & 6 & -1 & 1 \\ 0 & 4 & -1 & -4 \\ 0 & -2 & 6 & -1 \end{vmatrix}$$

We have added 4 times row 1 to row 2, and -3 times row 1 to row 4.

$$= +2\begin{vmatrix} 1 & 1 & -1 & 0 \\ 0 & 0 & 17 & -2 \\ 0 & 0 & 11 & -6 \\ 0 & -2 & 6 & -1 \end{vmatrix}$$

We have added 3 times row 4 to row 2, and 2 times row 4 to row 3.

$$= -2\begin{vmatrix} 1 & 1 & -1 & 0 \\ 0 & -2 & 6 & -1 \\ 0 & 0 & 11 & -6 \\ 0 & 0 & 17 & -2 \end{vmatrix}$$

We have interchanged rows 2 and 4.

$$= -22\begin{vmatrix} 1 & 1 & -1 & 0 \\ 0 & -2 & 6 & -1 \\ 0 & 0 & 1 & -\frac{6}{11} \\ 0 & 0 & 17 & -2 \end{vmatrix}$$

We have divided row 3 by 11.

$$= -22\begin{vmatrix} 1 & 1 & -1 & 0 \\ 0 & -2 & 6 & -1 \\ 0 & 0 & 1 & -\frac{6}{11} \\ 0 & 0 & 0 & \frac{80}{11} \end{vmatrix}$$

We have added -17 times row 3 to row 4.

$$= (-22)(1)(-2)(1)(\tfrac{80}{11}) = 320.$$

If the square matrix A has only *integer* entries, it is always possible to carry out the reduction to echelon form without introducing any fractions. In the computation of determinants (as opposed to the solution of linear systems), we have the additional flexibility of using elementary *column* operations; their effects are precisely analogous to those of elementary row operations as described in Theorem 1. In Example 2 we illustrate this by finishing differently the evaluation shown in Example 1.

EXAMPLE 2

$$\begin{vmatrix} 2 & 2 & -2 & 0 \\ -4 & 2 & 3 & 1 \\ 0 & 4 & -1 & -4 \\ 3 & 1 & 3 & -1 \end{vmatrix} = -2\begin{vmatrix} 1 & 1 & -1 & 0 \\ 0 & -2 & 6 & -1 \\ 0 & 0 & 11 & -6 \\ 0 & 0 & 17 & -2 \end{vmatrix} \qquad \text{(As in Example 1.)}$$

$$= -2\begin{vmatrix} 1 & 1 & -1 & 0 \\ 0 & -2 & 5 & -1 \\ 0 & 0 & 5 & -6 \\ 0 & 0 & 15 & -2 \end{vmatrix} \qquad \text{We have added column 4 to column 3.}$$

$$= -2\begin{vmatrix} 1 & 1 & -1 & 0 \\ 0 & -2 & 5 & -1 \\ 0 & 0 & 5 & -6 \\ 0 & 0 & 0 & 16 \end{vmatrix} \qquad \text{We have added } -3 \text{ times row 3 to row 4.}$$

$$= (-2)(1)(-2)(5)(16) = 320.$$

Yet another alternative is to reduce only the first $n - 1$ rows of the $n \times n$ matrix A. We then directly calculate the 2×2 determinant that remains in the lower right-hand corner. We get $\det A$ by multiplying this 2×2 determinant by the preceding factors and diagonal elements. Thus

$$\begin{vmatrix} 2 & 2 & -2 & 0 \\ -4 & 2 & 3 & 1 \\ 0 & 4 & -1 & -4 \\ 3 & 1 & 3 & -1 \end{vmatrix} = -2\begin{vmatrix} 1 & 1 & -1 & 0 \\ 0 & -2 & 6 & -1 \\ 0 & 0 & 11 & -6 \\ 0 & 0 & 17 & -2 \end{vmatrix}$$

$$= (-2)(1)(-2)\begin{vmatrix} 11 & -6 \\ 17 & -2 \end{vmatrix} = (4)(-22 + 102) = 320.$$

COMPUTATIONAL EFFICIENCY

Example 1 illustrates the *method of elimination* for evaluating determinants. Whether one is working with pencil and paper or with a computer, most of the time is spent on multiplications and divisions; additions and subtractions are much easier and more rapid. So let us count the number of multiplication-division operations required to evaluate an $n \times n$ determinant by the method of elimination.

To obtain the $n - 1$ zeros in the first column, all n^2 elements of the matrix except the n entries in the first row must be changed, and each of these $n^2 - n$ new elements requires a multiplication-division operation. When we clear out the second column, however, we effectively work on an $(n - 1) \times (n - 1)$ submatrix, and so $(n - 1)^2 - (n - 1)$ additional such operations are required. At an intermediate stage in the elimination—when we are working on a lower right $k \times k$ submatrix—we see that $k^2 - k$ operations are required to clear out the next column. Hence the total number of multiplication-division operations required to reduce an $n \times n$ matrix to echelon form is

$$(n^2 - n) + \cdots + (3^2 - 3) + (2^2 - 2) + (1^2 - 1)$$
$$= (1^2 + 2^2 + \cdots + n^2) - (1 + 2 + \cdots + n).$$

If we use the known identities

$$1 + 2 + \cdots + n = \frac{n(n+1)}{2}$$

and

$$1^2 + 2^2 + \cdots + n^2 = \frac{n(n+1)(2n+1)}{6}$$

for the sum of the first n positive integers and the sum of their squares, we find that the total number of operations is

$$\frac{1}{6}\, n(n+1)(2n+1) - \frac{1}{2}\, n(n+1) = \frac{1}{3}\,(n^3 - n).$$

If n is larger than 3 then n^3 is *much* larger than n, so the total number of multiplication-division operations is approximately $n^3/3$. Therefore, we finally see that *the evaluation of an $n \times n$ determinant by the method of elimination requires about $n^3/3$ operations.*

Now let us count the number of operations required to evaluate an $n \times n$ determinant using cofactor expansions. If $n = 5$, for instance, then the cofactor expansion along a row or column requires computation of *five* 4×4 determinants. A cofactor expansion of each of these five 4×4 determinants involves *four* 3×3 determinants. Each of these four 3×3 determinants leads to *three* 2×2 determinants, and finally each of these 2×2 determinants requires *two* multiplications for its evaluation. Hence the total number of multiplications required to evaluate the original 5×5 determinant is

$$5 \cdot 4 \cdot 3 \cdot 2 = 5! = 120.$$

In general, *the number of multiplications required to evaluate an $n \times n$ determinant completely by cofactor expansions is*

$$n! = n \cdot (n-1) \cdots 3 \cdot 2 \cdot 1 \qquad (n \text{ factorial}).$$

The point to all this is that if n is fairly large, then $n!$ is much larger than the (approximate) number $n^3/3$ of operations required in the method of elimination. To see how much larger, look at the table in Figure 2.1. For instance, suppose we want to

n	6	10	25	50
$\frac{1}{3}n^3$	72	333	5208	41,667
$n!$	720	3,628,800	1.55×10^{25}	3.04×10^{64}

2.1 Operation counts for evaluating an $n \times n$ determinant by elimination and by cofactor expansion.

evaluate a 25×25 determinant using a fairly powerful microcomputer capable of performing 50,000 arithmetic operations per second. Using the method of elimination it would take only about a tenth of a second. But by complete cofactor expansion it would take about

$$\frac{1.55 \times 10^{25}}{5 \times 10^{4}} \approx 3.10 \times 10^{20} \qquad \text{(seconds);}$$

that is, about 10^{13} (10 trillion) years! Thus the evaluation of large determinants by cofactor expansion is quite impractical, and the method of elimination is always used instead.

DETERMINANTS AND INVERTIBILITY

We began this chapter with the remark that a 2×2 matrix A is invertible if and only if its determinant is nonzero: $|A| \neq 0$. Now we want to show that this result also holds for $n \times n$ matrices. This connection between determinants and invertibility is closely related to the fact that the determinant function "respects" matrix multiplication in the sense that

$$|AB| = |A||B| \tag{4}$$

if A and B are $n \times n$ matrices. Our first step is to show that Equation (4) holds if A is an *elementary matrix* obtained from the $n \times n$ identity matrix I by performing a single elementary row operation.

Lemma: *Multiplication by an Elementary Matrix*

If B is an $n \times n$ matrix and E is an $n \times n$ elementary matrix then

$$|EB| = |E||B|. \tag{5}$$

Proof This is really just a restatement of Theorem 1. For instance, suppose that E is obtained from I by multiplying the pth row by c, so that $|E| = c$. Then Theorem 5 in Section 1.5 tells us that the product EB is the result of multiplying the pth row of B by c. Therefore

$$|EB| = c|B| = |E||B|,$$

so we have verified Equation (5) for the first of the three types of elementary matrices. The verifications for the other two types are similar (see Problem 29). ■

Now let A be an $n \times n$ matrix whose invertibility we want to discuss, and let R be the *reduced* echelon form of A. If the elementary matrices $F_1, F_2, \ldots, F_k$ correspond to the elementary row operations that reduce A to R, then

$$F_k \cdots F_2 F_1 A = R \tag{6}$$

by Theorem 5 in Section 1.5. Recalling that every elementary matrix is invertible (Section 1.5), we can rewrite Equation (6) as

$$A = E_1 E_2 \cdots E_k R \tag{7}$$

where each $E_i = (F_i)^{-1}$ is an elementary matrix. It now follows by k applications of the lemma that

$$|A| = |E_1||E_2| \cdots |E_k||R|. \tag{8}$$

This relation is the key both to the proof of (4) and to the proof of the following theorem.

> ***Theorem 2:*** *Determinants and Invertibility*
> The $n \times n$ matrix A is invertible if and only if $\det A \neq 0$.

Proof If (as above) R is the reduced echelon form of A, then Theorem 6 in Section 1.5 implies that

$$A \text{ is invertible} \quad \text{if and only if} \quad R = I. \tag{9}$$

Because R is a *square* reduced echelon matrix, we see that *either* R is the identity matrix I and $|R| = 1$, *or* R has an all-zero row and, consequently, $|R| = 0$. Therefore

$$R = I \quad \text{if and only if} \quad |R| \neq 0. \tag{10}$$

Finally, because $|E| \neq 0$ if E is an elementary matrix, it follows immediately from Equation (8) that

$$|R| \neq 0 \quad \text{if and only if} \quad |A| \neq 0. \tag{11}$$

Combining the statements in (9), (10), and (11), we see that A is invertible if and only if $|A| \neq 0$. ∎

So now we can add the statement $\det A \neq 0$ to the list of equivalent properties of nonsingular matrices stated in Theorem 7 of Section 1.5. Indeed, some texts *define* the square matrix A to be nonsingular if and only if $\det A \neq 0$.

EXAMPLE 3 According to Problem 35 in Section 2.2, the determinant of the matrix

$$V = \begin{bmatrix} 1 & a & a^2 \\ 1 & b & b^2 \\ 1 & c & c^2 \end{bmatrix}$$

is

$$|V| = (b - a)(c - a)(c - b).$$

Note that $|V| \neq 0$ if and only if the three numbers a, b, and c are *distinct*. Hence it follows from Theorem 2 that V is invertible if and only if a, b, and c are distinct. For instance, with $a = -2$, $b = 3$, and $c = -4$ we see that the matrix

$$\begin{bmatrix} 1 & -2 & 4 \\ 1 & 3 & 9 \\ 1 & -4 & 16 \end{bmatrix}$$

is invertible.

Theorem 3: *Determinants and Matrix Products*

If A and B are $n \times n$ matrices then

$$|AB| = |A||B|. \tag{4}$$

Proof If R is the reduced echelon form of A, then we see that

$$A = E_1E_2 \cdots E_kR \tag{7}$$

where E_1, $E_2, \ldots,$ and E_k are elementary matrices. Hence

$$AB = E_1E_2 \cdots E_kRB.$$

We now take the determinant of both sides, using the lemma stated earlier to "split off" the elementary matrices:

$$\begin{aligned} |AB| &= |E_1||E_2E_3 \cdots E_kRB| && \text{(lemma once)} \\ &= |E_1||E_2||E_3 \cdots E_kRB| && \text{(lemma twice)} \\ &= |E_1E_2||E_3 \cdots E_kRB|. && \text{(lemma thrice)} \end{aligned}$$

After $2k - 1$ steps we get

$$|AB| = |E_1E_2 \cdots E_k||RB|. \tag{12}$$

The remainder of the proof depends on whether or not A is invertible.

If A *is* invertible then $R = I$, so Equation (7) yields

$$A = E_1E_2 \cdots E_k$$

and also that $RB = IB = B$. In this case the meaning of Equation (12) is precisely that $|AB| = |A||B|$.

If A is *not* invertible then $|A| = 0$ by Theorem 2. Also, as we noted previously, the reduced echelon form R of A has an all-zero row in this case. Hence it follows from the definition of matrix multiplication that the product RB has an all-zero row, and therefore $|RB| = 0$. In this case Equation (12) implies that $|AB| = 0$. Because both $|A| = 0$ and $|AB| = 0$, the equation $|AB| = |A||B|$ holds, and the proof is complete. ■

The fact that $|AB| = |A||B|$ seems so natural that we might fail to note that it is also quite remarkable. Contrast the simplicity of the equation $|AB| = |A||B|$ with the complexity of the seemingly unrelated definitions of determinants and matrix products. For another contrast, we can mention that $|A + B|$ is generally *not* equal to $|A| + |B|$ (see Problem 23).

As a first application of Theorem 3 we can calculate the determinant of the *inverse* of an invertible matrix A:

$$AA^{-1} = I,$$

so

$$|A||A^{-1}| = |AA^{-1}| = |I| = 1,$$

and therefore

$$|A^{-1}| = \frac{1}{|A|}. \tag{13}$$

Now $|A| \neq 0$ because A is invertible. Thus $\det(A^{-1})$ *is the reciprocal of* $\det A$.

EXAMPLE 4 In Example 1 we found the determinant of

$$A = \begin{bmatrix} 2 & 2 & -2 & 0 \\ -4 & 2 & 3 & 1 \\ 0 & 4 & -1 & -4 \\ 3 & 1 & 3 & -1 \end{bmatrix}$$

to be $|A| = 320 \neq 0$. Hence A is invertible, and *without* finding A^{-1} we know from Equation (13) that $|A^{-1}| = 1/320$.

2.3 PROBLEMS

Use the method of elimination to evaluate the determinants in Problems 1–20.

1. $\begin{vmatrix} -2 & 2 & -4 \\ 3 & 0 & 1 \\ 1 & -2 & 2 \end{vmatrix}$

2. $\begin{vmatrix} 1 & 6 & 4 \\ 4 & 3 & 1 \\ 3 & -2 & -4 \end{vmatrix}$

3. $\begin{vmatrix} 2 & 1 & -2 \\ 5 & 1 & 3 \\ 4 & 3 & -2 \end{vmatrix}$

4. $\begin{vmatrix} 1 & 4 & 5 \\ 4 & 2 & 5 \\ -3 & 3 & -1 \end{vmatrix}$

5. $\begin{vmatrix} 3 & 4 & 3 \\ 3 & 2 & 1 \\ -3 & 2 & 4 \end{vmatrix}$

6. $\begin{vmatrix} 1 & -3 & -3 \\ -1 & 1 & 2 \\ 2 & -3 & -3 \end{vmatrix}$

7. $\begin{vmatrix} 1 & 4 & 2 \\ 4 & 2 & 1 \\ 2 & -2 & -5 \end{vmatrix}$

8. $\begin{vmatrix} 3 & 2 & -3 \\ 0 & 3 & 2 \\ 2 & 3 & -5 \end{vmatrix}$

9. $\begin{vmatrix} -4 & 4 & -1 \\ -1 & -2 & 2 \\ 1 & 4 & 3 \end{vmatrix}$

10. $\begin{vmatrix} 4 & 2 & -2 \\ 3 & 1 & -5 \\ -5 & -4 & 3 \end{vmatrix}$

11. $\begin{vmatrix} -2 & 5 & 4 \\ 5 & 3 & 1 \\ 1 & 4 & 5 \end{vmatrix}$

12. $\begin{vmatrix} 2 & 4 & -2 \\ -5 & -4 & -1 \\ -4 & 2 & 1 \end{vmatrix}$

13. $\begin{vmatrix} 2 & 3 & 3 & 1 \\ 0 & 4 & 3 & -3 \\ 2 & -1 & -1 & -3 \\ 0 & -4 & -3 & 2 \end{vmatrix}$

14. $\begin{vmatrix} 1 & 4 & 4 & 1 \\ 0 & 1 & -2 & 2 \\ 3 & 3 & 1 & 4 \\ 0 & 1 & -3 & -2 \end{vmatrix}$

15. $\begin{vmatrix} 1 & 0 & 0 & 3 \\ 0 & 1 & -2 & 0 \\ -2 & 3 & -2 & 3 \\ 0 & -3 & 3 & 3 \end{vmatrix}$

16. $\begin{vmatrix} 1 & 2 & 1 & -1 \\ 2 & 1 & 3 & 3 \\ 0 & 1 & -2 & 3 \\ -1 & 4 & -2 & 4 \end{vmatrix}$

17. $\begin{vmatrix} 0 & 1 & 1 & 1 \\ 3 & -1 & -1 & -1 \\ -1 & 2 & -3 & -2 \\ 2 & 3 & -2 & -3 \end{vmatrix}$

18. $\begin{vmatrix} 1 & 3 & 1 & 3 \\ -2 & -3 & 1 & 4 \\ 1 & -1 & 0 & 1 \\ 4 & -1 & 4 & 0 \end{vmatrix}$

19. $\begin{vmatrix} 1 & -1 & 1 & -1 \\ 1 & -1 & 3 & 2 \\ 4 & 2 & 1 & 3 \\ 3 & 3 & 1 & -4 \end{vmatrix}$

20. $\begin{vmatrix} 3 & 1 & -2 & 1 \\ 1 & 1 & -3 & 2 \\ 2 & 0 & 2 & 3 \\ 3 & 3 & 1 & -3 \end{vmatrix}$

21. Suppose that A is a 2×2 matrix with $|A| = 2$. Let $B = 3A$ and $C = 6B^{-1}$. Find $|C|$.

22. Suppose that A is a 3×3 matrix with $|A| = 4$. Let $B = 2A$ and $C = 4B^{-1}$. Find $|C|$.

23. If $A = \begin{bmatrix} a & b \\ c & d \end{bmatrix}$ and $B = I$ (the 2×2 identity matrix), show that $|A + B| = |A| + |B|$ if and only if $a + d = 0$.

24. Suppose that $A^2 = A$. Prove that $|A| = 0$ or $|A| = 1$.

25. Suppose that $A^n = 0$ (the zero matrix) for some positive integer n. Prove that $|A| = 0$.

26. The square matrix A is called **orthogonal** provided that $A^T = A^{-1}$. Show that the determinant of such a matrix must be either $+1$ or -1.

27. The matrices A and B are said to be **similar** provided that $A = P^{-1}BP$ for some invertible matrix P. Show that if A and B are similar then $|A| = |B|$.

28. The matrix A is said to be **skew-symmetric** provided that $A^T = -A$.
(a) Prove that if A is a 3×3 skew-symmetric matrix then $|A| = 0$.
(b) Find a 2×2 skew-symmetric matrix A such that $|A| \neq 0$.

29. Show that $|EB| = |E||B|$ if the elementary matrix E is obtained from the identity matrix by:
(a) Interchanging two rows;
(b) Adding a multiple of one row to another.

30. Deduce from Theorems 2 and 3 that if A and B are $n \times n$ invertible matrices, then AB is invertible if and only if both A and B are invertible.

31. Let A and B be $n \times n$ matrices. Suppose it is known that *either* $AB = I$ *or* $BA = I$. Use the result of Problem 30 to conclude that $B = A^{-1}$.

32. Show that

$$\begin{vmatrix} 2 & 1 \\ 1 & 2 \end{vmatrix} = 3 \quad \text{and} \quad \begin{vmatrix} 2 & 1 & 0 \\ 1 & 2 & 1 \\ 0 & 1 & 2 \end{vmatrix} = 4.$$

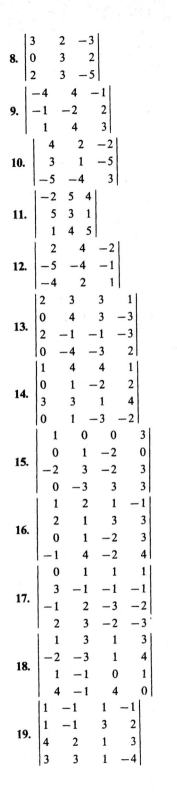

33. Expand along the first row and use the results of Problem 32 to show that

$$\begin{vmatrix} 2 & 1 & 0 & 0 \\ 1 & 2 & 1 & 0 \\ 0 & 1 & 2 & 1 \\ 0 & 0 & 1 & 2 \end{vmatrix} = 5.$$

34. Consider the $n \times n$ determinant

$$B_n = \begin{vmatrix} 2 & 1 & 0 & 0 & \cdots & 0 & 0 \\ 1 & 2 & 1 & 0 & \cdots & 0 & 0 \\ 0 & 1 & 2 & 1 & \cdots & 0 & 0 \\ \vdots & \vdots & \vdots & \vdots & \ddots & \vdots & \vdots \\ 0 & 0 & 0 & 0 & \cdots & 2 & 1 \\ 0 & 0 & 0 & 0 & \cdots & 1 & 2 \end{vmatrix}$$

in which each entry on the main diagonal is a 2, each entry on the two adjacent diagonals is a 1, and every other entry is zero.

(a) Expand along the first row to show that

$$B_n = 2B_{n-1} - B_{n-2}.$$

(b) Prove by induction on n that $B_n = n + 1$ for $n \geq 2$.

2.4 Cramer's Rule and Inverse Matrices

We stated Cramer's rule for the solution of a system of two equations in two unknowns in Section 2.1. Now that we know how to work with $n \times n$ determinants, we can generalize Cramer's rule to give explicit formulas for the solution of a system of n linear equations in n unknowns.

Suppose that we need to solve the $n \times n$ linear system

$$A\mathbf{x} = \mathbf{b} \tag{1}$$

where

$$A = [a_{ij}], \qquad \mathbf{x} = \begin{bmatrix} x_1 \\ x_2 \\ \vdots \\ x_n \end{bmatrix} \quad \text{and} \quad \mathbf{b} = \begin{bmatrix} b_1 \\ b_2 \\ \vdots \\ b_n \end{bmatrix}. \tag{2}$$

We assume that the coefficient matrix A is invertible, so we know in advance that a unique solution $\mathbf{x}$ of (1) exists. The question is how to write $\mathbf{x}$ explicitly in terms of the coefficients a_{ij} and the constants b_i. In the following discussion we think of $\mathbf{x}$ as a fixed (though as yet unknown) vector.

If we denote by $\mathbf{a}_1, \mathbf{a}_2, \ldots, \mathbf{a}_n$ the column vectors of the $n \times n$ matrix A, then

$$A = [\mathbf{a}_1 \quad \mathbf{a}_2 \quad \cdots \quad \mathbf{a}_n]. \tag{3}$$

By Fact 1 in Section 1.5, we can rewrite Equation (1) as

$$x_1\mathbf{a}_1 + x_2\mathbf{a}_2 + \cdots + x_n\mathbf{a}_n = \mathbf{b}.$$

Thus the constant vector $\mathbf{b}$ is expressed in terms of the entries $x_1, x_2, \dots, x_n$ of the solution vector $\mathbf{x}$ and the column vectors of A by

$$\mathbf{b} = \sum_{j=1}^{n} x_j \mathbf{a}_j. \tag{4}$$

The trick for finding the ith unknown x_i is to compute the determinant of the matrix

$$[\mathbf{a}_1 \quad \cdots \quad \mathbf{b} \quad \cdots \quad \mathbf{a}_n] = \begin{bmatrix} a_{11} & \cdots & b_1 & \cdots & a_{1n} \\ a_{21} & \cdots & b_2 & \cdots & a_{2n} \\ \vdots & \ddots & \vdots & \ddots & \vdots \\ a_{n1} & \cdots & b_n & \cdots & a_{nn} \end{bmatrix} \tag{5}$$

that we obtain by replacing the ith column $\mathbf{a}_i$ of A with the constant vector $\mathbf{b}$. Using Equation (4) to substitute for $\mathbf{b}$, we find that

$$\begin{aligned} |\mathbf{a}_1 \quad \cdots \quad \mathbf{b} \quad \cdots \quad \mathbf{a}_n| &= \left|\mathbf{a}_1 \quad \cdots \quad \sum_{j=1}^{n} x_j \mathbf{a}_j \quad \cdots \quad \mathbf{a}_n\right| \\ &= \sum_{j=1}^{n} |\mathbf{a}_1 \quad \cdots \quad x_j \mathbf{a}_j \quad \cdots \quad \mathbf{a}_n| \qquad \text{(by Property 4 of determinants)} \\ &= \sum_{j=1}^{n} x_j |\mathbf{a}_1 \quad \cdots \quad \mathbf{a}_j \quad \cdots \quad \mathbf{a}_n| \qquad \text{(by Property 1 of determinants).} \end{aligned}$$

Note that in the jth term of this summation, the vector $\mathbf{a}_j$ appears in the ith position. Thus we have found that

$$\begin{aligned} |\mathbf{a}_1 \quad \cdots \quad \mathbf{b} \quad \cdots \quad \mathbf{a}_n| = {} & x_1 |\mathbf{a}_1 \quad \mathbf{a}_2 \quad \cdots \quad \mathbf{a}_1 \quad \cdots \quad \mathbf{a}_n| \\ & + x_2 |\mathbf{a}_1 \quad \mathbf{a}_2 \quad \cdots \quad \mathbf{a}_2 \quad \cdots \quad \mathbf{a}_n| \\ & \vdots \\ & + x_i |\mathbf{a}_1 \quad \mathbf{a}_2 \quad \cdots \quad \mathbf{a}_i \quad \cdots \quad \mathbf{a}_n| \\ & \vdots \\ & + x_n |\mathbf{a}_1 \quad \mathbf{a}_2 \quad \cdots \quad \mathbf{a}_n \quad \cdots \quad \mathbf{a}_n|. \end{aligned}$$

Of the n determinants on the right-hand side here, all but the ith one have two identical columns and therefore are equal to zero. The coefficient of x_i in the ith term is simply

$$|A| = |\mathbf{a}_1 \quad \mathbf{a}_2 \quad \cdots \quad \mathbf{a}_i \quad \cdots \quad \mathbf{a}_n|.$$

Consequently a result of our computation is that

$$|\mathbf{a}_1 \quad \cdots \quad \mathbf{b} \quad \cdots \quad \mathbf{a}_n| = x_i |A|. \tag{6}$$

We get the desired simple formula for x_i after we divide each side by $|A| \neq 0$.

Theorem 1: *Cramer's Rule*

Consider the $n \times n$ linear system $A\mathbf{x} = \mathbf{b}$ with

$$A = [\mathbf{a}_1 \quad \mathbf{a}_2 \quad \cdots \quad \mathbf{a}_n].$$

If $|A| \neq 0$, then the ith entry of the unique solution $\mathbf{x} = (x_1, x_2, \ldots, x_n)$ is given by

$$x_i = \frac{|\mathbf{a}_1 \quad \cdots \quad \mathbf{b} \quad \cdots \quad \mathbf{a}_n|}{|A|} = \frac{1}{|A|}\begin{vmatrix} a_{11} & \cdots & b_1 & \cdots & a_{1n} \\ a_{21} & \cdots & b_2 & \cdots & a_{2n} \\ \vdots & \ddots & \vdots & \ddots & \vdots \\ a_{n1} & \cdots & b_n & \cdots & a_{nn} \end{vmatrix} \tag{7}$$

where in the last expression the constant vector $\mathbf{b}$ replaces the ith column vector $\mathbf{a}_i$ of A.

For instance, the unique solution (x_1, x_2, x_3) of the 3×3 system

$$\begin{aligned} a_{11}x_1 + a_{12}x_2 + a_{13}x_3 &= b_1 \\ a_{21}x_1 + a_{22}x_2 + a_{23}x_3 &= b_2 \\ a_{31}x_1 + a_{32}x_2 + a_{33}x_3 &= b_3 \end{aligned} \tag{8}$$

with $|A| = |a_{ij}| \neq 0$ is given by the formulas

$$\begin{aligned} x_1 &= \frac{1}{|A|}\begin{vmatrix} b_1 & a_{12} & a_{13} \\ b_2 & a_{22} & a_{23} \\ b_3 & a_{32} & a_{33} \end{vmatrix}, \\ x_2 &= \frac{1}{|A|}\begin{vmatrix} a_{11} & b_1 & a_{13} \\ a_{21} & b_2 & a_{23} \\ a_{31} & b_3 & a_{33} \end{vmatrix}, \\ x_3 &= \frac{1}{|A|}\begin{vmatrix} a_{11} & a_{12} & b_1 \\ a_{21} & a_{22} & b_2 \\ a_{31} & a_{32} & b_3 \end{vmatrix}. \end{aligned} \tag{9}$$

EXAMPLE 1 Use Cramer's rule to solve the system

$$\begin{aligned} x_1 + 4x_2 + 5x_3 &= 2 \\ 4x_1 + 2x_2 + 5x_3 &= 3 \\ -3x_1 + 3x_2 - x_3 &= 1. \end{aligned}$$

Solution We find that

$$|A| = \begin{vmatrix} 1 & 4 & 5 \\ 4 & 2 & 5 \\ -3 & 3 & -1 \end{vmatrix} = 29,$$

and then the formulas in (9) yield

$$x_1 = \frac{1}{29}\begin{vmatrix} 2 & 4 & 5 \\ 3 & 2 & 5 \\ 1 & 3 & -1 \end{vmatrix} = \frac{33}{29},$$

$$x_2 = \frac{1}{29}\begin{vmatrix} 1 & 2 & 5 \\ 4 & 3 & 5 \\ -3 & 1 & -1 \end{vmatrix} = \frac{35}{29},$$

and

$$x_3 = \frac{1}{29}\begin{vmatrix} 1 & 4 & 2 \\ 4 & 2 & 3 \\ -3 & 3 & 1 \end{vmatrix} = -\frac{23}{29}.$$

Note that the solution of an $n \times n$ linear system using Cramer's rule requires the evaluation of $n + 1$ determinants, each of size $n \times n$. Even if we use the method of elimination of Section 2.3, each of these $n + 1$ determinants requires approximately $n^3/3$ multiplication-division operations, so the whole solution requires approximately $(n + 1)(n^3/3) \approx n^4/3$ operations. But the solution of the system by Gaussian elimination followed by back substitution as in Section 1.2 requires only about $n^3/3$ operations and is therefore preferable to Cramer's rule for large systems. Consequently Cramer's rule is primarily of theoretical importance and is seldom used for the numerical solution of systems with more than two or three unknowns.

INVERSES AND THE ADJOINT MATRIX

We now use Cramer's rule to develop an explicit formula for the inverse A^{-1} of the invertible matrix A. First we need to rewrite Cramer's rule more concisely. Expansion of the determinant in the numerator in Equation (7) along its ith column yields

$$x_i = \frac{1}{|A|}(b_1A_{1i} + b_2A_{2i} + \cdots + b_nA_{ni}), \tag{10}$$

because the cofactor of b_p is simply the cofactor A_{pi} of a_{pi} in $|A|$. The formula in Equation (10) gives the solution vector

$$\mathbf{x} = \begin{bmatrix} x_1 \\ x_2 \\ \vdots \\ x_n \end{bmatrix} = \frac{1}{|A|}\begin{bmatrix} b_1A_{11} + b_2A_{21} + \cdots + b_nA_{n1} \\ b_1A_{12} + b_2A_{22} + \cdots + b_nA_{n2} \\ \vdots \\ b_1A_{1n} + b_2A_{2n} + \cdots + b_nA_{nn} \end{bmatrix}.$$

Then the definition of matrix multiplication yields

$$\mathbf{x} = \frac{1}{|A|}\begin{bmatrix} A_{11} & A_{21} & \cdots & A_{n1} \\ A_{12} & A_{22} & \cdots & A_{n2} \\ \vdots & \vdots & \ddots & \vdots \\ A_{1n} & A_{2n} & \cdots & A_{nn} \end{bmatrix}\begin{bmatrix} b_1 \\ b_2 \\ \vdots \\ b_n \end{bmatrix} \tag{11}$$

for the solution $\mathbf{x}$ of $A\mathbf{x} = \mathbf{b}$.

Observe that the double subscripts in (11) are reversed from their usual order; the element in the ith row and jth column is A_{ji} (rather than A_{ij}). We therefore see in (11) the *transpose* of the **cofactor matrix** $[A_{ij}]$ of the $n \times n$ matrix A. The transpose of the cofactor matrix of A is called the **adjoint matrix** of A and is denoted by

$$\text{adj } A = [A_{ij}]^T = [A_{ji}]. \tag{12}$$

With the aid of this notation, Cramer's rule as expressed in Equation (11) can be written in the especially simple form

$$\mathbf{x} = \frac{[A_{ji}]\mathbf{b}}{|A|} = \frac{(\text{adj } A)\mathbf{b}}{|A|}. \tag{13}$$

The fact that the formula in (13) gives the unique solution $\mathbf{x}$ of $A\mathbf{x} = \mathbf{b}$ implies that

$$A\,\frac{(\text{adj } A)\mathbf{b}}{|A|} = \mathbf{b} \tag{14}$$

for every n-vector $\mathbf{b}$. If we write

$$C = \frac{\text{adj } A}{|A|} \tag{15}$$

for brevity, then

$$AC\mathbf{b} = \mathbf{b} \tag{16}$$

for every n-vector $\mathbf{b}$. From this it follows (one column at a time, as we use Fact 2 in Section 1.5) that

$$ACB = B \tag{17}$$

for every matrix B having n rows. In particular, with $B = I$ (the $n \times n$ identity matrix), we see that

$$AC = I. \tag{18}$$

Therefore we have discovered that the matrix C as defined in Equation (15) is the inverse matrix A^{-1} of A.

Theorem 2: *The Inverse Matrix*
The inverse of the invertible matrix A is given by the formula

$$A^{-1} = \frac{\text{adj } A}{|A|} = \frac{[A_{ij}]^T}{|A|} \tag{19}$$

where, as usual, A_{ij} is the ijth cofactor of A; that is, A_{ij} is the product of $(-1)^{i+j}$ and the ijth minor of A.

EXAMPLE 2 Apply the formula in (19) to find the inverse of the matrix

$$A = \begin{bmatrix} 1 & 4 & 5 \\ 4 & 2 & 5 \\ -3 & 3 & -1 \end{bmatrix}$$

of Example 1, in which we found that $|A| = 29$.

Solution First we calculate the cofactors of A, arranging our computations in a natural 3×3 array:

$$A_{11} = +\begin{vmatrix} 2 & 5 \\ 3 & -1 \end{vmatrix} = -17, \quad A_{12} = -\begin{vmatrix} 4 & 5 \\ -3 & -1 \end{vmatrix} = -11, \quad A_{13} = +\begin{vmatrix} 4 & 2 \\ -3 & 3 \end{vmatrix} = 18,$$

$$A_{21} = -\begin{vmatrix} 4 & 5 \\ 3 & -1 \end{vmatrix} = 19, \quad A_{22} = +\begin{vmatrix} 1 & 5 \\ -3 & -1 \end{vmatrix} = 14, \quad A_{23} = -\begin{vmatrix} 1 & 4 \\ -3 & 3 \end{vmatrix} = -15,$$

$$A_{31} = +\begin{vmatrix} 4 & 5 \\ 2 & 5 \end{vmatrix} = 10, \quad A_{32} = -\begin{vmatrix} 1 & 5 \\ 4 & 5 \end{vmatrix} = 15, \quad A_{33} = +\begin{vmatrix} 1 & 4 \\ 4 & 2 \end{vmatrix} = -14.$$

(Note the familiar checkerboard pattern of signs.) Thus the cofactor matrix of A is

$$[A_{ij}] = \begin{bmatrix} -17 & -11 & 18 \\ 19 & 14 & -15 \\ 10 & 15 & -14 \end{bmatrix}.$$

We next interchange rows and columns to obtain the adjoint matrix

$$\text{adj } A = [A_{ij}]^T = \begin{bmatrix} -17 & 19 & 10 \\ -11 & 14 & 15 \\ 18 & -15 & -14 \end{bmatrix}.$$

Finally, in accord with Equation (19), we divide by $|A| = 29$ to get the inverse matrix

$$A^{-1} = \frac{1}{29}\begin{bmatrix} -17 & 19 & 10 \\ -11 & 14 & 15 \\ 18 & -15 & -14 \end{bmatrix}.$$

Just like Cramer's rule, the adjoint formula for the inverse matrix is computationally inefficient and is therefore of more theoretical than practical importance. The Gaussian elimination technique of Section 1.5 (or a version thereof) should always be used to find inverses of 4×4 and larger matrices.

2.4 PROBLEMS

Use Cramer's rule to solve each of the linear systems in Problems 1-10.

1. $\begin{aligned} x_1 - 2x_2 + 2x_3 &= 3 \\ 3x_1 \qquad + x_3 &= -1 \\ x_1 - x_2 + 2x_3 &= 2 \end{aligned}$

2. $\begin{aligned} 4x_1 + 3x_2 + x_3 &= 3 \\ 3x_1 - 2x_2 + 4x_3 &= -2 \\ x_1 + x_2 \qquad &= 2 \end{aligned}$

3. $\begin{aligned} 5x_1 + 2x_2 - 2x_3 &= 1 \\ x_1 + 5x_2 - 3x_3 &= -2 \\ 5x_1 - 3x_2 + 4x_3 &= 2 \end{aligned}$

4. $\begin{aligned} 5x_1 + 4x_2 - 2x_3 &= 4 \\ 2x_1 \qquad + 3x_3 &= 2 \\ 2x_1 - x_2 + x_3 &= 1 \end{aligned}$

5. $\begin{aligned} 3x_1 - x_2 - 5x_3 &= 3 \\ 4x_1 - 4x_2 - 3x_3 &= -4 \\ x_1 \qquad - 5x_3 &= 2 \end{aligned}$

6. $\begin{aligned} x_1 + 4x_2 + 2x_3 &= 3 \\ 4x_1 + 2x_2 + x_3 &= 1 \\ 2x_1 - 2x_2 - 5x_3 &= -3 \end{aligned}$

7. $\begin{aligned} 2x_1 \qquad - 5x_3 &= -3 \\ 4x_1 - 5x_2 + 3x_3 &= 3 \\ -2x_1 + x_2 + x_3 &= 1 \end{aligned}$

8. $\begin{aligned} 3x_1 + 4x_2 - 3x_3 &= 5 \\ 3x_1 - 2x_2 + 4x_3 &= 7 \\ 3x_1 + 2x_2 - x_3 &= 3 \end{aligned}$

9. $\begin{aligned} 2x_1 + 3x_2 - 5x_3 &= 1 \\ 3x_2 + 2x_3 &= -1 \\ 3x_1 + 2x_2 - 3x_3 &= 1 \end{aligned}$

10. $\begin{aligned} 5x_1 - 2x_2 + 4x_3 &= 2 \\ 4x_1 - 3x_2 + 4x_3 &= 1 \\ 5x_1 \qquad + x_3 &= 3 \end{aligned}$

Use the method of Example 2 to find the inverse A^{-1} of each matrix A given in Problems 11-20.

11. $\begin{bmatrix} -2 & 2 & -4 \\ 3 & 0 & 1 \\ 1 & -2 & 2 \end{bmatrix}$

12. $\begin{bmatrix} 0 & -1 & -2 \\ -5 & -1 & -3 \\ 2 & 2 & 0 \end{bmatrix}$

13. $\begin{bmatrix} -5 & -2 & 2 \\ 1 & 5 & -3 \\ 5 & -3 & 4 \end{bmatrix}$

14. $\begin{bmatrix} 2 & 0 & 3 \\ -5 & -4 & 2 \\ 2 & -1 & 1 \end{bmatrix}$

15. $\begin{bmatrix} 3 & 5 & 2 \\ -2 & 3 & -4 \\ -5 & 0 & -5 \end{bmatrix}$

16. $\begin{bmatrix} -4 & 4 & 3 \\ 3 & -1 & -5 \\ 1 & 0 & -5 \end{bmatrix}$

17. $\begin{bmatrix} -4 & 1 & 5 \\ -2 & 4 & 5 \\ -3 & -3 & -1 \end{bmatrix}$

18. $\begin{bmatrix} 3 & 4 & -3 \\ 3 & 2 & -1 \\ -3 & 2 & -4 \end{bmatrix}$

19. $\begin{bmatrix} -3 & -2 & 3 \\ 0 & 3 & 2 \\ 2 & 3 & -5 \end{bmatrix}$

20. $\begin{bmatrix} 2 & 4 & -3 \\ 2 & -3 & -1 \\ -5 & 0 & -3 \end{bmatrix}$

21. Let A be a 3×3 upper triangular matrix with nonzero determinant. Show by explicit computation that A^{-1} is also upper triangular.

22. Let A be an $n \times n$ matrix with $\det A = 1$ and with all elements of A integers.
(a) Show that A^{-1} has only integer entries.
(b) Suppose that $\mathbf{b}$ is an n-vector with only integer entries. Show that the solution vector $\mathbf{x}$ of $A\mathbf{x} = \mathbf{b}$ has only integer entries.

23. The square matrix A is said to be **symmetric** provided that $A^T = A$. Show that the inverse of a nonsingular symmetric matrix is also symmetric.

24. Figure 2.2 shows an acute triangle with angles A, B, and C and opposite sides a, b, and c. By dropping a perpendicular from each vertex to the opposite side, derive the equations

$$c \cos B + b \cos C = a$$

$$c \cos A + a \cos C = b$$

$$a \cos B + b \cos A = c.$$

Regarding these as linear equations in the unknowns cos A, cos B, and cos C, use Cramer's rule to derive the **law of cosines** by solving for

$$\cos A = \frac{b^2 + c^2 - a^2}{2bc}.$$

Thus

$$a^2 = b^2 + c^2 - 2bc \cos A.$$

Note that the case $A = \pi/2$ (90°) reduces to the Pythagorean theorem.

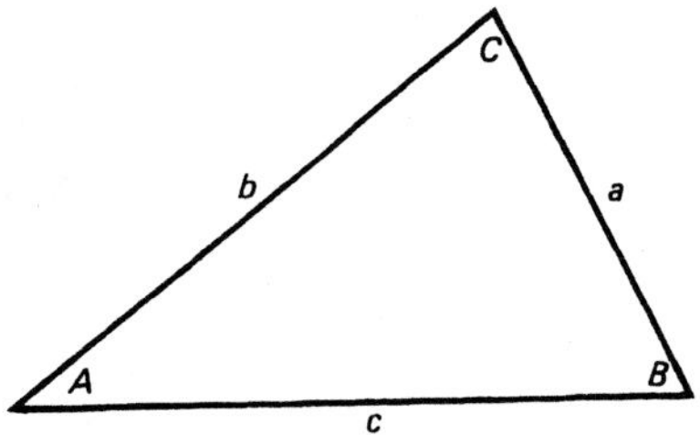

2.2 The triangle of Problem 24.

*2.5

Determinants and Curve Fitting

In Section 1.6 we introduced the application of linear algebra to the problem of finding a curve of specified type that passes through a given (finite) collection of points in the xy-plane. Here we show how to use determinants to solve curve-fitting problems.

Let us begin with the very simple problem of finding the equation

$$Ax + By + C = 0 \tag{1}$$

of the straight line through two given points (x_1, y_1) and (x_2, y_2). We assert that the desired equation can be written immediately in the form

$$\begin{vmatrix} x & y & 1 \\ x_1 & y_1 & 1 \\ x_2 & y_2 & 1 \end{vmatrix} = 0. \tag{2}$$

The reason is twofold: First, because the coordinates x_1, y_1, x_2, and y_2 are given constants, we see by expanding the determinant along its first row that Equation (2) has an x-term, a y-term, and a constant term. Thus it has the form in (1) and therefore represents a straight line L. Second, if we substitute either $x = x_1$, $y = y_1$ or $x = x_2$, $y = y_2$ in (2), then the determinant vanishes because it has two identical rows. Hence the two given points (x_1, y_1) and (x_2, y_2) satisfy the equation in (2) and therefore lie on the line L (see Figure 2.3).

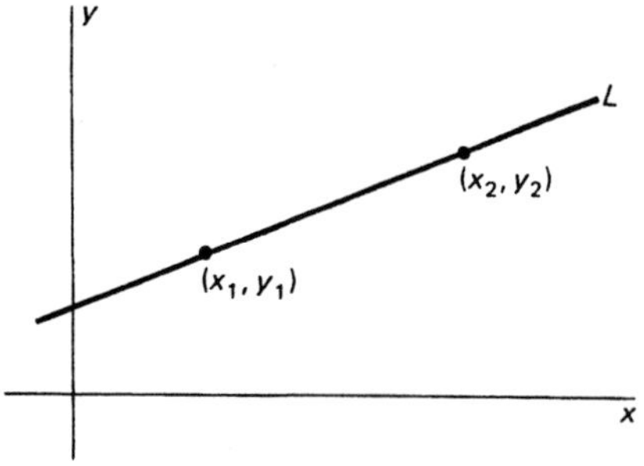

2.3 The straight line L through the two given points (x_1, y_1) and (x_2, y_2).

EXAMPLE 1 To find the straight line through the points (2, 3) and (5, 10), we substitute $x_1 = 2$, $y_1 = 3$ and $x_2 = 5$, $y_2 = 10$ in Equation (2) and simplify:

$$\begin{vmatrix} x & y & 1 \\ 2 & 3 & 1 \\ 5 & 10 & 1 \end{vmatrix} = 0;$$

$$x\begin{vmatrix} 3 & 1 \\ 10 & 1 \end{vmatrix} - y\begin{vmatrix} 2 & 1 \\ 5 & 1 \end{vmatrix} + \begin{vmatrix} 2 & 3 \\ 5 & 10 \end{vmatrix} = 0.$$

This yields

$$7x - 3y - 5 = 0$$

as the equation of the desired straight line.

The determinant approach to a curve-fitting problem consists of constructing a determinant in which the first row contains the appropriate variables for the desired equation and the remaining rows represent the values of those terms for the given data points. For instance, suppose that we want to find a *quadratic* function $y = f(x)$ of the form

$$y = Ax^2 + Bx + C \tag{3}$$

that fits three given points (x_1, y_1), (x_2, y_2), and (x_3, y_3). The graph of Equation (3) is a parabola through the three points (as in Figure 2.4). To find the coefficients A, B, and C, we set up the determinant equation

$$\begin{vmatrix} y & x^2 & x & 1 \\ y_1 & x_1^2 & x_1 & 1 \\ y_2 & x_2^2 & x_2 & 1 \\ y_3 & x_3^2 & x_3 & 1 \end{vmatrix} = 0. \tag{4}$$

If we think of expanding this determinant along its first row, we see that the resulting equation will contain terms involving y, x^2, x, and a constant, and hence will be of the form in (3). Moreover, if we substitute $x = x_i$, $y = y_i$ (for $i = 1, 2,$ or 3) in Equation (4),

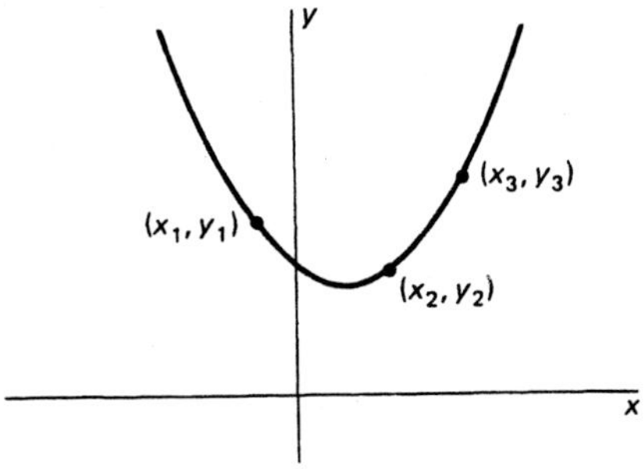

2.4 The parabola through the three given points (x_1, y_1), (x_2, y_2), and (x_3, y_3).

then the determinant will have two identical rows. Therefore each of the three given points satisfies Equation (4).

EXAMPLE 2 Suppose that the three given points (x_1, y_1), (x_2, y_2), and (x_3, y_3) are (1, 3), (2, 3), and (3, 7). Then Equation (4) becomes

$$\begin{vmatrix} y & x^2 & x & 1 \\ 3 & 1 & 1 & 1 \\ 3 & 4 & 2 & 1 \\ 7 & 9 & 3 & 1 \end{vmatrix} = 0.$$

When we expand along the first row and evaluate the four 3×3 determinants (any way we wish), we get the equation

$$-2y + 4x^2 - 12x + 14 = 0.$$

In the form of Equation (3), the parabola through the three given points is therefore described by

$$y = 2x^2 - 6x + 7.$$

In Section 1.6 (see Equation (5) there) we saw that the general equation of a circle in the xy-plane is

$$x^2 + y^2 + Ax + By + C = 0. \tag{5}$$

In order to find the circle that passes through three given points (x_1, y_1), (x_2, y_2), and (x_3, y_3), we set up the determinant equation

$$\begin{vmatrix} x^2 + y^2 & x & y & 1 \\ x_1^2 + y_1^2 & x_1 & y_1 & 1 \\ x_2^2 + y_2^2 & x_2 & y_2 & 1 \\ x_3^2 + y_3^2 & x_3 & y_3 & 1 \end{vmatrix} = 0. \tag{6}$$

The reason for the entry $x^2 + y^2$ is to guarantee that the equation we get will contain x^2- and y^2-terms *with equal coefficients* as in Equation (5), as well as terms containing x and y and a constant term.

EXAMPLE 3 Suppose that the three given points (x_1, y_1), (x_2, y_2), and (x_3, y_3) are $(-1, 5)$, $(5, -3)$, and $(6, 4)$. Then Equation (6) is

$$\begin{vmatrix} x^2 + y^2 & x & y & 1 \\ 26 & -1 & 5 & 1 \\ 34 & 5 & -3 & 1 \\ 52 & 6 & 4 & 1 \end{vmatrix} = 0.$$

After we expand along the first row and evaluate the four 3×3 determinants, we get the equation

$$50(x^2 + y^2) - 200x - 100y - 1000 = 0,$$

indeed of the form in (5). When we divide by 50 and then complete the square (as in Example 2 of Section 1.6), we finally obtain the equation

$$(x - 2)^2 + (y - 1)^2 = 25.$$

Thus the circle through the three given points has center located at (2,1) and radius 5.

Now we can discuss the fitting of conic sections (perhaps with the orbits of comets, planets, or satellites in mind). A **conic section** is the intersection of a plane with a cone. As indicated in Figure 2.5, there are three types of nontrivial conic sections—ellipses, parabolas, and hyperbolas. When oriented in standard fashion in the xy-plane, these three types of conic sections have the shapes shown in Figures 2.6, 2.7, and 2.8. Here we are mainly interested in the ellipse with **semiaxes** a and b (indicated in Figure 2.6). In Section 10.7 of Edwards and Penney, *Calculus and Analytic Geometry*, 2nd ed. (Englewood Cliffs, N.J.: Prentice Hall, 1986) it is shown that the equation of *any* conic section in the xy-plane—not necessarily one in some standard position, but even one that has been translated or rotated in the plane—is a second degree equation of the form

$$Ax^2 + Bxy + Cy^2 + Dx + Ey + F = 0. \tag{7}$$

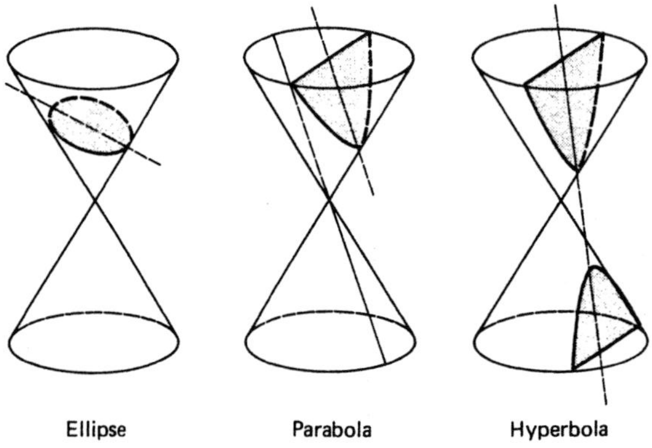

2.5 The conic sections.

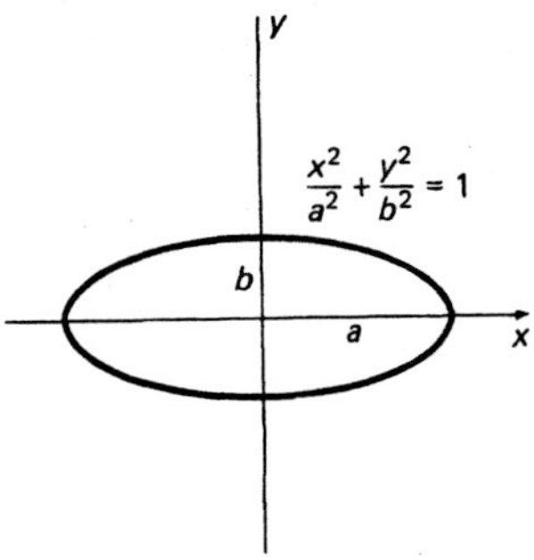

2.6 An ellipse.

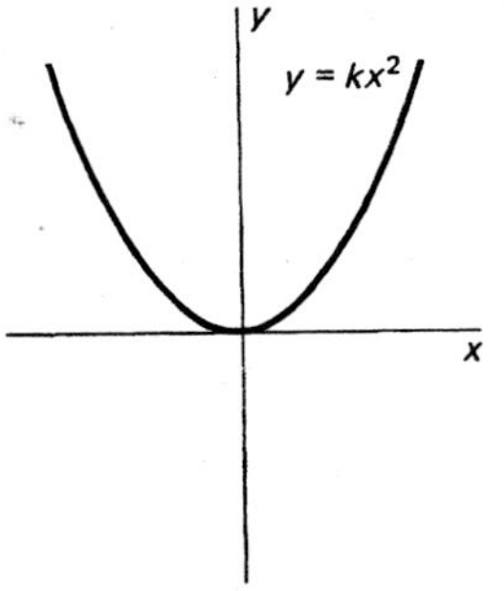

2.7 A parabola.

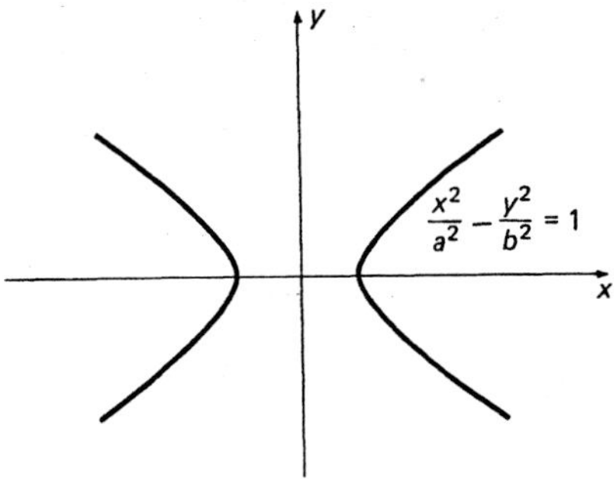

2.8 A hyperbola.

If we divide each term in Equation (7) by F and write $a = A/F$, $b = B/F$, and so forth, then we get the equation

$$ax^2 + bxy + cy^2 + dx + ey + 1 = 0. \tag{8}$$

In this form the general equation of a conic section involves *five* "arbitrary constants." If we knew five different points on a conic section, we could substitute their coordinates in Equation (8), thereby obtaining a system of five equations that we could hope to solve for the five coefficients a, b, c, d, and e. Indeed, this approach leads to an algebraic proof of the famous theorem of classical plane geometry to the effect that any *five* (distinct and noncollinear) points in the plane lie on a unique conic section.

To find the conic section that passes through five such points (x_i, y_i) $(i = 1, 2, 3, 4, 5)$, we set up the determinant equation

$$\begin{vmatrix} x^2 & xy & y^2 & x & y & 1 \\ x_1^2 & x_1y_1 & y_1^2 & x_1 & y_1 & 1 \\ x_2^2 & x_2y_2 & y_2^2 & x_2 & y_2 & 1 \\ x_3^2 & x_3y_3 & y_3^2 & x_3 & y_3 & 1 \\ x_4^2 & x_4y_4 & y_4^2 & x_4 & y_4 & 1 \\ x_5^2 & x_5y_5 & y_5^2 & x_5 & y_5 & 1 \end{vmatrix} = 0. \tag{9}$$

Observe that if we expand along the first row, we get one term of each type appearing in Equation (7). Furthermore, if we substitute the coordinates of one of the five given points in the first row, then the resulting determinant has two identical rows, so Equation (9) is satisfied.

EXAMPLE 4 Suppose that we are tracking a comet approaching the sun, measuring distance in *astronomical units* (1 A.U. is the average radius of the earth's orbit, about 93 million miles). Assume that five observations of the comet yield the five points (1, 9.265), (2, 10.892), (3, 12.331), (4, 13.625), and (5, 14.799) on its orbit. When we substitute these five points in the lower five rows of the 6×6 determinant in (9), we get the equation

$$\begin{vmatrix} x^2 & xy & y^2 & x & y & 1 \\ 1.000 & 9.265 & 85.837 & 1.000 & 9.265 & 1.000 \\ 4.000 & 21.784 & 118.635 & 2.000 & 10.892 & 1.000 \\ 9.000 & 36.992 & 152.043 & 3.000 & 12.331 & 1.000 \\ 16.000 & 54.500 & 185.638 & 4.000 & 13.625 & 1.000 \\ 25.000 & 73.994 & 219.006 & 5.000 & 14.799 & 1.000 \end{vmatrix} = 0. \tag{10}$$

No one would want to expand this determinant along its first row by hand. We used a personal computer with a determinant program to obtain the equation

$$(0.01413)x^2 - (0.01667)xy + (0.00926)y^2$$
$$- (0.04340)x - (0.05787)y - 0.07535 = 0. \tag{11}$$

This is the equation of the orbit of our comet. Actually, the original data points in Example 4 were chosen in advance to lie on the ellipse with equation

$$2929x^2 - 3456xy + 1921y^2 - 9000x - 12000y - 15625 = 0, \tag{12}$$

and the reader can verify that the equation in (12) is very nearly a constant multiple of the equation in (11). Figure 2.9 shows an accurate computer plot of the elliptical graph of Equation (12) and the original five points that determine it. In Section 8.1 we will see how linear algebra can be used to analyze Equation (12) to ascertain precisely what ellipse it describes. It turns out that the ellipse of Figure 2.9 is obtained as follows. Begin with the ellipse of Figure 2.10, having semiaxes $a = 13$ and $b = 5$. First translate it 12 units to the right; then rotate it counterclockwise through an angle $\alpha = \sin^{-1}(\frac{4}{5}) \approx 53°$. It follows, for instance, that the comet's point of closest approach to the sun (at the origin) is 1 A.U. and that its greatest distance from the sun is 25 A.U.

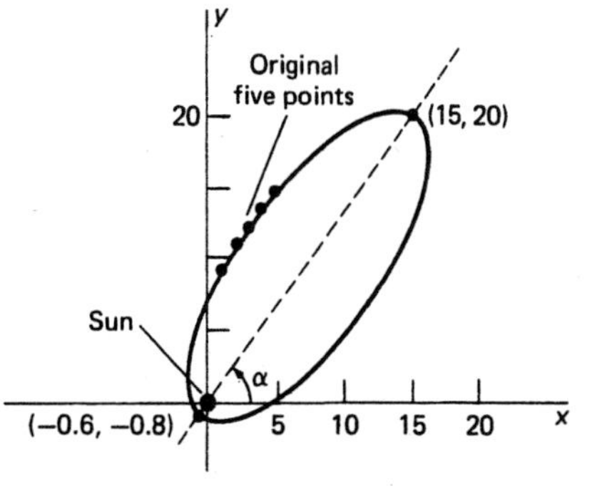

2.9 The elliptical orbit of the comet of Example 4.

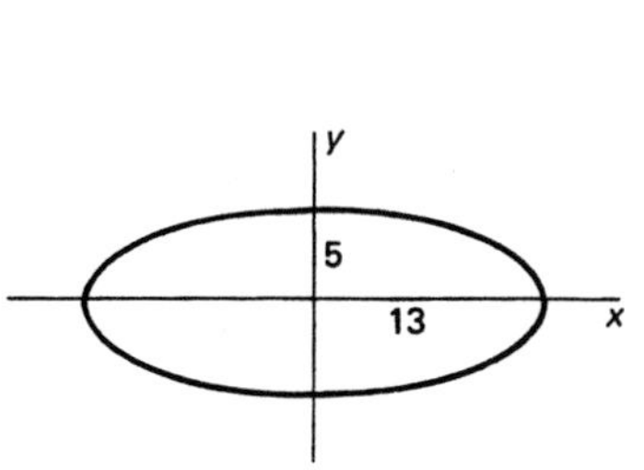

2.10 The ellipse in standard position.

2.5 PROBLEMS

In Problems 1 and 2 use Equation (2) to find the straight line through the two given points.

1. (1, 1) and (3, 7)

2. (−1, 11) and (2, −10)

In Problems 3-6 use Equation (4) to find the parabola $y = Ax^2 + Bx + C$ through the three given points.

3. (0, 3), (1, 1), and (2, −5)

4. (−1, 1), (1, 5), and (2, 16)

5. (1, 3), (2, 3), and (3, 5)

6. (−1, −1), (3, −13), and (5, 5)

In Problems 7-10 use Equation (6) to find the equation of the circle that passes through the three given points.

7. (−1, −1), (6, 6), and (7, 5)

8. (3, −4), (5, 10), and (−9, 12)

9. (1, 0), (0, −5), and (−5, −4)

10. (0, 0), (10, 0), and (−7, 7)

11. In Section 1.6 we discussed the equation

$$Ax^2 + Bxy + Cy^2 = 1$$

of a *central* conic section—that is, one that may be rotated but is not translated. Explain why the equation

$$\begin{vmatrix} x^2 & xy & y^2 & 1 \\ x_1^2 & x_1y_1 & y_1^2 & 1 \\ x_2^2 & x_2y_2 & y_2^2 & 1 \\ x_3^2 & x_3y_3 & y_3^2 & 1 \end{vmatrix} = 0$$

describes the central conic that passes through the three points (x_1, y_1), (x_2, y_2), and (x_3, y_3).

In Problems 12–15 use the determinant equation of Problem 11 to find the equation of the central conic that passes through the three given points.

12. (0, 5), (5, 0), and (5, 5)

13. (0, 5), (5, 0), and (10, 10)

14. (0, 1), (1, 0), and (10, 10)

15. (0, 4), (3, 0), and (5, 5)

AREA AND VOLUME DETERMINANTS

Another type of geometric application of determinants involves their use to express concisely the areas of certain plane figures and the volumes of certain solids in space. For instance, consider the plane parallelogram P (see Figure 2.11) that is determined by the vectors $\mathbf{v}_1 = (x_1, y_1)$ and $\mathbf{v}_2 = (x_2, y_2)$. According to Problem 17, the area A of P is given by

$$A = \pm\begin{vmatrix} x_1 & y_1 \\ x_2 & y_2 \end{vmatrix}. \tag{13}$$

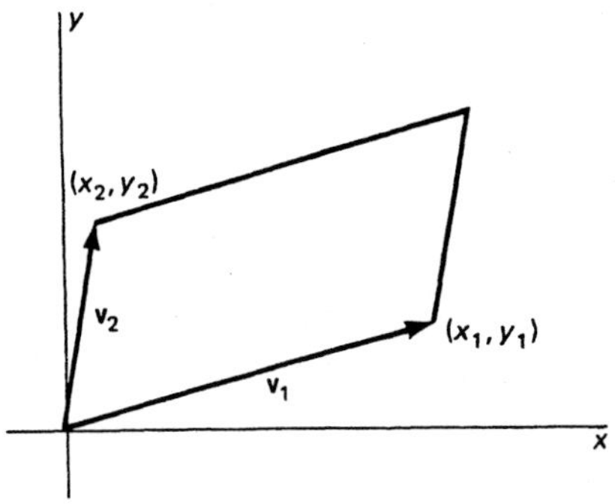

2.11 A parallelogram in the plane.

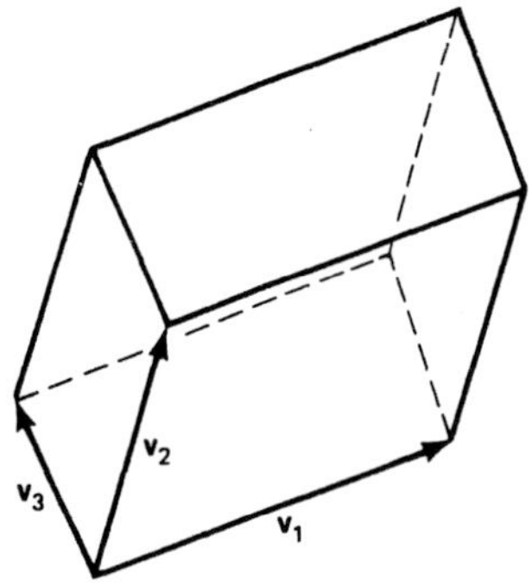

2.12 A parallelepiped in space.

The choice of sign in (13) depends upon the order in which the vertices $\mathbf{v}_1$ and $\mathbf{v}_2$ are labeled. Similarly, three vectors $\mathbf{v}_1 = (x_1, y_1, z_1)$, $\mathbf{v}_2 = (x_2, y_2, z_2)$, and $\mathbf{v}_3 = (x_3, y_3, z_3)$ in space determine a *parallelepiped* having one vertex at the origin (see Figure 2.12). In Section 14-2 of Edwards and Penney, *Calculus and Analytic Geometry*, 2nd ed. (Englewood Cliffs, N.J.: Prentice Hall, 1986), it is shown that the volume V of this parallelepiped is given by

$$V = \pm \begin{vmatrix} x_1 & y_1 & z_1 \\ x_2 & y_2 & z_2 \\ x_3 & y_3 & z_3 \end{vmatrix}. \tag{14}$$

The choice of sign in (14) depends upon the order in which the vertices $\mathbf{v}_1$, $\mathbf{v}_2$, $\mathbf{v}_3$ are labeled.

16. Figure 2.13 shows a triangle OAB in the plane with one vertex at the origin. Show that its area A is given by

$$A = \frac{1}{2}\begin{vmatrix} x_1 & y_1 \\ x_2 & y_2 \end{vmatrix}.$$

Suggestion: Use the fact that the area of a trapezoid is equal to half the product of its altitude and the sum of its two parallel sides.

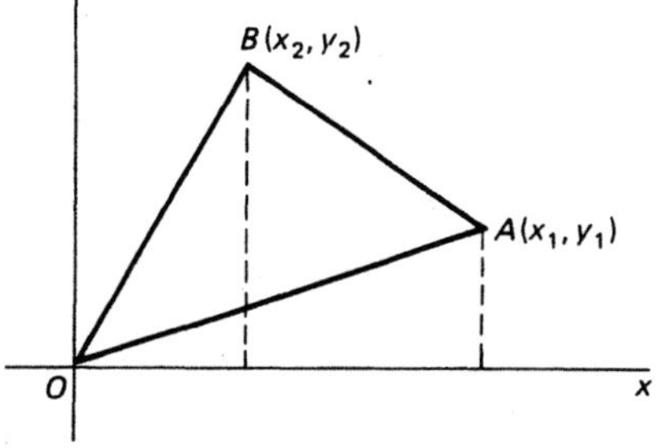

2.13 A special triangle in the plane.

17. Derive the formula in Equation (13) from the result in Problem 16.

18. Figure 2.14 shows a more general triangle ABC in the plane. Note that the vertices are labeled so that the boundary of the triangle is traced out counterclockwise from A to B to C and back to A. Deduce from the result in Problem 16 that its area is

$$\frac{1}{2}\begin{vmatrix} x_1 & y_1 & 1 \\ x_2 & y_2 & 1 \\ x_3 & y_3 & 1 \end{vmatrix}$$

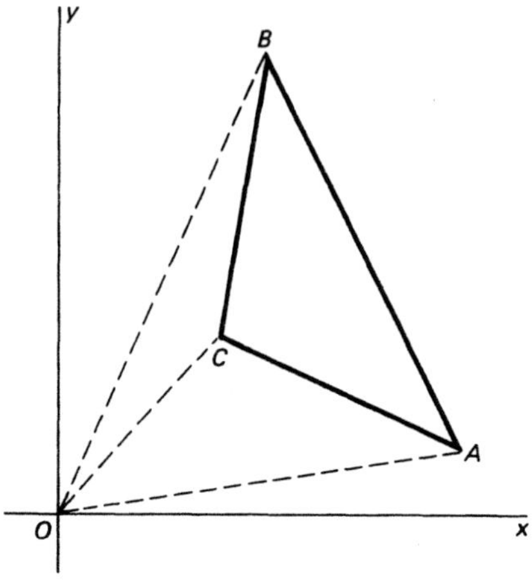

2.14 A more general triangle in the plane.

CHAPTER REVIEW QUESTIONS

1. How is the determinant of an $n \times n$ matrix defined inductively in terms of determinants of $(n-1) \times (n-1)$ matrices? Does this definition work in the case $n = 2$ if one defines the determinant of a 1×1 matrix $A = [a]$ by $\det A = a$?

2. What is the difference between a minor and a cofactor of a matrix? How is that difference related to the familiar checkerboard of signs?

3. What is the effect on $\det A$ of each of the three types of elementary row operations on the square matrix A?

4. Suppose that the $n \times n$ matrix A has been reduced by elementary row operations to the following "partial echelon" form:

$$\left[\begin{array}{ccccc|c} a_{11} & * & * & \cdots & * & \\ 0 & a_{22} & * & \cdots & * & \\ 0 & 0 & & & & C \\ \vdots & \vdots & & \ddots & \vdots & \\ 0 & 0 & & & a_{kk} & \\ \hline & & 0 & & & B \end{array}\right].$$

Explain why it follows that

$$|A| = a_{11}a_{22}\cdots a_{kk}|B|.$$

5. Explain why you know without doing any work that

(a) $\begin{vmatrix} 1 & 2 & 3 & 4 \\ 0 & 0 & 5 & 6 \\ 0 & 0 & 7 & 8 \\ 0 & 0 & 9 & 10 \end{vmatrix} = 0;$

(b) $\begin{vmatrix} 0 & 1 & 5 & 6 \\ 2 & 0 & 7 & 8 \\ 0 & 0 & 0 & 4 \\ 0 & 0 & 3 & 0 \end{vmatrix} = 24;$

(c) $\begin{vmatrix} 0 & 0 & 3 \\ 0 & 2 & 5 \\ 1 & 4 & 6 \end{vmatrix} = -6.$

6. Use determinants to answer this question: Is it possible to express an invertible matrix as a product of square matrices that are not all invertible?

7. If A is an $n \times n$ matrix, k is a constant, and $B = kA$, what is the relation between $|A|$ and $|B^{-1}|$?

8. If A is an $n \times n$ matrix, what is the relationship between the cofactor matrix of A and the adjoint matrix of A?

9. Suppose that $\mathbf{b}$ is the kth column vector of the invertible matrix A. Explain why Cramer's rule implies that the unique solution of $A\mathbf{x} = \mathbf{b}$ is given by $x_k = 1$, $x_j = 0$ for $j \neq k$.

10. Suppose that the matrix A has the form

$$A = \left[\begin{array}{c|c} B & D \\ \hline 0 & C \end{array}\right]$$

where B is $p \times p$ and C is $q \times q$. Does it necessarily follow that $|A| = |B||C|$?

Suggestion: Think of reducing A to echelon form by elementary row operations.

11. Does the adjoint formula (Theorem 2 in Section 2.4) for A^{-1} imply that $(A^T)^{-1} = (A^{-1})^T$?

3

Vectors in the Plane and in Space

3.1*

The Vector Space $\mathbf{R}^2$

The **coordinate plane** $\mathbf{R}^2$ is the set of all ordered pairs (x, y) of real numbers. The elements of $\mathbf{R}^2$—these ordered pairs—are called **points**. We write $P(x_0, y_0)$ to signify that the point P of $\mathbf{R}^2$ is the particular ordered pair (x_0, y_0). The location of the point P in the plane $\mathbf{R}^2$ is visualized in reference to the perpendicular **coordinate axes** shown in Figure 3.1—the horizontal x-axis and the vertical y-axis. Each axis is regarded as a copy of the real line $\mathbf{R}$, and the **origin** $(0, 0)$ where they intersect is the location of the zero point on each axis. The point $P(x_0, y_0)$ with ***x*-coordinate** x_0 and ***y*-coordinate** y_0 then corresponds (by perpendicular projection) to the pair of numbers x_0 on the x-axis and y_0 on the y-axis.

The location of the point P can also be specified by means of the *arrow* or directed line segment (also shown in Figure 3.1) that points from the origin (its *initial point*) to P (its *terminal point*). In physics arrows are often used to represent *vector quantities* such as force and velocity, that possess both magnitude and direction. For instance, the *velocity vector* $\mathbf{v}$ of a point moving in the plane may be represented by an arrow that points in the direction of its motion, with the length of the arrow equal to the speed of the moving point. If, as in Figure 3.2, we locate this arrow with its initial

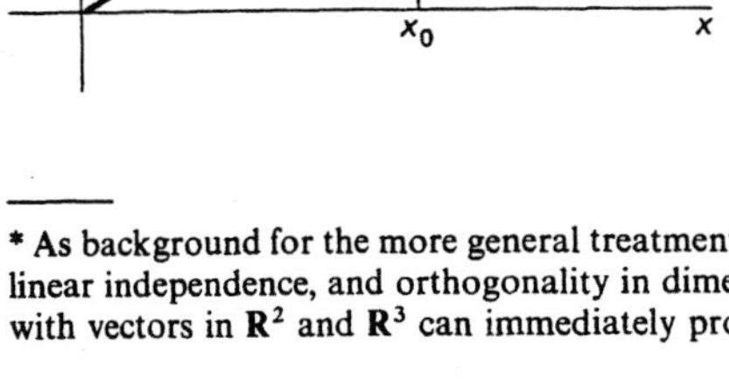

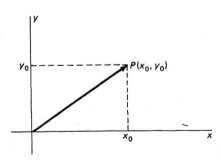

3.1 The point P with coordinates (x_0, y_0)

---

* As background for the more general treatment in Chapters 4 and 5, this chapter introduces vector spaces, linear independence, and orthogonality in dimensions two and three. Readers who are sufficiently familar with vectors in $\mathbf{R}^2$ and $\mathbf{R}^3$ can immediately prcceed to Chapter 4 without loss of continuity.

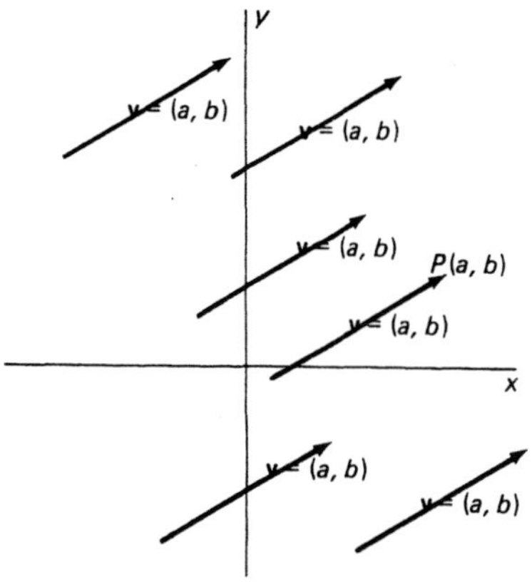

3.2 These arrows all represent the same vector $\mathbf{v} = (a, b)$.

point at the origin, then its direction and length are determined by its terminal point (a, b). But the arrow is merely a pictorial object; the mathematical object associated with the vector $\mathbf{v}$ is simply the point (a, b). For this reason it is customary to use the words *point* and *vector* interchangeably for elements of the plane $\mathbf{R}^2$ and thus to refer either to the *point* (a, b) or the *vector* (a, b).

> ***Definition:*** *Vector*
>
> A **vector** $\mathbf{v}$ in the plane $\mathbf{R}^2$ is simply an ordered pair (a, b) of real numbers. We write $\mathbf{v} = (a, b)$ and call a and b the **components** of the vector $\mathbf{v}$.

Thus "a vector is a point is a vector," but vector terminology often aids us in visualizing geometric relationships between different points. The directed line segment $\overrightarrow{OP}$ from the origin O to the point $P(a, b)$ is one representation of the vector $\mathbf{v} = (a, b)$. For this reason we sometimes call $\mathbf{v}$ the **position vector** of the point P (though they really are the same thing—the pair (a, b)). As indicated in Figure 3.2, any other directed line segment with the same direction *and* the same length can equally well represent the vector $\mathbf{v}$. What is important about an arrow is usually not where it is, but how long it is and which way it points.

As in Section 1.4, we adopt the convention that the vector $\mathbf{v}$ with first component v_1 and the second component v_2 may be written as either

$$\mathbf{v} = (v_1, v_2) \qquad \text{or} \qquad \mathbf{v} = \begin{bmatrix} v_1 \\ v_2 \end{bmatrix}.$$

Then the following definitions of addition of vectors and of multiplication of vectors by scalars are consistent with the matrix operations defined in Section 1.4.

> ***Definition:*** *Addition of Vectors*
>
> The **sum** $\mathbf{u} + \mathbf{v}$ of the two vectors $\mathbf{u} = (u_1, u_2)$ and $\mathbf{v} = (v_1, v_2)$ is the vector
>
> $$\mathbf{u} + \mathbf{v} = (u_1 + v_1, u_2 + v_2). \tag{1}$$

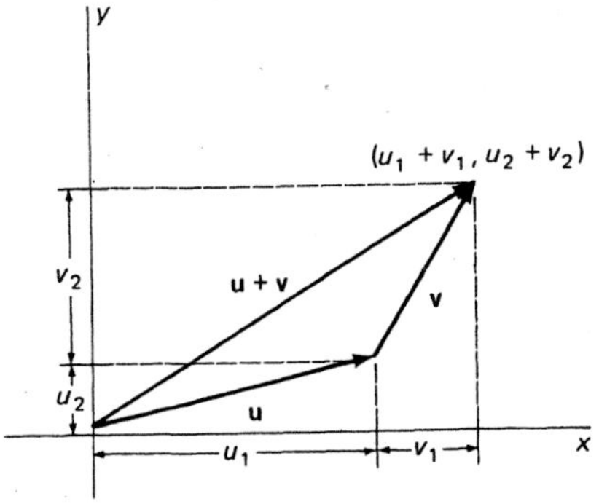

3.3 The triangle law of vector addition.

Thus we add vectors by adding corresponding components—that is, by *componentwise addition.* For instance, the sum of the vectors $\mathbf{u} = (4, 3)$ and $\mathbf{v} = (-5, 2)$ is

$$(4, 3) + (-5, 2) = (4 - 5, 3 + 2) = (-1, 5).$$

The geometric representation of vectors as arrows often converts an algebraic relation into a picture that is readily understood and remembered. Addition of vectors is defined algebraically in Equation (1). The geometric interpretation of vector addition is the **triangle law of addition** illustrated in Figure 3.3, where the labeled lengths indicate why this interpretation is valid. An equivalent interpretation is the **parallelogram law of addition** illustrated in Figure 3.4.

Multiplication of a vector by a scalar (real number) is also defined in a componentwise manner.

> ***Definition:*** *Multiplication of a Vector by a Scalar*
>
> If $\mathbf{u} = (u_1, u_2)$ is a vector and c is a real number, then the **scalar multiple** $c\mathbf{u}$ is the vector
>
> $$c\mathbf{u} = (cu_1, cu_2). \qquad (2)$$

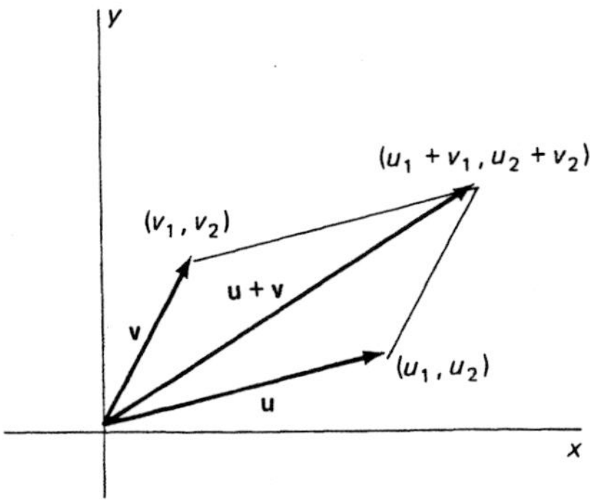

3.4 The parallelogram law of vector addition.

For instance, if $\mathbf{u} = (1, -2)$ then $3\mathbf{u} = (3, -6)$.

The **length** $|\mathbf{u}|$ of the vector $\mathbf{u} = (u_1, u_2)$ is defined to be the distance from the point (u_1, u_2) to the origin. The Pythagorean theorem for right triangles then yields

$$|\mathbf{u}| = \sqrt{(u_1)^2 + (u_2)^2}. \tag{3}$$

For instance, if $\mathbf{u} = (3, 4)$ then

$$|\mathbf{u}| = \sqrt{(3)^2 + (4)^2} = \sqrt{25} = 5.$$

Note that

$$\begin{aligned} |c\mathbf{u}| &= \sqrt{(cu_1)^2 + (cu_2)^2} \\ &= |c|\sqrt{(u_1)^2 + (u_2)^2} = |c| \cdot |\mathbf{u}|. \end{aligned} \tag{4}$$

Thus the length of $c\mathbf{u}$ is $|c|$ times the length of $\mathbf{u}$. The geometric interpretation of scalar multiplication is that $c\mathbf{u}$ is the vector of length $|c| \cdot |\mathbf{u}|$, with the same direction as $\mathbf{u}$ if $c > 0$ but the opposite direction if $c < 0$. See Figure 3.5.

In particular, the **negative** of the vector $\mathbf{u}$ is the vector

$$-\mathbf{u} = (-1)\mathbf{u} = (-u_1, -u_2), \tag{5}$$

with the same length as $\mathbf{u}$ but with the opposite direction. The **difference** $\mathbf{u} - \mathbf{v}$ of the vectors $\mathbf{u} = (u_1, u_2)$ and $\mathbf{v} = (v_1, v_2)$ is now easy to define:

$$\mathbf{u} - \mathbf{v} = \mathbf{u} + (-\mathbf{v}) = (u_1 - v_1, u_2 - v_2). \tag{6}$$

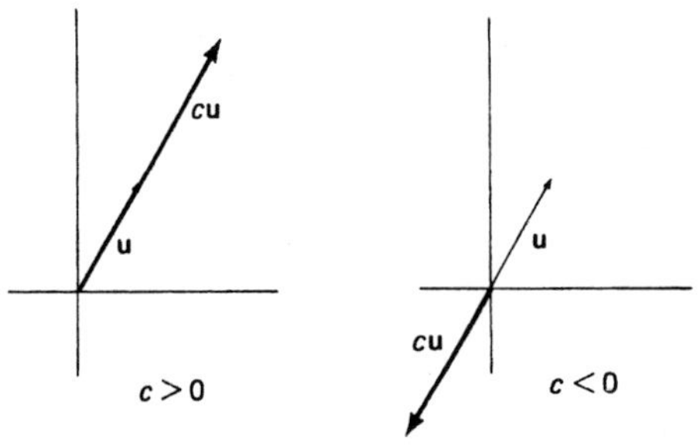

3.5 The vector $c\mathbf{u}$ may have the same direction as $\mathbf{u}$ or the opposite direction.

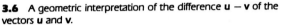

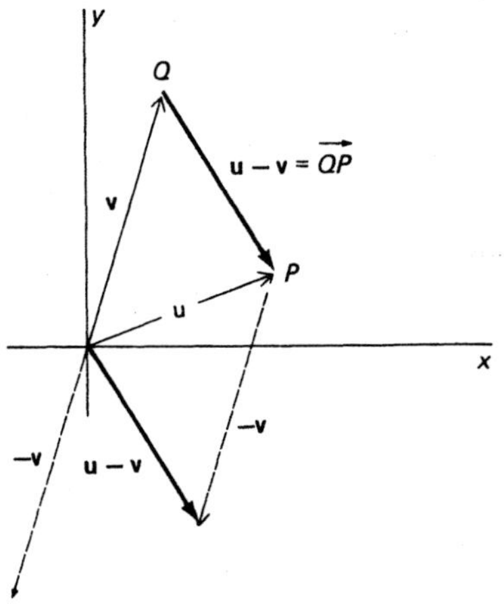

3.6 A geometric interpretation of the difference **u** − **v** of the vectors **u** and **v**.

If we think of (u_1, u_2) and (v_1, v_2) as position vectors of the points P and Q, respectively, then $\mathbf{u} - \mathbf{v}$ is represented by the arrow $\overrightarrow{QP}$ from Q to P. See Figure 3.6.

EXAMPLE 1 If $\mathbf{u} = (4, -3)$ and $\mathbf{v} = (-2, 3)$ then

$$\begin{aligned} |\mathbf{u}| &= \sqrt{(4)^2 + (-3)^2} = \sqrt{25} = 5, \\ \mathbf{u} + \mathbf{v} &= (4 + (-2), (-3) + 3) = (2, 0), \\ \mathbf{u} - \mathbf{v} &= (4 - (-2), (-3) - 3) = (6, -6), \\ 3\mathbf{u} &= (3 \cdot (4), 3 \cdot (-3)) = (12, -9), \\ -2\mathbf{v} &= (-2 \cdot (-2), -2 \cdot (3)) = (4, -6), \end{aligned}$$

and

$$2\mathbf{u} + 4\mathbf{v} = (2(4) + 4(-2), 2(-3) + 4(3)) = (0, 6).$$

The **zero vector** $\mathbf{0} = (0, 0)$ plays a special role. It acts like the real number 0 in that

$$\mathbf{u} + \mathbf{0} = \mathbf{u} \tag{7}$$

for any and every vector **u**.

The following theorem summarizes the algebraic properties of vector addition and multiplication of vectors by scalars.

> ***Theorem 1:*** $\mathbf{R}^2$ *as a Vector Space*
>
> If $\mathbf{u}$, $\mathbf{v}$, and $\mathbf{w}$ are vectors in $\mathbf{R}^2$ and r and s are real numbers, then:
>
> **(a)** $\mathbf{u} + \mathbf{v} = \mathbf{v} + \mathbf{u}$ (commutativity)
>
> **(b)** $\mathbf{u} + (\mathbf{v} + \mathbf{w}) = (\mathbf{u} + \mathbf{v}) + \mathbf{w}$ (associativity)
>
> **(c)** $\mathbf{u} + \mathbf{0} = \mathbf{0} + \mathbf{u} = \mathbf{u}$ (zero element)
>
> **(d)** $\mathbf{u} + (-\mathbf{u}) = (-\mathbf{u}) + \mathbf{u} = \mathbf{0}$ (additive inverse)
>
> **(e)** $r(\mathbf{u} + \mathbf{v}) = r\mathbf{u} + r\mathbf{v}$ (distributivity)
>
> **(f)** $(r + s)\mathbf{u} = r\mathbf{u} + s\mathbf{u}$
>
> **(g)** $r(s\mathbf{u}) = (rs)\mathbf{u}$
>
> **(h)** $1(\mathbf{u}) = \mathbf{u}$ (multiplicative identity).

Each of Properties (a)–(h) is easy to verify by working with components. For instance, if $\mathbf{u} = (u_1, u_2)$ and $\mathbf{v} = (v_1, v_2)$, then

$$\begin{aligned} r(\mathbf{u} + \mathbf{v}) &= r(u_1 + v_1, u_2 + v_2) \\ &= (ru_1 + rv_1, ru_2 + rv_2) \\ &= (ru_1, ru_2) + (rv_1, rv_2) \\ &= r\mathbf{u} + r\mathbf{v}; \end{aligned}$$

thus we have verified Property (e).

The properties listed in Theorem 1 may be summarized by saying that $\mathbf{R}^2$ is a *vector space*. By definition, a **vector space** is a set V of elements that can be added together and can be multiplied by scalars: If $\mathbf{u}$ and $\mathbf{v}$ are elements of V and r is a scalar, then $\mathbf{u} + \mathbf{v}$ and $r\mathbf{u}$ are also elements of V, and these two operations of addition and scalar multiplication satisfy properties (a)–(h) of Theorem 1. Thus the coordinate plane $\mathbf{R}^2$ is our first explicit example of a vector space. Here you should pause to note that the set $\mathbf{R}$ of real numbers, together with ordinary addition and multiplication, also satisfies all these properties, and hence that $\mathbf{R}$ is a second example of a vector space. In Chapter 4 we will study more general vector spaces.

THE UNIT VECTORS $\mathbf{i}$ AND $\mathbf{j}$

A **unit vector** is one with length 1. If $\mathbf{a} = (a_1, a_2)$ and $\mathbf{a} \neq \mathbf{0}$, then

$$\mathbf{u} = \frac{\mathbf{a}}{|\mathbf{a}|} \tag{8}$$

is the unit vector with the same direction as $\mathbf{a}$. Why? Because

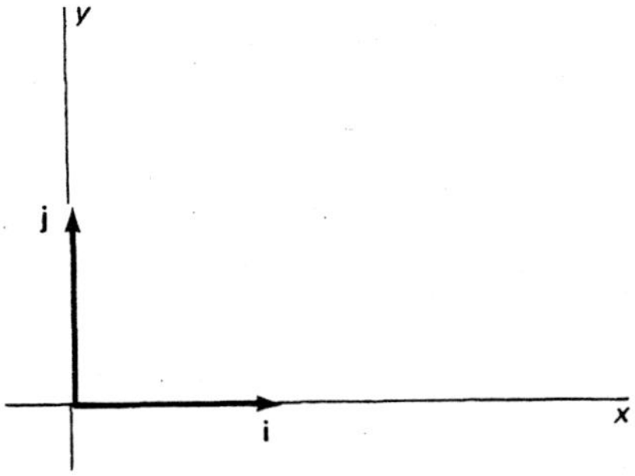

3.7 The unit vectors **i** and **j**.

$$|\mathbf{u}| = \sqrt{\left(\frac{a_1}{|\mathbf{a}|}\right)^2 + \left(\frac{a_2}{|\mathbf{a}|}\right)^2}$$
$$= \frac{1}{|\mathbf{a}|}\sqrt{(a_1)^2 + (a_2)^2} = 1.$$

For example, if $\mathbf{a} = (3, -4)$, then $|\mathbf{a}| = 5$. Hence $\mathbf{u} = (\frac{3}{5}, -\frac{4}{5})$ is a unit vector that has the same direction as **a**.

The two particular unit vectors

$$\mathbf{i} = (1, 0) \quad \text{and} \quad \mathbf{j} = (0, 1) \tag{9}$$

shown in Figure 3.7 play a special role. The first points in the positive x-direction, the second in the positive y-direction. Together they provide a useful alternative notation for vectors. For if $\mathbf{a} = (a_1, a_2)$, then

$$\begin{aligned}\mathbf{a} &= (a_1, 0) + (0, a_2) \\ &= a_1(1, 0) + a_2(0, 1) = a_1\mathbf{i} + a_2\mathbf{j}\end{aligned} \tag{10}$$

Thus every vector is a **linear combination** of the two vectors **i** and **j**. Such linear combinations of vectors may be manipulated exactly like combinations of real numbers. For instance, if

$$\mathbf{a} = a_1\mathbf{i} + a_2\mathbf{j} \quad \text{and} \quad \mathbf{b} = b_1\mathbf{i} + b_2\mathbf{j}$$

then

$$\begin{aligned}\mathbf{a} + \mathbf{b} &= (a_1\mathbf{i} + a_2\mathbf{j}) + (b_1\mathbf{i} + b_2\mathbf{j}) \\ &= (a_1 + b_1)\mathbf{i} + (a_2 + b_2)\mathbf{j}\end{aligned}$$

and

$$\begin{aligned}c\mathbf{a} &= c(a_1\mathbf{i} + a_2\mathbf{j}) \\ &= (ca_1)\mathbf{i} + (ca_2)\mathbf{j}.\end{aligned}$$

EXAMPLE 2 If $\mathbf{a} = 2\mathbf{i} - 3\mathbf{j}$ and $\mathbf{b} = 3\mathbf{i} + 4\mathbf{j}$, then

$$\begin{aligned} 5\mathbf{a} - 3\mathbf{b} &= 5(2\mathbf{i} - 3\mathbf{j}) - 3(3\mathbf{i} + 4\mathbf{j}) \\ &= (10 - 9)\mathbf{i} + (-15 - 12)\mathbf{j} = \mathbf{i} - 27\mathbf{j}. \end{aligned}$$

LINEAR INDEPENDENCE IN $\mathbf{R}^2$

Suppose that $\mathbf{u} = (u_1, u_2)$ and $\mathbf{v} = (v_1, v_2)$ are two vectors such that the points (u_1, u_2) and (v_1, v_2) lie on the same straight line through the origin. Figure 3.8 shows a case in which both points are in the first quadrant. From the similarity of the indicated right triangles we find that

$$\frac{u_1}{v_1} = \frac{u_2}{v_2} = \frac{|\mathbf{u}|}{|\mathbf{v}|}.$$

It follows that

$$\mathbf{u} = (u_1, u_2) = \left(\frac{u_1}{v_1} v_1, \frac{u_2}{v_2} v_2\right) = \frac{|\mathbf{u}|}{|\mathbf{v}|} \mathbf{v}.$$

That is,

$$\mathbf{u} = c\mathbf{v}, \tag{11}$$

where $c = |\mathbf{u}|/|\mathbf{v}|$. Thus the vector $\mathbf{u}$ is a *scalar multiple* of the vector $\mathbf{v}$.

Two vectors $\mathbf{u}$ and $\mathbf{v}$ are said to be **linearly dependent** if one of them is a scalar multiple of the other—either

$$\mathbf{u} = c\mathbf{v} \quad \text{or} \quad \mathbf{v} = c\mathbf{u} \tag{12}$$

for some scalar c. Note that if $\mathbf{u} = \mathbf{0}$ while $\mathbf{v} \neq \mathbf{0}$, then $\mathbf{u} = 0\mathbf{v}$, but $\mathbf{v}$ is not a scalar multiple of $\mathbf{u}$. (Why?) Thus if precisely one of the two vectors $\mathbf{u}$ and $\mathbf{v}$ is the zero vector, then $\mathbf{u}$ and $\mathbf{v}$ are linearly dependent, but only one of the two relations in (12) holds.

If $\mathbf{u}$ and $\mathbf{v}$ are linearly dependent vectors with $\mathbf{u} = c\mathbf{v}$ (for instance), then

$$1 \cdot \mathbf{u} + (-c) \cdot \mathbf{v} = \mathbf{0}.$$

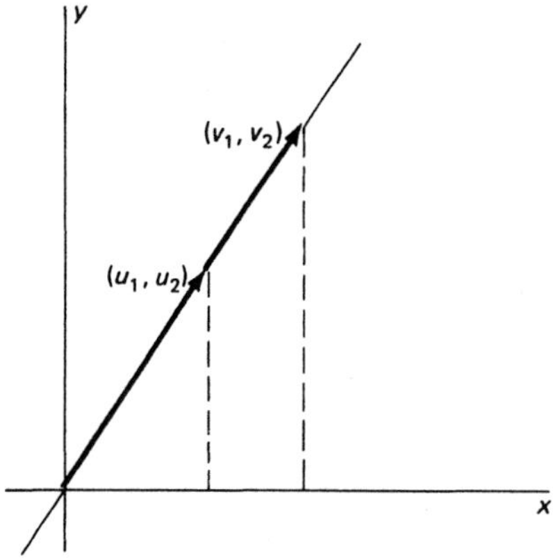

3.8 Two linearly dependent vectors **u** and **v**.

Thus there exist scalars a and b *not both zero* such that

$$a\mathbf{u} + b\mathbf{v} = \mathbf{0}. \tag{13}$$

Conversely, suppose that Equation (13) holds with a and b not both zero. If $a \neq 0$ (for instance) then we can solve for

$$\mathbf{u} = -\frac{b}{a}\mathbf{v} = c\mathbf{v}$$

with $c = -b/a$, so it follows that $\mathbf{u}$ and $\mathbf{v}$ are linearly dependent. Therefore we have proved the following theorem.

> ***Theorem 2:*** *Two Linearly Dependent Vectors*
>
> The two vectors $\mathbf{u}$ and $\mathbf{v}$ are linearly dependent if and only if there exist scalars a and b *not both zero* such that
>
> $$a\mathbf{u} + b\mathbf{v} = \mathbf{0}. \tag{13}$$

The most interesting pairs of vectors are those that are not linearly dependent. The two vectors $\mathbf{u}$ and $\mathbf{v}$ are said to be **linearly independent** provided that they are *not* linearly dependent. Thus $\mathbf{u}$ and $\mathbf{v}$ are linearly independent if and only if neither is a scalar multiple of the other. By Theorem 2 this is equivalent to the following statement:

> The two vectors $\mathbf{u}$ and $\mathbf{v}$ are linearly independent if and only if the relation
>
> $$a\mathbf{u} + b\mathbf{v} = \mathbf{0} \tag{13}$$
>
> implies that $a = b = 0$.

Thus the vectors $\mathbf{u}$ and $\mathbf{v}$ are linearly independent provided that no *nontrivial* linear combination of them is equal to the zero vector.

EXAMPLE 3 If $\mathbf{u} = (3, -2)$, $\mathbf{v} = (-6, 4)$, and $\mathbf{w} = (5, -7)$, then $\mathbf{u}$ and $\mathbf{v}$ are linearly dependent because $\mathbf{v} = -2\mathbf{u}$. On the other hand, $\mathbf{u}$ and $\mathbf{w}$ are linearly independent. Here is an argument to establish this fact: Suppose that there were scalars a and b such that

$$a\mathbf{u} + b\mathbf{w} = \mathbf{0}.$$

Then

$$a(3, -2) + b(5, -7) = \mathbf{0},$$

and thus we get the simultaneous equations

$$\begin{aligned} 3a + 5b &= 0 \\ -2a - 7b &= 0. \end{aligned}$$

It is now easy to show that $a = b = 0$ is the (unique) solution of this system. This shows that whenever

$$a\mathbf{u} + b\mathbf{w} = \mathbf{0},$$

it follows that $a = b = 0$. Therefore $\mathbf{u}$ and $\mathbf{w}$ are linearly independent.

Alternatively, one could prove that $\mathbf{u}$ and $\mathbf{w}$ are linearly independent by showing that neither is a scalar multiple of the other (because $\frac{5}{3} \neq \frac{7}{2}$).

A **basis** for $\mathbf{R}^2$ is a pair $\mathbf{u}$, $\mathbf{v}$ of vectors such that every vector $\mathbf{w}$ in $\mathbf{R}^2$ can be expressed as a linear combination

$$\mathbf{w} = a\mathbf{u} + b\mathbf{v} \tag{14}$$

of $\mathbf{u}$ and $\mathbf{v}$. That is, given any vector $\mathbf{w}$ in $\mathbf{R}^2$, there exist scalars a and b such that Equation (14) holds. Equation (10) implies that the unit vectors $\mathbf{i}$, $\mathbf{j}$ constitute one basis for $\mathbf{R}^2$.

WARNING When in Chapter 4 we define the concept of a basis for a general vector space, we will require in advance that the vectors involved be linearly independent. In the case of $\mathbf{R}^2$ it is clear geometrically that two linearly dependent vectors $\mathbf{u}$ and $\mathbf{v}$ cannot constitute a basis for $\mathbf{R}^2$. The reason is that if $\mathbf{u}$ and $\mathbf{v}$ are linearly dependent, then they lie on some particular straight line L through the origin. But every linear combination $a\mathbf{u} + b\mathbf{v}$ of $\mathbf{u}$ and $\mathbf{v}$ must also lie on L, and so no vector $\mathbf{w}$ lying off the line L can be a linear combination of $\mathbf{u}$ and $\mathbf{v}$. Consequently, the linearly dependent pair $\mathbf{u}$, $\mathbf{v}$ cannot be a basis for $\mathbf{R}^2$. The following theorem guarantees the converse of this statement: *Any* linearly independent pair of vectors in $\mathbf{R}^2$ is a basis for $\mathbf{R}^2$.

> ***Theorem 3:*** *Basis for* $\mathbf{R}^2$
>
> If the vectors $\mathbf{u}$ and $\mathbf{v}$ in $\mathbf{R}^2$ are linearly independent, then they constitute a basis for $\mathbf{R}^2$.

PROOF Let $\mathbf{u} = (u_1, u_2)$ and $\mathbf{v} = (v_1, v_2)$. Given any third vector $\mathbf{w} = (w_1, w_2)$, we need show only that there exist numbers a and b such that

$$\mathbf{w} = a\mathbf{u} + b\mathbf{v}. \tag{14}$$

That is,

$$a\begin{bmatrix} u_1 \\ u_2 \end{bmatrix} + b\begin{bmatrix} v_1 \\ v_2 \end{bmatrix} = \begin{bmatrix} w_1 \\ w_2 \end{bmatrix};$$

in matrix notation,

$$\begin{bmatrix} u_1 & v_1 \\ u_2 & v_2 \end{bmatrix}\begin{bmatrix} a \\ b \end{bmatrix} = \begin{bmatrix} w_1 \\ w_2 \end{bmatrix}. \tag{15}$$

The six numbers u_1, u_2, v_1, v_2, w_1, and w_2 are given, so (15) is a 2×2 linear system in the two unknowns a and b. If we can show that the coefficient matrix

$$A = \begin{bmatrix} u_1 & v_1 \\ u_2 & v_2 \end{bmatrix}$$

is invertible, then it will follow that the system in (15) has the (unique) solution

$$\begin{bmatrix} a \\ b \end{bmatrix} = A^{-1}\begin{bmatrix} w_1 \\ w_2 \end{bmatrix}, \tag{16}$$

and the proof will be complete.

To see that A is invertible, we note first that because $\mathbf{u}$ and $\mathbf{v}$ are linearly independent, the homogeneous system

$$A\begin{bmatrix} a \\ b \end{bmatrix} = a\mathbf{u} + b\mathbf{v} = \mathbf{0} = \begin{bmatrix} 0 \\ 0 \end{bmatrix}$$

has only the trivial solution $a = b = 0$. It therefore follows from Theorem 7 in Section 1.5 that A is invertible. Hence A^{-1} exists, so a and b are given by the formula in (16). ■

REMARK 1 Figure 3.9 provides a geometric interpretation of the linear combination $\mathbf{w} = a\mathbf{u} + b\mathbf{v}$ of Theorem 3. The multiple $a\mathbf{u}$ is the projection parallel to $\mathbf{v}$ of $\mathbf{w}$ onto the line of $\mathbf{u}$, whereas the multiple $b\mathbf{v}$ is the projection parallel to $\mathbf{u}$ of $\mathbf{w}$ onto the line of $\mathbf{v}$.

REMARK 2 It is worth showing directly that if $\mathbf{u}$ and $\mathbf{v}$ are linearly independent, then the expression

$$\mathbf{w} = a\mathbf{u} + b\mathbf{v} \tag{17}$$

is *unique*—it is the *only* way of expressing $\mathbf{w}$ as a linear combination of $\mathbf{u}$ and $\mathbf{v}$. For suppose that

$$\mathbf{w} = c\mathbf{u} + d\mathbf{v} \tag{18}$$

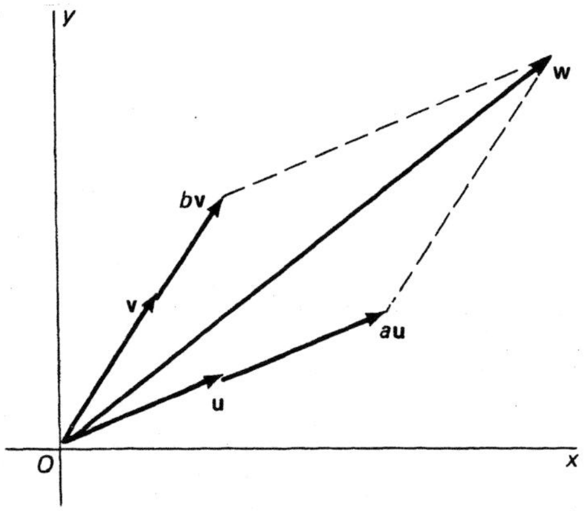

3.9 The vector **w** as a linear combination of the two vectors **u** and **v**.

is any way whatsoever of expressing $\mathbf{w}$ as a linear combination of $\mathbf{u}$ and $\mathbf{v}$. Then subtraction of the expressions in (18) from those in (17) yields

$$(a - c)\mathbf{u} + (b - d)\mathbf{v} = \mathbf{0}.$$

Because $\mathbf{u}$ and $\mathbf{v}$ are linearly independent it follows that $a - c = b - d = 0$ and thus that $c = a$ and $d = b$. Therefore the expression on the right-hand side in (18) is the same as that in (17), and this shows the uniqueness of the coefficients a and b.

EXAMPLE 4 Express the vector $\mathbf{w} = (11, 4)$ as a linear combination of the vectors $\mathbf{u} = (3, -2)$ and $\mathbf{v} = (-2, 7)$.

Solution We want to find numbers a and b such that

$$a\mathbf{u} + b\mathbf{v} = \mathbf{w};$$

$$a\begin{bmatrix} 3 \\ -2 \end{bmatrix} + b\begin{bmatrix} -2 \\ 7 \end{bmatrix} = \begin{bmatrix} 11 \\ 4 \end{bmatrix};$$

$$\begin{bmatrix} 3 & -2 \\ -2 & 7 \end{bmatrix}\begin{bmatrix} a \\ b \end{bmatrix} = \begin{bmatrix} 11 \\ 4 \end{bmatrix}.$$

Using either Gaussian elimination or Cramer's rule, we readily solve this 2×2 system for $a = 5$, $b = 2$. Thus $\mathbf{w} = 5\mathbf{u} + 2\mathbf{v}$.

3.1 PROBLEMS

In Problems 1-8, find $|\mathbf{a}|$, $|-2\mathbf{b}|$, $|\mathbf{a} - \mathbf{b}|$, $\mathbf{a} + \mathbf{b}$, and $3\mathbf{a} - 2\mathbf{b}$.

1. $\mathbf{a} = (1, -2)$, $\mathbf{b} = (-3, 2)$

2. $\mathbf{a} = (3, 4)$, $\mathbf{b} = (-4, 3)$

3. $\mathbf{a} = (-2, -2)$, $\mathbf{b} = (-3, -4)$

4. $\mathbf{a} = -2(4, 7)$, $\mathbf{b} = -3(-4, -2)$

5. $\mathbf{a} = \mathbf{i} + 3\mathbf{j}$, $\mathbf{b} = 2\mathbf{i} - 5\mathbf{j}$

6. $\mathbf{a} = 2\mathbf{i} - 5\mathbf{j}$, $\mathbf{b} = \mathbf{i} - 6\mathbf{j}$

7. $\mathbf{a} = 4\mathbf{i}$, $\mathbf{b} = -7\mathbf{j}$

8. $\mathbf{a} = -\mathbf{i} - \mathbf{j}$, $\mathbf{b} = 2\mathbf{i} + 2\mathbf{j}$

In Problems 9-12, find both a unit vector $\mathbf{u}$ with the same direction as $\mathbf{a}$ and a unit vector $\mathbf{v}$ with the direction opposite that of $\mathbf{a}$.

9. $\mathbf{a} = (-3, -4)$

10. $\mathbf{a} = (5, -12)$

11. $\mathbf{a} = 8\mathbf{i} + 15\mathbf{j}$

12. $\mathbf{a} = 7\mathbf{i} - 24\mathbf{j}$

In Problems 13-16, find the vector $\mathbf{a}$ represented by the arrow $\overrightarrow{PQ}$ in the plane.

13. $P = (3, 2)$, $Q = (3, -2)$

14. $P = (-3, 5)$, $Q = (-3, 6)$

15. $P = (-4, 7)$, $Q = (4, -7)$

16. $P = (1, -1)$, $Q = (-4, -1)$

In Problems 17-20, determine whether the given vectors $\mathbf{u}$ and $\mathbf{v}$ are linearly dependent or linearly independent.

17. $\mathbf{u} = (0, 2)$, $\mathbf{v} = (0, 3)$

18. $\mathbf{u} = (0, 2)$, $\mathbf{v} = (3, 0)$

19. $\mathbf{u} = (2, 2)$, $\mathbf{v} = (2, -2)$

20. $\mathbf{u} = (2, -2)$, $\mathbf{v} = (-2, 2)$

In Problems 21–26, express **w** as a linear combination of **u** and **v**.

21. $\mathbf{u} = (1, -2)$, $\mathbf{v} = (-1, 3)$, $\mathbf{w} = (1, 0)$

22. $\mathbf{u} = (3, 4)$, $\mathbf{v} = (2, 3)$, $\mathbf{w} = (0, -1)$

23. $\mathbf{u} = (5, 7)$, $\mathbf{v} = (2, 3)$, $\mathbf{w} = (1, 1)$

24. $\mathbf{u} = (4, 1)$, $\mathbf{v} = (-2, -1)$, $\mathbf{w} = (2, -2)$

25. $\mathbf{u} = (7, 5)$, $\mathbf{v} = (3, 4)$, $\mathbf{w} = (5, -2)$

26. $\mathbf{u} = (5, -2)$, $\mathbf{v} = (-6, 4)$, $\mathbf{w} = (5, 6)$

27. Suppose that **u**, **v**, and **w** denote arbitrary fixed vectors in $\mathbf{R}^2$. Show by componentwise computations that
(a) $\mathbf{u} + \mathbf{v} = \mathbf{v} + \mathbf{u}$;
(b) $\mathbf{u} + (\mathbf{v} + \mathbf{w}) = (\mathbf{u} + \mathbf{v}) + \mathbf{w}$.

28. Let **u** be a vector in $\mathbf{R}^2$ and let r and s be scalars. Show that
(a) $(r + s)\mathbf{u} = r\mathbf{u} + s\mathbf{u}$;
(b) $r(s\mathbf{u}) = (rs)\mathbf{u}$.

29. Prove that the vectors $\mathbf{u} = (u_1, u_2)$ and $\mathbf{v} = (v_1, v_2)$ are linearly independent if and only if

$$\begin{vmatrix} u_1 & v_1 \\ u_2 & v_2 \end{vmatrix} \neq 0.$$

30. Three vectors **u**, **v**, and **w** are called *linearly dependent* provided that there exist scalars a, b, and c *not all zero* such that

$$a\mathbf{u} + b\mathbf{v} + c\mathbf{w} = \mathbf{0}.$$

Use Theorem 3 to prove that *any* three arbitrary vectors in $\mathbf{R}^2$ are linearly dependent.

3.2

The Vector Space $\mathbf{R}^3$

Rectangular coordinates in the plane generalize in a natural way to rectangular coordinates in space. A point in space is determined by giving its location relative to three mutually perpendicular *coordinate axes* passing through the origin O. We draw the x-, y-, and z-axes as shown in Figure 3.10, with arrows indicating the positive direction along each axis. With this configuration of axes, our rectangular coordinate system is said to be *right-handed*: If the curled fingers of the right hand point in the direction of a 90° rotation from the positive x-axis to the positive y-axis, then the thumb points in the direction of the positive z-axis.

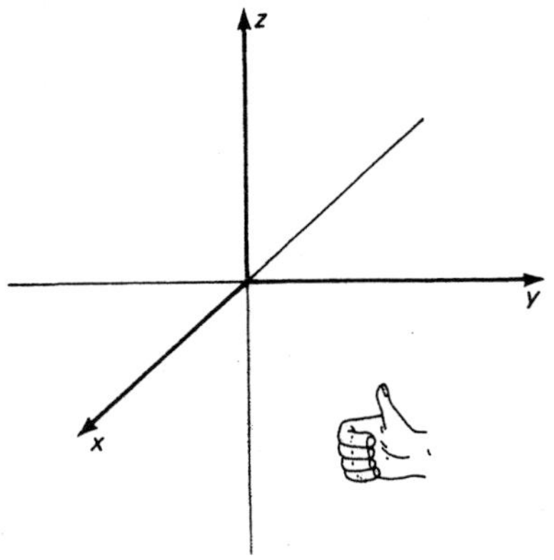

3.10 The right-handed rectangular coordinate system.

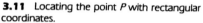

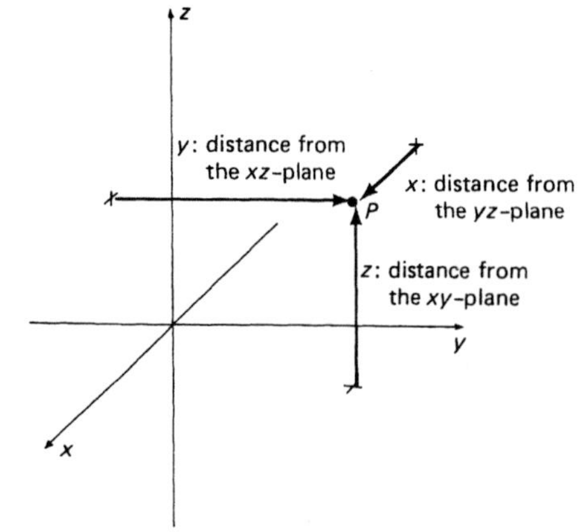

3.11 Locating the point P with rectangular coordinates.

The three coordinate axes taken in pairs determine three *coordinate planes*:

- The (horizontal) xy-plane, where $z = 0$;
- The (vertical) yz-plane, where $x = 0$; and
- The (vertical) xz-plane, where $y = 0$.

The point P in the plane is said to have **rectangular coordinates** (x, y, z) if (see Figure 3.11)

- x is its signed distance from the yz-plane,
- y is its signed distance from the xz-plane, and
- z is its signed distance from the xy-plane.

In this case we may describe the location of the point P by simply calling it $P(x, y, z)$. There is a one-to-one correspondence between points P in space and ordered triples (x, y, z) of real numbers.

Motivated by this standard approach to rectangular coordinates in space, we define **three-dimensional coordinate space $\mathbf{R}^3$** to be the set of all ordered triples (x, y, z) of real numbers. The elements of $\mathbf{R}^3$ are called (three-dimensional) **vectors**. The point $P(x, y, z)$ determines the vector $\mathbf{v} = (x, y, z)$ in $\mathbf{R}^3$, and $\mathbf{v}$ is represented geometrically (as in Figure 3.12) by the position vector $\overrightarrow{OP}$ from the origin to P (or by any parallel translate of this arrow). As in the two-dimensional case, we regard

$$\mathbf{v} = (x, y, z) \quad \text{and} \quad \mathbf{v} = \begin{bmatrix} x \\ y \\ z \end{bmatrix}$$

as equivalent symbols denoting the vector $\mathbf{v}$ with **components** x, y, and z.

We define addition of vectors in $\mathbf{R}^3$ and multiplication of vectors by scalars just as in Section 3.1—that is, in a componentwise manner, taking into account that our

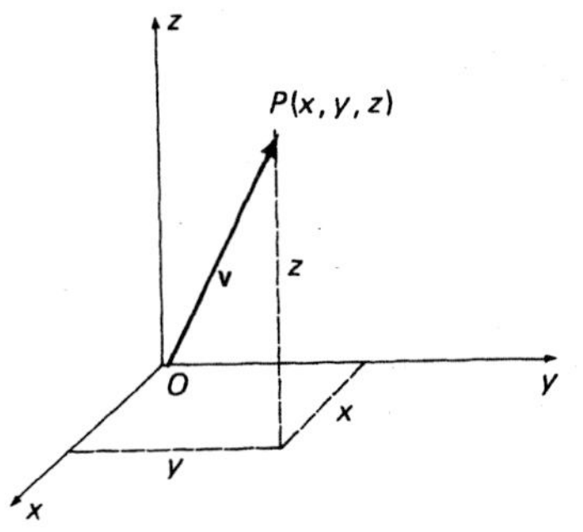

3.12 The directed segment $\overrightarrow{OP}$ representing the vector $\mathbf{v} = (x, y, z)$.

vectors now have three components rather than two. The **sum** of the vectors $\mathbf{a} = (a_1, a_2, a_3)$ and $\mathbf{b} = (b_1, b_2, b_3)$ is thus the vector

$$\mathbf{a} + \mathbf{b} = (a_1 + b_1, a_2 + b_2, a_3 + b_3). \tag{1}$$

Because arrows representing **a** and **b** lie in a plane (though not necessarily the xy-plane) if their initial points coincide, addition of vectors in $\mathbf{R}^3$ satisfies the same *parallelogram law* as in the two-dimensional case (Figure 3.13).

If c is a real number, then the **scalar multiple** $c\mathbf{a}$ of $\mathbf{a} = (a_1, a_2, a_3)$ is the vector

$$c\mathbf{a} = (ca_1, ca_2, ca_3). \tag{2}$$

The length $|\mathbf{a}|$ of **a** is defined to be

$$|\mathbf{a}| = \sqrt{(a_1)^2 + (a_2)^2 + (a_3)^2}, \tag{3}$$

analogous to the length of a two-dimensional vector. It follows that the length of the scalar multiple $c\mathbf{a}$ is $|c|$ times the length of **a** and that $c\mathbf{a}$ has the same direction as **a** if $c > 0$ and the opposite direction if $c < 0$.

EXAMPLE 1 If $\mathbf{a} = (3, 4, 12)$ and $\mathbf{b} = (-4, 3, 0)$, then

$$\mathbf{a} + \mathbf{b} = (3 + (-4), 4 + 3, 12 + 0) = (-1, 7, 12),$$

$$|\mathbf{a}| = \sqrt{3^2 + 4^2 + 12^2} = \sqrt{169} = 13,$$

$$2\mathbf{a} = (2 \cdot 3, 2 \cdot 4, 2 \cdot 12) = (6, 8, 24),$$

and

$$2\mathbf{a} - 3\mathbf{b} = (2(3) - 3(-4), 2(4) - 3(3), 2(12) - 3(0))$$
$$= (18, -1, 24).$$

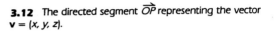

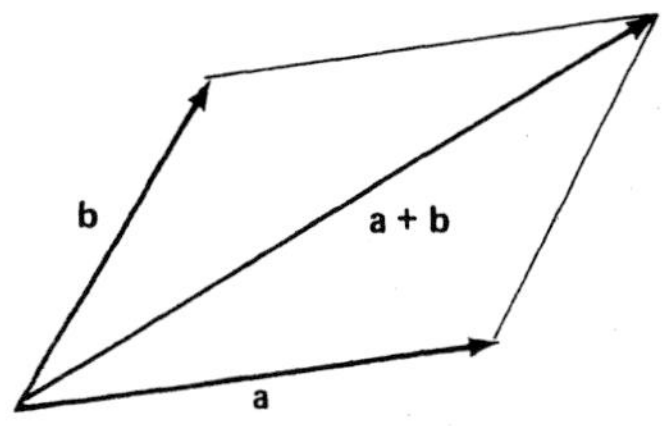

3.13 The parallelogram law for addition of vectors.

With vector addition and multiplication by scalars defined as in (1) and (2), $\mathbf{R}^3$ is a **vector space**. That is, these operations satisfy the conditions in (a)–(h) of the following theorem.

> ***Theorem 1*: $\mathbf{R}^3$ *as a Vector Space***
>
> If $\mathbf{u}$, $\mathbf{v}$, and $\mathbf{w}$ are vectors in $\mathbf{R}^3$ and r and s are real numbers, then:
>
> **(a)** $\mathbf{u} + \mathbf{v} = \mathbf{v} + \mathbf{u}$ (commutativity)
>
> **(b)** $\mathbf{u} + (\mathbf{v} + \mathbf{w}) = (\mathbf{u} + \mathbf{v}) + \mathbf{w}$ (associativity)
>
> **(c)** $\mathbf{u} + \mathbf{0} = \mathbf{0} + \mathbf{u} = \mathbf{u}$ (zero element)
>
> **(d)** $\mathbf{u} + (-\mathbf{u}) = (-\mathbf{u}) + \mathbf{u} = \mathbf{0}$ (additive inverse)
>
> **(e)** $r(\mathbf{u} + \mathbf{v}) = r\mathbf{u} + r\mathbf{v}$ (distributivity)
>
> **(f)** $(r + s)\mathbf{u} = r\mathbf{u} + s\mathbf{u}$
>
> **(g)** $r(s\mathbf{u}) = (rs)\mathbf{u}$
>
> **(h)** $1(\mathbf{u}) = \mathbf{u}$ (multiplicative identity).

Both the statement and the proof of this theorem are the same as those of Theorem 1 in Section 3.1, except that our vectors now have three components instead of two. Of course $\mathbf{0} = (0, 0, 0)$ denotes the **zero vector** in (c) and (d), and $-\mathbf{u} = (-1)\mathbf{u}$ in (d).

Any vector in $\mathbf{R}^3$ can be expressed in terms of the three **basic unit vectors**

$$\mathbf{i} = (1, 0, 0), \quad \mathbf{j} = (0, 1, 0), \quad \text{and} \quad \mathbf{k} = (0, 0, 1). \tag{4}$$

When represented by arrows with their initial points at the origin, these three vectors form a right-handed triple of vectors pointing in the positive directions along the three coordinate axes (as shown in Figure 3.14).

Any vector $\mathbf{a} = (a_1, a_2, a_3)$ in $\mathbf{R}^3$ can be expressed as the *linear combination*

$$\mathbf{a} = a_1\mathbf{i} + a_2\mathbf{j} + a_3\mathbf{k} \tag{5}$$

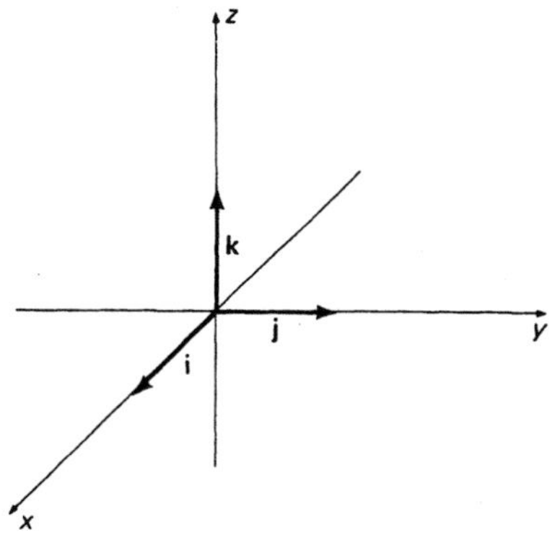

3.14 The basic unit vectors **i**, **j**, and **k**.

of the basic unit vectors **i**, **j**, and **k**. As in the two-dimensional case, the usefulness of this representation is that algebraic operations involving vectors can be carried out simply by collecting coefficients of **i**, **j**, and **k**. For instance,

$$\begin{aligned}\mathbf{a} + \mathbf{b} &= (a_1\mathbf{i} + a_2\mathbf{j} + a_3\mathbf{k}) + (b_1\mathbf{i} + b_2\mathbf{j} + b_3\mathbf{k}) \\ &= (a_1 + b_1)\mathbf{i} + (a_2 + b_2)\mathbf{j} + (a_3 + b_3)\mathbf{k}\end{aligned}$$

and

$$\begin{aligned}c\mathbf{a} &= c(a_1\mathbf{i} + a_2\mathbf{j} + a_3\mathbf{k}) \\ &= ca_1\mathbf{i} + ca_2\mathbf{j} + ca_3\mathbf{k}.\end{aligned}$$

You should note that everything we have said as yet in this section about the vector space $\mathbf{R}^3$ is in direct analogy to what we said in Section 3.1 about the vector space $\mathbf{R}^2$.

LINEAR DEPENDENCE IN $\mathbf{R}^3$

In Section 3.1 we said that the vectors $\mathbf{u} = (u_1, u_2)$ and $\mathbf{v} = (v_1, v_2)$ are linearly dependent provided that one is a scalar multiple of the other, in which case the points (u_1, u_2) and (v_1, v_2) lie on the same line through the origin. For *three* vectors $\mathbf{u} = (u_1, u_2, u_3)$, $\mathbf{v} = (v_1, v_2, v_3)$, and $\mathbf{w} = (w_1, w_2, w_3)$, the analogous condition is that the three points (u_1, u_2, u_3), (v_1, v_2, v_3), and (w_1, w_2, w_3) lie in the same *plane* through the origin in $\mathbf{R}^3$. Given **u**, **v**, and **w**, how can we determine whether the vectors **u**, **v**, and **w** are *coplanar*? The key to the answer is the following observation: If r and s are scalars, then the parallelogram law of addition implies that the vectors **u**, **v**, and $r\mathbf{u} + s\mathbf{v}$ are coplanar; specifically, they lie in the plane through the origin that's determined by the parallelogram with vertices **0**, $r\mathbf{u}$, $s\mathbf{v}$, and $r\mathbf{u} + s\mathbf{v}$. Thus any linear combination of **u** and **v** is coplanar with **u** and **v**. This is the motivation for our next definition.

> ***Definition:*** *Linearly Dependent Vectors in* $\mathbf{R}^3$
>
> The three vectors **u**, **v**, and **w** in $\mathbf{R}^3$ are said to be linearly dependent provided that one of them is a linear combination of the other two—that is, either
>
> $$\begin{aligned}\mathbf{w} &= r\mathbf{u} + s\mathbf{v} \quad \text{or} \\ \mathbf{u} &= r\mathbf{v} + s\mathbf{w} \quad \text{or} \qquad (6) \\ \mathbf{v} &= r\mathbf{u} + s\mathbf{w}\end{aligned}$$
>
> for appropriate scalars r and s.

Note that each of the three equations in (6) implies that there exist three scalars a, b, and c *not all zero* such that

$$a\mathbf{u} + b\mathbf{v} + c\mathbf{w} = \mathbf{0}. \tag{7}$$

For if $\mathbf{w} = r\mathbf{u} + s\mathbf{v}$ (for instance) then

$$r\mathbf{u} + s\mathbf{v} + (-1)\mathbf{w} = \mathbf{0},$$

so we can take $a = r$, $b = s$, and $c = -1 \neq 0$. Conversely, suppose that (7) holds with a, b, and c not all zero. If $c \neq 0$ (for instance) then we can solve for

$$\mathbf{w} = -\frac{a}{c}\mathbf{u} - \frac{b}{c}\mathbf{v} = r\mathbf{u} + s\mathbf{v}$$

with $r = -a/c$ and $s = -b/c$, so it follows that the three vectors $\mathbf{u}$, $\mathbf{v}$, and $\mathbf{w}$ are linearly dependent. Therefore we have proved the following theorem.

Theorem 2: *Three Linearly Dependent Vectors*

The three vectors $\mathbf{u}$, $\mathbf{v}$, and $\mathbf{w}$ in $\mathbf{R}^3$ are linearly dependent if and only if there exist scalars a, b, and c *not all zero* such that

$$a\mathbf{u} + b\mathbf{v} + c\mathbf{w} = \mathbf{0}. \tag{7}$$

The three vectors $\mathbf{u}$, $\mathbf{v}$, and $\mathbf{w}$ are called **linearly independent** provided that they are *not* linearly dependent. Thus $\mathbf{u}$, $\mathbf{v}$, and $\mathbf{w}$ are linearly independent if and only if neither of them is a linear combination of the other two. As a consequence of Theorem 2, this is equivalent to the following statement:

The vectors $\mathbf{u}$, $\mathbf{v}$, and $\mathbf{w}$ are linearly independent if and only if the relation

$$a\mathbf{u} + b\mathbf{v} + c\mathbf{w} = \mathbf{0} \tag{7}$$

implies that $a = b = c = 0$.

Thus the three vectors $\mathbf{u}$, $\mathbf{v}$, and $\mathbf{w}$ are linearly independent provided that no *nontrivial* linear combination of them is equal to the zero vector.

Given two vectors, one can see at a glance whether either is a scalar multiple of the other. By contrast, it is not evident at a glance whether or not three given vectors in $\mathbf{R}^3$ are linearly independent. The following theorem provides one way to resolve this question.

Theorem 3: *Three Linearly Independent Vectors*

The vectors $\mathbf{u} = (u_1, u_2, u_3)$, $\mathbf{v} = (v_1, v_2, v_3)$, and $\mathbf{w} = (w_1, w_2, w_3)$ are linearly independent if and only if

$$\begin{vmatrix} u_1 & v_1 & w_1 \\ u_2 & v_2 & w_2 \\ u_3 & v_3 & w_3 \end{vmatrix} \neq 0. \tag{8}$$

Proof We want to show that **u**, **v**, and **w** are linearly independent if and only if the matrix

$$A = \begin{bmatrix} u_1 & v_1 & w_1 \\ u_2 & v_2 & w_2 \\ u_3 & v_3 & w_3 \end{bmatrix}$$

—with column vectors **u**, **v**, and **w**—has nonzero determinant. By Theorem 2, the vectors **u**, **v**, and **w** are linearly independent if and only if the equation

$$a\begin{bmatrix} u_1 \\ u_2 \\ u_3 \end{bmatrix} + b\begin{bmatrix} v_1 \\ v_2 \\ v_3 \end{bmatrix} + c\begin{bmatrix} w_1 \\ w_2 \\ w_3 \end{bmatrix} = \mathbf{0}$$

implies that $a = b = c = 0$; that is, if and only if the system

$$\begin{bmatrix} u_1 & v_1 & w_1 \\ u_2 & v_2 & w_2 \\ u_3 & v_3 & w_3 \end{bmatrix}\begin{bmatrix} a \\ b \\ c \end{bmatrix} = \begin{bmatrix} 0 \\ 0 \\ 0 \end{bmatrix} \tag{9}$$

with unknowns a, b, and c has only the trivial solution. But Theorem 7 in Section 1.5 implies that this is so if and only if the coefficient matrix A is invertible, and Theorem 2 in Section 2.3 implies that A is invertible if and only if $|A| \neq 0$. Therefore, **u**, **v**, and **w** are linearly independent if and only if $|A| \neq 0$. ■

Hence, in order to determine whether or not three given vectors **u**, **v**, and **w** are linearly independent, we can calculate the determinant in (8). In practice, however, it is usually more efficient to set up and solve the linear system in (9). If we obtain only the trivial solution $a = b = c = 0$, then the three given vectors are linearly independent. But if we find a nontrivial solution, we then can express one of the vectors as a linear combination of the other two and thus see *how* the three vectors are linearly dependent.

EXAMPLE 2 To determine whether the three vectors $\mathbf{u} = (1, 2, -3)$, $\mathbf{v} = (3, 1, -2)$, and $\mathbf{w} = (5, -5, 6)$ are linearly independent or dependent, we need to solve the system

$$a\mathbf{u} + b\mathbf{v} + c\mathbf{w} = \begin{bmatrix} 1 & 3 & 5 \\ 2 & 1 & -5 \\ -3 & -2 & 6 \end{bmatrix}\begin{bmatrix} a \\ b \\ c \end{bmatrix} = \begin{bmatrix} 0 \\ 0 \\ 0 \end{bmatrix}.$$

By Gaussian elimination we readily reduce this system to the echelon form

$$\begin{bmatrix} 1 & 3 & 5 \\ 0 & 1 & 3 \\ 0 & 0 & 0 \end{bmatrix}\begin{bmatrix} a \\ b \\ c \end{bmatrix} = \begin{bmatrix} 0 \\ 0 \\ 0 \end{bmatrix}.$$

Therefore, we can choose $c = 1$, and it follows that $b = -3c = -3$ and $a = -3b - 5c = 4$. Therefore

$$4\mathbf{u} + (-3)\mathbf{v} + \mathbf{w} = \mathbf{0},$$

and hence **u**, **v**, and **w** are linearly dependent with $\mathbf{w} = -4\mathbf{u} + 3\mathbf{v}$.

A **basis** for $\mathbf{R}^3$ is a triple $\mathbf{u}, \mathbf{v}, \mathbf{w}$ of vectors such that every vector $\mathbf{t}$ in $\mathbf{R}^3$ can be expressed as a linear combination

$$\mathbf{t} = a\mathbf{u} + b\mathbf{v} + c\mathbf{w} \tag{10}$$

of the three vectors $\mathbf{u}$, $\mathbf{v}$, and $\mathbf{w}$. That is, given any vector $\mathbf{t}$ in $\mathbf{R}^3$, there exist scalars a, b, and c such that Equation (10) holds. Equation (5) implies that the unit vectors $\mathbf{i}, \mathbf{j}, \mathbf{k}$ constitute a basis for $\mathbf{R}^3$. The following theorem says that any three *linearly independent* vectors constitute a basis for $\mathbf{R}^3$.

> ***Theorem 4***: *Basis for* $\mathbf{R}^3$
> If the vectors $\mathbf{u}$, $\mathbf{v}$, and $\mathbf{w}$ in $\mathbf{R}^3$ are linearly independent, then they constitute a basis for $\mathbf{R}^3$.

PROOF Let $\mathbf{u} = (u_1, u_2, u_3)$, $\mathbf{v} = (v_1, v_2, v_3)$, and $\mathbf{w} = (w_1, w_2, w_3)$. Given any fourth vector $\mathbf{t} = (t_1, t_2, t_3)$, we must show that there exist scalars a, b, and c such that

$$\mathbf{t} = a\mathbf{u} + b\mathbf{v} + c\mathbf{w}; \tag{10}$$

that is, such that the system

$$\begin{bmatrix} u_1 & v_1 & w_1 \\ u_2 & v_2 & w_2 \\ u_3 & v_3 & w_3 \end{bmatrix} \begin{bmatrix} a \\ b \\ c \end{bmatrix} = \begin{bmatrix} t_1 \\ t_2 \\ t_3 \end{bmatrix} \tag{11}$$

has a solution (a, b, c). But by Theorem 3 the fact that $\mathbf{u}$, $\mathbf{v}$, and $\mathbf{w}$ are linearly independent implies that the coefficient matrix A in (11) has nonzero determinant and is therefore invertible. Hence there is a (unique) solution, which may be obtained by multiplying both sides in (11) by A^{-1}. ■

EXAMPLE 3 In order to express the vector $\mathbf{t} = (4, 20, 23)$ as a combination of the linearly independent vectors $\mathbf{u} = (1, 3, 2)$, $\mathbf{v} = (2, 8, 7)$, and $\mathbf{w} = (1, 7, 9)$, we need to solve the system

$$\begin{bmatrix} 1 & 2 & 1 \\ 3 & 8 & 7 \\ 2 & 7 & 9 \end{bmatrix} \begin{bmatrix} a \\ b \\ c \end{bmatrix} = \begin{bmatrix} 4 \\ 20 \\ 23 \end{bmatrix}$$

that we obtain by substitution in Equation (11). The echelon form found by Gaussian elimination is

$$\begin{bmatrix} 1 & 2 & 1 \\ 0 & 1 & 2 \\ 0 & 0 & 1 \end{bmatrix} \begin{bmatrix} a \\ b \\ c \end{bmatrix} = \begin{bmatrix} 4 \\ 4 \\ 3 \end{bmatrix},$$

so $c = 3$, $b = 4 - 2c = -2$, and $a = 4 - 2b - c = 5$. Thus

$$\mathbf{t} = 5\mathbf{u} - 2\mathbf{v} + 3\mathbf{w}.$$

SUBSPACES OF $\mathbf{R}^3$

As yet we have used the words *line* and *plane* in an informal or intuitive way. It is now time for us to say precisely what is meant by a line or plane *through the origin* in $\mathbf{R}^3$. Each is an example of a *subspace* of $\mathbf{R}^3$.

The nonempty subset V of $\mathbf{R}^3$ is called a **subspace** of $\mathbf{R}^3$ provided that V itself is a vector space under the operations of vector addition and multiplication of vectors by scalars. Suppose that the nonempty subset V of $\mathbf{R}^3$ is **closed** under these operations —that is, that the sum of any two vectors in V is also in V and every scalar multiple of a vector in V is also in V. Then the vectors in V automatically satisfy properties (a) through (h) of Theorem 1 because these properties are "inherited" from $\mathbf{R}^3$; they hold for *all* vectors in $\mathbf{R}^3$, including those in V. Consequently we see that a nonempty subset V of $\mathbf{R}^3$ is a **subspace** of $\mathbf{R}^3$ if and only if it satisfies the following two conditions:

(i) If $\mathbf{u}$ and $\mathbf{v}$ are vectors in V, then $\mathbf{u} + \mathbf{v}$ is also in V (closure under addition).

(ii) If $\mathbf{u}$ is a vector in V and c is a scalar, then $c\mathbf{u}$ is in V (closure under multiplication by scalars).

It is immediate that $V = \mathbf{R}^3$ is a subspace: $\mathbf{R}^3$ is a subspace of itself. At the opposite extreme, the subset $V = \{\mathbf{0}\}$ containing only the zero vector is also a subspace of $\mathbf{R}^3$, because $\mathbf{0} + \mathbf{0} = \mathbf{0}$ and $c\mathbf{0} = \mathbf{0}$ for every scalar c. Thus $V = \{\mathbf{0}\}$ satisfies conditions (i) and (ii). The subspaces $\{\mathbf{0}\}$ and $\mathbf{R}^3$ are sometimes called the *trivial* subspaces of $\mathbf{R}^3$ (because the verification that they *are* subspaces is quite trivial). All subspaces other than $\{\mathbf{0}\}$ and $\mathbf{R}^3$ itself are called **proper subspaces** of $\mathbf{R}^3$.

Now we want to show that the proper subspaces of $\mathbf{R}^3$ are what we customarily call lines and planes through the origin. Let V be a subspace of $\mathbf{R}^3$ that is neither $\{\mathbf{0}\}$ nor $\mathbf{R}^3$ itself. There are two cases to consider, depending on whether or not V contains two linearly independent vectors.

CASE 1: Suppose that V does *not* contain two linearly independent vectors. If $\mathbf{u}$ is a fixed nonzero vector in V, then by condition (ii) above every scalar multiple $c\mathbf{u}$ is also in V. Conversely, if $\mathbf{v}$ is any other vector in V, then $\mathbf{u}$ and $\mathbf{v}$ are linearly dependent, so it follows that $\mathbf{v} = c\mathbf{u}$ for some scalar c (see Problem 29). Thus the subspace V is the set of all scalar multiples of the fixed nonzero vector $\mathbf{u}$ and is therefore what we call a **line** through the origin in $\mathbf{R}^3$ (see Figure 3.15).

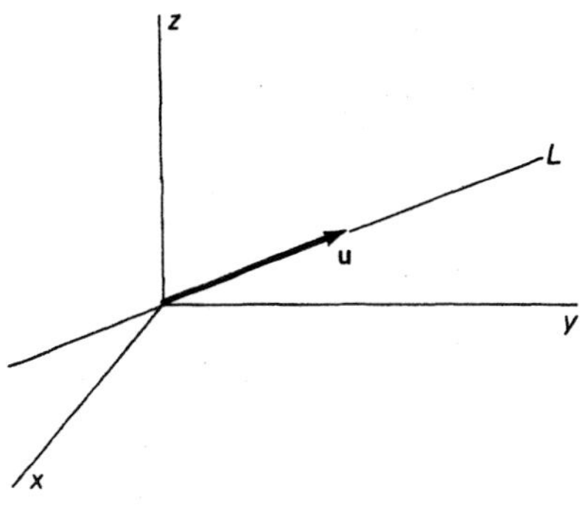

3.15 The line L spanned by the vector $\mathbf{u}$.

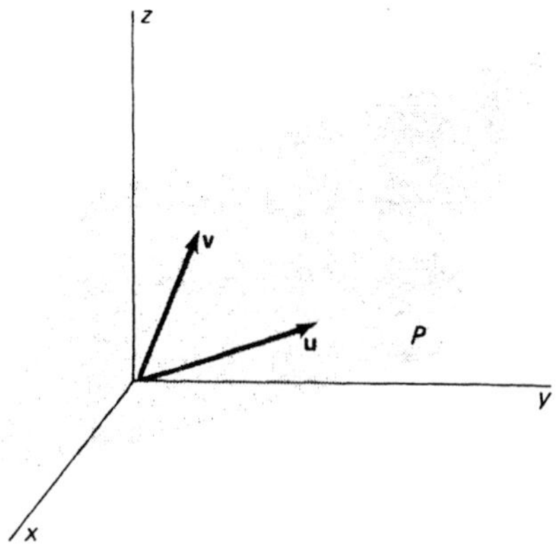

3.16 The plane P spanned by the vectors **u** and **v**.

CASE 2: Suppose that V contains two linearly independent vectors **u** and **v**. It then follows from conditions (i) and (ii) that V contains every linear combination $a\mathbf{u} + b\mathbf{v}$ of **u** and **v** (see Problem 28). Conversely, let **w** be any other vector in V. If **u**, **v**, **w** were linearly independent, then by Theorem 4 V would be all of $\mathbf{R}^3$. Therefore, **u**, **v**, **w** are linearly dependent, so it follows that there exist scalars a and b such that $\mathbf{w} = a\mathbf{u} + b\mathbf{v}$ (see Problem 31). Thus the subspace V is the set of all linear combinations $a\mathbf{u} + b\mathbf{v}$ of the two linearly independent vectors **u** and **v** and is therefore what we call a **plane** through the origin in $\mathbf{R}^3$ (see Figure 3.16).

Subspaces of the coordinate plane $\mathbf{R}^2$ are defined similarly—they are the nonempty subsets of $\mathbf{R}^2$ that are closed under addition and multiplication by scalars. In Problem 30 we ask you to show that every proper subspace of $\mathbf{R}^2$ is a line through the origin.

EXAMPLE 4 Let V be the set of all vectors (x, y) in $\mathbf{R}^2$ such that $y = x$. Given **u** and **v** in V, we may write $\mathbf{u} = (u, u)$ and $\mathbf{v} = (v, v)$. Then $\mathbf{u} + \mathbf{v} = (u + v, u + v)$ and $c\mathbf{u} = (cu, cu)$ are in V. It follows that V is a subspace of $\mathbf{R}^2$.

EXAMPLE 5 Let V be the set of all vectors (x, y) in $\mathbf{R}^2$ such that $x + y = 1$. Then $\mathbf{u} = (1, 0)$ and $\mathbf{v} = (0, 1)$ are in V, but the vector $\mathbf{u} + \mathbf{v} = (1, 1)$ is not. It follows that V is not a subspace of $\mathbf{R}^2$.

Example 5 illustrates the fact that lines that do not pass through the origin are not subspaces of $\mathbf{R}^2$. In Section 3.4 we discuss general lines and planes in $\mathbf{R}^3$. Because every subspace must contain the zero vector (see Problem 27), only lines and planes that pass through the origin are subspaces of $\mathbf{R}^3$.

3.2 PROBLEMS

In Problems 1–4, find $|\mathbf{a} - \mathbf{b}|$, $2\mathbf{a} + \mathbf{b}$, and $3\mathbf{a} - 4\mathbf{b}$.

1. $\mathbf{a} = (2, 5, -4)$, $\mathbf{b} = (1, -2, -3)$

2. $\mathbf{a} = (-1, 0, 2)$, $\mathbf{b} = (3, 4, -5)$

3. $\mathbf{a} = 2\mathbf{i} - 3\mathbf{j} + 5\mathbf{k}$, $\mathbf{b} = 5\mathbf{i} + 3\mathbf{j} - 7\mathbf{k}$

4. $\mathbf{a} = 2\mathbf{i} - \mathbf{j}$, $\mathbf{b} = \mathbf{j} - 3\mathbf{k}$

In Problems 5–8, apply Theorem 3 (that is, calculate a determinant) to determine whether the given vectors $\mathbf{u}$, $\mathbf{v}$, and $\mathbf{w}$ are linearly dependent or independent.

5. $\mathbf{u} = (3, -1, 2)$, $\mathbf{v} = (5, 4, -6)$, $\mathbf{w} = (8, 3, -4)$

6. $\mathbf{u} = (5, -2, 4)$, $\mathbf{v} = (2, -3, 5)$, $\mathbf{w} = (4, 5, -7)$

7. $\mathbf{u} = (1, -1, 2)$, $\mathbf{v} = (3, 0, 1)$, $\mathbf{w} = (1, -2, 2)$

8. $\mathbf{u} = (1, 1, 0)$, $\mathbf{v} = (4, 3, 1)$, $\mathbf{w} = (3, -2, -4)$

In Problems 9–14, use the method of Example 2 to determine whether the given vectors $\mathbf{u}$, $\mathbf{v}$, and $\mathbf{w}$ are linearly independent or dependent. If they are linearly dependent, find scalars a, b, and c *not all zero* such that $a\mathbf{u} + b\mathbf{v} + c\mathbf{w} = \mathbf{0}$.

9. $\mathbf{u} = (2, 0, 1)$, $\mathbf{v} = (-3, 1, -1)$, $\mathbf{w} = (0, -2, -1)$

10. $\mathbf{u} = (5, 5, 4)$, $\mathbf{v} = (2, 3, 1)$, $\mathbf{w} = (4, 1, 5)$

11. $\mathbf{u} = (1, 1, -2)$, $\mathbf{v} = (-2, -1, 6)$, $\mathbf{w} = (3, 7, 2)$

12. $\mathbf{u} = (1, 1, 0)$, $\mathbf{v} = (5, 1, 3)$, $\mathbf{w} = (0, 1, 2)$

13. $\mathbf{u} = (2, 0, 3)$, $\mathbf{v} = (5, 4, -2)$, $\mathbf{w} = (2, -1, 1)$

14. $\mathbf{u} = (1, 4, 5)$, $\mathbf{v} = (4, 2, 5)$, $\mathbf{w} = (-3, 3, -1)$

In Problems 15–18, express the vector $\mathbf{t}$ as a linear combination of the vectors $\mathbf{u}$, $\mathbf{v}$, and $\mathbf{w}$.

15. $\mathbf{t} = (2, -7, 9)$, $\mathbf{u} = (1, -2, 2)$, $\mathbf{v} = (3, 0, 1)$, $\mathbf{w} = (1, -1, 2)$

16. $\mathbf{t} = (5, 30, -21)$, $\mathbf{u} = (5, 2, -2)$, $\mathbf{v} = (1, 5, -3)$, $\mathbf{w} = (5, -3, 4)$

17. $\mathbf{t} = (0, 0, 19)$, $\mathbf{u} = (1, 4, 3)$, $\mathbf{v} = (-1, -2, 2)$, $\mathbf{w} = (4, 4, 1)$

18. $\mathbf{t} = (7, 7, 7)$, $\mathbf{u} = (2, 5, 3)$, $\mathbf{v} = (4, 1, -1)$, $\mathbf{w} = (1, 1, 5)$

In Problems 19–22, show that the given set V is closed under addition and under multiplication by scalars and is therefore a subspace of $\mathbf{R}^3$.

19. V is the set of all (x, y, z) such that $x = 0$.

20. V is the set of all (x, y, z) such that $x + y + z = 0$.

21. V is the set of all (x, y, z) such that $2x = 3y$.

22. V is the set of all (x, y, z) such that $z = 2x + 3y$.

In Problems 23–26, show that the given set V is not a subspace of $\mathbf{R}^3$.

23. V is the set of all (x, y, z) such that $y = 1$.

24. V is the set of all (x, y, z) such that $x + y + z = 3$.

25. V is the set of all (x, y, z) such that $z \geqq 0$.

26. V is the set of all (x, y, z) such that $xyz = 1$.

27. Show that every subspace V of $\mathbf{R}^3$ contains the zero vector $\mathbf{0}$.

28. Suppose that V is a subspace of $\mathbf{R}^3$. Show that V is closed under the operation of taking linear combinations of pairs of vectors. That is, show that if $\mathbf{u}$ and $\mathbf{v}$ are in V and a and b are scalars, then $a\mathbf{u} + b\mathbf{v}$ is in V.

29. Suppose that the vectors $\mathbf{u}$ and $\mathbf{v}$ in $\mathbf{R}^3$ are linearly dependent and that $\mathbf{u} \neq \mathbf{0}$. Show that $\mathbf{v} = c\mathbf{u}$ for some scalar c.

30. Suppose that V is a proper subspace of $\mathbf{R}^2$ and that $\mathbf{u}$ is a nonzero vector in V. Show that V is the set of all scalar multiples of $\mathbf{u}$ and therefore that V is a line through the origin.

31. Suppose that $\mathbf{u}$, $\mathbf{v}$, and $\mathbf{w}$ are vectors in $\mathbf{R}^3$ such that $\mathbf{u}$ and $\mathbf{v}$ are linearly independent but $\mathbf{u}$, $\mathbf{v}$, and $\mathbf{w}$ are linearly dependent. Show that there exist scalars a and b such that $\mathbf{w} = a\mathbf{u} + b\mathbf{v}$.

32. Let V_1 and V_2 be subspaces of $\mathbf{R}^3$. Their *intersection* $V = V_1 \cap V_2$ is the set of all vectors that lie both in V_1 and in V_2. Show that V is a subspace of $\mathbf{R}^3$.

3.3

Orthogonality and the Dot Product

In Section 3.2 we discussed the *algebra* of vectors in $\mathbf{R}^3$. The *Euclidean geometry* of space involves the concepts of *distance* and *angle*, both of which stem from the definition of the *length* of a vector.

Recall that the **length** $|\mathbf{v}|$ of the vector $\mathbf{v} = (a, b, c)$ is the nonnegative number

$$|\mathbf{v}| = \sqrt{a^2 + b^2 + c^2}. \tag{1}$$

The **distance** $d(P, Q)$ between the points P and Q with position vectors $\mathbf{a} = \overrightarrow{OP}$ and $\mathbf{b} = \overrightarrow{OQ}$ is defined to be

$$d(P, Q) = |\mathbf{a} - \mathbf{b}| = |\overrightarrow{PQ}|, \tag{2}$$

where $\overrightarrow{PQ}$ is the vector obtained by subtracting the coordinates of P from those of Q. For instance, the distance between the points $P(3, 1, 2)$ and $Q(7, 5, 9)$ is

$$d(P, Q) = \{(7-3)^2 + (5-1)^2 + (9-2)^2\}^{1/2} = \sqrt{81} = 9.$$

Figure 3.17 shows a triangle in space whose sides are represented by the vectors $\mathbf{a} = (a_1, a_2, a_3)$, $\mathbf{b} = (b_1, b_2, b_3)$, and $\mathbf{a} - \mathbf{b}$. According to the Pythagorean theorem of elementary geometry (or the law of cosines of elementary trigonometry), the vectors $\mathbf{a}$ and $\mathbf{b}$ are *perpendicular* if and only if the square of the hypotenuse is equal to the sum of the squares of the two legs:

$$|\mathbf{a} - \mathbf{b}|^2 = |\mathbf{a}|^2 + |\mathbf{b}|^2.$$

When we substitute the components of $\mathbf{a}$ and $\mathbf{b}$ we find that

$$(a_1 - b_1)^2 + (a_2 - b_2)^2 + (a_3 - b_3)^2$$
$$= \{(a_1)^2 + (a_2)^2 + (a_3)^2\} + \{(b_1)^2 + (b_2)^2 + (b_3)^2\}.$$

Then subtraction of the right-hand side from both sides yields

$$-2(a_1 b_1 + a_2 b_2 + a_3 b_3) = 0.$$

We therefore see that the vectors $\mathbf{a} = (a_1, a_2, a_3)$ and $\mathbf{b} = (b_1, b_2, b_3)$ are perpendicular if and only if

$$a_1 b_1 + a_2 b_2 + a_3 b_3 = 0. \tag{3}$$

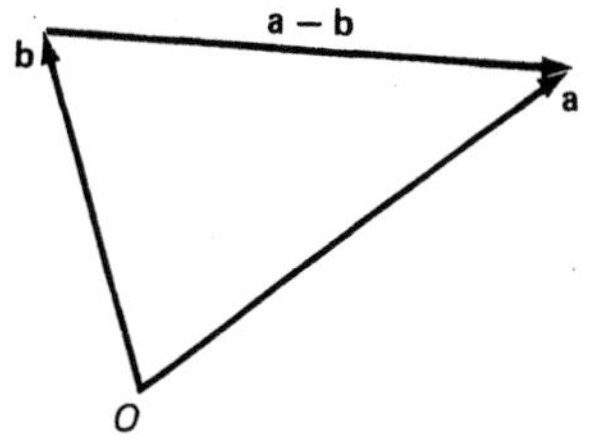

3.17 The triangle determined by the vectors **a** and **b**.

The combination of components appearing in (3) provides an important way of forming a *product* of two vectors.

> ***Definition:*** *The Dot Product*
> The **dot product** $\mathbf{a} \cdot \mathbf{b}$ of the vectors $\mathbf{a} = (a_1, a_2, a_3)$ and $\mathbf{b} = (b_1, b_2, b_3)$ is defined as follows:
>
> $$\mathbf{a} \cdot \mathbf{b} = a_1 b_1 + a_2 b_2 + a_3 b_3. \tag{4}$$

Note that the dot product of two vectors is a *real number*, not a vector. (For this reason the dot product is sometimes called the *scalar product.*) If $a_3 = b_3 = 0$, we may think of $\mathbf{a}$ and $\mathbf{b}$ as vectors in the xy-plane. Thus the dot product of the vectors $\mathbf{a} = (a_1, a_2)$ and $\mathbf{b} = (b_1, b_2)$ in $\mathbf{R}^2$ is given by

$$\mathbf{a} \cdot \mathbf{b} = a_1 b_1 + a_2 b_2. \tag{4'}$$

Motivated by the discussion leading to Equation (3), we say that the two vectors $\mathbf{a}$ and $\mathbf{b}$ are **orthogonal** (or **perpendicular**) provided that

$$\mathbf{a} \cdot \mathbf{b} = 0. \tag{5}$$

Note that the zero vector $\mathbf{0}$ is orthogonal to every vector $\mathbf{a}$ because $\mathbf{a} \cdot \mathbf{0} = 0$ for every choice of $\mathbf{a}$.

EXAMPLE 1 The vectors $\mathbf{a} = (3, -2, 1)$ and $\mathbf{b} = (3, 4, -1)$ are orthogonal because

$$\mathbf{a} \cdot \mathbf{b} = (3)(3) + (-2)(4) + (1)(-1) = 9 - 8 - 1 = 0.$$

The vectors $\mathbf{c} = (5, -2, 4)$ and $\mathbf{d} = (1, 6, -2)$ are not orthogonal because

$$\mathbf{c} \cdot \mathbf{d} = (5)(1) + (-2)(6) + (4)(-2) = 5 - 12 - 8 = -15 \neq 0.$$

Each of the properties of the dot product listed in Theorem 1 is easy to establish. Simply substitute the components of the vectors involved and then apply familiar properties of real numbers.

> ***Theorem 1:*** *Properties of the Dot Product*
> If $\mathbf{a}$, $\mathbf{b}$, and $\mathbf{c}$ are vectors and r is a real number, then
>
> **(i)** $\mathbf{a} \cdot \mathbf{a} = |\mathbf{a}|^2 \geq 0$,
> **(ii)** $\mathbf{a} \cdot \mathbf{b} = \mathbf{b} \cdot \mathbf{a}$, (commutativity)
> **(iii)** $\mathbf{a} \cdot (\mathbf{b} + \mathbf{c}) = \mathbf{a} \cdot \mathbf{b} + \mathbf{a} \cdot \mathbf{c}$, (distributivity)
> **(iv)** $(r\mathbf{a}) \cdot \mathbf{b} = r(\mathbf{a} \cdot \mathbf{b}) = \mathbf{a} \cdot (r\mathbf{b})$.
>
> In connection with part (i), note that $\mathbf{a} \cdot \mathbf{a} = 0$ if and only if $\mathbf{a} = \mathbf{0}$.

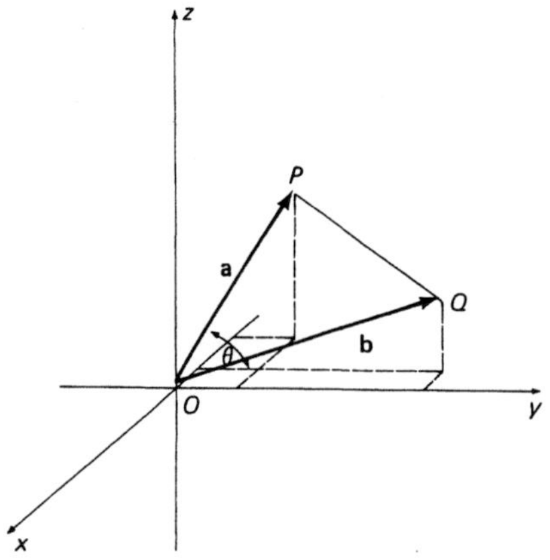

3.18 The angle θ between the vectors **a** and **b**.

The definition in (4) is algebraic, but the dot product has an important geometric interpretation. Let the vectors **a** and **b** be represented by the position vectors $\overrightarrow{OP}$ and $\overrightarrow{OQ}$, respectively. Then the **angle** θ between **a** and **b** is the angle at the origin O in the triangle OPQ of Figure 3.18. The vectors **a** and **b** are *collinear* if $\theta = 0°$ or $\theta = 180°$ (and then the triangle is degenerate), and are *orthogonal* if $\theta = 90°$. We regard the zero vector as both collinear with *and* orthogonal to *every* vector.

Theorem 2: *Interpretation of the Dot Product*

If θ is the angle between the vectors **a** and **b**, then

$$\mathbf{a} \cdot \mathbf{b} = |\mathbf{a}||\mathbf{b}| \cos \theta. \tag{6}$$

Proof If either $\mathbf{a} = \mathbf{0}$ or $\mathbf{b} = \mathbf{0}$, then Equation (6) reduces to $0 = 0$ and there is nothing more to prove. If the nonzero vectors **a** and **b** are collinear, then $\mathbf{b} = r\mathbf{a}$, either with $r > 0$ and $\theta = 0°$ or with $r < 0$ and $\theta = 180°$. In either of these two cases both sides of (6) reduce to $r|\mathbf{a}|^2$ and again there is nothing more to prove.

So we turn our attention to the general case in which the vectors $\mathbf{a} = \overrightarrow{OP}$ and $\mathbf{b} = \overrightarrow{OQ}$ are nonzero and not collinear. Then

$$\begin{aligned} |\overrightarrow{PQ}|^2 &= |\mathbf{a} - \mathbf{b}|^2 = (\mathbf{a} - \mathbf{b}) \cdot (\mathbf{a} - \mathbf{b}) \\ &= \mathbf{a} \cdot \mathbf{a} - \mathbf{a} \cdot \mathbf{b} - \mathbf{b} \cdot \mathbf{a} + \mathbf{b} \cdot \mathbf{b} \\ &= |\mathbf{a}|^2 + |\mathbf{b}|^2 - 2(\mathbf{a} \cdot \mathbf{b}). \end{aligned}$$

(Note the extensive use of the properties listed in Theorem 1.) On the other hand, $c = |\overrightarrow{PQ}|$ is the side of the triangle OPQ (Figure 3.18) opposite the angle θ included by the sides $a = |\mathbf{a}|$ and $b = |\mathbf{b}|$. The law of cosines (stated and derived in Problem 24 of Section 2.4) then implies that

$$c^2 = a^2 + b^2 - 2ab \cos \theta.$$

Therefore

$$|\overrightarrow{PQ}|^2 = |\mathbf{a}|^2 + |\mathbf{b}|^2 - 2|\mathbf{a}||\mathbf{b}| \cos \theta.$$

Finally, comparison of our two expressions for $|\overrightarrow{PQ}|^2$ yields Equation (6). ■

Theorem 2 tells us that the angle between the nonzero vectors **a** and **b** is the angle between 0° and 180° (inclusive) such that

$$\cos \theta = \frac{\mathbf{a} \cdot \mathbf{b}}{|\mathbf{a}||\mathbf{b}|}. \tag{7}$$

EXAMPLE 2 Find the angles in the triangle of Figure 3.19. This triangle has vertices at $A(2, -1, 0)$, $B(5, -4, 3)$, and $C(1, -3, 2)$.

Solution We apply Equation (7) with θ the angle at the vertex A, $\mathbf{a} = \overrightarrow{AB} = (3, -3, 3)$, and $\mathbf{b} = \overrightarrow{AC} = (-1, -2, 2)$. This gives

$$\begin{aligned}\cos \angle A &= \frac{(3, -3, 3)\cdot(-1, -2, 2)}{\sqrt{27}\sqrt{9}} \\ &= \tfrac{1}{3}\sqrt{3} \approx 0.5774,\end{aligned}$$

so $\angle A \approx 54.74°$. Similarly,

$$\begin{aligned}\cos \angle B &= \frac{\overrightarrow{BA}\cdot\overrightarrow{BC}}{|\overrightarrow{BA}||\overrightarrow{BC}|} \\ &= \frac{(-3, 3, -3)\cdot(-4, 1, -1)}{\sqrt{27}\sqrt{18}} \\ &= \tfrac{1}{3}\sqrt{6} \approx 0.8165,\end{aligned}$$

so $\angle B \approx 35.26°$. Then $\angle C = 180° - \angle A - \angle B = 90°$. As a check, note that

$$\overrightarrow{CA}\cdot\overrightarrow{CB} = (1, 2, -2)\cdot(4, -1, 1) = 0,$$

so the angle at C is, indeed, a right angle.

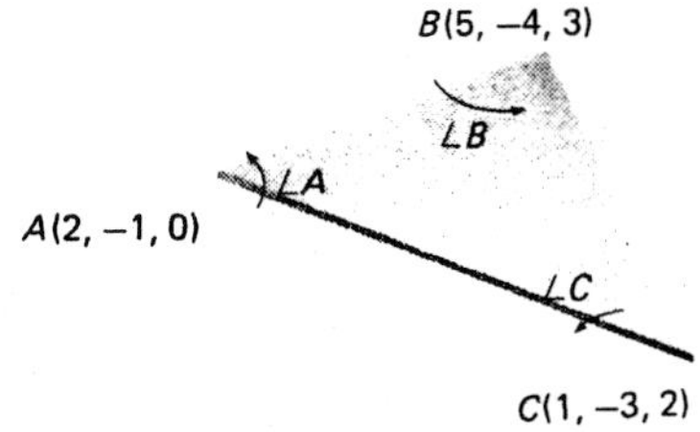

3.19 The triangle of Example 2.

ORTHOGONALITY AND LINEAR INDEPENDENCE

The following theorem means that if three vectors are **mutually orthogonal**—that is, each two of them forms an orthogonal pair—then the three form a particularly convenient kind of basis for $\mathbf{R}^3$.

> ***Theorem 3***: *Orthogonal Basis Vectors*
>
> If the three nonzero vectors **a**, **b**, and **c** are mutually orthogonal, then they are linearly independent. Any vector **v** in $\mathbf{R}^3$ may be expressed as a linear combination of **a**, **b**, and **c** by means of the formula
>
> $$\mathbf{v} = \frac{\mathbf{v}\cdot\mathbf{a}}{\mathbf{a}\cdot\mathbf{a}}\mathbf{a} + \frac{\mathbf{v}\cdot\mathbf{b}}{\mathbf{b}\cdot\mathbf{b}}\mathbf{b} + \frac{\mathbf{v}\cdot\mathbf{c}}{\mathbf{c}\cdot\mathbf{c}}\mathbf{c}. \tag{8}$$
>
> Note that if $\mathbf{a} = \mathbf{i}$, $\mathbf{b} = \mathbf{j}$, and $\mathbf{c} = \mathbf{k}$, then the formula in (8) reduces to the familiar $\mathbf{v} = v_1\mathbf{i} + v_2\mathbf{j} + v_3\mathbf{k}$.

Proof To show that the vectors **a**, **b**, and **c** are linearly independent, suppose that

$$r\mathbf{a} + s\mathbf{b} + t\mathbf{c} = \mathbf{0} \tag{9}$$

for some scalars r, s, and t. When we form the dot product of **a** with each side of this equation, we get

$$r(\mathbf{a}\cdot\mathbf{a}) + s(\mathbf{b}\cdot\mathbf{a}) + t(\mathbf{c}\cdot\mathbf{a}) = 0.$$

Now $\mathbf{a}\cdot\mathbf{a} = |\mathbf{a}|^2 \neq 0$, but $\mathbf{b}\cdot\mathbf{a} = \mathbf{c}\cdot\mathbf{a} = 0$ because the vectors are mutually orthogonal. It now follows that $r = 0$. Similarly, by forming the dot product of the terms in (9) with **b** and with **c**, we find that $s = 0$ and $t = 0$. Thus Equation (9) implies that $r = s = t = 0$, and therefore the three vectors **a**, **b**, and **c** are indeed linearly independent.

Hence Theorem 4 in Section 3.2 implies that the vectors **a**, **b**, and **c** form a basis for $\mathbf{R}^3$, so any vector **v** in $\mathbf{R}^3$ can be expressed as a linear combination

$$\mathbf{v} = r\mathbf{a} + s\mathbf{b} + t\mathbf{c}. \tag{10}$$

When we form the dot product of **a** with each side in (10), we get

$$\mathbf{v}\cdot\mathbf{a} = r(\mathbf{a}\cdot\mathbf{a}) + s(\mathbf{b}\cdot\mathbf{a}) + t(\mathbf{c}\cdot\mathbf{a}) = r(\mathbf{a}\cdot\mathbf{a}).$$

Because $\mathbf{a}\cdot\mathbf{a} \neq 0$, it follows that $r = (\mathbf{v}\cdot\mathbf{a})/(\mathbf{a}\cdot\mathbf{a})$. Similarly, by forming the dot product of both sides in (10) with **b** and with **c**, we find that $s = (\mathbf{v}\cdot\mathbf{b})/(\mathbf{b}\cdot\mathbf{b})$ and that $t = (\mathbf{v}\cdot\mathbf{c})/(\mathbf{c}\cdot\mathbf{c})$. We get the formula in (8) when we substitute these values of r, s, and t in Equation (10). ■

Three vectors **a**, **b**, and **c** as in Theorem 3 are said to constitute an **orthogonal basis** for $\mathbf{R}^3$. If, in addition to being mutually orthogonal, **a**, **b**, and **c** are *unit* vectors

($|\mathbf{a}| = |\mathbf{b}| = |\mathbf{c}| = 1$), then the three vectors are said to form an **orthonormal basis** for $\mathbf{R}^3$. In this case Equation (8) takes the especially simple form

$$\mathbf{v} = (\mathbf{v}\cdot\mathbf{a})\mathbf{a} + (\mathbf{v}\cdot\mathbf{b})\mathbf{b} + (\mathbf{v}\cdot\mathbf{c})\mathbf{c}. \tag{11}$$

The familiar orthonormal basis for $\mathbf{R}^3$ consists of the standard unit vectors **i**, **j**, and **k**. If $\mathbf{v} = (v_1, v_2, v_3)$, then $\mathbf{v}\cdot\mathbf{i} = v_1$, $\mathbf{v}\cdot\mathbf{j} = v_2$, and $\mathbf{v}\cdot\mathbf{k} = v_3$. So we again get $\mathbf{v} = v_1\mathbf{i} + v_2\mathbf{j} + v_3\mathbf{k}$.

EXAMPLE 3 To express the vector $\mathbf{v} = (3, -11, -17)$ as a linear combination of the orthogonal basis vectors $\mathbf{a} = (1, 1, -1)$, $\mathbf{b} = (2, 1, 3)$, and $\mathbf{c} = (4, -5, -1)$, we calculate the dot products

$$\mathbf{a}\cdot\mathbf{a} = 3, \qquad \mathbf{b}\cdot\mathbf{b} = 14, \qquad \mathbf{c}\cdot\mathbf{c} = 42,$$

$$\mathbf{v}\cdot\mathbf{a} = 9, \qquad \mathbf{v}\cdot\mathbf{b} = -56, \qquad \mathbf{v}\cdot\mathbf{c} = 84.$$

Then the formula in (8) yields

$$\begin{aligned}\mathbf{v} &= \frac{9}{3}\mathbf{a} + \frac{-56}{14}\mathbf{b} + \frac{84}{42}\mathbf{c}\\ &= 3\mathbf{a} - 4\mathbf{b} + 2\mathbf{c}.\end{aligned}$$

The simplicity of this computation—in comparison with the solution of three simultaneous equations in three unknowns in Example 3 of Section 3.2 (to express a given vector in terms of *non*orthogonal basis vectors)—shows what is "particularly convenient" about an orthogonal basis for $\mathbf{R}^3$.

ORTHOGONAL PROJECTIONS

If **a** and **b** are linearly independent vectors in $\mathbf{R}^3$, then—according to the discussion at the end of Section 3.2—the set $r\mathbf{a} + s\mathbf{b}$ of all linear combinations of **a** and **b** is a plane W through the origin. We will call W the plane **spanned** by the vectors **a** and **b**.

As indicated in Figure 3.20, we would like to express **b** as a sum

$$\mathbf{b} = \mathbf{b}_{\parallel} + \mathbf{b}_{\perp} \tag{12}$$

of a vector $\mathbf{b}_{\parallel}$ parallel to **a** and a vector $\mathbf{b}_{\perp}$ orthogonal to **a**. From the right triangle with angle θ in Figure 3.20 we see that the length of the vector $\mathbf{b}_{\parallel}$ is $\pm|\mathbf{b}|\cos\theta$, and that it points in the direction of the unit vector $\pm\mathbf{a}/|\mathbf{a}|$; we take the plus signs if θ is

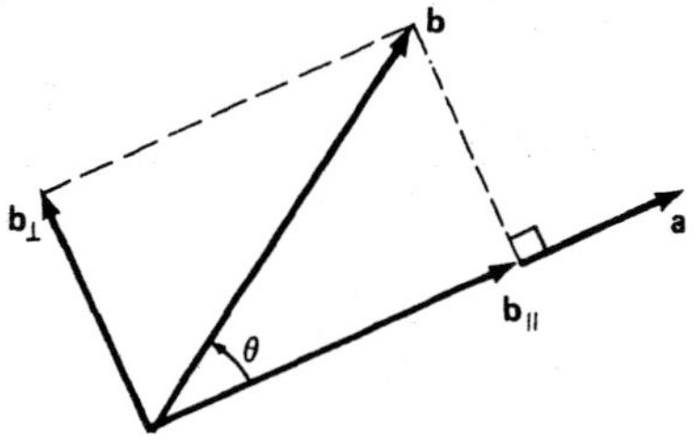

3.20 The vectors $\mathbf{b}_{\parallel}$ and $\mathbf{b}_{\perp}$.

acute and the minus signs if θ is obtuse. On the basis of these observations, we *define* the vector $\mathbf{b}_{\parallel}$ as follows:

$$\mathbf{b}_{\parallel} = (\pm|\mathbf{b}|\cos\theta)\left(\pm\frac{\mathbf{a}}{|\mathbf{a}|}\right)$$

$$= |\mathbf{b}|\cdot\frac{\mathbf{a}\cdot\mathbf{b}}{|\mathbf{a}||\mathbf{b}|}\cdot\frac{\mathbf{a}}{|\mathbf{a}|} = \frac{\mathbf{a}\cdot\mathbf{b}}{|\mathbf{a}|^2}\mathbf{a}.$$

The vector

$$\mathbf{b}_{\parallel} = \frac{\mathbf{a}\cdot\mathbf{b}}{\mathbf{a}\cdot\mathbf{a}}\mathbf{a} \tag{13}$$

is the **orthogonal projection** of the vector **b** onto the line determined by the vector **a**.

Motivated by Equation (12), we now *define*

$$\mathbf{b}_{\perp} = \mathbf{b} - \mathbf{b}_{\parallel} = \mathbf{b} - \frac{\mathbf{a}\cdot\mathbf{b}}{\mathbf{a}\cdot\mathbf{a}}\mathbf{a}, \tag{14}$$

and note immediately that

$$\mathbf{a}\cdot\mathbf{b}_{\perp} = \mathbf{a}\cdot\mathbf{b} - \frac{\mathbf{a}\cdot\mathbf{b}}{\mathbf{a}\cdot\mathbf{a}}\mathbf{a}\cdot\mathbf{a} = 0,$$

so $\mathbf{b}_{\perp}$ is, indeed, orthogonal to **a**.

EXAMPLE 4 If $\mathbf{a} = (2, 1, -2)$ and $\mathbf{b} = (4, -5, 3)$, then $\mathbf{a}\cdot\mathbf{a} = 9$ and $\mathbf{a}\cdot\mathbf{b} = -3$, so the formulas in (13) and (14) yield

$$\mathbf{b}_{\parallel} = -\frac{3}{9}(2, 1, -2) = \left(-\frac{2}{3}, -\frac{1}{3}, \frac{2}{3}\right)$$

and

$$\mathbf{b}_{\perp} = (4, -5, 3) - \left(-\frac{2}{3}, -\frac{1}{3}, \frac{2}{3}\right)$$

$$= \left(\frac{14}{3}, -\frac{14}{3}, \frac{7}{3}\right).$$

Now let **u**, **v**, and **w** be three given vectors such that **u** and **v** are linearly independent. We would like to find the *orthogonal projection* **p** of **w** into the plane W through the origin and spanned by **u** and **v** (see Figure 3.21). This is not merely a geometric problem that one may or may not find interesting; we will see in Chapter 5 that it is a practical problem with important and wide-ranging applications.

The first step in finding **p** is to replace **u** and **v** with *orthogonal* vectors **a** and **b** that span the same plane W. We may take $\mathbf{a} = \mathbf{u}$. Then the formula in (14), with **u** and **v** playing the roles of the vectors **a** and **b** there, yields the vector

$$\mathbf{b} = \mathbf{v} - \frac{\mathbf{u}\cdot\mathbf{v}}{\mathbf{u}\cdot\mathbf{u}}\mathbf{u} \tag{15}$$

that lies in the plane W and is orthogonal to $\mathbf{a} = \mathbf{u}$.

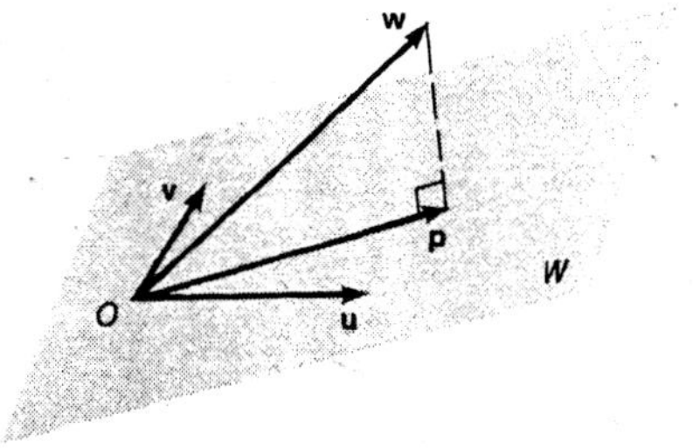

3.21 The projection **p** of **w** into the plane *W* spanned by **u** and **v**.

Now let **c** be a nonzero vector that is orthogonal to both **a** and **b**. (We could take **c** to be the cross-product vector defined later in this section, but here we do not need to know **c** specifically.) Then the three vectors **a**, **b**, **c** form an orthogonal basis for $\mathbf{R}^3$, so Equation (8) yields

$$\mathbf{w} = \frac{\mathbf{w}\cdot\mathbf{a}}{\mathbf{a}\cdot\mathbf{a}}\mathbf{a} + \frac{\mathbf{w}\cdot\mathbf{b}}{\mathbf{b}\cdot\mathbf{b}}\mathbf{b} + \frac{\mathbf{w}\cdot\mathbf{c}}{\mathbf{c}\cdot\mathbf{c}}\mathbf{c}. \tag{16}$$

Observe that the sum of the first two terms on the right-hand side is a vector in the plane W spanned by **a** and **b**, whereas the third term is a vector orthogonal to W (see Problem 29). Hence the vector

$$\mathbf{p} = \frac{\mathbf{w}\cdot\mathbf{a}}{\mathbf{a}\cdot\mathbf{a}}\mathbf{a} + \frac{\mathbf{w}\cdot\mathbf{b}}{\mathbf{b}\cdot\mathbf{b}}\mathbf{b} \tag{17}$$

is a vector in the plane W such that $\mathbf{w} - \mathbf{p}$ is orthogonal to W (as indicated in Figure 3.21). Because there can be only one such vector (see Problem 30), we see finally that the **orthogonal projection** of the vector **w** into the plane spanned by the *orthogonal* vectors **a** and **b** is the vector **p** given by the formula in Equation (17).

EXAMPLE 5 Given $\mathbf{u} = (2, 1, -2)$, $\mathbf{v} = (5, 1, 1)$, and $\mathbf{w} = (3, 9, 6)$, find the orthogonal projection **p** of **w** into the plane W spanned by **u** and **v**. Then calculate the (perpendicular) distance $|\mathbf{w} - \mathbf{p}|$ from the point **w** to the plane W.

Solution We let $\mathbf{a} = \mathbf{u} = (2, 1, -2)$ and apply (15) to write

$$\begin{aligned}\mathbf{b} &= \mathbf{v} - \frac{\mathbf{u}\cdot\mathbf{v}}{\mathbf{u}\cdot\mathbf{u}}\mathbf{u} \\ &= (5, 1, 1) - \frac{9}{9}(2, 1, -2) = (3, 0, 3).\end{aligned}$$

Then **a** and **b** are orthogonal vectors in W, so the formula in (17) gives the orthogonal projection of **w** into the plane W:

$$\begin{aligned}\mathbf{p} &= \frac{\mathbf{w}\cdot\mathbf{a}}{\mathbf{a}\cdot\mathbf{a}}\mathbf{a} + \frac{\mathbf{w}\cdot\mathbf{b}}{\mathbf{b}\cdot\mathbf{b}}\mathbf{b} \\ &= \frac{3}{9}(2, 1, -2) + \frac{27}{18}(3, 0, 3) = \frac{1}{6}(31, 2, 23).\end{aligned}$$

Thus the point $\mathbf{p} = \frac{1}{6}(31, 2, 23)$ is the orthogonal projection of $\mathbf{w}$, and hence the perpendicular distance from the point $\mathbf{w}$ to the plane W is

$$\begin{aligned} |\mathbf{w} - \mathbf{p}| &= |(3, 9, 6) - \tfrac{1}{6}(31, 2, 23)| \\ &= \tfrac{1}{6}\{(18 - 31)^2 + (54 - 2)^2 + (36 - 23)^2\}^{1/2} \approx 9.19. \end{aligned}$$

THE CROSS PRODUCT

Let $\mathbf{a} = (a_1, a_2, a_3)$ and $\mathbf{b} = (b_1, b_2, b_3)$ be linearly independent vectors, and suppose that we seek a nonzero vector $\mathbf{c} = (x, y, z)$ that is orthogonal both to $\mathbf{a}$ and to $\mathbf{b}$. Then $\mathbf{c}$ must satisfy the two orthogonality conditions

$$\begin{aligned} \mathbf{a} \cdot \mathbf{c} &= a_1 x + a_2 y + a_3 z = 0, \\ \mathbf{b} \cdot \mathbf{c} &= b_1 x + b_2 y + b_3 z = 0. \end{aligned} \tag{18}$$

Because $\mathbf{a}$ and $\mathbf{b}$ are linearly independent, one of the three determinants

$$\begin{vmatrix} a_1 & a_2 \\ b_1 & b_2 \end{vmatrix}, \quad \begin{vmatrix} a_2 & a_3 \\ b_2 & b_3 \end{vmatrix}, \quad \begin{vmatrix} a_1 & a_3 \\ b_1 & b_3 \end{vmatrix}$$

must be nonzero (see Problem 31). Suppose, for instance, that

$$\Delta = \begin{vmatrix} a_1 & a_2 \\ b_1 & b_2 \end{vmatrix} \neq 0.$$

Then we can rewrite the equations in (18) in the form

$$\begin{aligned} a_1 x + a_2 y &= -a_3 z \\ b_1 x + b_2 y &= -b_3 z, \end{aligned} \tag{19}$$

choose z arbitrarily, and use Cramer's rule to solve for x and y. This gives

$$\begin{aligned} x &= \frac{1}{\Delta}\begin{vmatrix} -a_3 z & a_2 \\ -b_3 z & b_2 \end{vmatrix} = \frac{z}{\Delta}\begin{vmatrix} a_2 & a_3 \\ b_2 & b_3 \end{vmatrix}, \\ y &= \frac{1}{\Delta}\begin{vmatrix} a_1 & -a_3 z \\ b_1 & -b_3 z \end{vmatrix} = \frac{z}{\Delta}\begin{vmatrix} a_3 & a_1 \\ b_3 & b_1 \end{vmatrix}. \end{aligned}$$

If we choose $z = \Delta$ to simplify these expressions for x and y, we have the nontrivial solution

$$x = \begin{vmatrix} a_2 & a_3 \\ b_2 & b_3 \end{vmatrix}, \quad y = \begin{vmatrix} a_3 & a_1 \\ b_3 & b_1 \end{vmatrix}, \quad z = \begin{vmatrix} a_1 & a_2 \\ b_1 & b_2 \end{vmatrix} \tag{20}$$

of the equations in (18). The resulting vector

$$\mathbf{c} = (a_2 b_3 - a_3 b_2, a_3 b_1 - a_1 b_3, a_1 b_2 - a_2 b_1) \tag{21}$$

is called the **cross product** $\mathbf{c} = \mathbf{a} \times \mathbf{b}$ of the vectors $\mathbf{a}$ and $\mathbf{b}$. Because $\mathbf{c}$ is a vector, the cross product is sometimes called the *vector product*. You can verify directly from (21) that $\mathbf{a} \times \mathbf{b}$ is orthogonal to both $\mathbf{a}$ and $\mathbf{b}$.

A common way of remembering the definition in (21) of the cross product $\mathbf{a} \times \mathbf{b}$ is to observe that it results from a formal expansion along the first row in the 3×3 determinant

$$\mathbf{a} \times \mathbf{b} = \begin{vmatrix} \mathbf{i} & \mathbf{j} & \mathbf{k} \\ a_1 & a_2 & a_3 \\ b_1 & b_2 & b_3 \end{vmatrix}. \tag{22}$$

EXAMPLE 6 The cross product of the vectors $\mathbf{a} = (3, -1, 2)$ and $\mathbf{b} = (2, 2, -1)$ is

$$\mathbf{a} \times \mathbf{b} = \begin{vmatrix} \mathbf{i} & \mathbf{j} & \mathbf{k} \\ 3 & -1 & 2 \\ 2 & 2 & -1 \end{vmatrix}$$

$$= \begin{vmatrix} -1 & 2 \\ 2 & -1 \end{vmatrix} \mathbf{i} - \begin{vmatrix} 3 & 2 \\ 2 & -1 \end{vmatrix} \mathbf{j} + \begin{vmatrix} 3 & -1 \\ 2 & 2 \end{vmatrix} \mathbf{k}$$

$$= -3\mathbf{i} + 7\mathbf{j} + 8\mathbf{k}.$$

You should pause here to verify (using the dot product) that $\mathbf{a} \times \mathbf{b} = (-3, 7, 8)$ is indeed orthogonal both to $\mathbf{a}$ and to $\mathbf{b}$.

Observe from (22) that the cross product is anticommutative:

$$\mathbf{b} \times \mathbf{a} = -\mathbf{a} \times \mathbf{b}. \tag{23}$$

As indicated in Figure 3.22, it turns out that the triple $\mathbf{a}$, $\mathbf{b}$, $\mathbf{a} \times \mathbf{b}$ is a *right-handed* triple of vectors, in exactly the same sense that $\mathbf{i}$, $\mathbf{j}$, $\mathbf{k}$ is a right-handed triple. In Problem 32 we outline a derivation of the formula

$$|\mathbf{a} \times \mathbf{b}| = |\mathbf{a}|\,|\mathbf{b}| \sin \theta \tag{24}$$

for the *length* of the cross product $\mathbf{a} \times \mathbf{b}$ in terms of the lengths of the vectors $\mathbf{a}$ and $\mathbf{b}$ and the angle θ between them. Whereas the definition of $\mathbf{a} \times \mathbf{b}$ in (21) is algebraic, it is uniquely determined geometrically by a knowledge of its direction and length.

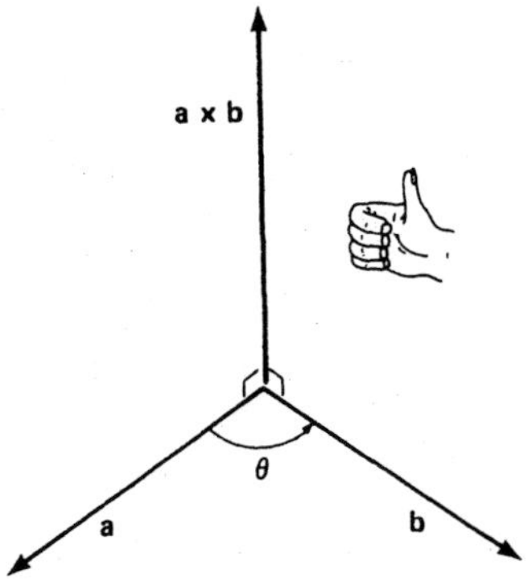

3.22 The vectors **a**, **b**, and **a** × **b** form—in that order—a right-handed triple.

3.3 PROBLEMS

In each of Problems 1-4, use the dot product to find the angle between the vectors **a** and **b**.

1. $\mathbf{a} = (2, 5, -4)$, $\mathbf{b} = (1, -2, -3)$

2. $\mathbf{a} = (-1, 0, 2)$, $\mathbf{b} = (3, 4, -5)$

3. $\mathbf{a} = \mathbf{i} + \mathbf{j} + \mathbf{k}$, $\mathbf{b} = \mathbf{j} - \mathbf{k}$

4. $\mathbf{a} = 2\mathbf{i} - 3\mathbf{j} + 5\mathbf{k}$, $\mathbf{b} = 5\mathbf{i} - 3\mathbf{j} - 7\mathbf{k}$

5. Find the three angles of the triangle with vertices $A(1, 1, 1)$, $B(3, -2, 3)$, and $C(3, 4, 6)$.

6. Find the angle between any longest diagonal of a cube and any edge it meets.

7. Show that the points (0, 0, 0), (1, 1, 0), (1, 0, 1), and (0, 1, 1) are the vertices of a regular tetrahedron (pyramid) by showing that each of the six edges has length $\sqrt{2}$. Then use the dot product to find the angle between any two edges.

8. The methane molecule CH_4 is arranged with the four hydrogen atoms at the vertices of a regular tetrahedron and with the carbon atom at the centroid of the tetrahedron. Suppose that the axes and scale are so chosen that the tetrahedron is the one of Problem 7, which has its centroid located at $(\frac{1}{2}, \frac{1}{2}, \frac{1}{2})$. Find the *bond angle* between the lines from the carbon atom to two of the hydrogen atoms.

In Problems 9-12, the three vectors **a**, **b**, and **c** are mutually orthogonal. Use Equation (8) to express **v** as a linear combination of them.

9. $\mathbf{a} = (1, 2, 1)$, $\mathbf{b} = (1, -1, 1)$, $\mathbf{c} = (1, 0, -1)$; $\mathbf{v} = (3, 4, 5)$

10. $\mathbf{a} = (2, 1, 1)$, $\mathbf{b} = (1, -3, 1)$, $\mathbf{c} = (4, -1, -7)$; $\mathbf{v} = (3, 4, 5)$

11. $\mathbf{a} = (2, 1, -1)$, $\mathbf{b} = (1, 1, 3)$, $\mathbf{c} = (4, -7, 1)$; $\mathbf{v} = (1, 1, 1)$

12. $\mathbf{a} = (2, 2, -1)$, $\mathbf{b} = (2, -1, 2)$, $\mathbf{c} = (3, -6, -6)$; $\mathbf{v} = (1, 0, 0)$

In Problems 13-16, express **b** in the form $\mathbf{b} = \mathbf{b}_{\parallel} + \mathbf{b}_{\perp}$, where $\mathbf{b}_{\parallel}$ is parallel to the vector **a** and $\mathbf{b}_{\perp}$ is orthogonal to **a**.

13. $\mathbf{a} = (1, 1, 1)$, $\mathbf{b} = (2, 3, 1)$

14. $\mathbf{a} = (1, 0, -1)$, $\mathbf{b} = (4, 3, -2)$

15. $\mathbf{a} = (2, 1, 1)$, $\mathbf{b} = (5, 1, 1)$

16. $\mathbf{a} = (0, 1, 3)$, $\mathbf{b} = (5, 8, 4)$

In Problems 17-20, find the orthogonal projection **p** of **w** into the plane spanned by the vectors **u** and **v**. In Problems 17 and 18, note that $\mathbf{u} \cdot \mathbf{v} = 0$, so you may choose $\mathbf{a} = \mathbf{u}$ and $\mathbf{b} = \mathbf{v}$ in the formula in Equation (17).

17. $\mathbf{u} = (1, 2, 1)$, $\mathbf{v} = (1, -1, 1)$, $\mathbf{w} = (1, 3, 2)$

18. $\mathbf{u} = (2, 2, -1)$, $\mathbf{v} = (2, -1, 2)$, $\mathbf{w} = (1, 2, 3)$

19. $\mathbf{u} = (1, 1, 1)$, $\mathbf{v} = (2, 3, 1)$, $\mathbf{w} = (3, 4, 5)$

20. $\mathbf{u} = (1, 0, -1)$, $\mathbf{v} = (4, 3, -2)$, $\mathbf{w} = (2, 3, -2)$

In Problems 21-24, use the cross product to find a nonzero vector **c** orthogonal both to **a** and to **b**.

21. $\mathbf{a} = (3, 2, 1)$, $\mathbf{b} = (4, 1, 3)$

22. $\mathbf{a} = (2, -1, 3)$, $\mathbf{b} = (5, 1, -1)$

23. $\mathbf{a} = (3, 4, 5)$, $\mathbf{b} = (1, 2, 3)$

24. $\mathbf{a} = (2, 7, -2)$, $\mathbf{b} = (3, -5, 2)$

25. Given **a**, show that the set W of all vectors **b** orthogonal to **a** is a subspace of $\mathbf{R}^3$.

26. Use the fact that $|\cos\theta| \leq 1$ for all θ to show that the **Cauchy-Schwarz inequality**

$$|\mathbf{a} \cdot \mathbf{b}| \leq |\mathbf{a}|\,|\mathbf{b}|$$

holds for all vectors **a** and **b** in $\mathbf{R}^3$.

27. Establish the **triangle inequality**

$$|\mathbf{a} + \mathbf{b}| \leq |\mathbf{a}| + |\mathbf{b}|$$

(for all **a** and **b** in $\mathbf{R}^3$) by first squaring both sides and then using the inequality of Problem 26.

28. Suppose that the vectors **a** and **b** are linearly independent and that the nonzero vector **c** is orthogonal to both **a** and **b**. Prove that the vectors **a**, **b**, and **c** are linearly independent.

29. Suppose that the plane V through the origin is spanned by the vectors **a** and **b**. The vector **w** is said to be *orthogonal* to V provided that **w** is orthogonal to every vector in V. Prove that if **w** is orthogonal to both **a** and **b**, then **w** is orthogonal to V.

30. Suppose that V is a plane in $\mathbf{R}^3$ and that P is a point of $\mathbf{R}^3$ not in V. Show that there is only one point Q of V such that $\overrightarrow{PQ}$ is orthogonal to V. *Suggestion*: To the contrary, suppose that there were two such points.

31. If the vectors $\mathbf{a} = (a_1, a_2, a_3)$ and $\mathbf{b} =$ $b_1, b_2, b_3)$ are linearly independent, show that at east one of the three 2×2 submatrices of the natrix

$$C = \begin{bmatrix} a_1 & a_2 & a_3 \\ b_1 & b_2 & b_3 \end{bmatrix}$$

ıas a nonzero determinant.

32. The identity

$$|\mathbf{a} \times \mathbf{b}|^2 = |\mathbf{a}|^2|\mathbf{b}|^2 - (\mathbf{a} \cdot \mathbf{b})^2 \qquad (25)$$

can be verified routinely (though tediously) by evaluating each side in terms of the components of **a** and **b** and then checking to see that the two sides agree. Under the assumption that this has been done, show that

$$|\mathbf{a} \times \mathbf{b}| = |\mathbf{a}||\mathbf{b}| \sin \theta$$

(where θ is the angle between **a** and **b**) by substituting $\mathbf{a} \cdot \mathbf{b} = |\mathbf{a}||\mathbf{b}| \cos \theta$ in (25).

3.4

Lines and Planes in Space

In elementary geometry a straight line in space is determined by any two points that lie on it. Here we take the alternative approach that a line in space is determined by a single point $\mathbf{p}_0$ on it and a vector $\mathbf{v}$ that determines the direction of the line.

By the **straight line** L that passes through the point $\mathbf{p}_0 = (x_0, y_0, z_0)$ and is parallel to the nonzero vector $\mathbf{v} = (a, b, c)$ is meant the set of all points $\mathbf{p} = (x, y, z)$ in $\mathbf{R}^3$ such that the vector $\overrightarrow{\mathbf{p}_0\mathbf{p}} = \mathbf{p} - \mathbf{p}_0$ is parallel to $\mathbf{v}$ (see Figure 3.23). Thus $\mathbf{p}$ lies on L if and only if

$$\mathbf{p} - \mathbf{p}_0 = t\mathbf{v};$$

that is, if and only if

$$\mathbf{p} = \mathbf{p}_0 + t\mathbf{v} \qquad (1)$$

for some scalar t. We can visualize the point $\mathbf{p}$ as moving along the line L, with $\mathbf{p}_0 + t\mathbf{v}$ being its location at time t; t can be any positive or negative real number, or zero. As illustrated in Figure 3.24, the line L is the **translate** by the vector $\mathbf{p}_0$ of the line through the origin with equation $\mathbf{p} = t\mathbf{v}$.

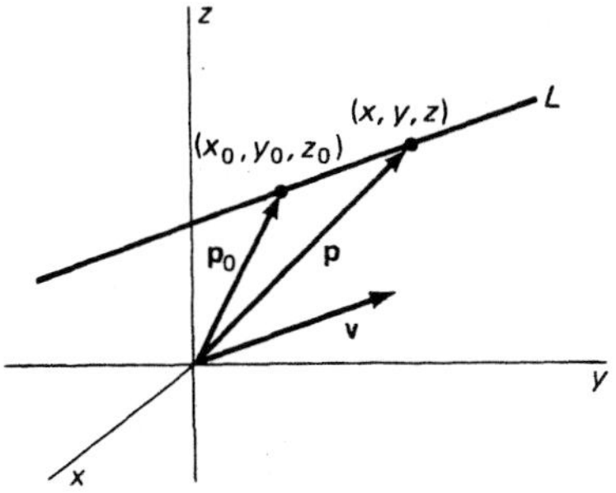

3.23 Finding the equation of the line L through the point $\mathbf{p}_0$ parallel to the vector $\mathbf{v}$.

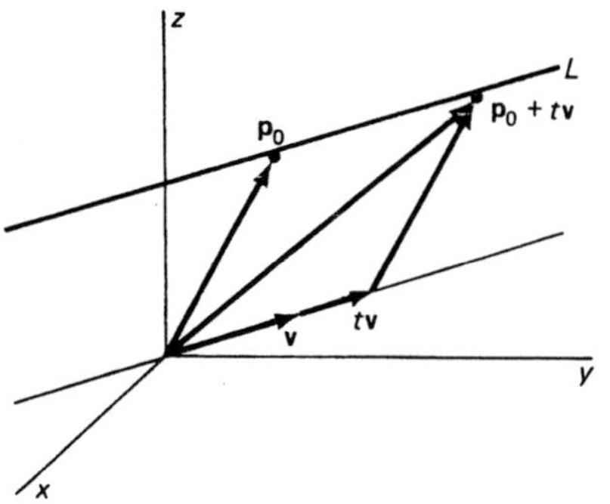

3.24 The line L as a translate of a line through the origin.

Equation (1) is a *vector equation* of the line L. By equating components of the vectors in (1) we get the scalar equations

$$x = x_0 + at$$
$$y = y_0 + bt \tag{2}$$
$$z = z_0 + ct.$$

These are **parametric equations** (with **parameter** t) of the line L through the point (x_0, y_0, z_0) that is parallel to the vector $\mathbf{v} = (a, b, c)$.

EXAMPLE 1 Write parametric equations of the line L that passes through the points $P_1(1, 2, 2)$ and $P_2(3, -1, 3)$.

Solution The line L is parallel to the vector $\mathbf{v} = \overrightarrow{P_1P_2} = (2, -3, 1)$, so we take $a = 2$, $b = -3$, and $c = 1$. With P_1 as the fixed point $\mathbf{p}_0$, the equations in (2) yield

$$x = 1 + 2t, \qquad y = 2 - 3t, \qquad z = 2 + t$$

as parametric equations of L. But if we take P_2 as the fixed point and $-2\mathbf{v} = (-4, 6, -2)$ as the direction vector, then we get from (2) the different parametric equations

$$x = 3 - 4t, \qquad y = -1 + 6t, \qquad z = 3 - 2t$$

of the same line L. Thus the parametric equations of a line are not unique.

Suppose that we want to determine the relationship between two given lines L_1 and L_2 with parametric equations

$$L_1: \quad x = x_1 + a_1 s, \qquad y = y_1 + b_1 s, \qquad z = z_1 + c_1 s \tag{3}$$

and

$$L_2: \quad x = x_2 + a_2 t, \qquad y = y_2 + b_2 t, \qquad z = z_2 + c_2 t. \tag{4}$$

(We use different symbols s and t because the parameters for the two lines have nothing to do with each other.) The lines L_1 and L_2 are parallel if and only if their direction vectors $\mathbf{v}_1 = (a_1, b_1, c_1)$ and $\mathbf{v}_2 = (a_2, b_2, c_2)$ are scalar multiples of each other, and we can see at a glance whether this is so. If L_1 and L_2 are parallel, we ask whether they are *distinct* lines, or if (3) and (4) are simply different parametrizations of the *same* line. If L_1 and L_2 are not parallel, we ask whether or not they intersect.

To answer these questions, we note that the point (x, y, z) lies on both lines, and hence is given both by the equations in (3) and by those in (4) if and only if there exist values of s and t satisfying the simultaneous equations

$$\begin{aligned} x_1 + a_1 s &= x_2 + a_2 t \\ y_1 + b_1 s &= y_2 + b_2 t \\ z_1 + c_1 s &= z_2 + c_2 t. \end{aligned} \tag{5}$$

This is a system of three linear equations in the two unknowns s and t. We know from Chapter 1 that any such linear system has either a unique solution, no solution, or infinitely many solutions. Figure 3.25 illustrates geometric situations corresponding to these three possibilities.

EXAMPLE 2 Consider the lines L_1 and L_2 with parametric equations

$$L_1: \qquad x = 1 + 2s, \qquad y = 2 - 3s, \qquad z = 2 + s$$

and

$$L_2: \qquad x = 3 + 4t, \qquad y = 1 - 6t, \qquad z = 5 + 2t.$$

Their respective direction vectors are $\mathbf{v}_1 = (2, -3, 1)$ and $\mathbf{v}_2 = (4, -6, 2)$. Because $\mathbf{v}_2 = 2\mathbf{v}_1$, we see immediately that L_1 and L_2 are parallel.

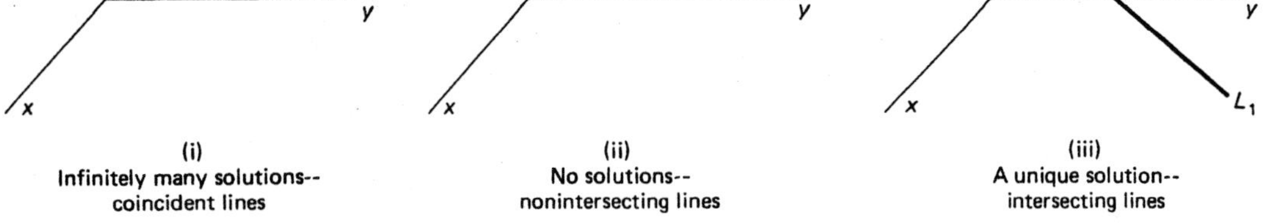

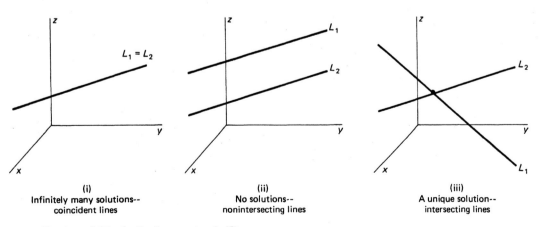

3.25 Three possibilities for the linear system in (5).

To determine whether or not the lines L_1 and L_2 are distinct, we write the system in (5),

$$\begin{aligned} 1 + 2s &= 3 + 4t \\ 2 - 3s &= 1 - 6t \\ 2 + s &= 5 + 2t; \end{aligned}$$

that is,

$$\begin{aligned} 2s - 4t &= 2 \\ -3s + 6t &= -1 \\ s - 2t &= 3. \end{aligned}$$

Using elementary row operations, we routinely reduce the augmented coefficient matrix

$$\begin{bmatrix} 2 & -4 & 2 \\ -3 & 6 & -1 \\ 1 & -2 & 3 \end{bmatrix}$$

of this system to the echelon form

$$\begin{bmatrix} 1 & -2 & 1 \\ 0 & 0 & 2 \\ 0 & 0 & 2 \end{bmatrix}.$$

The equation $0 \cdot s + 0 \cdot t = 2$ is inconsistent, so our linear system has no solution. Therefore the parallel lines L_1 and L_2 do not intersect, and hence are distinct straight lines.

PLANES IN $\mathbf{R}^3$

A plane $\mathscr{P}$ in space is determined by a point $\mathbf{p}_0 = (x_0, y_0, z_0)$ through which $\mathscr{P}$ passes and a line through $\mathbf{p}_0$ orthogonal to $\mathscr{P}$. Alternatively, we may be given the point $\mathbf{p}_0$ on $\mathscr{P}$ and a vector $\mathbf{n} = (a, b, c)$ that is orthogonal to the plane $\mathscr{P}$. By the plane $\mathscr{P}$ through the point $\mathbf{p}_0$ with **normal vector n** (as in Figure 3.26) is meant the set of all points $\mathbf{p} = (x, y, z)$ in $\mathbf{R}^3$ such that the vectors $\mathbf{n}$ and $\overrightarrow{\mathbf{p}_0\mathbf{p}} = \mathbf{p} - \mathbf{p}_0$ are orthogonal, in which case

$$\mathbf{n} \cdot (\mathbf{p} - \mathbf{p}_0) = 0. \tag{6}$$

If we substitute $\mathbf{n} = (a, b, c)$, $\mathbf{p} = (x, y, z)$, and $\mathbf{p}_0 = (x_0, y_0, z_0)$ in Equation (6) and then multiply out the dot product, we get the **point-normal equation**

$$a(x - x_0) + b(y - y_0) + c(z - z_0) = 0 \tag{7}$$

of the plane through the point $\mathbf{p}_0 = (x_0, y_0, z_0)$ with normal vector $\mathbf{n} = (a, b, c)$. In this context the word *normal* is a common synonym for the words *perpendicular* and *orthogonal.*

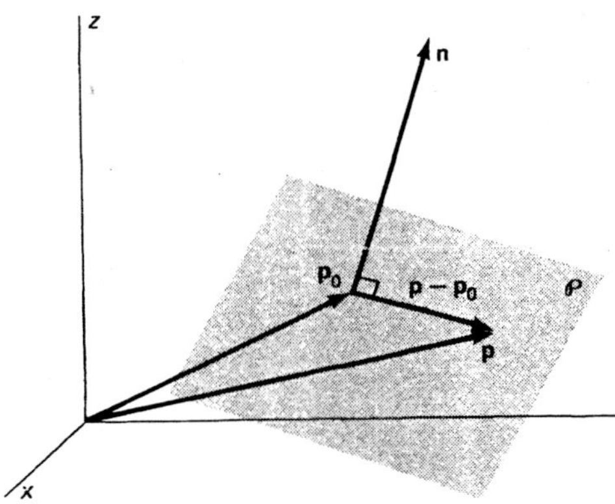

3.26 Because **n** is normal to P, it follows that **n** is normal to $\overrightarrow{\mathbf{p}_0\mathbf{p}}$.

EXAMPLE 3 The point-normal equation of the plane through $\mathbf{p}_0 = (-1, 5, 2)$ with normal vector $\mathbf{n} = (1, -3, 2)$ is

$$(1)(x + 1) + (-3)(y - 5) + (2)(z - 2) = 0,$$

which may be simplified to

$$x - 3y + 2z = -12.$$

Note that the coefficients of x, y, and z in the last equation are the components of the normal vector. This is always the case, because Equation (7) can be written in the form

$$ax + by + cz = d, \tag{8}$$

where $d = ax_0 + by_0 + cz_0$. Conversely, *every linear equation in x, y, and z of the form in* (8) *represents a plane in space* (provided that the coefficients a, b, and c are not all zero). For if $a \neq 0$ (for instance), we can choose y_0 and z_0 arbitrarily, then solve the equation $ax_0 + by_0 + cz_0 = d$ for x_0. With these values, Equation (8) takes the form

$$ax + by + cz = ax_0 + by_0 + cz_0;$$

that is,

$$a(x - x_0) + b(y - y_0) + c(z - z_0) = 0,$$

which is the point-normal equation of the plane through (x_0, y_0, z_0) with normal vector (a, b, c).

Given a plane with nonhomogeneous equation

$$ax + by + cz = d \tag{8}$$

with $d \neq 0$, the parallel plane through the origin has the homogeneous equation

$$ax + by + cz = 0. \tag{9}$$

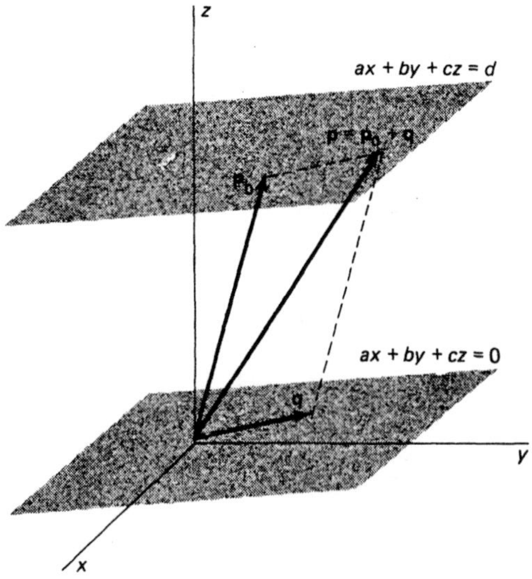

3.27 The plane $ax + by + cz = d$ as a translate of a plane through the origin.

If $\mathbf{p}_0 = (x_0, y_0, z_0)$ is a fixed point of the plane with the equation in (8), then it is readily verified (essentially by the computation of the preceding paragraph) that $\mathbf{p}$ satisfies Equation (8) if and only if $\mathbf{q} = \mathbf{p} - \mathbf{p}_0$ satisfies Equation (9). The relation

$$\mathbf{p} = \mathbf{p}_0 + \mathbf{q} \tag{10}$$

between $\mathbf{p}$ and $\mathbf{q}$ says simply that the plane in (8) is the **translate** by the vector $\mathbf{p}_0$ of the plane through the origin with the equation in (9) (see Figure 3.27). Thus we see that every plane in $\mathbf{R}^3$ is a translate of a plane through the origin, just as every line is a translate of a line through the origin.

EXAMPLE 4 Find an equation of the plane through the three points $P(2, 4, -3)$, $Q(3, 7, -1)$, and $R(4, 3, 0)$.

Solution We want an equation for this plane of the form in Equation (8):

$$ax + by + cz - d = 0.$$

When we substitute for x, y, z in this equation the coordinates of P, then of Q, and finally of R, we get the homogeneous linear system

$$\begin{aligned} 2a + 4b - 3c - d &= 0 \\ 3a + 7b - c - d &= 0 \\ 4a + 3b \phantom{{}-3c} - d &= 0 \end{aligned}$$

of three equations in the four unknowns a, b, c, and d. Using elementary row operations we reduce the coefficient matrix

$$\begin{bmatrix} 2 & 4 & -3 & -1 \\ 3 & 7 & -1 & -1 \\ 4 & 3 & 0 & -1 \end{bmatrix}$$

of this homogeneous system to the echelon form

$$\begin{bmatrix} 1 & 3 & 2 & 0 \\ 0 & 1 & 27 & 4 \\ 0 & 0 & 47 & 7 \end{bmatrix}.$$

We take $d = t$ as the free variable; then back substitution yields

$$c = -\frac{7}{47}t, \qquad b = -27c - 4d = \frac{1}{47}t,$$

and

$$a = -3b - 2c = \frac{11}{47}t.$$

To eliminate fractions we choose the parametric value $t = 47$. This gives $a = 11$, $b = 1$, $c = -7$, and $d = 47$, so an equation of the plane through the points P, Q, and R is

$$11x + y - 7z = 47.$$

In Problem 33 we suggest an alternative approach that employs the cross product of Section 3.3.

Now consider two planes with given equations

$$\begin{aligned} a_1x + b_1y + c_1z &= d_1, \\ a_2x + b_2y + c_2z &= d_2. \end{aligned} \tag{11}$$

If the two normal vectors $\mathbf{n}_1 = (a_1, b_1, c_1)$ and $\mathbf{n}_2 = (a_2, b_2, c_2)$ are scalar multiples of each other, then the two planes either coincide or are parallel and nonintersecting. For instance, the planes with equations

$$\begin{aligned} 2x - y + 3z &= 5, \\ 4x - 2y + 6z &= 10 \end{aligned}$$

coincide because the two equations are equivalent, whereas the parallel planes with equations

$$\begin{aligned} 2x - y + 3z &= 5, \\ 4x - 2y + 6z &= 9 \end{aligned}$$

do not intersect because the two equations obviously are inconsistent.

If the two planes in (11) are not parallel, then they intersect in a straight line that can be determined as in Example 5 (page 158).

REMARK Note how the preceding geometrical analysis makes it obvious that the two linear equations in (11) have either no solution (if the two planes are distinct and parallel) or infinitely many solutions (if they coincide or are not parallel). Similarly, consider how a picture of possible configurations of three planes in space (draw several sketches for yourself) makes it "obvious" that three linear equations in three unknowns have either a unique solution, no solution, or infinitely many solutions. If (for instance) the first two planes intersect in a line L, then the system has

- A unique solution if the third plane intersects L in a single point;
- No solution if the third plane is parallel to L;
- Infinitely many solutions if the third plane contains L.

EXAMPLE 5 Find the line of intersection of the planes with equations

$$\begin{aligned} 2x + 3y - z &= -3, \\ 4x + 5y + z &= 1. \end{aligned}$$

Solution The given equations constitute a system of two linear equations in three unknowns, and the set of all solutions (x, y, z) is the line of intersection of the two planes. We readily reduce the augmented coefficient matrix

$$\begin{bmatrix} 2 & 3 & -1 & -3 \\ 4 & 5 & 1 & 1 \end{bmatrix}$$

to the echelon form

$$\begin{bmatrix} 2 & 3 & -1 & -3 \\ 0 & -1 & 3 & 7 \end{bmatrix}.$$

We take $z = t$, then back substitution yields $y = -7 + 3t$ and $x = 9 - 4t$. Thus our line has parametric equations

$$\begin{aligned} x &= 9 - 4t \\ y &= -7 + 3t \\ z &= t, \end{aligned}$$

and hence it is the line through the point $\mathbf{p}_0 = (9, -7, 0)$ with direction vector $\mathbf{v} = (-4, 3, 1)$.

LINES, PLANES, AND SUBSPACES

Recall that a *subspace* of $\mathbf{R}^3$ is a subset that is closed under the operations of vector addition and multiplication by scalars. In Section 3.2 we showed that every *proper* subspace W of $\mathbf{R}^3$ *either* is the set $\{t\mathbf{v}\}$ of all scalar multiples of some (fixed) nonzero vector $\mathbf{v}$ *or* is the set $\{s\mathbf{u} + t\mathbf{v}\}$ of all linear combinations of some (fixed) pair of linearly independent vectors $\mathbf{u}$ and $\mathbf{v}$. Naturally enough, subspaces of the former type are called **1-dimensional** subspaces of $\mathbf{R}^3$ and subspaces of the latter type are called **2-dimensional** subspaces of $\mathbf{R}^3$.

Clearly the 1-dimensional subspace $W = \{t\mathbf{v}\}$ is simply the line through the origin (0, 0, 0) with direction vector $\mathbf{v}$. Thus the 1-dimensional subspaces of $\mathbf{R}^3$ are precisely the lines through the origin.

Similarly, geometric intuition indicates that the 2-dimensional subspaces of $\mathbf{R}^3$ are precisely the planes through the origin. To prove this, we must show that every 2-dimensional subspace of $\mathbf{R}^3$ is a plane through the origin and, conversely, that every such plane is a 2-dimensional subspace.

Given a 2-dimensional subspace $W = \{s\mathbf{u} + t\mathbf{v}\}$, let $\mathbf{n}$ be the cross product vector $\mathbf{u} \times \mathbf{v}$ introduced in Section 3.3. Then $\mathbf{n}$ is orthogonal both to $\mathbf{u}$ and to $\mathbf{v}$, and it follows that W is simply the plane through the origin with normal vector $\mathbf{n}$ (see Problem 34).

Conversely, let $\mathscr{P}$ be a plane through the origin. Then $\mathscr{P}$ is the graph of a homogeneous linear equation

$$ax + by + cz = 0.$$

If $a \neq 0$ (for instance) then the solution set of this equation is described by

$$y = s, \qquad z = t, \qquad x = -\frac{b}{a}s - \frac{c}{a}t;$$

in vector notation,

$$\begin{bmatrix} x \\ y \\ z \end{bmatrix} = \begin{bmatrix} -\frac{b}{a}s - \frac{c}{a}t \\ s \\ t \end{bmatrix} = s\begin{bmatrix} -b/a \\ 1 \\ 0 \end{bmatrix} + t\begin{bmatrix} -c/a \\ 0 \\ 1 \end{bmatrix}.$$

Thus the plane $\mathscr{P}$ is simply the set $\{s\mathbf{u} + t\mathbf{v}\}$ of all linear combinations of the linearly independent vectors $\mathbf{u} = (-b/a, 1, 0)$ and $\mathbf{v} = (-c/a, 0, 1)$, and is therefore a 2-dimensional subspace of $\mathbf{R}^3$.

Thus every line or plane through the origin is a proper subspace of $\mathbf{R}^3$, and every line or plane not passing through the origin is a translate of such a subspace. It follows that the solution set of every linear equation

$$ax + by + cz = d$$

(a plane, in this case), and of every pair

$$a_1x + b_1y + c_1z = d_1,$$

$$a_2x + b_2y + c_2z = d_2$$

of linear equations (a line in this case, provided the two equations are consistent but not equivalent), is a translate of a subspace of $\mathbf{R}^3$. In Chapter 4 we define subspaces of n-dimensional space, and we will see there that the solution set of any linear system $A\mathbf{x} = \mathbf{b}$ of m equations in n unknowns is a translate of a subspace of $\mathbf{R}^n$.

3.4 PROBLEMS

In Problems 1–8, write parametric equations of the indicated straight line.

1. Through $P(0, 0, 0)$ and parallel to $\mathbf{v} = (1, 2, 3)$.

2. Through $P(3, -4, 5)$ and parallel to $\mathbf{v} = (-2, 7, 3)$.

3. Through $P(4, 13, -3)$ and parallel to $\mathbf{v} = (2, 0, -3)$.

4. Through $P_1(0, 0, 0)$ and $P_2(-6, 3, 5)$.

5. Through $P_1(3, 5, 7)$ and $P_2(-6, -8, 10)$.

6. Through the origin and orthogonal to the plane with equation $x + y + z = 1$.

7. Through $P(2, -3, 4)$ and orthogonal to the plane with equation $2x - y + 3z = 4$.

8. Through $P(2, -1, 5)$ and parallel to the line with parametric equations $x = 3t$, $y = 2 + t$, $z = 2 - t$.

In Problems 9–16, write an equation (in the form $ax + by + cz = d$) of the indicated plane.

9. Through $P(5, 7, -6)$ with normal vector $\mathbf{n} = (2, 2, -1)$.

10. Through $P(10, 4, -3)$ with normal vector $\mathbf{n} = (7, 11, 0)$.

11. Through $P(1, -3, 2)$ with normal vector $\mathbf{n} = \overrightarrow{OP}$.

12. Through $P(5, 7, -6)$ and parallel to the xz-plane.

13. Through the origin and parallel to the plane with equation $3x + 4y - z = 10$.

14. Through $P(5, 1, 4)$ and parallel to the plane with equation $x + y - 2z = 0$.

15. Through the origin and the points $P(1, 1, 1)$ and $Q(1, -1, 3)$.

16. Through the points $A(1, 0, -1)$, $B(3, 3, 2)$, and $C(4, 5, -1)$.

In Problems 17–20, the parametric equations of two lines are given. Determine whether or not the two lines intersect.

17. $x = 5 + 3s$, $y = -3 - 2s$, $z = 4 + s$;
$x = 3 - t$, $y = -4 + 3t$, $z = 5 - 2t$

18. $x = 4 + s$, $y = -2 - 2s$, $z = 6 + 2s$;
$x = -4 + 3t$, $y = 4 - t$, $z = -2 + 2t$

19. $x = 1 + s$, $y = 2 - 2s$, $z = 3 + 2s$;
$x = 3 - t$, $y = 2 + 2t$, $z = 1 - 2t$

20. $x = 2 + s$, $y = 3 + 2s$, $z = 3 - 2s$;
$x = 3 + 2t$, $y = 2 - t$, $z = 2 + t$

In Problems 21–24, find parametric equations of the line of intersection of the planes with the given equations.

21. $x + y + z = 1$ and $2x - y + z = 5$

22. $2x + y + z = 4$ and $3x - y + z = 3$

23. $x + y - 2z = 0$ and $2x + z = 10$

24. $x = 10$ and $x + y + z = 0$

25. Find an equation of the plane through $P(1, 1, 1)$ that intersects the xy-plane in the same line as does the plane with equation $3x + 2y - 5z = 6$.

26. Find an equation of the plane through $P(1, 3, -2)$ and the line of intersection of the two planes with equations $x - y + z = 1$ and $x + y - z = 1$.

27. Show that the lines $x = 1 + s$, $y = -1 + 2s$, $z = 2 + s$ and $x = 2 + t$, $y = 2 + 3t$, $z = 4 + 2t$ intersect. Then find an equation of the (only) plane containing both these lines.

28. Show that the line of intersection of the planes

$$x + 2y - z = 2 \quad \text{and} \quad 3x + 2y + 2z = 7$$

is parallel to the line $x = 1 + 6t$, $y = 3 - 5t$, $z = 2 - 4t$. Then find an equation of the (only) plane that contains both these lines.

29. Find the point of intersection of the plane with equation $3x - 2y + z = 44$ and the line with parametric equations $x = 3 + 2t$, $y = 1 - 3t$, $z = 5 + 4t$.

30. Show that the perpendicular distance from the point $P_0(x_0, y_0, z_0)$ to the plane with equation $ax + by + cz = d$ is

$$D = \frac{|ax_0 + by_0 + cz_0 - d|}{\sqrt{a^2 + b^2 + c^2}}.$$

Suggestion: Write parametric equations of the line through P_0 orthogonal to the given plane P. Let $P_1(x_1, y_1, z_1)$ be the point of L, corresponding to $t = t_1$, at which the line intersects P. Solve for t_1, and finally compute $D = |\overrightarrow{P_0P_1}|$.

31. Use the formula of Problem 30 to find the perpendicular distance between the given point and the given plane.
(a) The origin and the plane with equation $x + 2y + 2z = 12$.
(b) The point $P(3, 2, 1)$ and the plane with equation $4x + 4y + 7z = 9$.

32. Use the formula of Problem 30 to show that the perpendicular distance between the two parallel planes

$$ax + by + cz = \alpha \quad \text{and} \quad ax + by + cz = \beta$$

is

$$D = \frac{|\alpha - \beta|}{\sqrt{a^2 + b^2 + c^2}}.$$

33. Rework Example 4 by first computing the normal vector $\mathbf{n} = \overrightarrow{PQ} \times \overrightarrow{PR}$ and then writing the point-normal equation of the plane through P with normal vector $\mathbf{n}$.

34. Let $\mathbf{u}$ and $\mathbf{v}$ be linearly independent vectors in $\mathbf{R}^3$. Show that the vector $\mathbf{w}$ is a linear combination $s\mathbf{u} + t\mathbf{v}$ of $\mathbf{u}$ and $\mathbf{v}$ if and only if it is orthogonal to the cross product vector $\mathbf{n} = \mathbf{u} \times \mathbf{v}$.

CHAPTER REVIEW QUESTIONS

1. What is the parallelogram law of addition?

2. What is meant by the statement that $\mathbf{R}^2$ is a vector space?

3. What is meant by the statement that the two vectors $\mathbf{a}$ and $\mathbf{b}$ are linearly dependent?

4. Suppose that the vectors $\mathbf{a}$ and $\mathbf{b}$ are linearly independent. Show that the vectors $\mathbf{a}$ and $\mathbf{a} + \mathbf{b}$ are linearly independent. What about the vectors $\mathbf{a} + \mathbf{b}$ and $\mathbf{a} - \mathbf{b}$?

5. If $\mathbf{a}$ and $\mathbf{b}$ are linearly independent vectors in $\mathbf{R}^3$, does it follow that the vectors $\mathbf{a}$, $\mathbf{a} + \mathbf{b}$, and $\mathbf{a} - \mathbf{b}$ are linearly independent?

6. If the vectors $\mathbf{a}$, $\mathbf{b}$, and $\mathbf{c}$ are linearly independent, does it follow that the vectors $\mathbf{a}$, $\mathbf{a} + \mathbf{b}$, and $\mathbf{a} + \mathbf{b} + \mathbf{c}$ are also linearly independent?

7. Given three specific vectors in $\mathbf{R}^3$, how can one determine whether or not they are linearly dependent? Whether they form a basis for $\mathbf{R}^3$?

8. What is a subspace of $\mathbf{R}^3$? Describe the various types of subspaces of $\mathbf{R}^3$.

9. Given two specific vectors in $\mathbf{R}^3$, what is the quickest way to determine whether or not they are orthogonal?

10. What is the geometric interpretation of the dot product of two vectors?

11. If you know that $\mathbf{a} \cdot \mathbf{b} = \mathbf{a} \cdot \mathbf{c} = \mathbf{b} \cdot \mathbf{c} = 0$ (but nothing else about the three vectors $\mathbf{a}$, $\mathbf{b}$, and $\mathbf{c}$), does it necessarily follow that $\mathbf{a}$, $\mathbf{b}$, $\mathbf{c}$ are linearly independent?

12. If $\mathbf{a}$ and $\mathbf{b}$ are orthogonal unit vectors, how does one find the orthogonal projection of a vector $\mathbf{v}$ into the plane spanned by $\mathbf{a}$ and $\mathbf{b}$?

13. How does one write parametric equations for the line through two given points P_1 and P_2?

14. How does one write an equation for the plane through three given points P_1, P_2, and P_3?

15. Given the parametric equations of a line L and the equation of a plane $\mathscr{P}$, what is the quickest way to determine whether or not L and $\mathscr{P}$ intersect?

16. Which lines and planes in $\mathbf{R}^3$ are subspaces of $\mathbf{R}^3$?

17. Is the solution set of two linear equations in three unknowns always a subspace of $\mathbf{R}^3$? Explain your answer.

4

Vector Spaces

4.1

The Vector Space $\mathbf{R}^n$ and Subspaces

In Chapter 3 we defined 3-dimensional space $\mathbf{R}^3$ to be the set of all triples (x, y, z) of real numbers. This definition provides a *mathematical model* of the physical space in which we live, because geometric intuition and experience require that the location of every point be specified uniquely by *three* coordinates.

In science fiction the fourth dimension often plays a rather exotic role. But there are quite common and ordinary situations where it is convenient to use four (or even more) coordinates rather than just two or three. For example, suppose we want to describe the motion of two points P and Q that are moving in the plane $\mathbf{R}^2$ under the action of some given physical law. (See Figure 4.1.) In order to tell where P and Q are at a given instant, we need to give two coordinates for P and two coordinates for Q. So let us write $P(x_1, x_2)$ and $Q(x_3, x_4)$ to indicate these *four* coordinates. Then the two points P and Q determine a quadruple or 4-tuple (x_1, x_2, x_3, x_4) of real numbers, and any such 4-tuple determines a possible pair of locations of P and Q. In this way the set of all pairs of points P and Q in the plane corresponds to the set of all 4-tuples of real numbers. By analogy with our definition of $\mathbf{R}^3$, we may define *4-dimensional space* $\mathbf{R}^4$ to be the set of all such 4-tuples (x_1, x_2, x_3, x_4). Then we can specify a pair of points P and Q in $\mathbf{R}^2$ by specifying a single *point* (x_1, x_2, x_3, x_4) in $\mathbf{R}^4$, and this viewpoint may simplify our analysis of the motions of the original points P and Q. For instance, it may turn out that their coordinates satisfy some single equation such as

$$3x_1 - 4x_2 + 2x_3 - 5x_4 = 0$$

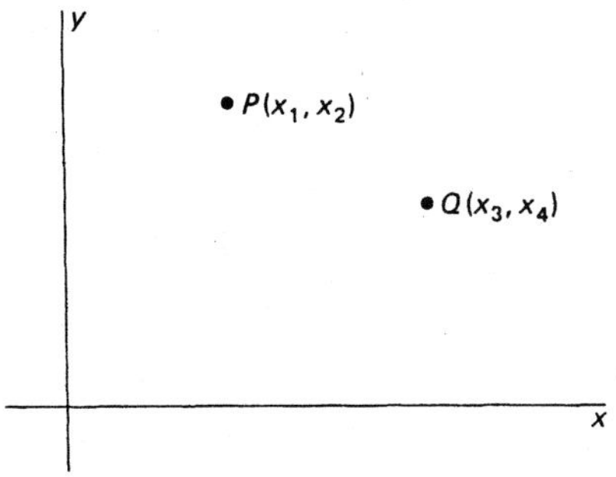

4.1 Two points in the plane $\mathbf{R}^2$ determine a single point (x_1, x_2, x_3, x_4) in $\mathbf{R}^4$.

that is better understood in terms of a single point in $\mathbf{R}^4$ than in terms of the separate points P and Q in $\mathbf{R}^2$. Finally, note that in this example the fourth dimension is quite tangible—it refers simply to the second coordinate x_4 of the point Q.

But the number 4 is no more special than the numbers 2 and 3. To describe similarly the motion of two points in $\mathbf{R}^3$, we would need 6 coordinates rather than 4. An efficient description of another physical situation might require 10 or even 100 coordinates. For general purposes, we want to be able to deal intelligently with n coordinates where n is any fixed positive integer.

An ***n*-tuple** of real numbers is an (ordered) list $(x_1, x_2, x_3, \ldots, x_n)$ of n real numbers. Thus $(1, 3, 4, 2)$ is a 4-tuple and $(0, -3, 7, 5, 2, -1)$ is a 6-tuple. A 2-tuple is an ordered pair and a 3-tuple is an ordered triple of real numbers, so the following definition generalizes our earlier definitions of the plane $\mathbf{R}^2$ and 3-space $\mathbf{R}^3$.

Definition: *n-Space* R^n

The ***n*-dimensional space** $\mathbf{R}^n$ is the set of all n-tuples $(x_1, x_2, x_3, \ldots, x_n)$ of real numbers.

The elements of n-space $\mathbf{R}^n$ are called **points** or **vectors**, and we ordinarily use boldface letters to denote vectors. The ith entry of the vector $\mathbf{x} = (x_1, x_2, x_3, \ldots, x_n)$ is called its ith **coordinate** or its ith **component**. For consistency with matrix operations we agree that

$$\mathbf{x} = (x_1, x_2, x_3, \ldots, x_n) = \begin{bmatrix} x_1 \\ x_2 \\ \vdots \\ x_n \end{bmatrix},$$

so the $n \times 1$ matrix, or *column* vector, is simply another notation for the same ordered list of n real numbers.

If $n > 3$ we cannot visualize vectors in $\mathbf{R}^n$ in the concrete way we can "see" vectors in $\mathbf{R}^2$ and $\mathbf{R}^3$. Nevertheless, we learned in Chapter 3 that the geometric properties of $\mathbf{R}^2$ and $\mathbf{R}^3$ stem ultimately from algebraic operations with vectors, and these algebraic operations can be defined for vectors in $\mathbf{R}^n$ by analogy with their definitions in dimensions 2 and 3.

If $\mathbf{u} = (u_1, u_2, \ldots, u_n)$ and $\mathbf{v} = (v_1, v_2, \ldots, v_n)$ are vectors in $\mathbf{R}^n$, then their **sum** is the vector $\mathbf{u} + \mathbf{v}$ given by

$$\mathbf{u} + \mathbf{v} = (u_1 + v_1, u_2 + v_2, \ldots, u_n + v_n). \tag{1}$$

Thus addition of vectors in $\mathbf{R}^n$ is defined in a componentwise manner, just as in $\mathbf{R}^2$ and $\mathbf{R}^3$, and we can visualize $\mathbf{u} + \mathbf{v}$ as a diagonal vector in a parallelogram determined by $\mathbf{u}$ and $\mathbf{v}$, as in Figure 4.2. If c is a scalar—a real number—then the **scalar multiple** $c\mathbf{u}$ is also defined in componentwise fashion:

$$c\mathbf{u} = (cu_1, cu_2, \ldots, cu_n). \tag{2}$$

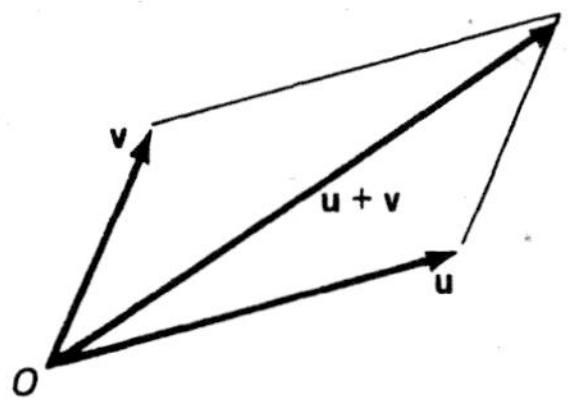

4.2 The parallelogram law for addition of vectors.

We can visualize $c\mathbf{u}$ as a vector collinear with $\mathbf{u}$, with only its length (and possibly its direction along the same line) altered by multiplication by the scalar c. See Figure 4.3.

In Sections 3.1 and 3.2 we saw that for vectors in $\mathbf{R}^2$ and $\mathbf{R}^3$ the operations in (1) and (2) satisfy a list of properties that constitute the definition of a *vector space*; the same is true for vectors in $\mathbf{R}^n$.

DEFINITION OF A VECTOR SPACE

Let V be a set of elements called *vectors*, in which the operations of addition of vectors and of multiplication of vectors by scalars are defined. That is, given vectors $\mathbf{u}$ and $\mathbf{v}$ in V and a scalar c, the vectors $\mathbf{u} + \mathbf{v}$ and $c\mathbf{u}$ are also in V (so V is *closed* under vector addition and multiplication by scalars). Then with these operations V is called a **vector space** provided that—given any vectors $\mathbf{u}$, $\mathbf{v}$, and $\mathbf{w}$ in V and any scalars a and b—the following properties hold true:

(a) $\mathbf{u} + \mathbf{v} = \mathbf{v} + \mathbf{u}$ (commutativity)

(b) $\mathbf{u} + (\mathbf{v} + \mathbf{w}) = (\mathbf{u} + \mathbf{v}) + \mathbf{w}$ (associativity)

(c) $\mathbf{u} + \mathbf{0} = \mathbf{0} + \mathbf{u} = \mathbf{u}$ (zero element)

(d) $\mathbf{u} + (-\mathbf{u}) = (-\mathbf{u}) + \mathbf{u} = \mathbf{0}$ (additive inverse)

(e) $a(\mathbf{u} + \mathbf{v}) = a\mathbf{u} + a\mathbf{v}$ (distributivity)

(f) $(a + b)\mathbf{u} = a\mathbf{u} + b\mathbf{u}$

(g) $a(b\mathbf{u}) = (ab)\mathbf{u}$

(h) $(1)\mathbf{u} = \mathbf{u}$

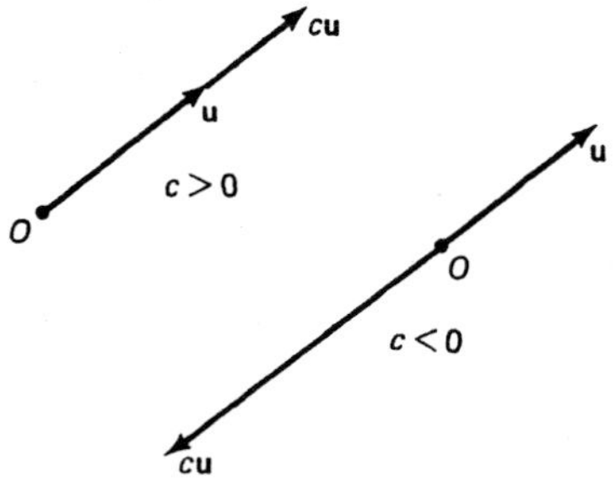

4.3 The vector $c\mathbf{u}$ may have the same direction as the vector $\mathbf{u}$ or the opposite direction.

In property (c) it is meant that there exists a **zero vector 0** in V such that $\mathbf{u} + \mathbf{0} = \mathbf{u}$. The zero vector in $\mathbf{R}^n$ is

$$\mathbf{0} = (0, 0, \ldots, 0).$$

Similarly, property (d) actually means that given the vector $\mathbf{u}$ in V, there exists a vector $-\mathbf{u}$ in V such that $\mathbf{u} + (-\mathbf{u}) = \mathbf{0}$. In $\mathbf{R}^n$ we clearly have

$$-\mathbf{u} = (-u_1, -u_2, \ldots, -u_n).$$

The fact that $\mathbf{R} = \mathbf{R}^1$ satisfies properties (a)–(h), with the real numbers playing the dual roles of scalars *and* vectors, means that the real line may be regarded as a vector space. If $n > 1$, then each of properties (a)–(h) may be readily verified for $\mathbf{R}^n$ by working with components and applying the corresponding properties of real numbers. For example, to verify the commutativity of vector addition in (a), we begin with Equation (1) and write

$$\begin{aligned}\mathbf{u} + \mathbf{v} &= (u_1 + v_1, u_2 + v_2, \ldots, u_n + v_n)\\ &= (v_1 + u_1, v_2 + u_2, \ldots, v_n + u_n)\\ &= \mathbf{v} + \mathbf{u}.\end{aligned}$$

Thus n-space $\mathbf{R}^n$ *is a vector space* with the operations defined in Equations (1) and (2). We will understand throughout that our scalars are the *real numbers*, though in more advanced treatments of linear algebra other scalars (such as the complex numbers) are sometimes used.

Observe that in the definition of a vector space nothing is said about the elements of V (the "vectors") being n-tuples. They can be any objects for which addition and multiplication by scalars are defined and satisfy properties (a)–(h). Although most of the vectors you will see in this text actually are n-tuples of real numbers, an example in which they are not may help to clarify the definition of a vector space.

EXAMPLE 1 Let $\mathcal{F}$ be the set of all real-valued functions defined on the real number line $\mathbf{R}$. Then each vector in $\mathcal{F}$ is a function $\mathbf{f}$ such that the real number $\mathbf{f}(x)$ is defined for all x in $\mathbf{R}$. Given $\mathbf{f}$ and $\mathbf{g}$ in $\mathcal{F}$ and a real number c, the functions $\mathbf{f} + \mathbf{g}$ and $c\mathbf{f}$ are defined in the natural way,

$$(\mathbf{f} + \mathbf{g})(x) = \mathbf{f}(x) + \mathbf{g}(x)$$

and

$$(c\mathbf{f})(x) = c(\mathbf{f}(x)).$$

Then each of properties (a)–(h) of a vector space follows readily from the corresponding property of the real numbers. For instance, if a is a scalar, then

$$\begin{aligned}\{a(\mathbf{f} + \mathbf{g})\}(x) &= a\{(\mathbf{f} + \mathbf{g})(x)\}\\ &= a\{\mathbf{f}(x) + \mathbf{g}(x)\}\\ &= a\mathbf{f}(x) + a\mathbf{g}(x)\\ &= (a\mathbf{f} + a\mathbf{g})(x).\end{aligned}$$

Thus $a(\mathbf{f} + \mathbf{g}) = a\mathbf{f} + a\mathbf{g}$, so $\mathcal{F}$ enjoys property (e).

After verification of the other seven properties we conclude that $\mathscr{F}$ is, indeed, a vector space—one that differs in a fundamental way from each of the vector spaces $\mathbf{R}^n$. We naturally call $\mathbf{R}^n$ an n-dimensional vector space, and in Section 4.3 we define the word *dimension* in such a way that the dimension of $\mathbf{R}^n$ actually *is* n. But the vector space F of functions turns out not to have dimension n for any integer n; it is an example of an infinite-dimensional vector space (see Section 4.5).

SUBSPACES

Let $W = \{\mathbf{0}\}$ be the subset of $\mathbf{R}^n$ that contains only the zero vector $\mathbf{0}$. Then W satisfies properties (a)–(h) of a vector space, because each reduces trivially to the equation $\mathbf{0} = \mathbf{0}$. Thus W is a subset of the vector space $V = \mathbf{R}^n$ that is itself a vector space.

> ***Definition:*** *Subspace*
> Let W be a nonempty subset of the vector space V. Then W is a **subspace** of V provided that W itself is a vector space with the operations of addition and multiplication by scalars as defined in V.

In order for the subset W to be a subspace of the vector space V, it first must be closed under the operations of vector addition and multiplication by scalars. Then it must satisfy properties (a)–(h) of a vector space. But W "inherits" all these properties from V, because the vectors in W all are vectors in V, and the vectors in V all satisfy properties (a)–(h). Hence, in order to determine whether the subset W is a vector space, we need only check the two closure conditions.

> ***Theorem 1:*** *Conditions for a Subspace*
> The nonempty subset W of the vector space V is a subspace of V if and only if it satisfies the following two conditions:
>
> **(i)** If $\mathbf{u}$ and $\mathbf{v}$ are vectors in W, then $\mathbf{u} + \mathbf{v}$ is also in W.
> **(ii)** If $\mathbf{u}$ is in W and c is a scalar, then the vector $c\mathbf{u}$ is also in W.

In Chapter 3 we saw that lines through the origin in $\mathbf{R}^2$ form subspaces of $\mathbf{R}^2$ and that lines and planes through the origin are subspaces of $\mathbf{R}^3$. The subspace W of the following example may be regarded as a "plane" through the origin in $\mathbf{R}^n$.

EXAMPLE 2 Let W be the subset of $\mathbf{R}^n$ consisting of all those vectors $(x_1, x_2, \ldots, x_n)$ whose coordinates satisfy the single homogeneous linear equation

$$a_1x_1 + a_2x_2 + \cdots + a_nx_n = 0,$$

where the given coefficients $a_1, a_2, \dots, a_n$ are not all zero. If $\mathbf{u} = (u_1, u_2, \dots, u_n)$ and $\mathbf{v} = (v_1, v_2, \dots, v_n)$ are vectors in W, then

$$\begin{aligned} &a_1(u_1 + v_1) + a_2(u_2 + v_2) + \cdots + a_n(u_n + v_n) \\ &\quad = (a_1u_1 + a_2u_2 + \cdots + a_nu_n) + (a_1v_1 + a_2v_2 + \cdots + a_nu_n) \\ &\quad = 0 + 0 = 0, \end{aligned}$$

so $\mathbf{u} + \mathbf{v} = (u_1 + v_1, \dots, u_n + v_n)$ is also in W. If c is a scalar, then

$$\begin{aligned} a_1(cu_1) + a_2(cu_2) + \cdots + a_n(cu_n) &= c(a_1u_1 + a_2u_2 + \cdots + a_nu_n) \\ &= (c)(0) = 0, \end{aligned}$$

so $c\mathbf{u} = (cu_1, cu_2, \dots, cu_n)$ is in W. Thus we have shown that W satisfies conditions (i) and (ii) of Theorem 1 and is therefore a subspace of $\mathbf{R}^n$.

In order to apply Theorem 1 to show that W *is* a subspace of the vector space V, we must show that W satisfies *both* conditions in the theorem. But to apply Theorem 1 to show that W is *not* a subspace of V, we need only show *either* that condition (i) fails *or* that condition (ii) fails.

EXAMPLE 3 Let W be the set of all those vectors (x_1, x_2, x_3, x_4) in $\mathbf{R}^4$ whose four coordinates are all nonnegative: $x_i \geq 0$ for $i = 1, 2, 3, 4$. Then it should be clear that the sum of two vectors in W is also a vector in W because the sum of two nonnegative numbers is nonnegative. Thus W satisfies condition (i) of Theorem 1. But if we take $\mathbf{u} = (1, 1, 1, 1)$ in W and $c = -1$, then we find that the scalar multiple

$$c\mathbf{u} = (-1)(1, 1, 1, 1) = (-1, -1, -1, -1)$$

is *not* in W. Thus W fails to satisfy condition (ii) and therefore is *not* a subspace of $\mathbf{R}^4$.

EXAMPLE 4 Let W be the set of all those vectors (x_1, x_2, x_3, x_4) in $\mathbf{R}^4$ such that $x_1x_4 = 0$. Now W satisfies condition (ii) of Theorem 1 because $x_1x_4 = 0$ implies that $(cx_1)(cx_4) = 0$ for any scalar c. But if we take the vectors $\mathbf{u} = (1, 1, 0, 0)$ and $\mathbf{v} = (0, 0, 1, 1)$ in W, we see that their sum $\mathbf{u} + \mathbf{v} = (1, 1, 1, 1)$ is *not* in W. Thus W does not satisfy condition (i) and therefore is *not* a subspace of $\mathbf{R}^4$.

Example 2 implies that the solution set of a homogeneous linear equation

$$a_1x_1 + a_2x_2 + \cdots + a_nx_n = 0$$

in n variables is always a *subspace* of $\mathbf{R}^n$. Theorem 2 further implies that the same is true of a *homogeneous* system of linear equations. Recall that any such system of m equations in n unknowns can be written in the form $A\mathbf{x} = \mathbf{0}$, where A is the $m \times n$ coefficient matrix and $\mathbf{x} = (x_1, x_2, \dots, x_n)$ is regarded as a column vector. The solution set of $A\mathbf{x} = \mathbf{0}$ is then the set of all vectors $\mathbf{x}$ in $\mathbf{R}^n$ that satisfy this equation; that is, the set of all its solution vectors.

> ***Theorem 2:*** *Solution Subspaces*
> If A is a (constant) $m \times n$ matrix, then the solution set of the homogeneous linear system
>
> $$A\mathbf{x} = \mathbf{0} \tag{3}$$
>
> is a subspace of $\mathbf{R}^n$.

Proof Let W denote the solution set of Equation (3). If $\mathbf{u}$ and $\mathbf{v}$ are vectors in W, then $A\mathbf{u} = A\mathbf{v} = \mathbf{0}$. Hence

$$A(\mathbf{u} + \mathbf{v}) = A\mathbf{u} + A\mathbf{v} = \mathbf{0} + \mathbf{0} = \mathbf{0}.$$

Thus the sum $\mathbf{u} + \mathbf{v}$ is also in W, and hence W satisfies condition (i) of Theorem 1. If c is a scalar, then

$$A(c\mathbf{u}) = c(A\mathbf{u}) = c\mathbf{0} = \mathbf{0},$$

so $c\mathbf{u}$ is in W if $\mathbf{u}$ is in W. Thus W also satisfies condition (ii) of Theorem 1. It therefore follows that W is a subspace of $\mathbf{R}^n$. ∎

Note that in order to conclude by Theorem 2 that the solution set of a linear system is a subspace, it is necessary for the system to be *homogeneous*. Indeed, the solution set of a nonhomogeneous linear system

$$A\mathbf{x} = \mathbf{b} \tag{4}$$

with $\mathbf{b} \neq \mathbf{0}$ is *never* a subspace. For if $\mathbf{u}$ were a solution vector of the system in (4), then

$$A(2\mathbf{u}) = 2(A\mathbf{u}) = 2\mathbf{b} \neq \mathbf{b}$$

because $\mathbf{b} \neq \mathbf{0}$. Thus the scalar multiple $2\mathbf{u}$ of the solution vector $\mathbf{u}$ is *not* a solution vector. Therefore Theorem 1 implies that the solution set of (4) is *not* a subspace.

Because the solution set of a *homogeneous* linear system is a subspace, we often call it the **solution space** of the system. The subspaces of $\mathbf{R}^n$ are the possible solution spaces of a homogeneous linear system with n unknowns, and this is one of the principal reasons for our interest in subspaces of $\mathbf{R}^n$.

At opposite extremes as subspaces of $\mathbf{R}^n$ lie the **zero subspace** $\{\mathbf{0}\}$ and $\mathbf{R}^n$ itself. Every other subspace of $\mathbf{R}^n$, each one that is neither $\{\mathbf{0}\}$ nor $\mathbf{R}^n$, is called a **proper subspace** of $\mathbf{R}^n$. The proper subspaces of $\mathbf{R}^n$ play the same role in $\mathbf{R}^n$ that lines and planes through the origin play in $\mathbf{R}^3$. In the following two sections we develop the tools that are needed to analyze the structure of a given proper subspace of $\mathbf{R}^n$. In particular, given the homogeneous system $A\mathbf{x} = \mathbf{0}$, we ask how we can describe its solution space in a concise and illuminating way, beyond the mere statement that it is the set of all solution vectors of the system. Example 5 illustrates one possible way of doing this.

EXAMPLE 5 In Example 4 of Section 1.4 we considered the homogeneous system

$$\begin{aligned} x_1 + 3x_2 - 15x_3 + 7x_4 &= 0 \\ x_1 + 4x_2 - 19x_3 + 10x_4 &= 0 \\ 2x_1 + 5x_2 - 26x_3 + 11x_4 &= 0. \end{aligned} \tag{5}$$

The reduced echelon form of the coefficient matrix of this system is

$$\begin{bmatrix} 1 & 0 & -3 & -2 \\ 0 & 1 & -4 & 3 \\ 0 & 0 & 0 & 0 \end{bmatrix}.$$

Hence x_1 and x_2 are the leading variables and x_3 and x_4 are free variables. Back substitution yields the general solution

$$x_3 = s, \qquad x_4 = t, \qquad x_2 = 4s - 3t, \qquad x_1 = 3s + 2t$$

in terms of arbitrary parameters s and t. Thus a typical solution vector of the system in (5) has the form

$$\mathbf{x} = \begin{bmatrix} x_1 \\ x_2 \\ x_3 \\ x_4 \end{bmatrix} = \begin{bmatrix} 3s + 2t \\ 4s - 3t \\ s \\ t \end{bmatrix} = s \begin{bmatrix} 3 \\ 4 \\ 1 \\ 0 \end{bmatrix} + t \begin{bmatrix} 2 \\ -3 \\ 0 \\ 1 \end{bmatrix}.$$

It follows that the solution space of the system in (5) may be described as the set of all linear combinations of the form

$$\mathbf{x} = s\mathbf{u} + t\mathbf{v} \tag{6}$$

where $\mathbf{u} = (3, 4, 1, 0)$ and $\mathbf{v} = (2, -3, 0, 1)$. Thus we have found the two particular solution vectors $\mathbf{u}$ and $\mathbf{v}$ of our system that completely determine its solution space (by the formula in (6)).

4.1 PROBLEMS

In Problems 1–14, a subset W of some n-space $\mathbf{R}^n$ is defined by means of a given condition imposed on the typical vector $(x_1, x_2, \ldots, x_n)$. Apply Theorem 1 to determine whether or not W is a subspace of $\mathbf{R}^n$.

1. W is the set of all vectors in $\mathbf{R}^3$ such that $x_3 = 0$.

2. W is the set of all vectors in $\mathbf{R}^3$ such that $x_1 = 5x_2$.

3. W is the set of all vectors in $\mathbf{R}^3$ such that $x_2 = 1$.

4. W is the set of all vectors in $\mathbf{R}^3$ such that $x_1 + x_2 + x_3 = 1$.

5. W is the set of all vectors in $\mathbf{R}^4$ such that $x_1 + 2x_2 + 3x_3 + 4x_4 = 0$.

6. W is the set of all vectors in $\mathbf{R}^4$ such that $x_1 = 3x_3$ and $x_2 = 4x_4$.

7. W is the set of all vectors in $\mathbf{R}^2$ such that $|x_1| = |x_2|$.

8. W is the set of all vectors in $\mathbf{R}^2$ such that $(x_1)^2 + (x_2)^2 = 0$.

9. W is the set of all vectors in $\mathbf{R}^2$ such that $(x_1)^2 + (x_2)^2 = 1$.

10. W is the set of all vectors in $\mathbf{R}^2$ such that $|x_1| + |x_2| = 1$.

11. W is the set of all vectors in $\mathbf{R}^4$ such that $x_1 + x_2 = x_3 + x_4$.

12. W is the set of all vectors in $\mathbf{R}^4$ such that $x_1x_2 = x_3x_4$.

13. W is the set of all vectors in $\mathbf{R}^4$ such that $x_1x_2x_3x_4 = 0$.

14. W is the set of those vectors in $\mathbf{R}^4$ whose components are all nonzero.

In Problems 15–18, apply the method of Example 5 to find two solution vectors $\mathbf{u}$ and $\mathbf{v}$ such that the solution space is the set of all linear combinations of the form $s\mathbf{u} + t\mathbf{v}$.

15. $$\begin{aligned} x_1 - 4x_2 + x_3 - 4x_4 &= 0 \\ x_1 + 2x_2 + x_3 + 8x_4 &= 0 \\ x_1 + x_2 + x_3 + 6x_4 &= 0 \end{aligned}$$

16. $$\begin{aligned} x_1 - 4x_2 - 3x_3 - 7x_4 &= 0 \\ 2x_1 - x_2 + x_3 + 7x_4 &= 0 \\ x_1 + 2x_2 + 3x_3 + 11x_4 &= 0 \end{aligned}$$

17. $$\begin{aligned} x_1 + 3x_2 + 8x_3 - x_4 &= 0 \\ x_1 - 3x_2 - 10x_3 + 5x_5 &= 0 \\ x_1 + 4x_2 + 11x_3 - 2x_4 &= 0 \end{aligned}$$

18. $$\begin{aligned} x_1 + 3x_2 + 2x_3 + 5x_4 - x_5 &= 0 \\ 2x_1 + 7x_2 + 4x_3 + 11x_4 + 2x_5 &= 0 \\ 2x_1 + 6x_2 + 5x_3 + 12x_4 - 7x_5 &= 0 \end{aligned}$$

In Problems 19–22, reduce the given system to echelon form to find a single solution vector $\mathbf{u}$ such that the solution space is the set of all scalar multiples of $\mathbf{u}$.

19. $$\begin{aligned} x_1 - 3x_2 - 5x_3 - 6x_4 &= 0 \\ 2x_1 + x_2 + 4x_3 - 4x_4 &= 0 \\ x_1 + 3x_2 + 7x_3 + x_4 &= 0 \end{aligned}$$

20. $$\begin{aligned} x_1 + 5x_2 + x_3 - 8x_4 &= 0 \\ 2x_1 + 5x_2 \qquad - 5x_4 &= 0 \\ 2x_1 + 7x_2 + x_3 - 9x_4 &= 0 \end{aligned}$$

21. $$\begin{aligned} x_1 + 7x_2 + 2x_3 - 3x_4 &= 0 \\ 2x_1 + 7x_2 + x_3 - 4x_4 &= 0 \\ 3x_1 + 5x_2 - x_3 - 5x_4 &= 0 \end{aligned}$$

22. $$\begin{aligned} x_1 + 3x_2 + 3x_3 + 3x_4 &= 0 \\ 2x_1 + 7x_2 + 5x_3 - x_4 &= 0 \\ 2x_1 + 7x_2 + 4x_3 - 4x_4 &= 0 \end{aligned}$$

23. Show that every subspace W of a vector space V contains the zero vector $\mathbf{0}$.

24. Apply the properties of a vector space V to show each of the following.
(a) $0\mathbf{u} = \mathbf{0}$ for every $\mathbf{u}$ in V.
(b) $c\mathbf{0} = \mathbf{0}$ for every scalar c.
(c) $(-1)\mathbf{u} = -\mathbf{u}$ for every $\mathbf{u}$ in V.
Do *not* assume that the vectors in V are n-tuples of real numbers.

25. Show that the nonempty subset W of a vector space V is a subspace of V if and only if for every pair of vectors $\mathbf{u}$ and $\mathbf{v}$ in W and every pair of scalars a and b, $a\mathbf{u} + b\mathbf{v}$ is also in W.

26. *Prove*: If $\mathbf{u}$ is a (fixed) vector in the vector space V, then the set W of all scalar multiples $c\mathbf{u}$ of $\mathbf{u}$ is a subspace of V.

27. Let $\mathbf{u}$ and $\mathbf{v}$ be (fixed) vectors in the vector space V. Show that the set W of all linear combinations $a\mathbf{u} + b\mathbf{v}$ of $\mathbf{u}$ and $\mathbf{v}$ is a subspace of V.

28. Suppose that A is an $n \times n$ matrix and that k is a (constant) scalar. Show that the set of all vectors $\mathbf{x}$ such that $A\mathbf{x} = k\mathbf{x}$ is a subspace of $\mathbf{R}^n$.

29. Let A be an $n \times n$ matrix, $\mathbf{b}$ be a nonzero vector, and $\mathbf{x}_0$ be a solution vector of the system $A\mathbf{x} = \mathbf{b}$. Show that $\mathbf{x}$ is a solution of the nonhomogeneous system $A\mathbf{x} = \mathbf{b}$ if and only if $\mathbf{y} = \mathbf{x} - \mathbf{x}_0$ is a solution of the homogeneous system $A\mathbf{y} = \mathbf{0}$.

30. Let U and V be subspaces of the vector space W. Their **intersection** $U \cap V$ is the set of all vectors that are both in U and in V. Show that $U \cap V$ is a subspace of W. If U and V are two planes through the origin in $\mathbf{R}^3$, what is $U \cap V$?

31. Let U and V be subspaces of the vector space W. Their **sum** $U + V$ is the set of all vectors $\mathbf{w}$ of the form

$$\mathbf{w} = \mathbf{u} + \mathbf{v}$$

where $\mathbf{u}$ is in U and $\mathbf{v}$ is in V. Show that $U + V$ is a subspace of W. If U and V are lines through the origin in $\mathbf{R}^3$, what is $U + V$?

4.2 Linear Combinations and Linear Independence

In Example 5 of Section 4.1 we solved the homogeneous linear system

$$\begin{aligned} x_1 + 3x_2 - 15x_3 + 7x_4 &= 0 \\ x_1 + 4x_2 - 19x_3 + 10x_4 &= 0 \\ 2x_1 + 5x_2 - 26x_3 + 11x_4 &= 0. \end{aligned} \tag{1}$$

We found that its solution space W consists of all those vectors $\mathbf{x}$ in $\mathbf{R}^4$ that have the form

$$\mathbf{x} = s(3, 4, 1, 0) + t(2, -3, 0, 1). \tag{2}$$

We therefore can visualize W as the plane in $\mathbf{R}^4$ determined by the vectors $\mathbf{v}_1 = (3, 4, 1, 0)$ and $\mathbf{v}_2 = (2, -3, 0, 1)$. The fact that every solution vector is a combination (as in (2)) of the particular solution vectors $\mathbf{v}_1$ and $\mathbf{v}_2$ gives us a quite tangible understanding of the solution space W of the system in (1).

More generally, we know from Theorem 2 in Section 4.1 that the solution set V of any $m \times n$ homogeneous linear system $A\mathbf{x} = \mathbf{0}$ is a subspace of $\mathbf{R}^n$. In order better to understand such a vector space V, we would like to find a minimal set of vectors $\mathbf{v}_1$, $\mathbf{v}_2, \ldots, \mathbf{v}_k$ in V such that *every* vector in V is a sum of scalar multiples of these particular vectors.

The vector $\mathbf{w}$ is called a **linear combination** of the vectors $\mathbf{v}_1, \mathbf{v}_2, \ldots, \mathbf{v}_k$ provided that there exist scalars $c_1, c_2, \ldots, c_k$ such that

$$\mathbf{w} = c_1\mathbf{v}_1 + c_2\mathbf{v}_2 + \cdots + c_k\mathbf{v}_k. \tag{3}$$

Given a vector $\mathbf{w}$ in $\mathbf{R}^n$, the problem of determining whether or not $\mathbf{w}$ is a linear combination of the vectors $\mathbf{v}_1, \mathbf{v}_2, \ldots, \mathbf{v}_k$ amounts to solving a linear system to see whether we can find scalars $c_1, c_2, \ldots, c_k$ so that (3) holds.

EXAMPLE 1 To determine whether the vector $\mathbf{w} = (2, -6, 3)$ in $\mathbf{R}^3$ is a linear combination of the vectors $\mathbf{v}_1 = (1, -2, -1)$ and $\mathbf{v}_2 = (3, -5, 4)$, we write the equation $c_1\mathbf{v}_1 + c_2\mathbf{v}_2 = \mathbf{w}$ in matrix form:

$$c_1\begin{bmatrix} 1 \\ -2 \\ -1 \end{bmatrix} + c_2\begin{bmatrix} 3 \\ -5 \\ 4 \end{bmatrix} = \begin{bmatrix} 2 \\ -6 \\ 3 \end{bmatrix}$$

—that is,

$$\begin{aligned} c_1 + 3c_2 &= 2 \\ -2c_1 - 5c_2 &= -6 \\ -c_1 + 4c_2 &= 3. \end{aligned}$$

The augmented coefficient matrix

$$\begin{bmatrix} 1 & 3 & 2 \\ -2 & -5 & -6 \\ -1 & 4 & 3 \end{bmatrix}$$

may be reduced by elementary row operations to the echelon form

$$\begin{bmatrix} 1 & 3 & 2 \\ 0 & 1 & -2 \\ 0 & 0 & 19 \end{bmatrix}.$$

We see now from the third row that our system is inconsistent, so the desired scalars c_1 and c_2 do not exist. Thus $\mathbf{w}$ is *not* a linear combination of $\mathbf{v}_1$ and $\mathbf{v}_2$.

EXAMPLE 2 To express the vector $\mathbf{w} = (-7, 7, 11)$ as a linear combination of the vectors $\mathbf{v}_1 = (1, 2, 1)$, $\mathbf{v}_2 = (-4, -1, 2)$, and $\mathbf{v}_3 = (-3, 1, 3)$, we write the equation $c_1\mathbf{v}_1 + c_2\mathbf{v}_2 + c_3\mathbf{v}_3 = \mathbf{w}$ in the form

$$c_1\begin{bmatrix} 1 \\ 2 \\ 1 \end{bmatrix} + c_2\begin{bmatrix} -4 \\ -1 \\ 2 \end{bmatrix} + c_3\begin{bmatrix} -3 \\ 1 \\ 3 \end{bmatrix} = \begin{bmatrix} -7 \\ 7 \\ 11 \end{bmatrix}$$

—that is,

$$\begin{aligned} c_1 - 4c_2 - 3c_3 &= -7 \\ 2c_1 - c_2 + c_3 &= 7 \\ c_1 + 2c_2 + 3c_3 &= 11. \end{aligned}$$

The reduced echelon form of the augmented coefficient matrix of this system is

$$\begin{bmatrix} 1 & 0 & 1 & 5 \\ 0 & 1 & 1 & 3 \\ 0 & 0 & 0 & 0 \end{bmatrix}.$$

Thus c_3 is a free variable. With $c_3 = t$, back substitution yields $c_1 = 5 - t$ and $c_2 = 3 - t$. For instance, $t = 1$ gives $c_1 = 4$, $c_2 = 2$, and $c_3 = 1$, so

$$\mathbf{w} = 4\mathbf{v}_1 + 2\mathbf{v}_2 + \mathbf{v}_3.$$

But $t = -2$ yields $c_1 = 7$, $c_2 = 5$, and $c_3 = -2$, so $\mathbf{w}$ can also be expressed as

$$\mathbf{w} = 7\mathbf{v}_1 + 5\mathbf{v}_2 - 2\mathbf{v}_3.$$

We have found not only that $\mathbf{w}$ can be expressed as a linear combination of the vectors $\mathbf{v}_1, \mathbf{v}_2, \mathbf{v}_3$, but also that this can be done in many different ways (one for each choice of the parameter t).

We began this section with the observation that every solution vector of the linear system in (1) is a linear combination of the vectors $\mathbf{v}_1$ and $\mathbf{v}_2$ that appear in the right-hand side of Equation (2). A brief way of saying this is that the vectors $\mathbf{v}_1$ and $\mathbf{v}$ span the solution space. More generally, suppose that $\mathbf{v}_1, \mathbf{v}_2, \ldots, \mathbf{v}_k$ are vectors in : vector space V. Then we say that the vectors $\mathbf{v}_1, \mathbf{v}_2, \ldots, \mathbf{v}_k$ **span** the vector space provided that *every* vector in V is a linear combination of these k vectors. We may als say that the set $S = \{\mathbf{v}_1, \mathbf{v}_2, \ldots, \mathbf{v}_k\}$ of vectors is a **spanning set** for V.

EXAMPLE 3 The familiar unit vectors $\mathbf{i} = (1, 0, 0)$, $\mathbf{j} = (0, 1, 0)$, and $\mathbf{k} = (0, 0, 1$ span $\mathbf{R}^3$ because every vector $\mathbf{x} = (x_1, x_2, x_3)$ in $\mathbf{R}^3$ can be expressed as the linea combination

$$\mathbf{x} = x_1\mathbf{i} + x_2\mathbf{j} + x_3\mathbf{k}$$

of these three vectors **i**, **j**, and **k**.

If the vectors $\mathbf{v}_1, \mathbf{v}_2, \ldots, \mathbf{v}_k$ in the vector space V do not span V, we can ask abou the subset of V consisting of all those vectors that are linear combinations of $\mathbf{v}$ $\mathbf{v}_2, \ldots, \mathbf{v}_k$. The following theorem implies that this subset is always a *subspace* of V.

Theorem 1: *The Span of a Set of Vectors*

Let $\mathbf{v}_1, \mathbf{v}_2, \ldots, \mathbf{v}_k$ be vectors in the vector space V. Then the set W of all linear combinations of $\mathbf{v}_1, \mathbf{v}_2, \ldots, \mathbf{v}_k$ is a subspace of V.

PROOF We must show that W is closed under addition of vectors and multiplicatio by scalars. If

$$\mathbf{u} = a_1\mathbf{v}_1 + a_2\mathbf{v}_2 + \cdots + a_k\mathbf{v}_k$$

and

$$\mathbf{v} = b_1\mathbf{v}_1 + b_2\mathbf{v}_2 + \cdots + b_k\mathbf{v}_k$$

are vectors in W, then

$$\mathbf{u} + \mathbf{v} = (a_1 + b_1)\mathbf{v}_1 + (a_2 + b_2)\mathbf{v}_2 + \cdots + (a_k + b_k)\mathbf{v}_k$$

and

$$c\mathbf{u} = (ca_1)\mathbf{v}_1 + (ca_2)\mathbf{v}_2 + \cdots + (ca_k)\mathbf{v}_k$$

for any scalar c. Thus $\mathbf{u} + \mathbf{v}$ and $c\mathbf{u}$ are linear combinations of $\mathbf{v}_1, \mathbf{v}_2, \ldots, \mathbf{v}_k$ an therefore are vectors in W. It is clear that W is nonempty, and hence W is a subspac of V. ∎

We say that the subspace W of Theorem 1 is the space **spanned** by the vectors $\mathbf{v}$ $\mathbf{v}_2, \ldots, \mathbf{v}_k$, or is the **span** of the set $S = \{\mathbf{v}_1, \mathbf{v}_2, \ldots, \mathbf{v}_k\}$ of vectors. We sometimes writ

$$W = \text{span}(S) = \text{span}\{\mathbf{v}_1, \mathbf{v}_2, \ldots, \mathbf{v}_k\}.$$

Thus Example 3 implies that $\mathbf{R}^3 = \text{span}\{\mathbf{i}, \mathbf{j}, \mathbf{k}\}$. The question as to whether a given vector $\mathbf{w}$ in $\mathbf{R}^n$ lies in the subspace $\text{span}\{\mathbf{v}_1, \mathbf{v}_2, \ldots, \mathbf{v}_k\}$ reduces to solving a linear system, as illustrated by Examples 1 and 2.

It is easy to verify that the space $W = \text{span}\{\mathbf{v}_1, \mathbf{v}_2, \ldots, \mathbf{v}_k\}$ of Theorem 1 is the smallest subspace of V that contains all the vectors $\mathbf{v}_1, \mathbf{v}_2, \ldots, \mathbf{v}_k$—meaning that every other subspace of V that contains these k vectors must also contain W (Problem 30).

LINEAR INDEPENDENCE

Henceforth, when we solve a homogeneous system of linear equations, we generally will seek a set $\mathbf{v}_1, \mathbf{v}_2, \ldots, \mathbf{v}_k$ of solution vectors that span the solution space W of the system. Perhaps the most concrete way to describe a subspace W of a vector space V is to give explicitly a set $\mathbf{v}_1, \mathbf{v}_2, \ldots, \mathbf{v}_k$ of vectors that span W. And this type of representation is most useful and desirable (as well as most aesthetically pleasing) when each vector $\mathbf{w}$ in W is expressible in a *unique* way as a linear combination of $\mathbf{v}_1, \mathbf{v}_2, \ldots, \mathbf{v}_k$. (For instance, each vector in $\mathbf{R}^3$ is a unique linear combination of the vectors $\mathbf{i}$, $\mathbf{j}$, and $\mathbf{k}$ of Example 3.) But Example 2 demonstrates that a vector $\mathbf{w}$ may well be expressed in many different ways as a linear combination of given vectors $\mathbf{v}_1, \mathbf{v}_2, \ldots, \mathbf{v}_k$.

Thus not all spanning sets enjoy the uniqueness property that we desire. Two questions arise: Given a subspace W of a vector space V, does there necessarily exist a spanning set with the uniqueness property that we desire? If so, how do we find one that does? The following definition provides the key to both answers.

***Definition*:** *Linear Independence*

The vectors $\mathbf{v}_1, \mathbf{v}_2, \ldots, \mathbf{v}_k$ in a vector space V are said to be **linearly independent** provided that the equation

$$c_1\mathbf{v}_1 + c_2\mathbf{v}_2 + \cdots + c_k\mathbf{v}_k = \mathbf{0} \tag{4}$$

has only the trivial solution $c_1 = c_2 = \cdots = c_k = 0$. That is, the only linear combination of $\mathbf{v}_1, \mathbf{v}_2, \ldots, \mathbf{v}_k$ that represents the zero vector $\mathbf{0}$ is the trivial combination $0\mathbf{v}_1 + 0\mathbf{v}_2 + \cdots + 0\mathbf{v}_k$.

EXAMPLE 4 The **standard unit vectors**

$$\begin{aligned} \mathbf{e}_1 &= (1, 0, 0, \ldots, 0), \\ \mathbf{e}_2 &= (0, 1, 0, \ldots, 0), \\ &\;\vdots \\ \mathbf{e}_n &= (0, 0, 0, \ldots, 1), \end{aligned}$$

in $\mathbf{R}^n$ are linearly independent. The reason is that the equation

$$c_1\mathbf{e}_1 + c_2\mathbf{e}_2 + \cdots + c_n\mathbf{e}_n = \mathbf{0}$$

quite evidently reduces to

$$(c_1, c_2, \ldots, c_n) = (0, 0, \ldots, 0),$$

and thus has only the trivial solution $c_1 = c_2 = \cdots = c_n = 0$.

EXAMPLE 5 To determine whether the vectors $\mathbf{v}_1 = (1, 2, 2, 1)$, $\mathbf{v}_2 = (2, 3, 4, 1)$, and $\mathbf{v}_3 = (3, 8, 7, 5)$ in $\mathbf{R}^4$ are linearly independent, we write the equation $c_1\mathbf{v}_1 + c_2\mathbf{v}_2 + c_3\mathbf{v}_3 = \mathbf{0}$ as the linear system

$$\begin{aligned} c_1 + 2c_2 + 3c_3 &= 0 \\ 2c_1 + 3c_2 + 8c_3 &= 0 \\ 2c_1 + 4c_2 + 7c_3 &= 0 \\ c_1 + c_2 + 5c_3 &= 0 \end{aligned}$$

and then solve for c_1, c_2, and c_3. The augmented coefficient matrix of this system reduces to the echelon form

$$\begin{bmatrix} 1 & 2 & 3 & 0 \\ 0 & 1 & -2 & 0 \\ 0 & 0 & 1 & 0 \\ 0 & 0 & 0 & 0 \end{bmatrix},$$

so we see that the only solution is $c_1 = c_2 = c_3 = 0$. Thus the vectors $\mathbf{v}_1$, $\mathbf{v}_2$, and $\mathbf{v}_3$ are linearly independent.

Observe that linear independence of the vectors $\mathbf{v}_1, \mathbf{v}_2, \ldots, \mathbf{v}_k$ actually is a property of the *set* $S = \{\mathbf{v}_1, \mathbf{v}_2, \ldots, \mathbf{v}_k\}$ whose elements are these vectors. Occasionally the phraseology "the set $S = \{\mathbf{v}_1, \mathbf{v}_2, \ldots, \mathbf{v}_k\}$ is linearly independent" is more convenient. For instance, *any subset of a linearly independent set* $S = \{\mathbf{v}_1, \mathbf{v}_2, \ldots, \mathbf{v}_k\}$ *is a linearly independent set of vectors* (Problem 29).

Now we show that *the coefficients in a linear combination of the linearly independent vectors* $\mathbf{v}_1, \mathbf{v}_2, \ldots, \mathbf{v}_k$ *are unique.* If both

$$\mathbf{w} = a_1\mathbf{v}_1 + a_2\mathbf{v}_2 + \cdots + a_k\mathbf{v}_k \tag{5}$$

and

$$\mathbf{w} = b_1\mathbf{v}_1 + b_2\mathbf{v}_2 + \cdots + b_k\mathbf{v}_k, \tag{6}$$

then

$$a_1\mathbf{v}_1 + a_2\mathbf{v}_2 + \cdots + a_k\mathbf{v}_k = b_1\mathbf{v}_1 + b_2\mathbf{v}_2 + \cdots + b_k\mathbf{v}_k,$$

so it follows that

$$(a_1 - b_1)\mathbf{v}_1 + (a_2 - b_2)\mathbf{v}_2 + \cdots + (a_k - b_k)\mathbf{v}_k = \mathbf{0}. \tag{7}$$

Because the vectors $\mathbf{v}_1, \mathbf{v}_2, \ldots, \mathbf{v}_k$ are linearly independent, each of the coefficients in (7) must vanish. Therefore $a_1 = b_1, a_2 = b_2, \ldots, a_k = b_k$, so we have shown that the linear combinations in (5) and (6) actually are identical. Hence if a vector $\mathbf{w}$ is in the set $\text{span}\{\mathbf{v}_1, \mathbf{v}_2, \ldots, \mathbf{v}_k\}$, then it can be expressed in only one way as a linear combination of these linearly independent vectors.

A set of vectors is called **linearly dependent** provided it is not linearly independent. Hence the vectors $\mathbf{v}_1, \mathbf{v}_2, \ldots, \mathbf{v}_k$ are linearly dependent if and only if there exist scalars $c_1, c_2, \ldots, c_k$ *not all zero* such that

$$c_1\mathbf{v}_1 + c_2\mathbf{v}_2 + \cdots + c_k\mathbf{v}_k = \mathbf{0}. \tag{8}$$

In short, a (finite) set of vectors is linearly dependent provided that some *nontrivial* linear combination of them equals the zero vector.

EXAMPLE 6 Let $\mathbf{v}_1 = (2, 1, 3)$, $\mathbf{v}_2 = (5, -2, 4)$, $\mathbf{v}_3 = (3, 8, -6)$, and $\mathbf{v}_4 = (2, 7, -4)$. Then the equation $c_1\mathbf{v}_1 + c_2\mathbf{v}_2 + c_3\mathbf{v}_3 + c_4\mathbf{v}_4 = \mathbf{0}$ is equivalent to the linear system

$$\begin{aligned} 2c_1 + 5c_2 + 3c_3 + 2c_4 &= 0 \\ c_1 - 2c_2 + 8c_3 + 7c_4 &= 0 \\ 3c_1 + 4c_2 - 6c_3 - 4c_4 &= 0 \end{aligned}$$

of three equations in four unknowns. Because this homogeneous system has more unknowns than equations, Theorem 3 in Section 1.3 implies that it has a nontrivial solution. Therefore we may conclude—without even solving explicitly for c_1, c_2, c_3, and c_4—that the vectors $\mathbf{v}_1$, $\mathbf{v}_2$, $\mathbf{v}_3$, and $\mathbf{v}_4$ are linearly dependent. (It happens that

$$2\mathbf{v}_1 - \mathbf{v}_2 + 3\mathbf{v}_3 - 4\mathbf{v}_4 = \mathbf{0},$$

as you can easily verify.)

The argument in Example 6 may be generalized in an obvious way to prove that *any set of more than n vectors in* $\mathbf{R}^n$ *is linearly dependent.* For if $k > n$, then Equation (8) is equivalent to a homogeneous linear system with more unknowns (k) than equations (n), so Theorem 3 in Section 1.3 yields a nontrivial solution.

We now look at the way in which the elements of a linearly dependent set of vectors $\mathbf{v}_1, \mathbf{v}_2, \ldots, \mathbf{v}_k$ "depend" on one another. We know that there exist scalars c_1, $c_2, \ldots, c_k$ not all zero such that

$$c_1\mathbf{v}_1 + c_2\mathbf{v}_2 + \cdots + c_k\mathbf{v}_k = \mathbf{0}. \tag{9}$$

Suppose that the pth coefficient is nonzero: $c_p \neq 0$. Then we can solve Equation (9) for $c_p\mathbf{v}_p$ and next divide by c_p to get

$$\mathbf{v}_p = a_1\mathbf{v}_1 + \cdots + a_{p-1}\mathbf{v}_{p-1} + a_{p+1}\mathbf{v}_{p+1} + \cdots + a_k\mathbf{v}_k \tag{10}$$

where $a_i = -c_i/c_p$ for $i \neq p$. Thus at least one of the linearly dependent vectors is a linear combination of the other $k - 1$. Conversely, suppose we are given a set of vectors $\mathbf{v}_1, \mathbf{v}_2, \ldots, \mathbf{v}_k$ with one of them dependent on the others as in Equation (10). Then we can transpose all the terms to the left-hand side to get an equation of the form in (9) with $c_p = 1 \neq 0$. This shows that the vectors are linearly dependent. Therefore we have proved that *the vectors* $\mathbf{v}_1, \mathbf{v}_2, \ldots, \mathbf{v}_k$ *are linearly dependent if and only if at least one of them is a linear combination of the others.*

For instance (as we saw in Chapter 3), two vectors are linearly dependent if and only if one of them is a scalar multiple of the other, in which case the two vectors are collinear. Three vectors are linearly dependent if and only if one of them is a linear combination of the other two, in which case the three vectors are coplanar.

In Theorem 3 of Section 3.2 we saw that the *determinant* provides a criterion for deciding whether three vectors in $\mathbf{R}^3$ are linearly independent: The vectors $\mathbf{v}_1, \mathbf{v}_2, \mathbf{v}_3$ in $\mathbf{R}^3$ are linearly independent if and only if the determinant of the 3×3 matrix

$$A = [\mathbf{v}_1 \quad \mathbf{v}_2 \quad \mathbf{v}_3]$$

is nonzero. The proof given there in the three-dimensional case generalizes readily to the n-dimensional case. Given n vectors $\mathbf{v}_1, \mathbf{v}_2, \ldots, \mathbf{v}_n$ in $\mathbf{R}^n$, we consider the $n \times n$ matrix

$$A = [\mathbf{v}_1 \quad \mathbf{v}_2 \quad \cdots \quad \mathbf{v}_n]$$

having these vectors as its column vectors. Then, by Theorem 2 in Section 2.3, $\det A \neq 0$ if and only if A is invertible, in which case the system $A\mathbf{c} = \mathbf{0}$ has only the trivial solution $c_1 = c_2 = \cdots = c_n = 0$, so the vectors $\mathbf{v}_1, \mathbf{v}_2, \ldots, \mathbf{v}_n$ must be linearly independent.

Theorem 2: *Independence of n Vectors in* $\mathbf{R}^n$

The n vectors $\mathbf{v}_1, \mathbf{v}_2, \ldots, \mathbf{v}_n$ in $\mathbf{R}^n$ are linearly independent if and only if the $n \times n$ matrix

$$A = [\mathbf{v}_1 \quad \mathbf{v}_2 \quad \cdots \quad \mathbf{v}_n]$$

with them as its column vectors has nonzero determinant.

We saw earlier that a set of *more* than n vectors in $\mathbf{R}^n$ is always linearly dependent. The following theorem shows us how the determinant provides a criterion in the case of *fewer* than n vectors in $\mathbf{R}^n$.

Theorem 3: *Fewer Than n Vectors in* $\mathbf{R}^n$

Consider k vectors $\mathbf{v}_1, \mathbf{v}_2, \ldots, \mathbf{v}_k$ in $\mathbf{R}^n$, with $k < n$. Let

$$A = [\mathbf{v}_1 \quad \mathbf{v}_2 \quad \cdots \quad \mathbf{v}_k]$$

be the $n \times k$ matrix having them as its column vectors. Then the vectors $\mathbf{v}_1, \mathbf{v}_2, \ldots, \mathbf{v}_k$ are linearly independent if and only if some $k \times k$ submatrix of A has nonzero determinant.

Rather than including a complete proof, we will simply illustrate the "if" part of Theorem 3 in the case $n = 5$, $k = 3$. Let $\mathbf{v}_1 = (a_1, a_2, a_3, a_4, a_5)$, $\mathbf{v}_2 = (b_1, b_2, b_3, b_4, b_5)$, and $\mathbf{v}_3 = (c_1, c_2, c_3, c_4, c_5)$ be three vectors in $\mathbf{R}^5$ such that the 5×3 matrix

$$A = \begin{bmatrix} a_1 & b_1 & c_1 \\ a_2 & b_2 & c_2 \\ a_3 & b_3 & c_3 \\ a_4 & b_4 & c_4 \\ a_5 & b_5 & c_5 \end{bmatrix}$$

has a 3×3 submatrix with nonzero determinant. Suppose, for instance, that

$$\begin{vmatrix} a_1 & b_1 & c_1 \\ a_3 & b_3 & c_3 \\ a_5 & b_5 & c_5 \end{vmatrix} \neq 0.$$

Then Theorem 2 implies that the three vectors $\mathbf{u}_1 = (a_1, a_3, a_5)$, $\mathbf{u}_2 = (b_1, b_3, b_5)$, and $\mathbf{u}_3 = (c_1, c_3, c_5)$ in $\mathbf{R}^3$ are linearly independent. Now suppose that $c_1\mathbf{v}_1 + c_2\mathbf{v}_2 + c_3\mathbf{v}_3 = \mathbf{0}$. Then by deleting the second and fourth components of each vector in this equation, we find that $c_1\mathbf{u}_1 + c_2\mathbf{u}_2 + c_3\mathbf{u}_3 = \mathbf{0}$. But the fact that $\mathbf{u}_1$, $\mathbf{u}_2$, $\mathbf{u}_3$ are linearly independent implies that $c_1 = c_2 = c_3 = 0$, and it now follows that $\mathbf{v}_1$, $\mathbf{v}_2$, $\mathbf{v}_3$ are linearly independent.

4.2 PROBLEMS

In Problems 1–8, determine whether the given vectors $\mathbf{v}_1, \mathbf{v}_2, \ldots, \mathbf{v}_n$ are linearly independent or linearly dependent. Do this essentially by inspection—that is, without solving a linear system of equations.

1. $\mathbf{v}_1 = (4, -2, 6, -4)$, $\mathbf{v}_2 = (6, -3, 9, -6)$

2. $\mathbf{v}_1 = (3, 9, -3, 6)$, $\mathbf{v}_2 = (2, 6, -1, 4)$

3. $\mathbf{v}_1 = (3, 4)$, $\mathbf{v}_2 = (6, -1)$, $\mathbf{v}_3 = (7, 5)$

4. $\mathbf{v}_1 = (4, -2, 2)$, $\mathbf{v}_2 = (5, 4, -3)$, $\mathbf{v}_3 = (4, 6, 5)$, $\mathbf{v}_4 = (-7, 9, 3)$

5. $\mathbf{v}_1 = (1, 0, 0)$, $\mathbf{v}_2 = (0, -2, 0)$, $\mathbf{v}_3 = (0, 0, 3)$

6. $\mathbf{v}_1 = (1, 0, 0)$, $\mathbf{v}_2 = (1, 1, 0)$, $\mathbf{v}_3 = (1, 1, 1)$

7. $\mathbf{v}_1 = (2, 1, 0, 0)$, $\mathbf{v}_2 = (3, 0, 1, 0)$, $\mathbf{v}_3 = (4, 0, 0, 1)$

8. $\mathbf{v}_1 = (1, 0, 3, 0)$, $\mathbf{v}_2 = (0, 2, 0, 4)$, $\mathbf{v}_3 = (1, 2, 3, 4)$

In Problems 9–16, express the indicated vector $\mathbf{w}$ as a linear combination of the given vectors $\mathbf{v}_1, \mathbf{v}_2, \ldots, \mathbf{v}_k$ if this is possible. If not, show it is impossible.

9. $\mathbf{w} = (1, 0, -7)$; $\mathbf{v}_1 = (5, 3, 4)$, $\mathbf{v}_2 = (3, 2, 5)$

10. $\mathbf{w} = (3, -1, -2)$; $\mathbf{v}_1 = (-3, 1, -2)$, $\mathbf{v}_2 = (6, -2, 3)$

11. $\mathbf{w} = (1, 0, 0, -1)$; $\mathbf{v}_1 = (7, -6, 4, 5)$, $\mathbf{v}_2 = (3, -3, 2, 3)$

12. $\mathbf{w} = (4, -4, 3, 3)$; $\mathbf{v}_1 = (7, 3, -1, 9)$, $\mathbf{v}_2 = (-2, -2, 1, -3)$

13. $\mathbf{w} = (5, 2, -2)$; $\mathbf{v}_1 = (1, 5, -3)$, $\mathbf{v}_2 = (5, -3, 4)$

14. $\mathbf{w} = (2, -3, 2, -3)$; $\mathbf{v}_1 = (1, 0, 0, 3)$, $\mathbf{v}_2 = (0, 1, -2, 0)$, $\mathbf{v}_3 = (0, -1, 1, 1)$

15. $\mathbf{w} = (4, 5, 6)$; $\mathbf{v}_1 = (2, -1, 4)$, $\mathbf{v}_2 = (3, 0, 1)$, $\mathbf{v}_3 = (1, 2, -1)$

16. $\mathbf{w} = (7, 7, 9, 11)$; $\mathbf{v}_1 = (2, 0, 3, 1)$, $\mathbf{v}_2 = (4, 1, 3, 2)$, $\mathbf{v}_3 = (1, 3, -1, 3)$

In Problems 17–22, three vectors $\mathbf{v}_1$, $\mathbf{v}_2$, and $\mathbf{v}_3$ are given. If they are linearly independent, show this; otherwise find a nontrivial linear combination of them that is equal to the zero vector.

17. $\mathbf{v}_1 = (1, 0, 1)$, $\mathbf{v}_2 = (2, -3, 4)$, $\mathbf{v}_3 = (3, 5, 2)$

18. $\mathbf{v}_1 = (2, 0, -3)$, $\mathbf{v}_2 = (4, -5, -6)$, $\mathbf{v}_3 = (-2, 1, 3)$

19. $\mathbf{v}_1 = (2, 0, 3, 0)$, $\mathbf{v}_2 = (5, 4, -2, 1)$, $\mathbf{v}_3 = (2, -1, 1, -1)$

20. $\mathbf{v}_1 = (1, 1, -1, 1)$, $\mathbf{v}_2 = (2, 1, 1, 1)$, $\mathbf{v}_3 = (3, 1, 4, 1)$

21. $\mathbf{v}_1 = (3, 0, 1, 2)$, $\mathbf{v}_2 = (1, -1, 0, 1)$, $\mathbf{v}_3 = (1, 2, 1, 0)$

22. $\mathbf{v}_1 = (3, 9, 0, 5)$, $\mathbf{v}_2 = (3, 0, 9, -7)$, $\mathbf{v}_3 = (4, 7, 5, 0)$

In Problems 23–26, the vectors $\{\mathbf{v}_i\}$ are known to be linearly independent. Apply the definition of linear independence to show that the vectors $\{\mathbf{u}_i\}$ are also linearly independent.

23. $\mathbf{u}_1 = \mathbf{v}_1 + \mathbf{v}_2$, $\mathbf{u}_2 = \mathbf{v}_1 - \mathbf{v}_2$

24. $\mathbf{u}_1 = \mathbf{v}_1 + \mathbf{v}_2$, $\mathbf{u}_2 = 2\mathbf{v}_1 + 3\mathbf{v}_2$

25. $\mathbf{u}_1 = \mathbf{v}_1$, $\mathbf{u}_2 = \mathbf{v}_1 + 2\mathbf{v}_2$, $\mathbf{u}_3 = \mathbf{v}_1 + 2\mathbf{v}_2 + 3\mathbf{v}_3$

26. $\mathbf{u}_1 = \mathbf{v}_2 + \mathbf{v}_3$, $\mathbf{u}_2 = \mathbf{v}_1 + \mathbf{v}_3$, $\mathbf{u}_3 = \mathbf{v}_1 + \mathbf{v}_2$

27. *Prove*: If the (finite) set S of vectors contains the zero vector, then S is linearly dependent.

28. *Prove*: If the set S of vectors is linearly dependent and the (finite) set T contains S, then T is also linearly dependent. You may assume that $S = \{\mathbf{v}_1, \mathbf{v}_2, \ldots, \mathbf{v}_k\}$ and that $T = \{\mathbf{v}_1, \mathbf{v}_2, \ldots, \mathbf{v}_m\}$ with $m > k$.

29. Show that if the (finite) set S of vectors is linearly independent, then any subset T of S is also linearly independent.

30. Suppose that the subspace U of the vector space V contains the vectors $\mathbf{v}_1, \mathbf{v}_2, \ldots, \mathbf{v}_k$. Show that U contains the subspace spanned by these vectors.

31. Let S and T be sets of vectors in a vector space such that S is a subset of span(T). Show that span(S) is also a subset of span(T).

32. Let $\mathbf{v}_1, \mathbf{v}_2, \ldots, \mathbf{v}_k$ be linearly independent vectors in the set S of vectors. *Prove*: If no set of more than k vectors in S is linearly independent, then every vector in S is a linear combination of $\mathbf{v}_1, \mathbf{v}_2, \ldots, \mathbf{v}_k$.

In Problems 33–35, let $\mathbf{v}_1, \mathbf{v}_2, \ldots, \mathbf{v}_k$ be vectors in $\mathbf{R}^n$ and let

$$A = [\mathbf{v}_1 \quad \mathbf{v}_2 \quad \cdots \quad \mathbf{v}_k]$$

be the $n \times k$ matrix with these vectors as its column vectors.

33. *Prove*: If some $k \times k$ submatrix of A is the $k \times k$ identity matrix, then $\mathbf{v}_1, \mathbf{v}_2, \ldots, \mathbf{v}_k$ are linearly independent.

34. Suppose that $k = n$, that the vectors $\mathbf{v}_1, \mathbf{v}_2, \ldots, \mathbf{v}_k$ are linearly independent, and that B is a nonsingular $n \times n$ matrix. Prove that the column vectors of the matrix AB are linearly independent.

35. Suppose that $k < n$, that the vectors $\mathbf{v}_1, \mathbf{v}_2, \ldots, \mathbf{v}_k$ are linearly independent, and that B is a nonsingular $k \times k$ matrix. Use Theorem 3 to show that the column vectors of AB are linearly independent.

4.3 Bases for Vector Spaces

An especially useful way of describing the solution space of a homogeneous linear system is to list explicitly a set S of solution vectors such that *every* solution vector is a unique linear combination of these particular ones. The following definition specifies the properties of such a set S of "basic" solution vectors, and the concept is equally important for vector spaces other than solution spaces.

Definition: *Basis*

A finite set S of vectors in a vector space V is called a **basis** for V provided that

(a) The vectors in S are linearly independent, and

(b) The vectors in S span V.

In short, a basis for the vector space V is a linearly independent spanning set of vectors in V. Thus if $S = \{\mathbf{v}_1, \mathbf{v}_2, \ldots, \mathbf{v}_n\}$ is a basis for S, then any vector $\mathbf{w}$ in V can be expressed as a linear combination

$$\mathbf{w} = c_1\mathbf{v}_1 + c_2\mathbf{v}_2 + \cdots + c_n\mathbf{v}_n \tag{1}$$

of the vectors in S, and we saw in Section 4.2 that the linear independence of S implies that the coefficients $c_1, c_2, \ldots, c_n$ in (1) are *unique*. That is, $\mathbf{w}$ cannot be expressed differently as a linear combination of the basis vectors $\mathbf{v}_1, \mathbf{v}_2, \ldots, \mathbf{v}_n$.

EXAMPLE 1 The **standard basis** for $\mathbf{R}^n$ consists of the unit vectors

$$\mathbf{e}_1 = (1, 0, 0, \ldots, 0), \mathbf{e}_2 = (0, 1, 0, \ldots, 0), \ldots,$$
$$\mathbf{e}_n = (0, 0, 0, \ldots, 1).$$

If $\mathbf{x} = (x_1, x_2, \ldots, x_n)$ is a vector in $\mathbf{R}^n$, then

$$\mathbf{x} = x_1\mathbf{e}_1 + x_2\mathbf{e}_2 + \cdots + x_n\mathbf{e}_n.$$

Thus the vectors $\mathbf{e}_1, \mathbf{e}_2, \ldots, \mathbf{e}_n$ span $\mathbf{R}^n$, and we noted in Example 4 of Section 4.2 that these *standard unit vectors* are linearly independent.

EXAMPLE 2 Let $\mathbf{v}_1, \mathbf{v}_2, \ldots, \mathbf{v}_n$ be n linearly independent vectors in $\mathbf{R}^n$. We saw in Section 4.2 that any set of more than n vectors in $\mathbf{R}^n$ is linearly dependent. Hence, given a vector $\mathbf{w}$ in $\mathbf{R}^n$, there exist scalars $c, c_1, c_2, \ldots, c_n$ not all zero such that

$$c\mathbf{w} + c_1\mathbf{v}_1 + c_2\mathbf{v}_2 + \cdots + c_n\mathbf{v}_n = \mathbf{0}. \tag{2}$$

If c were zero, then (2) would imply that the vectors $\mathbf{v}_1, \mathbf{v}_2, \ldots, \mathbf{v}_n$ are linearly dependent. Hence $c \neq 0$, so Equation (2) can be solved for $\mathbf{w}$ as a linear combination of $\mathbf{v}_1, \mathbf{v}_2, \ldots, \mathbf{v}_n$. Thus the linearly independent vectors $\mathbf{v}_1, \mathbf{v}_2, \ldots, \mathbf{v}_n$ *also* span $\mathbf{R}^n$ and therefore constitute a basis for $\mathbf{R}^n$.

Example 2 shows that *any set of n linearly independent vectors in* $\mathbf{R}^n$ *is a basis for* $\mathbf{R}^n$. By Theorem 2 in Section 4.2, we therefore can determine whether n given vectors $\mathbf{v}_1, \mathbf{v}_2, \ldots, \mathbf{v}_n$ form a basis for $\mathbf{R}^n$ by calculating the determinant of the $n \times n$ matrix

$$A = [\mathbf{v}_1 \quad \mathbf{v}_2 \quad \cdots \quad \mathbf{v}_n]$$

with these vectors as its column vectors. They constitute a basis for $\mathbf{R}^n$ if and only if $\det A \neq 0$.

EXAMPLE 3 Let $\mathbf{v}_1 = (1, -1, -2, -3)$, $\mathbf{v}_2 = (1, -1, 2, 3)$, $\mathbf{v}_3 = (1, -1, -3, -2)$, and $\mathbf{v}_4 = (0, 3, -1, 2)$. Then we find that

$$\begin{vmatrix} 1 & 1 & 1 & 0 \\ -1 & -1 & -1 & 3 \\ -2 & 2 & -3 & -1 \\ -3 & 3 & -2 & 2 \end{vmatrix} = 30 \neq 0,$$

so it follows that $\{\mathbf{v}_1, \mathbf{v}_2, \mathbf{v}_3, \mathbf{v}_4\}$ is a basis for $\mathbf{R}^4$.

Theorem 1 has the following import: Just as in $\mathbf{R}^n$, a basis for *any* vector space V contains the largest possible number of linearly independent vectors in V.

> ***Theorem 1:*** *Bases as Maximal Linearly Independent Sets*
> Let $S = \{\mathbf{v}_1, \mathbf{v}_2, \ldots, \mathbf{v}_n\}$ be a basis for the vector space V. Then any set of more than n vectors in V is linearly dependent.

Proof We need to show that if $m > n$, then any set $T = \{\mathbf{w}_1, \mathbf{w}_2, \ldots, \mathbf{w}_m\}$ of m vectors in V is linearly dependent. Because the basis S spans V, each vector $\mathbf{w}_j$ in T can be expressed as a linear combination of $\mathbf{v}_1, \mathbf{v}_2, \ldots, \mathbf{v}_n$:

$$\begin{aligned} \mathbf{w}_1 &= a_{11}\mathbf{v}_1 + a_{21}\mathbf{v}_2 + \cdots + a_{n1}\mathbf{v}_n \\ \mathbf{w}_2 &= a_{12}\mathbf{v}_1 + a_{22}\mathbf{v}_2 + \cdots + a_{n2}\mathbf{v}_n \\ &\;\,\vdots \\ \mathbf{w}_m &= a_{1m}\mathbf{v}_1 + a_{2m}\mathbf{v}_2 + \cdots + a_{nm}\mathbf{v}_n. \end{aligned} \tag{3}$$

Now we need to find scalars $c_1, c_2, \ldots, c_m$ not all zero such that

$$c_1\mathbf{w}_1 + c_2\mathbf{w}_2 + \cdots + c_m\mathbf{w}_m = \mathbf{0}. \tag{4}$$

Substituting in (4) the expressions in (3) for each $\mathbf{w}_j$, we get

$$\begin{aligned} &c_1(a_{11}\mathbf{v}_1 + a_{21}\mathbf{v}_2 + \cdots + a_{n1}\mathbf{v}_n) \\ &+ c_2(a_{12}\mathbf{v}_1 + a_{22}\mathbf{v}_2 + \cdots + a_{n2}\mathbf{v}_n) + \cdots \\ &+ c_m(a_{1m}\mathbf{v}_1 + a_{2m}\mathbf{v}_2 + \cdots + a_{nm}\mathbf{v}_n) = \mathbf{0}. \end{aligned} \tag{5}$$

Because the vectors $\mathbf{v}_1, \mathbf{v}_2, \ldots, \mathbf{v}_n$ are linearly independent, the coefficient in (5) of each $\mathbf{v}_i$ must vanish:

$$\begin{aligned} a_{11}c_1 + a_{12}c_2 + \cdots + a_{1m}c_m &= 0 \\ a_{21}c_1 + a_{22}c_2 + \cdots + a_{2m}c_m &= 0 \\ &\;\,\vdots \\ a_{n1}c_1 + a_{n2}c_2 + \cdots + a_{nm}c_m &= 0. \end{aligned} \tag{6}$$

But because $m > n$, this is a homogeneous linear system with more unknowns than equations and therefore has a nontrivial solution $(c_1, c_2, \ldots, c_m)$. Then $c_1, c_2, \ldots, c_m$

are scalars not all zero such that (4) holds, so we have shown that the set T of more than n vectors is linearly dependent. ■

Now let $S = \{\mathbf{v}_1, \mathbf{v}_2, \ldots, \mathbf{v}_n\}$ and $T = \{\mathbf{w}_1, \mathbf{w}_2, \ldots, \mathbf{w}_m\}$ be two different bases for the same vector space V. Because S is a basis and T is linearly independent, Theorem 1 implies that $m \leq n$. Now reverse the roles of S and T; the fact that T is a basis and S is linearly independent implies similarly that $n \leq m$. Hence $m = n$, so we have proved the following theorem for any vector space with a finite basis.

> ***Theorem 2:*** *The Dimension of a Vector Space*
>
> Any two bases for a vector space consist of the same number of vectors.

A nonzero vector space V is called **finite-dimensional** provided that there exists a basis for V consisting of a finite number of vectors from V. In this case the number n of vectors in each basis for V is called the **dimension** of V, denoted by $n = \dim V$. Then V is an *n-dimensional* vector space. The standard basis of Example 1 shows that $\mathbf{R}^n$ is, indeed, an n-dimensional vector space.

Note that the zero vector space $\{\mathbf{0}\}$ has no basis because it contains *no* linearly independent set of vectors. (Sometimes it is convenient to adopt the convention that the null set is a basis for $\{\mathbf{0}\}$.) Here we define $\dim\{\mathbf{0}\}$ to be zero. A nonzero vector space that has no finite basis is called **infinite-dimensional**. Infinite-dimensional vector spaces are discussed in Section 4.5, but we include an illustrative example of one here.

EXAMPLE 4 Let $\mathscr{P}$ be the set of all polynomials of the form

$$p(x) = a_0 + a_1x + a_2x^2 + \cdots + a_nx^n,$$

where the largest exponent $n \geq 0$ that appears is the *degree* of the polynomial $p(x)$, and the coefficients $a_0, a_1, a_2, \ldots, a_n$ are real numbers. We add polynomials in $\mathscr{P}$ and multiply them by scalars in the usual way—that is, by collecting coefficients of like powers of x. For instance, if

$$p(x) = 3 + 2x + 5x^3 \quad \text{and} \quad q(x) = 7 + 4x + 3x^2 + 9x^4,$$

then

$$\begin{aligned}(p + q)(x) &= (3 + 7) + (2 + 4)x + (0 + 3)x^2 + (5 + 0)x^3 + (0 + 9)x^4 \\ &= 10 + 6x + 3x^2 + 5x^3 + 9x^4\end{aligned}$$

and

$$(7p)(x) = 7(3 + 2x + 5x^3) = 21 + 14x + 35x^3.$$

It is readily verified that with these operations $\mathscr{P}$ is a vector space. But $\mathscr{P}$ has no finite basis. For if $p_1, p_2, \ldots, p_n$ are elements of $\mathscr{P}$, then the degree of any linear combination of them is at most the maximum of *their* degrees. Hence no polynomial in $\mathscr{P}$ of higher degree lies in $\text{span}\{p_1, p_2, \ldots, p_n\}$. Thus no finite subset of $\mathscr{P}$ spans $\mathscr{P}$, and therefore $\mathscr{P}$ is an infinite-dimensional vector space.

Here our concern is with finite-dimensional vector spaces, and we note first that any proper subspace W of a finite-dimensional vector space V is itself finite-dimensional, with $\dim W < \dim V$. For if $\dim V = n$, let $k \leq n$ be the largest integer such that W contains k linearly independent vectors $\mathbf{v}_1, \mathbf{v}_2, \ldots, \mathbf{v}_k$. Then by the same argument as in Example 2, we see that $\{\mathbf{v}_1, \mathbf{v}_2, \ldots, \mathbf{v}_k\}$ is a basis for W, so W is finite-dimensional with $\dim W = k$, and $k < n$ because W is a proper subspace.

Moreover, an n-dimensional vector space V contains proper subspaces of each dimension $k = 1, 2, \ldots, n-1$. For instance, if $\{\mathbf{v}_1, \mathbf{v}_2, \ldots, \mathbf{v}_n\}$ is a basis for V and $k < n$, then $W = \text{span}\{\mathbf{v}_1, \mathbf{v}_2, \ldots, \mathbf{v}_k\}$ is a subspace of dimension k. Thus $\mathbf{R}^4$ contains proper subspaces of dimensions 1, 2, and 3; $\mathbf{R}^5$ contains proper subspaces of dimensions 1, 2, 3, and 4; and so on. The proper subspaces of $\mathbf{R}^n$ of dimensions $1, 2, \ldots, n-1$ are the higher-dimensional analogues of lines and planes through the origin in $\mathbf{R}^3$.

Suppose that V is an n-dimensional vector space and that $S = \{\mathbf{v}_1, \mathbf{v}_2, \ldots, \mathbf{v}_n\}$ is a set of n vectors in V. Then, in order to show that S is a basis for V, it is not necessary to prove *both* that S is linearly independent *and* that S spans V, because it turns out (for n vectors in an n-dimensional vector space) that either property of S implies the other. For instance, if $S = \{\mathbf{v}_1, \mathbf{v}_2, \ldots, \mathbf{v}_n\}$ is a set of n linearly independent vectors in V, then Theorem 1 and the argument of Example 2 (once again) imply that S spans V and hence is a basis for V. This proves part (a) of Theorem 3. The remaining parts are left to the problems (see Problems 27–32).

Theorem 3: *Independent Sets, Spanning Sets, and Bases*

Let V be an n-dimensional vector space and let S be a subset of V. Then

(a) If S is linearly independent and consists of n vectors, then S is a basis for V;

(b) If S spans V and consists of n vectors, then S is a basis for V;

(c) If S is linearly independent, then S is contained in a basis for V;

(d) If S spans V, then S contains a basis for V.

Part (c) of Theorem 3 is often applied in the following form: If W is a k-dimensional subspace of the n-dimensional vector space V, then any basis $\{\mathbf{v}_1, \mathbf{v}_2, \ldots, \mathbf{v}_k\}$ for W can be "extended" to a basis $\{\mathbf{v}_1, \mathbf{v}_2, \ldots, \mathbf{v}_n\}$ for V, consisting of the original basis vectors for W together with $n-k$ additional vectors $\mathbf{v}_{k+1}, \mathbf{v}_{k+2}, \ldots, \mathbf{v}_n$.

BASES FOR SOLUTION SPACES

We consider now the homogeneous linear system

$$A\mathbf{x} = \mathbf{0} \tag{7}$$

in which A is an $m \times n$ matrix, so the system consists of m equations in the n variables $x_1, x_2, \ldots, x_n$. Its solution space W is then a subspace of $\mathbf{R}^n$. We want to determine the dimension of W and, moreover, to find an explicit basis for W. Thus we seek a maximal set of linearly independent solution vectors of (7).

Recall the Gaussian elimination method of Section 1.2. We use elementary row operations to reduce the coefficient matrix A to an echelon matrix E and note the (nonzero) *leading entries* in the rows of E. The *leading variables* are those that correspond to the columns of E containing the leading entries. The remaining variables (if any) are the *free variables*. If there are no free variables, then our system has only the trivial solution, so $W = \{\mathbf{0}\}$. If there are free variables, we set each of them (separately) equal to a parameter and solve (by back substitution) for the leading variables as linear combinations of these parameters. The solution space W is then the set of all solution vectors obtained in this manner (for all possible values of the parameters).

To illustrate the general situation, let us suppose that the leading variables are the first r variables $x_1, x_2, \ldots, x_r$, so the $k = n - r$ variables $x_{r+1}, x_{r+2}, \ldots, x_n$ are free variables. The reduced system $E\mathbf{x} = \mathbf{0}$ then takes the form

$$\begin{aligned} b_{11}x_1 + b_{12}x_2 + \cdots + b_{1r}x_r + \cdots + b_{1n}x_n &= 0 \\ b_{22}x_2 + \cdots + b_{2r}x_r + \cdots + b_{2n}x_n &= 0 \\ &\vdots \\ b_{rr}x_r + \cdots + b_{rn}x_n &= 0 \end{aligned} \tag{8}$$

(plus k trivial equations of the form $0 = 0$). We set

$$x_{r+1} = t_1, \qquad x_{r+2} = t_2, \ldots, x_n = t_k \tag{9}$$

and then solve (by back substitution) the equations in (8) for the leading variables

$$\begin{aligned} x_1 &= c_{11}t_1 + c_{12}t_2 + \cdots + c_{1k}t_k \\ x_2 &= c_{21}t_1 + c_{22}t_2 + \cdots + c_{2k}t_k \\ &\vdots \\ x_r &= c_{r1}t_1 + c_{r2}t_2 + \cdots + c_{rk}t_k. \end{aligned} \tag{10}$$

The typical solution vector $(x_1, x_2, \ldots, x_n)$ is given in terms of the k parameters $t_1, t_2, \ldots, t_k$ by the equations in (9) and (10).

We now choose k particular solution vectors $\mathbf{v}_1, \mathbf{v}_2, \ldots, \mathbf{v}_k$ as follows: To get $\mathbf{v}_j$ we set the jth parameter t_j equal to 1 and set all other parameters equal to zero. Then

$$\mathbf{v}_j = (c_{1j}, c_{2j}, \ldots, c_{rj}, 0, \ldots, 1, \ldots, 0), \tag{11}$$

with the 1 appearing as the $(r + j)$th entry. The vectors $\mathbf{v}_1, \mathbf{v}_2, \ldots, \mathbf{v}_k$ are the column vectors of the $n \times k$ matrix

$$\begin{bmatrix} c_{11} & c_{12} & \cdots & c_{1k} \\ c_{21} & c_{22} & \cdots & c_{2k} \\ \vdots & \vdots & \ddots & \vdots \\ c_{r1} & c_{r2} & \cdots & c_{rk} \\ 1 & 0 & \cdots & 0 \\ 0 & 1 & \cdots & 0 \\ \vdots & \vdots & \ddots & \vdots \\ 0 & 0 & \cdots & 1 \end{bmatrix}. \tag{12}$$

Because of the presence of the lower $k \times k$ identity matrix, it is clear that the vectors $\mathbf{v}_1, \mathbf{v}_2, \ldots, \mathbf{v}_k$ are linearly independent (see Problem 36). But Equations (9) and (10) show that the typical solution vector $\mathbf{x}$ is a linear combination

$$\mathbf{x} = t_1\mathbf{v}_1 + t_2\mathbf{v}_2 + \cdots + t_k\mathbf{v}_k. \tag{13}$$

Therefore the vectors $\mathbf{v}_1, \mathbf{v}_2, \ldots, \mathbf{v}_k$ defined in (11) form a basis for the solution space W of the original system in (7).

The following algorithm summarizes the steps in this procedure.

Algorithm: *A Basis for the Solution Space*

To find a basis for the solution space W of the homogeneous linear system $A\mathbf{x} = \mathbf{0}$, carry out the following steps.

1. Reduce the coefficient matrix A to echelon form.
2. Identify the r leading variables and the $k = n - r$ free variables. If $k = 0$ then $W = \{\mathbf{0}\}$.
3. Set the free variables equal to parameters $t_1, t_2, \ldots, t_k$ and then solve by back substitution for the leading variables in terms of these parameters.
4. Let $\mathbf{v}_j$ be the solution vector obtained by setting t_j equal to 1 and the other parameters equal to zero. Then $\{\mathbf{v}_1, \mathbf{v}_2, \ldots, \mathbf{v}_k\}$ is a basis for W.

EXAMPLE 5 Find a basis for the solution space of the homogeneous linear system

$$\begin{aligned} 3x_1 + 6x_2 - x_3 - 5x_4 + 5x_5 &= 0 \\ 2x_1 + 4x_2 - x_3 - 3x_4 + 2x_5 &= 0 \\ 3x_1 + 6x_2 - 2x_3 - 4x_4 + x_5 &= 0. \end{aligned} \tag{14}$$

Solution We readily reduce the coefficient matrix A to the echelon form

$$E = \begin{bmatrix} 1 & 2 & 0 & -2 & 3 \\ 0 & 0 & 1 & -1 & 4 \\ 0 & 0 & 0 & 0 & 0 \end{bmatrix}.$$

The leading entries are in the first and third columns, so the leading variables are x_1 and x_3; the free variables are x_2, x_4, and x_5. To avoid subscripts we use r, s, and t rather than t_1, t_2, and t_3 to denote the three parameters. Thus we set

$$x_2 = r, \qquad x_4 = s, \qquad \text{and} \qquad x_5 = t. \tag{15}$$

Then back substitution in the reduced system

$$\begin{aligned} x_1 + 2x_2 \qquad - 2x_4 + 3x_5 &= 0 \\ x_3 - x_4 + 4x_5 &= 0 \end{aligned}$$

yields

$$x_1 = -2r + 2s - 3t \quad \text{and} \quad x_3 = s - 4t. \tag{16}$$

The equations in (15) and (16) give the typical solution vector $(x_1, x_2, x_3, x_4, x_5)$ in terms of the parameters r, s, and t.

With $r = 1$ and $s = t = 0$,

We obtain $\mathbf{v}_1 = (-2, 1, 0, 0, 0)$.

With $s = 1$ and $r = t = 0$,

We obtain $\mathbf{v}_2 = (2, 0, 1, 1, 0)$.

With $t = 1$ and $r = s = 0$,

We obtain $\mathbf{v}_3 = (-3, 0, -4, 0, 1)$.

Thus the solution space of the system in (14) is a 3-dimensional subspace of $\mathbf{R}^5$ with basis $\{\mathbf{v}_1, \mathbf{v}_2, \mathbf{v}_3\}$.

4.3 PROBLEMS

In Problems 1–8, determine whether or not the given vectors in $\mathbf{R}^n$ form a basis for $\mathbf{R}^n$.

1. $\mathbf{v}_1 = (4, 7)$, $\mathbf{v}_2 = (5, 6)$

2. $\mathbf{v}_1 = (3, -1, 2)$, $\mathbf{v}_2 = (6, -2, 4)$, $\mathbf{v}_3 = (5, 3, -1)$

3. $\mathbf{v}_1 = (1, 7, -3)$, $\mathbf{v}_2 = (2, 1, 4)$, $\mathbf{v}_3 = (6, 5, 1)$, $\mathbf{v}_4 = (0, 7, 13)$

4. $\mathbf{v}_1 = (3, -7, 5, 2)$, $\mathbf{v}_2 = (1, -1, 3, 4)$, $\mathbf{v}_3 = (7, 11, 3, 13)$

5. $\mathbf{v}_1 = (0, 7, -3)$, $\mathbf{v}_2 = (0, 5, 4)$, $\mathbf{v}_3 = (0, 5, 10)$

6. $\mathbf{v}_1 = (0, 0, 1)$, $\mathbf{v}_2 = (0, 1, 2)$, $\mathbf{v}_3 = (1, 2, 3)$

7. $\mathbf{v}_1 = (0, 0, 1)$, $\mathbf{v}_2 = (7, 4, 11)$, $\mathbf{v}_3 = (5, 3, 13)$

8. $\mathbf{v}_1 = (2, 0, 0, 0)$, $\mathbf{v}_2 = (0, 3, 0, 0)$, $\mathbf{v}_3 = (0, 0, 7, 6)$, $\mathbf{v}_4 = (0, 0, 4, 5)$

In Problems 9–11, find a basis for the indicated subspace of $\mathbf{R}^3$.

9. The plane with equation $x - 2y + 5z = 0$.

10. The plane with equation $y = z$.

11. The line of intersection of the planes described in Problems 9 and 10.

In Problems 12–14, find a basis for the indicated subspace of $\mathbf{R}^4$.

12. The set of all vectors of the form (a, b, c, d) for which $a = b + c + d$.

13. The set of all vectors of the form (a, b, c, d) such that $a = 3c$ and $b = 4d$.

14. The set of all vectors of the form (a, b, c, d) for which $a + 2b = c + 3d = 0$.

In Problems 15–26, find a basis for the solution space of the given homogeneous linear system.

15. $$\begin{aligned} x_1 - 2x_2 + 3x_3 &= 0 \\ 2x_1 - 3x_2 - x_3 &= 0 \end{aligned}$$

16. $$\begin{aligned} x_1 + 3x_2 + 4x_3 &= 0 \\ 3x_1 + 8x_2 + 7x_3 &= 0 \end{aligned}$$

17. $$\begin{aligned} x_1 - 3x_2 + 2x_3 - 4x_4 &= 0 \\ 2x_1 - 5x_2 + 7x_3 - 3x_4 &= 0 \end{aligned}$$

18. $$\begin{aligned} x_1 + 3x_2 + 4x_3 + 5x_4 &= 0 \\ 2x_1 + 6x_2 + 9x_3 + 5x_4 &= 0 \end{aligned}$$

19. $$\begin{aligned} x_1 - 3x_2 - 9x_3 - 5x_4 &= 0 \\ 2x_1 + x_2 - 4x_3 + 11x_4 &= 0 \\ x_1 + 3x_2 + 3x_3 + 13x_4 &= 0 \end{aligned}$$

20. $$\begin{aligned} x_1 - 3x_2 - 10x_3 + 5x_4 &= 0 \\ x_1 + 4x_2 + 11x_3 - 2x_4 &= 0 \\ x_1 + 3x_2 + 8x_3 - x_4 &= 0 \end{aligned}$$

21. $$\begin{aligned} x_1 - 4x_2 - 3x_3 - 7x_4 &= 0 \\ 2x_1 - x_2 + x_3 + 7x_4 &= 0 \\ x_1 + 2x_2 + 3x_3 + 11x_4 &= 0 \end{aligned}$$

22. $$\begin{aligned} x_1 - 2x_2 - 3x_3 - 16x_4 &= 0 \\ 2x_1 - 4x_2 + x_3 + 17x_4 &= 0 \\ x_1 - 2x_2 + 3x_3 + 26x_4 &= 0 \end{aligned}$$

23. $$\begin{aligned} x_1 + 5x_2 + 13x_3 + 14x_4 &= 0 \\ 2x_1 + 5x_2 + 11x_3 + 12x_4 &= 0 \\ 2x_1 + 7x_2 + 17x_3 + 19x_4 &= 0 \end{aligned}$$

24. $$\begin{aligned} x_1 + 3x_2 - 4x_3 - 8x_4 + 6x_5 &= 0 \\ x_1 + 2x_3 + x_4 + 3x_5 &= 0 \\ 2x_1 + 7x_2 - 10x_3 - 19x_4 + 13x_5 &= 0 \end{aligned}$$

25. $$\begin{aligned} x_1 + 2x_2 + 7x_3 - 9x_4 + 31x_5 &= 0 \\ 2x_1 + 4x_2 + 7x_3 - 11x_4 + 34x_5 &= 0 \\ 3x_1 + 6x_2 + 5x_3 - 11x_4 + 29x_5 &= 0 \end{aligned}$$

26. $$\begin{aligned} 3x_1 + x_2 - 3x_3 + 11x_4 + 10x_5 &= 0 \\ 5x_1 + 8x_2 + 2x_3 - 2x_4 + 7x_5 &= 0 \\ 2x_1 + 5x_2 - x_4 + 14x_5 &= 0 \end{aligned}$$

27. Suppose that S is a set of n linearly independent vectors in the n-dimensional vector space V. Prove that S is a basis for V.

28. Suppose that S is a set of n vectors that span the n-dimensional vector space V. Prove that S is a basis for V.

29. Let $\{\mathbf{v}_1, \mathbf{v}_2, \ldots, \mathbf{v}_k\}$ be a basis for the proper subspace W of the vector space V, and suppose that the vector $\mathbf{v}$ of V is not in W. Show that the vectors $\mathbf{v}_1, \mathbf{v}_2, \ldots, \mathbf{v}_k, \mathbf{v}$ are linearly independent.

30. Use the result of Problem 29 to prove that every linearly independent set of vectors in a finite-dimensional vector space V is contained in a basis for V.

31. Suppose that the vectors $\mathbf{v}_1, \mathbf{v}_2, \ldots, \mathbf{v}_k, \mathbf{v}_{k+1}$ span the vector space V and that $\mathbf{v}_{k+1}$ is a linear combination of $\mathbf{v}_1, \mathbf{v}_2, \ldots, \mathbf{v}_k$. Show that the vectors $\mathbf{v}_1, \mathbf{v}_2, \ldots, \mathbf{v}_k$ span V.

32. Use the result of Problem 31 to prove that every spanning set for a finite-dimensional vector space V contains a basis for V.

33. Let S be a linearly independent set of vectors in the finite-dimensional vector space V. Then S is called a **maximal linearly independent set** provided that if any other vector is adjoined to S, then the resulting set is linearly dependent. Prove that every maximal linearly independent set in V is a basis for V.

34. Let S be a finite set of vectors that span the vector space V. Then S is called a **minimal spanning set** provided that no proper subset of S spans V. Prove that every minimal spanning set in V is a basis for V.

35. Let S be a finite set of vectors that span the vector space V. Then S is called a **uniquely spanning set** provided that each vector in V can be expressed in one and only one way as a linear combination of the vectors in S. Prove that every uniquely spanning set in V is a basis for V.

36. Apply the definition of linear independence to show directly that the column vectors of the matrix in (12) are linearly independent.

4.4 Row and Column Spaces

In numerous examples we have observed the phenomenon of "disappearing equations" that sometimes occurs when we solve a linear system using the method of Gaussian elimination. The appearance in this process of a trivial equation $0 = 0$ means that one of the original equations was redundant. For instance, in the system

$$\begin{aligned} x - 2y + 2z &= 0 \\ x + 4y + 3z &= 0 \\ 2x + 2y + 5z &= 0, \end{aligned}$$

the third equation provides no additional information about a solution (x, y, z) because it is merely the sum of the first two equations.

Given a homogeneous linear system, it is natural to ask how many of the equations are "irredundant," and which ones they are. We will see that an answer to this question leads to a natural and simple relation between the number of irredundant equations, the number of unknowns, and the number of linearly independent solutions.

The individual equations of the homogeneous linear system $A\mathbf{x} = \mathbf{0}$ correspond to the rows of the coefficient matrix A. Given an $m \times n$ matrix $A = [a_{ij}]$, the **row vectors** of A are the m vectors

$$\begin{aligned} \mathbf{r}_1 &= (a_{11}, a_{12}, \ldots, a_{1n}) \\ \mathbf{r}_2 &= (a_{21}, a_{22}, \ldots, a_{2n}) \\ &\vdots \\ \mathbf{r}_m &= (a_{m1}, a_{m2}, \ldots, a_{mn}) \end{aligned} \tag{1}$$

in $\mathbf{R}^n$. The subspace of $\mathbf{R}^n$ spanned by the m row vectors $\mathbf{r}_1, \mathbf{r}_2, \ldots, \mathbf{r}_m$ is called the **row space** Row(A) of the matrix A. The *dimension* of the row space Row(A) is called the **row rank** of the matrix A.

EXAMPLE 1 Consider the 4×5 echelon matrix

$$A = \begin{bmatrix} 1 & -3 & 2 & 5 & 3 \\ 0 & 0 & 1 & -4 & 2 \\ 0 & 0 & 0 & 1 & 7 \\ 0 & 0 & 0 & 0 & 0 \end{bmatrix}.$$

Its row vectors are $\mathbf{r}_1 = (1, -3, 2, 5, 3)$, $\mathbf{r}_2 = (0, 0, 1, -4, 2)$, $\mathbf{r}_3 = (0, 0, 0, 1, 7)$, and $\mathbf{r}_4 = (0, 0, 0, 0, 0)$. We want to show that the row vectors that are not zero are linearly independent. To this end we calculate the linear combination

$$c_1\mathbf{r}_1 + c_2\mathbf{r}_2 + c_3\mathbf{r}_3 = (c_1, -3c_1, 2c_1 + c_2, 5c_1 - 4c_2 + c_3, 3c_1 + 2c_2 + 7c_3).$$

If $c_1\mathbf{r}_1 + c_2\mathbf{r}_2 + c_3\mathbf{r}_3 = \mathbf{0}$, then the first component gives $c_1 = 0$, next the third component $2c_1 + c_2 = 0$ yields $c_2 = 0$, and finally the fourth component $5c_1 - 4c_2 + c_3 = 0$ yields $c_3 = 0$. Thus the vectors $\mathbf{r}_1$, $\mathbf{r}_2$, and $\mathbf{r}_3$ are linearly independent and therefore form a basis for the row space Row(A). Hence Row(A) is a 3-dimensional subspace of $\mathbf{R}^5$, and the row rank of A is 3.

It should be apparent that the method used in Example 1 applies to any *echelon* matrix $E = [e_{ij}]$. If the first column of E is not all zero, then its *nonzero* row vectors $\mathbf{r}_1$, $\mathbf{r}_2, \ldots, \mathbf{r}_k$ have the forms

$$\begin{aligned} \mathbf{r}_1 &= (e_{11}, \ldots, e_{1p}, \ldots, e_{1q}, \ldots), \\ \mathbf{r}_2 &= (0, \ldots, 0, e_{2p}, \ldots, e_{2q}, \ldots), \\ \mathbf{r}_3 &= (0, \ldots, \quad 0, \ldots, \quad e_{3q}, \ldots), \end{aligned}$$

and so forth (where e_{11}, e_{2p}, and e_{3q} denote nonzero leading entries). Then the equation

$$c_1\mathbf{r}_1 + c_2\mathbf{r}_2 + \cdots + c_k\mathbf{r}_k = \mathbf{0}$$

implies that

$$c_1e_{11} = 0, \qquad c_1e_{1p} + c_2e_{2p} = 0, \qquad c_1e_{1q} + c_2e_{2q} + c_3e_{3q} = 0,$$

and so forth. We can therefore conclude in turn that $c_1 = 0, c_2 = 0, \ldots, c_k = 0$. Thus the row vectors $\mathbf{r}_1, \mathbf{r}_2, \ldots, \mathbf{r}_k$ are linearly independent, and hence we have the following result.

> ***Theorem 1:*** *Row Space of an Echelon Matrix*
> The nonzero row vectors of an echelon matrix are linearly independent and therefore form a basis for its row space.

We investigate the row space of an arbitrary matrix A by reducing A to an echelon matrix E. The following theorem then guarantees that A and E have the same row space. Recall that two matrices are (row) *equivalent* provided that each can be transformed to the other by elementary row operations.

> ***Theorem 2:*** *Row Spaces of Equivalent Matrices*
> If two matrices A and B are equivalent, then they have the same row space.

PROOF Because A can be transformed to B by elementary row operations, it follows that each row vector of B is a linear combination of the row vectors of A; the fact that this is obviously true if A is transformed into B by a single row operation implies its truth for any (finite) number of row operations. But then each vector in Row(B) is a linear combination of linear combinations of row vectors of A and hence is a linear combination of row vectors of A, which means that it is also a vector in Row(A). Therefore the fact that A can be transformed to B implies that Row(A) contains Row(B).

But elementary row operations are "reversible," so B can also be transformed to A by row operations. Hence the same argument shows that Row(B) contains Row(A). Finally, the fact that each of the two row spaces Row(A) and Row(B) contains the other means that they are, indeed, identical. ■

Theorems 1 and 2 together provide a routine procedure for finding a basis for the row space of a given matrix, thereby determining its row rank.

Algorithm 1: *A Basis for the Row Space*
To find a basis for the row space of a matrix A, use elementary row operations to reduce A to an echelon matrix E. Then the nonzero row vectors of E form a basis for Row(A).

EXAMPLE 2 To find a basis for the row space of the matrix

$$A = \begin{bmatrix} 1 & 2 & 1 & 3 & 2 \\ 3 & 4 & 9 & 0 & 7 \\ 2 & 3 & 5 & 1 & 8 \\ 2 & 2 & 8 & -3 & 5 \end{bmatrix}, \tag{2}$$

we reduce it to the echelon form

$$E = \begin{bmatrix} 1 & 2 & 1 & 3 & 2 \\ 0 & 1 & -3 & 5 & -4 \\ 0 & 0 & 0 & 1 & -7 \\ 0 & 0 & 0 & 0 & 0 \end{bmatrix}. \tag{3}$$

Then the nonzero row vectors $\mathbf{v}_1 = (1, 2, 1, 3, 2)$, $\mathbf{v}_2 = (0, 1, -3, 5, -4)$, and $\mathbf{v}_3 = (0, 0, 0, 1, -7)$ form a basis for the row space of A. Thus Row(A) is a 3-dimensional subspace of $\mathbf{R}^5$ and the row rank of A is 3.

In Example 2, note that Algorithm 1 does *not* tell us that the first three row vectors of the matrix A itself are linearly independent. We know that *some* three row vectors of A span Row(A), but without further investigation we do not know *which* three.

Now we turn our attention from row vectors to column vectors. Given an $m \times n$ matrix $A = [a_{ij}]$, the **column vectors** of A are the n vectors

$$\mathbf{c}_1 = \begin{bmatrix} a_{11} \\ a_{21} \\ \vdots \\ a_{m1} \end{bmatrix}, \quad \mathbf{c}_2 = \begin{bmatrix} a_{12} \\ a_{22} \\ \vdots \\ a_{m2} \end{bmatrix}, \ldots, \mathbf{c}_n = \begin{bmatrix} a_{1n} \\ a_{2n} \\ \vdots \\ a_{mn} \end{bmatrix} \tag{4}$$

in $\mathbf{R}^m$. The subspace of $\mathbf{R}^m$ spanned by the n column vectors $\mathbf{c}_1, \mathbf{c}_2, \ldots, \mathbf{c}_n$ is called the **column space** Col(A) of the matrix A. The *dimension* of the space Col(A) is called the **column rank** of the matrix A.

EXAMPLE 3 Consider the 4×5 echelon matrix

$$E = \begin{bmatrix} 1 & 2 & 1 & 3 & 2 \\ 0 & 1 & -3 & 5 & -4 \\ 0 & 0 & 0 & 1 & -7 \\ 0 & 0 & 0 & 0 & 0 \end{bmatrix}. \tag{5}$$

Its five column vectors $\mathbf{c}_1, \mathbf{c}_2, \mathbf{c}_3, \mathbf{c}_4, \mathbf{c}_5$ all lie in the subspace $\mathbf{R}^3 = \{(x_1, x_2, x_3, 0)\}$ of $\mathbf{R}^4$. The column vectors that contain the leading entries in the nonzero rows of E are

$$\mathbf{c}_1 = \begin{bmatrix} 1 \\ 0 \\ 0 \\ 0 \end{bmatrix}, \quad \mathbf{c}_2 = \begin{bmatrix} 2 \\ 1 \\ 0 \\ 0 \end{bmatrix}, \quad \text{and} \quad \mathbf{c}_4 = \begin{bmatrix} 3 \\ 5 \\ 1 \\ 0 \end{bmatrix}. \tag{6}$$

Note that

$$a_1\mathbf{c}_1 + a_2\mathbf{c}_2 + a_4\mathbf{c}_4 = (a_1 + 2a_2 + 3a_4, a_2 + 5a_4, a_4, 0).$$

Hence $a_1\mathbf{c}_1 + a_2\mathbf{c}_2 + a_4\mathbf{c}_4 = \mathbf{0}$ readily implies that $a_1 = a_2 = a_4 = 0$. Thus the vectors $\mathbf{c}_1$, $\mathbf{c}_2$, and $\mathbf{c}_4$ are linearly independent and therefore form a basis for $\mathbf{R}^3 = \{(x_1, x_2, x_3, 0)\}$. Hence Col($E$) is a 3-dimensional subspace of $\mathbf{R}^4$ and the column rank of E is 3.

To find the column rank of an arbitrary $m \times n$ matrix A we begin in the same way as when finding the row rank. First we use elementary row operations to reduce A to an echelon matrix E. But the relationship between the column spaces of A and E is far more subtle than that between their row spaces; the reason is that elementary row operations generally do *not* preserve column spaces.

To analyze this situation, let us denote by $\mathbf{c}_1, \mathbf{c}_2, \ldots, \mathbf{c}_n$ the column vectors of the original matrix A, and by $\mathbf{c}_1^*, \mathbf{c}_2^*, \ldots, \mathbf{c}_n^*$ the column vectors of the echelon matrix to which we have reduced A. Suppose that E has k nonzero rows. Then each column vector of E has the form $\mathbf{c}_j^* = (*, \ldots, *, 0, \ldots, 0)$ with $m - k$ final zeros. Hence the column space Col(E) is contained in $\mathbf{R}^k$ (considered as the subspace of $\mathbf{R}^m$ for which $x_{k+1} = \cdots = x_m = 0$).

We are particularly interested in those columns of E that contain the nonzero leading entries in the nonzero rows of E. These k columns are called the **pivot columns** of E. The echelon matrix E has the general form

$$E = \begin{bmatrix} d_1 & * & * & * & \cdots & * & * & * \\ 0 & d_2 & * & * & \cdots & * & * & * \\ 0 & 0 & 0 & d_3 & \cdots & * & * & * \\ \vdots & \vdots & \vdots & \vdots & \ddots & \vdots & \vdots & \vdots \\ 0 & 0 & 0 & 0 & \cdots & d_k & * & * \\ 0 & 0 & 0 & 0 & \cdots & 0 & 0 & 0 \\ \vdots & \vdots & \vdots & \vdots & \ddots & \vdots & \vdots & \vdots \\ 0 & 0 & 0 & 0 & \cdots & 0 & 0 & 0 \end{bmatrix}, \tag{7}$$

where $d_1, d_2, \ldots, d_k$ are the nonzero leading entries. Hence the k pivot column vectors of E look like

$$\begin{bmatrix} d_1 \\ 0 \\ 0 \\ \vdots \\ 0 \\ 0 \\ \vdots \\ 0 \end{bmatrix}, \quad \begin{bmatrix} * \\ d_2 \\ 0 \\ \vdots \\ 0 \\ 0 \\ \vdots \\ 0 \end{bmatrix}, \quad \begin{bmatrix} * \\ * \\ d_3 \\ \vdots \\ 0 \\ 0 \\ \vdots \\ 0 \end{bmatrix}, \ldots, \begin{bmatrix} * \\ * \\ * \\ \vdots \\ d_k \\ 0 \\ \vdots \\ 0 \end{bmatrix}. \tag{8}$$

Because of the upper triangular pattern visible here, it should be apparent that the argument in Example 3 can be used to show that these k pivot vectors form a basis for

Col(E). Thus *the column rank of the echelon matrix E is equal to the number k of its nonzero rows, and hence is equal to its row rank.*

Now comes the subtle part. We want to show that the column rank of the original matrix A also is k. Note first that the homogeneous linear systems

$$A\mathbf{x} = \mathbf{0} \quad \text{and} \quad E\mathbf{x} = \mathbf{0} \tag{9}$$

have the same solution set because the matrices A and E are equivalent. If $\mathbf{x} = (x_1, x_2, \ldots, x_n)$, then the left-hand sides in (9) are linear combinations of column vectors:

$$\begin{aligned} A\mathbf{x} &= x_1\mathbf{c}_1 + x_2\mathbf{c}_2 + \cdots + x_n\mathbf{c}_n, \\ E\mathbf{x} &= x_1\mathbf{c}_1^* + x_2\mathbf{c}_2^* + \cdots + x_n\mathbf{c}_n^*. \end{aligned} \tag{10}$$

Because $\mathbf{x}$ satisfies *either* both *or* neither of the systems in (9), it follows that

$$x_1\mathbf{c}_1 + x_2\mathbf{c}_2 + \cdots + x_n\mathbf{c}_n = \mathbf{0}$$

if and only if

$$x_1\mathbf{c}_1^* + x_2\mathbf{c}_2^* + \cdots + x_n\mathbf{c}_n^* = \mathbf{0}.$$

Hence every linear dependence between column vectors of E is mirrored in a linear dependence *with the same coefficients* between the corresponding column vectors of A. In particular, because the k pivot column vectors of E are linearly independent, it follows that the corresponding k column vectors of A are linearly independent. And because the k pivot column vectors of E span Col(E), it follows that the corresponding k column vectors of A span Col(A). Thus the latter k vectors form a basis for the column space of A, and the column rank of A is k. Consequently we have established the following method for finding a basis for the column space of a given matrix.

Algorithm 2: *A Basis for the Column Space*

To find a basis for the column space of a matrix A, use elementary row operations to reduce A to an echelon matrix E. Then the column vectors of A that correspond to the pivot columns of E form a basis for Col(A).

EXAMPLE 4 Consider again the 4×5 matrix

$$A = \begin{bmatrix} 1 & 2 & 1 & 3 & 2 \\ 3 & 4 & 9 & 0 & 7 \\ 2 & 3 & 5 & 1 & 8 \\ 2 & 2 & 8 & -3 & 5 \end{bmatrix}$$

of Example 2, in which we reduced it to the echelon matrix

$$E = \begin{bmatrix} 1 & 2 & 1 & 3 & 2 \\ 0 & 1 & -3 & 5 & -4 \\ 0 & 0 & 0 & 1 & -7 \\ 0 & 0 & 0 & 0 & 0 \end{bmatrix}.$$

The pivot columns of E are its first, second, and fourth columns, so the 3-dimensional column space of A has a basis consisting of its first, second, and fourth column vectors $\mathbf{c}_1 = (1, 3, 2, 2)$, $\mathbf{c}_2 = (2, 4, 3, 2)$, and $\mathbf{c}_4 = (3, 0, 1, -3)$.

The fact that Algorithm 2 provides a basis for Col(A) consisting of column vectors of A itself (rather than the echelon matrix E) enables us to apply it to the problem of extracting a maximal linearly independent subset from a given set of vectors in $\mathbf{R}^n$.

EXAMPLE 5 Find a subset of the vectors $\mathbf{v}_1 = (1, -1, 2, 2)$, $\mathbf{v}_2 = (-3, 4, 1, -2)$, $\mathbf{v}_3 = (0, 1, 7, 4)$, and $\mathbf{v}_4 = (-5, 7, 4, -2)$ that forms a basis for the subspace W of $\mathbf{R}^4$ spanned by these four vectors.

Solution It is not clear at the outset whether W is 2-dimensional, 3-dimensional, or 4-dimensional. To apply Algorithm 2, we arrange the given vectors as the *column* vectors of the matrix

$$A = \begin{bmatrix} 1 & -3 & 0 & -5 \\ -1 & 4 & 1 & 7 \\ 2 & 1 & 7 & 4 \\ 2 & -2 & 4 & -2 \end{bmatrix},$$

which reduces readily to the echelon matrix

$$E = \begin{bmatrix} 1 & -3 & 0 & -5 \\ 0 & 1 & 1 & 2 \\ 0 & 0 & 0 & 0 \\ 0 & 0 & 0 & 0 \end{bmatrix}.$$

The pivot columns of E are its first two columns, so the first two column vectors $\mathbf{v}_1 = (1, -1, 2, 2)$ and $\mathbf{v}_2 = (-3, 4, 1, -2)$ of A form a basis for the column space W. In particular, we see that W is 2-dimensional.

We have seen that the row rank *and* the column rank of an echelon matrix E *both* equal the number of rows of E that are not all zeros. But if A is any matrix that reduces by row operations to the echelon matrix E, then—according to Algorithm 1—the row rank of A is equal to the row rank of E, while Algorithm 2 implies that the column rank of A is equal to the column rank of E. We therefore have the following fundamental result.

> ***Theorem 3:*** *Equality of Row Rank and Column Rank*
> The row rank and the column rank of any matrix are equal.

For instance, if A is a 5×7 matrix and Row(A) is a 3-dimensional subspace of $\mathbf{R}^7$, then Theorem 3 tells us that Col(A) must be a 3-dimensional subspace of $\mathbf{R}^5$.

To see what an extraordinary theorem this is, think of a random 11×17 matrix A, possibly printed by a computer that uses a random number generator to produce independently the 187 entries in A. If it turns out that precisely 9 (no more) of the 11 row vectors of A are linearly independent, then Theorem 3 implies that precisely 9 (no more) of the 17 column vectors of A are linearly independent.

The common value of the row rank and the column rank of the matrix A is simply called the **rank** of A and is denoted by rank(A). The rank of A provides a meaning for the number of irredundant equations in the homogeneous linear system

$$A\mathbf{x} = \mathbf{0}. \tag{11}$$

Indeed, the individual scalar equations in (11) correspond to the column vectors of the transpose matrix A^T, whose rank r equals that of A (Why?). Then the r column vectors of A^T that form a basis for Col(A^T) correspond to the r equations in (11) that are irredundant; the remaining equations are linear combinations of these irredundant ones and hence are redundant.

The solution space of the homogeneous system $A\mathbf{x} = \mathbf{0}$ is sometimes called the **null space** of A, denoted by Null(A). Note that if A is an $m \times n$ matrix, then Null(A) and Row(A) are subspaces of $\mathbf{R}^n$, whereas Col(A) is a subspace of $\mathbf{R}^m$. If $r = \text{rank}(A)$, then the r column vectors of A that form a basis for Col(A) correspond to the r leading variables in a solution of $A\mathbf{x} = \mathbf{0}$ by Gaussian elimination. Moreover, we know from the algorithm in Section 4.3 that the dimension of the solution space Null(A) is equal to the number $n - r$ of free variables. We therefore obtain the important identity

$$\text{rank}(A) + \dim \text{Null}(A) = n \tag{12}$$

for any $m \times n$ matrix A. For instance, if A is the matrix of Example 4 with rank 3 and $n = 5$, then the dimension of the null space of A is $5 - 3 = 2$

For another typical application of Equation (12), consider a homogeneous system of five linear equations in seven unknowns. If the 5×7 coefficient matrix of the system has rank 3, so only 3 of the 5 equations are irredundant, then (because $n = 7$) the system has $7 - 3 = 4$ linearly independent solutions.

If A is an $m \times n$ matrix with rank m, then Equation (12) implies that the system $A\mathbf{x} = \mathbf{0}$ has $n - m$ linearly independent solutions. Thus $\text{rank}(A) = m$ is the condition under which the "conventional wisdom" about the relation between the numbers of equations, unknowns, and solutions is valid.

NONHOMOGENEOUS LINEAR SYSTEMS

It follows immediately from Equation (10) and the definition of Col(A) that *the nonhomogeneous linear system* $A\mathbf{x} = \mathbf{b}$ *is consistent if and only if the vector* $\mathbf{b}$ *is in the column space of* A. In the problems below we outline some of the applications to nonhomogeneous systems of the results in this section.

If we can find a single particular solution $\mathbf{x}_0$ of the nonhomogeneous system

$$A\mathbf{x} = \mathbf{b}, \tag{13}$$

then the determination of its solution set reduces to solving the associated homogeneous system

$$A\mathbf{x} = \mathbf{0}. \tag{14}$$

For then Problem 29 in Section 4.1 implies that the solution set of (13) is the set of all vectors $\mathbf{x}$ of the form

$$\mathbf{x} = \mathbf{x}_0 + \mathbf{x}_h$$

where $\mathbf{x}_h$ is a solution of (14). Hence if $\mathbf{x}_1, \mathbf{x}_2, \ldots, \mathbf{x}_r$ is a basis for the solution space of (14), then the solution set of the nonhomogeneous system is the set of all vectors of the form

$$\mathbf{x} = \mathbf{x}_0 + c_1\mathbf{x}_1 + c_2\mathbf{x}_2 + \cdots + c_r\mathbf{x}_r.$$

We may describe this solution set as the *translate* by the vector $\mathbf{x}_0$ of the r-dimensional solution space of the corresponding homogeneous system.

4.4 PROBLEMS

In Problems 1–12, find both a basis for the row space and a basis for the column space of the given matrix A.

1. $\begin{bmatrix} 1 & 2 & 3 \\ 1 & 5 & -9 \\ 2 & 5 & 2 \end{bmatrix}$

2. $\begin{bmatrix} 5 & 2 & 4 \\ 2 & 1 & 1 \\ 4 & 1 & 5 \end{bmatrix}$

3. $\begin{bmatrix} 1 & -4 & -3 & -7 \\ 2 & -1 & 1 & 7 \\ 1 & 2 & 3 & 11 \end{bmatrix}$

4. $\begin{bmatrix} 1 & -3 & -9 & -5 \\ 2 & 1 & 4 & 11 \\ 1 & 3 & 3 & 13 \end{bmatrix}$

5. $\begin{bmatrix} 1 & 1 & 1 & 1 \\ 3 & 1 & -3 & 4 \\ 2 & 5 & 11 & 12 \end{bmatrix}$

6. $\begin{bmatrix} 1 & 4 & 9 & 2 \\ 2 & 2 & 6 & -3 \\ 2 & 7 & 16 & 3 \end{bmatrix}$

7. $\begin{bmatrix} 1 & 1 & -1 & 7 \\ 1 & 4 & 5 & 16 \\ 1 & 3 & 3 & 13 \\ 2 & 5 & 4 & 23 \end{bmatrix}$

8. $\begin{bmatrix} 1 & -2 & -3 & -5 \\ 1 & 4 & 9 & 2 \\ 1 & 3 & 7 & 1 \\ 2 & 2 & 6 & -3 \end{bmatrix}$

9. $\begin{bmatrix} 1 & 3 & 3 & 9 \\ 2 & 7 & 4 & 8 \\ 2 & 7 & 5 & 12 \\ 2 & 8 & 3 & 2 \end{bmatrix}$

10. $\begin{bmatrix} 1 & 2 & 3 & 1 & 3 \\ 1 & 3 & 4 & 3 & 6 \\ 2 & 2 & 4 & 3 & 5 \\ 2 & 1 & 3 & 2 & 3 \end{bmatrix}$

11. $\begin{bmatrix} 1 & 1 & 3 & 3 & 1 \\ 2 & 3 & 7 & 8 & 2 \\ 2 & 3 & 7 & 8 & 3 \\ 3 & 1 & 7 & 5 & 4 \end{bmatrix}$

12. $\begin{bmatrix} 1 & 1 & 3 & 3 & 0 \\ -1 & 0 & -2 & -1 & 1 \\ 2 & 3 & 7 & 8 & 1 \\ -2 & 4 & 0 & 6 & 7 \end{bmatrix}$

In Problems 13–16, a set S of vectors in $\mathbf{R}^4$ is given. Find a subset of S that forms a basis for the subspace of $\mathbf{R}^4$ spanned by S.

13. $\mathbf{v}_1 = (1, 3, -2, 4)$, $\mathbf{v}_2 = (2, -1, 3, 2)$, $\mathbf{v}_3 = (5, 1, 4, 8)$

14. $\mathbf{v}_1 = (1, -1, 2, 3)$, $\mathbf{v}_2 = (2, 3, 4, 1)$, $\mathbf{v}_3 = (1, 1, 2, 1)$, $\mathbf{v}_4 = (4, 1, 8, 7)$

15. $\mathbf{v}_1 = (3, 2, 2, 2)$, $\mathbf{v}_2 = (2, 1, 2, 1)$, $\mathbf{v}_3 = (4, 3, 2, 3)$, $\mathbf{v}_4 = (1, 2, 3, 4)$

16. $\mathbf{v}_1 = (5, 4, 2, 2)$, $\mathbf{v}_2 = (3, 1, 2, 3)$, $\mathbf{v}_3 = (7, 7, 2, 1)$, $\mathbf{v}_4 = (1, -1, 2, 4)$, $\mathbf{v}_5 = (5, 4, 6, 7)$

Let $S = \{\mathbf{v}_1, \mathbf{v}_2, \ldots, \mathbf{v}_k\}$ be a basis for the subspace W of $\mathbf{R}^n$. Then a basis T for $\mathbf{R}^n$ that contains S can be found by applying the method of Example 5 to the vectors

$$\mathbf{v}_1, \mathbf{v}_2, \ldots, \mathbf{v}_k, \mathbf{e}_1, \mathbf{e}_2, \ldots, \mathbf{e}_n.$$

Do this in Problems 17–20.

17. Find a basis T for $\mathbf{R}^3$ that contains the vectors $\mathbf{v}_1 = (1, 2, 2)$ and $\mathbf{v}_2 = (2, 3, 3)$.

18. Find a basis T for $\mathbf{R}^3$ that contains the vectors $\mathbf{v}_1 = (3, 2, -1)$ and $\mathbf{v}_2 = (2, -2, 1)$.

19. Find a basis T for $\mathbf{R}^4$ that contains the vectors $\mathbf{v}_1 = (1, 1, 1, 1)$ and $\mathbf{v}_2 = (2, 3, 3, 3)$.

20. Find a basis T for $\mathbf{R}^4$ that contains the vectors $\mathbf{v}_1 = (3, 2, 3, 3)$ and $\mathbf{v}_2 = (5, 4, 5, 5)$.

Given a homogeneous system $A\mathbf{x} = \mathbf{0}$ of (scalar) linear equations, we say that a subset of these equations is *irredundant* provided that the corresponding column vectors of the transpose A^T are linearly independent. In Problems 21–24, extract from each given system a maximal subset of irredundant equations.

21. $$\begin{aligned} x_1 - 3x_2 + 2x_3 &= 0 \\ 2x_1 + 3x_2 + 2x_3 &= 0 \\ 4x_1 - 3x_2 + 6x_3 &= 0 \end{aligned}$$

22. $$\begin{aligned} 3x_1 + 2x_2 + 2x_3 + 2x_4 &= 0 \\ 2x_1 + 3x_2 + 3x_3 + 3x_4 &= 0 \\ 8x_1 + 7x_2 + 7x_3 + 7x_4 &= 0 \end{aligned}$$

23. $$\begin{aligned} x_1 + 2x_2 - x_3 + 2x_4 &= 0 \\ 3x_1 - x_2 + 3x_3 + x_4 &= 0 \\ 5x_1 + 3x_2 + x_3 + 5x_4 &= 0 \\ 2x_1 + 5x_3 + 4x_4 &= 0 \end{aligned}$$

24. $$\begin{aligned} 3x_1 + 2x_2 + 2x_3 &= 0 \\ 2x_1 + 3x_2 + 3x_3 &= 0 \\ 7x_1 + 8x_2 + 8x_3 &= 0 \\ 8x_1 + 7x_2 + 7x_3 &= 0 \\ 5x_1 + 6x_2 + 5x_3 &= 0 \end{aligned}$$

25. Explain why the rank of a matrix A is equal to the rank of its transpose A^T.

26. Explain why the $n \times n$ matrix A is invertible if and only if its rank is n.

27. Let A be a 3×5 matrix whose three row vectors are linearly independent. Prove that, for each $\mathbf{b}$ in $\mathbf{R}^3$, the nonhomogeneous system $A\mathbf{x} = \mathbf{b}$ has a solution.

28. Let A be a 5×3 matrix that has three linearly independent row vectors. Suppose that $\mathbf{b}$ is a vector in $\mathbf{R}^5$ such that the nonhomogeneous system $A\mathbf{x} = \mathbf{b}$ has a solution. Prove that this solution is unique.

29. Let A be an $m \times n$ matrix with $m < n$. Given $\mathbf{b}$ in $\mathbf{R}^m$, note that any solution of $A\mathbf{x} = \mathbf{b}$ expresses $\mathbf{b}$ as a linear combination of the column vectors of A. Then prove that no such solution is unique.

30. Given the $m \times n$ matrix A with $m > n$, show that there exists a vector $\mathbf{b}$ in $\mathbf{R}^m$ such that the system $A\mathbf{x} = \mathbf{b}$ has no solution.

31. (Existence of Solutions) Let A be an $m \times n$ matrix. Prove that the system $A\mathbf{x} = \mathbf{b}$ is consistent for every $\mathbf{b}$ in $\mathbf{R}^m$ if and only if the rank of A is equal to m.

32. (Uniqueness of Solutions) Let A be an $m \times n$ matrix and suppose that the system $A\mathbf{x} = \mathbf{b}$ is consistent. Prove that its solution is unique if and only if the rank of A is equal to n.

33. Prove that the pivot column vectors in (8) are linearly independent.

34. Let A be a matrix with rank r, and suppose that A can be reduced to echelon form *without row interchanges*. Show that the first r row vectors of A are linearly independent.

35. Deduce from Theorem 3 in Section 4.2 that the rank of the matrix A is the largest integer r such that A has a nonsingular $r \times r$ submatrix.

*4.5

General Vector Spaces

In the previous four sections of this chapter, almost all the specific vector spaces appearing in our examples and problems have been vector spaces of n-tuples of real numbers. Thus we have confined our attention largely to Euclidean spaces and their subspaces. In this section we discuss examples of some other types of vector spaces that play important roles in various branches of mathematics and their applications.

EXAMPLE 1 Given fixed positive integers m and n, let M_{mn} denote the set of all $m \times n$ matrices with real number entries. Then M_{mn} is a vector space with the usual operations of addition of matrices and multiplication of matrices by scalars (real numbers). That is, these operations satisfy properties (a)–(h) in the definition of a vector space (Section 4.1). In particular, the zero element in M_{mn} is the $m \times n$ matrix 0 whose elements are all zeros, and the negative $-A$ of the matrix A is (as usual) the matrix whose elements are the negatives of the corresponding entries of A.

Given positive integers i and j with $1 \le i \le m$ and $1 \le j \le n$, let E_{ij} denote the $m \times n$ matrix whose only nonzero entry is the number 1 in the ith row and the jth column. Then it should be clear that the mn elements $\{E_{ij}\}$ of M_{mn} form a basis for M_{mn}, so M_{mn} is a finite-dimensional vector space of dimension mn.

For instance, in the case of the vector space M_{22} of all 2×2 matrices, these alleged basis elements are the four matrices

$$E_{11} = \begin{bmatrix} 1 & 0 \\ 0 & 0 \end{bmatrix}, \qquad E_{12} = \begin{bmatrix} 0 & 1 \\ 0 & 0 \end{bmatrix},$$

$$E_{21} = \begin{bmatrix} 0 & 0 \\ 1 & 0 \end{bmatrix}, \quad \text{and} \quad E_{22} = \begin{bmatrix} 0 & 0 \\ 0 & 1 \end{bmatrix}.$$

Then any matrix in M_{22} can be expressed as

$$\begin{bmatrix} a & b \\ c & d \end{bmatrix} = aE_{11} + bE_{12} + cE_{21} + dE_{22},$$

so the set $\{E_{11}, E_{12}, E_{21}, E_{22}\}$ spans M_{22}. Moreover,

$$aE_{11} + bE_{12} + cE_{21} + dE_{22} = \begin{bmatrix} a & b \\ c & d \end{bmatrix} = \begin{bmatrix} 0 & 0 \\ 0 & 0 \end{bmatrix}$$

implies immediately that $a = b = c = d = 0$, so the set $\{E_{11}, E_{12}, E_{21}, E_{22}\}$ is also linearly independent, and therefore forms a basis for M_{22}. Thus we have shown that M_{22} is a 4-dimensional vector space.

EXAMPLE 2 Let C denote the subset of M_{22} consisting of all 2×2 matrices of the form

$$\begin{bmatrix} a & -b \\ b & a \end{bmatrix}. \tag{1}$$

Obviously the sum of any two such matrices is such a matrix, as is any scalar multiple of such a matrix. Thus C is closed under the operations of addition of matrices and multiplication by scalars, and is therefore a *subspace* of M_{22}.

To determine the dimension of the subspace C, we consider the two special matrices

$$\mathrm{Re} = \begin{bmatrix} 1 & 0 \\ 0 & 1 \end{bmatrix} \quad \text{and} \quad \mathrm{Im} = \begin{bmatrix} 0 & -1 \\ 1 & 0 \end{bmatrix} \tag{2}$$

in C. Here Re is another notation for the 2×2 identity matrix I, whereas the matrix Im is not so familiar. The matrices Re and Im are linearly independent—obviously neither is a scalar multiple of the other—and

$$\begin{bmatrix} a & -b \\ b & a \end{bmatrix} = a\,\mathrm{Re} + \mathrm{b}\,\mathrm{Im}, \tag{3}$$

so these two matrices span C. Thus {Re, Im} is a basis for C, and so C is a 2-dimensional subspace of the 4-dimensional vector space M_{22} of 2×2 matrices.

Now observe that

$$(\mathrm{Im})^2 = \begin{bmatrix} 0 & -1 \\ 1 & 0 \end{bmatrix}\begin{bmatrix} 0 & -1 \\ 1 & 0 \end{bmatrix} = \begin{bmatrix} -1 & 0 \\ 0 & -1 \end{bmatrix} = -\mathrm{Re}. \tag{4}$$

It follows that the matrix product of any two elements $a\,\mathrm{Re} + b\,\mathrm{Im}$ and $c\,\mathrm{Re} + d\,\mathrm{Im}$ of C is given by

$$\begin{aligned}(a\,\mathrm{Re} + b\,\mathrm{Im})(c\,\mathrm{Re} + d\,\mathrm{Im}) &= ac(\mathrm{Re})^2 + bc\,\mathrm{Im}\,\mathrm{Re} + ad\,\mathrm{Re}\,\mathrm{Im} + bd(\mathrm{Im})^2 \\ &= (ac - bd)\mathrm{Re} + (ad + bc)\mathrm{Im}. \end{aligned} \tag{5}$$

This explicit formula for the product of two matrices in C shows that, in addition to being closed under matrix addition and multiplication by scalars, the subspace C of M_{22} also is *closed under matrix multiplication.*

If you feel that the idea of a space of matrices being closed under matrix multiplication is a rather complex one, you are quite correct! Indeed, the vector space C can be taken as a "model" for the set of all *complex numbers* of the form $a + bi$, where a and b are real numbers and $i = \sqrt{-1}$ denotes the "imaginary" square root of -1 (so that $i^2 = -1$). Because $(\mathrm{Im})^2 = -\mathrm{Re}$, the matrix Im plays the role of i and the matrix

$$\begin{bmatrix} a & -b \\ b & a \end{bmatrix} = a\,\mathrm{Re} + b\,\mathrm{Im}$$

corresponds to the complex number $a + bi$. And the matrix multiplication formula in (5) is then analogous to the formula

$$(a + bi)(c + di) = (ac - bd) + (ad + bc)i$$

for the multiplication of complex numbers. In addition to providing a concrete interpretation of complex numbers in terms of real numbers, the matrix model C

provides a convenient way to manipulate complex numbers in computer programming languages (such as APL) in which matrix operations are "built in" but complex operations are not.

FUNCTION SPACES

In Example 1 of Section 4.1 we introduced the vector space $\mathcal{F}$ of all real-valued functions defined on the real line $\mathbf{R}$. If $\mathbf{f}$ and $\mathbf{g}$ are elements of $\mathcal{F}$ and c is a scalar, then

$$(\mathbf{f} + \mathbf{g})(x) = \mathbf{f}(x) + \mathbf{g}(x)$$

and (6)

$$(c\mathbf{f})(x) = c(\mathbf{f}(x))$$

for all x in $\mathbf{R}$. The zero element in $\mathcal{F}$ is the function $\mathbf{0}$ such that $\mathbf{0}(x) = 0$ for all x. We frequently refer to a function in $\mathcal{F}$ by simply specifying its formula. For instance, by "the function x^2" we mean that function whose value at each x in $\mathbf{R}$ is x^2.

The functions $\mathbf{f}_1, \mathbf{f}_2, \ldots, \mathbf{f}_k$ in $\mathcal{F}$ are linearly dependent provided that there exist scalars $c_1, c_2, \ldots, c_k$ not all zero such that

$$c_1\mathbf{f}_1(x) + c_2\mathbf{f}_2(x) + \cdots + c_k\mathbf{f}_k(x) = 0$$

for all x in $\mathbf{R}$. We often can determine whether or not two given functions are linearly dependent simply by observing whether or not one is a scalar multiple of the other.

EXAMPLE 3 The functions e^x and e^{-2x} are linearly independent because either of the equations $e^x = ae^{-2x}$ or $e^{-2x} = be^x$ would imply that e^{3x} is a constant, which obviously is not so. By contrast, the functions $\sin 2x$ and $\sin x \cos x$ are linearly dependent because of the trigonometric identity $\sin 2x = 2 \sin x \cos x$. The three functions 1, $\cos^2 x$, and $\sin^2 x$ are linearly dependent because the fundamental identity $\cos^2 x + \sin^2 x = 1$ can be written in the form

$$(-1)(1) + (1)(\cos^2 x) + (1)(\sin^2 x) = 0.$$

A subspace of $\mathcal{F}$ is called a **function space**. An example of a function space is the vector space $\mathcal{P}$ of all polynomials in $\mathcal{F}$ (Example 4 in Section 4.3). A function $\mathbf{p}(x)$ in $\mathcal{F}$ is called a **polynomial of degree** $n \geq 0$ if it can be expressed in the form

$$\mathbf{p}(x) = a_0 + a_1x + a_2x^2 + \cdots + a_nx^n \tag{7}$$

with $a_n \neq 0$. Polynomials are added and multiplied by scalars in the usual manner—by collecting coefficients of like powers of x. Clearly any linear combination of polynomials is a polynomial, so $\mathcal{P}$ is, indeed, a subspace of $\mathcal{F}$.

EXAMPLE 4 Given $n \geq 0$, denote by $\mathcal{P}_n$ the set of all polynomials of degree at most n. That is, $\mathcal{P}_n$ consists of all polynomials of degrees 0, 1, 2, ..., n. Any linear combination of two polynomials of degree at most n is again a polynomial of degree at most n, so $\mathscr{P}_n$ is a subspace of $\mathscr{P}$ (and of $\mathscr{F}$). The formula in (7) shows that the $n + 1$ polynomials

$$1, x, x^2, x^3, \ldots, x^n \tag{8}$$

span $\mathscr{P}_n$. To show that these "monomials" are linearly independent, suppose that

$$c_0 + c_1x + c_2x^2 + \cdots + c_nx^n = 0 \tag{9}$$

for all x in $\mathbf{R}$. If $a_0, a_1, \ldots, a_n$ are fixed *distinct* real numbers, then each a_i satisfies Equation (9). In matrix notation this means that

$$\begin{bmatrix} 1 & a_0 & a_0^2 & \cdots & a_0^n \\ 1 & a_1 & a_1^2 & \cdots & a_1^n \\ 1 & a_2 & a_2^2 & \cdots & a_2^n \\ \vdots & \vdots & \vdots & \ddots & \vdots \\ 1 & a_n & a_n^2 & \cdots & a_n^n \end{bmatrix} \begin{bmatrix} c_0 \\ c_1 \\ c_2 \\ \vdots \\ c_n \end{bmatrix} = \begin{bmatrix} 0 \\ 0 \\ 0 \\ \vdots \\ 0 \end{bmatrix}. \tag{10}$$

The coefficient matrix in (10) is a Vandermonde matrix V, and Problems 35–37 in Section 2.2 imply that any Vandermonde matrix is nonsingular. Therefore the system $V\mathbf{c} = \mathbf{0}$ has only the trivial solution $\mathbf{c} = \mathbf{0}$, so it follows from (10) that $c_0 = c_1 = c_2 = \ldots = c_n = 0$. Thus we have proved that the $n + 1$ monomials $1, x, x^2, \ldots, x^n$ are linearly independent, and hence constitute a basis for $\mathscr{P}_n$. Consequently $\mathscr{P}_n$ is an $(n + 1)$-dimensional vector space.

The fact that the monomials in (8) are linearly independent implies that the coefficients in a polynomial are unique. That is, if

$$a_0 + a_1x + \cdots + a_nx^n = b_0 + b_1x + \cdots + b_nx^n$$

for all x, then $a_0 = b_0, a_1 = b_1, \ldots,$ and $a_n = b_n$. This *identity principle* for polynomials is often used without proof in elementary algebra. A typical application is the method of *partial-fraction decomposition* illustrated in Example 5.

EXAMPLE 5 Find constants A, B, and C such that

$$\frac{6x}{(x-1)(x+1)(x+2)} = \frac{A}{x-1} + \frac{B}{x+1} + \frac{C}{x+2} \tag{11}$$

for all x (other than $x = 1, -1,$ or -2).

Solution Multiplication of each side of the equation in (11) by the denominator on the left-hand side yields

$$6x = A(x+1)(x+2) + B(x-1)(x+2) + C(x-1)(x+1);$$

$$6x = (2A - 2B - C) + (3A + B)x + (A + B + C)x^2.$$

Then the identity principle for polynomials yields the linear equations

$$\begin{aligned} 2A - 2B - C &= 0 \\ 3A + B \quad\;\; &= 6 \\ A + B + C &= 0 \end{aligned}$$

that we readily solve for $A = 1$, $B = 3$, and $C = -4$. Therefore

$$\frac{6x}{(x-1)(x+1)(x+2)} = \frac{1}{x-1} + \frac{3}{x+1} - \frac{4}{x+2}$$

if $x \neq 1, -1, -2$.

EXAMPLE 6 Show that the four polynomials

$$1, \quad x, \quad 3x^2 - 1, \quad \text{and} \quad 5x^3 - 3x \tag{12}$$

form a basis for $\mathscr{P}_3$.

Solution In order to show simultaneously that these four polynomials span $\mathscr{P}_3$ and are linearly independent, it suffices to see that every polynomial

$$p(x) = b_0 + b_1x + b_2x^2 + b_3x^3 \tag{13}$$

in $\mathscr{P}_3$ can be expressed uniquely as a linear combination

$$\begin{aligned} &c_0(1) + c_1(x) + c_2(3x^2 - 1) + c_3(5x^3 - 3x) \\ &\quad = (c_0 - c_2) + (c_1 - 3c_3)x + (3c_2)x^2 + (5c_3)x^3 \end{aligned} \tag{14}$$

of the polynomials in (12). But upon comparing the coefficients in (13) and (14), we see that we need only observe that the linear system

$$\begin{bmatrix} 1 & 0 & -1 & 0 \\ 0 & 1 & 0 & -3 \\ 0 & 0 & 3 & 0 \\ 0 & 0 & 0 & 5 \end{bmatrix} \begin{bmatrix} c_0 \\ c_1 \\ c_2 \\ c_3 \end{bmatrix} = \begin{bmatrix} b_0 \\ b_1 \\ b_2 \\ b_3 \end{bmatrix}$$

obviously has a unique solution for c_0, c_1, c_2, c_3 in terms of b_0, b_1, b_2, b_3.

Because the vector space $\mathscr{P}$ of all polynomials contains $n + 1$ linearly independent functions for every integer $n \geq 0$, it follows that $\mathscr{P}$ is an infinite-dimensional vector space. So too is any function space, such as $\mathscr{F}$ itself, that contains $\mathscr{P}$. Another important function space is the set $\mathscr{C}^{(0)}$ of all continuous functions on $\mathbf{R}$; $\mathscr{C}^{(0)}$ is a subspace of $\mathscr{F}$ because every linear combination of continuous functions is again a continuous function. Every polynomial is a continuous function, so $\mathscr{C}^{(0)}$ contains $\mathscr{P}$ and is therefore an infinite-dimensional vector space. Similarly, the set $\mathscr{C}^{(k)}$ of all functions in $\mathscr{F}$ that have continuous kth order derivatives is an infinite-dimensional function space.

LINEAR DIFFERENTIAL EQUATIONS*

Linear algebra has extensive applications in the study of differential equations. Here we indicate briefly the connection between these two branches of mathematics by

* The remainder of this section is for those readers who have studied elementary differential calculus.

discussing the second order linear differential equation of the form

$$y'' + p(x)y' + q(x)y = 0, \tag{15}$$

where y' and y'' denote the first and second derivatives of the function $y(x)$. We assume that the coefficient functions $p(x)$ and $q(x)$ are given continuous functions defined on **R**. A **solution** of (15) is then a function $y(x)$ in the function space $\mathscr{C}^{(2)}$ that satisfies (15) for all x.

EXAMPLE 7 A specific differential equation of the form in (15) is

$$y'' - 5y' + 6y = 0. \tag{16}$$

Here $p(x) = -5$ and $q(x) = 6$ are constants. It is easy to verify by direct substitution in (16) that the two functions

$$y_1(x) = e^{2x} \quad \text{and} \quad y_2(x) = e^{3x} \tag{17}$$

are both solutions of the given differential equation.

Given a differential equation, we generally try to determine the set of all its solutions. In the case of a linear differential equation of the form in (15), this set of solutions is always a vector space of functions. To see why, suppose that $y_1(x)$ and $y_2(x)$ are two solutions of (15). If $y(x) = c_1y_1(x) + c_2y_2(x)$ is a linear combination of y_1 and y_2, then

$$\begin{aligned} y'' &+ p(x)y' + q(x)y \\ &= (c_1y_1 + c_2y_2)'' + p(x)(c_1y_1 + c_2y_2)' + q(x)(c_1y_1 + c_2y_2) \\ &= c_1(y_1'' + p(x)y_1' + q(x)y_1) + c_2(y_2'' + p(x)y_2' + q(x)y_2) \\ &= c_1 \cdot 0 + c_2 \cdot 0 = 0 \end{aligned}$$

because y_1 and y_2 satisfy Equation (15). Thus any linear combination of two solutions is also a solution, and this is why the differential equation is said to be *linear*. It follows that the set S of all solutions of a given second order linear differential equation of this form is a vector space; S is called the **solution space** of the equation. The following fundamental result in the theory of differential equations provides the key to understanding the solution space S.

Theorem 1: *Solutions of Differential Equations*
Suppose that the coefficient functions $p(x)$ and $q(x)$ in (15) are continuous on **R**. Then, given numbers a and b, there exists a unique solution $y(x)$ of the differential equation that satisfies the initial conditions

$$y(0) = a \quad \text{and} \quad y'(0) = b. \tag{18}$$

If we take $a = 1$ and $b = 0$ in (18), we get a solution $y_1(x)$ such that

$$y_1(0) = 1 \quad \text{and} \quad y_1'(0) = 0. \tag{19}$$

If we take $a = 0$ and $b = 1$, we get a second solution such that

$$y_2(0) = 0 \quad \text{and} \quad y_2'(0) = 1. \tag{20}$$

We assert that these two particular solutions of (15) must be linearly independent. For if

$$c_1 y_1(x) + c_2 y_2(x) = 0,$$

then differentiation yields

$$c_1 y_1'(x) + c_2 y_2'(x) = 0.$$

Substitution of $x = 0$ in these two equations then gives

$$0 = c_1 y_1(0) + c_2 y_2(0) = c_1 \cdot 1 + c_2 \cdot 0 = c_1$$

and

$$0 = c_1 y_1'(x) + c_2 y_2'(0) = c_1 \cdot 0 + c_2 \cdot 1 = c_2.$$

Thus y_1 and y_2 are linearly independent.

Moreover, the solutions $y_1(x)$ and $y_2(x)$ span the solution space S of the differential equation. To see why this is so, let $y(x)$ be any solution and let $c_1 = y(0)$ and $c_2 = y'(0)$. If

$$\phi(x) = c_1 y_1(x) + c_2 y_2(x),$$

then essentially the same computation as in the preceding paragraph shows that $\phi(0) = c_1$ and $\phi'(0) = c_2$. Thus the two solutions $y(x)$ and $\phi(x)$ satisfy the same initial conditions. Therefore the uniqueness part of Theorem 1 implies that they are actually the same function,

$$y(x) = \phi(x) = c_1 y_1(x) + c_2 y_2(x),$$

so $y(x)$ is a linear combination of $y_1(x)$ and $y_2(x)$. We may now conclude that $y_1(x)$ and $y_2(x)$ constitute a basis for S. This proves the next theorem.

Theorem 2: *Solution Spaces of Differential Equations*

If $p(x)$ and $q(x)$ are continuous on $\mathbf{R}$, then the solution space S of the second order linear differential equation

$$y'' + p(x)y' + q(x)y = 0 \tag{15}$$

is a 2-dimensional vector space.

The import of Theorem 2 is this: If you can find just two linearly independent solutions of a differential equation of the form in (15), then you in effect have found them all! For these two particular solutions must form a basis for the 2-dimensional solution space, and therefore any solution must be a linear combination of these two.

EXAMPLE 7 (continued) The two solutions $y_1(x) = e^{2x}$ and $y_2(x) = e^{3x}$ of the differential equation $y'' - 5y' + 6y = 0$ are obviously linearly independent (neither being a scalar multiple of the other). Hence they form a basis for the solution space, so every solution is of the form

$$y(x) = c_1e^{2x} + c_2e^{3x}. \tag{21}$$

For instance, suppose we seek the particular solution such that

$$y(0) = 5 \quad \text{and} \quad y'(0) = 12.$$

Then we need to choose c_1 and c_2 in (21) so that

$$\begin{aligned} y(0) &= c_1 + c_2 = 5 \\ &\text{and} \\ y'(0) &= 2c_1 + 3c_2 = 12; \end{aligned} \tag{22}$$

the latter equation is a consequence of the fact that

$$y'(x) = 2c_1e^{2x} + 3c_2e^{3x}.$$

The solution of the linear system in (22) is $c_1 = 3$, $c_2 = 2$, so the desired particular solution is

$$y(x) = 3e^{2x} + 2e^{3x}.$$

In the case of a second order linear differential equation

$$y'' + py' + qy = 0$$

with *constant* coefficients p and q, there are routine procedures for finding two linearly independent solutions, so that computations like those in Example 7 can be carried out. For instance, see Section 18-5 of Edwards and Penney, *Calculus and Analytic Geometry*, 2nd ed. (Englewood Cliffs, N.J.: Prentice-Hall, 1986) or Section 2.3 of Edwards and Penney, *Elementary Differential Equations with Applications* (Englewood Cliffs, N.J.: Prentice-Hall, 1985).

Finally, the theory of second order linear differential equations outlined in this subsection generalizes in a natural way to nth order linear differential equations of the form

$$y^{(n)} + p_1(x)y^{(n-1)} + \cdots + p_{n-1}(x)y' + p_n(x)y = 0. \tag{23}$$

If the coefficient functions $p_1(x), \ldots, p_n(x)$ in such a differential equation are continuous on $\mathbf{R}$, then the solution space of the differential equation is an n-dimensional function space. In some of the problems below we outline the use of this fact to find solutions of given differential equations satisfying specified initial conditions.

4.5 PROBLEMS

In Problems 1–4, determine whether or not the indicated set of 3×3 matrices is a subspace of M_{33}.

1. The set of all diagonal 3×3 matrices.

2. The set of all symmetric 3×3 matrices (that is, matrices $A = [a_{ij}]$ such that $a_{ij} = a_{ji}$ for $1 \le i \le 3$, $1 \le j \le 3$).

3. The set of all nonsingular 3×3 matrices.

4. The set of all singular 3×3 matrices.

In Problems 5–8, determine whether or not each indicated set of functions is a subspace of the space $\mathscr{F}$ of all real-valued functions on **R**.

5. The set of all f such that $f(0) = 0$.

6. The set of all f such that $f(x) \neq 0$ for all x.

7. The set of all f such that $f(0) = 0$ and $f(1) = 1$.

8. The set of all f such that $f(-x) = -f(x)$ for all x.

In Problems 9–12, a condition on the coefficients of a polynomial $a_0 + a_1x + a_2x^2 + a_3x^3$ is given. Determine whether or not the set of all such polynomials satisfying this condition is a subspace of the space $\mathscr{P}$ of all polynomials.

9. $a_3 \neq 0$

10. $a_0 = a_1 = 0$

11. $a_0 + a_1 + a_2 + a_3 = 0$

12. a_0, a_1, a_2, and a_3 are all integers

In Problems 13–18, determine whether the given functions are linearly independent.

13. $\sin x$ and $\cos x$

14. e^x and xe^x

15. $1 + x$, $1 - x$, and $1 - x^2$

16. $1 + x$, $x + x^2$, and $1 - x^2$

17. $\cos 2x$, $\sin^2 x$, and $\cos^2 x$

18. $2\cos x + 3\sin x$ and $4\cos x + 5\sin x$

In Problems 19–22, use the method of Example 5 to find the constants A, B, and C in the indicated partial-fraction decompositions.

19. $\dfrac{x-5}{(x-2)(x-3)} = \dfrac{A}{x-2} + \dfrac{B}{x-3}$

20. $\dfrac{2}{x(x^2-1)} = \dfrac{A}{x} + \dfrac{B}{x-1} + \dfrac{C}{x+1}$

21. $\dfrac{8}{x(x^2+4)} = \dfrac{A}{x} + \dfrac{Bx+C}{x^2+4}$

22. $\dfrac{2x}{(x+1)(x+2)(x+3)}$

$$= \frac{A}{x+1} + \frac{B}{x+2} + \frac{C}{x+3}$$

In Problems 23–26, a second order linear differential equation, two functions $y_1(x)$ and $y_2(x)$, and a pair of initial conditions are given. First verify by substitution that $y_1(x)$ and $y_2(x)$ are both solutions of the differential equation. Then use the method of the continuation of Example 7 to find a solution $y(x)$ that satisfies the indicated initial conditions.

23. $y'' - 3y' + 2y = 0$; $y_1(x) = e^x$, $y_2(x) = e^{2x}$; $y(0) = 1$, $y'(0) = -1$

24. $y'' - y' - 6y = 0$; $y_1(x) = e^{3x}$, $y_2(x) = e^{-2x}$; $y(0) = 7$, $y'(0) = 11$

25. $y'' + 4y = 0$; $y_1(x) = \cos 2x$, $y_2(x) = \sin 2x$; $y(0) = 4$, $y'(0) = 6$

26. $y'' - 2y' + y = 0$; $y_1(x) = e^x$, $y_2(x) = xe^x$; $y(0) = 5$, $y'(0) = 2$

27. (a) Show that the functions $y_1(x) = e^x$ and $y_2(x) = e^{-x}$ form a basis for the solution space S of the differential equation $y'' - y = 0$.
(b) Show that the functions

$$y_3(x) = \cosh x = \frac{1}{2}(e^x + e^{-x})$$

and

$$y_4(x) = \sinh x = \frac{1}{2}(e^x - e^{-x})$$

form another basis for the solution space S.

28. Let f, g, and h be twice-differentiable functions on $\mathbf{R}$. Then the function

$$W(x) = \begin{vmatrix} f(x) & g(x) & h(x) \\ f'(x) & g'(x) & h'(x) \\ f''(x) & g''(x) & h''(x) \end{vmatrix}$$

is called the **Wronskian** of f, g, and h. If f, g, and h are linearly dependent, deduce from the equation

$$c_1 f(x) + c_2 g(x) + c_3 h(x) = 0$$

(with c_1, c_2, and c_3 not all zero), together with the two equations obtained by differentiating it twice, that $W(x) = 0$ for all x. Therefore, in order to show that three given functions are linearly independent, it suffices to show that their Wronskian is *not* identically zero.

29. (a) Use the result of Problem 28 to show that the functions $y_1(x) = e^x$, $y_2(x) = e^{-x}$, and $y_3(x) = e^{-2x}$ are linearly independent solutions of the third order linear differential equation

$$y^{(3)} + 2y'' - y' - 2y = 0$$

and therefore form a basis for its solution space.
(b) Find a particular solution $y(x)$ that satisfies the initial conditions $y(0) = 0$, $y'(0) = 7$, and $y''(0) = 3$.

30. Repeat Problem 29, except use the solutions $y_1(x) = e^x$, $y_2(x) = \cos 2x$, and $y_3(x) = \sin 2x$ of the differential equation

$$y^{(3)} - y'' + 4y' - 4y = 0$$

and the initial conditions $y(0) = 1$, $y'(0) = 5$, $y''(0) = -5$.

31. Let V be the set of all infinite sequences $\{x_n\} = \{x_1, x_2, x_3, \ldots\}$ of real numbers. Let addition of elements of V and multiplication by scalars be defined as follows:

$$\{x_n\} + \{y_n\} = \{x_n + y_n\}$$

and

$$c\{x_n\} = \{cx_n\}.$$

(a) Show that V is a vector space with these operations.
(b) Prove that V is infinite-dimensional.

32. Let V be the vector space of Problem 31 and let the subset W consist of those elements $\{x_n\}$ of V such that $x_n = x_{n-1} + x_{n-2}$ for $n \geq 2$. Thus a typical element of W is the *Fibonacci sequence*

$$\{1, 1, 2, 3, 5, 8, 13, 21, 34, 55, \ldots\}.$$

(a) Show that W is a subspace of V.
(b) Prove that W is 2-dimensional.

33. Motivated by Example 2, let us define a function or transformation T from the set of all complex numbers to the space of all 2×2 matrices of the form in (1) as follows. Given a complex number $z = a + bi$, let

$$T(z) = \begin{bmatrix} a & -b \\ b & a \end{bmatrix}.$$

(a) Suppose that z_1 and z_2 are complex numbers and c_1 and c_2 are real numbers. Show that

$$T(c_1 z_1 + c_2 z_2) = c_1 T(z_1) + c_2 T(z_2).$$

(b) Show that

$$T(z_1 z_2) = T(z_1)T(z_2)$$

for all complex numbers z_1 and z_2. Note the complex multiplication on the left in contrast with the matrix multiplication on the right.
(c) Prove that if z is an arbitrary nonzero complex number, then

$$T(z^{-1}) = \{T(z)\}^{-1},$$

where $z^{-1} = 1/z$ and $\{T(z)\}^{-1}$ is the inverse of the matrix $T(z)$.

34. Let A and B be 4×4 (real) matrices partitioned into 2×2 submatrices or "blocks:"

$$A = \begin{bmatrix} A_{11} & A_{12} \\ A_{21} & A_{22} \end{bmatrix}, \qquad B = \begin{bmatrix} B_{11} & B_{12} \\ B_{21} & B_{22} \end{bmatrix}.$$

Then verify that AB can be calculated in "blockwise" fashion:

$$AB = \begin{bmatrix} A_{11}B_{11} + A_{12}B_{21} & A_{11}B_{12} + A_{12}B_{22} \\ A_{21}B_{11} + A_{22}B_{21} & A_{21}B_{12} + A_{22}B_{22} \end{bmatrix}.$$

35. Given a 2×2 matrix $M = [z_{ij}]$ whose entries are complex numbers, let $T(M)$ denote the 4×4 matrix of real numbers given in block form by

$$T(M) = \begin{bmatrix} T(z_{11}) & T(z_{12}) \\ T(z_{21}) & T(z_{22}) \end{bmatrix}.$$

The transformation T on the right-hand side is the one we defined in Problem 33. Suppose that M and N are 2×2 complex matrices. Use Problems 33(b) and 34 to show that

$$T(MN) = T(M)T(N).$$

Hence one can find the product of the 2×2 complex matrices M and N by calculating the product of the 4×4 real matrices $T(M)$ and $T(N)$. For instance, if

$$M = \begin{bmatrix} 1+i & 2+i \\ 1+2i & 1+3i \end{bmatrix}$$

and

$$N = \begin{bmatrix} 3-i & 1-2i \\ 2-i & 3-2i \end{bmatrix},$$

then

$$T(M)T(N) = \left[\begin{array}{cc:cc} 1 & -1 & 2 & -1 \\ 1 & 1 & 1 & 2 \\ \hdashline 1 & -2 & 1 & -3 \\ 2 & 1 & 3 & 1 \end{array}\right] \times \left[\begin{array}{cc:cc} 3 & 1 & 1 & 2 \\ -1 & 3 & -2 & 1 \\ \hdashline 2 & 1 & 3 & 2 \\ -1 & 2 & -2 & 3 \end{array}\right]$$

$$= \left[\begin{array}{cc:cc} 9 & -2 & 11 & 2 \\ 2 & 9 & -2 & 11 \\ \hdashline 10 & -10 & 14 & -7 \\ 10 & 10 & 7 & 14 \end{array}\right].$$

Therefore

$$MN = \begin{bmatrix} 9+2i & 11-2i \\ 10+10i & 14+7i \end{bmatrix}.$$

If M is a nonsingular 2×2 complex matrix, it can be shown that $T(M^{-1}) = \{T(M)\}^{-1}$. The $n \times n$ versions of these results are sometimes used to carry out complex matrix operations in computer languages that support only real arithmetic.

CHAPTER REVIEW QUESTIONS

1. Suppose that the subset W of $\mathbf{R}^n$ has the property that if $\mathbf{u}$ and $\mathbf{v}$ are vectors in W and a and b are scalars, then $a\mathbf{u} + b\mathbf{v}$ is in W. Does it follow that W is a subspace of $\mathbf{R}^n$?

2. Is there a subset of $\mathbf{R}^n$ that is closed under multiplication by scalars but does not contain the zero vector?

3. Give an example of a subset of $\mathbf{R}^n$ (you choose n) that is closed under addition of vectors but is not closed under multiplication of vectors by scalars.

4. Give an example of a subset of $\mathbf{R}^n$ (you choose n) that is closed under multiplication by scalars but is not closed under addition of vectors.

5. Under what conditions is the solution set of the linear system $A\mathbf{x} = \mathbf{b}$ (where A is an $m \times n$ matrix) a subspace of $\mathbf{R}^n$?

6. Suppose that k vectors in $\mathbf{R}^n$ are given (numerically). Describe a computational procedure by which you can determine whether or not these k vectors are linearly independent. No determinants are allowed.

7. State in one sentence why it is true that any $n + 1$ vectors in $\mathbf{R}^n$ are linearly dependent.

8. Suppose that S is a set of vectors in $\mathbf{R}^n$ such that every vector in $\mathbf{R}^n$ can be expressed in one and only one way as a linear combination of vectors in S. Does it follow that S is a basis for $\mathbf{R}^n$?

9. Let S be a set of four vectors such that any three of them are linearly independent. Does it follow that the four vectors are linearly independent?

10. The *union* of the two subspaces W_1 and W_2 of $\mathbf{R}^n$ is the set of all those vectors that are in either W_1 or W_2 (or both). Under what conditions is W also a subspace of $\mathbf{R}^n$? What about the set V of all vectors of the form $c_1\mathbf{v}_1 + c_2\mathbf{v}_2$ where c_1 and c_2 are scalars, $\mathbf{v}_1$ is in W_1, and $\mathbf{v}_2$ is in W_2?

11. Let S and T be two linearly independent sets of vectors such that no vector in either set is a linear combination of vectors in the other set. Does it follow that the union of S and T is a linearly independent set?

12. What fact about linear systems of equations is the key to the proof that any two bases for a finite-dimensional vector space have the same number of elements?

13. Does every set of vectors that spans $\mathbf{R}^n$ contain a basis for $\mathbf{R}^n$?

14. Given a basis S for a subspace W of $\mathbf{R}^n$, does it follow that S is contained in some basis for $\mathbf{R}^n$?

15. Given a homogeneous linear system $A\mathbf{x} = \mathbf{0}$, what is the quickest way to find the dimension of its solution space?

16. Given a spanning set S for a subspace W of $\mathbf{R}^n$, how can you extract from S a basis for W?

17. Suppose that the matrix A is row-equivalent to the echelon matrix E having k nonzero row vectors. Must the first k rows of A form a basis for the row space of E? Must the k pivot columns of E form a basis for the column space of A?

18. If the matrices A and B are row-equivalent, what is the relationship between their column spaces?

19. The pivot columns of a matrix A are those that correspond to the pivot columns of its reduced echelon form E. Why is it true that every column vector of A is a linear combination of its pivot column vectors?

20. Let A be a 5×7 matrix.
(a) What is the largest possible rank that A might have?
(b) Does there exist a vector $\mathbf{b}$ in $\mathbf{R}^5$ such that the system $A\mathbf{x} = \mathbf{b}$ has a unique solution?
(c) If the rank of A is 4, is the system $A\mathbf{x} = \mathbf{b}$ consistent for every $\mathbf{b}$ in $\mathbf{R}^5$?
(d) If the rank of A is 3, what is the dimension of the solution space of $A\mathbf{x} = \mathbf{0}$?

21. Let U and V be subspaces of $\mathbf{R}^n$ such that every vector in $\mathbf{R}^n$ is the sum of a vector in U and a vector in V. Let S and T be bases for U and V, respectively. Under what condition is the union of S and T a basis for $\mathbf{R}^n$?

5

Orthogonality and Least Squares

5.1

Orthogonal Vectors in $\mathbf{R}^n$

In Section 3.3 we observed that the geometrical concepts of *distance* and *angle* in 3-dimensional space may be based on the definition of the dot product of two vectors in $\mathbf{R}^3$. In this section we show that the same is true in n-dimensional space $\mathbf{R}^n$.

The **dot product** of the two vectors $\mathbf{u} = (u_1, u_2, \ldots, u_n)$ and $\mathbf{v} = (v_1, v_2, \ldots, v_n)$ in $\mathbf{R}^n$ is defined to be

$$\mathbf{u} \cdot \mathbf{v} = u_1 v_1 + u_2 v_2 + \cdots + u_n v_n. \tag{1}$$

Note that this definition is a direct generalization of the definition of the dot product of two vectors in $\mathbf{R}^3$. And just as in $\mathbf{R}^3$, it follows almost immediately from the formula in (1) that if $\mathbf{u}$, $\mathbf{v}$, and $\mathbf{w}$ are vectors in $\mathbf{R}^n$ and c is a scalar, then

$$\mathbf{u} \cdot \mathbf{v} = \mathbf{v} \cdot \mathbf{u} \qquad \text{(symmetry)} \tag{2}$$

$$\mathbf{u} \cdot (\mathbf{v} + \mathbf{w}) = \mathbf{u} \cdot \mathbf{v} + \mathbf{u} \cdot \mathbf{w} \qquad \text{(distributivity)} \tag{3}$$

$$(c\mathbf{u}) \cdot \mathbf{v} = c(\mathbf{u} \cdot \mathbf{v}) \qquad \text{(homogeneity)} \tag{4}$$

$$\mathbf{u} \cdot \mathbf{u} \geq 0; \quad \mathbf{u} \cdot \mathbf{u} = 0 \quad \text{if and only if} \quad \mathbf{u} = \mathbf{0}. \qquad \text{(positivity)} \tag{5}$$

Therefore the dot product in $\mathbf{R}^n$ is an example of an *inner product.*

Definition*: *Inner Product

An **inner product** on a vector space V is a function that associates with each pair of vectors $\mathbf{u}$ and $\mathbf{v}$ in V a scalar $\langle \mathbf{u}, \mathbf{v} \rangle$ such that, if $\mathbf{u}$, $\mathbf{v}$, and $\mathbf{w}$ are vectors and c is a scalar, then

(i) $\langle \mathbf{u}, \mathbf{v} \rangle = \langle \mathbf{v}, \mathbf{u} \rangle$;

(ii) $\langle \mathbf{u}, \mathbf{v} + \mathbf{w} \rangle = \langle \mathbf{u}, \mathbf{v} \rangle + \langle \mathbf{u}, \mathbf{w} \rangle$;

(iii) $\langle c\mathbf{u}, \mathbf{v} \rangle = c\langle \mathbf{u}, \mathbf{v} \rangle$;

(iv) $\langle \mathbf{u}, \mathbf{u} \rangle \geq 0$; $\langle \mathbf{u}, \mathbf{u} \rangle = 0$ if and only if $\mathbf{u} = \mathbf{0}$.

The dot product on $\mathbf{R}^n$ is sometimes called the **Euclidean inner product**, and with this inner product $\mathbf{R}^n$ is sometimes called **Euclidean *n*-dimensional space**. We can use any of the notations in

$$\mathbf{u} \cdot \mathbf{v} = \langle \mathbf{u}, \mathbf{v} \rangle = \mathbf{u}^T \mathbf{v}$$

for the dot product (recall in the last expression that $\mathbf{u}^T = (u_1, u_2, \ldots, u_n)$ represents the *column* vector with the indicated entries). Here we will use the notation $\mathbf{u} \cdot \mathbf{v}$. In Section 5.5 we discuss more general inner products, and there we will see that what is done in this section with the Euclidean inner product can be done with any inner product on any finite-dimensional vector space.

The **length** $|\mathbf{u}|$ of the vector $\mathbf{u} = (u_1, u_2, \ldots, u_n)$ is defined as follows:

$$\mathbf{u} = \sqrt{(\mathbf{u} \cdot \mathbf{u})} = (u_1^2 + u_2^2 + \cdots + u_n^2)^{1/2}. \tag{6}$$

Note that the case $n = 2$ is a consequence of the familiar Pythagorean formula in the plane.

Theorem 1 gives one of the most important inequalities in mathematics. Many proofs are known, but none of them seems direct and well motivated.

Theorem 1: *The Cauchy-Schwarz Inequality*

If $\mathbf{u}$ and $\mathbf{v}$ are vectors in $\mathbf{R}^n$ then

$$|\mathbf{u} \cdot \mathbf{v}| \leq |\mathbf{u}||\mathbf{v}|. \tag{7}$$

Proof If $\mathbf{u} = \mathbf{0}$, then $|\mathbf{u} \cdot \mathbf{v}| = |\mathbf{u}| = 0$, so the inequality is satisfied trivially. If $\mathbf{u} \neq \mathbf{0}$, then we let $a = \mathbf{u} \cdot \mathbf{u}$, $b = 2\mathbf{u} \cdot \mathbf{v}$, and $c = \mathbf{v} \cdot \mathbf{v}$. For any real number x, the positivity property of the dot product then yields

$$\begin{aligned} 0 &\leq (x\mathbf{u} + \mathbf{v}) \cdot (x\mathbf{u} + \mathbf{v}) \\ &= (\mathbf{u} \cdot \mathbf{u})x^2 + 2(\mathbf{u} \cdot \mathbf{v})x + (\mathbf{v} \cdot \mathbf{v}), \end{aligned}$$

so that

$$0 \leq ax^2 + bx + c.$$

Thus the quadratic equation $ax^2 + bx + c = 0$ either has no real roots or has a repeated real root. Hence the quadratic formula

$$x = \frac{-b \pm \sqrt{b^2 - 4ac}}{2a}$$

implies that the discriminant $b^2 - 4ac$ cannot be positive; that is, $b^2 \leq 4ac$, so

$$4(\mathbf{u} \cdot \mathbf{v})^2 \leq 4(\mathbf{u} \cdot \mathbf{u})(\mathbf{v} \cdot \mathbf{v}).$$

We get the Cauchy-Schwarz inequality in (7) when we take square roots, remembering that the numbers $|\mathbf{u}| = (\mathbf{u} \cdot \mathbf{u})^{1/2}$ and $|\mathbf{v}| = (\mathbf{v} \cdot \mathbf{v})^{1/2}$ are nonnegative. ■

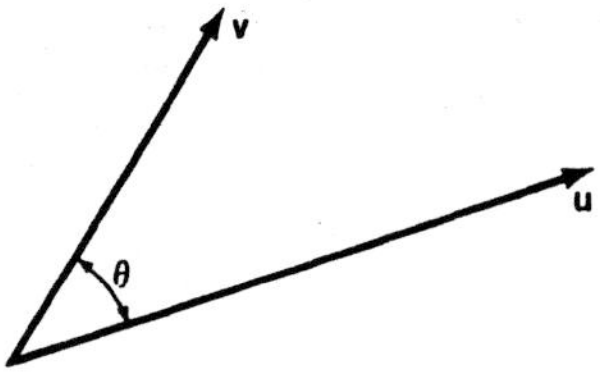

5.1 The angle θ between the vectors **u** and **v**.

The Cauchy-Schwarz inequality enables us to *define* the angle θ between the nonzero vectors **u** and **v**. (See Figure 5.1.) Division by the positive number $|\mathbf{u}||\mathbf{v}|$ in (7) yields $|\mathbf{u}\cdot\mathbf{v}|/(|\mathbf{u}||\mathbf{v}|) \leq 1$, so

$$-1 \leq \frac{\mathbf{u}\cdot\mathbf{v}}{|\mathbf{u}||\mathbf{v}|} \leq +1. \tag{8}$$

Hence there is a unique angle θ between 0 and π radians, inclusive (that is, between 0° and 180°), such that

$$\cos\theta = \frac{\mathbf{u}\cdot\mathbf{v}}{|\mathbf{u}||\mathbf{v}|}. \tag{9}$$

Thus we obtain the same geometric interpretation

$$\mathbf{u}\cdot\mathbf{v} = |\mathbf{u}||\mathbf{v}|\cos\theta \tag{10}$$

of the dot product in $\mathbf{R}^n$ that we saw (for $n = 3$) in Theorem 2 of Section 3.3.

On the basis of (10) we call the vectors **u** and **v** **orthogonal** provided that

$$\mathbf{u}\cdot\mathbf{v} = 0. \tag{11}$$

If **u** and **v** are nonzero vectors this means that $\cos\theta = 0$, so $\theta = \pi/2$ (90°). Note that $\mathbf{u} = \mathbf{0}$ satisfies (11) for all **v**, so the zero vector is orthogonal to *every* vector.

EXAMPLE 1 Find the angle θ_n in $\mathbf{R}^n$ between the x_1-axis and the line through the origin and the point $(1, 1, \ldots, 1)$.

Solution We take $\mathbf{u} = (1, 0, 0, \ldots, 0)$ on the x_1-axis and $\mathbf{v} = (1, 1, \ldots, 1)$. Then $|\mathbf{u}| = 1$, $|\mathbf{v}| = \sqrt{n}$, and $\mathbf{u}\cdot\mathbf{v} = 1$, so the formula in (9) gives

$$\cos\theta_n = \frac{\mathbf{u}\cdot\mathbf{v}}{|\mathbf{u}||\mathbf{v}|} = \frac{1}{\sqrt{n}}.$$

For instance, if

$$n = 3, \quad \text{then} \quad \theta_3 = \cos^{-1}\left(\frac{1}{\sqrt{3}}\right) \approx 0.9553 \quad (55°);$$

$$n = 4, \quad \text{then} \quad \theta_4 = \cos^{-1}\left(\frac{1}{\sqrt{4}}\right) \approx 1.0472 \quad (60°);$$

$$n = 5, \quad \text{then} \quad \theta_5 = \cos^{-1}\left(\frac{1}{\sqrt{5}}\right) \approx 1.1071 \quad (63°);$$

$$n = 100, \quad \text{then} \quad \theta_{100} = \cos^{-1}\left(\frac{1}{10}\right) \approx 1.4706 \quad (84°).$$

It is interesting to note that θ_n increases as n increases. Indeed, θ_n approaches $\cos^{-1}(0) = \pi/2$ (90°) as n increases without bound (so that $1/\sqrt{n}$ approaches zero).

In addition to angles, the dot product provides a definition of distance in $\mathbf{R}^n$. The **distance** $d(\mathbf{u}, \mathbf{v})$ between the points (vectors) $\mathbf{u} = (u_1, u_2, \ldots, u_n)$ and $\mathbf{v} = (v_1, v_2, \ldots, v_n)$ is defined to be

$$\begin{aligned} d(\mathbf{u}, \mathbf{v}) &= |\mathbf{u} - \mathbf{v}| \\ &= [(u_1 - v_1)^2 + (u_2 - v_2)^2 + \cdots + (u_n - v_n)^2]^{1/2}. \end{aligned} \tag{12}$$

EXAMPLE 2 The distance between the points $\mathbf{u} = (1, -1, -2, 3, 5)$ and $\mathbf{v} = (4, 3, 4, 5, 9)$ in $\mathbf{R}^5$ is

$$|\mathbf{u} - \mathbf{v}| = \sqrt{3^2 + 4^2 + 6^2 + 2^2 + 4^2} = \sqrt{81} = 9.$$

The *triangle inequality* of Theorem 2 relates the three sides of the triangle shown in Figure 5.2.

Theorem 2: *The Triangle Inequality*
If $\mathbf{u}$ and $\mathbf{v}$ are vectors in $\mathbf{R}^n$, then

$$|\mathbf{u} + \mathbf{v}| \le |\mathbf{u}| + |\mathbf{v}|. \tag{13}$$

PROOF We apply the Cauchy-Schwarz inequality to find that

$$\begin{aligned} |\mathbf{u} + \mathbf{v}|^2 &= (\mathbf{u} + \mathbf{v}) \cdot (\mathbf{u} + \mathbf{v}) \\ &= \mathbf{u} \cdot \mathbf{u} + 2\mathbf{u} \cdot \mathbf{v} + \mathbf{v} \cdot \mathbf{v} \\ &\le \mathbf{u} \cdot \mathbf{u} + 2|\mathbf{u}||\mathbf{v}| + \mathbf{v} \cdot \mathbf{v} \\ &= |\mathbf{u}|^2 + 2|\mathbf{u}||\mathbf{v}| + |\mathbf{v}|^2, \end{aligned} \tag{14}$$

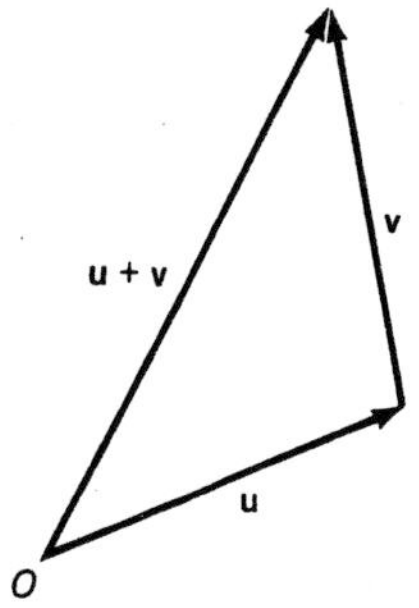

5.2 The triangle of the triangle inequality.

and therefore

$$|\mathbf{u} + \mathbf{v}|^2 \le (|\mathbf{u}| + |\mathbf{v}|)^2.$$

We now get (13) when we take square roots. ■

If the vectors **u** and **v** are orthogonal, then $\mathbf{u} \cdot \mathbf{v} = 0$, so line (14) in the proof of the triangle inequality yields the **Pythagorean formula**

$$|\mathbf{u} + \mathbf{v}|^2 = |\mathbf{u}|^2 + |\mathbf{v}|^2 \tag{15}$$

for a *right* triangle in $\mathbf{R}^n$ (see Figure 5.3).

The following theorem states a simple relationship between orthogonality and linear independence.

> ***Theorem 3:*** *Orthogonality and Linear Independence*
> If the nonzero vectors $\mathbf{v}_1, \mathbf{v}_2, \ldots, \mathbf{v}_k$ are mutually orthogonal—that is, each two of them are orthogonal—then they are linearly independent.

Proof Suppose that

$$c_1\mathbf{v}_1 + c_2\mathbf{v}_2 + \cdots + c_k\mathbf{v}_k = \mathbf{0}$$

where, as usual, $c_1, c_2, \ldots, c_k$ are scalars. When we take the dot product of each side of this equation with $\mathbf{v}_i$, we find that

$$c_i\mathbf{v}_i \cdot \mathbf{v}_i = c_i|\mathbf{v}_i|^2 = 0.$$

Now $|\mathbf{v}_i| \neq 0$ because $\mathbf{v}_i$ is a nonzero vector. It follows that $c_i = 0$. Thus $c_1 = c_2 = \cdots = c_k = 0$, and therefore the mutually orthogonal nonzero vectors $\mathbf{v}_1, \mathbf{v}_2, \ldots, \mathbf{v}_k$ are linearly independent. ■

In particular, any set of n mutually orthogonal nonzero vectors in $\mathbf{R}^n$ constitutes a basis for $\mathbf{R}^n$. Such a basis is called an **orthogonal basis**. For instance, the standard unit vectors $\mathbf{e}_1, \mathbf{e}_2, \ldots, \mathbf{e}_n$ form an orthogonal basis for $\mathbf{R}^n$.

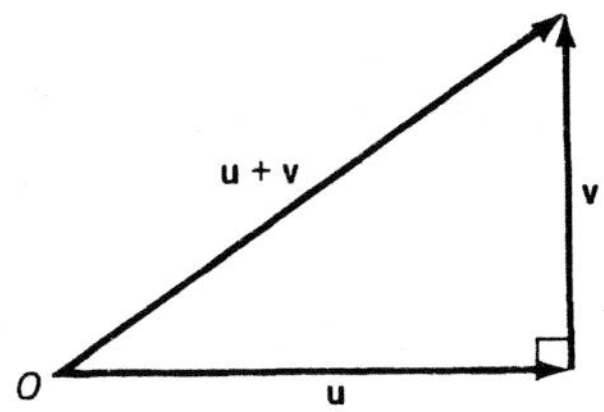

5.3 A right triangle in $\mathbf{R}^n$.

ORTHOGONAL COMPLEMENTS

Now we want to relate orthogonality to the solution of systems of linear equations. Consider the homogeneous linear system

$$A\mathbf{x} = \mathbf{0} \tag{16}$$

of m equations in n unknowns. If $\mathbf{v}_1, \mathbf{v}_2, \ldots, \mathbf{v}_m$ are the row vectors of the $m \times n$ coefficient matrix A, then the system looks like

$$\begin{bmatrix} \text{———} \mathbf{v}_1 \text{———} \\ \text{———} \mathbf{v}_2 \text{———} \\ \vdots \\ \text{———} \mathbf{v}_m \text{———} \end{bmatrix} \begin{bmatrix} | \\ \mathbf{x} \\ | \end{bmatrix} = \begin{bmatrix} \mathbf{v}_1 \cdot \mathbf{x} \\ \mathbf{v}_2 \cdot \mathbf{x} \\ \vdots \\ \mathbf{v}_m \cdot \mathbf{x} \end{bmatrix} = \begin{bmatrix} 0 \\ 0 \\ \vdots \\ 0 \end{bmatrix}.$$

Consequently it is clear that $\mathbf{x}$ is a solution vector of $A\mathbf{x} = \mathbf{0}$ if and only if $\mathbf{x}$ is orthogonal to each row vector of A. But in the latter event $\mathbf{x}$ is orthogonal to every linear combination of row vectors of A because

$$\begin{aligned} \mathbf{x} \cdot (c_1\mathbf{v}_1 + c_2\mathbf{v}_2 + \cdots + c_k\mathbf{v}_k) \\ &= c_1\mathbf{x}_1 \cdot \mathbf{v}_1 + c_2\mathbf{x}_2 \cdot \mathbf{v}_2 + \cdots + c_k\mathbf{x}_k \cdot \mathbf{v}_k \\ &= (c_1)(0) + (c_2)(0) + \cdots + (c_k)(0) = 0. \end{aligned}$$

Thus we have shown that *the vector* $\mathbf{x}$ *in* $\mathbf{R}^n$ *is a solution vector* of $A\mathbf{x} = \mathbf{0}$ *if and only if* $\mathbf{x}$ *is orthogonal to each vector in the row space Row(A) of the matrix A*. This situation motivates the following definition.

> ***Definition:*** *The Orthogonal Complement of a Subspace*
> The vector $\mathbf{u}$ is **orthogonal** to the subspace V of $\mathbf{R}^n$ provided that $\mathbf{u}$ is orthogonal to every vector in V. The **orthogonal complement** $V^\perp$ (read "V perp") of V is the set of all those vectors in $\mathbf{R}^n$ that are orthogonal to the subspace V.

If $\mathbf{u}_1$ and $\mathbf{u}_2$ are vectors in $V^\perp$, $\mathbf{v}$ is in V, and c_1 and c_2 are scalars, then

$$\begin{aligned} (c_1\mathbf{u}_1 + c_2\mathbf{u}_2) \cdot \mathbf{v} &= c_1\mathbf{u}_1 \cdot \mathbf{v} + c_2\mathbf{u}_2 \cdot \mathbf{v} \\ &= (c_1)(0) + (c_2)(0) = 0. \end{aligned}$$

Thus any linear combination of vectors in $V^\perp$ is orthogonal to every vector in V and hence is a vector in $V^\perp$. Therefore *the orthogonal complement* $V^\perp$ *of a subspace* V *is itself a subspace of* $\mathbf{R}^n$. The standard picture of two complementary subspaces V and $V^\perp$ consists of an orthogonal line and plane through the origin in $\mathbf{R}^3$ (see Figure 5.4). The proofs of the remaining parts of Theorem 4 are left to the problems.

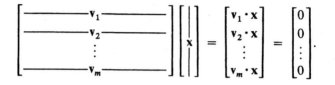

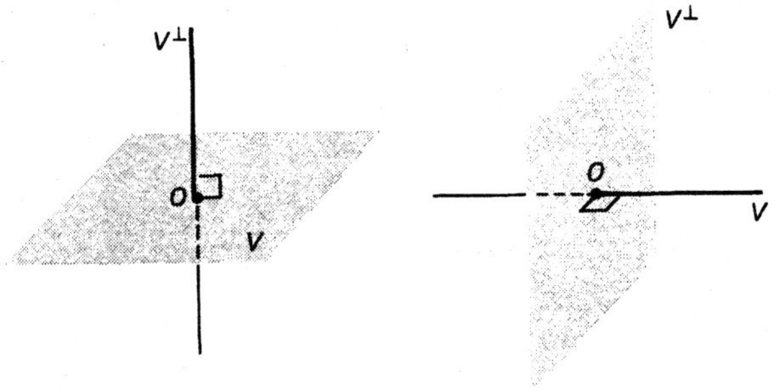

5.4 Orthogonal complements.

> ***Theorem 4:*** *Properties of Orthogonal Complements*
> Let V be a subspace of $\mathbf{R}^n$. Then
>
> 1. Its orthogonal complement $V^\perp$ is also a subspace of $\mathbf{R}^n$;
> 2. The only vector that lies in both V and $V^\perp$ is the zero vector;
> 3. The orthogonal complement of $V^\perp$ is V—that is, $(V^\perp)^\perp = V$;
> 4. If S is a spanning set for V, then the vector $\mathbf{u}$ is in $V^\perp$ if and only if $\mathbf{u}$ is orthogonal to every vector in S.

In our discussion of the homogeneous linear system $A\mathbf{x} = \mathbf{0}$ in (16), we showed that a vector space lies in the null space of A—that is, in the solution space of $A\mathbf{x} = \mathbf{0}$—if and only if it is orthogonal to each vector in the row space of A. In the language of orthogonal complements, this proves Theorem 5.

> ***Theorem 5:*** *The Row Space and the Null Space*
> Let A be an $m \times n$ matrix. Then the row space Row(A) and the null space Null(A) are orthogonal complements in $\mathbf{R}^n$. That is,
>
> $$\text{If} \quad V = \text{Row}(A), \quad \text{then} \quad V^\perp = \text{Null}(A). \tag{17}$$

Now suppose that a subspace V of $\mathbf{R}^n$ is given, with $\mathbf{v}_1, \mathbf{v}_2, \ldots, \mathbf{v}_m$ a set of vectors that span V. For instance, these vectors may form a given basis for V. Then the implication in (17) provides the following algorithm for finding a basis for the orthogonal complement $V^\perp$ of V.

1. Let A be the $m \times n$ matrix with row vectors $\mathbf{v}_1, \mathbf{v}_2, \ldots, \mathbf{v}_m$.
2. Reduce A to echelon form and use the algorithm of Section 4.3 to find a basis $\{\mathbf{u}_1, \mathbf{u}_2, \ldots, \mathbf{u}_k\}$ for the solution space Null(A) of $A\mathbf{x} = \mathbf{0}$. Because $V^\perp = \text{Null}(A)$, this will be a basis for the orthogonal complement of V.

EXAMPLE 3 Let V be the 1-dimensional subspace of $\mathbf{R}^3$ spanned by the vector $\mathbf{v}_1 = (1, -3, 5)$. Then

$$A = [1 \quad -3 \quad 5]$$

and our linear system $A\mathbf{x} = \mathbf{0}$ consists of the single equation

$$x_1 - 3x_2 + 5x_3 = 0.$$

If $x_2 = s$ and $x_3 = t$, then $x_1 = 3s - 5t$. With $s = 1$ and $t = 0$ we get the solution vector $\mathbf{u}_1 = (3, 1, 0)$, whereas with $s = 0$ and $t = 1$ we get the solution vector $\mathbf{u}_2 = (-5, 0, 1)$. Thus the orthogonal complement $V^\perp$ is the 2-dimensional subspace of $\mathbf{R}^3$ having $\mathbf{u}_1 = (3, 1, 0)$ and $\mathbf{u}_2 = (-5, 0, 1)$ as basis vectors.

EXAMPLE 4 Let V be the 2-dimensional subspace of $\mathbf{R}^5$ that has $\mathbf{v}_1 = (1, 2, 1, -3, -3)$ and $\mathbf{v}_2 = (2, 5, 6, -10, -12)$ as basis vectors. The matrix

$$A = \begin{bmatrix} 1 & 2 & 1 & -3 & -3 \\ 2 & 5 & 6 & -10 & -12 \end{bmatrix}$$

with row vectors $\mathbf{v}_1$ and $\mathbf{v}_2$ has reduced echelon form

$$E = \begin{bmatrix} 1 & 0 & -7 & 5 & 9 \\ 0 & 1 & 4 & -4 & -6 \end{bmatrix}.$$

Hence the solution space of $A\mathbf{x} = \mathbf{0}$ is described parametrically by

$$x_3 = r, \qquad x_4 = s, \qquad x_5 = t,$$

$$x_2 = -4r + 4s + 6t,$$

$$x_1 = 7r - 5s - 9t.$$

Then the choice

$$r = 1, \quad s = 0, \quad t = 0 \quad \text{yields} \quad \mathbf{u}_1 = (7, -4, 1, 0, 0);$$

$$r = 0, \quad s = 1, \quad t = 0 \quad \text{yields} \quad \mathbf{u}_2 = (-5, 4, 0, 1, 0);$$

$$r = 0, \quad s = 0, \quad t = 1 \quad \text{yields} \quad \mathbf{u}_3 = (-9, 6, 0, 0, 1).$$

Thus the orthogonal complement $V^\perp$ is the 3-dimensional subspace of $\mathbf{R}^5$ with basis $\{\mathbf{u}_1, \mathbf{u}_2, \mathbf{u}_3\}$.

Observe that $\dim V + \dim V^\perp = 3$ in Example 3, but $\dim V + \dim V^\perp = 5$ in Example 4. It is no coincidence that in each case the dimensions of V and $V^\perp$ add up to the dimension n of the Euclidean space containing them. To see why, suppose that V is a subspace of $\mathbf{R}^n$ and let A be an $m \times n$ matrix whose row vectors span V. Then Equation (12) in Section 4.4 implies that

$$\text{rank}(A) + \dim \text{Null}(A) = n.$$

But

$$\dim V = \dim \text{Row}(A) = \text{rank}(A)$$

and

$$\dim V^{\perp} = \dim \text{Null}(A)$$

by Theorem 5, so it follows that

$$\dim V + \dim V^{\perp} = n. \tag{18}$$

Moreover, it should be apparent intuitively that if

$$\{\mathbf{v}_1, \mathbf{v}_2, \ldots, \mathbf{v}_m\} \text{ is a basis for } V$$

and

$$\{\mathbf{u}_1, \mathbf{u}_2, \ldots, \mathbf{u}_k\} \text{ is a basis for } V^{\perp},$$

then

$$\{\mathbf{v}_1, \mathbf{v}_2, \ldots, \mathbf{v}_m, \mathbf{u}_1, \mathbf{u}_2, \ldots, \mathbf{u}_k\} \text{ is a basis for } \mathbf{R}^n.$$

That is, *the union of a basis for V and a basis for $V^{\perp}$ is a basis for* $\mathbf{R}^n$. In Problem 34 of this section we ask you to prove that this is so.

5.1 PROBLEMS

In Problems 1–4, determine whether the given vectors are mutually orthogonal.

1. $\mathbf{v}_1 = (2, 1, 2, 1)$, $\mathbf{v}_2 = (3, -6, 1, -2)$, $\mathbf{v}_3 = (3, -1, -5, 5)$

2. $\mathbf{v}_1 = (3, -2, 3, -4)$, $\mathbf{v}_2 = (6, 3, 4, 6)$, $\mathbf{v}_3 = (17, -12, -21, 3)$

3. $\mathbf{v}_1 = (5, 2, -4, -1)$, $\mathbf{v}_2 = (3, -5, 1, 1)$, $\mathbf{v}_3 = (3, 0, 8, -17)$

4. $\mathbf{v}_1 = (1, 2, 3, -2, 1)$, $\mathbf{v}_2 = (3, 2, 3, 6, -4)$, $\mathbf{v}_3 = (6, 2, -4, 1, 4)$

In Problems 5–8, the three vertices A, B, and C of a triangle are given. Prove that each triangle is a right triangle by showing that its sides a, b, and c satisfy the Pythagorean relation $a^2 + b^2 = c^2$.

5. $A(6, 6, 5, 8)$, $B(6, 8, 6, 5)$, $C(5, 7, 4, 6)$

6. $A(3, 5, 1, 3)$, $B(4, 2, 6, 4)$, $C(1, 3, 4, 2)$

7. $A(4, 5, 3, 5, -1)$, $B(3, 4, -1, 4, 4)$, $C(1, 3, 1, 3, 1)$

8. $A(2, 8, -3, -1, 2)$, $B(-2, 5, 6, 2, 12)$, $C(-5, 3, 2, -3, 5)$

9–12. Find the acute angles (in degrees) of each of the right triangles of Problems 5–8, respectively.

In Problems 13–22, the given vectors span a subspace V of the indicated Euclidean space. Find a basis for the orthogonal complement $V^{\perp}$ of V.

13. $\mathbf{v}_1 = (1, -2, 3)$

14. $\mathbf{v}_1 = (1, 5, -3)$

15. $\mathbf{v}_1 = (1, -2, -3, 5)$

16. $\mathbf{v}_1 = (1, 7, -6, -9)$

17. $\mathbf{v}_1 = (1, 3, 2, 4)$, $\mathbf{v}_2 = (2, 7, 7, 3)$

18. $\mathbf{v}_1 = (1, -3, 3, 5)$, $\mathbf{v}_2 = (2, -5, 9, 3)$

19. $\mathbf{v}_1 = (1, 2, 5, 2, 3)$, $\mathbf{v}_2 = (3, 7, 11, 9, 5)$

20. $\mathbf{v}_1 = (2, 5, 5, 4, 3)$, $\mathbf{v}_2 = (3, 7, 8, 8, 8)$

21. $\mathbf{v}_1 = (1, 2, 3, 1, 3)$, $\mathbf{v}_2 = (1, 3, 4, 3, 6)$, $\mathbf{v}_3 = (2, 2, 4, 3, 5)$

22. $\mathbf{v}_1 = (1, 1, 1, 1, 3)$, $\mathbf{v}_2 = (2, 3, 1, 4, 7)$, $\mathbf{v}_3 = (5, 3, 7, 1, 5)$

23. Prove: For arbitrary vectors $\mathbf{u}$ and $\mathbf{v}$,
(a) $|\mathbf{u} + \mathbf{v}|^2 + |\mathbf{u} - \mathbf{v}|^2 = 2|\mathbf{u}|^2 + 2|\mathbf{v}|^2$;
(b) $|\mathbf{u} + \mathbf{v}|^2 - |\mathbf{u} - \mathbf{v}|^2 = 4\mathbf{u} \cdot \mathbf{v}$.

24. Given mutually orthogonal vectors $\mathbf{v}_1, \mathbf{v}_2, \ldots, \mathbf{v}_k$, show that

$$|\mathbf{v}_1 + \mathbf{v}_2 + \cdots + \mathbf{v}_k|^2 = |\mathbf{v}_1|^2 + |\mathbf{v}_2|^2 + \cdots + |\mathbf{v}_k|^2.$$

25. Suppose that A, B, and C are the unit points on distinct coordinate axes in $\mathbf{R}^n$ (for example, perhaps $A = \mathbf{e}_1$, $B = \mathbf{e}_2$, and $C = \mathbf{e}_3$). Show that ABC is an equilateral triangle.

26. Prove that $|\mathbf{u} \cdot \mathbf{v}| = |\mathbf{u}||\mathbf{v}|$ if and only if the vectors $\mathbf{u}$ and $\mathbf{v}$ are linearly dependent.

In Problems 27–29, V denotes a subspace of $\mathbf{R}^n$.

27. Show that the only vector that lies in both V and $V^\perp$ is the zero vector.

28. Prove that if $W = V^\perp$ then $W^\perp = V$.

29. Let S be a spanning set for V. Show that the vector $\mathbf{u}$ is in $V^\perp$ if and only if $\mathbf{u}$ is orthogonal to every vector in S.

30. Suppose that the vectors $\mathbf{u}$ and $\mathbf{v}$ are orthogonal and that $\mathbf{u} + \mathbf{v} = \mathbf{0}$. Show that $\mathbf{u} = \mathbf{v} = \mathbf{0}$.

31. Let S and T be two sets of vectors in $\mathbf{R}^n$ such that each vector in S is orthogonal to every vector in T. Prove that each vector in span(S) is orthogonal to every vector in span(T).

32. Let $S = \{\mathbf{u}_1, \mathbf{u}_2\}$ and $T = \{\mathbf{v}_1, \mathbf{v}_2\}$ be linearly independent sets of vectors such that each $\mathbf{u}_i$ in S is orthogonal to every vector $\mathbf{v}_j$ in T. Then use the results of Problems 30 and 31 to show that the four vectors $\mathbf{u}_1$, $\mathbf{u}_2$, $\mathbf{v}_1$, $\mathbf{v}_2$ are linearly independent.

33. Let $S = \{\mathbf{u}_1, \mathbf{u}_2, \ldots, \mathbf{u}_k\}$ and $T = \{\mathbf{v}_1, \mathbf{v}_2, \ldots, \mathbf{v}_m\}$ be linearly independent sets of vectors such that each $\mathbf{u}_i$ in S is orthogonal to every vector $\mathbf{v}_j$ in T. Then generalize Problem 32 to show that the $k + m$ vectors $\mathbf{u}_1, \mathbf{u}_2, \ldots, \mathbf{u}_k, \mathbf{v}_1, \mathbf{v}_2, \ldots, \mathbf{v}_m$ are linearly independent.

34. Deduce from the result of Problem 33 that if V is a subspace of $\mathbf{R}^n$, then the union of a basis for V and a basis for $V^\perp$ is a basis for $\mathbf{R}^n$.

35. Let A be an $m \times n$ matrix and $\mathbf{b}$ a vector in $\mathbf{R}^m$. Combine the observations listed below to prove that *the nonhomogeneous linear system $A\mathbf{x} = \mathbf{b}$ is consistent if and only if $\mathbf{b}$ is orthogonal to the solution space of the homogeneous system $A^T\mathbf{y} = \mathbf{0}$.*
(a) $A\mathbf{x} = \mathbf{b}$ is consistent if and only if $\mathbf{b}$ is in Col(A).
(b) $\mathbf{b}$ is in Col(A) if and only if $\mathbf{b}$ is orthogonal to $\{\text{Col}(A)\}^\perp = \{\text{Row}(A^T)\}^\perp$.
(c) $\{\text{Row}(A^T)\}^\perp = \text{Null}(A^T)$.

5.2

Orthogonal Projections and Least Squares Solutions

In this section we discuss the concept of an *approximate solution* to a linear system that is inconsistent and hence has no (exact) solution. For instance, consider the system

$$\begin{aligned} x_1 + x_2 &= 4 \\ 2x_1 + x_2 &= 8 \\ x_1 + 2x_2 &= 5 \end{aligned} \tag{1}$$

of $m = 3$ equations in $n = 2$ unknowns. If this system were consistent, the first and second equations would yield $x_1 = 4$, whereas the first and third equations would yield $x_2 = 1$. But $2x_1 + x_2 = (2)(4) + (1) = 9$ rather than 8, so these values do not satisfy the second equation. Thus the system in (1) is inconsistent.

Many important practical problems lead to inconsistent linear systems!* Given such a system, it is common practice to seek a vector $\mathbf{x}$ that is "as close as possible" to being a solution vector of the system.

---

* For example, one of us (D.E.P.) once had the problem of determining the quantitative meaning of six terms such as "slight erosion" and "moderate erosion" as used by a variety of geological observers in different regions of the Southern Piedmont over several decades. Analysis of silt deposition led to 36 equations in six unknowns, *no 7 of which were consistent*!

To explain what the phrase "as close as possible" should mean in this context, let us interpret the system in (1) geometrically. Its coefficient matrix

$$A = \begin{bmatrix} 1 & 1 \\ 2 & 1 \\ 1 & 2 \end{bmatrix} = [\mathbf{a}_1 \quad \mathbf{a}_2] = \begin{bmatrix} A_1 \\ A_2 \\ A_3 \end{bmatrix} \tag{2}$$

has column vectors $\mathbf{a}_1 = (1, 2, 1)$ and $\mathbf{a}_2 = (1, 1, 2)$ in $\mathbf{R}^3$ and has row vectors $A_1 = [1 \quad 1]$, $A_2 = [2 \quad 1]$, and $A_3 = [1 \quad 2]$. The column vectors $\mathbf{a}_1$ and $\mathbf{a}_2$ span a plane V through the origin in $\mathbf{R}^3$, and the fact that the system is inconsistent means simply that the vector $\mathbf{b} = (4, 8, 5)$ in (1) is *not* in V.

As indicated in Figure 5.5, we can write

$$\mathbf{b} = \mathbf{p} + \mathbf{q} \tag{3}$$

where $\mathbf{p}$ is the *orthogonal projection* of $\mathbf{b}$ into the plane V and $\mathbf{q}$ is orthogonal to V. Because $\mathbf{p}$ is in V and the linearly independent vectors $\mathbf{a}_1$ and $\mathbf{a}_2$ span V, there exist unique numbers $\bar{x}_1$ and $\bar{x}_2$ such that $\mathbf{p} = \bar{x}_1\mathbf{a}_1 + \bar{x}_2\mathbf{a}_2$. That is,

$$\mathbf{p} = A\bar{\mathbf{x}} \tag{4}$$

where $\bar{\mathbf{x}} = (\bar{x}_1, \bar{x}_2)$ is regarded as a 2×1 column vector.

The orthogonal projection $\mathbf{p}$ of the point $\mathbf{b}$ into V is the point of the plane V closest to $\mathbf{b}$. That is, the distance $|\mathbf{p} - \mathbf{b}|$ is smaller for $\mathbf{p}$ than for any other point of the plane V. Equivalently, its square $|\mathbf{p} - \mathbf{b}|^2$ is minimal. We see from (4) that $\mathbf{p} = (A_1\bar{\mathbf{x}}, A_2\bar{\mathbf{x}}, A_3\bar{\mathbf{x}})$ where A_1, A_2, A_3 are the rows of A, so

$$|\mathbf{p} - \mathbf{b}|^2 = (A_1\bar{\mathbf{x}} - b_1)^2 + (A_2\bar{\mathbf{x}} - b_2)^2 + (A_3\bar{\mathbf{x}} - b_3)^2. \tag{5}$$

Note that the three quantities whose *squares* appear on the right-hand side in (5) are simply the differences between the left-hand and right-hand sides that result when we substitute $\bar{x}_1$ and $\bar{x}_2$ in the three equations of the original system in (1). If we write

$$E_i = |A_i\bar{\mathbf{x}} - b_i|$$

for the "error" in the ith equation ($i = 1, 2, 3$), and $E = |\mathbf{p} - \mathbf{b}|$ for the distance from $\mathbf{p}$ to $\mathbf{b}$, then Equation (5) may be written in the form

$$E^2 = (E_1)^2 + (E_2)^2 + (E_3)^2. \tag{6}$$

Hence the fact that $E^2 = |\mathbf{p} - \mathbf{b}|^2$ is minimal means that the choice $\bar{\mathbf{x}} = (\bar{x}_1, \bar{x}_2)$ yields the "least sum of squares of errors" in (6). This is what we mean when we say

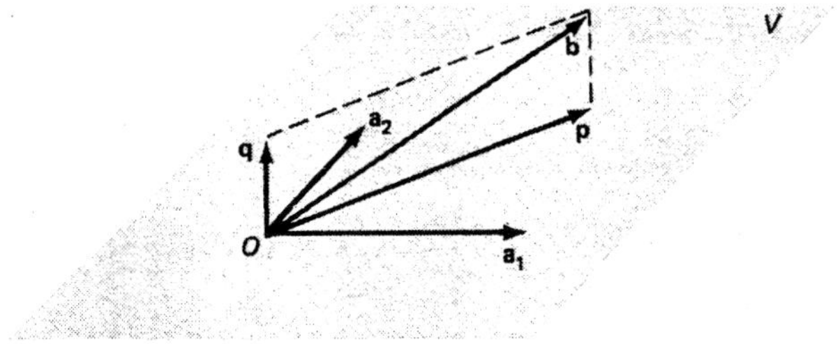

5.5 Geometric interpretation of the equation in (3).

(informally) that $\bar{\mathbf{x}} = (\bar{x}_1, \bar{x}_2)$ is as close as possible to being a solution of the inconsistent system in (1).

We return to the particular system in (1) in Example 1 of this section, but only after we have developed the necessary machinery for dealing with the general nonhomogeneous linear system

$$A\mathbf{x} = \mathbf{b}. \tag{7}$$

We assume throughout that the $m \times n$ coefficient matrix A has rank n, which means that its n column vectors $\mathbf{a}_1, \mathbf{a}_2, \ldots, \mathbf{a}_n$ are *linearly independent* and hence form a basis for the column space V of A.

Our interest here is in the situation when the system in (7) is *inconsistent.* Because (7) may be rewritten as

$$x_1\mathbf{a}_1 + x_2\mathbf{a}_2 + \cdots + x_n\mathbf{a}_n = \mathbf{b},$$

its inconsistency means simply that $\mathbf{b}$ is *not* in the n-dimensional subspace V of $\mathbf{R}^m$. Thus $m > n$, and so our inconsistent system $A\mathbf{x} = \mathbf{b}$ has more equations than unknowns. Such linear systems sometimes are called **overdetermined**. Motivated by the discussion above of the particular system in (1), we want to find the orthogonal projection $\mathbf{p}$ of $\mathbf{b}$ into $V = \text{Col}(A)$.

ORTHOGONAL PROJECTION PROBLEM:

Given a vector $\mathbf{b}$ in $\mathbf{R}^m$ that does not lie in the subspace V with basis vectors $\mathbf{a}_1$, $\mathbf{a}_2, \ldots, \mathbf{a}_n$, find vectors $\mathbf{p}$ in V and $\mathbf{q}$ orthogonal to V such that

$$\mathbf{b} = \mathbf{p} + \mathbf{q}. \tag{8}$$

In principle this is an easy problem. If $\{\mathbf{u}_1, \mathbf{u}_2, \ldots, \mathbf{u}_k\}$ is a basis for the orthogonal complement $V^\perp$ of dimension $k = m - n$, then (as we remarked at the end of Section 5.1) the vectors $\mathbf{a}_1, \mathbf{a}_2, \ldots, \mathbf{a}_n, \mathbf{u}_1, \mathbf{u}_2, \ldots, \mathbf{u}_k$ form a basis for $\mathbf{R}^m$. Hence there exist scalars $\bar{x}_1, \bar{x}_2, \ldots, \bar{x}_m$ such that

$$\mathbf{b} = \bar{x}_1\mathbf{a}_1 + \cdots + \bar{x}_n\mathbf{a}_n + \bar{x}_{n+1}\mathbf{u}_1 + \cdots + \bar{x}_m\mathbf{u}_k.$$

Then obviously (8) holds with

$$\mathbf{p} = \bar{x}_1\mathbf{a}_1 + \bar{x}_2\mathbf{a}_2 + \cdots + \bar{x}_n\mathbf{a}_n \tag{9}$$

and

$$\mathbf{q} = \mathbf{b} - \mathbf{p} = \bar{x}_{n+1}\mathbf{u}_1 + \cdots + \bar{x}_m\mathbf{u}_k.$$

Moreover, the decomposition

$$\mathbf{b} = \mathbf{p} + \mathbf{q}$$

of $\mathbf{b}$ into the sum of a vector $\mathbf{p}$ in V and a vector $\mathbf{q}$ orthogonal to V is unique (see Problem 24). The unique vector $\mathbf{p}$ defined in (9) is called the **orthogonal projection** of the vector $\mathbf{b}$ into the subspace V.

In practice, we need an algorithm for the explicit computation of $\mathbf{p}$. Note first that if A is the $m \times n$ matrix with column vectors $\mathbf{a}_1, \mathbf{a}_2, \ldots, \mathbf{a}_n$, then (9) implies that

$$\mathbf{p} = A\bar{\mathbf{x}}. \tag{10}$$

Now let $\mathbf{y}$ be an arbitary vector in $\mathbf{R}^n$. Then the vector

$$A\mathbf{y} = y_1\mathbf{a}_1 + y_2\mathbf{a}_2 + \cdots + y_n\mathbf{a}_n$$

lies in V and is therefore orthogonal to

$$\mathbf{q} = \mathbf{p} - \mathbf{b} = A\bar{\mathbf{x}} - \mathbf{b}.$$

If we write the dot product $(A\mathbf{y})\cdot\mathbf{q}$ in the form $(A\mathbf{y})^T\mathbf{q}$, it is easy to see that

$$(A\mathbf{y})^T(A\bar{\mathbf{x}} - \mathbf{b}) = 0;$$

$$\mathbf{y}^T A^T(A\bar{\mathbf{x}} - \mathbf{b}) = 0;$$

$$\mathbf{y}^T(A^T A\bar{\mathbf{x}} - A^T\mathbf{b}) = 0.$$

Because this last result holds for *every* $\mathbf{y}$ in $\mathbf{R}^n$, it follows that $A^T A\bar{\mathbf{x}} - A^T\mathbf{b} = \mathbf{0}$; that is, that

$$A^T A\bar{\mathbf{x}} = A^T\mathbf{b}. \tag{11}$$

The system in (11) is called the **normal system** associated with the system $A\mathbf{x} = \mathbf{b}$. Note that it is obtained by multiplying each term in the equation $A\bar{\mathbf{x}} = \mathbf{b}$ on the left by the transpose matrix A^T. According to Theorem 2 (found at the end of this section), the assumption that the $m \times n$ matrix A has rank n implies that the $n \times n$ matrix $A^T A$ is nonsingular. Consequently the normal system in (11) has the unique solution

$$\bar{\mathbf{x}} = (A^T A)^{-1} A^T\mathbf{b}. \tag{12}$$

Once $\bar{\mathbf{x}}$ has been found, the orthogonal projection $\mathbf{p}$ of $\mathbf{b}$ into $V = \text{Col}(A)$ is given (from Equation (10)) by

$$\mathbf{p} = A\bar{\mathbf{x}} = A(A^T A)^{-1} A^T\mathbf{b}. \tag{13}$$

Equations (12) and (13) should *not* be memorized. The best practice is always to begin with the normal system $A^T A\bar{\mathbf{x}} = A^T\mathbf{b}$ and solve directly for $\bar{\mathbf{x}}$. With large systems Gaussian elimination will ordinarily be more efficient than first finding the inverse matrix $(A^T A)^{-1}$ and then using Equation (12) to find $\bar{\mathbf{x}}$. At the last step compute the orthogonal projection by use of the formula $\mathbf{p} = A\bar{\mathbf{x}}$.

EXAMPLE 1 For the inconsistent system in (1) at the beginning of this section we have

$$A = \begin{bmatrix} 1 & 1 \\ 2 & 1 \\ 1 & 2 \end{bmatrix} \quad \text{and} \quad \mathbf{b} = \begin{bmatrix} 4 \\ 8 \\ 5 \end{bmatrix}.$$

Hence the normal system $A^T A\bar{\mathbf{x}} = A^T\mathbf{b}$ is

$$\begin{bmatrix} 1 & 2 & 1 \\ 1 & 1 & 2 \end{bmatrix}\begin{bmatrix} 1 & 1 \\ 2 & 1 \\ 1 & 2 \end{bmatrix}\begin{bmatrix} \bar{x}_1 \\ \bar{x}_2 \end{bmatrix} = \begin{bmatrix} 1 & 2 & 1 \\ 1 & 1 & 2 \end{bmatrix}\begin{bmatrix} 4 \\ 8 \\ 5 \end{bmatrix}$$

—that is,

$$\begin{bmatrix} 6 & 5 \\ 5 & 6 \end{bmatrix}\begin{bmatrix} \bar{x}_1 \\ \bar{x}_2 \end{bmatrix} = \begin{bmatrix} 25 \\ 22 \end{bmatrix}.$$

Then

$$(A^T A)^{-1} = \begin{bmatrix} 6 & 5 \\ 5 & 6 \end{bmatrix}^{-1} = \frac{1}{11}\begin{bmatrix} 6 & -5 \\ -5 & 6 \end{bmatrix},$$

so

$$\begin{bmatrix} \bar{x}_1 \\ \bar{x}_2 \end{bmatrix} = \frac{1}{11}\begin{bmatrix} 6 & -5 \\ -5 & 6 \end{bmatrix}\begin{bmatrix} 25 \\ 22 \end{bmatrix} = \frac{1}{11}\begin{bmatrix} 40 \\ 7 \end{bmatrix}.$$

Thus $\bar{\mathbf{x}} = (\frac{40}{11}, \frac{7}{11})$, and then the orthogonal projection of $\mathbf{b}$ into $V = \text{Col}(A)$ is

$$\mathbf{p} = A\bar{\mathbf{x}} = \frac{1}{11}\begin{bmatrix} 1 & 1 \\ 2 & 1 \\ 1 & 2 \end{bmatrix}\begin{bmatrix} 40 \\ 7 \end{bmatrix} = \frac{1}{11}\begin{bmatrix} 47 \\ 87 \\ 54 \end{bmatrix}.$$

Hence $\mathbf{p} = (4\frac{3}{11}, 7\frac{10}{11}, 4\frac{10}{11})$ is the point of the plane V closest to $\mathbf{b} = (4, 8, 5)$. Note that the "least sum of squares of errors" in (5) is

$$|\mathbf{p} - \mathbf{b}|^2 = (\tfrac{3}{11})^2 + (-\tfrac{1}{11})^2 + (-\tfrac{1}{11})^2 = \tfrac{1}{11}.$$

EXAMPLE 2 Suppose that V is the line through the origin in $\mathbf{R}^m$ determined by the single nonzero vector $\mathbf{a}$ (see Figure 5.6). This situation corresponds to the equation

$$\mathbf{a}x = \mathbf{b}.$$

With $A = \mathbf{a}$ and $n = 1$, the normal system in (11) reduces to the single scalar equation

$$\mathbf{a}^T\mathbf{a}\bar{x} = \mathbf{a}^T\mathbf{b}.$$

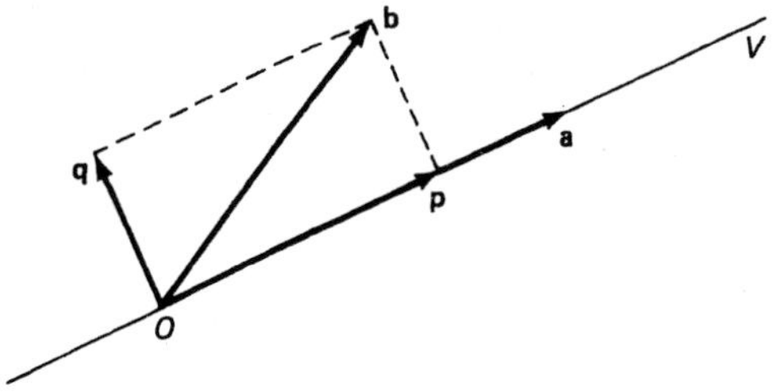

5.6 Orthogonal projection into a line.

Hence $\bar{x} = \mathbf{a}^T\mathbf{b}/\mathbf{a}^T\mathbf{a}$, so the orthogonal projection of the vector $\mathbf{b}$ into the line determined by $\mathbf{a} \neq \mathbf{0}$ is

$$\mathbf{p} = \mathbf{a}\bar{x} = \frac{\mathbf{a}^T\mathbf{b}}{\mathbf{a}^T\mathbf{a}}\mathbf{a} = \frac{\mathbf{a}\cdot\mathbf{b}}{\mathbf{a}\cdot\mathbf{a}}\mathbf{a}. \tag{14}$$

Note that this agrees with Equation (13) in Section 3.3. For instance, if $\mathbf{a} = (2, 1, 3, -1, 5)$ and $\mathbf{b} = (-3, 2, 4, 8, 6)$ in $\mathbf{R}^5$, then $\mathbf{a}\cdot\mathbf{a} = 40$ and $\mathbf{a}\cdot\mathbf{b} = 30$, so the orthogonal projection of $\mathbf{b}$ into the line determined by $\mathbf{a}$ is $\mathbf{p} = \frac{3}{4}\mathbf{a}$.

> ***Theorem 1:*** *Orthogonal Projection as Closest Point*
> Let V be a subspace of $\mathbf{R}^m$ and suppose that $\mathbf{b}$ is not in V. Then the orthogonal projection $\mathbf{p}$ of $\mathbf{b}$ into V is closer to $\mathbf{b}$ than is any other vector in V.

Proof Let $\mathbf{v}$ be an arbitrary vector in V. Then the Pythagorean formula (Equation (15) in Section 5.1) for the right triangle indicated in Figure 5.7 yields

$$|\mathbf{v} - \mathbf{b}|^2 = |\mathbf{v} - \mathbf{p}|^2 + |\mathbf{p} - \mathbf{b}|^2.$$

Hence

$$|\mathbf{p} - \mathbf{b}|^2 = |\mathbf{v} - \mathbf{b}|^2 - |\mathbf{v} - \mathbf{p}|^2 \leq |\mathbf{v} - \mathbf{b}|^2.$$

Thus $|\mathbf{p} - \mathbf{b}| \leq |\mathbf{v} - \mathbf{b}|$, and $|\mathbf{p} - \mathbf{b}| < |\mathbf{v} - \mathbf{b}|$ unless $\mathbf{p} = \mathbf{v}$. ■

To apply Theorem 1 to the $m \times n$ linear system $A\mathbf{x} = \mathbf{b}$ (where A has rank n), let $A_1, A_2, \ldots, A_m$ denote the m rows of A. Then the system of equations is

$$\begin{aligned} A_1\mathbf{x} &= b_1 \\ A_2\mathbf{x} &= b_2 \\ &\vdots \\ A_m\mathbf{x} &= b_m. \end{aligned} \tag{15}$$

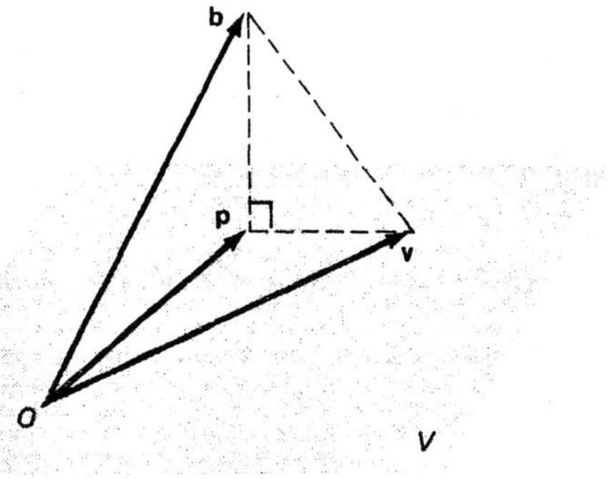

5.7 Illustration for the proof of Theorem 1.

A typical vector $\mathbf{v}$ in $V = \text{Col}(A)$ may be expressed as

$$\mathbf{v} = A\mathbf{x} = (A_1\mathbf{x}, A_2\mathbf{x}, \ldots, A_m\mathbf{x})$$

for some $\mathbf{x}$ in $\mathbf{R}^n$. For this $\mathbf{x}$, the "error" in the ith equation in (15) is $E_i = |A_i\mathbf{x} - b_i|$, so the total "error squared" is

$$E^2 = (E_1)^2 + (E_2)^2 + \cdots + (E_m)^2;$$

that is,

$$|\mathbf{v} - \mathbf{b}|^2 = (A_1\mathbf{x} - b_1)^2 + (A_2\mathbf{x} - b_2)^2 + \cdots + (A_m\mathbf{x} - b_m)^2. \tag{16}$$

Then Theorem 1 means that this "error squared" is *least* when $\mathbf{v} = \mathbf{p}$, and hence $\mathbf{x}$ is the solution $\bar{\mathbf{x}}$ of the normal system $A^TA\bar{\mathbf{x}} = A^T\mathbf{b}$. This fact is the motivation for the following definition.

Definition*: *Least Squares Solution

Let the $m \times n$ matrix A have rank n. Then by the **least squares solution** of the system $A\mathbf{x} = \mathbf{b}$ is meant the solution $\bar{\mathbf{x}}$ of the corresponding normal system $A^TA\bar{\mathbf{x}} = A^T\mathbf{b}$.

If the system $A\mathbf{x} = \mathbf{b}$ is inconsistent, then, of course, its least squares solution is not actually a solution. But if the system *is* consistent, then its least squares solution is its (unique) actual solution (see Problem 26).

EXAMPLE 3 Find the least squares solution of the linear system

$$\begin{aligned} 2x_1 + x_2 - 2x_3 &= 6 \\ x_1 \qquad - x_3 &= 3 \\ x_1 + x_2 \qquad &= 9 \\ x_1 + x_2 - x_3 &= 6. \end{aligned} \tag{17}$$

Solution Though we will not pause to verify it, the 4×3 coefficient matrix A in (17) has rank 3. First we calculate

$$A^TA = \begin{bmatrix} 2 & 1 & 1 & 1 \\ 1 & 0 & 1 & 1 \\ -2 & -1 & 0 & -1 \end{bmatrix} \begin{bmatrix} 2 & 1 & -2 \\ 1 & 0 & -1 \\ 1 & 1 & 0 \\ 1 & 1 & -1 \end{bmatrix} = \begin{bmatrix} 7 & 4 & -6 \\ 4 & 3 & -3 \\ -6 & -3 & 6 \end{bmatrix}$$

and

$$A^T\mathbf{b} = \begin{bmatrix} 2 & 1 & 1 & 1 \\ 1 & 0 & 1 & 1 \\ -2 & -1 & 0 & -1 \end{bmatrix} \begin{bmatrix} 6 \\ 3 \\ 9 \\ 6 \end{bmatrix} = \begin{bmatrix} 30 \\ 21 \\ -21 \end{bmatrix}.$$

Thus the normal system $A^TA\bar{\mathbf{x}} = A^T\mathbf{b}$ is

$$\begin{bmatrix} 7 & 4 & -6 \\ 4 & 3 & -3 \\ -6 & -3 & 6 \end{bmatrix} \begin{bmatrix} \bar{x}_1 \\ \bar{x}_2 \\ \bar{x}_3 \end{bmatrix} = \begin{bmatrix} 30 \\ 21 \\ -21 \end{bmatrix}.$$

Now the augmented coefficient matrix

$$\left[\begin{array}{ccc:c} 7 & 4 & -6 & 30 \\ 4 & 3 & -3 & 21 \\ -6 & -3 & 6 & -21 \end{array}\right]$$

reduces readily to the echelon form

$$\left[\begin{array}{ccc:c} 1 & 1 & 0 & 9 \\ 0 & 1 & 3 & 15 \\ 0 & 0 & 1 & 4 \end{array}\right].$$

By back substitution we find that $\bar{x}_3 = 4$, $\bar{x}_2 = 3$, and $\bar{x}_1 = 6$. Thus the least squares solution of the system in (17) is $\bar{\mathbf{x}} = (6, 3, 4)$. Also

$$\mathbf{p} = A\bar{\mathbf{x}} = \begin{bmatrix} 2 & 1 & -2 \\ 1 & 0 & -1 \\ 1 & 1 & 0 \\ 1 & 1 & -1 \end{bmatrix} \begin{bmatrix} 6 \\ 3 \\ 4 \end{bmatrix} = \begin{bmatrix} 7 \\ 2 \\ 9 \\ 5 \end{bmatrix},$$

so the orthogonal projection of $\mathbf{b} = (6, 3, 9, 6)$ into $V = \text{Col}(A)$ is $\mathbf{p} = (7, 2, 9, 5)$.

Finally we verify the nonsingularity of the $n \times n$ matrix A^TA needed to assure that the normal system $A^TA\bar{\mathbf{x}} = A^T\mathbf{b}$ has a unique solution.

> ***Theorem 2:*** *Nonsingularity of A^TA*
> If the $m \times n$ matrix A has rank n, then the $n \times n$ matrix A^TA is nonsingular.

Proof In order to prove that the square matrix A^TA is nonsingular, it suffices (by Theorem 7 in Section 1.5) to show that the system $A^TA\mathbf{x} = \mathbf{0}$ has only the trivial solution $\mathbf{x} = \mathbf{0}$. So suppose that $A^TA\mathbf{x} = \mathbf{0}$. Then the vector $A\mathbf{x}$ is both in the column space Col(A) of A and in the null space Null(A^T) of A^T. But $\text{Null}(A^T) = \{\text{Col}(A)\}^\perp$ by Theorem 5 in Section 5.1. Thus the vector $A\mathbf{x}$ lies *both* in the subspace Col(A) of $\mathbf{R}^m$ *and* in its orthogonal complement $\{\text{Col}(A)\}^\perp$. Consequently Theorem 4 in Section 5.1 implies that $A\mathbf{x} = \mathbf{0}$; that is, that

$$x_1\mathbf{a}_1 + x_2\mathbf{a}_2 + \cdots + x_n\mathbf{a}_n = \mathbf{0}.$$

But the column vectors $\mathbf{a}_1, \mathbf{a}_2, \ldots, \mathbf{a}_n$ of A are linearly independent because A has rank n. Hence $x_1 = x_2 = \cdots = x_n = 0$, so $\mathbf{x} = \mathbf{0}$ as desired. ■

5.2 PROBLEMS

In Problems 1–6, find the point **p** of the line spanned by **a** that is closest to **b**.

1. $\mathbf{a} = (1, 1, 1)$, $\mathbf{b} = (4, 5, 6)$

2. $\mathbf{a} = (1, 2, 3)$, $\mathbf{b} = (7, 7, 7)$

3. $\mathbf{a} = (1, 0, 1, 1)$, $\mathbf{b} = (4, -3, 5, 3)$

4. $\mathbf{a} = (2, 1, 0, -2)$, $\mathbf{b} = (7, 6, -5, 1)$

5. $\mathbf{a} = (1, -1, 1, 2, -3)$, $\mathbf{b} = (10, 0, 0, 5, -4)$

6. $\mathbf{a} = (4, 5, -5, 3, 1, 2)$, $\mathbf{b} = (15, 24, -12, 2, 0, -3)$

In Problems 7–16, find the least squares solution $\bar{\mathbf{x}}$ of each given linear system $A\mathbf{x} = \mathbf{b}$. Also find the orthogonal projection **p** of **b** into the column space of A.

7. $$\begin{aligned} x_1 + x_2 &= 3 \\ x_1 - x_2 &= 1 \\ 2x_1 - x_2 &= 2 \end{aligned}$$

8. $$\begin{aligned} x_1 + 2x_2 &= 2 \\ x_1 + x_2 &= 2 \\ 3x_1 + x_2 &= 3 \end{aligned}$$

9. $$\begin{aligned} x_1 + x_2 &= 3 \\ x_1 - x_2 &= 0 \\ 3x_1 - x_2 &= 8 \end{aligned}$$

10. $$\begin{aligned} x_1 + x_2 &= 3 \\ 2x_1 - x_2 &= 3 \\ x_1 - 2x_2 &= 1 \end{aligned}$$

11. $$\begin{aligned} x_1 + x_2 &= 3 \\ x_1 - x_2 &= 0 \\ 2x_1 + x_2 &= 6 \\ x_1 + 2x_2 &= 3 \end{aligned}$$

12. $$\begin{aligned} x_1 + 2x_2 &= 4 \\ x_1 - x_2 &= 0 \\ x_1 + x_2 &= 4 \\ 3x_1 + 2x_2 &= 8 \end{aligned}$$

13. $$\begin{aligned} x_1 - 2x_2 + 2x_3 &= 0 \\ 2x_1 \qquad - x_3 &= 3 \\ x_1 - x_2 \qquad &= 0 \\ x_2 - x_3 &= 0 \end{aligned}$$

14. $$\begin{aligned} x_1 - x_2 - x_3 &= 0 \\ x_1 - 2x_2 - 3x_3 &= -2 \\ 3x_1 - 2x_2 + x_3 &= 2 \\ x_2 + 3x_3 &= 4 \end{aligned}$$

15. $$\begin{aligned} x_1 - x_2 \qquad &= 5 \\ x_2 - 2x_3 &= -5 \\ x_1 + 2x_2 - x_3 &= 0 \\ x_1 \qquad - 2x_3 &= 0 \end{aligned}$$

16. $$\begin{aligned} x_1 - x_2 + x_3 &= 5 \\ x_3 &= 0 \\ 3x_1 + x_2 - 2x_3 &= 15 \\ 3x_1 - x_2 + x_3 &= 10 \end{aligned}$$

In Problems 17–22, let V be the solution space of the given homogeneous linear equation or equations. First find a basis for V, and then find the orthogonal projection **p** of **b** onto V.

17. $x_1 - 3x_2 + 2x_3 = 0$; $\mathbf{b} = (14, 14, 28)$

18. $x_1 + 3x_2 - 4x_3 = 0$; $\mathbf{b} = (13, 13, 26)$

19. $x_1 - 2x_2 + 3x_3 - 4x_4 = 0$; $\mathbf{b} = (3, -3, 3, -3)$

20. $x_1 + 2x_2 + 2x_3 + 2x_3 = 0$; $\mathbf{b} = (13, 13, 13, 13)$

21. $x_1 + x_2 + x_3 + x_4 = 0$; $2x_1 + 3x_2 + 3x_3 + x_4 = 0$; $\mathbf{b} = (11, 11, 0, 22)$

22. $x_1 - x_2 + x_3 - x_4 = 0$, $3x_1 - 2x_2 + 4x_3 - x_4 = 0$; $\mathbf{b} = (5, 5, 5, 5)$

23. Show that the least squares solution of the linear system

$$x = b_1, \quad x = b_2, \quad \ldots, \quad x = b_m$$

of m equations in the single variable x is the average

$$\bar{x} = \frac{1}{m}(b_1 + b_2 + \cdots + b_m).$$

24. Let $\mathbf{p}_1$ and $\mathbf{p}_2$ be vectors in the subspace V of $\mathbf{R}^m$ and let the vectors $\mathbf{q}_1$ and $\mathbf{q}_2$ be orthogonal to V. Show that if $\mathbf{p}_1 + \mathbf{q}_1 = \mathbf{p}_2 + \mathbf{q}_2$ then $\mathbf{p}_1 = \mathbf{p}_2$ and $\mathbf{q}_1 = \mathbf{q}_2$. Hence the decomposition $\mathbf{b} = \mathbf{p} + \mathbf{q}$ of a vector **b** into components parallel to and orthogonal to V is unique.

25. Suppose that the $m \times n$ matrix A has rank n and that the vector **b** is orthogonal to the column space of A. Show that the least squares solution of $A\mathbf{x} = \mathbf{b}$ is $\bar{\mathbf{x}} = \mathbf{0}$.

26. Let A be an $m \times n$ matrix of rank n and let **b** be a vector in $\mathbf{R}^m$ such that the system $A\mathbf{x} = \mathbf{b}$ is

consistent. *Prove*: If $\mathbf{x}^*$ is its actual solution and $\bar{\mathbf{x}}$ is its least squares solution, then $\bar{\mathbf{x}} = \mathbf{x}^*$.

27. Suppose that the n column vectors $\mathbf{a}_1, \mathbf{a}_2, \ldots, \mathbf{a}_n$ of the $m \times n$ matrix A are mutually orthogonal. Given $\mathbf{b}$ in $\mathbf{R}^m$, show that the orthogonal projection of $\mathbf{b}$ into the column space of A is

$$\mathbf{p} = \frac{\mathbf{a}_1 \cdot \mathbf{b}}{\mathbf{a}_1 \cdot \mathbf{a}_1}\mathbf{a}_1 + \frac{\mathbf{a}_2 \cdot \mathbf{b}}{\mathbf{a}_2 \cdot \mathbf{a}_2}\mathbf{a}_2 + \cdots + \frac{\mathbf{a}_n \cdot \mathbf{b}}{\mathbf{a}_n \cdot \mathbf{a}_n}\mathbf{a}_n.$$

In Problems 28 and 29, three mutually orthogonal vectors $\mathbf{a}_1$, $\mathbf{a}_2$, and $\mathbf{a}_3$ in $\mathbf{R}^4$ are given. Use the formula in Problem 27 to find the orthogonal projection $\mathbf{p}$ of $\mathbf{b}$ into the subspace of $\mathbf{R}^4$ spanned by $\mathbf{a}_1, \mathbf{a}_2, \mathbf{a}_3$.

28. $\mathbf{a}_1 = (1, 1, 1, 1)$, $\mathbf{a}_2 = (1, -1, 1, -1)$, $\mathbf{a}_3 = (1, 1, -1, -1)$; $\mathbf{b} = (2, 4, 8, -6)$

29. $\mathbf{a}_1 = (1, 0, 1, 0)$, $\mathbf{a}_2 = (0, 1, 0, 1)$, $\mathbf{a}_3 = (1, 0, -1, 0)$; $\mathbf{b} = (7, 3, 5, 9)$

30. Prove the following generalization of Theorem 2: If the $m \times n$ matrix A has rank r, then so does the $n \times n$ matrix A^TA. *Suggestion*: Show that A and A^TA have the same null space. Note that $\mathbf{x} \cdot (A^TA\mathbf{x}) = (A\mathbf{x}) \cdot (A\mathbf{x})$. (Why?)

*5.3

Least Squares Curve Fitting

The problem of fitting curves or equations to empirical data is ubiquitous in the natural, social, engineering, and management sciences. Consequently, *curve fitting* is the most common application of least squares solutions of overdetermined linear systems.

Suppose that the outcome of a number of measurements or observations is a collection of pairs of data points $(x_1, y_1), (x_2, y_2), \ldots, (x_n, y_n)$. For example,

- y_i might be the yield from an acre of corn to which x_i pounds of fertilizer had been applied;
- y_i might be the weekly sales of a product when the price is set at x_i dollars per unit;
- y_i might be the volume of a sample of gas when its temperature is x_i;
- y_i might be the size of a certain population after x_i years.

The goal in curve fitting is to find a functional relationship $y = f(x)$ that represents these data points as well as possible.

Under many circumstances it is plausible (at least as a working hypothesis) to expect the relationship between the x-values and the y-values to be linear:

$$y = a + bx, \tag{1}$$

at least approximately, for some particular choice of the constants a and b. But in practice, the empirically observed points are not likely to lie precisely on a straight line. Even with the best of theories and the most careful measurements, there is unavoidable discrepancy between prediction and reality. Hence a graph of the data points, together with a straight line that appears to fit them well, might look like Figure 5.8.

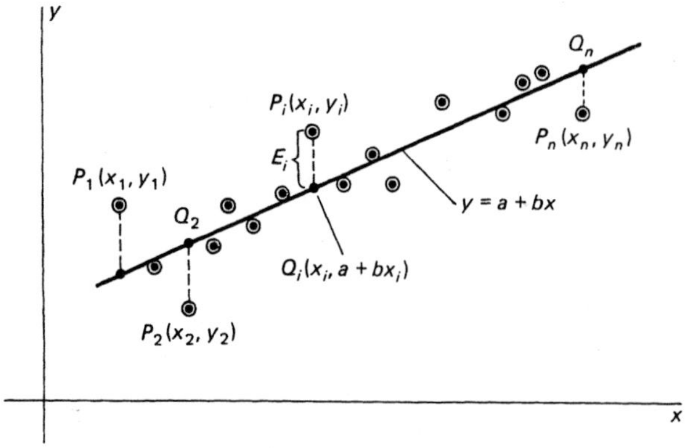

5.8 Fitting the best straight line to the data points (x_i, y_i), $1 \leq i \leq n$.

Our problem then is to choose the constants a and b in (1) so that the straight line $y = a + bx$ best fits the given points (in some sense yet to be specified). If we substitute the given data pairs $(x_1, y_1), (x_2, y_2), \ldots, (x_n, y_n)$ into the equation, we get the (probably inconsistent) linear system

$$\begin{aligned} a + bx_1 &= y_1 \\ a + bx_2 &= y_2 \\ &\vdots \\ a + bx_n &= y_n \end{aligned} \tag{2}$$

of n equations in the two unknowns a and b. This system is of the form

$$A\mathbf{x} = \mathbf{b} \tag{3}$$

with

$$\mathbf{x} = \begin{bmatrix} a \\ b \end{bmatrix}, \qquad A = \begin{bmatrix} 1 & x_1 \\ 1 & x_2 \\ \vdots & \vdots \\ 1 & x_n \end{bmatrix}, \qquad \mathbf{b} = \begin{bmatrix} y_1 \\ y_2 \\ \vdots \\ y_n \end{bmatrix}. \tag{4}$$

The associated normal system

$$A^T A\mathbf{x} = A^T\mathbf{b} \tag{5}$$

of Section 5.2 is then

$$\begin{bmatrix} 1 & 1 & \cdots & 1 \\ x_1 & x_2 & \cdots & x_n \end{bmatrix} \begin{bmatrix} 1 & x_1 \\ 1 & x_2 \\ \vdots & \vdots \\ 1 & x_n \end{bmatrix} \begin{bmatrix} a \\ b \end{bmatrix} = \begin{bmatrix} 1 & 1 & \cdots & 1 \\ x_1 & x_2 & \cdots & x_n \end{bmatrix} \begin{bmatrix} y_1 \\ y_2 \\ \vdots \\ y_n \end{bmatrix}. \tag{6}$$

Upon performing the indicated matrix multiplications, we get the **normal equations**

$$\begin{aligned} na + (\textstyle\sum x_i)b &= \textstyle\sum y_i \\ (\textstyle\sum x_i)a + (\textstyle\sum x_i^2)b &= \textstyle\sum x_i y_i \end{aligned} \tag{7}$$

(each summation from $i = 1$ to $i = n$) for the problem of fitting the line $y = a + bx$ to the n given data points.

The solution $\mathbf{x} = (a, b)$ of the normal equations in (7) is the least squares solution of the original linear system in (2). The resulting error in the ith equation is the vertical distance $E_i = y_i - (a + bx_i)$ indicated in Figure 5.8; this is the discrepancy between the observed value y_i and the value $a + bx_i$ predicted by the equation $y = a + bx$ for $x = x_i$. According to Theorem 1 in Section 5.2, the least squares solution $\mathbf{x} = (a, b)$ provides the straight line $y = a + bx$ that minimizes the sum

$$\sum_{i=1}^{n} (E_i)^2 = \sum_{i=1}^{n} [y_i - (a + bx_i)]^2 \tag{8}$$

of the squares of these discrepancies. This is the sense in which the *least squares straight line* best fits the given data.

In practice there is no need to memorize or use directly the normal equations in (7). Instead we recommend that the system $A\mathbf{x} = \mathbf{b}$ described in Equations (2)–(4) be set up explicitly and the normal system $A^T A\mathbf{x} = A^T\mathbf{b}$ then be solved for $\mathbf{x} = (a, b)$.

Algorithm: *The Least Squares Straight Line*

To find the straight line $y = a + bx$ that best fits the data points (x_1, y_1), $(x_2, y_2), \ldots, (x_n, y_n)$, find the least squares solution $\mathbf{x} = (a, b)$ of the system

$$\begin{bmatrix} 1 & x_1 \\ 1 & x_2 \\ \vdots & \vdots \\ 1 & x_n \end{bmatrix} \begin{bmatrix} a \\ b \end{bmatrix} = \begin{bmatrix} y_1 \\ y_2 \\ \vdots \\ y_n \end{bmatrix}. \tag{9}$$

EXAMPLE 1 Find the straight line that best fits these data.

x	−1	1	2	4
y	2	4	6	12

Solution With these data Equation (9) is

$$\begin{bmatrix} 1 & -1 \\ 1 & 1 \\ 1 & 2 \\ 1 & 4 \end{bmatrix} \begin{bmatrix} a \\ b \end{bmatrix} = \begin{bmatrix} 2 \\ 4 \\ 6 \\ 12 \end{bmatrix}.$$

Multiplication by A^T yields the normal system

$$\begin{bmatrix} 1 & 1 & 1 & 1 \\ -1 & 1 & 2 & 4 \end{bmatrix} \begin{bmatrix} 1 & -1 \\ 1 & 1 \\ 1 & 2 \\ 1 & 4 \end{bmatrix} \begin{bmatrix} a \\ b \end{bmatrix} = \begin{bmatrix} 1 & 1 & 1 & 1 \\ -1 & 1 & 2 & 4 \end{bmatrix} \begin{bmatrix} 2 \\ 4 \\ 6 \\ 12 \end{bmatrix},$$

which we simplify to

$$\begin{bmatrix} 4 & 6 \\ 6 & 22 \end{bmatrix} \begin{bmatrix} a \\ b \end{bmatrix} = \begin{bmatrix} 24 \\ 62 \end{bmatrix}.$$

We now find it easy to solve for $a = 3$ and $b = 2$. Thus the least squares straight line has equation

$$y = 3 + 2x.$$

Note that this linear equation "predicts" the values $y(-1) = 1$, $y(1) = 5$, $y(2) = 7$, and $y(4) = 11$, so in this case each discrepancy from the given data is $+1$ or -1.

EXAMPLE 2 As a step toward determining the selling price that would maximize its profits, a perfume company wished to express its weekly sales y (in thousands of bottles) as a linear function of the price x (in dollars per bottle). In order to do this, it test-sold the perfume in four similar cities, with the following results.

	City 1	*City 2*	*City 3*	*City 4*
x	6.25	6.75	8.00	8.75
y	6.03	5.62	4.78	4.34

With these data Equation (9) is

$$\begin{bmatrix} 1 & 6.25 \\ 1 & 6.75 \\ 1 & 8.00 \\ 1 & 8.75 \end{bmatrix} \begin{bmatrix} a \\ b \end{bmatrix} = \begin{bmatrix} 6.03 \\ 5.62 \\ 4.78 \\ 4.34 \end{bmatrix}.$$

We multiply each side on the left by A^T and retain two decimal places to obtain the normal system

$$\begin{bmatrix} 4.00 & 29.75 \\ 29.75 & 225.19 \end{bmatrix} \begin{bmatrix} a \\ b \end{bmatrix} = \begin{bmatrix} 20.77 \\ 151.84 \end{bmatrix},$$

which has the solution $a = 10.20$, $b = -0.67$. Thus the least squares straight line has equation

$$y = 10.20 - (0.67)x.$$

This result indicates that each increase of \$1 per bottle in the selling price will decrease the weekly sales by about 670 bottles.

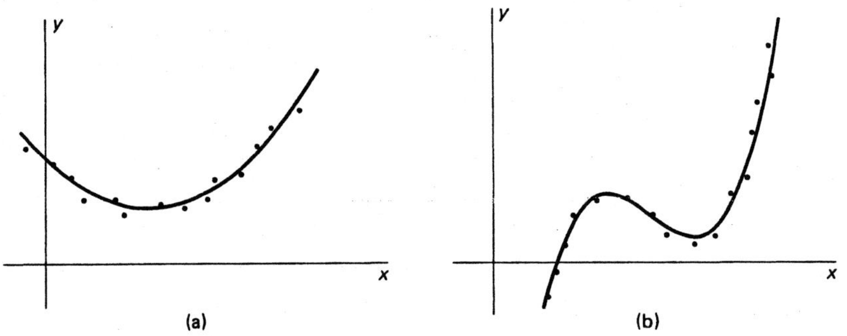

5.9 Nonlinear data plots.

Sometimes it is clear that we should *not* seek a straight line fit. For example, the appearance of the data points plotted in Figure 5.9(a) suggests a quadratic relationship,

$$y = a + bx + cx^2,$$

while the appearance of the data plot in Figure 5.9(b) suggests a cubic relationship,

$$y = a + bx + cx^2 + dx^3.$$

So suppose that we wish to find the polynomial

$$y = a_0 + a_1x + a_2x^2 + \cdots + a_kx^k \tag{10}$$

of degree k that best fits the data points $(x_1, y_1), (x_2, y_2), \ldots, (x_n, y_n)$. When we substitute each of these data points in (1) we get the linear system

$$\begin{bmatrix} 1 & x_1 & x_1^2 & \cdots & x_1^k \\ 1 & x_2 & x_2^2 & \cdots & x_2^k \\ \vdots & \vdots & \vdots & \ddots & \vdots \\ 1 & x_n & x_n^2 & \cdots & x_n^k \end{bmatrix} \begin{bmatrix} a_0 \\ a_1 \\ \vdots \\ a_k \end{bmatrix} = \begin{bmatrix} y_1 \\ y_2 \\ \vdots \\ y_n \end{bmatrix} \tag{11}$$

with the coefficients $a_0, a_1, \ldots, a_k$ in (10) as unknowns. If some $k + 1$ of the values $x_1, x_2, \ldots, x_n$ are distinct, then it follows from Problem 37 in Section 2.2 and from Theorem 3 in Section 4.2 that the column vectors of the coefficient matrix A in (11) are linearly independent. Then Theorem 2 in Section 5.2 implies that the normal system $A^T A\mathbf{x} = A^T\mathbf{b}$ has a unique solution $\mathbf{x} = (a_0, a_1, \ldots, a_k)$. With these coefficients in (10) we get the *least squares polynomial of degree k* that best fits the given data points.

EXAMPLE 3 Find the quadratic polynomial

$$y = a + bx + cx^2$$

that best fits these data.

x	−2	−1	1	2
y	6	0	8	17

Solution Here $k = 2$ and $n = 4$. With the given data and (a, b, c) in place of (a_0, a_1, a_2), Equation (11) is

$$\begin{bmatrix} 1 & -2 & 4 \\ 1 & -1 & 1 \\ 1 & 1 & 1 \\ 1 & 2 & 4 \end{bmatrix} \begin{bmatrix} a \\ b \\ c \end{bmatrix} = \begin{bmatrix} 6 \\ 0 \\ 8 \\ 17 \end{bmatrix}.$$

Multiplication of both sides on the left by A^T yields the normal system

$$\begin{bmatrix} 4 & 0 & 10 \\ 0 & 10 & 0 \\ 10 & 0 & 34 \end{bmatrix} \begin{bmatrix} a \\ b \\ c \end{bmatrix} = \begin{bmatrix} 31 \\ 30 \\ 100 \end{bmatrix},$$

which we solve readily for $a = \frac{3}{2}$, $b = 3$, and $c = \frac{5}{2}$. Thus our least squares quadratic polynomial is

$$\begin{aligned} y &= \frac{3}{2} + 3x + \frac{5}{2}x^2 \\ &= \frac{1}{2}(3 + 6x + 5x^2). \end{aligned}$$

This polynomial predicts the values $y(-2) = 5.5$, $y(-1) = 1$, $y(1) = 7$, and $y(2) = 17.5$. Thus the discrepancies between the given and predicted values are 0.5, -1, 1, and -0.5, respectively.

Our first three examples deal with fitting a curve $y = f(x)$ to given data points in the plane. Suppose now that we are given data points (x_1, y_1, z_1), $(x_1, y_2, z_2), \ldots, (x_n, y_n, z_n)$ in *space*, and we wish to find the plane with equation

$$z = a + bx + cy \tag{12}$$

that best fits these points. Substitution of the given data in (12) yields the linear system

$$\begin{bmatrix} 1 & x_1 & y_1 \\ 1 & x_2 & y_2 \\ \vdots & \vdots & \vdots \\ 1 & x_n & y_n \end{bmatrix} \begin{bmatrix} a \\ b \\ c \end{bmatrix} = \begin{bmatrix} z_1 \\ z_2 \\ \vdots \\ z_n \end{bmatrix} \tag{13}$$

in the coefficients a, b, c. This is a system of the form $A\mathbf{x} = \mathbf{b}$ with $\mathbf{x} = (a, b, c)$. With the solution $\mathbf{x} = (a, b, c)$ of the corresponding normal system $A^TA\mathbf{x} = A^T\mathbf{b}$ we get the *least squares plane* that best fits the given data, in the sense that the sum

$$\sum_{i=1}^{n} [z_i - (a + bx_i + cy_i)]^2$$

of the squares of the (vertical) distances from the data points to this plane is minimal. Some examples of least squares planes are included in the problems for this section.

Although the polynomial in (10) is a nonlinear function of x, the problem of finding a least squares polynomial is a linear problem because the coefficients a_0, $a_1, \ldots, a_k$ that must be found appear linearly. But the methods of this section may also be adapted to certain curve-fitting problems in which the "undetermined parameters" appear nonlinearly. For instance, consider a population that numbers $P(t)$ individuals at time t. Under the common assumption of *natural population growth*, this population will be described by an exponential function:

$$P(t) = P_0 e^{kt}. \tag{14}$$

If we are given population data $(t_1, P_1), (t_2, P_2), \ldots, (t_n, P_n)$ specifying the population at n distinct times, then we would like to determine the values of the *initial population* P_0 and the *growth rate constant* k so that the function $P = P_0 e^{kt}$ best fits the given data. If we take the (natural) logarithm of each side in (15), we get the equation

$$\log P = \log P_0 + kt. \tag{15}$$

Note that $\log P_0$ and k appear *linearly* in this equation. When we substitute the n given data pairs in (15), we obtain the linear system

$$\begin{bmatrix} 1 & t_1 \\ 1 & t_2 \\ \vdots & \vdots \\ 1 & t_n \end{bmatrix} \begin{bmatrix} \log P_0 \\ k \end{bmatrix} = \begin{bmatrix} \log P_1 \\ \log P_2 \\ \vdots \\ \log P_n \end{bmatrix} \tag{16}$$

in the unknowns $\log P_0$ and k. This system is of the form $A\mathbf{x} = \mathbf{b}$ with $\mathbf{x} = (\log P_0, k)$. We find the best values of P_0 and k by solving the corresponding normal system $A^T A\mathbf{x} = A^T\mathbf{b}$.

EXAMPLE 4 The U.S. Census population data (in millions) for the years 1930 through 1980 are shown next.

Year	1930	1940	1950	1960	1970	1980
Population	123.20	131.67	150.70	179.32	203.21	226.51

If we take $t = 0$ in 1930, then we have the six data pairs (0, 123.20), (10, 131.67), (20, 150.70), (30, 179.32), (40, 203.21), and (50, 226.51). Figure 5.10 shows these points plotted in the tP-plane. Figure 5.11 shows a plot on semilog graph paper ($\log P$ is plotted against t). The fact that the points in Figure 5.11 appear to lie approximately on a straight line indicates that the data may fit a natural exponential model, as in (14).

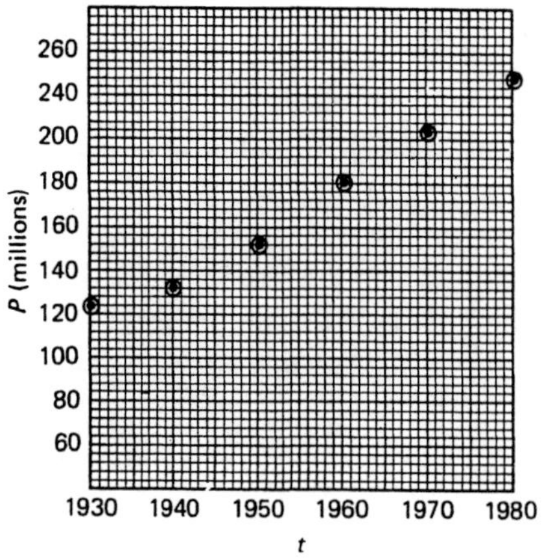

5.10 A plot of P against t

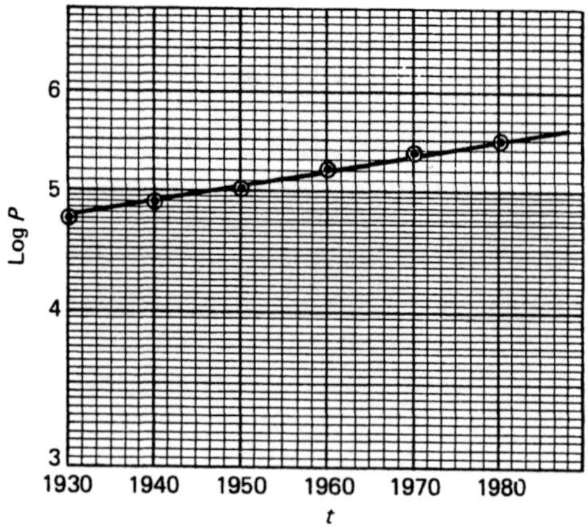

5.11 A plot of log P against t

When we substitute the given population data in (16) we get the linear system

$$\begin{bmatrix} 1 & 0 \\ 1 & 10 \\ 1 & 20 \\ 1 & 30 \\ 1 & 40 \\ 1 & 50 \end{bmatrix} \begin{bmatrix} \log P_0 \\ k \end{bmatrix} = \begin{bmatrix} 4.81 \\ 4.88 \\ 5.02 \\ 5.19 \\ 5.31 \\ 5.42 \end{bmatrix}$$

in $\log P_0$ and k. (Though we show only two decimal places, we retain ten significant figures in the intermediate computations.) After we multiply each side on the left by A^T, we obtain the corresponding normal system

$$\begin{bmatrix} 6 & 150 \\ 150 & 5500 \end{bmatrix} \begin{bmatrix} \log P_0 \\ k \end{bmatrix} = \begin{bmatrix} 30.64 \\ 788.49 \end{bmatrix},$$

whose solution is $\log P_0 = 4.7830$, $k = 0.0129$. Then $P_0 = \exp(4.7830) \approx 119.47$, so our exponential fit to the given population data is

$$P(t) = (119.47)e^{(0.0129)t}.$$

The value $k = 0.0129$ corresponds to an average annual growth rate of 1.29%. The following table compares the actual and predicted populations:

Year	1930	1940	1950	1960	1970	1980	1990
Predicted	119.47	135.92	154.63	175.93	200.15	227.71	259.06
Actual	123.20	131.67	150.70	179.32	203.21	226.51	?
Percent error	3.0	−3.2	−2.6	1.8	1.4	−0.6	?

The agreement is reasonable but not spectacular, due to changes in birth and death rates that have occurred during these decades. In particular, because of lower birth rates during the 1970s and 1980s, the 1990 census will probably show a population somewhat smaller than the predicted 259 million.

5.3 PROBLEMS

In each of Problems 1–10, find the straight line $y = a + bx$ that best fits the given data.

1.

x	1	2	3
y	2	2	4

2.

x	1	2	3
y	2	3	5

3.

x	−1	1	3
y	2	5	10

4.

x	0	2	6
y	8	4	0

5.

x	0	1	2	3
y	2	4	6	9

6.

x	0	1	2	3
y	3	6	9	15

7.

x	−1	1	3	5
y	2	4	8	14

8.

x	−1	1	3	5
y	12	8	2	−6

9.

x	2	3	4	6
y	2	5	9	15

10.

x	2	3	4	6
y	0	−5	−15	−25

In each of Problems 11–14, find the function of the form $y = a + bx^2$ that best fits the given data.

11.

x	−1	0	1	2
y	2	6	2	−4

12.

x	−1	0	1	2
y	8	2	8	16

13.

x	−1	1	3
y	1	1	12

14.

x	1	2	3
y	4	6	14

In each of Problems 15–20, find the quadratic function $y = a + bx + cx^2$ that best fits the given data.

15.

x	−2	−1	1	2
y	0	0	6	12

16.

x	-2	-1	1	2
y	2	0	6	16

17.

x	-2	-1	1	2
y	3	-1	3	16

18.

x	0	1	2	3
y	2	0	4	12

19.

x	0	1	2	3
y	2	4	8	16

20.

x	0	1	2	3
y	4	8	0	-12

In each of Problems 21–24, find the plane with equation of the form $z = a + bx + cy$ that best fits the given data.

21.

x	0	1	2	0
y	1	0	1	2
z	2	3	4	1

22.

x	1	-1	2	0
y	-1	1	0	2
z	4	2	3	1

23.

x	1	-1	1	0
y	-1	1	0	1
z	5	2	4	3

24.

x	0	1	0	2
y	0	0	1	2
z	0	2	2	5

In the next two problems, find the best fit of the form $y = ae^{kx}$.

25.

x	-1	1	2	3
y	0.1	2.3	10	45

26.

x	0	1	2	3
y	50	7	1	0.1

In Problems 27 and 28, find the best fit of the form $y = ax^k$. Note that

$$\log y = \log a + k \log x$$

is linear in $\log a$ and k.

27.

x	5	10	15	20
y	5.7	7.5	8.9	9.9

28.

x	1	2	3	4
y	10	2.5	1.1	0.6

29. In order to find a linear relation $y = a + bx$ between the price x per box (in cents) and the weekly sales y (in thousands of cases), a soap manufacturer test-sold soap in three cities at different prices, with the following results.

x	79	89	99
y	110	95	85

What weekly sales should be expected if the price is set at 69¢ per box?

30. The per capita consumption of cigarettes in 1930 and the lung cancer death rate (deaths per million males) for 1950 in the Scandinavian countries were as follows.

Country	Cigarette consumption	Deaths from lung cancer
Denmark	350	165
Finland	1100	350
Norway	250	95
Sweden	300	120

Fit these data to a straight line to estimate the 1950 male lung cancer death rate for Australia, in which the 1930 per capita cigarette consumption was 470. (The actual death rate was 170.) What lung cancer death rate might you expect in a country in which no cigarettes at all are smoked?

31. The total cost y (in dollars) for printing x copies of a certain booklet is known for three lot sizes; here are the details.

x	700	2700	3700
y	2700	4200	5000

Express the total cost as the sum of a fixed cost and an additional cost per booklet printed. What, then, should 2000 copies cost?

32. The systolic blood pressure p (in millimeters of mercury) of a healthy child is essentially a linear function $p = a + b \log w$ of the natural logarithm of his or her weight w in pounds. The numbers m and b are constants. Determine them from the following experimental data.

w	41	67	78	93	125
p	89	100	103	107	110

What should the systolic blood pressure of a healthy 100-pound child be?

33. Show that the normal equations for fitting a parabola with equation $y = a + bx + cx^2$ to given data points (x_i, y_i) are

$$\begin{aligned} na + (\textstyle\sum x_i)b + (\sum x_i^2)c &= \textstyle\sum y_i \\ (\textstyle\sum x_i)a + (\sum x_i^2)b + (\sum x_i^3)c &= \textstyle\sum x_i y_i \\ (\textstyle\sum x_i^2)a + (\sum x_i^3)b + (\sum x_i^4)c &= \textstyle\sum x_i^2 y_i. \end{aligned}$$

34. Show that the normal equations for fitting a plane with equation $z = a + bx + cy$ to given data points (x_i, y_i, z_i) are

$$\begin{aligned} na + (\textstyle\sum x_i)b + (\sum y_i)c &= \textstyle\sum z_i \\ (\textstyle\sum x_i)a + (\sum x_i^2)b + (\sum x_i y_i)c &= \textstyle\sum x_i z_i \\ (\textstyle\sum y_i)a + (\sum x_i y_i)b + (\sum y_i^2)c &= \textstyle\sum y_i z_i. \end{aligned}$$

5.4

Orthogonal Bases and the Gram-Schmidt Algorithm

In Section 5.2 we discussed the problem of finding the orthogonal projection $\mathbf{p}$ of the vector $\mathbf{b}$ into the subspace V of $\mathbf{R}^m$. If the vectors $\mathbf{v}_1, \mathbf{v}_2, \ldots, \mathbf{v}_n$ form a basis for V, and the $m \times n$ matrix A has these basis vectors as its column vectors, then the orthogonal projection $\mathbf{p}$ is given by

$$\mathbf{p} = A\mathbf{x} \tag{1}$$

where $\mathbf{x}$ is the (unique) solution of the normal system

$$A^T A\mathbf{x} = A^T\mathbf{b}. \tag{2}$$

The formula for $\mathbf{p}$ takes an especially simple and attractive form when the basis vectors $\mathbf{v}_1, \mathbf{v}_2, \ldots, \mathbf{v}_n$ are mutually orthogonal.

> ***Definition**: Orthogonal Basis*
>
> An **orthogonal basis** for the subspace V of $\mathbf{R}^m$ is a basis consisting of vectors $\mathbf{v}_1, \mathbf{v}_2, \ldots, \mathbf{v}_n$ that are mutually orthogonal, so that $\mathbf{v}_i \cdot \mathbf{v}_j = 0$ if $i \neq j$. If in addition these basis vectors are unit vectors, so that $\mathbf{v}_i \cdot \mathbf{v}_i = 1$ for $i = 1, 2, \ldots, n$, then the orthogonal basis is called an **orthonormal basis**.

EXAMPLE 1 The vectors

$$\mathbf{v}_1 = (1, 1, 0), \qquad \mathbf{v}_2 = (1, -1, 2), \qquad \mathbf{v}_3 = (-1, 1, 1)$$

form an orthogonal basis for $\mathbf{R}^3$. We can "normalize" this orthogonal basis by dividing each basis vector by its length: If

$$\mathbf{w}_i = \frac{\mathbf{v}_i}{|\mathbf{v}_i|} \qquad (i = 1, 2, 3),$$

then the vectors

$$\mathbf{w}_1 = \left(\frac{1}{\sqrt{2}}, \frac{1}{\sqrt{2}}, 0\right), \mathbf{w}_2 = \left(\frac{1}{\sqrt{6}}, -\frac{1}{\sqrt{6}}, \frac{2}{\sqrt{6}}\right), \mathbf{w}_3 = \left(-\frac{1}{\sqrt{3}}, \frac{1}{\sqrt{3}}, \frac{1}{\sqrt{3}}\right)$$

form an orthonormal basis for $\mathbf{R}^3$.

Now suppose that the column vectors $\mathbf{v}_1, \mathbf{v}_2, \ldots, \mathbf{v}_n$ of the $m \times n$ matrix A form an *orthogonal* basis for the subspace V of $\mathbf{R}^m$. Then

$$A^T A = [\mathbf{v}_i \cdot \mathbf{v}_j] = \begin{bmatrix} \mathbf{v}_1 \cdot \mathbf{v}_1 & 0 & \cdots & 0 \\ 0 & \mathbf{v}_2 \cdot \mathbf{v}_2 & \cdots & 0 \\ \vdots & \vdots & \ddots & \vdots \\ 0 & 0 & \cdots & \mathbf{v}_n \cdot \mathbf{v}_n \end{bmatrix}. \tag{3}$$

Thus the coefficient matrix in the normal system in (2) is a diagonal matrix, so the normal equations simplify to

$$\begin{aligned} (\mathbf{v}_1 \cdot \mathbf{v}_1)x_1 &= \mathbf{v}_1 \cdot \mathbf{b} \\ (\mathbf{v}_2 \cdot \mathbf{v}_2)x_2 &= \mathbf{v}_2 \cdot \mathbf{b} \\ &\vdots \\ (\mathbf{v}_n \cdot \mathbf{v}_n)x_n &= \mathbf{v}_n \cdot \mathbf{b} \end{aligned} \tag{4}$$

Consequently the solution $\mathbf{x} = (x_1, x_2, \ldots, x_n)$ of the normal system $A^T A\mathbf{x} = A^T\mathbf{b}$ is given by

$$x_i = \frac{\mathbf{v}_i \cdot \mathbf{b}}{\mathbf{v}_i \cdot \mathbf{v}_i} \qquad (i = 1, 2, \ldots, n). \tag{5}$$

When we substitute this solution in Equation (1),

$$\mathbf{p} = A\mathbf{x} = x_1\mathbf{v}_1 + x_2\mathbf{v}_2 + \cdots + x_n\mathbf{v}_n,$$

we get the following result.

Theorem 1: *Projection into an Orthogonal Basis*

Suppose that the vectors $\mathbf{v}_1, \mathbf{v}_2, \ldots, \mathbf{v}_n$ form an orthogonal basis for the subspace V of $\mathbf{R}^n$. Then the orthogonal projection $\mathbf{p}$ of the vector $\mathbf{b}$ into V is given by

$$\mathbf{p} = \frac{\mathbf{v}_1 \cdot \mathbf{b}}{\mathbf{v}_1 \cdot \mathbf{v}_1}\mathbf{v}_1 + \frac{\mathbf{v}_2 \cdot \mathbf{b}}{\mathbf{v}_2 \cdot \mathbf{v}_2}\mathbf{v}_2 + \cdots + \frac{\mathbf{v}_n \cdot \mathbf{b}}{\mathbf{v}_n \cdot \mathbf{v}_n}\mathbf{v}_n. \tag{6}$$

Note that if the basis $\mathbf{v}_1, \mathbf{v}_2, \ldots, \mathbf{v}_n$ is orthonormal rather than merely orthogonal, then the formula for the orthogonal projection $\mathbf{p}$ simplifies still further:

$$\mathbf{p} = (\mathbf{v}_1 \cdot \mathbf{b})\mathbf{v}_1 + (\mathbf{v}_2 \cdot \mathbf{b})\mathbf{v}_2 + \cdots + (\mathbf{v}_n \cdot \mathbf{b})\mathbf{v}_n.$$

If $n = 1$ and $\mathbf{v} = \mathbf{v}_1$, then the formula in (6) reduces to the formula

$$\mathbf{p} = \frac{\mathbf{v} \cdot \mathbf{b}}{\mathbf{v} \cdot \mathbf{v}} \mathbf{v} \tag{7}$$

for the **component of b parallel to v**. The **component of b orthogonal to v** is then

$$\mathbf{q} = \mathbf{b} - \mathbf{p} = \mathbf{b} - \frac{\mathbf{v} \cdot \mathbf{b}}{\mathbf{v} \cdot \mathbf{v}} \mathbf{v}. \tag{8}$$

Theorem 1 may also be stated without symbolism: *The orthogonal projection* **p** *of the vector* **b** *into the subspace V is the sum of the components of* **b** *parallel to the orthogonal basis vectors* $\mathbf{v}_1, \mathbf{v}_2, \ldots, \mathbf{v}_n$ *for V.*

EXAMPLE 2 The vectors

$$\mathbf{v}_1 = (1, 1, 0, 1), \qquad \mathbf{v}_2 = (1, -2, 3, 1), \qquad \mathbf{v}_3 = (-4, 3, 3, 1)$$

are mutually orthogonal, and hence form an orthogonal basis for a 3-dimensional subspace V of $\mathbf{R}^4$. To find the orthogonal projection $\mathbf{p}$ of $\mathbf{b} = (0, 7, 0, 7)$ into V we use the formula in (6) and get

$$\begin{aligned} \mathbf{p} &= \frac{\mathbf{v}_1 \cdot \mathbf{b}}{\mathbf{v}_1 \cdot \mathbf{v}_1} \mathbf{v}_1 + \frac{\mathbf{v}_2 \cdot \mathbf{b}}{\mathbf{v}_2 \cdot \mathbf{v}_2} \mathbf{v}_2 + \frac{\mathbf{v}_3 \cdot \mathbf{b}}{\mathbf{v}_3 \cdot \mathbf{v}_3} \mathbf{v}_3 \\ &= \frac{14}{3}(1, 1, 0, 1) + \frac{-7}{15}(1, -2, 3, 1) + \frac{28}{35}(-4, 3, 3, 1); \end{aligned}$$

therefore

$$\mathbf{p} = (1, 8, 1, 5).$$

The component of the vector **b** orthogonal to the subspace V is

$$\mathbf{q} = \mathbf{b} - \mathbf{p} = (0, 7, 0, 7) - (1, 8, 1, 5) = (-1, -1, -1, 2).$$

Example 2 illustrates how useful orthogonal bases can be for computational purposes. There is a standard process that is used to transform a given *linearly independent* set of vectors $\mathbf{v}_1, \mathbf{v}_2, \ldots, \mathbf{v}_n$ in $\mathbf{R}^m$ into a *mutually orthogonal* set of vectors $\mathbf{u}_1, \mathbf{u}_2, \ldots, \mathbf{u}_n$ that span the same subspace of $\mathbf{R}^m$. We begin with

$$\mathbf{u}_1 = \mathbf{v}_1. \tag{9}$$

To get the second vector $\mathbf{u}_2$, we subtract from $\mathbf{v}_2$ its component parallel to $\mathbf{u}_1$. That is,

$$\mathbf{u}_2 = \mathbf{v}_2 - \frac{\mathbf{u}_1 \cdot \mathbf{v}_2}{\mathbf{u}_1 \cdot \mathbf{u}_1} \mathbf{u}_1 \tag{10}$$

is the component of $\mathbf{v}_2$ orthogonal to $\mathbf{u}_1$. At this point it is clear that $\mathbf{u}_1$ and $\mathbf{u}_2$ form an orthogonal basis for the 2-dimensional subspace V_2 spanned by $\mathbf{v}_1$ and $\mathbf{v}_2$. To get the third vector $\mathbf{u}_3$, we subtract from $\mathbf{v}_3$ its components parallel to $\mathbf{u}_1$ and $\mathbf{u}_2$. Thus

$$\mathbf{u}_3 = \mathbf{v}_3 - \frac{\mathbf{u}_1 \cdot \mathbf{v}_3}{\mathbf{u}_1 \cdot \mathbf{u}_1}\mathbf{u}_1 - \frac{\mathbf{u}_2 \cdot \mathbf{v}_3}{\mathbf{u}_2 \cdot \mathbf{u}_2}\mathbf{u}_2 \tag{11}$$

is the component of $\mathbf{v}_3$ orthogonal to the subspace V_2 spanned by $\mathbf{u}_1$ and $\mathbf{u}_2$. Having defined $\mathbf{u}_1, \mathbf{u}_2, \ldots, \mathbf{u}_k$ in this manner, we take $\mathbf{u}_{k+1}$ to be the component of $\mathbf{v}_{k+1}$ orthogonal to the subspace V_k spanned by $\mathbf{u}_1, \mathbf{u}_2, \ldots, \mathbf{u}_k$. This process for constructing the mutually orthogonal vectors $\mathbf{u}_1, \mathbf{u}_2, \ldots, \mathbf{u}_n$ is summarized in the following algorithm.

Algorithm: *Gram-Schmidt Orthogonalization*

To replace the linearly independent vectors $\mathbf{v}_1, \mathbf{v}_2, \ldots, \mathbf{v}_n$ one by one with mutually orthogonal vectors $\mathbf{u}_1, \mathbf{u}_2, \ldots, \mathbf{u}_n$ that span the same subspace of $\mathbf{R}^m$, begin with

$$\mathbf{u}_1 = \mathbf{v}_1. \tag{12}$$

For $k = 1, 2, \ldots, n-1$ in turn, take

$$\begin{aligned}\mathbf{u}_{k+1} = \mathbf{v}_{k+1} &- \frac{\mathbf{u}_1 \cdot \mathbf{v}_{k+1}}{\mathbf{u}_1 \cdot \mathbf{u}_1}\mathbf{u}_1 \\ &- \frac{\mathbf{u}_2 \cdot \mathbf{v}_{k+1}}{\mathbf{u}_2 \cdot \mathbf{u}_2}\mathbf{u}_2 - \cdots - \frac{\mathbf{u}_k \cdot \mathbf{v}_{k+1}}{\mathbf{u}_k \cdot \mathbf{u}_k}\mathbf{u}_k. \end{aligned} \tag{13}$$

The formula in (13) means that we get $\mathbf{u}_{k+1}$ from $\mathbf{v}_{k+1}$ by subtracting from $\mathbf{v}_{k+1}$ its components parallel to the mutually orthogonal vectors $\mathbf{u}_1, \mathbf{u}_2, \ldots, \mathbf{u}_k$ previously constructed, and hence $\mathbf{u}_{k+1}$ is orthogonal to each of the first k vectors. If we assume inductively that the vectors $\mathbf{u}_1, \mathbf{u}_2, \ldots, \mathbf{u}_k$ span the same subspace as the original k vectors $\mathbf{v}_1, \mathbf{v}_2, \ldots, \mathbf{v}_k$, then it also follows from (13) that the vectors $\mathbf{u}_1, \mathbf{u}_2, \ldots, \mathbf{u}_{k+1}$ span the same subspace as the vectors $\mathbf{v}_1, \mathbf{v}_2, \ldots, \mathbf{v}_{k+1}$. If we begin with a basis $\mathbf{v}_1, \mathbf{v}_2, \ldots, \mathbf{v}_n$ for the subspace V of $\mathbf{R}^n$, the final result of carrying out the Gram-Schmidt algorithm is therefore an *orthogonal* basis $\mathbf{u}_1, \mathbf{u}_2, \ldots, \mathbf{u}_n$ for V.

Theorem 2: *Existence of Orthogonal Bases*

Every nonzero subspace of $\mathbf{R}^m$ has an orthogonal basis.

As a final step, one can convert the orthogonal basis to an *orthonormal* basis by dividing each of the orthogonal basis vectors $\mathbf{u}_1, \mathbf{u}_2, \ldots, \mathbf{u}_n$ by its length.

In numerical applications of the Gram-Schmidt algorithm, the calculations involved often can be simplified by multiplying each vector $\mathbf{u}_k$ (as it is found) by an appropriate scalar factor to eliminate unwanted fractions. We do this in the two examples that follow.

EXAMPLE 3 To apply the Gram-Schmidt algorithm beginning with the basis

$$\mathbf{v}_1 = (3, 1, 1), \qquad \mathbf{v}_2 = (1, 3, 1), \qquad \mathbf{v}_3 = (1, 1, 3)$$

for $\mathbf{R}^3$, we first take

$$\mathbf{u}_1 = \mathbf{v}_1 = (3, 1, 1).$$

Then

$$\mathbf{u}_2 = \mathbf{v}_2 - \frac{\mathbf{u}_1 \cdot \mathbf{v}_2}{\mathbf{u}_1 \cdot \mathbf{u}_1}\mathbf{u}_1 = (1, 3, 1) - \frac{7}{11}(3, 1, 1)$$

$$= \left(-\frac{10}{11}, \frac{26}{11}, \frac{4}{11}\right) = \frac{2}{11}(-5, 13, 2).$$

We delete the scalar factor $\frac{2}{11}$ (or multiply by $\frac{11}{2}$) and instead use $\mathbf{u}_2 = (-5, 13, 2)$. Next,

$$\mathbf{u}_3 = \mathbf{v}_3 - \frac{\mathbf{u}_1 \cdot \mathbf{v}_3}{\mathbf{u}_1 \cdot \mathbf{u}_1}\mathbf{u}_1 - \frac{\mathbf{u}_2 \cdot \mathbf{v}_3}{\mathbf{u}_2 \cdot \mathbf{u}_2}\mathbf{u}_2$$

$$= (1, 1, 3) - \frac{7}{11}(3, 1, 1) - \frac{14}{198}(-5, 13, 2)$$

$$= \left(-\frac{55}{99}, -\frac{55}{99}, \frac{220}{99}\right) = -\frac{5}{9}(1, 1, -4).$$

We delete the scalar factor $-\frac{5}{9}$ and thereby choose $\mathbf{u}_3 = (1, 1, -4)$. Thus our final result is the orthogonal basis

$$\mathbf{u}_1 = (3, 1, 1), \qquad \mathbf{u}_2 = (-5, 13, 2), \qquad \mathbf{u}_3 = (1, 1, -4)$$

for $\mathbf{R}^3$.

EXAMPLE 4 Find an orthogonal basis for the subspace V of $\mathbf{R}^4$ that has basis vectors

$$\mathbf{v}_1 = (2, 1, 2, 1), \qquad \mathbf{v}_2 = (2, 2, 1, 0), \qquad \mathbf{v}_3 = (1, 2, 1, 0).$$

Solution We begin with

$$\mathbf{u}_1 = \mathbf{v}_1 = (2, 1, 2, 1).$$

Then

$$\mathbf{u}_2 = \mathbf{v}_2 - \frac{\mathbf{u}_1 \cdot \mathbf{v}_2}{\mathbf{u}_1 \cdot \mathbf{u}_1}\mathbf{u}_1 = (2, 2, 1, 0) - \frac{8}{10}(2, 1, 2, 1)$$

$$= \left(\frac{2}{5}, \frac{6}{5}, -\frac{3}{5}, -\frac{4}{5}\right) = \frac{1}{5}(2, 6, -3, -4).$$

We delete the scalar factor $\frac{1}{5}$ and instead take $\mathbf{u}_2 = (2, 6, -3, -4)$. Next,

$$\begin{aligned}\mathbf{u}_3 &= \mathbf{v}_3 - \frac{\mathbf{u}_1 \cdot \mathbf{v}_3}{\mathbf{u}_1 \cdot \mathbf{u}_1}\mathbf{u}_1 - \frac{\mathbf{u}_2 \cdot \mathbf{v}_3}{\mathbf{u}_2 \cdot \mathbf{u}_2}\mathbf{u}_2 \\ &= (1, 2, 1, 0) - \frac{6}{10}(2, 1, 2, 1) - \frac{11}{65}(2, 6, -3, -4) \\ &= \left(-\frac{70}{130}, \frac{50}{130}, \frac{40}{130}, \frac{10}{130}\right) = \frac{1}{13}(-7, 5, 4, 1).\end{aligned}$$

We delete the scalar factor $\frac{1}{13}$ and instead take $\mathbf{u}_3 = (-7, 5, 4, 1)$. Thus our orthogonal basis for the subspace V consists of the vectors

$$\mathbf{u}_1 = (2, 1, 2, 1), \qquad \mathbf{u}_2 = (2, 6, -3, -4), \qquad \mathbf{u}_3 = (-7, 5, 4, 1).$$

5.4 PROBLEMS

In Problems 1–22, a basis $\{\mathbf{v}_i\}$ for a subspace V of $\mathbf{R}^n$ is given. Apply the Gram-Schmidt algorithm to transform the given basis into an orthogonal basis $\{\mathbf{u}_i\}$ for V. If a vector $\mathbf{b}$ is given, use the orthogonal basis to find the orthogonal projection $\mathbf{p}$ of $\mathbf{b}$ into V.

1. $\mathbf{v}_1 = (3, 2)$, $\mathbf{v}_2 = (2, 3)$

2. $\mathbf{v}_1 = (3, 5)$, $\mathbf{v}_2 = (4, 7)$

3. $\mathbf{v}_1 = (3, 1, 2)$, $\mathbf{v}_2 = (2, 1, 3)$; $\mathbf{b} = (0, 27, 0)$

4. $\mathbf{v}_1 = (2, 2, 3)$, $\mathbf{v}_2 = (4, 3, 5)$; $\mathbf{b} = (0, 0, 9)$

5. $\mathbf{v}_1 = (2, 2, 2, 1)$, $\mathbf{v}_2 = (1, 2, 2, 2)$; $\mathbf{b} = (25, 0, 0, 25)$

6. $\mathbf{v}_1 = (2, -1, 1, 0)$, $\mathbf{v}_2 = (3, 1, 0, 1)$; $\mathbf{b} = (0, 0, 0, 41)$

7. $\mathbf{v}_1 = (1, 1, 0)$, $\mathbf{v}_2 = (1, 0, 1)$, $\mathbf{v}_3 = (0, 1, 1)$

8. $\mathbf{v}_1 = (2, 1, 1)$, $\mathbf{v}_2 = (1, 3, 1)$, $\mathbf{v}_3 = (1, 1, 4)$

9. $\mathbf{v}_1 = (2, 1, 1)$, $\mathbf{v}_2 = (1, 2, 1)$, $\mathbf{v}_3 = (1, 1, 2)$

10. $\mathbf{v}_1 = (1, 2, 2)$, $\mathbf{v}_2 = (2, 1, 2)$, $\mathbf{v}_3 = (2, 2, 1)$

11. $\mathbf{v}_1 = (1, 1, 0, 1)$, $\mathbf{v}_2 = (1, 0, 1, 1)$, $\mathbf{v}_3 = (0, 1, 1, 1)$; $\mathbf{b} = (7, 0, 7, 0)$

12. $\mathbf{v}_1 = (1, 1, 0, 0)$, $\mathbf{v}_2 = (2, 0, 1, 0)$, $\mathbf{v}_3 = (3, 1, 0, 1)$; $\mathbf{b} = (0, 10, 0, 10)$

13. $\mathbf{v}_1 = (2, 1, 0, 0)$, $\mathbf{v}_2 = (3, 0, 1, 0)$, $\mathbf{v}_3 = (4, 1, 0, 1)$; $\mathbf{b} = (0, 0, 0, 9)$

14. $\mathbf{v}_1 = (1, 1, 1, 0)$, $\mathbf{v}_2 = (2, 1, 0, 1)$, $\mathbf{v}_3 = (3, 0, 1, 1)$; $\mathbf{b} = (3, 3, 3, 3)$

15. $\mathbf{v}_1 = (2, 1, 1, 0)$, $\mathbf{v}_2 = (3, 1, 0, 1)$, $\mathbf{v}_3 = (4, 0, 1, 1)$

16. $\mathbf{v}_1 = (2, 2, 1, 1)$, $\mathbf{v}_2 = (2, 1, 2, 1)$, $\mathbf{v}_3 = (1, 2, 2, 1)$

17. $\mathbf{v}_1 = (2, 1, 1, 1)$, $\mathbf{v}_2 = (2, 2, 1, 0)$, $\mathbf{v}_3 = (1, 2, 0, 1)$

18. $\mathbf{v}_1 = (1, -1, 1, -1)$, $\mathbf{v}_2 = (1, 3, 1, -1)$, $\mathbf{v}_3 = (2, 0, 1, 1)$

19. $\mathbf{v}_1 = (1, 0, 1, 1, 0)$, $\mathbf{v}_2 = (0, 1, 0, 1, 1)$, $\mathbf{v}_3 = (1, 1, 0, 0, 1)$

20. $\mathbf{v}_1 = (1, 0, 2, 0, 0)$, $\mathbf{v}_2 = (1, 1, 0, 2, 0)$, $\mathbf{v}_3 = (0, 1, 0, 0, 2)$

21. $\mathbf{v}_1 = (1, 0, 0, 1, 0)$, $\mathbf{v}_2 = (0, 2, 0, 1, 1)$, $\mathbf{v}_3 = (0, 0, 3, 0, 1)$

22. $\mathbf{v}_1 = (1, 2, 3, 2, 1)$, $\mathbf{v}_2 = (1, 1, 1, 0, 0)$, $\mathbf{v}_3 = (0, 0, 1, 1, 1)$

23. Describe an algorithm for finding an orthogonal basis for the solution space of a given homogeneous system $A\mathbf{x} = \mathbf{0}$.

24. Let $\mathbf{v}_1, \mathbf{v}_2, \ldots, \mathbf{v}_k$ be k mutually orthogonal vectors in $\mathbf{R}^n$ with $k < n$. Describe an algorithm for finding an orthogonal basis for $\mathbf{R}^n$ that contains the given vectors $\mathbf{v}_1, \mathbf{v}_2, \ldots, \mathbf{v}_k$.

25. Let $\{\mathbf{u}_1, \mathbf{u}_2, \ldots, \mathbf{u}_n\}$ be an orthonormal basis for a subspace U of $\mathbf{R}^m$, and suppose that

$$\mathbf{v} = a_1\mathbf{u}_1 + a_2\mathbf{u}_2 + \cdots + a_n\mathbf{u}_n$$

and

$$\mathbf{w} = b_1\mathbf{u}_1 + b_2\mathbf{u}_2 + \cdots + b_n\mathbf{u}_n.$$

Show that

$$\mathbf{v}\cdot\mathbf{w} = a_1b_1 + a_2b_2 + \cdots + a_nb_n$$

and, in particular, that

$$|\mathbf{v}|^2 = a_1^2 + a_2^2 + \cdots + a_n^2.$$

These formulas describe a way in which an orthonormal basis for a vector space is like the standard unit basis $\{\mathbf{e}_1, \mathbf{e}_2, \ldots, \mathbf{e}_n\}$ for $\mathbf{R}^n$.

*5.5

Inner Product Spaces

Recall from Section 5.1 that an **inner product** on a vector space V is a function that associates with each (ordered) pair of vectors $\mathbf{u}$ and $\mathbf{v}$ in V a scalar $\langle \mathbf{u}, \mathbf{v}\rangle$ such that

(i) $\langle \mathbf{u}, \mathbf{v}\rangle = \langle \mathbf{v}, \mathbf{u}\rangle$;

(ii) $\langle \mathbf{u}, \mathbf{v} + \mathbf{w}\rangle = \langle \mathbf{u}, \mathbf{v}\rangle + \langle \mathbf{u}, \mathbf{w}\rangle$;

(iii) $\langle c\mathbf{u}, \mathbf{v}\rangle = c\langle \mathbf{u}, \mathbf{v}\rangle$;

(iv) $\langle \mathbf{u}, \mathbf{u}\rangle \geq 0$; $\langle \mathbf{u}, \mathbf{u}\rangle = 0$ if and only if $\mathbf{u} = \mathbf{0}$.

An **inner product space** is a vector space V together with a specified inner product $\langle \mathbf{u}, \mathbf{v}\rangle$ on V.

The Euclidean inner product—that is, the dot product $\langle \mathbf{u}, \mathbf{v}\rangle = \mathbf{u}\cdot\mathbf{v}$—is only one example of an inner product on the vector space $\mathbf{R}^n$ of n-tuples of real numbers. To see how other inner products on $\mathbf{R}^n$ can be defined, let A be a fixed $n \times n$ matrix. Given (column) vectors $\mathbf{u}$ and $\mathbf{v}$ in $\mathbf{R}^n$, let us define the "product" $\langle \mathbf{u}, \mathbf{v}\rangle$ of these two vectors to be

$$\langle \mathbf{u}, \mathbf{v}\rangle = \mathbf{u}^T A\mathbf{v}. \tag{1}$$

Note that $\langle \mathbf{u}, \mathbf{v}\rangle$ is a 1×1 matrix—that is, $\langle \mathbf{u}, \mathbf{v}\rangle$ is a scalar. Then

$$\begin{aligned}\langle \mathbf{u}, \mathbf{v} + \mathbf{w}\rangle &= \mathbf{u}^T A(\mathbf{v} + \mathbf{w})\\ &= \mathbf{u}^T A\mathbf{v} + \mathbf{u}^T A\mathbf{w}\\ &= \langle \mathbf{u}, \mathbf{v}\rangle + \langle \mathbf{u}, \mathbf{w}\rangle\end{aligned}$$

and

$$\begin{aligned}\langle c\mathbf{u}, \mathbf{v}\rangle &= (c\mathbf{u}^T)A\mathbf{v}\\ &= c\mathbf{u}^T A\mathbf{v} = c\langle \mathbf{u}, \mathbf{v}\rangle,\end{aligned}$$

so we see immediately that $\langle \mathbf{u}, \mathbf{v}\rangle = \mathbf{u}^T A\mathbf{v}$ satisfies properties (ii) and (iii) of an inner product.

In order to verify properties (i) and (iv) we must impose appropriate conditions on the matrix A. Suppose first that A is *symmetric*: $A = A^T$. Because $\mathbf{u}^T A\mathbf{v}$ is a real number, it follows that $(\mathbf{u}^T A\mathbf{v})^T = \mathbf{u}^T A\mathbf{v}$. Consequently

$$\begin{aligned}\langle \mathbf{u}, \mathbf{v}\rangle &= \mathbf{u}^T A\mathbf{v} = (\mathbf{u}^T A\mathbf{v})^T \\ &= \mathbf{v}^T A^T\mathbf{u} = \mathbf{v}^T A\mathbf{u} = \langle \mathbf{v}, \mathbf{u}\rangle.\end{aligned}$$

Thus the inner product $\langle \mathbf{u}, \mathbf{v}\rangle = \mathbf{u}^T A\mathbf{v}$ satisfies property (i) provided that the matrix A is symmetric.

The symmetric $n \times n$ matrix A is said to be **positive definite** if $\mathbf{u}^T A\mathbf{u} > 0$ for every nonzero n-vector $\mathbf{u}$, in which case $\langle \mathbf{u}, \mathbf{v}\rangle = \mathbf{u}^T A\mathbf{v}$ satisfies property (iv) of an inner product. Then our discussion shows that *if the $n \times n$ matrix A is (symmetric and) positive definite, then*

$$\langle \mathbf{u}, \mathbf{v}\rangle = \mathbf{u}^T A\mathbf{v} \tag{1}$$

defines an inner product on $\mathbf{R}^n$. The familiar dot product $\mathbf{u}\cdot\mathbf{v} = \mathbf{u}^T\mathbf{v} = \mathbf{u}^T I\mathbf{v}$ is simply the special case in which $A = I$, the $n \times n$ identity matrix.

In Section 8.2 we will state criteria for determining whether a given symmetric $n \times n$ matrix A is positive definite, and hence whether $\langle \mathbf{u}, \mathbf{v}\rangle = \mathbf{u}^T A\mathbf{v}$ defines an inner product on $\mathbf{R}^n$. In the case of a symmetric 2×2 matrix

$$A = \begin{bmatrix} a & b \\ b & c \end{bmatrix} \tag{2}$$

this question can be answered by a simple technique of completing the square, as in Example 1 of this section. Note that if $\mathbf{u} = (u_1, u_2)$ and $\mathbf{v} = (v_1, v_2)$ then

$$\langle \mathbf{u}, \mathbf{v}\rangle = \mathbf{u}^T A\mathbf{v} = \begin{bmatrix} u_1 & u_2 \end{bmatrix}\begin{bmatrix} a & b \\ b & c \end{bmatrix}\begin{bmatrix} v_1 \\ v_2 \end{bmatrix},$$

so that

$$\langle \mathbf{u}, \mathbf{v}\rangle = au_1v_1 + bu_1v_2 + bu_2v_1 + cu_2v_2. \tag{3}$$

EXAMPLE 1 Consider the symmetric 2×2 matrix

$$A = \begin{bmatrix} 3 & 2 \\ 2 & 4 \end{bmatrix}.$$

Then

$$\langle \mathbf{u}, \mathbf{v}\rangle = \mathbf{u}^T A\mathbf{v} = 3u_1v_1 + 2u_1v_2 + 2u_2v_1 + 4u_2v_2$$

automatically satisfies properties (i)–(iii) of an inner product on $\mathbf{R}^2$. If $\mathbf{u} = (x, y)$, then (3) gives

$$\langle \mathbf{u}, \mathbf{u}\rangle = \mathbf{u}^T A\mathbf{u} = 3x^2 + 4xy + 4y^2 = (x + 2y)^2 + 2x^2.$$

It is therefore clear that $\mathbf{u}^T A\mathbf{u} \geq 0$ and that $\mathbf{u}^T A\mathbf{v} = 0$ if and only if $x + 2y = 0 = x$; that is, if and only if $x = y = 0$. Thus the symmetric matrix A is positive definite, and so $\langle \mathbf{u}, \mathbf{v} \rangle = \mathbf{u}^T A \mathbf{v}$ defines an inner product on $\mathbf{R}^2$. Note that if $\mathbf{u} = (3, 1)$ and $\mathbf{v} = (1, 4)$, then $\mathbf{u} \cdot \mathbf{v} = 7$, whereas

$$\langle \mathbf{u}, \mathbf{v} \rangle = \begin{bmatrix} 3 & 1 \end{bmatrix} \begin{bmatrix} 3 & 2 \\ 2 & 4 \end{bmatrix} \begin{bmatrix} 1 \\ 4 \end{bmatrix} = 51.$$

Thus the inner product $\langle \mathbf{u}, \mathbf{v} \rangle = \mathbf{u}^T A \mathbf{v}$ is quite different from the Euclidean inner product on $\mathbf{R}^2$.

Essentially everything that has been done with the Euclidean inner product on $\mathbf{R}^n$ in the first four sections of this chapter can be done with an arbitrary inner product space V (with an occasional proviso that the vector space V be finite-dimensional). Given an arbitrary inner product $\langle \mathbf{u}, \mathbf{v} \rangle$ on a vector space V, the **length** (or **norm**) of the vector $\mathbf{u}$ (with respect to this inner product) is defined to be

$$\|\mathbf{u}\| = \sqrt{\langle \mathbf{u}, \mathbf{u} \rangle}. \tag{4}$$

For instance, the length of $\mathbf{u} = (3, 1)$ with respect to the inner product of Example 1 is given by

$$\|\mathbf{u}\|^2 = \begin{bmatrix} 3 & 1 \end{bmatrix} \begin{bmatrix} 3 & 2 \\ 2 & 4 \end{bmatrix} \begin{bmatrix} 3 \\ 1 \end{bmatrix} = 43.$$

Thus $\|\mathbf{u}\| = \sqrt{43}$, whereas the Euclidean length of $\mathbf{u} = (3, 1)$ is $|\mathbf{u}| = \sqrt{\mathbf{u} \cdot \mathbf{u}} = \sqrt{10}$.

The proof of Theorem 1 in Section 5.1 translates (see Problem 19) into a proof of the **Cauchy-Schwarz inequality**

$$|\langle \mathbf{u}, \mathbf{v} \rangle| \le \|\mathbf{u}\| \, \|\mathbf{v}\| \tag{5}$$

for an arbitrary inner product on any vector space V. Just as in the discussion of Equations (8) and (9) of Section 5.1, it follows that the angle θ between the nonzero vectors $\mathbf{u}$ and $\mathbf{v}$ can be defined in this way:

$$\cos \theta = \frac{\langle \mathbf{u}, \mathbf{v} \rangle}{\|\mathbf{u}\| \, \|\mathbf{v}\|}. \tag{6}$$

Consequently we say that the vectors $\mathbf{u}$ and $\mathbf{v}$ are **orthogonal** provided that $\langle \mathbf{u}, \mathbf{v} \rangle = 0$. The **triangle inequality**

$$\|\mathbf{u} + \mathbf{v}\| \le \|\mathbf{u}\| + \|\mathbf{v}\| \tag{7}$$

for an arbitrary inner product space follows from the Cauchy-Schwarz inequality just as in Theorem 2 of Section 5.1. And it follows just as in Theorem 3 of the same section that any finite set of mutually orthogonal vectors in an inner product space is a linearly independent set.

The techniques of Section 5.4 are of special interest in the more general setting of inner product spaces. The Gram-Schmidt orthogonalization algorithm can be used to convert a basis $\{\mathbf{v}_1, \mathbf{v}_2, \ldots, \mathbf{v}_n\}$ for a finite-dimensional inner product space V into an orthogonal basis $\{\mathbf{u}_1, \mathbf{u}_2, \ldots, \mathbf{u}_n\}$. The analogues for this purpose of the formulas in Equations (12) and (13) in Section 5.4 are

$$\mathbf{u}_1 = \mathbf{v}_1 \tag{8}$$

and

$$\mathbf{u}_{k+1} = \mathbf{v}_{k+1} - \frac{\langle \mathbf{u}_1, \mathbf{v}_{k+1} \rangle}{\langle \mathbf{u}_1, \mathbf{u}_1 \rangle}\mathbf{u}_1 - \frac{\langle \mathbf{u}_2, \mathbf{v}_{k+1} \rangle}{\langle \mathbf{u}_2, \mathbf{u}_2 \rangle}\mathbf{u}_2 - \cdots - \frac{\langle \mathbf{u}_k, \mathbf{v}_{k+1} \rangle}{\langle \mathbf{u}_k, \mathbf{u}_k \rangle}\mathbf{u}_k \tag{9}$$

for $k = 1, 2, \ldots, n-1$ in turn. Thus $\mathbf{u}_{k+1}$ is obtained by subtracting from $\mathbf{v}_{k+1}$ each of its components parallel (with respect to the given inner product) to the previously constructed orthogonal vectors $\mathbf{u}_1, \mathbf{u}_2, \ldots, \mathbf{u}_k$.

Now let $\{\mathbf{u}_1, \mathbf{u}_2, \ldots, \mathbf{u}_n\}$ be an orthogonal basis for the (finite-dimensional) subspace W of the inner product space V. Given any vector $\mathbf{b}$ in V, we define (in analogy with the formula in Equation (6) of Section 5.4) the **orthogonal projection $\mathbf{p}$** of $\mathbf{b}$ into the subspace W to be

$$\mathbf{p} = \frac{\langle \mathbf{u}_1, \mathbf{b} \rangle}{\langle \mathbf{u}_1, \mathbf{u}_1 \rangle}\mathbf{u}_1 + \frac{\langle \mathbf{u}_2, \mathbf{b} \rangle}{\langle \mathbf{u}_2, \mathbf{u}_2 \rangle}\mathbf{u}_2 + \cdots + \frac{\langle \mathbf{u}_n, \mathbf{b} \rangle}{\langle \mathbf{u}_n, \mathbf{u}_n \rangle}\mathbf{u}_n. \tag{10}$$

It is readily verified (see Problem 20) that $\mathbf{q} = \mathbf{b} - \mathbf{p}$ is orthogonal to every vector in W, and it follows that $\mathbf{p}$ and $\mathbf{q}$ are the unique vectors parallel to and orthogonal to W (respectively) such that $\mathbf{b} = \mathbf{p} + \mathbf{q}$. Finally, the triangle inequality can be used (as in Theorem 1 of Section 5.2) to show that the orthogonal projection $\mathbf{p}$ of $\mathbf{b}$ into W is the point of the subspace W closest to $\mathbf{b}$. If $\mathbf{b}$ itself is a vector in W, then $\mathbf{p} = \mathbf{b}$, and the right-hand side in (10) expresses $\mathbf{b}$ as a linear combination of the orthogonal basis vectors $\mathbf{u}_1, \mathbf{u}_2, \ldots, \mathbf{u}_n$.

INNER PRODUCTS AND FUNCTION SPACES*

Some of the most interesting and important applications involving orthogonal bases and projections are to vector spaces of functions. In Section 4.5 we introduced the vector space $\mathscr{F}$ of all real-valued functions on the real line $\mathbf{R}$ as well as various infinite-dimensional subspaces of $\mathscr{F}$, including the space $\mathscr{P}$ of all polynomials and the space of all continuous functions on $\mathbf{R}$.

Here we want to discuss the infinite-dimensional vector space $\mathscr{C}[a, b]$ consisting of all continuous functions defined on the closed interval $[a, b]$, with the usual vector space operations

$$(f + g)(x) = f(x) + g(x) \quad \text{and} \quad (cf)(x) = cf(x).$$

When it is unnecessary to refer explicitly to the interval $[a, b]$, we will simply write $\mathscr{C} = \mathscr{C}[a, b]$.

* The remainder of this section is for those readers who have studied elementary calculus.

To provide the vector space $\mathscr{C}[a, b]$ with an inner product, we define

$$\langle f, g\rangle = \int_a^b f(x)g(x)\,dx \tag{11}$$

for any two functions f and g in $\mathscr{C}[a, b]$. The fact that $\langle f, g\rangle$ satisfies properties (i)–(iii) of an inner product follows from familiar elementary facts about integrals. For instance,

$$\begin{aligned}\langle f, g + h\rangle &= \int_a^b f(x)\{g(x) + h(x)\}\,dx \\ &= \int_a^b f(x)g(x)\,dx + \int_a^b f(x)h(x)\,dx \\ &= \langle f, g\rangle + \langle f, h\rangle.\end{aligned}$$

It is also true (though perhaps not so obvious) that if f is a continuous function such that

$$\langle f, f\rangle = \int_a^b \{f(x)\}^2\,dx = 0,$$

then it follows that $f(x) \equiv 0$ on $[a, b]$; that is, f is the zero function in $\mathscr{C}[a, b]$. Therefore, $\langle f, g\rangle$ as defined in (11) also satisfies Property (iv) and hence is an inner product on $\mathscr{C}[a, b]$.

The **norm** $\|f\|$ of the function f in $\mathscr{C}$ is defined to be

$$\|f\| = \sqrt{\langle f, f\rangle} = \left(\int_a^b \{f(x)\}^2\,dx\right)^{1/2}. \tag{12}$$

Then the Cauchy-Schwarz and triangle inequalities for $\mathscr{C}[a, b]$ take the forms

$$\left|\int_a^b f(x)g(x)\,dx\right| \leq \left(\int_a^b \{f(x)\}^2\,dx\right)^{1/2}\left(\int_a^b \{g(x)\}^2\,dx\right)^{1/2} \tag{13}$$

and

$$\left(\int_a^b \{f(x) + g(x)\}^2\,dx\right)^{1/2} \leq \left(\int_a^b \{f(x)\}^2\,dx\right)^{1/2} + \left(\int_a^b \{g(x)\}^2\,dx\right)^{1/2}, \tag{14}$$

respectively. It may surprise you to observe that these inequalities involving integrals follow immediately from the general inequalities in (5) and (7), which do not explicitly involve definite integrals.

EXAMPLE 2 Let $\mathscr{P}_n$ denote the subspace of $\mathscr{C}[-1, 1]$ consisting of all polynomials of degree at most n. As we saw in Example 4 of Section 4.5, $\mathscr{P}_n$ is an $(n + 1)$-dimensional vector space, with basis elements

$$q_0(x) = 1,\ q_1(x) = x,\ q_2(x) = x^2, \ldots, q_n(x) = x^n.$$

We want to apply the Gram-Schmidt algorithm to convert $\{q_0, q_1, \ldots, q_n\}$ into an orthogonal basis $\{p_0, p_1, \ldots, p_n\}$ for $\mathscr{P}_n$. According to (8) and (9), we begin with

$$p_0(x) = q_0(x) = 1, \tag{15}$$

and first calculate

$$\langle p_0, p_0 \rangle = \int_{-1}^{1} 1 \cdot 1 \, dx = 2,$$

$$\langle p_0, q_1 \rangle = \int_{-1}^{1} 1 \cdot x \, dx = 0.$$

Then

$$p_1 = q_1 - \frac{\langle p_0, q_1 \rangle}{\langle p_0, p_0 \rangle} p_0 = q_1 - \frac{0}{2} p_0 = q_1,$$

so

$$p_1(x) = x. \tag{16}$$

Next,

$$\langle p_1, p_1 \rangle = \langle p_0, q_2 \rangle = \int_{-1}^{1} x^2 \, dx = \frac{2}{3}$$

and

$$\langle p_1, q_2 \rangle = \int_{-1}^{1} x^3 \, dx = 0,$$

so

$$\begin{aligned} p_2 &= q_2 - \frac{\langle p_0, q_2 \rangle}{\langle p_0, p_0 \rangle} p_0 - \frac{\langle p_1, q_2 \rangle}{\langle p_1, p_1 \rangle} p_1 \\ &= q_2 - \frac{\frac{2}{3}}{2} p_0 - \frac{0}{\frac{2}{3}} p_1 = q_2 - \frac{1}{3} p_0, \end{aligned}$$

and hence

$$p_2(x) = x^2 - \frac{1}{3} = \frac{1}{3}(3x^2 - 1). \tag{17}$$

To go one step further, we compute the integrals

$$\langle p_0, q_3 \rangle = \int_{-1}^{1} x^3 \, dx = 0,$$

$$\langle p_1, q_3 \rangle = \int_{-1}^{1} x^4 \, dx = \frac{2}{5},$$

$$\langle p_2, q_3 \rangle = \int_{-1}^{1} x^3\left(x^2 - \frac{1}{3}\right) dx = 0,$$

and

$$\langle p_2, p_2 \rangle = \int_{-1}^{1} \left(x^2 - \frac{1}{3}\right)^2 dx = \frac{8}{45}.$$

Then

$$\begin{aligned} p_3 &= q_3 - \frac{\langle p_0, q_3 \rangle}{\langle p_0, p_0 \rangle} p_0 - \frac{\langle p_1, q_3 \rangle}{\langle p_1, p_1 \rangle} p_1 - \frac{\langle p_2, q_3 \rangle}{\langle p_2, p_2 \rangle} p_2 \\ &= q_3 - \frac{0}{2} p_0 - \frac{\frac{2}{5}}{\frac{2}{3}} p_1 - \frac{0}{\frac{8}{45}} p_2 = q_3 - \frac{3}{5} p_1, \end{aligned}$$

so

$$p_3(x) = x^3 - \frac{3}{5} x = \frac{1}{5}(5x^3 - 3x). \qquad (18)$$

The orthogonal polynomials in (15)–(18) are constant multiples of the famous **Legendre polynomials.** The first six Legendre polynomials are

$$\begin{aligned} P_0(x) &= 1, \\ P_1(x) &= x, \\ P_2(x) &= \frac{1}{2}(3x^2 - 1), \\ P_3(x) &= \frac{1}{2}(5x^3 - 3x), \\ P_4(x) &= \frac{1}{8}(35x^4 - 30x^2 + 3), \\ P_5(x) &= \frac{1}{8}(63x^5 - 70x^3 + 15x). \end{aligned} \qquad (19)$$

For reasons that need not concern us here, the constant multipliers are chosen so that

$$P_0(1) = P_1(1) = P_2(1) = \cdots = 1.$$

Given a function f in $\mathscr{C}[-1, 1]$, the orthogonal projection p of f into $\mathscr{P}_n$ is given (see the formula in (10)) in terms of Legendre polynomials by

$$p(x) = \frac{\langle P_0, f \rangle}{\langle P_0, P_0 \rangle} P_0(x) + \frac{\langle P_1, f \rangle}{\langle P_1, P_1 \rangle} P_1(x) + \cdots + \frac{\langle P_n, f \rangle}{\langle P_n, P_n \rangle} P_n(x).$$

Then $p(x)$ is the nth degree **least squares polynomial** approximation to $f(x)$ on $[-1, 1]$. It is the nth degree polynomial that minimizes the **mean square error**

$$\|f - p\|^2 = \int_{-1}^{1} \{f(x) - p(x)\}^2 \, dx.$$

EXAMPLE 3 Let $\mathscr{T}_N$ denote the subspace of $\mathscr{C}[-\pi, \pi]$ that consists of all "trigonometric polynomials" of the form

$$a_0 + \sum_{n=1}^{N} (a_n \cos nx + b_n \sin nx). \tag{20}$$

Then $\mathscr{T}_N$ is spanned by the $2N + 1$ functions

$$1, \cos x, \sin x, \cos 2x, \sin 2x, \ldots, \cos Nx, \sin Nx. \tag{21}$$

By standard techniques of integral calculus we find that

$$\langle 1, \cos nx \rangle = \int_{-\pi}^{\pi} \cos nx \, dx = 0,$$

$$\langle 1, \sin nx \rangle = \int_{-\pi}^{\pi} \sin nx \, dx = 0,$$

$$\langle \cos mx, \sin nx \rangle = \int_{-\pi}^{\pi} \cos mx \sin nx \, dx = 0$$

for all positive integers m and n, and that

$$\langle \sin mx, \sin nx \rangle = \int_{-\pi}^{\pi} \sin mx \sin nx \, dx = 0,$$

$$\langle \cos mx, \cos nx \rangle = \int_{-\pi}^{\pi} \cos mx \cos nx \, dx = 0$$

if $m \neq n$. Thus the $2N + 1$ nonzero functions in (21) are mutually orthogonal and hence are linearly independent. It follows that $\mathscr{T}_N$ is a $(2N + 1)$-dimensional subspace of $\mathscr{C}[-\pi, \pi]$ with the functions in (21) constituting an orthogonal basis.

To find the norms of these basis functions, we calculate the integrals

$$\langle 1, 1 \rangle = \int_{-\pi}^{\pi} 1 \, dx = 2\pi,$$

$$\begin{aligned}\langle \cos nx, \cos nx \rangle &= \int_{-\pi}^{\pi} \cos^2 nx \, dx \\ &= \int_{-\pi}^{\pi} \frac{1}{2}(1 + \cos 2nx) \, dx \\ &= \frac{1}{2}\left[x + \frac{1}{2n} \sin 2nx\right]_{-\pi}^{\pi} = \pi\end{aligned}$$

and, similarly,

$$\langle \sin nx, \sin nx \rangle = \int_{-\pi}^{\pi} \sin^2 nx \, dx = \pi.$$

Thus

$$\|1\| = \sqrt{2\pi} \quad \text{and} \quad \|\cos nx\| = \|\sin nx\| = \sqrt{\pi} \tag{22}$$

for all n.

Now suppose that $f(x)$ is an arbitrary continuous function in $\mathscr{C}[-\pi, \pi]$. According to the formula in (10), the orthogonal projection $p(x)$ of $f(x)$ into the subspace $\mathscr{T}_N$ is the sum of the $2N + 1$ orthogonal projections of $f(x)$ onto the orthogonal basis elements in (21). These orthogonal projections are given by

$$\frac{\langle f(x), 1\rangle}{\langle 1, 1\rangle} = a_0$$

where

$$a_0 = \frac{\langle f(x), 1\rangle}{\langle 1, 1\rangle} = \frac{1}{2\pi}\int_{-\pi}^{\pi} f(x)\,dx; \tag{23}$$

$$\frac{\langle f(x), \cos nx\rangle}{\langle \cos nx, \cos nx\rangle} \cos nx = a_n \cos nx$$

where

$$a_n = \frac{\langle f(x), \cos nx\rangle}{\langle \cos nx, \cos nx\rangle} = \frac{1}{\pi}\int_{-\pi}^{\pi} f(x) \cos nx\,dx; \tag{24}$$

and

$$\frac{\langle f(x), \sin nx\rangle}{\langle \sin nx, \sin nx\rangle} \sin nx = b_n \sin nx$$

where

$$b_n = \frac{\langle f(x), \sin nx\rangle}{\langle \sin nx, \sin nx\rangle} = \frac{1}{\pi}\int_{-\pi}^{\pi} f(x) \sin nx\,dx. \tag{25}$$

Consequently the orthogonal projection $p(x)$ of the function $f(x)$ into $\mathscr{T}_N$ is given by

$$p(x) = a_0 + \sum_{n=1}^{N} (a_n \cos nx + b_n \sin nx), \tag{26}$$

where the coefficients are given by the formulas in Equations (23)–(25). These constants $a_0, a_1, b_1, a_2, b_2, \ldots$ are called the **Fourier coefficients** of the function $f(x)$ on $[-\pi, \pi]$. The fact that the orthogonal projection p is the element of $\mathscr{T}_N$ closest to f means that the Fourier coefficients of f minimize the mean square error

$$\|f - p\|^2 = \int_{-\pi}^{\pi} \left\{ f(x) - a_0 - \sum_{n=1}^{N} (a_n \cos nx + b_n \sin nx) \right\}^2 dx.$$

This is the sense in which the trigonometric polynomial $p(x)$ is the "best least squares approximation" (in $\mathscr{T}_N$) to the given continuous function $f(x)$.

Finally, we remark that $p(x)$ in (26) is a (finite) partial sum of the infinite series

$$a_0 + \sum_{n=1}^{\infty} (a_n \cos nx + b_n \sin nx).$$

With the coefficients given in (23)–(25), this infinite series is known as the **Fourier series** of f on $[-\pi, \pi]$.

EXAMPLE 4 Given $f(x) = x$ on $[-\pi, \pi]$, find the orthogonal projection p of f into $\mathscr{T}_4$.

Solution The formula in (23) yields

$$a_0 = \frac{1}{2\pi}\int_{-\pi}^{\pi} x\,dx = \frac{1}{2\pi}\left[\frac{1}{2}x^2\right]_{-\pi}^{\pi} = 0.$$

To find a_n and b_n for $n > 0$ we need the integral formulas

$$\int u \cos u\,du = \cos u + u \sin u + C$$

and

$$\int u \sin u\,du = \sin u - u \cos u + C.$$

Then the formula in (24) yields

$$\begin{aligned} a_n &= \frac{1}{\pi}\int_{-\pi}^{\pi} x \cos nx\,dx = \frac{1}{n^2\pi}\int_{-n\pi}^{n\pi} u \cos u\,du \qquad (u = nx) \\ &= \frac{1}{n^2\pi}\Big[\cos u + u \sin u\Big]_{-n\pi}^{n\pi} = 0 \end{aligned}$$

for all positive integers n. And the formula in (25) yields

$$\begin{aligned} b_n &= \frac{1}{\pi}\int_{-\pi}^{\pi} x \sin nx\,dx = \frac{1}{n^2\pi}\int_{-n\pi}^{n\pi} u \sin u\,du \qquad (u = nx) \\ &= \frac{1}{n^2\pi}\Big[\sin u - u \cos u\Big]_{-n\pi}^{n\pi} = -\frac{2}{n}\cos n\pi = \frac{2}{n}(-1)^{n+1} \end{aligned}$$

for all positive integers n. Substituting these values for $n \le 4$ in (26), we get the desired orthogonal projection

$$p(x) = 2\left(\sin x - \frac{1}{2}\sin 2x + \frac{1}{3}\sin 3x - \frac{1}{4}\sin 4x\right).$$

This is the "trigonometric polynomial of degree 4" that (in the least squares sense) best approximates $f(x) = x$ on the interval $[-\pi, \pi]$.

5.5 PROBLEMS

For each 2×2 matrix A given in Problems 1–6, show that $\langle \mathbf{u}, \mathbf{v} \rangle = \mathbf{u}^T A \mathbf{v}$ is an inner product on $\mathbf{R}^2$. Given $\mathbf{u} = (x, y)$, write $\mathbf{u}^T A \mathbf{u}$ as a sum of squares as in Example 1.

1. $\begin{bmatrix} 2 & 0 \\ 0 & 3 \end{bmatrix}$

2. $\begin{bmatrix} 1 & 1 \\ 1 & 3 \end{bmatrix}$

3. $\begin{bmatrix} 2 & -2 \\ -2 & 3 \end{bmatrix}$

4. $\begin{bmatrix} 1 & 3 \\ 3 & 10 \end{bmatrix}$

5. $\begin{bmatrix} 4 & 6 \\ 6 & 11 \end{bmatrix}$

6. $\begin{bmatrix} 9 & -3 \\ -3 & 2 \end{bmatrix}$

In each of Problems 7–10, apply the Gram-Schmidt algorithm to the vectors $\mathbf{e}_1 = (1, 0)$ and $\mathbf{e}_2 = (0, 1)$ to obtain vectors $\mathbf{u}_1$ and $\mathbf{u}_2$ that are orthogonal with respect to the inner product $\langle \mathbf{u}, \mathbf{v} \rangle = \mathbf{u}^T A \mathbf{v}$.

7. A is the matrix of Problem 3.

8. A is the matrix of Problem 4.

9. A is the matrix of Problem 5.

10. A is the matrix of Problem 6.

For each 3×3 matrix A given in Problems 11 and 12, show that $\langle \mathbf{u}, \mathbf{v} \rangle = \mathbf{u}^T A \mathbf{v}$ is an inner product on $\mathbf{R}^3$. Given $\mathbf{u} = (x, y, z)$, write $\mathbf{u}^T A \mathbf{u}$ as a sum of squares.

11. $\begin{bmatrix} 2 & 1 & 1 \\ 1 & 2 & 0 \\ 1 & 0 & 1 \end{bmatrix}$

12. $\begin{bmatrix} 2 & 2 & 0 \\ 2 & 5 & 2 \\ 0 & 2 & 4 \end{bmatrix}$

In Problems 13 and 14, apply the Gram-Schmidt algorithm to the vectors $\mathbf{e}_1 = (1, 0, 0)$, $\mathbf{e}_2 = (0, 1, 0)$, and $\mathbf{e}_3 = (0, 0, 1)$ to obtain vectors $\mathbf{u}_1$, $\mathbf{u}_2$, and $\mathbf{u}_3$ that are mutually orthogonal with respect to the inner product $\langle \mathbf{u}, \mathbf{v} \rangle = \mathbf{u}^T A \mathbf{v}$.

13. A is the matrix of Problem 11.

14. A is the matrix of Problem 12.

15. Show that

$$\langle p, q \rangle = p(0)q(0) + p(1)q(1) + p(2)q(2)$$

defines an inner product on the space $\mathcal{P}_2$ of polynomials of degree at most 2.

16. Apply the Gram-Schmidt algorithm to the basis $\{1, x, x^2\}$ for $\mathcal{P}_2$ to construct a basis $\{p_0, p_1, p_2\}$ that is orthogonal with respect to the inner product of Problem 15.

17. Show that the symmetric 2×2 matrix

$$A = \begin{bmatrix} a & b \\ b & c \end{bmatrix}$$

is positive definite if both $a > 0$ and $ac - b^2 > 0$. *Suggestion*: Write $ax^2 + 2bxy + cy^2$ as a sum of squares in the form $a(x + \alpha y)^2 + \beta y^2$.

18. If the nonzero vectors $\mathbf{v}_1, \mathbf{v}_2, \ldots, \mathbf{v}_n$ in an inner product space V are mutually orthogonal, prove that they are linearly independent.

19. Translate the proof of Theorem 1 in Section 5.1 into a proof of the Cauchy-Schwarz inequality for an arbitrary inner product space.

20. Let $\mathbf{p}$ be the orthogonal projection (defined in Equation (10)) of $\mathbf{b}$ into the subspace W spanned by the orthogonal vectors $\mathbf{u}_1, \mathbf{u}_2, \ldots, \mathbf{u}_n$. Show that $\mathbf{q} = \mathbf{b} - \mathbf{p}$ is orthogonal to W.

21. Let $\mathcal{W}$ be the subspace of $\mathcal{C}[0, 1]$ consisting of all functions of the form $f(x) = a + be^x$. Apply the Gram-Schmidt algorithm to the basis $\{1, e^x\}$ to obtain the orthogonal basis $\{p_1, p_2\}$, where

$$p_1(x) = 1 \quad \text{and} \quad p_2(x) = e^x - e + 1.$$

22. Show that the orthogonal projection of the function $f(x) = x$ into the subspace $\mathcal{W}$ of Problem 21 is

$$p(x) = -\frac{1}{2} + \frac{e^x}{e - 1} \approx (0.5820)e^x - 0.5000.$$

This is the best (least squares) approximation to $f(x) = x$ by a function on $[0, 1]$ of the form $a + be^x$. *Suggestion*: The antiderivative of xe^x is $(x - 1)e^x + C$.

23. Continue the computations in Example 2 to derive the constant multiple

$$p_4(x) = \tfrac{1}{35}(35x^4 - 30x^2 + 3)$$

of the Legendre polynomial of degree 4.

24. The orthogonal projection of $f(x) = x^3$ into $\mathscr{P}_3$ is the function f itself. Use this fact to express x^3 as a linear combination of the Legendre polynomials $P_0(x)$, $P_1(x)$, $P_2(x)$, and $P_3(x)$ listed in (19).

25. This problem deals with orthogonal polynomials in $\mathscr{C}[0, 1]$ rather than $\mathscr{C}[-1, 1]$. Apply the Gram-Schmidt algorithm to transform the basis $\{1, x, x^2\}$ for $\mathscr{P}_2$ into the orthogonal basis $\{p_0, p_1, p_2\}$ where

$$p_0(x) = 1, \qquad p_1(x) = \frac{1}{2}(2x - 1),$$

and

$$p_3(x) = \frac{1}{6}(6x^2 - 6x + 1).$$

26. Let $f(x) = e^x$ on $[0, 1]$. Use the orthogonal polynomials $p_0(x)$ and $p_1(x)$ of Problem 25 to show that the orthogonal projection of $f(x)$ into $\mathscr{P}_1$ is

$$\begin{aligned} p(x) &= (4e - 10) + 6(3 - e)x \\ &\approx 0.8731 + (1.6903)x. \end{aligned}$$

This is the best linear approximation to e^x on the interval $[0, 1]$. Verify the following entries:

x	0.00	0.25	0.50	0.75	1.00
e^x	1.00	1.28	1.65	2.12	2.72
$p(x)$	0.87	1.30	1.72	2.14	2.56

27. (a) Suppose that $g(x)$ is an *even* function—that is, $g(-x) = g(x)$ for all x. Substitute $u = -x$ on $[-\pi, 0]$ to show that

$$\int_{-\pi}^{\pi} g(x)\,dx = 2\int_0^{\pi} g(x)\,dx.$$

(b) Suppose that $g(x)$ is an *odd* function, meaning that $g(-x) = -g(x)$ for all x. Show that

$$\int_{-\pi}^{\pi} g(x)\,dx = 0.$$

28. Use the results in Problem 27 to show the following.

(a) If $f(x)$ is an even function then the orthogonal projection of $f(x)$ into $\mathscr{T}_n$ contains only cosine terms.

(b) If $f(x)$ is an odd function then the orthogonal projection of $f(x)$ into $\mathscr{T}_n$ contains only sine terms.

29. Use the results of the preceding two problems to show that the orthogonal projection of $f(x) = |x|$ into $\mathscr{T}_5$ is

$$p(x) = \frac{\pi}{2} - \frac{4}{\pi}\left(\cos x + \frac{1}{9}\cos 3x + \frac{1}{25}\cos 5x\right).$$

30. Let f be an arbitrary function in $\mathscr{C}[0, 1]$. This problem outlines a "brute force" method for finding the orthogonal projection p of f into the n-dimensional subspace $\mathscr{P}_{n-1}$ of polynomials of degree at most $n - 1$, *without* first finding an orthogonal basis for $\mathscr{P}_{n-1}$. If $f = p + q$ where q is orthogonal to $\mathscr{P}_{n-1}$, then $\langle q(x), x^k\rangle = 0$ for $k = 0, 1, 2, \ldots, n - 1$. So let

$$b_k = \langle f(x), x^k\rangle = \langle p(x), x^k\rangle.$$

If

$$p(x) = c_0 + c_1 x + c_2 x^2 + \cdots + c_{n-1}x^{n-1},$$

then expansion of $\langle p(x), x^k\rangle$ yields the equation

$$\begin{aligned} x_0\langle 1, x^k\rangle + c_1\langle x, x^k\rangle + \cdots + c_{n-1}\langle x^{n-1}, x^k\rangle \\ = b_k \end{aligned}$$

for $k = 0, 1, 2, \ldots, n - 1$. Show that this system of n linear equations in the n components of $\mathbf{c} = (c_0, c_1, \ldots, c_{n-1})$ takes the form

$$H\mathbf{c} = \mathbf{b},$$

where H is the $n \times n$ **Hilbert matrix**

$$H = \begin{bmatrix} 1 & \frac{1}{2} & \frac{1}{3} & \cdots & \frac{1}{n} \\ \frac{1}{2} & \frac{1}{3} & \frac{1}{4} & \cdots & \frac{1}{n+1} \\ \vdots & \vdots & \vdots & \ddots & \vdots \\ \frac{1}{n} & \frac{1}{n+1} & \frac{1}{n+2} & \cdots & \frac{1}{2n-1} \end{bmatrix}.$$

The Hilbert matrix H is nonsingular so, in principle, one can find the orthogonal projection $p(x)$ by solving the equation $H\mathbf{c} = \mathbf{b}$ for $\mathbf{c}$ in terms of the known vector $\mathbf{b} = (b_0, b_1, \ldots, b_{n-1})$. But if

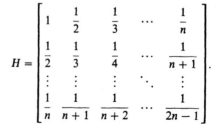

n is fairly large ($n \geq 10$, for example), then the equation $H\mathbf{c} = \mathbf{b}$ is notoriously difficult to solve numerically. The Hilbert matrix has the unfortunate property that a limited-precision solution of the system by Gaussian elimination leads to unacceptably large roundoff errors. Consequently the brute force method for finding $p(x)$ is ineffective as a practical matter. Therefore orthogonal polynomials *must* be used for the accurate determination of least squares polynomial approximations to arbitrary continuous functions.

31. The 3×3 Hilbert matrix

$$H = \begin{bmatrix} 1 & \frac{1}{2} & \frac{1}{3} \\ \frac{1}{2} & \frac{1}{3} & \frac{1}{4} \\ \frac{1}{3} & \frac{1}{4} & \frac{1}{5} \end{bmatrix}$$

is not so bad; show that

$$H^{-1} = \begin{bmatrix} 9 & -36 & 30 \\ -36 & 192 & -180 \\ 30 & -180 & 180 \end{bmatrix}.$$

Then use the method of Problem 30 to derive the least squares approximation

$$\begin{aligned} p(x) &= (39e - 105) + (588 - 216e)x \\ &\quad + (210e - 570)x^2 \\ &\approx 1.0130 + (0.8511)x + (0.8392)x^2 \end{aligned}$$

to $f(x) = e^x$ on $[0, 1]$. Compare the following values with those listed in Problem 26.

x	0.000	0.250	0.500	0.750	1.000
e^x	1.000	1.294	1.649	2.117	2.718
$p(x)$	1.013	1.278	1.648	2.123	2.703
$T_2(x)$	1.000	1.281	1.542	2.031	2.500

The final line shows the corresponding values of the Taylor polynomial

$$T_2(x) = 1 + x + \tfrac{1}{2}x^2,$$

a much inferior approximation on the whole interval than the least squares polynomial $p(x)$.

CHAPTER REVIEW QUESTIONS

1. What single operation on vectors underlies both the concept of distance and the concept of angles in $\mathbf{R}^n$?

2. What are the properties of an inner product on a vector space?

3. State the inequality needed in order to define the angle between two vectors in $\mathbf{R}^n$.

4. If $|\mathbf{u} + \mathbf{v}|^2 = |\mathbf{u}|^2 + |\mathbf{v}|^2$, does it follow that the vectors $\mathbf{u}$ and $\mathbf{v}$ are orthogonal?

5. If S is a set of mutually orthogonal vectors, does it follow that S is a linearly independent set of vectors?

6. Given a basis for a subspace V of $\mathbf{R}^n$, tell how to find a basis for the orthogonal complement of V.

7. Given a matrix A, what is the relationship between the row space of A and the null space of A?

8. Given a subspace V of $\mathbf{R}^n$ and a vector $\mathbf{b}$ in $\mathbf{R}^n$, define the orthogonal projection $\mathbf{p}$ of $\mathbf{b}$ into V, and explain why $\mathbf{p}$ is unique.

9. Let A be an $m \times n$ matrix of rank n and let $\mathbf{p}$ be the orthogonal projection of $\mathbf{b}$ into $V = \text{Col}(A)$. Explain why there is a unique vector $\mathbf{x}$ in $\mathbf{R}^n$ such that $\mathbf{p} = A\mathbf{x}$. What "sum of squares" does $\mathbf{x}$ minimize?

10. Given a linear system $A\mathbf{x} = \mathbf{b}$, what is the associated normal system?

11. What is a least squares solution of a linear system $A\mathbf{x} = \mathbf{b}$? When is a least squares solution actually a solution of $A\mathbf{x} = \mathbf{b}$?

12. Under what condition on the matrix A does it follow that the square matrix A^TA is invertible?

13. Given points (x_1, y_1), (x_2, y_2), $\ldots$, (x_n, y_n) in $\mathbf{R}^2$, tell how to find the least squares line $y = a + bx$ that best fits these points. Precisely what "sum of squares" does this line $y = a + bx$ minimize?

14. Explain why every subspace of $\mathbf{R}^n$ has an orthogonal basis. How is one actually constructed?

15. Explain how the existence of an orthogonal basis for a subspace V simplifies the problem of finding the orthogonal projection of a given vector $\mathbf{b}$ into V.

16. Given a set of mutually orthogonal nonzero vectors in $\mathbf{R}^n$, explain how to enlarge this set to an orthogonal basis for $\mathbf{R}^n$.

17. Suppose that the Gram-Schmidt algorithm is applied to the set $S = \{\mathbf{v}_1, \mathbf{v}_2, \ldots, \mathbf{v}_n\}$ of vectors, and that the result is the set $T = \{\mathbf{u}_1, \mathbf{u}_2, \ldots, \mathbf{u}_n\}$. Explain why the set T is linearly dependent if and only if $\mathbf{u}_k = \mathbf{0}$ for some k. Does this imply that the original set S was linearly dependent?

18. Let S and T be bases for the finite-dimensional subspaces U and V of an inner product space W, and suppose that each vector in S is orthogonal to each vector in T. Explain why it follows that the only vector that belongs both to U and to V is the zero vector. Does this fact imply that the union of the sets S and T is a linearly independent set of vectors? Explain.

6

Eigenvalues and Eigenvectors

6.1 Introduction

Given a square matrix A, let us pose the following question: Does there exist a nonzero vector $\mathbf{v}$ such that the result $A\mathbf{v}$ of multiplying $\mathbf{v}$ by the matrix A is simply a scalar multiple of $\mathbf{v}$? Thus we ask whether or not there exist a nonzero vector $\mathbf{v}$ *and* a scalar λ such that

$$A\mathbf{v} = \lambda\mathbf{v}. \tag{1}$$

Section 6.3 and Chapter 8 are devoted to interesting applications in which this question arises. The following definition provides the terminology that we use in discussing Equation (1).

> ***Definition:*** *Eigenvalues and Eigenvectors*
> The real number λ is said to be an **eigenvalue** of the $n \times n$ matrix A provided that there exists a *nonzero* vector $\mathbf{v}$ such that
>
> $$A\mathbf{v} = \lambda\mathbf{v}, \tag{1}$$
>
> in which case the vector $\mathbf{v}$ is called an **eigenvector** of the matrix A. We also say that the eigenvector $\mathbf{v}$ is **associated** with the eigenvalue λ, or that the eigenvalue λ **corresponds** to the eigenvector $\mathbf{v}$.

The prefix *eigen* is a German word which (in some contexts) may be translated as *proper*, so eigenvalues are sometimes called *proper values.* Eigenvalues and eigenvectors are also called *characteristic values* and *characteristic vectors* in some books.

EXAMPLE 1 Consider the 2×2 matrix

$$A = \begin{bmatrix} 5 & -6 \\ 2 & -2 \end{bmatrix}.$$

If $\mathbf{v} = (2, 1)$, then

$$A\mathbf{v} = \begin{bmatrix} 5 & -6 \\ 2 & -2 \end{bmatrix}\begin{bmatrix} 2 \\ 1 \end{bmatrix} = \begin{bmatrix} 4 \\ 2 \end{bmatrix} = 2\mathbf{v}.$$

Thus $\mathbf{v} = (2, 1)$ is an eigenvector of A associated with the eigenvalue $\lambda = 2$. If $\mathbf{v} = (3, 2)$, then

$$A\mathbf{v} = \begin{bmatrix} 5 & -6 \\ 2 & -2 \end{bmatrix}\begin{bmatrix} 3 \\ 2 \end{bmatrix} = \begin{bmatrix} 3 \\ 2 \end{bmatrix} = 1\mathbf{v},$$

so $\mathbf{v} = (3, 2)$ is an eigenvector of A associated with the eigenvalue $\lambda = 1$. In summary, we see that the scalars $\lambda_1 = 2$ and $\lambda_2 = 1$ are both eigenvalues of the matrix A; they correspond to the eigenvectors $\mathbf{v}_1 = (2, 1)$ and $\mathbf{v}_2 = (3, 2)$, respectively.

Eigenvalues and eigenvectors have a simple geometric interpretation. Suppose that λ is an eigenvalue of the matrix A with associated eigenvector $\mathbf{v}$, so that $A\mathbf{v} = \lambda\mathbf{v}$. Then the length $|A\mathbf{v}|$ of the vector $A\mathbf{v}$ is $\pm\lambda|\mathbf{v}|$, depending on the sign of λ. Thus if $\lambda > 0$ then multiplication of $\mathbf{v}$ by the matrix A expands or contracts the vector $\mathbf{v}$ while preserving its direction, but if $\lambda < 0$ then multiplication of $\mathbf{v}$ by A reverses the direction of $\mathbf{v}$ (see Figure 6.1).

REMARK 1 If $\mathbf{v} = \mathbf{0}$, then the equation $A\mathbf{v} = \lambda\mathbf{v}$ holds for every scalar λ and hence is of no significance. This is why only *nonzero* vectors qualify as eigenvectors in the definition.

REMARK 2 Let λ and $\mathbf{v}$ be an eigenvalue and associated eigenvector of the matrix A. If k is any nonzero scalar and $\mathbf{u} = k\mathbf{v}$, then

$$\begin{aligned} A\mathbf{u} &= A(k\mathbf{v}) = k(A\mathbf{v}) \\ &= k(\lambda\mathbf{v}) = \lambda(k\mathbf{v}) = \lambda\mathbf{u}, \end{aligned}$$

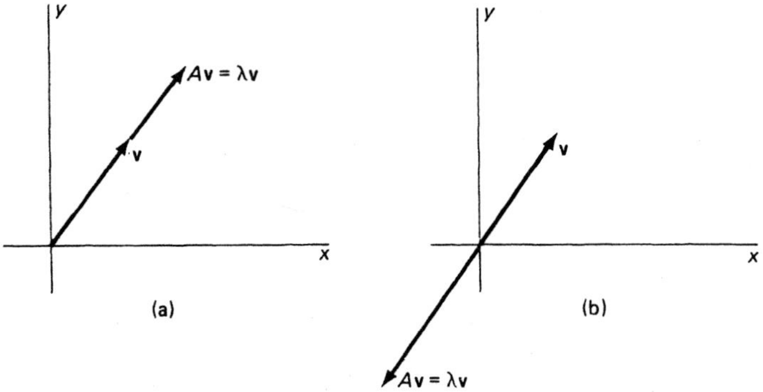

6.1 (a) A positive eigenvalue; (b) A negative eigenvalue.

so $\mathbf{u} = k\mathbf{v}$ is also an eigenvector associated with λ. Thus *any nonzero scalar multiple of an eigenvector is also an eigenvector and is associated with the same eigenvalue.* In Example 1, for instance, $\mathbf{u}_1 = -3\mathbf{v}_1 = (-6, -3)$ is an eigenvector associated with $\lambda_1 = 2$, and $\mathbf{u}_2 = 4\mathbf{v}_2 = (12, 8)$ is an eigenvector associated with $\lambda_2 = 1$.

THE CHARACTERISTIC EQUATION

We now attack the problem of finding the eigenvalues and eigenvectors of a given $n \times n$ square matrix A. According to the definition, the nonzero vector $\mathbf{v}$ is an eigenvector of A associated with the eigenvalue λ exactly when

$$A\mathbf{v} = \lambda\mathbf{v} = \lambda I\mathbf{v};$$

that is, when

$$(A - \lambda I)\mathbf{v} = \mathbf{0}. \tag{2}$$

For a fixed value of λ, Equation (2) is a homogeneous linear system of n equations in the n components of $\mathbf{v}$. By Theorem 2 in Section 2.3 and Theorem 7 in Section 1.5, this system has a nontrivial solution $\mathbf{v} \neq \mathbf{0}$ if and only if the determinant

$$\det(A - \lambda I) = |A - \lambda I|$$

of its coefficient matrix is *zero*. The equation $|A - \lambda I| = 0$ is called the **characteristic equation** of the square matrix A, and we have proved that there exists an eigenvalue $\mathbf{v}$ associated with λ if and only if λ satisfies this equation.

> ***Theorem 1:*** *The Characteristic Equation*
>
> The real number λ is an eigenvalue of the $n \times n$ matrix A if and only if λ satisfies the characteristic equation
>
> $$|A - \lambda I| = 0. \tag{3}$$

Now let us see just what sort of equation the characteristic equation in (3) is. Note that the matrix

$$A - \lambda I = \begin{bmatrix} a_{11} - \lambda & a_{12} & \cdots & a_{1n} \\ a_{21} & a_{22} - \lambda & \cdots & a_{2n} \\ \vdots & \vdots & \ddots & \vdots \\ a_{n1} & a_{n2} & \cdots & a_{nn} - \lambda \end{bmatrix} \tag{4}$$

is obtained simply by subtracting λ from each diagonal element of A. If we think of expanding the determinant by minors, we see that $|A - \lambda I|$ is a *polynomial* in the variable λ, and that the highest power of λ comes from the product of the diagonal elements of the matrix in (4). Therefore the characteristic equation of the $n \times n$ matrix A takes the form

$$(-1)^n \lambda^n + c_{n-1}\lambda^{n-1} + \cdots + c_1\lambda + c_0 = 0, \tag{5}$$

an nth degree polynomial equation in λ.

According to the fundamental theorem of algebra, every nth degree polynomial equation in one variable has n solutions (counting multiple solutions), but some of them may be complex. In more advanced treatments the complex solutions (if any) of the characteristic equation are sometimes called *complex eigenvalues*, but in this book we consider only real eigenvalues. Hence we can conclude that *an $n \times n$ matrix A has at most n eigenvalues.* It has exactly n eigenvalues if its characteristic equation has n distinct real solutions; otherwise, A has fewer than n eigenvalues.

Algorithm: *Eigenvalues and Eigenvectors*

To find the eigenvalues and associated eigenvectors of the $n \times n$ matrix A:

1. First solve the characteristic equation

$$|A - \lambda I| = 0.$$

2. Then, for *each* eigenvalue λ thereby found, solve the linear system

$$(A - \lambda I)\mathbf{v} = \mathbf{0}$$

to find the eigenvectors associated with λ.

Solving the characteristic equation is almost always easier said than done. In the examples that follow and in the problems, we have chosen matrices for which the characteristic polynomial $|A - \lambda I|$ readily factors to reveal the eigenvalues.

EXAMPLE 2 Find the eigenvalues and associated eigenvectors of the matrix

$$A = \begin{bmatrix} 5 & 7 \\ -2 & -4 \end{bmatrix}.$$

Solution Here

$$A - \lambda I = \begin{bmatrix} 5-\lambda & 7 \\ -2 & -4-\lambda \end{bmatrix}, \tag{6}$$

so the characteristic equation of A is

$$\begin{aligned} 0 &= |A - \lambda I| \\ &= (5-\lambda)(-4-\lambda) - (-2)(7) \\ &= (\lambda - 5)(\lambda + 4) + 14 = \lambda^2 - \lambda - 6: \end{aligned}$$

$$(\lambda + 2)(\lambda - 3) = 0.$$

Thus the matrix A has the two eigenvalues -2 and 3. To distinguish them we write $\lambda_1 = -2$ and $\lambda_2 = 3$. To find the associated eigenvectors, we must *separately* substitute each eigenvalue in (6) and then solve the resulting system $(A - \lambda I)\mathbf{v} = \mathbf{0}$.

- The case $\lambda_1 = -2$: With $\mathbf{v} = (x, y)$, the system $(A - \lambda I)\mathbf{v} = \mathbf{0}$ is

$$\begin{bmatrix} 7 & 7 \\ -2 & -2 \end{bmatrix}\begin{bmatrix} x \\ y \end{bmatrix} = \begin{bmatrix} 0 \\ 0 \end{bmatrix}.$$

  Each of the two scalar equations here is a multiple of the equation $x + y = 0$, and any nontrivial solution $\mathbf{v} = (x, y)$ of this equation is a nonzero multiple of $(1, -1)$. Hence (to within a constant multiple) the only eigenvector associated with $\lambda_1 = -2$ is $\mathbf{v}_1 = (1, -1)$.
- The case $\lambda_2 = 3$: With $\mathbf{v} = (x, y)$, the system $(A - \lambda I)\mathbf{v} = \mathbf{0}$ is

$$\begin{bmatrix} 2 & 7 \\ -2 & -7 \end{bmatrix}\begin{bmatrix} x \\ y \end{bmatrix} = \begin{bmatrix} 0 \\ 0 \end{bmatrix}.$$

  Again we have only a single equation, $2x + 7y = 0$, and any nontrivial solution of this equation will suffice. The choice $y = -2$ yields $x = 7$, so (to within a constant multiple) the only eigenvector associated with $\lambda_2 = 3$ is $\mathbf{v}_2 = (7, -2)$.

Finally, note that it is not enough to say simply that the given matrix A has eigenvalues -2 and 3 and has eigenvectors $(1, -1)$ and $(7, -2)$. To give complete information we must say which eigenvector is associated with each eigenvalue.

The next example shows that a matrix can fail to have any (real) eigenvalues at all.

EXAMPLE 3 The characteristic equation of the matrix

$$A = \begin{bmatrix} 3 & 5 \\ -5 & -3 \end{bmatrix}$$

is

$$\begin{vmatrix} 3-\lambda & 5 \\ -5 & -3-\lambda \end{vmatrix} = (3-\lambda)(-3-\lambda) + 25$$

$$= \lambda^2 + 16 = 0.$$

But the equation $\lambda^2 + 16 = 0$ has no real solutions (its solutions are the pure imaginary numbers $4i$ and $-4i$). Thus the given matrix A has no eigenvalues.

EXAMPLE 4 The 2×2 identity matrix I has characteristic equation

$$\begin{vmatrix} 1-\lambda & 0 \\ 0 & 1-\lambda \end{vmatrix} = (1-\lambda)^2 = 0,$$

so I has the single eigenvalue $\lambda = 1$. The equation $(I - 1I)\mathbf{v} = \mathbf{0}$ is

$$\begin{bmatrix} 0 & 0 \\ 0 & 0 \end{bmatrix}\begin{bmatrix} x \\ y \end{bmatrix} = \begin{bmatrix} 0 \\ 0 \end{bmatrix},$$

so *every* nonzero vector $\mathbf{v} = (x, y)$ is an eigenvector of I. In particular, the single eigenvalue $\lambda = 1$ corresponds to the *two* linearly independent eigenvectors $\mathbf{v}_1 = (1, 0)$ and $\mathbf{v}_2 = (0, 1)$.

EXAMPLE 5 The characteristic equation of the matrix

$$A = \begin{bmatrix} 2 & 3 \\ 0 & 2 \end{bmatrix}$$

is $(2 - \lambda)^2 = 0$, so A has the single eigenvalue $\lambda = 2$. The equation $(A - 2I)\mathbf{v} = \mathbf{0}$ is

$$\begin{bmatrix} 0 & 3 \\ 0 & 0 \end{bmatrix}\begin{bmatrix} x \\ y \end{bmatrix} = \begin{bmatrix} 0 \\ 0 \end{bmatrix}.$$

Thus x is arbitrary but $y = 0$, so the eigenvalue $\lambda = 2$ corresponds (to within a constant multiple) to the single eigenvector $\mathbf{v} = (1, 0)$.

Examples 2–5 illustrate the four possibilities for a 2×2 matrix A. It may have either

- Two distinct eigenvalues, each corresponding to a single eigenvector;
- One eigenvalue corresponding to a single eigenvector;
- One eigenvalue corresponding to two linearly independent eigenvectors; or
- No eigenvalues.

The characteristic equation of a 3×3 matrix is (by Equation (5)) of the form

$$-\lambda^3 + c_2\lambda^2 + c_1\lambda + c_0 = 0. \tag{7}$$

Because every such cubic equation has at least one real solution, every 3×3 matrix has (in contrast with 2×2 matrices) at least one (real) eigenvalue. A 3×3 matrix may have one, two, or three distinct eigenvalues, and a single eigenvalue of a 3×3 matrix may correspond to one, two, or three linearly independent eigenvectors. The remaining two examples of this section illustrate some of the possibilities. The next example shows also that, whereas the zero vector $\mathbf{0}$ cannot be an eigenvector of a matrix, there is nothing to prevent $\lambda = 0$ from being an eigenvalue.

EXAMPLE 6 Find the eigenvalues and associated eigenvectors of the matrix

$$A = \begin{bmatrix} 3 & 0 & 0 \\ -4 & 6 & 2 \\ 16 & -15 & -5 \end{bmatrix}.$$

Solution The matrix $A - \lambda I$ is

$$A - \lambda I = \begin{bmatrix} 3-\lambda & 0 & 0 \\ -4 & 6-\lambda & 2 \\ 16 & -15 & -5-\lambda \end{bmatrix}. \tag{8}$$

Upon expansion of the determinant along its first row, we find that

$$\begin{aligned} |A - \lambda I| &= (3-\lambda)[(6-\lambda)(-5-\lambda) + 30] \\ &= (3-\lambda)(\lambda^2 - \lambda) = \lambda(\lambda - 1)(3 - \lambda). \end{aligned}$$

Hence the characteristic equation $|A - \lambda I| = 0$ yields the three eigenvalues $\lambda_1 = 0$, $\lambda_2 = 1$, and $\lambda_3 = 3$. To find the associated eigenvectors we must solve the system $(A - \lambda I)\mathbf{v} = \mathbf{0}$ separately for each of these three eigenvalues.

- For $\lambda_1 = 0$: We write $\mathbf{v} = (x, y, z)$ and substitute $\lambda = 0$ in the coefficient matrix in (8) to obtain the system

$$\begin{bmatrix} 3 & 0 & 0 \\ -4 & 6 & 2 \\ 16 & -15 & -5 \end{bmatrix} \begin{bmatrix} x \\ y \\ z \end{bmatrix} = \begin{bmatrix} 0 \\ 0 \\ 0 \end{bmatrix}.$$

  From the first of the three equations here, $3x = 0$, we see that $x = 0$. Then each of the remaining two equations is a multiple of the equation $3y + z = 0$. The choice $y = 1$ yields $z = -3$. Thus the eigenvector $\mathbf{v}_1 = (0, 1, -3)$ is associated with $\lambda_1 = 0$.

- For $\lambda_2 = 1$: Substitution of $\lambda = 1$ in the coefficient matrix in (8) yields the system

$$\begin{bmatrix} 2 & 0 & 0 \\ -4 & 5 & 2 \\ 16 & -15 & -6 \end{bmatrix} \begin{bmatrix} x \\ y \\ z \end{bmatrix} = \begin{bmatrix} 0 \\ 0 \\ 0 \end{bmatrix}$$

  for $\mathbf{v} = (x, y, z)$. The first equation $2x = 0$ implies that $x = 0$. Then the third equation is a multiple of the second equation, $5y + 2z = 0$. The choice $y = 2$ yields $z = -5$, so the eigenvector $\mathbf{v}_2 = (0, 2, -5)$ is associated with $\lambda_2 = 1$.

- For $\lambda_3 = 3$: Substitution of $\lambda = 3$ in the coefficient matrix in (8) yields the system

$$\begin{bmatrix} 0 & 0 & 0 \\ -4 & 3 & 2 \\ 16 & -15 & -8 \end{bmatrix} \begin{bmatrix} x \\ y \\ z \end{bmatrix} = \begin{bmatrix} 0 \\ 0 \\ 0 \end{bmatrix}.$$

  In this case the first equation yields no information. But the result of adding 4 times the second equation to the third equation is $-3y = 0$, so $y = 0$. Consequently the second and third equations are both multiples of the equation $2x - z = 0$. The choice $x = 1$ yields $z = 2$, so the eigenvector $\mathbf{v}_3 = (1, 0, 2)$ is associated with $\lambda_3 = 3$.

In summary, we have found the eigenvectors $\mathbf{v}_1 = (0, 1, -3)$, $\mathbf{v}_2 = (0, 2, -5)$, and $\mathbf{v}_3 = (1, 0, 2)$ associated with the distinct eigenvalues $\lambda_1 = 0$, $\lambda_2 = 1$, and $\lambda_3 = 3$, respectively.

REMARK Substitution of $\lambda = 0$ in the characteristic equation $|A - \lambda I| = 0$ yields $|A| = 0$. Therefore $\lambda = 0$ is an eigenvalue of the matrix A if and only if A is singular: $|A| = 0$.

Let λ be a fixed eigenvalue of the matrix A. Then the set of all eigenvectors associated with A is the set of all nonzero solution vectors of the system

$$(A - \lambda I)\mathbf{v} = \mathbf{0}. \tag{9}$$

The solution space of this system is called the **eigenspace** of A associated with the eigenvalue λ; it consists of all eigenvectors associated with λ *together with* the zero vector. In Example 6 we found (to within a constant multiple) only a single eigenvector associated with each eigenvector λ; in this case the eigenspace of λ is 1-dimensional. In the case of an eigenspace of higher dimension, we generally want to find a basis for the solution space of Equation (9).

EXAMPLE 7 Find bases for the eigenspaces of the matrix

$$A = \begin{bmatrix} 4 & -2 & 1 \\ 2 & 0 & 1 \\ 2 & -2 & 3 \end{bmatrix}.$$

Solution Here we have

$$A - \lambda I = \begin{bmatrix} 4-\lambda & -2 & 1 \\ 2 & -\lambda & 1 \\ 2 & -2 & 3-\lambda \end{bmatrix}. \tag{10}$$

We expand along the first row to obtain

$$\begin{aligned} |A - \lambda I| &= (4-\lambda)(\lambda^2 - 3\lambda + 2) - (-2)(4 - 2\lambda) + (1)(-4 + 2\lambda) \\ &= -\lambda^3 + 7\lambda^2 - 16\lambda + 12. \end{aligned}$$

Thus to find the eigenvalues we need to solve the cubic equation

$$\lambda^3 - 7\lambda^2 + 16\lambda - 12 = 0. \tag{11}$$

We look (hopefully) for integer solutions. The factor theorem of algebra implies that if the polynomial equation

$$\lambda^n + c_{n-1}\lambda^{n-1} + \cdots + c_1\lambda + c_0 = 0$$

with integer coefficients and leading coefficient 1 has an integer solution, then that integer is a divisor of the constant c_0. In the case of the cubic equation in (11), the possibilities for such a solution are ± 1, ± 2, ± 3, ± 4, ± 6, and ± 12. We substitute these numbers successively in (11), and thereby find that $+1$ and -1 are not solutions but that $\lambda = +2$ is a solution. Hence $\lambda - 2$ is a factor of the cubic polynomial in (11). Next, the long division

$$\begin{array}{r|l} & \lambda^2 - 5\lambda \ + 6 \\ \hline \lambda - 2 & \lambda^3 - 7\lambda^2 + 16\lambda - 12 \\ & \lambda^3 - 2\lambda^2 \\ \hline & \quad -5\lambda^2 + 16\lambda - 12 \\ & \quad -5\lambda^2 + 10\lambda \\ \hline & \qquad\qquad 6\lambda - 12 \\ & \qquad\qquad 6\lambda - 12 \\ \hline & \qquad\qquad\qquad 0 \end{array}$$

shows that

$$\begin{aligned} \lambda^3 - 7\lambda^2 + 16\lambda - 12 &= (\lambda - 2)(\lambda^2 - 5\lambda + 6) \\ &= (\lambda - 2)(\lambda - 2)(\lambda - 3) \\ &= (\lambda - 2)^2(\lambda - 3). \end{aligned}$$

Thus we see finally that the given matrix A has the repeated eigenvalue $\lambda = 2$ and the eigenvalue $\lambda = 3$.

- For $\lambda = 2$: The system $(A - \lambda I)\mathbf{v} = \mathbf{0}$ is

$$\begin{bmatrix} 2 & -2 & 1 \\ 2 & -2 & 1 \\ 2 & -2 & 1 \end{bmatrix} \begin{bmatrix} x \\ y \\ z \end{bmatrix} = \begin{bmatrix} 0 \\ 0 \\ 0 \end{bmatrix},$$

which reduces to the single equation $2x - 2y + z = 0$. This equation obviously has a 2-dimensional solution space. With $y = 1$ and $z = 0$, we get $x = 1$, and hence obtain the basis eigenvector $\mathbf{v}_1 = (1, 1, 0)$. With $y = 0$ and $z = 2$, we get $x = -1$ and hence the basis eigenvector $\mathbf{v}_2 = (-1, 0, 2)$. The 2-dimensional eigenspace of A associated with the repeated eigenvalue $\lambda = 2$ has basis $\{\mathbf{v}_1, \mathbf{v}_2\}$.

- For $\lambda = 3$: The system $(A - \lambda I)\mathbf{v} = \mathbf{0}$ is

$$\begin{bmatrix} 1 & -2 & 1 \\ 2 & -3 & 1 \\ 2 & -2 & 0 \end{bmatrix} \begin{bmatrix} x \\ y \\ z \end{bmatrix} = \begin{bmatrix} 0 \\ 0 \\ 0 \end{bmatrix}.$$

The last equation here implies that $x = y$, and then each of the first two equations yields $x = y = z$. It follows that the eigenspace of A associated with $\lambda = 3$ is 1-dimensional and has $\mathbf{v}_3 = (1, 1, 1)$ as a basis eigenvector.

REMARK The typical higher-degree polynomial is not so easy to factor as the one in Example 7. Hence a numerical technique such as Newton's method is often needed to solve the characteristic equation. Moreover, for an $n \times n$ matrix with n greater than about 4, the amount of labor required to find the characteristic equation by expanding the determinant $|A - \lambda I|$ is generally prohibitive; because of the presence of the variable λ, row and column elimination methods do not work as they do with numerical determinants. Consequently specialized techniques, beyond the scope of the present discussion, are often required to find the eigenvalues and eigenvectors of the large matrices that occur in many applications. Problems 34 and 35 at the end of this section outline a numerical technique that sometimes is useful with matrices of moderate size.

6.1 PROBLEMS

In Problems 1–26, find the eigenvalues and associated eigenvectors of the given matrix A. Find a basis for each eigenspace of dimension 2 or larger.

1. $\begin{bmatrix} 4 & -2 \\ 1 & 1 \end{bmatrix}$

2. $\begin{bmatrix} 5 & -6 \\ 3 & -4 \end{bmatrix}$

3. $\begin{bmatrix} 8 & -6 \\ 3 & -1 \end{bmatrix}$

4. $\begin{bmatrix} 4 & -3 \\ 2 & -1 \end{bmatrix}$

5. $\begin{bmatrix} 10 & -9 \\ 6 & -5 \end{bmatrix}$

6. $\begin{bmatrix} 6 & -4 \\ 3 & -1 \end{bmatrix}$

7. $\begin{bmatrix} 10 & -8 \\ 6 & -4 \end{bmatrix}$

8. $\begin{bmatrix} 7 & -6 \\ 12 & -10 \end{bmatrix}$

9. $\begin{bmatrix} 8 & -10 \\ 2 & -1 \end{bmatrix}$

10. $\begin{bmatrix} 9 & -10 \\ 2 & 0 \end{bmatrix}$

11. $\begin{bmatrix} 19 & -10 \\ 21 & -10 \end{bmatrix}$

12. $\begin{bmatrix} 13 & -15 \\ 6 & -6 \end{bmatrix}$

13. $\begin{bmatrix} 2 & 0 & 0 \\ 2 & -2 & -1 \\ -2 & 6 & 3 \end{bmatrix}$

14. $\begin{bmatrix} 5 & 0 & 0 \\ 4 & -4 & -2 \\ -2 & 12 & 6 \end{bmatrix}$

15. $\begin{bmatrix} 2 & -2 & 0 \\ 2 & -2 & -1 \\ -2 & 2 & 3 \end{bmatrix}$

16. $\begin{bmatrix} 1 & 0 & -1 \\ -2 & 3 & -1 \\ -6 & 6 & 0 \end{bmatrix}$

17. $\begin{bmatrix} 3 & 5 & -2 \\ 0 & 2 & 0 \\ 0 & 2 & 1 \end{bmatrix}$

18. $\begin{bmatrix} 1 & 0 & 0 \\ -6 & 8 & 2 \\ 12 & -15 & -3 \end{bmatrix}$

19. $\begin{bmatrix} 3 & 6 & -2 \\ 0 & 1 & 0 \\ 0 & 0 & 1 \end{bmatrix}$

20. $\begin{bmatrix} 1 & 0 & 0 \\ -4 & 7 & 2 \\ 10 & -15 & -4 \end{bmatrix}$

21. $\begin{bmatrix} 4 & -3 & 1 \\ 2 & -1 & 1 \\ 0 & 0 & 2 \end{bmatrix}$

22. $\begin{bmatrix} 5 & -6 & 3 \\ 6 & -7 & 3 \\ 6 & -6 & 2 \end{bmatrix}$

23. $\begin{bmatrix} 1 & 2 & 2 & 2 \\ 0 & 2 & 2 & 2 \\ 0 & 0 & 3 & 2 \\ 0 & 0 & 0 & 4 \end{bmatrix}$

24. $\begin{bmatrix} 1 & 0 & 4 & 0 \\ 0 & 1 & 4 & 0 \\ 0 & 0 & 3 & 0 \\ 0 & 0 & 0 & 3 \end{bmatrix}$

25. $\begin{bmatrix} 1 & 0 & 1 & 0 \\ 0 & 1 & 1 & 0 \\ 0 & 0 & 2 & 0 \\ 0 & 0 & 0 & 2 \end{bmatrix}$

26. $\begin{bmatrix} 4 & 0 & 0 & -3 \\ 0 & 2 & 0 & 0 \\ 0 & 0 & -1 & 0 \\ 6 & 0 & 0 & -5 \end{bmatrix}$

27. Suppose that λ is an eigenvalue of the matrix A with associated eigenvector **v** and that n is a positive integer. Show that λ^n is an eigenvalue of A^n with associated eigenvector **v**.

28. Show that λ is an eigenvalue of the invertible matrix A if and only if λ^{-1} is an eigenvalue of A^{-1}. Are the associated eigenvectors the same?

29. (a) Suppose that A is a square matrix. Use the characteristic equation to show that A and A^T have the same eigenvalues.
(b) Give an example of a 2×2 matrix A such that A and A^T do not have the same eigenvectors.

30. Show that the eigenvalues of a triangular $n \times n$ matrix are its diagonal elements.

31. Suppose that the characteristic equation $|A - \lambda I| = 0$ is written as a polynomial equation (Equation (5)). Show that the constant term is $c_0 = \det A$. *Suggestion*: Substitute an appropriate value for λ.

32. If $A = [a_{ij}]$ is an $n \times n$ matrix, then the **trace** tr A of A is defined to be

$$\operatorname{tr} A = a_{11} + a_{22} + \cdots + a_{nn},$$

the sum of the diagonal elements of A. It can be proved that the coefficient of λ^{n-1} in Equation (5) is $c_{n-1} = (-1)^{n-1}(\operatorname{tr} A)$. Show explicitly that this is true in the case of a 2×2 matrix.

33. Suppose that the $n \times n$ matrix A has n (real) eigenvalues $\lambda_1, \lambda_2, \ldots, \lambda_n$. Assuming the general result stated in Problem 32, prove that

$$\begin{aligned} \lambda_1 + \lambda_2 + \cdots + \lambda_n &= \operatorname{tr} A \\ &= a_{11} + a_{22} + \cdots + a_{nn}. \end{aligned}$$

34. According to the results stated in Problems 31 and 32, the characteristic polynomial

$$p(\lambda) = |A - \lambda I|$$

of a 3×3 matrix A is given by

$$p(\lambda) = -\lambda^3 + (\operatorname{tr} A)\lambda^2 + c_1\lambda + (\det A).$$

The remaining coefficient c_1 can be found by substituting $\lambda = 1$ and then calculating the two determinants $|A|$ and $p(1) = |A - I|$. Use this method to find the characteristic equation, eigenvalues, and associated eigenvectors of the matrix

$$A = \begin{bmatrix} 32 & -67 & 47 \\ 7 & -14 & 13 \\ -7 & 15 & -6 \end{bmatrix}.$$

35. According to the results stated in Problems 31 and 32, the characteristic polynomial

$$p(\lambda) = |A - \lambda I|$$

of a 4×4 matrix A is given by

$$p(\lambda) = \lambda^4 - (\operatorname{tr} A)\lambda^3 + c_2\lambda^2 + c_1\lambda + (\det A).$$

The remaining coefficients c_1 and c_2 can be found by substituting $\lambda = \pm 1$ and calculating the three determinants $|A|$, $p(1) = |A - I|$, and $p(-1) = |A + I|$. Use this method to find the characteristic equation, eigenvalues, and associated eigenvectors of the matrix

$$A = \begin{bmatrix} 22 & -9 & -8 & -8 \\ 10 & -7 & -14 & 2 \\ 10 & 0 & 8 & -10 \\ 29 & -9 & -3 & -15 \end{bmatrix}.$$

6.2 Diagonalization of Matrices

Given an $n \times n$ matrix A, we may ask *how many* linearly independent eigenvectors the matrix A has. In Section 6.1 we saw several examples (with $n = 2$ and $n = 3$) in which the $n \times n$ matrix A has n linearly independent eigenvectors—the largest possible number, because any $n+1$ vectors in $\mathbf{R}^n$ must be linearly dependent. By contrast, in Example 3 of Section 6.1 we saw that the matrix

$$A = \begin{bmatrix} 3 & 5 \\ -5 & -3 \end{bmatrix}$$

has no (real) eigenvalues and hence no eigenvectors at all. In Example 5 of Section 6.1 we saw that the 2×2 matrix

$$A = \begin{bmatrix} 2 & 3 \\ 0 & 2 \end{bmatrix}$$

has the single eigenvalue $\lambda = 2$ corresponding to the single eigenvector $\mathbf{v} = (1, 0)$.

Something very nice happens when the $n \times n$ matrix A does have n linearly independent eigenvectors. Suppose that the eigenvalues $\lambda_1, \lambda_2, \ldots, \lambda_n$ (not necessarily distinct) of A correspond to the n linearly independent eigenvectors $\mathbf{v}_1, \mathbf{v}_2, \ldots, \mathbf{v}_n$, respectively. Let

$$P = \begin{bmatrix} | & | & & | \\ \mathbf{v}_1 & \mathbf{v}_2 & \cdots & \mathbf{v}_n \\ | & | & & | \end{bmatrix} \tag{1}$$

be the $n \times n$ matrix having these eigenvectors as its *column* vectors. Then

$$AP = A \begin{bmatrix} | & | & & | \\ \mathbf{v}_1 & \mathbf{v}_2 & \cdots & \mathbf{v}_n \\ | & | & & | \end{bmatrix}$$

$$= \begin{bmatrix} | & | & & | \\ A\mathbf{v}_1 & A\mathbf{v}_2 & \cdots & A\mathbf{v}_n \\ | & | & & | \end{bmatrix},$$

and hence

$$AP = \begin{bmatrix} | & | & & | \\ \lambda_1\mathbf{v}_1 & \lambda_2\mathbf{v}_2 & \cdots & \lambda_n\mathbf{v}_n \\ | & | & & | \end{bmatrix} \tag{2}$$

because $A\mathbf{v}_j = \lambda_j\mathbf{v}_j$ for each $j = 1, 2, \ldots, n$. Thus the product matrix AP has column vectors $\lambda_1\mathbf{v}_1, \lambda_2\mathbf{v}_2, \ldots, \lambda_n\mathbf{v}_n$.

Now consider the diagonal matrix

$$D = \begin{bmatrix} \lambda_1 & 0 & \cdots & 0 \\ 0 & \lambda_2 & \cdots & 0 \\ \vdots & \vdots & \ddots & \vdots \\ 0 & 0 & \cdots & \lambda_n \end{bmatrix}, \tag{3}$$

whose diagonal elements are the eigenvalues corresponding (in the same order) to the eigenvectors forming the columns of P. Then

$$PD = \begin{bmatrix} | & | & & | \\ \mathbf{v}_1 & \mathbf{v}_2 & \cdots & \mathbf{v}_n \\ | & | & & | \end{bmatrix} \begin{bmatrix} \lambda_1 & 0 & \cdots & 0 \\ 0 & \lambda_2 & \cdots & 0 \\ \vdots & \vdots & \ddots & \vdots \\ 0 & 0 & \cdots & \lambda_n \end{bmatrix}$$

$$= \begin{bmatrix} | & | & & | \\ \lambda_1\mathbf{v}_1 & \lambda_2\mathbf{v}_2 & \cdots & \lambda_n\mathbf{v}_n \\ | & | & & | \end{bmatrix} \tag{4}$$

because the product of the ith row of P and the jth column of D is simply the product of λ_j and the ith component of $\mathbf{v}_j$.

Finally, upon comparing the results in (2) and (4), we see that

$$AP = PD. \tag{5}$$

But the matrix P is invertible because its n column vectors are linearly independent. So we may multiply on the right by P^{-1} to obtain

$$A = PDP^{-1}. \tag{6}$$

Equation (6) expresses the $n \times n$ matrix A having n linearly independent eigenvectors in terms of the *eigenvector matrix* P and the diagonal *eigenvalue matrix* D. It can be rewritten as $D = P^{-1}AP$, but the form in (6) is the one that should be memorized.

EXAMPLE 1 In Example 1 of Section 6.1 we saw that the matrix

$$A = \begin{bmatrix} 5 & -6 \\ 2 & -2 \end{bmatrix}$$

has eigenvalues $\lambda_1 = 2$ and $\lambda_2 = 1$ corresponding to the linearly independent eigenvectors $\mathbf{v}_1 = (2, 1)$ and $\mathbf{v}_2 = (3, 2)$, respectively. Then

$$P = \begin{bmatrix} 2 & 3 \\ 1 & 2 \end{bmatrix}, \quad D = \begin{bmatrix} 2 & 0 \\ 0 & 1 \end{bmatrix}, \quad \text{and} \quad P^{-1} = \begin{bmatrix} 2 & -3 \\ -1 & 2 \end{bmatrix}.$$

So

$$PDP^{-1} = \begin{bmatrix} 2 & 3 \\ 1 & 2 \end{bmatrix} \begin{bmatrix} 2 & 0 \\ 0 & 1 \end{bmatrix} \begin{bmatrix} 2 & -3 \\ -1 & 2 \end{bmatrix}$$

$$= \begin{bmatrix} 4 & 3 \\ 2 & 2 \end{bmatrix} \begin{bmatrix} 2 & -3 \\ -1 & 2 \end{bmatrix} = \begin{bmatrix} 5 & -6 \\ 2 & -2 \end{bmatrix} = A,$$

in accord with Equation (6).

The following definition embodies the precise relationship in (6) between the original matrix A and the diagonal matrix D.

> ***Definition*:** *Similar Matrices*
>
> The $n \times n$ matrices A and B are called **similar** provided that there exists an invertible matrix P such that
>
> $$B = P^{-1}AP. \tag{7}$$

Note that this relationship between A and B is symmetric, for if $B = P^{-1}AP$, then $A = Q^{-1}BQ$ for some invertible matrix Q—just take $Q = P^{-1}$.

An $n \times n$ matrix A is called **diagonalizable** if it is similar to a diagonal matrix D; that is, there exists a diagonal matrix D and an invertible matrix P such that $A = PDP^{-1}$, and so

$$P^{-1}AP = D. \tag{8}$$

The process of finding the diagonalizing matrix P and the diagonal matrix D in (8) is called **diagonalization** of the matrix A. In Example 1 we showed that the matrices

$$A = \begin{bmatrix} 5 & -6 \\ 2 & -2 \end{bmatrix} \quad \text{and} \quad D = \begin{bmatrix} 2 & 0 \\ 0 & 1 \end{bmatrix}$$

are similar, and hence that the 2×2 matrix A is diagonalizable.

Now we ask under what conditions a given square matrix is diagonalizable. In deriving Equation (6), we showed that *if* the $n \times n$ matrix A has n linearly independent eigenvectors, *then* A is diagonalizable. The converse of this statement is true also.

> ***Theorem 1*:** *Criterion for Diagonalizability*
>
> The $n \times n$ matrix A is diagonalizable if and only if it has n linearly independent eigenvectors.

Proof It remains only to show that if the $n \times n$ matrix A is diagonalizable, then it has n linearly independent eigenvectors. So suppose that A is similar to the diagonal matrix D with diagonal elements $d_1, d_2, \ldots, d_n$, and let

$$P = [\mathbf{v}_1 \quad \mathbf{v}_2 \quad \cdots \quad \mathbf{v}_n]$$

be an invertible matrix such that $D = P^{-1}AP$. Then

$$\begin{aligned} AP &= A[\mathbf{v}_1 \quad \mathbf{v}_2 \quad \cdots \quad \mathbf{v}_n] \\ &= [A\mathbf{v}_1 \quad A\mathbf{v}_2 \quad \cdots \quad A\mathbf{v}_n], \end{aligned}$$

and

$$PD = [d_1\mathbf{v}_1 \quad d_2\mathbf{v}_2 \quad \cdots \quad d_n\mathbf{v}_n]$$

by essentially the same computation as in Equation (4). But $AP = PD$ because $D = P^{-1}AP$, so it follows that

$$A\mathbf{v}_j = d_j\mathbf{v}_j$$

for each $j = 1, 2, \ldots, n$. Thus the vectors $\mathbf{v}_1, \mathbf{v}_2, \ldots, \mathbf{v}_n$ are eigenvectors of A associated with the eigenvalues $d_1, d_2, \ldots, d_n$, respectively. And it follows from Theorem 2 in Section 2.3 and Theorem 2 in Section 4.2 that these n eigenvectors of the matrix A are linearly independent, because they are the column vectors of the invertible matrix P. ■

REMARK It is important to remember not only the fact that an $n \times n$ matrix A having n linearly independent eigenvectors is diagonalizable, but also the specific diagonalization $A = PDP^{-1}$ in Equation (6), where the matrix P has the n eigenvectors as its columns, and the corresponding eigenvalues are the diagonal elements of the diagonal matrix D.

EXAMPLE 2 In Example 5 of Section 6.1 we saw that the matrix

$$A = \begin{bmatrix} 2 & 3 \\ 0 & 2 \end{bmatrix}$$

has only one eigenvalue, $\lambda = 2$, and that (to within a constant multiple) only the single eigenvector $\mathbf{v} = (1, 0)$ is associated with this eigenvalue. Thus the 2×2 matrix A does *not* have $n = 2$ linearly independent eigenvectors. Hence Theorem 1 implies that A is not diagonalizable.

EXAMPLE 3 In Example 6 of Section 6.1 we found that the matrix

$$A = \begin{bmatrix} 3 & 0 & 0 \\ -4 & 6 & 2 \\ 16 & -15 & -5 \end{bmatrix}$$

has the following eigenvalues and associated eigenvectors:

$$\lambda_1 = 3: \quad \mathbf{v}_1 = (1, 0, 2)$$
$$\lambda_2 = 1: \quad \mathbf{v}_2 = (0, 2, -5)$$
$$\lambda_3 = 0: \quad \mathbf{v}_3 = (0, 1, -3).$$

It is obvious (why?) that the three eigenvectors $\mathbf{v}_1$, $\mathbf{v}_2$, $\mathbf{v}_3$ are linearly independent, so Theorem 1 implies that the 3×3 matrix A is diagonalizable. In particular, the inverse of the eigenvector matrix

$$P = [\mathbf{v}_1 \quad \mathbf{v}_2 \quad \mathbf{v}_3] = \begin{bmatrix} 1 & 0 & 0 \\ 0 & 2 & 1 \\ 2 & -5 & -3 \end{bmatrix}$$

is

$$P^{-1} = \begin{bmatrix} 1 & 0 & 0 \\ -2 & 3 & 1 \\ 4 & -5 & -2 \end{bmatrix},$$

and the diagonal eigenvalue matrix is

$$D = \begin{bmatrix} \lambda_1 & 0 & 0 \\ 0 & \lambda_2 & 0 \\ 0 & 0 & \lambda_3 \end{bmatrix} = \begin{bmatrix} 3 & 0 & 0 \\ 0 & 1 & 0 \\ 0 & 0 & 0 \end{bmatrix}.$$

Therefore Equation (6) in the form $P^{-1}AP = D$ yields the diagonalization

$$P^{-1}AP = \begin{bmatrix} 1 & 0 & 0 \\ -2 & 3 & 1 \\ 4 & -5 & -2 \end{bmatrix} \begin{bmatrix} 3 & 0 & 0 \\ -4 & 6 & 2 \\ 16 & -15 & -5 \end{bmatrix} \begin{bmatrix} 1 & 0 & 0 \\ 0 & 2 & 1 \\ 2 & -5 & -3 \end{bmatrix}$$
$$= \begin{bmatrix} 3 & 0 & 0 \\ 0 & 1 & 0 \\ 0 & 0 & 0 \end{bmatrix}$$

of the matrix A.

The following theorem tells us that any set of eigenvectors associated with *distinct* eigenvalues (as in Example 3) is automatically linearly independent.

> ***Theorem 2:*** *Eigenvectors Associated with Distinct Eigenvalues*
> Suppose that the eigenvectors $\mathbf{v}_1, \mathbf{v}_2, \ldots, \mathbf{v}_k$ are associated with the distinct eigenvalues $\lambda_1, \lambda_2, \ldots, \lambda_k$ of the matrix A. Then these k eigenvectors are linearly independent.

PROOF Our proof will be by induction on k. The theorem is certainly true in the case $k = 1$, because any single (nonzero) eigenvector constitutes a linearly independent set. Now assume inductively that any set of $k - 1$ eigenvectors associated with distinct eigenvalues is linearly independent. Supposing that

$$c_1\mathbf{v}_1 + c_2\mathbf{v}_2 + \cdots + c_k\mathbf{v}_k = \mathbf{0}, \tag{9}$$

we need to show that $c_1 = c_2 = \cdots = c_k = 0$. To do this we will multiply in Equation (9) by the matrix $A - \lambda_1 I$. First note that

$$(A - \lambda_1 I)\mathbf{v}_j = A\mathbf{v}_j - \lambda_1\mathbf{v}_j = \begin{cases} \mathbf{0} & \text{if } j = 1, \\ (\lambda_j - \lambda_1)\mathbf{v}_j & \text{if } j > 1, \end{cases}$$

because $A\mathbf{v}_j = \lambda_j\mathbf{v}_j$ for each j. Therefore the result of multiplying Equation (9) by $A - \lambda_1 I$ is

$$c_2(\lambda_2 - \lambda_1)\mathbf{v}_2 + \cdots + c_k(\lambda_k - \lambda_1)\mathbf{v}_k = \mathbf{0}. \tag{10}$$

But the $k - 1$ eigenvectors $\mathbf{v}_2, \mathbf{v}_3, \ldots, \mathbf{v}_k$ are linearly independent by the inductive assumption. Because $\lambda_j - \lambda_1 \neq 0$ for each $j > 1$, it therefore follows from Equation (10) that $c_2 = c_3 = \cdots = c_k = 0$. But then Equation (9) reduces to $c_1\mathbf{v}_1 = \mathbf{0}$, so it now follows (because $\mathbf{v}_1 \neq \mathbf{0}$) that $c_1 = 0$ as well. Thus we have shown that all the coefficients in Equation (9) must vanish, and hence that the k eigenvectors $\mathbf{v}_1$, $\mathbf{v}_2, \ldots, \mathbf{v}_k$ are linearly independent. Theorem 2 now follows by induction. ■

If the $n \times n$ matrix A has n distinct eigenvalues, then by Theorem 2 the n associated eigenvectors are linearly independent, so Theorem 1 implies that the matrix A is diagonalizable. Thus we have the sufficient condition for diagonalizability given in Theorem 3.

> ***Theorem 3:*** *An $n \times n$ Matrix with n Distinct Eigenvalues*
> If the $n \times n$ matrix A has n distinct eigenvalues, then it is diagonalizable.

In general, however, an $n \times n$ matrix A can be expected to have fewer than n distinct eigenvalues $\lambda_1, \lambda_2, \ldots, \lambda_k$. If $k < n$, then we may *attempt* to diagonalize A by carrying out the following procedure.

STEP 1: Find a basis S_i for the eigenspace associated with each eigenvalue λ_i.

STEP 2: Form the union S of the bases $S_1, S_2, \ldots, S_k$. According to Theorem 4 in this section, the set S of eigenvectors of A is linearly independent.

STEP 3: If S contains n eigenvectors $\mathbf{v}_1, \mathbf{v}_2, \ldots, \mathbf{v}_n$, then the matrix

$$P = [\mathbf{v}_1 \quad \mathbf{v}_2 \quad \cdots \quad \mathbf{v}_n]$$

diagonalizes A. That is, $P^{-1}AP = D$, where the diagonal elements of D are the eigenvalues (repeated as necessary) corresponding to the k eigenvectors $\mathbf{v}_1, \mathbf{v}_2, \ldots, \mathbf{v}_n$.

If the set S—obtained by "merging" the bases for all the eigenspaces of A—contains fewer than n eigenvectors, then it can be proved that the matrix A is not diagonalizable.

EXAMPLE 4 In Example 7 of Section 6.1 we saw that the matrix

$$A = \begin{bmatrix} 4 & -2 & 1 \\ 2 & 0 & 1 \\ 2 & -2 & 3 \end{bmatrix}$$

has only two distinct eigenvalues, $\lambda_1 = 2$ and $\lambda_2 = 3$. We found that the eigenvalue $\lambda_1 = 2$ corresponds to a 2-dimensional eigenspace with basis vectors $\mathbf{v}_1 = (1, 1, 0)$ and $\mathbf{v}_2 = (-1, 0, 2)$, and that $\lambda_2 = 3$ corresponds to a 1-dimensional eigenspace with basis vector $\mathbf{v}_3 = (1, 1, 1)$. By Theorem 4 (or by explicit verification), these three eigenvectors are linearly independent, so Theorem 1 implies that the 3×3 matrix A is diagonalizable. The diagonalizing matrix

$$P = [\mathbf{v}_1 \quad \mathbf{v}_2 \quad \mathbf{v}_3] = \begin{bmatrix} 1 & -1 & 1 \\ 1 & 0 & 1 \\ 0 & 2 & 1 \end{bmatrix}$$

has inverse matrix

$$P^{-1} = \begin{bmatrix} -2 & 3 & -1 \\ -1 & 1 & 0 \\ 2 & -2 & 1 \end{bmatrix},$$

so we obtain the diagonalization

$$P^{-1}AP = \begin{bmatrix} -2 & 3 & -1 \\ -1 & 1 & 0 \\ 2 & -2 & 1 \end{bmatrix} \begin{bmatrix} 4 & -2 & 1 \\ 2 & 0 & 1 \\ 2 & -2 & 3 \end{bmatrix} \begin{bmatrix} 1 & -1 & 1 \\ 1 & 0 & 1 \\ 0 & 2 & 1 \end{bmatrix}$$

$$= \begin{bmatrix} 2 & 0 & 0 \\ 0 & 2 & 0 \\ 0 & 0 & 3 \end{bmatrix} = D$$

of the matrix A.

> ***Theorem 4:*** *Complete Independence of Eigenvectors*
> Let $\lambda_1, \lambda_2, \ldots, \lambda_k$ be the distinct eigenvalues of the $n \times n$ matrix A. For each $i = 1, 2, \ldots, k$, let S_i be a basis for the eigenspace associated with λ_i. Then the union S of the bases $S_1, S_2, \ldots, S_k$ is a linearly independent set of eigenvectors of A.

PROOF To simplify the notation we will illustrate the proof with the typical case $k = 3$, with A having three distinct eigenvalues λ_1, λ_2, and λ_3. Let

$$S_1 = \{\mathbf{u}_1, \mathbf{u}_2, \ldots, \mathbf{u}_p\},$$
$$S_2 = \{\mathbf{v}_1, \mathbf{v}_2, \ldots, \mathbf{v}_q\}, \qquad \text{and}$$
$$S_3 = \{\mathbf{w}_1, \mathbf{w}_2, \ldots, \mathbf{w}_r\}$$

be bases for the eigenspaces associated with the eigenvalues λ_1, λ_2, and λ_3. Assuming that a linear combination of the vectors in $S = S_1 \cup S_2 \cup S_3$ vanishes—

$$\begin{aligned} a_1\mathbf{u}_1 + a_2\mathbf{u}_2 + \cdots + a_p\mathbf{u}_p \\ + b_1\mathbf{v}_1 + b_2\mathbf{v}_2 + \cdots + b_q\mathbf{v}_q \\ + c_1\mathbf{w}_1 + c_2\mathbf{w}_2 + \cdots + c_r\mathbf{w}_r = \mathbf{0} \end{aligned} \tag{11}$$

—we need to show that the coefficients are all zero. If we write

$$\mathbf{u} = a_1\mathbf{u}_1 + a_2\mathbf{u}_2 + \cdots + a_p\mathbf{u}_p,$$
$$\mathbf{v} = b_1\mathbf{v}_1 + b_2\mathbf{v}_2 + \cdots + b_q\mathbf{v}_q, \qquad \text{and}$$
$$\mathbf{w} = c_1\mathbf{w}_1 + c_2\mathbf{w}_2 + \cdots + c_r\mathbf{w}_r,$$

then Equation (11) takes the simple form

$$\mathbf{u} + \mathbf{v} + \mathbf{w} = \mathbf{0}. \tag{12}$$

But the vectors $\mathbf{u}$, $\mathbf{v}$, and $\mathbf{w}$ either are zero vectors or are eigenvectors associated with the distinct eigenvalues λ_1, λ_2, and λ_3. In the latter event Theorem 2 would imply that $\mathbf{u}$, $\mathbf{v}$, and $\mathbf{w}$ are linearly independent. Therefore Equation (12) implies that $\mathbf{u} = \mathbf{v} = \mathbf{w} = \mathbf{0}$. Finally, the fact that the $\{\mathbf{u}_i\}$ are linearly independent implies that $a_1 = a_2 = \cdots = a_p = 0$; the fact that the $\{\mathbf{v}_i\}$ are linearly independent implies that $b_1 = b_2 = \cdots = b_q = 0$; similarly, $c_1 = c_2 = \cdots = c_r = 0$. Thus we have shown that the coefficients in (11) all vanish, and hence that the vectors in $S = S_1 \cup S_2 \cup S_3$ are linearly independent. ■

6.2 PROBLEMS

In Problems 1–28, determine whether or not the given matrix A is diagonalizable. If it is, find a diagonalizing matrix P and a diagonal matrix D such that $P^{-1}AP = D$.

1. $\begin{bmatrix} 5 & -4 \\ 2 & -1 \end{bmatrix}$

2. $\begin{bmatrix} 6 & -6 \\ 4 & -4 \end{bmatrix}$

3. $\begin{bmatrix} 5 & -3 \\ 2 & 0 \end{bmatrix}$

4. $\begin{bmatrix} 5 & -4 \\ 3 & -2 \end{bmatrix}$

5. $\begin{bmatrix} 9 & -8 \\ 6 & -5 \end{bmatrix}$

6. $\begin{bmatrix} 10 & -6 \\ 12 & -7 \end{bmatrix}$

7. $\begin{bmatrix} 6 & -10 \\ 2 & -3 \end{bmatrix}$

8. $\begin{bmatrix} 11 & -15 \\ 6 & -8 \end{bmatrix}$

9. $\begin{bmatrix} -1 & 4 \\ -1 & 3 \end{bmatrix}$

10. $\begin{bmatrix} 3 & -1 \\ 1 & 1 \end{bmatrix}$

11. $\begin{bmatrix} 5 & 1 \\ -9 & -1 \end{bmatrix}$

12. $\begin{bmatrix} 11 & 9 \\ -16 & -13 \end{bmatrix}$

13. $\begin{bmatrix} 1 & 3 & 0 \\ 0 & 2 & 0 \\ 0 & 0 & 2 \end{bmatrix}$

14. $\begin{bmatrix} 2 & -2 & 1 \\ 2 & -2 & 1 \\ 2 & -2 & 1 \end{bmatrix}$

15. $\begin{bmatrix} 3 & -3 & 1 \\ 2 & -2 & 1 \\ 0 & 0 & 1 \end{bmatrix}$

16. $\begin{bmatrix} 3 & -2 & 0 \\ 0 & 1 & 0 \\ -4 & 4 & 1 \end{bmatrix}$

17. $\begin{bmatrix} 7 & -8 & 3 \\ 6 & -7 & 3 \\ 2 & -2 & 2 \end{bmatrix}$

18. $\begin{bmatrix} 6 & -5 & 2 \\ 4 & -3 & 2 \\ 2 & -2 & 3 \end{bmatrix}$

19. $\begin{bmatrix} 1 & 1 & -1 \\ -2 & 4 & -1 \\ -4 & 4 & 1 \end{bmatrix}$

20. $\begin{bmatrix} 2 & 0 & 0 \\ -6 & 11 & 2 \\ 6 & -15 & 0 \end{bmatrix}$

21. $\begin{bmatrix} 0 & 1 & 0 \\ -1 & 2 & 0 \\ -1 & 1 & 1 \end{bmatrix}$

22. $\begin{bmatrix} 2 & -2 & 1 \\ -1 & 2 & 0 \\ -5 & 7 & -1 \end{bmatrix}$

23. $\begin{bmatrix} -2 & 4 & -1 \\ -3 & 5 & -1 \\ -1 & 1 & 1 \end{bmatrix}$

24. $\begin{bmatrix} 3 & -2 & 1 \\ 1 & 0 & 1 \\ -1 & 1 & 2 \end{bmatrix}$

25. $\begin{bmatrix} 1 & 0 & -2 & 0 \\ 0 & 1 & -2 & 0 \\ 0 & 0 & -1 & 0 \\ 0 & 0 & 0 & -1 \end{bmatrix}$

26. $\begin{bmatrix} 1 & 0 & 0 & 1 \\ 0 & 1 & 0 & 1 \\ 0 & 0 & 1 & 1 \\ 0 & 0 & 0 & 2 \end{bmatrix}$

27. $\begin{bmatrix} 1 & 1 & 0 & 0 \\ 0 & 1 & 1 & 0 \\ 0 & 0 & 1 & 1 \\ 0 & 0 & 0 & 2 \end{bmatrix}$

28. $\begin{bmatrix} 1 & 1 & 0 & 1 \\ 0 & 1 & 1 & 1 \\ 0 & 0 & 2 & 1 \\ 0 & 0 & 0 & 2 \end{bmatrix}$

29. Prove: If the matrices A and B are similar and the matrices B and C are similar, then the matrices A and C are similar.

30. Suppose that the matrices A and B are similar and that n is a positive integer. Prove that the matrices A^n and B^n are similar.

31. Suppose that the invertible matrices A and B are similar. Prove that their inverses A^{-1} and B^{-1} are also similar.

32. Show that if the $n \times n$ matrices A and B are similar, then they have the same characteristic equation and therefore have the same eigenvalues.

33. Suppose that the $n \times n$ matrices A and B are similar and that each has n real eigenvalues. Show that $\det A = \det B$ and that $\operatorname{tr} A = \operatorname{tr} B$. See Problems 32 and 33 in Section 6.1.

34. Consider the 2×2 matrix

$$A = \begin{bmatrix} a & b \\ c & d \end{bmatrix}$$

and let $\Delta = (a-d)^2 + 4bc$. Then show that
(a) A is diagonalizable if $\Delta > 0$;
(b) A is not diagonalizable if $\Delta < 0$;
(c) If $\Delta = 0$, then A may be diagonalizable or it may not be.

35. Let A be a 3×3 matrix with three distinct eigenvalues. Tell how to construct six different invertible matrices $P_1, P_2, \ldots, P_6$ and six different diagonal matrices $D_1, D_2, \ldots, D_6$ such that $P_i D_i (P_i)^{-1} = A$ for each $i = 1, 2, \ldots, 6$.

36. Prove: If the diagonalizable matrices A and B have the same eigenvalues (with the same multiplicities), then A and B are similar.

37. Given: The diagonalizable matrix A. Show that the eigenvalues of A^2 are the squares of the eigenvalues of A, but that A and A^2 have the same eigenvectors.

38. Suppose that the $n \times n$ matrix A has n linearly independent eigenvectors associated with a single eigenvalue λ. Show that A is a diagonal matrix.

39. Let λ_i be an eigenvalue of the $n \times n$ matrix A, and assume that the characteristic equation of A has only real solutions. The **algebraic multiplicity** of λ_i is the largest positive integer $p(i)$ such that $(\lambda - \lambda_i)^{p(i)}$ is a factor of the characteristic polynomial $|A - \lambda I|$. The **geometric multiplicity** of λ_i is the dimension $q(i)$ of the eigenspace associated with λ_i. It can be shown that $p(i) \geq q(i)$ for every eigenvalue λ_i. Taking this as already established, prove that the given matrix A is diagonalizable if and only if the geometric multiplicity of each eigenvalue is equal to its algebraic multiplicity.

*6.3 Applications Involving Powers of Matrices

In this section we discuss applications that depend on an ability to compute the matrix A^k for large values of k given the $n \times n$ matrix A. If A is diagonalizable, then A^k can be found directly by a method that avoids the labor of calculating the powers A^2, A^3, A^4, ... by successive matrix multiplications.

Recall from Section 6.2 that if the $n \times n$ matrix A has n linearly independent eigenvectors $\mathbf{v}_1, \mathbf{v}_2, \ldots, \mathbf{v}_n$ associated with the eigenvalues $\lambda_1, \lambda_2, \ldots, \lambda_n$ (not necessarily distinct), then

$$A = PDP^{-1}, \tag{1}$$

where

$$P = \begin{bmatrix} | & | & & | \\ \mathbf{v}_1 & \mathbf{v}_2 & \cdots & \mathbf{v}_n \\ | & | & & | \end{bmatrix}$$

and

$$D = \begin{bmatrix} \lambda_1 & 0 & \cdots & 0 \\ 0 & \lambda_2 & \cdots & 0 \\ \vdots & \vdots & \ddots & \vdots \\ 0 & 0 & \cdots & \lambda_n \end{bmatrix}. \tag{2}$$

Note that (1) yields

$$A^2 = (PDP^{-1})(PDP^{-1}) = PD(P^{-1}P)DP^{-1} = PD^2P^{-1}$$

because $P^{-1}P = I$. More generally, for each positive integer k,

$$\begin{aligned} A^k &= (PDP^{-1})^k \\ &= (PDP^{-1})(PDP^{-1})\cdots(PDP^{-1})(PDP^{-1}) \\ &= PD(P^{-1}P)D\cdots(P^{-1}P)DP^{-1}; \end{aligned}$$

$$A^k = PD^kP^{-1}. \tag{3}$$

But the kth power D^k of the diagonal matrix D is easily computed:

$$D^k = \begin{bmatrix} \lambda_1^k & 0 & \cdots & 0 \\ 0 & \lambda_2^k & \cdots & 0 \\ \vdots & \vdots & \ddots & \vdots \\ 0 & 0 & \cdots & \lambda_n^k \end{bmatrix}.$$

Consequently the formula in (3) gives a quick and effective way to calculate any desired power of the diagonalizable matrix A once its eigenvalues and associated eigenvectors—and hence the matrices P and D—have been found.

EXAMPLE 1 Find A^5 if

$$A = \begin{bmatrix} 4 & -2 & 1 \\ 2 & 0 & 1 \\ 2 & -2 & 3 \end{bmatrix}.$$

Solution In Example 7 of Section 6.1 we found that the 3×3 matrix A has the eigenvalue $\lambda_1 = 3$ with associated eigenvector $\mathbf{v}_1 = (1, 1, 1)$, and the repeated eigenvalue $\lambda_2 = 2$ with associated eigenvectors $\mathbf{v}_2 = (1, 1, 0)$ and $\mathbf{v}_3 = (-1, 0, 2)$. Therefore $A = PDP^{-1}$ with

$$P = \begin{bmatrix} 1 & 1 & -1 \\ 1 & 1 & 0 \\ 1 & 0 & 2 \end{bmatrix} \quad \text{and} \quad D = \begin{bmatrix} 3 & 0 & 0 \\ 0 & 2 & 0 \\ 0 & 0 & 2 \end{bmatrix}.$$

We first calculate

$$P^{-1} = \begin{bmatrix} 2 & -2 & 1 \\ -2 & 3 & -1 \\ -1 & 1 & 0 \end{bmatrix}$$

and

$$D^5 = \begin{bmatrix} 243 & 0 & 0 \\ 0 & 32 & 0 \\ 0 & 0 & 32 \end{bmatrix}.$$

Then the formula in (3) yields

$$A^5 = \begin{bmatrix} 1 & 1 & -1 \\ 1 & 1 & 0 \\ 1 & 0 & 2 \end{bmatrix} \begin{bmatrix} 243 & 0 & 0 \\ 0 & 32 & 0 \\ 0 & 0 & 32 \end{bmatrix} \begin{bmatrix} 2 & -2 & 1 \\ -2 & 3 & -1 \\ -1 & 1 & 0 \end{bmatrix}$$

$$= \begin{bmatrix} 243 & 32 & -32 \\ 243 & 32 & 0 \\ 243 & 0 & 64 \end{bmatrix} \begin{bmatrix} 2 & -2 & 1 \\ -2 & 3 & -1 \\ -1 & 1 & 0 \end{bmatrix}$$

$$= \begin{bmatrix} 454 & -422 & 211 \\ 422 & -390 & 211 \\ 422 & -422 & 243 \end{bmatrix}.$$

TRANSITION MATRICES

We want to apply this method of computing A^k to the analysis of a certain type of physical system that can be described by means of the following kind of mathematical model. Suppose that the sequence

$$\mathbf{x}_0, \mathbf{x}_1, \mathbf{x}_2, \ldots, \mathbf{x}_k, \ldots \tag{4}$$

of n-vectors is defined by its **initial vector** $\mathbf{x}_0$ and an $n \times n$ **transition matrix** A in the following manner:

$$\mathbf{x}_{k+1} = A\mathbf{x}_k \qquad \text{for each } k \geq 0. \tag{5}$$

We envision a physical system—such as a population with n specified subpopulations—that evolves through a sequence of successive *states* described by the vectors in (4). Then our goal is to calculate the kth *state vector* $\mathbf{x}_k$. But using (5) repeatedly we find that

$$\mathbf{x}_1 = A\mathbf{x}_0, \quad \mathbf{x}_2 = A\mathbf{x}_1 = A^2\mathbf{x}_0, \quad \mathbf{x}_3 = A\mathbf{x}_2 = A^3\mathbf{x}_0,$$

and in general that

$$\mathbf{x}_k = A^k\mathbf{x}_0. \tag{6}$$

Thus our task amounts to calculating the kth power A^k of the transition matrix A.

EXAMPLE 2 Let us analyze afresh the metropolitan area population that we discussed in Example 1 of Section 1.7. The constant total population of 1 million persons is divided between a city and its suburbs. Let C_k denote the city population and S_k denote the suburban population after k years. We suppose that each year 15% of the people in the city move to the suburbs, whereas 10% of the people in the suburbs move to the city. As in Equations (3) and (4) of Section 1.7, it follows that

$$\begin{aligned} C_{k+1} &= (0.85)C_k + (0.10)S_k \\ S_{k+1} &= (0.15)C_k + (0.90)S_k \end{aligned} \tag{7}$$

for each $k \geq 0$. Thus for such k,

$$\mathbf{x}_{k+1} = A\mathbf{x}_k \quad \text{and hence} \quad \mathbf{x}_k = A^k\mathbf{x}_0,$$

where

$$\mathbf{x}_k = \begin{bmatrix} C_k \\ S_k \end{bmatrix} \quad \text{and} \quad A = \begin{bmatrix} 0.85 & 0.10 \\ 0.15 & 0.90 \end{bmatrix}. \tag{8}$$

The characteristic equation of the transition matrix A is

$$\begin{aligned} \left(\frac{17}{20} - \lambda\right)\left(\frac{9}{10} - \lambda\right) - \left(\frac{3}{20}\right)\left(\frac{1}{10}\right) &= 0; \\ (17 - 20\lambda)(9 - 10\lambda) - 3 &= 0; \\ 200\lambda^2 - 350\lambda + 150 &= 0; \\ 4\lambda^2 - 7\lambda + 3 &= 0; \\ (\lambda - 1)(4\lambda - 3) &= 0. \end{aligned}$$

Thus the eigenvalues of A are $\lambda_1 = 1$ and $\lambda_2 = 0.75$. For $\lambda_1 = 1$, the system $(A - \lambda I)\mathbf{v} = \mathbf{0}$ is

$$\begin{bmatrix} -0.15 & 0.10 \\ 0.15 & -0.10 \end{bmatrix}\begin{bmatrix} x \\ y \end{bmatrix} = \begin{bmatrix} 0 \\ 0 \end{bmatrix},$$

so an associated eigenvector is $\mathbf{v}_1 = (2, 3)$. For $\lambda_2 = 0.75$, the system $(A - \lambda I)\mathbf{v} = \mathbf{0}$ is

$$\begin{bmatrix} 0.10 & 0.10 \\ 0.15 & 0.15 \end{bmatrix}\begin{bmatrix} x \\ y \end{bmatrix} = \begin{bmatrix} 0 \\ 0 \end{bmatrix},$$

so an associated eigenvector is $\mathbf{v}_2 = (-1, 1)$. It follows that $A = PDP^{-1}$ where

$$P = \begin{bmatrix} 2 & -1 \\ 3 & 1 \end{bmatrix}, \qquad D = \begin{bmatrix} 1 & 0 \\ 0 & \frac{3}{4} \end{bmatrix},$$

and

$$P^{-1} = \tfrac{1}{5}\begin{bmatrix} 1 & 1 \\ -3 & 2 \end{bmatrix}.$$

Now suppose that our goal is to determine the long-term distribution of population between the city and its suburbs. Note first that $(\frac{3}{4})^k$ is "negligible" when k is sufficiently large; for instance, $(\frac{3}{4})^{40} \approx 0.00001$. It follows that if $k \geq 40$, then the formula $A^k = PD^kP^{-1}$ yields

$$\begin{aligned} A^k &= \begin{bmatrix} 2 & -1 \\ 3 & 1 \end{bmatrix}\begin{bmatrix} 1 & 0 \\ 0 & (\frac{3}{4})^k \end{bmatrix}(\tfrac{1}{5})\begin{bmatrix} 1 & 1 \\ -3 & 2 \end{bmatrix} \\ &\approx \tfrac{1}{5}\begin{bmatrix} 2 & -1 \\ 3 & 1 \end{bmatrix}\begin{bmatrix} 1 & 0 \\ 0 & 0 \end{bmatrix}\begin{bmatrix} 1 & 1 \\ -3 & 2 \end{bmatrix} \\ &= \tfrac{1}{5}\begin{bmatrix} 2 & 0 \\ 3 & 0 \end{bmatrix}\begin{bmatrix} 1 & 1 \\ -3 & 2 \end{bmatrix} = \tfrac{1}{5}\begin{bmatrix} 2 & 2 \\ 3 & 3 \end{bmatrix}. \end{aligned} \tag{9}$$

Hence it follows that if k is sufficiently large, then

$$\begin{aligned}\mathbf{x}_k = A^k\mathbf{x}_0 &\approx \tfrac{1}{5}\begin{bmatrix}2 & 2\\ 3 & 3\end{bmatrix}\begin{bmatrix}C_0\\ S_0\end{bmatrix}\\ &= (C_0 + S_0)\begin{bmatrix}0.4\\ 0.6\end{bmatrix} = \begin{bmatrix}0.4\\ 0.6\end{bmatrix},\end{aligned}$$

because $C_0 + P_0 = 1$ (million), the constant total population of the metropolitan area. Thus our analysis shows that irrespective of the initial distribution of population between the city and its suburbs, the long-term distribution consists of 40% in the city and 60% in the suburbs.

REMARK The result in Example 2—that the long-term situation is independent of the initial situation—is characteristic of a general class of common problems. Note that the transition matrix A in (8) has the property that *the sum of the elements in each column is* 1. An $n \times n$ matrix with nonnegative entries having this property is called a **stochastic matrix.** It can be proved that if A is a stochastic matrix having only positive entries, then $\lambda_1 = 1$ is one eigenvalue of A and that $|\lambda_i| < 1$ for the others (see Problems 29 and 30). Moreover, as $k \to \infty$, the matrix A^k approaches the constant matrix

$$[\mathbf{v}_1 \quad \mathbf{v}_1 \quad \cdots \quad \mathbf{v}_1],$$

each of whose identical columns is the eigenvector of A associated with $\lambda_1 = 1$ having the sum of its elements equal to 1. The 2×2 stochastic matrix A of Example 2 illustrates this general result, with $\lambda_1 = 1$, $\lambda_2 = \frac{3}{4}$, and $\mathbf{v}_1 = (\frac{2}{5}, \frac{3}{5})$.

PREDATOR-PREY MODELS

In Example 2 of Section 1.7 we considered a predator-prey population consisting of the foxes and rabbits living in a certain forest. Initially there are F_0 foxes and R_0 rabbits, and after k months there are F_k foxes and R_k rabbits. We assume that the transition from each month to the next is described by the equations

$$\begin{aligned}F_{k+1} &= (0.4)F_k + (0.3)R_k\\ R_{k+1} &= \quad -rF_k + (1.2)R_k,\end{aligned} \tag{10}$$

where the constant $r > 0$ is the "capture rate" representing the average number of rabbits consumed monthly by each fox. Thus

$$\mathbf{x}_{k+1} = A\mathbf{x}_k \quad \text{and hence} \quad \mathbf{x}_k = A^k\mathbf{x}_0 \tag{11}$$

where

$$\mathbf{x}_k = \begin{bmatrix}F_k\\ R_k\end{bmatrix} \quad \text{and} \quad A = \begin{bmatrix}0.4 & 0.3\\ -r & 1.2\end{bmatrix}. \tag{12}$$

We want to investigate the long-term behavior of the fox and rabbit populations for different values of the capture rate r.

The characteristic equation of the transition matrix A in (12) is

$$(0.4 - \lambda)(1.2 - \lambda) + (0.3)r = 0;$$
$$(4 - 10\lambda)(12 - 10\lambda) + 30r = 0;$$
$$100\lambda^2 - 160\lambda + (48 + 30r) = 0.$$

The quadratic formula then yields the equation

$$\begin{aligned} \lambda &= \frac{1}{200}[160 \pm \sqrt{(160)^2 - (400)(48 + 30r)}] \\ &= \frac{1}{10}(8 \pm \sqrt{16 - 30r}) \end{aligned} \tag{13}$$

giving the eigenvalues of A in terms of the capture rate r. Examples 3, 4, and 5 illustrate three possibilities (for different values of r) for what may happen to the fox and rabbit populations as k increases:

- F_k and R_k may approach constant nonzero values. This is the case of *stable limiting populations* that coexist in equilibrium with one another.
- F_k and R_k may both approach zero. This is the case of *mutual extinction* of the two species.
- F_k and R_k may both increase without bound. This is the case of a *population explosion*.

EXAMPLE 3 (Stable Limiting Population) If $r = 0.4$, then Equation (13) gives the eigenvalues $\lambda_1 = 1$ and $\lambda_2 = 0.6$. For $\lambda_1 = 1$, the system $(A - \lambda I)\mathbf{v} = \mathbf{0}$ is

$$\begin{bmatrix} -0.6 & 0.3 \\ -0.4 & 0.2 \end{bmatrix} \begin{bmatrix} x \\ y \end{bmatrix} = \begin{bmatrix} 0 \\ 0 \end{bmatrix},$$

so an associated eigenvector is $\mathbf{v}_1 = (1, 2)$. For $\lambda_2 = 0.6$, the system $(A - \lambda I)\mathbf{v} = \mathbf{0}$ is

$$\begin{bmatrix} -0.2 & 0.3 \\ -0.4 & 0.6 \end{bmatrix} \begin{bmatrix} x \\ y \end{bmatrix} = \begin{bmatrix} 0 \\ 0 \end{bmatrix},$$

so an associated eigenvector is $\mathbf{v}_2 = (3, 2)$. It follows that $A = PDP^{-1}$ where

$$P = \begin{bmatrix} 1 & 3 \\ 2 & 2 \end{bmatrix}, \quad D = \begin{bmatrix} 1 & 0 \\ 0 & 0.6 \end{bmatrix}, \quad \text{and} \quad P^{-1} = -\tfrac{1}{4}\begin{bmatrix} 2 & -3 \\ -2 & 1 \end{bmatrix}.$$

We are now ready to calculate A^k. If k is sufficiently large that $(0.6)^k \approx 0$ (for instance, $(0.6)^{25} \approx 0.000003$), then the formula $A^k = PD^kP^{-1}$ yields

$$
\begin{aligned}
A^k &= \begin{bmatrix} 1 & 3 \\ 2 & 2 \end{bmatrix} \begin{bmatrix} 1 & 0 \\ 0 & (0.6)^k \end{bmatrix} \left(-\tfrac{1}{4}\right) \begin{bmatrix} 2 & -3 \\ -2 & 1 \end{bmatrix} \\
&\approx -\tfrac{1}{4} \begin{bmatrix} 1 & 3 \\ 2 & 2 \end{bmatrix} \begin{bmatrix} 1 & 0 \\ 0 & 0 \end{bmatrix} \begin{bmatrix} 2 & -3 \\ -2 & 1 \end{bmatrix} \\
&= -\tfrac{1}{4} \begin{bmatrix} 1 & 0 \\ 2 & 0 \end{bmatrix} \begin{bmatrix} 2 & -3 \\ -2 & 1 \end{bmatrix} \\
&= \tfrac{1}{4} \begin{bmatrix} -2 & 3 \\ -4 & 6 \end{bmatrix}.
\end{aligned}
$$

Hence it follows that if k is sufficiently large, then

$$
\mathbf{x}_k = A^k \mathbf{x}_0 = \tfrac{1}{4} \begin{bmatrix} -2 & 3 \\ -4 & 6 \end{bmatrix} \begin{bmatrix} F_0 \\ R_0 \end{bmatrix} = \tfrac{1}{4} \begin{bmatrix} 3R_0 - 2F_0 \\ 6R_0 - 4F_0 \end{bmatrix}
$$

—that is,

$$
\begin{bmatrix} F_k \\ R_k \end{bmatrix} = \alpha \begin{bmatrix} 1 \\ 2 \end{bmatrix} \qquad \text{where} \quad \alpha = \tfrac{1}{4}(3R_0 - 2F_0). \tag{14}
$$

Assuming the initial populations are such that $\alpha > 0$ (that is, $3R_0 > 2F_0$), (14) implies that as k increases the fox and rabbit populations approach a stable situation in which there are twice as many rabbits as foxes. For instance, if $F_0 = R_0 = 100$, then when k is sufficiently large, there will be 25 foxes and 50 rabbits.

EXAMPLE 4 (Mutual Extinction) If $r = 0.5$, then Equation (13) gives the eigenvalues $\lambda_1 = 0.9$ and $\lambda_2 = 0.7$. For $\lambda_1 = 0.9$, the system $(A - \lambda I)\mathbf{v} = \mathbf{0}$ is

$$
\begin{bmatrix} -0.5 & 0.3 \\ -0.5 & 0.3 \end{bmatrix} \begin{bmatrix} x \\ y \end{bmatrix} = \begin{bmatrix} 0 \\ 0 \end{bmatrix},
$$

so an associated eigenvector is $\mathbf{v}_1 = (3, 5)$. For $\lambda_2 = 0.7$, the system $(A - \lambda I)\mathbf{v} = \mathbf{0}$ is

$$
\begin{bmatrix} -0.3 & 0.3 \\ -0.5 & 0.5 \end{bmatrix} \begin{bmatrix} x \\ y \end{bmatrix} = \begin{bmatrix} 0 \\ 0 \end{bmatrix},
$$

so an associated eigenvector is $\mathbf{v}_2 = (1, 1)$. It follows that $A = PDP^{-1}$, with

$$
P = \begin{bmatrix} 3 & 1 \\ 5 & 1 \end{bmatrix}, \qquad D = \begin{bmatrix} 0.9 & 0 \\ 0 & 0.7 \end{bmatrix}, \quad \text{and} \quad P^{-1} = -\tfrac{1}{2} \begin{bmatrix} 1 & -1 \\ -5 & 3 \end{bmatrix}.
$$

Now both $(0.9)^k$ and $(0.7)^k$ approach 0 as k increases without bound ($k \to +\infty$). Hence if k is sufficiently large, then the formula $A^k = PD^kP^{-1}$ yields

$$
\begin{aligned}
A^k &= \begin{bmatrix} 3 & 1 \\ 5 & 1 \end{bmatrix} \begin{bmatrix} (0.9)^k & 0 \\ 0 & (0.7)^k \end{bmatrix} \left(-\tfrac{1}{2}\right) \begin{bmatrix} 1 & -1 \\ -5 & 3 \end{bmatrix} \\
&\approx -\tfrac{1}{2} \begin{bmatrix} 3 & 1 \\ 5 & 1 \end{bmatrix} \begin{bmatrix} 0 & 0 \\ 0 & 0 \end{bmatrix} \begin{bmatrix} 1 & -1 \\ -5 & 3 \end{bmatrix} = \begin{bmatrix} 0 & 0 \\ 0 & 0 \end{bmatrix},
\end{aligned}
$$

so

$$\begin{bmatrix} F_k \\ R_k \end{bmatrix} = A^k \begin{bmatrix} F_0 \\ R_0 \end{bmatrix} \approx \begin{bmatrix} 0 & 0 \\ 0 & 0 \end{bmatrix} \begin{bmatrix} F_0 \\ R_0 \end{bmatrix} = \begin{bmatrix} 0 \\ 0 \end{bmatrix}. \tag{15}$$

Thus F_k and R_k both approach zero as $k \to +\infty$, so both the foxes and the rabbits die out—mutual extinction occurs.

EXAMPLE 5 (Population Explosion) If $r = 0.325$, then Equation (13) gives the eigenvalues $\lambda_1 = 1.05$ and $\lambda_2 = 0.55$. For $\lambda_1 = 1.05$, the system $(A - \lambda I)\mathbf{v} = \mathbf{0}$ is

$$\begin{bmatrix} -0.650 & 0.30 \\ -0.325 & 0.15 \end{bmatrix} \begin{bmatrix} x \\ y \end{bmatrix} = \begin{bmatrix} 0 \\ 0 \end{bmatrix}.$$

Each equation is a multiple of $-13x + 6y = 0$, so an associated eigenvector is $\mathbf{v}_1 = (6, 13)$. For $\lambda_2 = 0.55$, the system $(A - \lambda I)\mathbf{v} = \mathbf{0}$ is

$$\begin{bmatrix} -0.150 & 0.30 \\ -0.325 & 0.65 \end{bmatrix} \begin{bmatrix} x \\ y \end{bmatrix} = \begin{bmatrix} 0 \\ 0 \end{bmatrix},$$

so an associated eigenvector is $\mathbf{v}_2 = (2, 1)$. It follows that $A = PDP^{-1}$ with

$$P = \begin{bmatrix} 6 & 2 \\ 13 & 1 \end{bmatrix}, \quad D = \begin{bmatrix} 1.05 & 0 \\ 0 & 0.55 \end{bmatrix}, \quad \text{and} \quad P^{-1} = -\tfrac{1}{20} \begin{bmatrix} 1 & -2 \\ -13 & 6 \end{bmatrix}.$$

Note that $(0.55)^k$ approaches zero but that $(1.05)^k$ increases without bound as $k \to +\infty$. It follows that if k is sufficiently large, then the formula $A^k = PDP^{-1}$ yields

$$\begin{aligned} A^k &= \begin{bmatrix} 6 & 2 \\ 13 & 1 \end{bmatrix} \begin{bmatrix} (1.05)^k & 0 \\ 0 & (0.55)^k \end{bmatrix} \left(-\tfrac{1}{20}\right) \begin{bmatrix} 1 & -2 \\ -13 & 6 \end{bmatrix} \\ &\approx -\tfrac{1}{20} \begin{bmatrix} 6 & 2 \\ 13 & 1 \end{bmatrix} \begin{bmatrix} (1.05)^k & 0 \\ 0 & 0 \end{bmatrix} \begin{bmatrix} 1 & -2 \\ -13 & 6 \end{bmatrix} \\ &= -\tfrac{1}{20} \begin{bmatrix} (6)(1.05)^k & 0 \\ (13)(1.05)^k & 0 \end{bmatrix} \begin{bmatrix} 1 & -2 \\ -13 & 6 \end{bmatrix}, \end{aligned}$$

and therefore

$$A^k \approx -\tfrac{1}{20}(1.05)^k \begin{bmatrix} 6 & -12 \\ 13 & -26 \end{bmatrix}. \tag{16}$$

Hence if k is sufficiently large, then

$$\begin{aligned} \mathbf{x}_k = A^k \mathbf{x}_0 &\approx -\tfrac{1}{20}(1.05)^k \begin{bmatrix} 6 & -12 \\ 13 & -26 \end{bmatrix} \begin{bmatrix} F_0 \\ R_0 \end{bmatrix} \\ &= -\tfrac{1}{20}(1.05)^k \begin{bmatrix} 6F_0 - 12R_0 \\ 13F_0 - 26R_0 \end{bmatrix}, \end{aligned}$$

and so

$$\begin{bmatrix} F_k \\ R_k \end{bmatrix} \approx (1.05)^k \gamma \begin{bmatrix} 6 \\ 13 \end{bmatrix} \quad \text{where} \quad \gamma = \tfrac{1}{20}(2R_0 - F_0). \tag{17}$$

If $\gamma > 0$ (that is, if $2R_0 > F_0$), then the factor $(1.05)^k$ in (17) implies that the fox and rabbit populations both increase at a rate of 5% per month, and thus each increases without bound as $k \to +\infty$. Moreover, when k is sufficiently large, the two populations maintain a constant ratio of 6 foxes for every 13 rabbits. It is also of interest to note that the monthly "population multiplier" is the larger eigenvalue $\lambda_1 = 1.05$ and that the limiting *ratio* of populations is determined by the associated eigenvector $\mathbf{v}_1 = (6, 13)$.

In summary, let us compare the results in Examples 3, 4, and 5. The critical capture rate $r = 0.4$ of Example 3 represents a monthly consumption of 0.4 rabbits per fox, resulting in stable limiting populations of both species. But if the foxes are greedier and consume more than 0.4 rabbits per fox monthly, then the result is extinction of both species (as in Example 4). If the rabbits become more skilled at evading foxes, so that less than 0.4 rabbits per fox are consumed each month, then both populations grow without bound, as in Example 5.

6.3 PROBLEMS

In Problems 1-10 a matrix A is given. Use the method of Example 1 to compute A^5.

1. $\begin{bmatrix} 3 & -2 \\ 1 & 0 \end{bmatrix}$

2. $\begin{bmatrix} 5 & -6 \\ 3 & -4 \end{bmatrix}$

3. $\begin{bmatrix} 6 & -6 \\ 4 & -4 \end{bmatrix}$

4. $\begin{bmatrix} 4 & -3 \\ 2 & -1 \end{bmatrix}$

5. $\begin{bmatrix} 5 & -4 \\ 3 & -2 \end{bmatrix}$

6. $\begin{bmatrix} 6 & -10 \\ 2 & -3 \end{bmatrix}$

7. $\begin{bmatrix} 1 & 3 & 0 \\ 0 & 2 & 0 \\ 0 & 0 & 2 \end{bmatrix}$

8. $\begin{bmatrix} 1 & -2 & 1 \\ 0 & 1 & 0 \\ 0 & -2 & 2 \end{bmatrix}$

9. $\begin{bmatrix} 1 & -3 & 1 \\ 0 & 2 & 0 \\ 0 & 0 & 2 \end{bmatrix}$

10. $\begin{bmatrix} 4 & -3 & 1 \\ 2 & -1 & 1 \\ 0 & 0 & 2 \end{bmatrix}$

Find A^{10} for each matrix A given in Problems 11-14.

11. $\begin{bmatrix} 1 & 0 & 0 \\ -6 & 5 & 2 \\ 21 & -15 & -6 \end{bmatrix}$

12. $\begin{bmatrix} 11 & -6 & -2 \\ 20 & -11 & -4 \\ 0 & 0 & 1 \end{bmatrix}$

13. $\begin{bmatrix} 1 & -1 & 1 \\ 2 & -2 & 1 \\ 4 & -4 & 1 \end{bmatrix}$

14. $\begin{bmatrix} 5 & -5 & -3 \\ 2 & -2 & -1 \\ 4 & -4 & -3 \end{bmatrix}$

In Problems 15-20, a city-suburban population transition matrix A (as in Example 2) is given. Find the resulting long-term distribution of a constant total population between the city and its suburbs.

15. $A = \begin{bmatrix} 0.9 & 0.1 \\ 0.1 & 0.9 \end{bmatrix}$

16. $A = \begin{bmatrix} 0.85 & 0.05 \\ 0.15 & 0.95 \end{bmatrix}$

17. $A = \begin{bmatrix} 0.75 & 0.15 \\ 0.25 & 0.85 \end{bmatrix}$

18. $A = \begin{bmatrix} 0.8 & 0.1 \\ 0.2 & 0.9 \end{bmatrix}$

19. $A = \begin{bmatrix} 0.9 & 0.05 \\ 0.1 & 0.95 \end{bmatrix}$

20. $A = \begin{bmatrix} 0.8 & 0.15 \\ 0.2 & 0.85 \end{bmatrix}$

Problems 21–23 deal with a fox-rabbit population as in Examples 3–5, except with the transition matrix

$$A = \begin{bmatrix} 0.6 & 0.5 \\ -r & 1.2 \end{bmatrix}$$

in place of the one used in the text.

21. If $r = 0.16$, show that in the long term the populations of foxes and rabbits are stable, with 5 foxes for each 4 rabbits.

22. If $r = 0.175$, show that in the long term the populations of foxes and rabbits both die out.

23. If $r = 0.135$, show that in the long term the fox and rabbit populations both increase at the rate of 5% per month, maintaining a constant ratio of 10 foxes for each 9 rabbits.

24. Suppose that the 2×2 matrix A has eigenvalues $\lambda_1 = 1$ and $\lambda_2 = -1$ with eigenvectors $\mathbf{v}_1 = (3, 4)$ and $\mathbf{v}_2 = (5, 7)$, respectively. Find the matrix A and the powers A^{99} and A^{100}.

25. Suppose that $|\lambda| = 1$ for each eigenvalue λ of the diagonalizable matrix A. Show that $A^n = I$ for every even positive integer n.

26. Suppose that

$$A = \begin{bmatrix} 0 & 1 \\ 1 & 0 \end{bmatrix}.$$

Show that $A^{2n} = I$ and that $A^{2n+1} = A$ for every positive integer n.

27. Suppose that

$$A = \begin{bmatrix} 0 & 1 \\ -1 & 0 \end{bmatrix}.$$

Show that $A^{4n} = I$, $A^{4n+1} = A$, $A^{4n+2} = -I$, and $A^{4n+3} = -A$ for every positive integer n.

28. The matrix

$$A = \begin{bmatrix} 1 & 1 \\ 0 & 1 \end{bmatrix}$$

is not diagonalizable. (Why not?) Write $A = I + B$. Show that $B^2 = 0$ and thence that

$$A^n = \begin{bmatrix} 1 & n \\ 0 & 1 \end{bmatrix}.$$

29. Consider the stochastic matrix

$$A = \begin{bmatrix} p & 1-q \\ 1-p & q \end{bmatrix}$$

where $0 < p < 1$ and $0 < q < 1$. Show that the eigenvalues of A are $\lambda_1 = 1$ and $\lambda_2 = p + q - 1$, so that $|\lambda_2| < 1$.

30. Suppose that A is an $n \times n$ stochastic matrix —the sum of the elements of each column vector is 1. If $\mathbf{v} = (1, 1, \ldots, 1)$, show that $A^T\mathbf{v} = \mathbf{v}$. Why does it follow that $\lambda = 1$ is an eigenvalue of A?

31. In his *Liber abaci* published in 1202, Leonardo Fibonacci* asked the following question: How many pairs of rabbits are produced from a single original pair in one year, if every month each pair begets a new pair, which is similarly productive beginning in the second succeeding month? The answer is provided by the **Fibonacci sequence**

$$1, 1, 2, 3, 5, 8, 13, 21, 34, 55, \ldots$$

in which each term is the sum of its two immediate predecessors. That is, the sequence is defined recursively as follows:

$$s_0 = 1 = s_1, \qquad s_{n+1} = s_n + s_{n-1} \qquad \text{for } n \geq 1.$$

* "Leonardo, son of Bonacci," 1175–1250?, one of the outstanding mathematicians of the middle ages. He is also known as Leonardo of Pisa (Leonardo Pisano).

Then s_n is the number of rabbit pairs present after n months. Note that if

$$\mathbf{x}_n = \begin{bmatrix} s_{n+1} \\ s_n \end{bmatrix} \quad \text{and} \quad A = \begin{bmatrix} 1 & 1 \\ 1 & 0 \end{bmatrix},$$

then

$$\mathbf{x}_n = A\mathbf{x}_{n-1} \quad \text{and so} \quad \mathbf{x}_n = A^n\mathbf{x}_0$$

where $\mathbf{x}_0 = (1, 1)$.

(a) Show that A has eigenvalues $\lambda_1 = \frac{1}{2}(1 + \sqrt{5})$ and $\lambda_2 = \frac{1}{2}(1 - \sqrt{5})$ with associated eigenvectors $\mathbf{v}_1 = (1 + \sqrt{5}, 2)$ and $\mathbf{v}_2 = (1 - \sqrt{5}, 2)$, respectively.

(b) Compute

$$\begin{bmatrix} s_{n+1} \\ s_n \end{bmatrix} = A^n\mathbf{x}_0 = PD^nP^{-1}\begin{bmatrix} 1 \\ 1 \end{bmatrix}$$

to derive the amazing formula

$$s_n = \frac{1}{\sqrt{5}}\left[\left(\frac{1+\sqrt{5}}{2}\right)^{n+1} - \left(\frac{1-\sqrt{5}}{2}\right)^{n+1}\right].$$

Thus after 1 year the number of rabbit pairs is

$$s_{12} = \frac{1}{\sqrt{5}}\left[\left(\frac{1+\sqrt{5}}{2}\right)^{13} - \left(\frac{1-\sqrt{5}}{2}\right)^{13}\right] = 233.$$

Show that there are 75,025 rabbit pairs after 2 years and over 2.5 trillion rabbit pairs after 5 years.

6.4 Symmetric Matrices and Orthogonal Eigenvectors

In Section 6.2 we saw that an $n \times n$ matrix is diagonalizable if and only if it has n linearly independent eigenvectors. An important class of matrices that satisfy this criterion are the symmetric matrices. (Recall that the square matrix $A = [a_{ij}]$ is **symmetric** provided that $A = A^T$—in other words, $a_{ij} = a_{ji}$ for $1 \le i \le n$ and $1 \le j \le n$.) In this section we will see that every symmetric $n \times n$ matrix has n eigenvectors that not only are linearly independent but also are mutually orthogonal with respect to the Euclidean inner (dot) product.

According to Theorem 2 in Section 6.2, any two eigenvectors $\mathbf{v}_1$ and $\mathbf{v}_2$ associated with distinct eigenvalues λ_1 and λ_2 of an $n \times n$ matrix A are linearly independent. But if the matrix A is symmetric, we can show that $\mathbf{v}_1$ and $\mathbf{v}_2$ are orthogonal and not merely linearly independent.

> ***Theorem 1:** Orthogonal Eigenvectors of Symmetric Matrices*
> Eigenvectors associated with distinct eigenvalues of a symmetric matrix are orthogonal.

PROOF Suppose that $\mathbf{v}_1$ and $\mathbf{v}_2$ are eigenvectors associated with the distinct eigenvalues λ_1 and λ_2 of the symmetric matrix A. Our goal is to show that $\mathbf{v}_1 \cdot \mathbf{v}_2 = \mathbf{v}_1^T\mathbf{v}_2 = 0$. Note first that the 1×1 matrix $\mathbf{v}_1^TA\mathbf{v}_2$ is obviously symmetric, so it follows that

$$\mathbf{v}_1^TA\mathbf{v}_2 = (\mathbf{v}_1^TA\mathbf{v}_2)^T = \mathbf{v}_2^TA^T\mathbf{v}_1 = \mathbf{v}_2^T\mathrm{A}\mathbf{v}_1 \tag{1}$$

because $A^T = A$. But

$$\mathbf{v}_1^T A \mathbf{v}_2 = \mathbf{v}_1^T \lambda_2 \mathbf{v}_2 = \lambda_2 \mathbf{v}_1^T \mathbf{v}_2 \tag{2}$$

and

$$\mathbf{v}_2^T A \mathbf{v}_1 = \mathbf{v}_2^T \lambda_1 \mathbf{v}_1 = \lambda_1 \mathbf{v}_1^T \mathbf{v}_2 \tag{3}$$

because $\mathbf{v}_2^T \mathbf{v}_1 = \mathbf{v}_1 \cdot \mathbf{v}_2 = \mathbf{v}_1^T \mathbf{v}_2$. Hence

$$\lambda_1 \mathbf{v}_1^T \mathbf{v}_2 = \lambda_2 \mathbf{v}_1^T \mathbf{v}_2,$$

so $(\lambda_1 - \lambda_2)\mathbf{v}_1^T \mathbf{v}_2 = 0$. Because $\lambda_1 \neq \lambda_2$, it now follows that $\mathbf{v}_1^T \mathbf{v}_2 = 0$, and therefore the eigenvectors $\mathbf{v}_1$ and $\mathbf{v}_2$ are orthogonal. ■

EXAMPLE 1 The characteristic equation of the symmetric matrix

$$A = \begin{bmatrix} 1 & 2 & 2 \\ 2 & 6 & 2 \\ 2 & 2 & 6 \end{bmatrix} \tag{4}$$

is

$$\lambda^3 - 13\lambda^2 + 36\lambda = \lambda(\lambda - 4)(\lambda - 9) = 0,$$

so the 3×3 matrix A has the three distinct eigenvalues $\lambda_1 = 9$, $\lambda_2 = 4$, and $\lambda_3 = 0$. With $\lambda_1 = 9$ the matrix

$$A - 9I = \begin{bmatrix} -8 & 2 & 2 \\ 2 & -3 & 2 \\ 2 & 2 & -3 \end{bmatrix}$$

has echelon form

$$\begin{bmatrix} 2 & -3 & 2 \\ 0 & 1 & -1 \\ 0 & 0 & 0 \end{bmatrix},$$

so an associated eigenvector is $\mathbf{v}_1 = (1, 2, 2)$. With $\lambda_2 = 4$ the matrix

$$A - 4I = \begin{bmatrix} -3 & 2 & 2 \\ 2 & 2 & 2 \\ 2 & 2 & 2 \end{bmatrix}$$

has echelon form

$$\begin{bmatrix} 1 & 1 & 1 \\ 0 & 1 & 1 \\ 0 & 0 & 0 \end{bmatrix},$$

so an associated eigenvector is $\mathbf{v}_2 = (0, 1, -1)$. With $\lambda_3 = 0$ the matrix

$$A - 0I = \begin{bmatrix} 1 & 2 & 2 \\ 2 & 6 & 2 \\ 2 & 2 & 6 \end{bmatrix}$$

has echelon form

$$\begin{bmatrix} 1 & 2 & 2 \\ 0 & 1 & -1 \\ 0 & 0 & 0 \end{bmatrix},$$

so an associated eigenvector is $\mathbf{v}_3 = (4, -1, -1)$. Note finally that

$$\mathbf{v}_1 \cdot \mathbf{v}_2 = \mathbf{v}_1 \cdot \mathbf{v}_3 = \mathbf{v}_2 \cdot \mathbf{v}_3 = 0$$

in accord with Theorem 1.

The eigenvectors $\mathbf{v}_1 = (1, 2, 2)$, $\mathbf{v}_2 = (0, 1, -1)$, and $\mathbf{v}_3 = (4, -1, -1)$ in Example 1 form an orthogonal basis for $\mathbf{R}^3$. If we divide each of these vectors by its length, we obtain the *unit* vectors

$$\mathbf{u}_1 = \left(\frac{1}{3}, \frac{2}{3}, \frac{2}{3}\right), \quad \mathbf{u}_2 = \left(0, \frac{1}{\sqrt{2}}, -\frac{1}{\sqrt{2}}\right), \quad \text{and} \quad \mathbf{u}_3 = \left(\frac{4}{\sqrt{18}}, -\frac{1}{\sqrt{18}}, -\frac{1}{\sqrt{18}}\right)$$

that form an *orthonormal* basis for $\mathbf{R}^3$ consisting of eigenvectors of the matrix A in (4). If $P = [\mathbf{u}_1 \quad \mathbf{u}_2 \quad \mathbf{u}_3]$ and D is the diagonal matrix determined by the corresponding eigenvalues of A,

$$P = \begin{bmatrix} \frac{1}{3} & 0 & \frac{4}{\sqrt{18}} \\ \frac{2}{3} & \frac{1}{\sqrt{2}} & -\frac{1}{\sqrt{18}} \\ \frac{2}{3} & -\frac{1}{\sqrt{2}} & -\frac{1}{\sqrt{18}} \end{bmatrix} \quad \text{and} \quad D = \begin{bmatrix} 9 & 0 & 0 \\ 0 & 4 & 0 \\ 0 & 0 & 0 \end{bmatrix}, \tag{5}$$

then Equation (6) in Section 6.2 implies that

$$A = PDP^{-1}, \quad \text{so} \quad P^{-1}AP = D. \tag{6}$$

The fact that the column vectors of the diagonalizing matrix P are orthonormal has important consequences. For instance, note that

$$P^T P = I, \tag{7}$$

because the ijth element of $P^T P$ is the dot product of the ith row of P^T and the jth column of P and hence is the dot product of the ith and jth columns of P. Thus the matrix P is invertible with $P^{-1} = P^T$; *its inverse matrix is simply its transpose.* Hence the matrix P in (5) is an example of an *orthogonal matrix.*

Definition: *Orthogonal Matrix*

An **orthogonal matrix** is an invertible square matrix A such that

$$A^{-1} = A^T. \tag{8}$$

Problems 22–24 deal with the proof of the following theorem.

> ***Theorem 2:*** *Properties of Orthogonal Matrices*
> The following properties of an $n \times n$ matrix A are equivalent.
>
> **(a)** A is orthogonal.
> **(b)** A^T is orthogonal.
> **(c)** The column vectors of A are orthonormal.
> **(d)** The row vectors of A are orthonormal.

The fact that the column vectors of a square matrix A are orthonormal if and only if its row vectors also are orthonormal is interesting and not entirely obvious. Because of (c) and (d), it might seem more perspicuous to call A an "orthonormal matrix," but the accepted terminology is *orthogonal matrix.*

Recall that the (square) matrix A is said to be *diagonalizable* provided that there exists an invertible matrix P such that $P^{-1}AP$ is a diagonal matrix D. The (square) matrix A is called **orthogonally diagonalizable** provided that there exists an *orthogonal* matrix P such that $P^{-1}AP = D$ is a diagonal matrix D, in which case

$$P^TAP = D \quad \text{and} \quad A = PDP^T \tag{9}$$

because $P^{-1} = P^T$. For instance, the matrix A of Example 1 is orthogonally diagonalizable because it is diagonalized by the orthogonal matrix P in (5).

According to Theorem 1 in Section 6.2, an $n \times n$ matrix is diagonalizable if and only if it has n linearly independent eigenvectors. The following theorem provides the analogous relationship between *orthogonal* diagonalizability and *orthogonal* eigenvectors.

> ***Theorem 3:*** *Criterion for Orthogonal Diagonalizability*
> The $n \times n$ matrix A is orthogonally diagonalizable if and only if it has n mutually orthogonal eigenvectors.

Proof Suppose first that A is orthogonally diagonalizable, so that there exists an orthogonal matrix P such that $P^{-1}AP = D$ is a diagonal matrix. Then, just as in the proof of Theorem 1 in Section 6.2, the fact that $AP = PD$ implies that each of the n column vectors of P is an eigenvector of A. But then these n eigenvectors of A are orthonormal by Theorem 2(c) and hence are mutually orthogonal.

Conversely, suppose that A has n mutually orthogonal eigenvectors $\mathbf{v}_1, \mathbf{v}_2, \ldots, \mathbf{v}_n$ associated with the eigenvalues $\lambda_1, \lambda_2, \ldots, \lambda_n$, respectively. Let $\mathbf{u}_i = \mathbf{v}_i/|\mathbf{v}_i|$ for each i, $1 \leq i \leq n$. Then the n eigenvectors $\mathbf{u}_1, \mathbf{u}_2, \ldots, \mathbf{u}_n$ of A are orthonormal. If

$$P = [\mathbf{u}_1 \quad \mathbf{u}_2 \quad \cdots \quad \mathbf{u}_n]$$

and D is the diagonal matrix with diagonal elements $\lambda_1, \lambda_2, \ldots, \lambda_n$, then it follows precisely as in Equations (1)-(6) of Section 6.2 that $P^{-1}AP = D$. But the matrix P is orthogonal (by Theorem 2) because its column vectors are orthonormal. Thus we have shown that A is orthogonally diagonalizable. ■

Now we ask under what conditions we can apply Theorem 3 to orthogonally diagonalize a given $n \times n$ matrix A. For instance, suppose that A is a matrix like the one in Example 1—it is symmetric *and* has n distinct eigenvalues $\lambda_1, \lambda_2, \ldots, \lambda_n$ corresponding to the eigenvectors $\mathbf{v}_1, \mathbf{v}_2, \ldots, \mathbf{v}_n$. Then Theorem 1 implies that these n eigenvectors are mutually orthogonal, so A is orthogonally diagonalizable by Theorem 3. In particular, the proof of Theorem 3 implies this: If

$$P = [\mathbf{u}_1 \quad \mathbf{u}_2 \quad \cdots \quad \mathbf{u}_n], \tag{10}$$

where $\mathbf{u}_i = \mathbf{v}_i/|\mathbf{v}_i|$ for each i, and if D is the diagonal matrix with diagonal elements $\lambda_1, \lambda_2, \ldots, \lambda_n$, then P is orthogonal and

$$P^{-1}AP = D \tag{11}$$

is a specific orthogonal diagonalization of A.

If the $n \times n$ matrix A has $k < n$ distinct eigenvalues $\lambda_1, \lambda_2, \ldots, \lambda_k$, then we can *attempt* to find an orthogonal diagonalization of A by carrying out the following procedure.

STEP 1: Find a basis for the eigenspace associated with each eigenvalue λ_i of A.

STEP 2: Apply the Gram–Schmidt algorithm of Section 5.4 to convert this basis into an *orthogonal* basis S_i for the eigenspace associated with λ_i.

STEP 3: Form the union S of the orthogonal bases $S_1, S_2, \ldots, S_k$. If the matrix A is symmetric, then it follows from Theorem 1 that the vectors in S are mutually orthogonal.

STEP 4: If S contains n mutually orthogonal eigenvectors $\mathbf{v}_1, \mathbf{v}_2, \ldots, \mathbf{v}_n$, then the matrix

$$P = [\mathbf{u}_1 \quad \mathbf{u}_2 \quad \cdots \quad \mathbf{u}_n],$$

where $\mathbf{u}_i = \mathbf{v}_i/|\mathbf{v}_i|$, orthogonally diagonalizes the matrix A as in Equations (10) and (11).

There are two ways in which this approach may fail to yield an orthogonal diagonalization of A. First, if A is not symmetric, then eigenvectors belonging to different eigenspaces may not be orthogonal. Second, even if the vectors in S are mutually orthogonal, there may be fewer than n of them.

EXAMPLE 2 Consider the symmetric 4×4 matrix

$$A = \begin{bmatrix} 4 & 0 & 0 & 0 \\ 0 & 3 & 0 & 1 \\ 0 & 0 & 4 & 0 \\ 0 & 1 & 0 & 3 \end{bmatrix}.$$

Utilizing the abundant zeros in A, we find readily that its characteristic polynomial is

$$(\lambda - 2)(\lambda - 4)^3 = 0.$$

Hence A has the distinct eigenvalues $\lambda_1 = 2$ and $\lambda_2 = 4$, the latter of multiplicity 3.

With $\lambda_1 = 2$ we find that

$$A - 2I = \begin{bmatrix} 2 & 0 & 0 & 0 \\ 0 & 1 & 0 & 1 \\ 0 & 0 & 2 & 0 \\ 0 & 1 & 0 & 1 \end{bmatrix},$$

so it is clear that $\mathbf{v}_1 = (0, 1, 0, -1)$ is an associated eigenvector.

With $\lambda_2 = 4$ we find that

$$A - 4I = \begin{bmatrix} 0 & 0 & 0 & 0 \\ 0 & -1 & 0 & 1 \\ 0 & 0 & 0 & 0 \\ 0 & 1 & 0 & -1 \end{bmatrix},$$

so the system $(A - 4I)\mathbf{v} = \mathbf{0}$ has leading variable x_2 and free variables x_1, x_3, and x_4. Hence the usual procedure yields the independent eigenvectors $\mathbf{v}_2 = (1, 0, 0, 0)$, $\mathbf{v}_3 = (0, 1, 0, 1)$, and $\mathbf{v}_4 = (0, 0, 1, 0)$ associated with the eigenvalue $\lambda_2 = 4$.

Obviously the eigenvectors $\mathbf{v}_1, \mathbf{v}_2, \mathbf{v}_3$, and $\mathbf{v}_4$ are already mutually orthogonal, so we do not need the Gram–Schmidt orthogonalization process. We normalize each of these eigenvectors and form the diagonalizing and diagonal matrices

$$P = \begin{bmatrix} 0 & 1 & 0 & 0 \\ \dfrac{1}{\sqrt{2}} & 0 & \dfrac{1}{\sqrt{2}} & 0 \\ 0 & 0 & 0 & 1 \\ -\dfrac{1}{\sqrt{2}} & 0 & \dfrac{1}{\sqrt{2}} & 0 \end{bmatrix} \quad \text{and} \quad D = \begin{bmatrix} 2 & 0 & 0 & 0 \\ 0 & 4 & 0 & 0 \\ 0 & 0 & 4 & 0 \\ 0 & 0 & 0 & 4 \end{bmatrix}.$$

Then P is an orthogonal matrix that diagonalizes the given matrix A: $P^{-1}AP = D$.

One of the most amazing results in linear algebra is the fact that the method outlined in Steps 1–4 above succeeds if and only if the matrix A is symmetric. This is a consequence of our next theorem.

Theorem 4: *Symmetry and Orthogonal Diagonalizability*
A square matrix is orthogonally diagonalizable if and only if it is symmetric.

The proof of necessity is quite simple. Suppose that A is orthogonally diagonalizable; hence there exists an orthogonal matrix P and a diagonal matrix D such that $A = PDP^T$. Then

$$\begin{aligned} A^T &= (PDP^T)^T \\ &= (P^T)^T D^T P^T = PDP^T = A, \end{aligned}$$

so it follows that A is symmetric. The proof of sufficiency is more difficult—we discuss it in the appendix to this section.

To see what is so remarkable about Theorem 4, consider the fact that symmetry is so transparent that one can tell at a glance whether or not a given matrix is symmetric. On the other hand, orthogonal diagonalizability is a rather complicated property of matrices involving a delicate mixture of the concepts of matrix multiplication, orthogonality, matrix inverses, and (implicitly) eigenvalues and eigenvectors. Theorem 4 says that a matrix A has this complicated property if and only if it has the simple property of symmetry!

Another important property of symmetric matrices involves their characteristic equations. In general, the characteristic equation of an $n \times n$ matrix A is an nth degree polynomial equation, which may well have some complex solutions. But this cannot happen if the matrix A is symmetric.

Theorem 5: *Characteristic Roots of Symmetric Matrices*
The characteristic equation of a symmetric matrix has only real solutions.

The proof of Theorem 5 is discussed in the appendix to this section. It turns out that if λ_i is an eigenvalue of the symmetric $n \times n$ matrix A, then the dimension of the associated eigenspace is equal to the multiplicity of λ_i as a zero of the characteristic polynomial $|A - \lambda I|$. Consequently, we get a complete set of n eigenvectors when we "merge" orthogonal bases for all of the eigenspaces of A, and Theorem 1 implies that these n eigenvectors are mutually orthogonal.

EXAMPLE 3 The characteristic equation of the symmetric matrix

$$A = \begin{bmatrix} 4 & 1 & 0 & 0 & 0 \\ 1 & 4 & 0 & 0 & 0 \\ 0 & 0 & 4 & 0 & 1 \\ 0 & 0 & 0 & 5 & 0 \\ 0 & 0 & 1 & 0 & 4 \end{bmatrix}$$

is

$$[(4-\lambda)^2 - 1](5-\lambda)[(4-\lambda)^2 - 1] = -(\lambda - 3)^2(\lambda - 5)^3 = 0.$$

Hence A has the eigenvalue $\lambda_1 = 3$ of multiplicity 2 and the eigenvalue $\lambda_2 = 5$ of multiplicity 3. Consequently, A has a 2-dimensional eigenspace associated with the eigenvalue $\lambda_1 = 3$ and a 3-dimensional eigenspace associated with the eigenvalue $\lambda_2 = 5$. In Problem 19 we ask you to complete this example by finding orthogonal bases for these two eigenspaces.

6.4 PROBLEMS

A *complete* set of eigenvectors for an $n \times n$ matrix A is a set of n linearly independent eigenvectors of A. Find a complete set of mutually orthogonal eigenvectors for each of the symmetric matrices in Problems 1–18.

1. $\begin{bmatrix} 3 & 1 \\ 1 & 3 \end{bmatrix}$

2. $\begin{bmatrix} 4 & 2 \\ 2 & 4 \end{bmatrix}$

3. $\begin{bmatrix} 9 & 2 \\ 2 & 6 \end{bmatrix}$

4. $\begin{bmatrix} 13 & 4 \\ 4 & 7 \end{bmatrix}$

5. $\begin{bmatrix} 1 & 3 & 0 \\ 3 & 1 & 0 \\ 0 & 0 & 2 \end{bmatrix}$

6. $\begin{bmatrix} 5 & 3 & 0 \\ 3 & 5 & 0 \\ 0 & 0 & 4 \end{bmatrix}$

7. $\begin{bmatrix} 3 & 0 & 3 \\ 0 & 6 & 0 \\ 3 & 0 & 3 \end{bmatrix}$

8. $\begin{bmatrix} 6 & -3 & 0 \\ -3 & 6 & 0 \\ 0 & 0 & 3 \end{bmatrix}$

9. $\begin{bmatrix} 4 & 1 & 2 \\ 1 & 1 & -1 \\ 2 & -1 & 4 \end{bmatrix}$

10. $\begin{bmatrix} 5 & 2 & 1 \\ 2 & 2 & -2 \\ 1 & -2 & 5 \end{bmatrix}$

11. $\begin{bmatrix} 4 & 1 & 4 \\ 1 & 7 & 1 \\ 4 & 1 & 4 \end{bmatrix}$

12. $\begin{bmatrix} 1 & 2 & 2 \\ 2 & 7 & 1 \\ 2 & 1 & 7 \end{bmatrix}$

13. $\begin{bmatrix} 4 & 1 & 1 \\ 1 & 4 & 1 \\ 1 & 1 & 4 \end{bmatrix}$

14. $\begin{bmatrix} 5 & 1 & 3 \\ 1 & 7 & 1 \\ 3 & 1 & 5 \end{bmatrix}$

15. $\begin{bmatrix} 2 & 0 & 0 & 0 \\ 0 & 1 & 0 & 1 \\ 0 & 0 & 2 & 0 \\ 0 & 1 & 0 & 1 \end{bmatrix}$

16. $\begin{bmatrix} 1 & 2 & 0 & 0 \\ 2 & 4 & 0 & 0 \\ 0 & 0 & 2 & 2 \\ 0 & 0 & 2 & 2 \end{bmatrix}$

17. $\begin{bmatrix} 1 & 0 & 1 & 0 \\ 0 & 1 & 0 & 1 \\ 1 & 0 & 1 & 0 \\ 0 & 1 & 0 & 1 \end{bmatrix}$

18. $\begin{bmatrix} 3 & 0 & 1 & 0 \\ 0 & 2 & 0 & 2 \\ 1 & 0 & 3 & 0 \\ 0 & 2 & 0 & 2 \end{bmatrix}$

19. Find a complete set of mutually orthogonal eigenvectors for the symmetric 5×5 matrix of Example 3.

20. Find the eigenvalues and the dimensions of the associated eigenspaces of the symmetric 6×6 matrix

$$A = \left[\begin{array}{ccc:ccc} 4 & 0 & 2 & & & \\ 0 & 4 & 0 & & 0 & \\ 2 & 0 & 4 & & & \\ \hdashline & & & 5 & 0 & 1 \\ & 0 & & 0 & 6 & 0 \\ & & & 1 & 0 & 5 \end{array}\right].$$

The characteristic polynomial of A is the product of the characteristic polynomials of the two nonzero 3×3 submatrices of A.

21. Prove that $|\det A| = 1$ if A is orthogonal.

22. Show that the matrix A is orthogonal if and only if its transpose A^T is orthogonal.

23. Show that an $n \times n$ matrix is orthogonal if and only if its column vectors are orthonormal.

24. Show that an $n \times n$ matrix is orthogonal if and only if its row vectors are orthonormal.

25. Prove that if A and B are orthogonal $n \times n$ matrices, then the product matrix AB is also orthogonal.

26. Two matrices A and B are said to be **orthogonally similar** provided that $B = P^{-1}AP$ for some orthogonal matrix P. Suppose that A and B are orthogonally similar. Prove that A is symmetric if and only if B is symmetric.

27. Show that if A is symmetric and n is a positive integer, then A^n is symmetric.

28. Suppose that A is a diagonalizable matrix whose eigenspaces are mutually orthogonal. Show that A is symmetric.

*Appendix to Section 6.4

Here we discuss the proofs of Theorems 4 and 5. The proof of Theorem 5 is more elementary, so we begin with it.

Suppose that $A = [a_{ij}]$ is a symmetric $n \times n$ matrix (with real entries) and that λ is a solution of the characteristic equation

$$|A - \lambda I| = 0. \tag{1}$$

Even though the coefficients in this nth degree polynomial equation are real, the solution λ could be a complex number: $\lambda = \alpha + \beta i$ where $i = \sqrt{-1}$ and α and β are the real and imaginary parts of λ. Recall that the **conjugate** of such a complex number is obtained by changing the sign of the imaginary part and is denoted by an overbar,

$$\bar{\lambda} = \alpha - \beta i.$$

The proof of Theorem 5 depends upon a few basic facts about matrices with complex entries and systems of linear equations with complex coefficients. The facts we need are complex analogues of familiar facts about real matrices and real linear systems. For instance, matrix products and determinants of matrices are defined for complex matrices in precisely the same way as for real matrices. In addition, the fundamental theorem about homogeneous $n \times n$ linear systems also carries over to the complex case. That is, if A is a complex $n \times n$ matrix, then the homogeneous system $A\mathbf{x} = \mathbf{0}$ has a nontrivial solution if and only if $\det A = |A| = 0$. In this case a solution is a complex n-vector—an n-tuple of complex numbers.

We want to apply the theorem just stated to the homogeneous linear system

$$(A - \lambda I)\mathbf{v} = \mathbf{0}, \tag{2}$$

where the coefficient matrix $A - \lambda I$ is complex if λ is complex. Then Equation (1) implies that this system has a nontrivial (complex) solution vector

$$\mathbf{v} = (x_1 + iy_1, x_2 + iy_2, \ldots, x_n + iy_n) \tag{3}$$

such that

$$A\mathbf{v} = \lambda\mathbf{v}. \tag{4}$$

We multiply each side in (4) by the $1 \times n$ matrix

$$\bar{\mathbf{v}}^T = [x_1 - iy_1 \quad x_2 - iy_2 \quad \ldots \quad x_n - iy_n] \tag{5}$$

that is the *conjugate transpose* of the $n \times 1$ matrix $\mathbf{v}$. The result is the equation

$$\bar{\mathbf{v}}^T A\mathbf{v} = \lambda\bar{\mathbf{v}}^T\mathbf{v}. \tag{6}$$

Note that $\bar{\mathbf{v}}^T A\mathbf{v}$ and $\bar{\mathbf{v}}^T\mathbf{v}$ are 1×1 matrices and thus are complex numbers. If we can show that in fact they are *real* numbers with $\bar{\mathbf{v}}^T\mathbf{v} \neq 0$, then Equation (6) will imply that λ is a quotient of two real numbers and hence is itself a real number.

The fact that $\bar{\mathbf{v}}^T\mathbf{v}$ is a nonzero real number is almost immediate because

$$\bar{\mathbf{v}}^T\mathbf{v} = \sum_{p=1}^{n} (x_p + iy_p)(x_p - iy_p) = \sum_{p=1}^{n} (x_p^2 + y_p^2) \tag{7}$$

and not all the entries in $\mathbf{v}$ are zero. To show that $\bar{\mathbf{v}}^T A\mathbf{v}$ is real, we first note that the definition of matrix multiplication implies that

$$\bar{\mathbf{v}}^T A\mathbf{v} = \sum_{p,q=1}^{n} a_{pq}(x_p - iy_p)(x_q + iy_q). \tag{8}$$

If $p = q$, then

$$a_{pp}(x_p - iy_p)(x_p + iy_p) = a_{pp}(x_p^2 + y_p^2), \tag{9}$$

so the "diagonal terms" in (8) are all real. If $p \neq q$, then the sum of the pqth and qpth terms in (8) is

$$\begin{aligned} &a_{pq}(x_p - iy_p)(x_q + iy_q) + a_{qp}(x_q - iy_q)(x_p + iy_p) \\ &\quad = a_{pq}(x_p y_q + ix_p y_q - ix_q y_p + y_p y_q) \\ &\qquad + a_{qp}(x_p x_q - ix_p y_q + ix_q y_p + y_p y_q) \\ &\quad = 2a_{pq}(x_p x_q + y_p y_q) \end{aligned} \tag{10}$$

because $a_{pq} = a_{qp}$ (this is where we use the hypothesis that A is symmetric). Thus all the imaginary terms in (8) cancel, and so $\bar{\mathbf{v}}^T A\mathbf{v}$ is a real number. Therefore

$$\lambda = \frac{\bar{\mathbf{v}}^T A\mathbf{v}}{\bar{\mathbf{v}}^T\mathbf{v}}$$

is real, and we have completed the proof of Theorem 5. ∎

Now we turn our attention to Theorem 4; we want to prove that every symmetric $n \times n$ matrix is orthogonally diagonalizable. The proof will be by induction on n, beginning with the fact that every symmetric 1×1 matrix $[a]$ is already a diagonal matrix.

Now assume that $n \geq 2$. We make the inductive assumption that every symmetric $(n-1) \times (n-1)$ matrix is orthogonally diagonalizable and suppose that A is a symmetric $n \times n$ matrix. Having already proved Theorem 5 (*without* assuming the truth of Theorem 4), we know that the symmetric matrix A has at least one (real) eigenvalue λ_1 (because by the fundamental theorem of algebra its characteristic equation must have at least one solution). Let $\mathbf{v}_1$ be an eigenvector of A associated with λ_1—and choose $\mathbf{v}_1$ of unit length: $|\mathbf{v}_1| = 1$. Then we can apply the Gram-Schmidt algorithm to find vectors $\mathbf{v}_2, \mathbf{v}_3, \ldots, \mathbf{v}_n$ such that the n vectors $\mathbf{v}_1, \mathbf{v}_2, \ldots, \mathbf{v}_n$ are orthonormal. Only the first of these vectors is guaranteed to be an eigenvector of A, but Theorem 2 in Section 6.4 implies that the $n \times n$ matrix

$$Q = [\mathbf{v}_1 \quad \mathbf{v}_2 \quad \cdots \quad \mathbf{v}_n] \tag{11}$$

is an orthogonal matrix, so $Q^{-1} = Q^T$.

Now we note that

$$\begin{aligned} AQ &= [A\mathbf{v}_1 \quad A\mathbf{v}_2 \quad \cdots \quad A\mathbf{v}_n] \\ &= [\lambda_1\mathbf{v}_1 \quad A\mathbf{v}_2 \quad \cdots \quad A\mathbf{v}_n] \end{aligned}$$

because $A\mathbf{v}_1 = \lambda_1\mathbf{v}_1$. Next we form the $n \times n$ matrix

$$B = Q^TAQ = \begin{bmatrix} \mathbf{v}_1^T \\ \mathbf{v}_2^T \\ \vdots \\ \mathbf{v}_n^T \end{bmatrix} [\lambda_1\mathbf{v}_1 \quad A\mathbf{v}_2 \quad \cdots \quad A\mathbf{v}_n]. \tag{12}$$

Because the vectors $\mathbf{v}_1, \mathbf{v}_2, \ldots, \mathbf{v}_n$ are orthonormal (and so $\mathbf{v}_i^T\mathbf{v}_1 = 0$ if $i > 1$), it follows immediately from the matrix multiplication indicated in (12) that B has the form

$$B = \begin{bmatrix} \lambda_1 & * & * & * \\ 0 & * & * & * \\ 0 & * & * & * \\ 0 & * & * & * \end{bmatrix}, \tag{13}$$

where the asterisks denote elements that may or may not be zero. But

$$B^T = (Q^TAQ)^T = Q^TA^TQ = Q^TAQ = B$$

because A is symmetric, and therefore B is symmetric as well. Hence the elements of its first row are the same as the elements of its first column. Consequently, B has the form

$$B = \begin{bmatrix} \lambda_1 & 0 & 0 & 0 \\ 0 & * & * & * \\ 0 & * & * & * \\ 0 & * & * & * \end{bmatrix} = \left[\begin{array}{c|ccc} \lambda_1 & 0 & 0 & 0 \\ \hline 0 & & & \\ 0 & & C & \\ 0 & & & \end{array}\right] \tag{14}$$

where C is a symmetric $(n-1) \times (n-1)$ matrix.

Our inductive assumption now comes into play: It implies that there is an orthogonal $(n-1) \times (n-1)$ matrix R such that $R^TCR = D_1$ is a diagonal matrix. The $n \times n$ matrix

$$S = \left[\begin{array}{c|ccc} 1 & 0 & 0 & 0 \\ \hline 0 & & & \\ 0 & & R & \\ 0 & & & \end{array}\right]$$

is orthogonal because its columns are orthonormal, and

$$S^TBS = \left[\begin{array}{c|ccc} 1 & 0 & 0 & 0 \\ \hline 0 & & & \\ 0 & & R^T & \\ 0 & & & \end{array}\right] \left[\begin{array}{c|ccc} \lambda_1 & 0 & 0 & 0 \\ \hline 0 & & & \\ 0 & & C & \\ 0 & & & \end{array}\right] \left[\begin{array}{c|ccc} 1 & 0 & 0 & 0 \\ \hline 0 & & & \\ 0 & & R & \\ 0 & & & \end{array}\right]$$

$$= \left[\begin{array}{c|ccc} \lambda_1 & 0 & 0 & 0 \\ \hline 0 & & & \\ 0 & & R^TCR & \\ 0 & & & \end{array}\right] = \left[\begin{array}{c|ccc} \lambda_1 & 0 & 0 & 0 \\ \hline 0 & & & \\ 0 & & D_1 & \\ 0 & & & \end{array}\right].$$

Thus

$$S^TBS = D \tag{15}$$

is a diagonal matrix.

Finally, the product $P = QS$ is an orthogonal matrix by Problem 25, and

$$P^TAP = S^T(Q^TAQ)S = S^TBS = D. \tag{16}$$

Hence P is an orthogonal matrix that diagonalizes our symmetric $n \times n$ matrix A, and therefore the proof of Theorem 4 is complete. ■

CHAPTER REVIEW QUESTIONS

1. Does there exist a matrix that has the zero vector $\mathbf{0}$ as an eigenvector?

2. Can a single eigenvector be associated with two distinct eigenvalues of a matrix?

3. What is the largest number of distinct eigenvalues that an $n \times n$ matrix can have? The least number?

4. Is a linear combination of eigenvectors of a matrix A necessarily an eigenvector of A? If not, what must be the relationship between the eigenvectors in order that any nontrivial linear combination of them also be an eigenvector?

5. Explain briefly why each eigenvalue λ of the matrix A satisfies the characteristic equation $|A - \lambda I| = 0$. Must every solution of this equation be an eigenvalue of A?

6. Enumerate the various possibilities for a 3×3 matrix A, as to how many eigenvalues A may have and how many eigenvectors may be associated with each eigenvalue.

7. What is the smallest number of distinct eigenvalues that a diagonalizable 4×4 matrix can have?

8. Can three linearly dependent eigenvectors of a matrix A be associated with three distinct eigenvalues of A?

9. Must a diagonalizable $n \times n$ matrix have n distinct eigenvalues? Must it have n linearly independent eigenvectors?

10. How can one determine whether or not a given matrix is diagonalizable?

11. Suppose that the $n \times n$ matrix A has n linearly independent eigenvectors. Write a formula that expresses A in terms of its eigenvectors and eigenvalues.

12. Explain a feasible method for computing the 100th power of a diagonalizable 3×3 matrix.

13. If the $n \times n$ matrices A and B are similar and A has n linearly independent eigenvectors, does it follow that B also has n linearly independent eigenvectors?

14. If one extracts several linearly independent eigenvectors from each of several different eigenspaces of a matrix, must the set of all these eigenvectors be linearly independent?

15. What is the relationship between two different eigenspaces of a symmetric matrix?

16. What is the smallest number of mutually orthogonal eigenvectors that an orthogonally diagonalizable 4×4 matrix can have?

17. Explain the simplest way to determine whether or not a given $n \times n$ matrix is orthogonally diagonalizable.

18. Suppose that the $n \times n$ matrix A has exactly two distinct eigenvalues and that the associated eigenspaces are orthogonal. Does it follow that these two eigenspaces are orthogonal complements of one another in $\mathbf{R}^n$?

19. Suppose that the $n \times n$ matrix A has exactly two distinct eigenvalues whose associated eigenspaces are orthogonal complements in $\mathbf{R}^n$. Does it follow that the matrix A is symmetric?

20. What is the smallest number of distinct eigenvalues that a symmetric 3×3 matrix can have?

21. Suppose that the eigenspaces of an $n \times n$ matrix A are mutually orthogonal. Under what condition on their dimensions does it follow that A is symmetric?

7

Linear Transformations

7.1 Matrix Transformations

Recall that a **function** F from the set V to the set W is a rule that assigns to each element x of V exactly one element $F(x)$ of W. If V and W are vector spaces, then F is a *vector-valued function* (of a vector variable) that associates with each vector $\mathbf{v}$ in V a vector $\mathbf{w} = F(\mathbf{v})$ in W. In this case the function F also is called a *mapping*, or a *transformation*, from the vector space V to the vector space W. We write $F: V \to W$ and call the vector $\mathbf{w} = F(\mathbf{v})$ the **image** of the vector $\mathbf{v}$ under the transformation F. In this chapter we will see that the study of matrices and linear systems is closely related to the study of a special class of vector space transformations known as *linear transformations.*

EXAMPLE 1 Let $\mathbf{v} = (x, y, z)$ be a typical vector in $\mathbf{R}^3$. Then the formula

$$F(\mathbf{v}) = (2x - y + z, x + 3y - 2z) \tag{1}$$

defines a transformation from $\mathbf{R}^3$ to $\mathbf{R}^2$. For instance, the image of the vector $\mathbf{v} = (3, 2, 1)$ is the vector $\mathbf{w} = F(\mathbf{v}) = (5, 7)$. Observe that if

$$A = \begin{bmatrix} 2 & -1 & 1 \\ 1 & 3 & -2 \end{bmatrix} \tag{2}$$

then

$$A\mathbf{v} = \begin{bmatrix} 2 & -1 & 1 \\ 1 & 3 & -2 \end{bmatrix} \begin{bmatrix} x \\ y \\ z \end{bmatrix} = \begin{bmatrix} 2x - y + z \\ x + 3y - 2z \end{bmatrix}. \tag{3}$$

Upon comparing (1) and (3) we see that the transformation $F: \mathbf{R}^3 \to \mathbf{R}^2$ is given by

$$F(\mathbf{v}) = A\mathbf{v}. \tag{4}$$

That is, the image of $\mathbf{v}$ is obtained by multiplying the 3-vector $\mathbf{v}$ by the 2×3 matrix A.

The formula in (4) implies that the transformation $F: \mathbf{R}^3 \to \mathbf{R}^2$ of Example 1 corresponds to multiplication by the 2×3 matrix A in (2). More generally, we can use any fixed $m \times n$ matrix A to define a transformation from $\mathbf{R}^n$ to $\mathbf{R}^m$. If $\mathbf{x}$ is a (column) vector in $\mathbf{R}^n$, then the $m \times 1$ product matrix $A\mathbf{x}$ is a (column) vector in $\mathbf{R}^m$. Hence the formula

$$T(\mathbf{x}) = A\mathbf{x} \tag{5}$$

defines the **matrix transformation** $T: \mathbf{R}^n \to \mathbf{R}^m$ that **corresponds** to the $m \times n$ matrix A; we may describe T as **multiplication by** A. To remember that the matrix transformation T corresponding to an $m \times n$ matrix A is one from $\mathbf{R}^n$ to $\mathbf{R}^m$ (rather than from $\mathbf{R}^m$ to $\mathbf{R}^n$), we need only observe that $\mathbf{x}$ must be an n-vector in order that the product $A\mathbf{x}$ be defined.

EXAMPLE 2 The 3×2 matrix

$$A = \begin{bmatrix} 1 & 2 \\ 3 & -2 \\ 4 & 3 \end{bmatrix}$$

defines the transformation $T: \mathbf{R}^2 \to \mathbf{R}^3$ given by

$$T(x, y) = \begin{bmatrix} 1 & 2 \\ 3 & -2 \\ 4 & 3 \end{bmatrix} \begin{bmatrix} x \\ y \end{bmatrix}$$

$$= \begin{bmatrix} x + 2y \\ 3x - 2y \\ 4x + 3y \end{bmatrix} = (x + 2y, 3x - 2y, 4x + 3y).$$

Here we write $T(x, y)$—rather than $T((x, y))$—for the image of the vector (x, y) under the transformation T.

Matrix transformations have important special properties. Suppose that the transformation $T: \mathbf{R}^n \to \mathbf{R}^m$ is defined by $T(\mathbf{x}) = A\mathbf{x}$, where A is a given $m \times n$ matrix. If $\mathbf{u}$ and $\mathbf{v}$ are n-vectors and c is a scalar, then

$$T(\mathbf{u} + \mathbf{v}) = A(\mathbf{u} + \mathbf{v}) = A\mathbf{u} + A\mathbf{v} = T(\mathbf{u}) + T(\mathbf{v}) \tag{6}$$

and

$$T(c\mathbf{u}) = A(c\mathbf{u}) = c(A\mathbf{u}) = cT(\mathbf{u}). \tag{7}$$

A transformation between vector spaces that enjoys these two properties is said to be *linear*.

> ***Definition:*** *Linear Transformation*
>
> If V and W are vector spaces, then the function $T: V \to W$ is a **linear transformation** provided that
>
> **(i)** $T(\mathbf{u} + \mathbf{v}) = T(\mathbf{u}) + T(\mathbf{v})$ and
>
> **(ii)** $T(c\mathbf{u}) = cT(\mathbf{u})$
>
> for all vectors $\mathbf{u}$ and $\mathbf{v}$ in V and for every scalar c.

Property (i) of this definition may be described by saying that the linear transformation T *preserves addition* of vectors—the image of the sum of two vectors is the sum of their images. Property (ii) says that T *preserves scalar multiplication.*

We may show that a given transformation $T:\mathbf{R}^n \to \mathbf{R}^m$ is linear *either* by verifying the two properties of the definition directly *or* by showing that T is a matrix transformation.

EXAMPLE 3 Let the transformation $T:\mathbf{R}^2 \to \mathbf{R}^2$ be defined as follows:

$$T(x, y) = (3x - 5y, 4x + 7y).$$

Then we note that

$$T(x, y) = \begin{bmatrix} 3 & -5 \\ 4 & 7 \end{bmatrix}\begin{bmatrix} x \\ y \end{bmatrix}.$$

Thus T is a matrix transformation, and is therefore linear (by the computations in (6) and (7)).

EXAMPLE 4 Let the transformation $T:\mathbf{R}^2 \to \mathbf{R}^2$ be defined to be

$$T(x, y) = (xy, x + y + 1).$$

If $\mathbf{u} = (1, 0)$ and $\mathbf{v} = (0, 1)$, then

$$T(\mathbf{u}) = T(\mathbf{v}) = (0, 2) \qquad \text{but}$$

$$T(\mathbf{u} + \mathbf{v}) = T(1, 1) = (1, 3) \neq T(\mathbf{u}) + T(\mathbf{v}).$$

Thus the transformation T does not preserve addition and, therefore, is *not* linear. Moreover,

$$T(2, 2) = (4, 5) \neq 2 \cdot T(1, 1),$$

so T does not preserve scalar multiplication either.

The meaning of the following theorem is that a transformation between vector spaces is linear if and only if it preserves linear combinations of pairs of vectors.

Theorem 1: *Linearity and Linear Combinations*

If V and W are vector spaces, then the transformation $T: V \to W$ is linear if and only if

$$T(c_1\mathbf{v}_1 + c_2\mathbf{v}_2) = c_1 T(\mathbf{v}_1) + c_2 T(\mathbf{v}_2) \tag{8}$$

for all pairs of vectors $\mathbf{v}_1$, $\mathbf{v}_2$ in V and all pairs c_1, c_2 of scalars.

PROOF If T is linear, then—applying in turn properties (i) and (ii) in the definition of linearity—we find that

$$\begin{aligned} T(c_1\mathbf{v}_1 + c_2\mathbf{v}_2) &= T(c_1\mathbf{v}_1) + T(c_2\mathbf{v}_2) \\ &= c_1 T(\mathbf{v}_1) + c_2 T(\mathbf{v}_2). \end{aligned}$$

Thus the linear transformation T has the property in (8). Conversely, suppose that the transformation T has the property in (8). Then with $c_1 = c_2 = 1$, we find that $T(\mathbf{v}_1 + \mathbf{v}_2) = T(\mathbf{v}_1) + T(\mathbf{v}_2)$, whereas with $c_1 = c$ and $c_2 = 0$, we find that $T(c\mathbf{v}_1) = cT(\mathbf{v}_1)$. Thus T preserves both addition and scalar multiplication, and therefore is linear. ■

By repeated application of Theorem 1 we see that if T is a linear transformation, then

$$T(c_1\mathbf{v}_1 + c_2\mathbf{v}_2 + \cdots + c_n\mathbf{v}_n) = c_1T(\mathbf{v}_1) + c_2T(\mathbf{v}_2) + \cdots + c_nT(\mathbf{v}_n). \tag{9}$$

Thus a linear transformation preserves *arbitrary* (finite) linear combinations.

The computations in (6) and (7) show that every matrix transformation is linear. Conversely, every linear transformation from $\mathbf{R}^n$ to $\mathbf{R}^m$ is a matrix transformation.

Theorem 2: *The Matrix of a Linear Transformation*

The function $T:\mathbf{R}^n \to \mathbf{R}^m$ is a linear transformation if and only if it is a matrix transformation, in which case the matrix A corresponding to T is given by

$$A = [T(\mathbf{e}_1) \quad T(\mathbf{e}_2) \quad \ldots \quad T(\mathbf{e}_n)]. \tag{10}$$

Thus *the jth column vector of A is the image $T(\mathbf{e}_j)$ of the jth standard unit basis vector $\mathbf{e}_j$.*

Proof If $T:\mathbf{R}^n \to \mathbf{R}^m$ is a matrix transformation defined by $T(\mathbf{x}) = A\mathbf{x}$, then we know by (6) and (7) that T is linear, so it remains only to verify Equation (10). But it follows immediately from the definition of matrix multiplication that $T(\mathbf{e}_j) = A\mathbf{e}_j$ is the jth column vector of A, as specified in (10).

Conversely, suppose that $T:\mathbf{R}^n \to \mathbf{R}^m$ is a linear transformation. Let the $m \times n$ matrix A be defined as in Equation (10):

$$A = [T(\mathbf{e}_1) \quad T(\mathbf{e}_2) \quad \ldots \quad T(\mathbf{e}_n)].$$

We want to show that $T(\mathbf{x}) = A\mathbf{x}$ for every vector $\mathbf{x} = (x_1, x_2, \ldots, x_n)$ in $\mathbf{R}^n$, and thus that T is the matrix transformation corresponding to A. But the linearity of T yields

$$\begin{aligned} T(\mathbf{x}) &= T(x_1\mathbf{e}_1 + x_2\mathbf{e}_2 + \cdots + x_n\mathbf{e}_n) \\ &= x_1T(\mathbf{e}_1) + x_2T(\mathbf{e}_2) + \cdots + x_nT(\mathbf{e}_n) \\ &= [T(\mathbf{e}_1) \quad T(\mathbf{e}_2) \quad \ldots \quad T(\mathbf{e}_n)]\begin{bmatrix} x_1 \\ x_2 \\ \vdots \\ x_n \end{bmatrix} \\ &= A\mathbf{x}, \end{aligned}$$

as desired. ■

An important consequence of Theorem 2 is that a *linear* transformation $T:\mathbf{R}^n \to \mathbf{R}^m$ is completely determined by its "action" on the standard unit basis vectors $\mathbf{e}_1, \mathbf{e}_2, \ldots, \mathbf{e}_n$.

EXAMPLE 5 Let $T:\mathbf{R}^3 \to \mathbf{R}^3$ be a linear transformation such that

$$T(\mathbf{e}_1) = (2, 1, 3), \qquad T(\mathbf{e}_2) = (-1, 0, 2), \quad \text{and} \quad T(\mathbf{e}_3) = (3, 4, -1).$$

Then according to (10) the matrix of T is

$$A = [T(\mathbf{e}_1) \quad T(\mathbf{e}_2) \quad T(\mathbf{e}_3)] = \begin{bmatrix} 2 & -1 & 3 \\ 1 & 0 & 4 \\ 3 & 2 & -1 \end{bmatrix}$$

Hence the image under T of $\mathbf{v} = (x, y, z)$ is

$$T(\mathbf{v}) = \begin{bmatrix} 2 & -1 & 3 \\ 1 & 0 & 4 \\ 3 & 2 & -1 \end{bmatrix} \begin{bmatrix} x \\ y \\ z \end{bmatrix},$$

so

$$T(x, y, z) = (2x - y + 3z, x + 4z, 3x + 2y - z).$$

GEOMETRIC TRANSFORMATIONS OF THE PLANE $\mathbf{R}^2$

Often a linear transformation $T:\mathbf{R}^n \to \mathbf{R}^n$ is described initially in geometrical terms; for instance, T might be the transformation of the plane $\mathbf{R}^2$ into itself that reflects each point in the x-axis. If the effect of T on each standard unit basis vector is evident, we can then apply Theorem 2 to construct the matrix of T and thereby obtain an algebraic description of T. In the next three examples we illustrate this procedure for some important geometric transformations of the plane $\mathbf{R}^2$.

EXAMPLE 6 A **reflection** in the line L through the origin is the transformation that maps each point in the plane to its mirror image through the line L. Figure 7.1 illustrates the reflection T in the x-axis, for which $T(x, y) = (x, -y)$. Obviously

$$T(\mathbf{e}_1) = \mathbf{e}_1 = (1, 0) \quad \text{and} \quad T(\mathbf{e}_2) = -\mathbf{e}_2 = (0, -1),$$

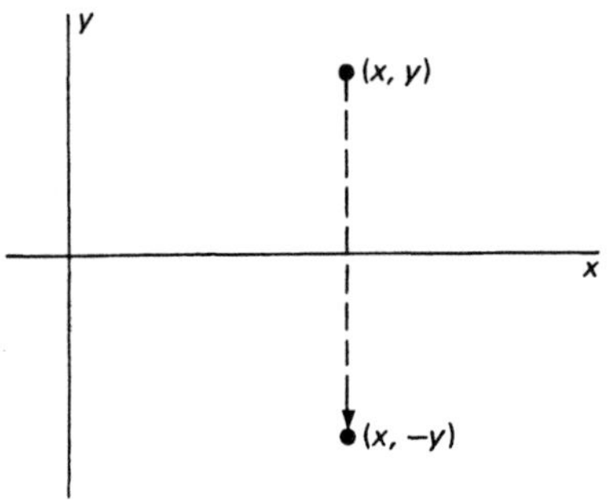

7.1 Reflection in the *x*-axis.

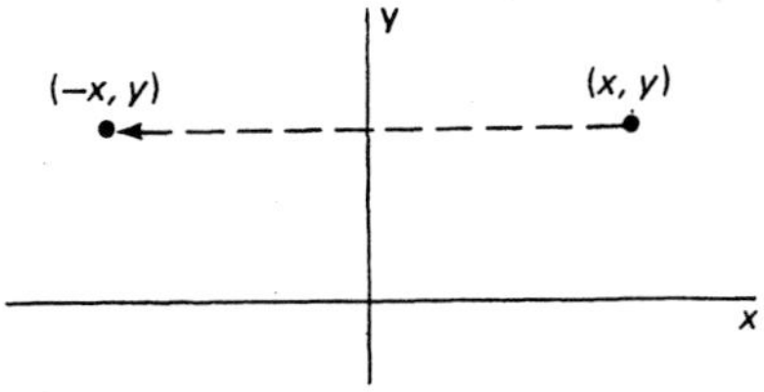

7.2 Reflection in the y-axis.

so the matrix of T is

$$A = \begin{bmatrix} 1 & 0 \\ 0 & -1 \end{bmatrix}. \tag{11}$$

As a check we note that

$$T(x, y) = \begin{bmatrix} 1 & 0 \\ 0 & -1 \end{bmatrix}\begin{bmatrix} x \\ y \end{bmatrix} = \begin{bmatrix} x \\ -y \end{bmatrix} = (x, -y).$$

You should be able to show similarly that the matrix of the reflection in the y-axis, illustrated in Figure 7.2, is

$$A = \begin{bmatrix} -1 & 0 \\ 0 & 1 \end{bmatrix}. \tag{12}$$

REMARK In Example 6 we first *assumed* that the geometric reflection T was a linear transformation. Then Theorem 2 provided us with the matrix A in (11). But the corresponding matrix transformation *is* a linear transformation of $\mathbf{R}^2$ and, moreover, we find that it carries out the desired geometric transformation. This result vindicates the initial assumption that T is linear. Alternatively, one could in advance use the geometric definition of T to show directly that T is a linear transformation.

EXAMPLE 7 Let T denote the counterclockwise **rotation** of the plane $\mathbf{R}^2$ through the angle θ, as indicated in Figure 7.3. Figure 7.4 shows the images under T of the unit basis vectors $\mathbf{e}_1$ and $\mathbf{e}_2$. It follows from elementary trigonometry that

$$T(\mathbf{e}_1) = (\cos\theta, \sin\theta) \qquad \text{and}$$

$$T(\mathbf{e}_2) = \left(\cos\left(\theta + \frac{\pi}{2}\right), \sin\left(\theta + \frac{\pi}{2}\right)\right) = (-\sin\theta, \cos\theta).$$

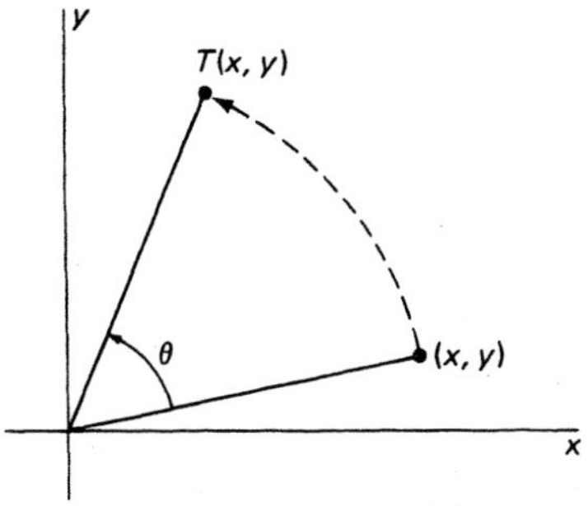

7.3 Rotation of $\mathbf{R}^2$ through the angle θ.

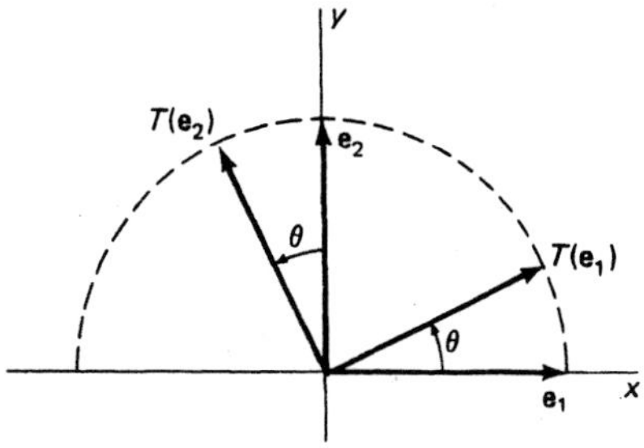

7.4 Rotation of the unit basis vectors.

It can be verified geometrically that T is a linear transformation, so Theorem 2 yields

$$A = [T(\mathbf{e}_1) \quad T(\mathbf{e}_2)] = \begin{bmatrix} \cos\theta & -\sin\theta \\ \sin\theta & \cos\theta \end{bmatrix} \tag{13}$$

for the matrix of T. If $\theta = 45°$, for instance, then

$$A = \begin{bmatrix} \dfrac{1}{\sqrt{2}} & \dfrac{-1}{\sqrt{2}} \\ \dfrac{1}{\sqrt{2}} & \dfrac{1}{\sqrt{2}} \end{bmatrix} = \frac{1}{\sqrt{2}}\begin{bmatrix} 1 & -1 \\ 1 & 1 \end{bmatrix}. \tag{14}$$

Hence the image $T(x, y) = (x', y')$ of the point (x, y) under the rotation of $\mathbf{R}^2$ through the angle $\theta = 45°$ is given by

$$\begin{bmatrix} x' \\ y' \end{bmatrix} = \frac{1}{\sqrt{2}}\begin{bmatrix} 1 & -1 \\ 1 & 1 \end{bmatrix}\begin{bmatrix} x \\ y \end{bmatrix} = \frac{1}{\sqrt{2}}\begin{bmatrix} x - y \\ x + y \end{bmatrix}.$$

Thus

$$x' = \frac{1}{\sqrt{2}}(x - y), \qquad y' = \frac{1}{\sqrt{2}}(x + y).$$

Sometimes a linear transformation $T:\mathbf{R}^n \to \mathbf{R}^n$ is described as the composition of a (finite) sequence $T_1, T_2, \ldots, T_k$ of linear transformations of $\mathbf{R}^n$. That is,

$$T(\mathbf{x}) = T_k(T_{k-1}(\ldots T_2(T_1(\mathbf{x}))\ldots))$$

for each $\mathbf{x}$ in $\mathbf{R}^n$. Thus $T(\mathbf{x})$ is the result of first applying to $\mathbf{x}$ the transformation T_1, then T_2, and so on. We accordingly write

$$T = T_k T_{k-1} \cdots T_2 T_1. \tag{15}$$

Now let A_i be the $n \times n$ matrix of the transformation T_i (for $i = 1, 2, \ldots, k$), so that $T_i(\mathbf{x}) = A_i\mathbf{x}$. Then

$$\begin{aligned} T(\mathbf{x}) &= T_k T_{k-1} \cdots T_2(T_1(\mathbf{x})) \\ &= T_k T_{k-1} \cdots T_2(A_1\mathbf{x}) \\ &\;\;\vdots \\ &= T_k(A_{k-1} \cdots A_2 A_1 \mathbf{x}); \\ T(\mathbf{x}) &= A_k A_{k-1} \cdots A_2 A_1 \mathbf{x}. \end{aligned}$$

Therefore the matrix of T is the product

$$A = A_k A_{k-1} \cdots A_2 A_1. \tag{16}$$

Thus *the matrix of the composition* $T = T_k \ldots T_2 T_1$ *is the product* $A = A_k \ldots A_2 A_1$ *of the matrices of the linear transformations* $T_1, T_2, \ldots, T_k$ *of* $\mathbf{R}^n$.

EXAMPLE 8 Let $T:\mathbf{R}^2 \to \mathbf{R}^2$ be the linear transformation of the plane that consists of reflection in the line $y = x$ (as in Figure 7.5). Then it is clear that

$$T(\mathbf{e}_1) = \mathbf{e}_2 = (0, 1) \quad \text{and} \quad T(\mathbf{e}_2) = \mathbf{e}_1 = (1, 0),$$

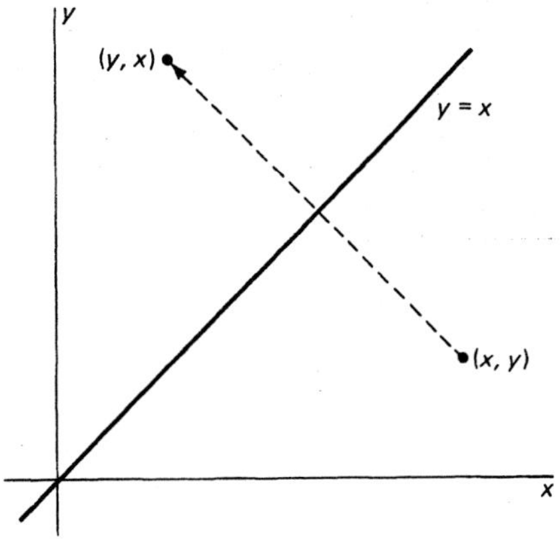

7.5 Reflection in the line $y = x$.

so the matrix of T is

$$A = [T(\mathbf{e}_1) \quad T(\mathbf{e}_2)] = \begin{bmatrix} 0 & 1 \\ 1 & 0 \end{bmatrix}. \tag{17}$$

Consequently $T(x, y) = (y, x)$.

For an alternative approach, it is geometrically evident that we can write $T = T_3 T_2 T_1$, where

- T_1 is the rotation through the angle $\theta = -45°$ that carries the line $y = x$ to the x-axis;
- T_2 is reflection in the x-axis;
- T_3 is the rotation through the angle $\theta = 45°$ that carries the x-axis back to the line $y = x$.

Then, from the computations in Examples 6 and 7, we find that the matrices of the transformations T_1, T_2, and T_3 are

$$A_1 = \frac{1}{\sqrt{2}}\begin{bmatrix} 1 & 1 \\ -1 & 1 \end{bmatrix}, \quad A_2 = \begin{bmatrix} 1 & 0 \\ 0 & -1 \end{bmatrix}, \quad \text{and} \quad A_3 = \frac{1}{\sqrt{2}}\begin{bmatrix} 1 & -1 \\ 1 & 1 \end{bmatrix}.$$

Hence the matrix of the reflection T is the product

$$\begin{aligned} A &= A_3 A_2 A_1 \\ &= \frac{1}{\sqrt{2}}\begin{bmatrix} 1 & -1 \\ 1 & 1 \end{bmatrix}\begin{bmatrix} 1 & 0 \\ 0 & -1 \end{bmatrix}\left(\frac{1}{\sqrt{2}}\right)\begin{bmatrix} 1 & 1 \\ -1 & 1 \end{bmatrix} \\ &= \frac{1}{2}\begin{bmatrix} 1 & -1 \\ 1 & 1 \end{bmatrix}\begin{bmatrix} 1 & 1 \\ 1 & -1 \end{bmatrix} \\ &= \frac{1}{2}\begin{bmatrix} 0 & 2 \\ 2 & 0 \end{bmatrix} = \begin{bmatrix} 0 & 1 \\ 1 & 0 \end{bmatrix}, \end{aligned}$$

in agreement with (17).

An effective way to analyze a linear transformation is to "decompose" or factor it into a composition of simpler linear transformations, ones for which the geometric effect is easy to visualize. Suppose, for instance, that the matrix A of the linear transformation $T:\mathbf{R}^2 \to \mathbf{R}^2$ is nonsingular. Then it follows from the proof of Theorem 6 in Section 1.5 that A can be expressed as a product of elementary matrices—

$$A = A_k A_{k-1} \cdots A_2 A_1. \tag{18}$$

But every elementary 2 × 2 matrix has one of the following forms:

$$\begin{bmatrix} c & 0 \\ 0 & 1 \end{bmatrix}, \quad \begin{bmatrix} 1 & 0 \\ 0 & c \end{bmatrix}, \quad \begin{bmatrix} 0 & 1 \\ 1 & 0 \end{bmatrix}, \quad \begin{bmatrix} 1 & c \\ 0 & 1 \end{bmatrix}, \quad \begin{bmatrix} 1 & 0 \\ c & 1 \end{bmatrix}. \tag{19}$$

Hence the transformation T can be factored as

$$T = T_k T_{k-1} \cdots T_2 T_1, \tag{20}$$

where each T_i corresponds to multiplication by a single elementary matrix of one of the forms listed in (19). It therefore remains only to analyze the geometric effect of such an "elementary transformation" of the plane.

The first elementary matrix in (19) corresponds to a transformation T such that $T(x, y) = (cx, y)$. We call such a transformation with $c > 0$ an **expansion** (or **compression**) **in the x-direction**. It is an expansion if $c > 1$ (see Figure 7.6), a compression if $0 < c < 1$. If $c = 1$, then the transformation T is the **identity transformation** of $\mathbf{R}^2$ that leaves each point fixed. If $c < 0$ but $c \neq -1$, then the factorization

$$\begin{bmatrix} c & 0 \\ 0 & 1 \end{bmatrix} = \begin{bmatrix} -1 & 0 \\ 0 & 1 \end{bmatrix} \begin{bmatrix} -c & 0 \\ 0 & 1 \end{bmatrix}$$

shows that T consists of an expansion or compression in the x-direction followed by reflection in the y-axis. If $c = -1$, then the same factorization shows that T is simply a reflection in the y-axis (see Example 6).

By a similar analysis we see that the second elementary matrix in (19) corresponds to an expansion (or compression) in the y-direction, followed if $c < 0$ and $c \neq -1$ by a reflection in the x-axis.

Our work in Example 8 shows that the third elementary matrix in (19) corresponds to a reflection of the plane in the line $y = x$.

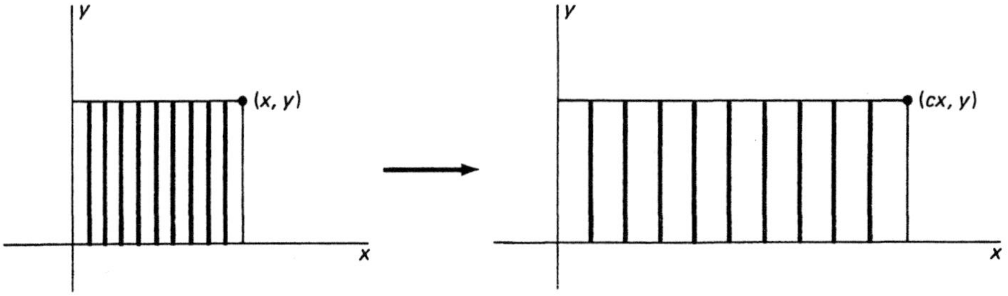

7.6 An expansion in the x-direction.

Figure 7.7 illustrates the effect of a transformation corresponding to the fourth variety of elementary matrix listed in (19). Each point (x, y) is moved parallel to the x-axis by a (signed) distance cy to the new position $(x + cy, y)$. The points on the x-axis are left fixed, and each point off the x-axis is moved an amount proportional to its distance from the x-axis. Such a transformation of the plane is called a **shear in the x-direction.** A **shear in the y-direction** is similar, except that each point is moved parallel to the y-axis (in an amount proportional to its distance from that axis), and is represented by the fifth type of elementary matrix listed in (19).

In summary we see that every plane linear transformation that corresponds to multiplication by an *elementary* matrix is one of the following:

- A reflection in one of the coordinate axes or in the line $y = x$;
- An expansion or compression in either the x-direction or the y-direction, perhaps followed by a reflection in a coordinate axis;
- A shear in either the x-direction or the y-direction.

Because every nonsingular matrix factors as a product of elementary matrices, this discussion proves the next theorem.

Theorem 3: *Linear Transformations of the Plane*
Suppose that the linear transformation $T: \mathbf{R}^2 \to \mathbf{R}^2$ corresponds to a nonsingular matrix A. Then T is a finite composition of reflections, expansions, compressions, and shears.

To describe explicitly the effect of a given linear transformation T as in Theorem 3, we need to express the matrix A as a product of elementary matrices. Because the matrix A is nonsingular, it can be reduced to the identity matrix I by a finite sequence of elementary row operations (Section 1.5). But each elementary row operation can be carried out by multiplication on the left by an appropriate elementary matrix. It follows that there exist elementary matrices $E_1, E_2, \ldots, E_k$ such that

$$E_k E_{k-1} \cdots E_2 E_1 A = I. \tag{21}$$

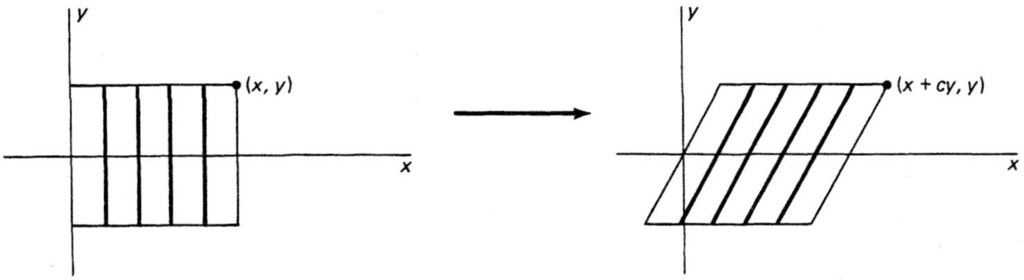

7.7 A shear in the x-direction (with $c > 0$).

Then the resulting equation

$$A = E_1^{-1}E_2^{-1}\cdots E_{k-1}^{-1}E_k^{-1} \tag{22}$$

expresses A as a product of elementary matrices (because the inverse of an elementary matrix is also an elementary matrix).

EXAMPLE 9 Suppose that $T:\mathbf{R}^2 \to \mathbf{R}^2$ is defined by $T(\mathbf{x}) = A\mathbf{x}$ where

$$A = \begin{bmatrix} 2 & 9 \\ 1 & 3 \end{bmatrix}.$$

First we reduce A to I as follows:

$$\begin{bmatrix} 2 & 9 \\ 1 & 3 \end{bmatrix} \xrightarrow{\text{SWAP}(R_1, R_2)} \begin{bmatrix} 1 & 3 \\ 2 & 9 \end{bmatrix}$$

$$\xrightarrow{(-2)R_1 + R_2} \begin{bmatrix} 1 & 3 \\ 0 & 3 \end{bmatrix}$$

$$\xrightarrow{(1/3)R_2} \begin{bmatrix} 1 & 3 \\ 0 & 1 \end{bmatrix}$$

$$\xrightarrow{(-3)R_2 + R_1} \begin{bmatrix} 1 & 0 \\ 0 & 1 \end{bmatrix}.$$

The four elementary matrices corresponding to the four indicated elementary row operations are

$$E_1 = \begin{bmatrix} 0 & 1 \\ 1 & 0 \end{bmatrix}, \quad E_2 = \begin{bmatrix} 1 & 0 \\ -2 & 1 \end{bmatrix},$$

$$E_3 = \begin{bmatrix} 1 & 0 \\ 0 & \frac{1}{3} \end{bmatrix}, \quad E_4 = \begin{bmatrix} 1 & -3 \\ 0 & 1 \end{bmatrix}.$$

Consequently,

$$\begin{aligned} A &= E_1^{-1}E_2^{-1}E_3^{-1}E_4^{-1} \\ &= \begin{bmatrix} 0 & 1 \\ 1 & 0 \end{bmatrix}\begin{bmatrix} 1 & 0 \\ 2 & 1 \end{bmatrix}\begin{bmatrix} 1 & 0 \\ 0 & 3 \end{bmatrix}\begin{bmatrix} 1 & 3 \\ 0 & 1 \end{bmatrix}. \end{aligned}$$

As we read the effect of each of these factors from right to left, we see finally that the geometric effect of the transformation T is the result of the following four geometric operations:

- First, a shear in the x-direction with $c = 3$;
- Next, an expansion in the y-direction with $c = 3$;
- Third, a shear in the y-direction with $c = 2$;
- Finally, a reflection in the line $y = x$.

7.1 PROBLEMS

In Problems 1–10, a transformation T from one Euclidean space to another is defined. Determine whether or not T is a linear transformation. If so, find the matrix A such that $T(\mathbf{x}) = A\mathbf{x}$. If not, tell why not.

1. $T(x, y) = (x + y, x - y)$

2. $T(x, y) = (2x + 3y, 3x - 2y)$

3. $T(x, y) = (x + 2y, 3)$

4. $T(x, y) = (xy, 3x - y)$

5. $T(x, y, z) = (x, y^2, z^3)$

6. $T(x, y, z) = (y + z, x + z, x^2 + y^2)$

7. $T(x, y) = (x - 3y, 3x - y, 2x + 5y)$

8. $T(x, y) = (2x + y, x + 5y, x - y)$

9. $T(x, y, z) = (2x - 3y + 4z, 3x - 5y - 7z)$

10. $T(x, y, z) = (3x - z, 2x - 4y)$

In Problems 11–16, the given transformation T is linear.

11. Given $T:\mathbf{R}^2 \to \mathbf{R}^2$ with $T(\mathbf{e}_1) = (3, 2)$ and $T(\mathbf{e}_2) = (4, 3)$, find $T(x, y)$.

12. Given $T:\mathbf{R}^2 \to \mathbf{R}^2$ with $T(\mathbf{e}_1) = (1, -2)$ and $T(\mathbf{e}_2) = (-3, 2)$, find $T(x, y)$.

13. Given $T:\mathbf{R}^2 \to \mathbf{R}^3$ with $T(\mathbf{e}_1) = (1, 2, 3)$ and $T(\mathbf{e}_2) = (4, 5, 6)$, find $T(x, y)$.

14. Given $T:\mathbf{R}^3 \to \mathbf{R}^2$ with $T(\mathbf{e}_1) = (1, -1)$, $T(\mathbf{e}_2) = (4, 3)$, and $T(\mathbf{e}_3) = (5, 0)$, find $T(x, y, z)$.

15. Given $T:\mathbf{R}^3 \to \mathbf{R}^3$ with $T(\mathbf{e}_1) = (1, 2, 0)$, $T(\mathbf{e}_2) = (3, 0, 4)$, and $T(\mathbf{e}_3) = (0, 5, 6)$, find $T(x, y, z)$.

16. Given $T:\mathbf{R}^4 \to \mathbf{R}^2$ with $T(\mathbf{e}_1) = (2, 0)$, $T(\mathbf{e}_2) = (0, 4)$, $T(\mathbf{e}_3) = (3, 0)$, and $T(\mathbf{e}_4) = (0, 5)$, find $T(u, v, x, y)$.

In Problems 17–22, find a 2×2 matrix A such that the linear transformation $T:\mathbf{R}^2 \to \mathbf{R}^2$ defined by $T(\mathbf{x}) = A\mathbf{x}$ carries out the indicated succession of geometric operations.

17. First an expansion by a factor of 2 in the x-direction; then a reflection in the x-axis.

18. First an expansion by a factor of 3 in the y-direction; then a reflection in the y-axis.

19. First a counterclockwise rotation through an angle of 90°; then a reflection in the line $y = x$.

20. First a reflection in the line $y = -x$; then a rotation through an angle of 180°.

21. First an expansion by a factor of 2 in the x-direction; then an expansion by a factor of 3 in the y-direction; then a reflection in the line $y = x$.

22. First a rotation through an angle of 45°; then an expansion by a factor of $\sqrt{2}$ in the x-direction; then an expansion by a factor of $2\sqrt{2}$ in the y-direction.

In Problems 23–30, first use the method of Example 9 to express the given 2×2 matrix A as a product of elementary matrices. Then describe the geometric effect of the plane transformation $T(\mathbf{x}) = A\mathbf{x}$ in terms of expansions, compressions, reflections, and shears.

23. $\begin{bmatrix} 2 & 0 \\ 0 & 3 \end{bmatrix}$

24. $\begin{bmatrix} 2 & 0 \\ 0 & -1 \end{bmatrix}$

25. $\begin{bmatrix} 0 & 2 \\ 3 & 0 \end{bmatrix}$

26. $\begin{bmatrix} 0 & 3 \\ -1 & 0 \end{bmatrix}$

27. $\begin{bmatrix} 1 & 1 \\ 1 & 2 \end{bmatrix}$

28. $\begin{bmatrix} 1 & 3 \\ 2 & 7 \end{bmatrix}$

29. $\begin{bmatrix} 1 & 2 \\ 2 & 7 \end{bmatrix}$

30. $\begin{bmatrix} 3 & 1 \\ 7 & 2 \end{bmatrix}$

31. Use matrices to show that the result of a reflection in the x-axis followed by a reflection in the y-axis is a counterclockwise rotation through an angle of 180°.

32. Use matrices to show that the result of a reflection in the line $y = x$ followed by a reflection in the line $y = -x$ is a counterclockwise rotation through an angle of 180°.

33. Let L be the straight line through the origin in $\mathbf{R}^2$ that forms the angle θ with the positive x-axis. Then the reflection T in the line L can be accomplished by a rotation through the angle $-\theta$ to move L to the x-axis, then a reflection in the x-axis, and finally a rotation through the angle θ to move L back to its original position. Use matrix multiplication and the trigonometric identities

$$\cos 2\theta = \cos^2 \theta - \sin^2 \theta,$$
$$\sin 2\theta = 2 \sin \theta \cos \theta$$

to show that the matrix of T is

$$A = \begin{bmatrix} \cos 2\theta & \sin 2\theta \\ \sin 2\theta & -\cos 2\theta \end{bmatrix}.$$

34. Let L be the line through the origin in $\mathbf{R}^2$ that makes an angle of $\theta/2$ with the positive x-axis. Use the matrix found in Problem 33 to show that the result of a reflection in the x-axis followed by a reflection in the line L is a counterclockwise rotation through the angle θ. Thus every rotation may be expressed as the composition of two reflections.

35. Suppose that the lines L_1 and L_2 through the origin in $\mathbf{R}^2$ make angles α and β, respectively, with the positive x-axis. Use the matrix of Problem 33 and the trigonometric identities

$$\cos(\alpha - \beta) = \cos \alpha \cos \beta + \sin \alpha \sin \beta,$$
$$\sin(\alpha - \beta) = \sin \alpha \cos \beta - \sin \beta \cos \alpha$$

to show that the result of a reflection in L_1 followed by a reflection in L_2 is a rotation through the angle $2(\beta - \alpha)$. Thus the composition of any two reflections is a rotation.

7.2 Properties of Linear Transformations

In Theorem 1 of Section 7.1 we saw that if V and W are vector spaces, then the transformation $T: V \to W$ is *linear* if and only if

$$T(a\mathbf{u} + b\mathbf{v}) = aT(\mathbf{u}) + bT(\mathbf{v}) \tag{1}$$

for every pair $\mathbf{u}$, $\mathbf{v}$ of vectors in V and every pair a, b of scalars. The following theorem lists some simple properties of linear transformations that are obtained by substituting appropriate values of a and b in Equation (1).

> ***Theorem 1:*** *Simple Consequences of Linearity*
> If V and W are vector spaces, $T: V \to W$ is a linear transformation, and $\mathbf{u}$ and $\mathbf{v}$ are vectors in V, then T has the following properties:
>
> **(i)** $T(\mathbf{0}) = \mathbf{0}$.
> **(ii)** $T(-\mathbf{v}) = -T(\mathbf{v})$.
> **(iii)** $T(\mathbf{u} - \mathbf{v}) = T(\mathbf{u}) - T(\mathbf{v})$.

Proof We obtain (i) by substitution of $a = b = 0$ in (1), (ii) by substitution of $a = 0$ and $b = -1$, and (iii) by substitution of $a = 1$ and $b = -1$. ■

EXAMPLE 1 Let $F:\mathbf{R}^2 \to \mathbf{R}^2$ be defined as follows:

$$F(x, y) = (x + y, 1).$$

Then $F(\mathbf{0}) = (0, 1) \neq \mathbf{0}$, so the transformation F does not satisfy the first property in Theorem 1. Therefore F cannot be linear.

Next, let $G:\mathbf{R}^2 \to \mathbf{R}^2$ be defined by

$$G(x, y) = |x| + |y|.$$

Then $G(1, 1) = G(-1, -1) = 2$, so $G(-1, -1) \neq -G(1, 1)$. Thus the transformation G does not satisfy the second property in Theorem 1. Hence G is not linear.

Let $T: V \to W$ be a linear transformation and let $\mathbf{v}_1, \mathbf{v}_2, \ldots, \mathbf{v}_n$ be vectors in V. If

$$\mathbf{v} = c_1\mathbf{v}_1 + c_2\mathbf{v}_2 + \cdots + c_n\mathbf{v}_n \tag{2}$$

then it follows by repeated application of (1) that

$$T(\mathbf{v}) = c_1 T(\mathbf{v}_1) + c_2 T(\mathbf{v}_2) + \cdots + c_n T(\mathbf{v}_n). \tag{3}$$

Thus a linear transformation "respects" linear combinations of vectors.

If the vector space V is n-dimensional and the vectors $\mathbf{v}_1, \mathbf{v}_2, \ldots, \mathbf{v}_n$ form a basis for V, then each vector $\mathbf{v}$ can be expressed as in (2), so its image $T(\mathbf{v})$ is determined by Equation (3). Thus *a linear transformation defined on V is completely determined by its values on a set of basis vectors for V.*

EXAMPLE 2 Suppose that we want to define a linear transformation $T:\mathbf{R}^2 \to \mathbf{R}^2$ such that

$$T(\mathbf{v}_1) = \mathbf{w}_1 \quad \text{and} \quad T(\mathbf{v}_2) = \mathbf{w}_2$$

where

$$\mathbf{v}_1 = (3, 5), \qquad \mathbf{v}_2 = (4, 7)$$

and

$$\mathbf{w}_1 = (2, 4), \qquad \mathbf{w}_2 = (-1, 3).$$

According to Theorem 2 in Section 7.1, there is a 2×2 matrix A such that T is defined by $T(\mathbf{x}) = A\mathbf{x}$. Then

$$\begin{aligned} A[\mathbf{v}_1 \quad \mathbf{v}_2] &= [A\mathbf{v}_1 \quad A\mathbf{v}_2] \\ &= [T(\mathbf{v}_1) \quad T(\mathbf{v}_2)] = [\mathbf{w}_1 \quad \mathbf{w}_2]. \end{aligned}$$

Thus

$$A\begin{bmatrix} 3 & 4 \\ 5 & 7 \end{bmatrix} = \begin{bmatrix} 2 & -1 \\ 4 & 3 \end{bmatrix},$$

so it follows that

$$A = \begin{bmatrix} 2 & -1 \\ 4 & 3 \end{bmatrix} \begin{bmatrix} 3 & 4 \\ 5 & 7 \end{bmatrix}^{-1}$$

$$= \begin{bmatrix} 2 & -1 \\ 4 & 3 \end{bmatrix} \begin{bmatrix} 7 & -4 \\ -5 & 3 \end{bmatrix} = \begin{bmatrix} 19 & -11 \\ 13 & -7 \end{bmatrix}.$$

Hence $T:\mathbf{R}^2 \to \mathbf{R}^2$ is defined for $\mathbf{v} = (x, y)$ by

$$T(\mathbf{v}) = \begin{bmatrix} 19 & -11 \\ 13 & -7 \end{bmatrix} \begin{bmatrix} x \\ y \end{bmatrix} = \begin{bmatrix} 19x - 11y \\ 13x - 7y \end{bmatrix},$$

and therefore $T(x, y) = (19x - 11y, 13x - 7y)$.

The expansions, compressions, shears, and reflections that we discussed in Section 7.1 are examples of *one-to-one* linear transformations of $\mathbf{R}^2$ *onto* $\mathbf{R}^2$. The linear transformation $T:V \to W$ is said to be **one-to-one** provided that no two different vectors in V have the same image in W. That is, $T(\mathbf{v}_1) = T(\mathbf{v}_2)$ implies that $\mathbf{v}_1 = \mathbf{v}_2$. The transformation T is called **onto** provided that every vector in W is the image of *at least* one vector in V. That is, for each $\mathbf{w}$ in W there exists $\mathbf{v}$ in V such that $\mathbf{w} = T(\mathbf{v})$.

EXAMPLE 3 The transformation $T_1:\mathbf{R}^2 \to \mathbf{R}^3$ defined by $T_1(x, y) = (x, y, 0)$ is one-to-one but not onto; for instance, (0, 0, 1) is not the image of any point in $\mathbf{R}^2$. The transformation $T_2:\mathbf{R}^3 \to \mathbf{R}^2$ defined by $T_2(x, y, z) = (x, y)$ is onto but not one-to-one; for instance, (0, 0, 0) and (0, 0, 1) are different points of $\mathbf{R}^3$ with the same image (0, 0).

If the linear transformation $T:V \to W$ is *both* one-to-one and onto, then each vector $\mathbf{w}$ in W is the image of *one and only one* vector $\mathbf{v}$ in V. That is, given $\mathbf{w}$ in W, there exists *exactly one* vector $\mathbf{v}$ in V such that $T(\mathbf{v}) = \mathbf{w}$. In this case the transformation T is called an **isomorphism**.

EXAMPLE 4 The linear transformation $T:\mathbf{R}^2 \to \mathbf{R}^2$ of Example 2 is defined by $T(\mathbf{x}) = A\mathbf{x}$ where

$$A = \begin{bmatrix} 19 & -11 \\ 13 & -7 \end{bmatrix}.$$

Now $\det A = 10$, so A is invertible and A^{-1} exists. It follows that, given $\mathbf{w}$ in $\mathbf{R}^2$, $\mathbf{v} = A^{-1}\mathbf{w}$ is a vector such that

$$T(\mathbf{v}) = A(A^{-1}\mathbf{w}) = \mathbf{w}.$$

Thus T is onto. If $T(\mathbf{v}_1) = T(\mathbf{v}_2)$, then

$$A\mathbf{v}_1 = A\mathbf{v}_2 \quad \text{yields} \quad A^{-1}(A\mathbf{v}_1) = A^{-1}(A\mathbf{v}_2),$$

so $\mathbf{v}_1 = \mathbf{v}_2$. Hence the transformation $T:\mathbf{R}^2 \to \mathbf{R}^2$ is also one-to-one, and is therefore an isomorphism.

We say that the vector space V is **isomorphic** to the vector space W provided that there exists an isomorphism $T: V \to W$. In this case the inverse mapping $T^{-1}: W \to V$ is defined because T is one-to-one and onto. Moreover, T^{-1} is also a linear transformation (Problem 27) and is therefore an isomorphism. Hence the fact that V is isomorphic to W implies that W is also isomorphic to V, and we simply say in such a case that the vector spaces V and W are **isomorphic**.

EXAMPLE 5 Given an n-dimensional vector space V, let $\{\mathbf{v}_1, \mathbf{v}_2, \ldots, \mathbf{v}_n\}$ be a basis for V. Then we can define a mapping $T: \mathbf{R}^n \to V$ by

$$T(x_1, x_2, \ldots, x_n) = x_1\mathbf{v}_1 + x_2\mathbf{v}_2 + \cdots + x_n\mathbf{v}_n. \tag{4}$$

It should be clear that T is a linear transformation. Moreover, the fact that every vector $\mathbf{v}$ in V can be expressed as a linear combination of the form in (4) implies that T is a mapping of $\mathbf{R}^n$ *on*to V. And the fact that $\mathbf{v}$ can be expressed in only one way as such a linear combination implies that T is also one-to-one. Thus T is an isomorphism, and so the n-dimensional vector space V is isomorphic to Euclidean n-space $\mathbf{R}^n$.

Example 5 implies that any two n-dimensional vector spaces are isomorphic, however different the individual vectors in the two spaces may appear. For instance, 3-dimensional Euclidean space $\mathbf{R}^3$ is isomorphic to the 3-dimensional vector space $\mathscr{P}_2$ of second degree polynomials with basis $\{1, x, x^2\}$. The fact that any n-dimensional vector space V is isomorphic to $\mathbf{R}^n$ means that, in regard to properties that involve only addition of vectors and multiplication of vectors by scalars, V is merely a "copy" of $\mathbf{R}^n$. In this sense any two finite-dimensional vector spaces of the same dimension are essentially the same!

KERNEL AND RANGE

Now we turn our attention to linear transformations that are not isomorphisms. Suppose that the linear transformation $T: V \to W$ is not one-to-one, so that there exist unequal vectors $\mathbf{v}_1$ and $\mathbf{v}_2$ in V such that $T(\mathbf{v}_1) = T(\mathbf{v}_2)$. If $\mathbf{v} = \mathbf{v}_1 - \mathbf{v}_2 \neq \mathbf{0}$, then

$$T(\mathbf{v}) = T(\mathbf{v}_1 - \mathbf{v}_2) = T(\mathbf{v}_1) - T(\mathbf{v}_2) = \mathbf{0}.$$

Thus the assumption that T is *not* one-to-one implies that there exists a *nonzero* vector $\mathbf{v}$ such that $T(\mathbf{v}) = \mathbf{0}$. The set of all those vectors $\mathbf{v}$ in V such that $T(\mathbf{v}) = \mathbf{0}$—including the zero vector itself—is called the **kernel** of the linear transformation T and is denoted by $\ker(T)$. Our argument shows that *the linear transformation $T: V \to W$ is one-to-one if and only if its kernel is the zero subspace of V.*

The **range** of the linear transformation $T: V \to W$ is the set of all those vectors in W that are images under T of vectors in V. Thus T is a mapping of V *on*to W if and only if the range of T is all of W.

EXAMPLE 6 Let $T: \mathbf{R}^3 \to \mathbf{R}^2$ be defined as follows: $T(x, y, z) = (x, 0)$ for all (x, y, z) in $\mathbf{R}^3$. Then the kernel of T is the set of all (x, y, z) in $\mathbf{R}^3$ such that $x = 0$; thus

$\ker(T)$ is the yz-plane in $\mathbf{R}^3$. The range of T is the set of all (x, y) in $\mathbf{R}^2$ such that $y = 0$, and thus is the x-axis in $\mathbf{R}^2$.

Note in Example 6 that both the kernel and the range of T are subspaces. The following theorem assures us that this will always be the case.

> ***Theorem 2:*** *Kernel and Range*
> If $T: V \to W$ is a linear transformation, then the kernel of T is a subspace of V and the range of T is a subspace of W.

Proof To show that $\ker(T)$ is a subspace of V, suppose that $\mathbf{v}_1$ and $\mathbf{v}_2$ are elements of $\ker(T)$ and that c_1 and c_2 are scalars. Then the fact that $T(\mathbf{v}_1) = T(\mathbf{v}_2) = \mathbf{0}$ implies that

$$\begin{aligned} T(c_1\mathbf{v}_1 + c_2\mathbf{v}_2) &= c_1 T(\mathbf{v}_1) + c_2 T(\mathbf{v}_2) \\ &= c_1\mathbf{0} + c_2\mathbf{0} = \mathbf{0}. \end{aligned}$$

Thus $c_1\mathbf{v}_1 + c_2\mathbf{v}_2$ is also in $\ker(T)$, so it follows that $\ker(T)$ is a subspace of V.

To show that the range of T is a subspace of W, suppose that $\mathbf{w}_1$ and $\mathbf{w}_2$ are elements of the range of T and that c_1 and c_2 are scalars. Let $\mathbf{v}_1$ and $\mathbf{v}_2$ be vectors in V such that $T(\mathbf{v}_1) = \mathbf{w}_1$ and $T(\mathbf{v}_2) = \mathbf{w}_2$. Then

$$\begin{aligned} T(c_1\mathbf{v}_1 + c_2\mathbf{v}_2) &= c_1 T(\mathbf{v}_1) + c_2 T(\mathbf{v}_2) \\ &= c_1\mathbf{w}_1 + c_2\mathbf{w}_2. \end{aligned}$$

Thus $c_1\mathbf{w}_1 + c_2\mathbf{w}_2$ is also in the range of T, so it follows that the range of T is a subspace of W. ■

If the range of the linear transformation T is finite-dimensional, then its *dimension* is called the **rank** of T, denoted by $\operatorname{rank}(T)$. For instance, in Example 6 the range of the transformation $T:\mathbf{R}^3 \to \mathbf{R}^2$ is one-dimensional, so $\operatorname{rank}(T) = 1$.

Let us consider the case in which $V = \mathbf{R}^n$ and $W = \mathbf{R}^m$. Let the linear transformation $T:\mathbf{R}^n \to \mathbf{R}^m$ correspond to the $m \times n$ matrix A, so that $T(\mathbf{x}) = A\mathbf{x}$ for each vector $\mathbf{x}$ in $\mathbf{R}^n$. Then the kernel of T is simply the solution space of the homogeneous linear system

$$A\mathbf{x} = \mathbf{0},$$

so

$$\ker(T) = \operatorname{Null}(A). \tag{5}$$

The range of T is the set of all vectors $\mathbf{y}$ in $\mathbf{R}^m$ such that the linear system

$$A\mathbf{x} = \mathbf{y}$$

has a solution. Hence the range of T is equal to the column space Col(A) of the matrix A, so

$$\text{rank}(T) = \dim \text{Col}(A) = \text{rank}(A). \tag{6}$$

Thus *the rank of a linear transformation between Euclidean spaces is equal to the rank of its matrix.*

In Section 4.4 we saw that the rank and the null space of any $m \times n$ matrix A satisfy the equality

$$\text{rank}(A) + \dim \text{Null}(A) = n. \tag{7}$$

When we substitute the information in (5) and (6) in Equation (7), we see that

$$\text{rank}(T) + \dim \ker(T) = n \tag{8}$$

for any linear transformation $T: \mathbf{R}^n \to \mathbf{R}^m$ between Euclidean spaces. The following theorem implies that the important equality in (8) holds for any linear transformation $T: V \to W$ such that the domain V is finite-dimensional.

Theorem 3: *Rank and Dimension*

Let V and W be vector spaces with V of dimension n. Then

$$\text{rank}(T) + \dim \ker(T) = n \tag{8}$$

for any linear transformation $T: V \to W$.

The proof of Theorem 3 follows the next example.

EXAMPLE 7 Let $T: \mathbf{R}^5 \to \mathbf{R}^4$ be the linear transformation corresponding to the 4×5 matrix

$$A = \begin{bmatrix} 1 & 2 & 1 & 3 & 2 \\ 3 & 4 & 9 & 0 & 7 \\ 2 & 3 & 5 & 1 & 8 \\ 2 & 2 & 8 & -3 & 5 \end{bmatrix}$$

of Example 2 in Section 4.4; A may be reduced to the echelon matrix

$$E = \begin{bmatrix} 1 & 2 & 1 & 3 & 2 \\ 0 & 1 & -3 & 5 & -4 \\ 0 & 0 & 0 & 1 & -7 \\ 0 & 0 & 0 & 0 & 0 \end{bmatrix}.$$

Note that the pivot columns of E are its first, second, and fourth columns. Hence Col(A) is generated by the corresponding column vectors $\mathbf{w}_1 = (1, 3, 2, 2)$, $\mathbf{w}_2 = (2, 4, 3, 2)$, and $\mathbf{w}_3 = (3, 0, 1, -3)$ of the matrix A of T. Thus the range of T is this

3-dimensional subspace Col(A) of $\mathbf{R}^4$, and rank(T) = 3. To determine ker(T) = Null(A), we set the free variables $x_3 = s$ and $x_5 = t$ and solve in the usual way for

$$x_4 = 7t, \qquad x_2 = 3s - 31t, \qquad x_1 = -7s + 39t.$$

With $s = 1$ and $t = 0$ we get the solution vector $\mathbf{v}_1 = (-7, 3, 1, 0, 0)$, whereas with $s = 0$ and $t = 1$ we get $\mathbf{v}_2 = (39, -31, 0, 7, 1)$. Thus ker($T$) = Null($A$) is the 2-dimensional subspace of $\mathbf{R}^5$ generated by $\mathbf{v}_1$ and $\mathbf{v}_2$, and Equation (8) reduces in this example to $3 + 2 = 5$.

PROOF OF THEOREM 3 If dim ker(T) = n, then ker(T) = V and the range of T is the zero subspace of W. In this special case the equality in (8) reduces to $0 + n = n$.

If dim ker(T) = $k < n$, let $S = \{\mathbf{v}_1, \mathbf{v}_2, \ldots, \mathbf{v}_k\}$ be a basis for ker(T). Choose vectors $\mathbf{v}_{k+1}, \mathbf{v}_{k+2}, \ldots, \mathbf{v}_n$ such that the vectors $\mathbf{v}_1, \mathbf{v}_2, \ldots, \mathbf{v}_n$ form a basis for V. (If the kernel of T is zero-dimensional, then $k = 0$ and we let S be the empty set.) We want to show that the $n - k$ vectors

$$\mathbf{w}_{k+1} = T(\mathbf{v}_{k+1}), \ldots, \mathbf{w}_n = T(\mathbf{v}_n) \tag{9}$$

form a basis for the range of T.

First we note that any vector in the range of T has the form

$$\begin{aligned} &T(c_1\mathbf{v}_1 + \cdots + c_k\mathbf{v}_k + c_{k+1}\mathbf{v}_{k+1} + \cdots + c_n\mathbf{v}_n) \\ &\quad = c_1T(\mathbf{v}_1) + \cdots + c_kT(\mathbf{v}_k) + c_{k+1}T(\mathbf{v}_{k+1}) + \cdots + c_nT(\mathbf{v}_n) \\ &\quad = c_{k+1}T(\mathbf{v}_{k+1}) + \cdots + c_nT(\mathbf{v}_n) \\ &\quad = c_{k+1}\mathbf{w}_{k+1} + \cdots + c_n\mathbf{w}_n \end{aligned}$$

because $T(\mathbf{v}_1) = \cdots = T(\mathbf{v}_k) = \mathbf{0}$. Thus the vectors $\mathbf{w}_{k+1}, \ldots, \mathbf{w}_n$ span the range of T.

It remains to see that these $n - k$ vectors are linearly independent. Assuming that

$$c_{k+1}\mathbf{w}_{k+1} + \cdots + c_n\mathbf{w}_n = \mathbf{0}, \tag{10}$$

we want to show that $c_{k+1} = \cdots = c_n = 0$. Now Equations (9) and (10) yield

$$T(c_{k+1}\mathbf{v}_{k+1} + \cdots + c_n\mathbf{v}_n) = \mathbf{0},$$

so $c_{k+1}\mathbf{v}_{k+1} + \cdots + c_n\mathbf{v}_n$ is in ker(T). Hence there exist scalars $c_1, c_2, \ldots, c_k$ such that

$$c_{k+1}\mathbf{v}_{k+1} + \cdots + c_n\mathbf{v}_n = c_1\mathbf{v}_1 + \cdots + c_k\mathbf{v}_k. \tag{11}$$

(If $k = 0$ then the right-hand side in (11) is the zero vector.) Because the vectors $\mathbf{v}_1, \mathbf{v}_2, \ldots, \mathbf{v}_n$ constitute a basis for V, the coefficients in (11) must all vanish. In particular, the coefficients in (10) must all vanish, so the vectors $\mathbf{w}_{k+1}, \ldots, \mathbf{w}_n$ are linearly independent.

Consequently these $n - k$ vectors form a basis for the range of T, and so rank(T) = $n - k$. Thus Equation (8) reduces to the identity $(n - k) + k = n$. ■

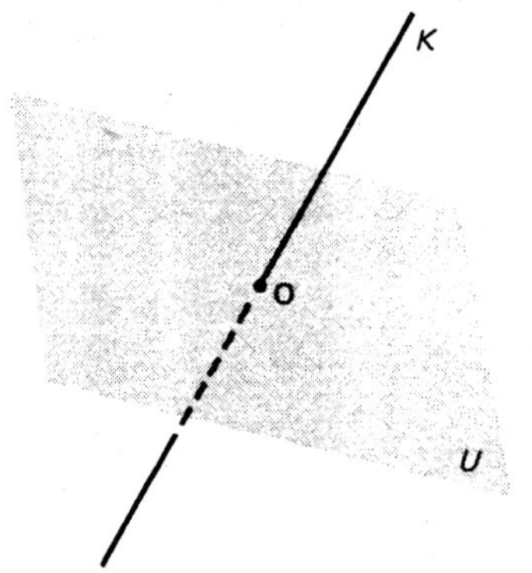

7.8 Complementary subspaces of V—the kernel of T and a copy of the range of T.

REMARK. In the notation of the proof of Theorem 3, let $K = \ker(T)$ with basis vectors $\mathbf{v}_1, \ldots, \mathbf{v}_k$, and let U be the subspace of V generated by the remaining basis vectors $\mathbf{v}_{k+1}, \ldots, \mathbf{v}_n$. Then it is not difficult to show (Problem 34) that

(i) K and U are "complementary" subspaces of V, in that $K + U = V$ and $K \cap U = \{\mathbf{0}\}$.

(ii) T is a one-to-one mapping of U onto the range of T in W.

Thus V is the sum of the kernel of T and a copy of the range of T, with these two subspaces intersecting in the zero vector (see Figure 7.8). Furthermore, if the projection $P: V \to U$ is defined by $P(\mathbf{k} + \mathbf{u}) = \mathbf{u}$ if $\mathbf{k}$ is in K and $\mathbf{u}$ is in U, then it follows readily that

$$T(\mathbf{v}) = T(P(\mathbf{v}))$$

for all $\mathbf{v}$ in V. Thus *a linear transformation T defined on a finite-dimensional vector space factors into a projection that "annihilates" the kernel of T, followed by an isomorphism onto the range of T.*

7.2 PROBLEMS

In Problems 1–4, a transformation $T: \mathbf{R}^2 \to \mathbf{R}^2$ is defined. Apply Theorem 1 to show that T is not linear.

1. $T(x, y) = (x + 1, y + 1)$
2. $T(x, y) = (2x + y, x + 3y - 1)$
3. $T(x, y) = (xy, x^2 + y^2)$
4. $T(x, y) = (|x|, |y|)$

In Problems 5–10, find the 2×2 matrix A of a linear transformation $T: \mathbf{R}^2 \to \mathbf{R}^2$ such that $T(\mathbf{v}_i) = \mathbf{w}_i$ for $i = 1, 2$.

5. $\mathbf{v}_1 = (2, 3)$, $\mathbf{v}_2 = (-1, -1)$; $\mathbf{w}_1 = (1, 0)$, $\mathbf{w}_2 = (0, 1)$
6. $\mathbf{v}_1 = (2, 3)$, $\mathbf{v}_2 = (-3, -4)$; $\mathbf{w}_1 = (0, 1)$, $\mathbf{w}_2 = (1, 0)$
7. $\mathbf{v}_1 = (2, -1)$, $\mathbf{v}_2 = (-1, 1)$; $\mathbf{w}_1 = (1, 1)$, $\mathbf{w}_2 = (-1, 1)$
8. $\mathbf{v}_1 = (3, 4)$, $\mathbf{v}_2 = (5, 7)$; $\mathbf{w}_1 = (2, 1)$, $\mathbf{w}_2 = (1, 2)$
9. $\mathbf{v}_1 = (3, 7)$, $\mathbf{v}_2 = (2, 5)$; $\mathbf{w}_1 = (1, 3)$, $\mathbf{w}_2 = (-3, 1)$
10. $\mathbf{v}_1 = (4, 3)$, $\mathbf{v}_2 = (5, 4)$; $\mathbf{w}_1 = (-3, 2)$, $\mathbf{w}_2 = (-3, -4)$

Problems 11 and 12 have the same instructions as Problems 5–10, except that T is a linear transformation from $\mathbf{R}^2$ to $\mathbf{R}^3$, so A will be a 3×2 matrix.

11. $\mathbf{v}_1 = (5, 3)$, $\mathbf{v}_2 = (3, 2)$; $\mathbf{w}_1 = (2, -1, 3)$, $\mathbf{w}_2 = (3, 2, -4)$

12. $\mathbf{v}_1 = (5, 4)$, $\mathbf{v}_2 = (6, 5)$; $\mathbf{w}_1 = (3, 2, 1)$, $\mathbf{w}_2 = (6, 5, 4)$

In Problems 13–24, the $m \times n$ matrix A of a linear transformation $T:\mathbf{R}^n \to \mathbf{R}^m$ is given. Determine the rank r of T and the dimension k of $\ker(T)$.

13. $\begin{bmatrix} 2 & 1 \\ 4 & 3 \end{bmatrix}$

14. $\begin{bmatrix} 3 & -2 \\ -3 & 2 \end{bmatrix}$

15. $\begin{bmatrix} 3 & 1 & -2 \\ -3 & -1 & 2 \end{bmatrix}$

16. $\begin{bmatrix} 1 & -2 & 4 \\ 2 & -3 & 9 \end{bmatrix}$

17. $\begin{bmatrix} 1 & 2 \\ 3 & 7 \\ 5 & 11 \end{bmatrix}$

18. $\begin{bmatrix} 1 & 2 \\ 3 & 6 \\ 5 & 10 \end{bmatrix}$

19. $\begin{bmatrix} 1 & 5 & 1 \\ 2 & 1 & -2 \\ 1 & 7 & 2 \end{bmatrix}$

20. $\begin{bmatrix} 1 & 3 & 2 \\ 1 & 4 & 1 \\ 2 & 7 & 3 \end{bmatrix}$

21. $\begin{bmatrix} 1 & -5 & 1 & -6 \\ 2 & -3 & 2 & 2 \\ 1 & 1 & 1 & 6 \end{bmatrix}$

22. $\begin{bmatrix} 1 & 5 & 11 & 2 \\ 2 & 1 & 4 & 8 \\ 1 & 7 & 15 & 1 \end{bmatrix}$

23. $\begin{bmatrix} 2 & 7 & 7 & 5 \\ 1 & 3 & 2 & 0 \\ 2 & 5 & 2 & -2 \end{bmatrix}$

24. $\begin{bmatrix} 1 & -2 & -2 & 8 & -1 \\ 2 & 3 & -1 & 3 & 11 \\ 1 & 1 & 1 & 4 & -4 \end{bmatrix}$

25. Let $T:\mathbf{R}^2 \to \mathbf{R}^2$ be defined by $T(\mathbf{x}) = A\mathbf{x}$ where

$$A = \begin{bmatrix} 2 & 4 \\ 3 & 6 \end{bmatrix}.$$

Show that the kernel and the range of T are both lines through the origin. For each, write an equation of the form $ax + by = 0$.

26. Let $T:\mathbf{R}^3 \to \mathbf{R}^3$ be defined by $T(\mathbf{x}) = A\mathbf{x}$ where

$$A = \begin{bmatrix} 1 & 2 & 2 \\ 1 & 3 & 5 \\ 2 & 5 & 7 \end{bmatrix}.$$

Show that the range of T is a plane and write the equation of that plane. Show that the kernel of T is a line and write parametric equations for the line.

27. Let the linear transformation $T:V \to W$ be one-to-one and onto, so that $T^{-1}:W \to V$ is defined. Show that T^{-1} is linear.

28. Show that any two n-dimensional vector spaces V and W are isomorphic.

In Problems 29–31, $T:V \to W$ is a linear transformation, the vector space V is n-dimensional, and the vector space W is m-dimensional.

29. Show that T cannot be one-to-one if $n > m$.

30. Show that T cannot be onto if $n < m$.

31. Suppose that $n = m$. Prove that T is one-to-one if and only if it is onto.

32. Suppose that $T:\mathbf{R}^n \to \mathbf{R}^n$ is defined by $T(\mathbf{x}) = A\mathbf{x}$. Show that T is an isomorphism if and only if the $n \times n$ matrix A is invertible.

33. Suppose that the linear transformation $T:V \to W$ is one-to-one. Show that the image of a linearly independent set of vectors in V is a linearly independent set in W.

34. Suppose that V is a finite-dimensional vector space, that W is a vector space, and that $T:V \to W$ is a linear transformation. If $K = \ker(T)$ and R is the range of T, show that there is a subspace U of V such that $K + U = V$ and $K \cap V = \{\mathbf{0}\}$. Then prove that T maps U one-to-one onto R.

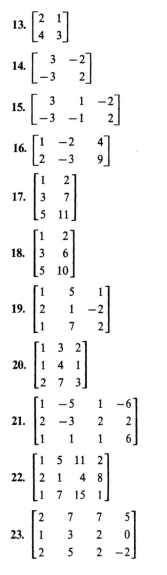

7.3

Coordinates and Change of Basis

In Euclidean space the idea of a coordinate system is closely related to the idea of a basis. Given a vector

$$\mathbf{v} = x_1\mathbf{e}_1 + x_2\mathbf{e}_2 + \cdots + x_n\mathbf{e}_n \tag{1}$$

in $\mathbf{R}^n$, we call the numbers $x_1, x_2, \ldots, x_n$ the *coordinates* of the vector $\mathbf{v}$. Thus the coordinates of a vector in $\mathbf{R}^n$ are the coefficients in its expression as a linear combination of the standard unit basis vectors $\mathbf{e}_1, \mathbf{e}_2, \ldots, \mathbf{e}_n$.

This idea of coordinates generalizes to arbitrary finite-dimensional vector spaces. Let $B = \{\mathbf{v}_1, \mathbf{v}_2, \ldots, \mathbf{v}_n\}$ be a basis for the n-dimensional vector space V. Then any vector $\mathbf{v}$ in V can be expressed in a unique way as a linear combination

$$\mathbf{v} = x_1\mathbf{v}_1 + x_2\mathbf{v}_2 + \cdots + x_n\mathbf{v}_n \tag{2}$$

of the basis vectors in B. The coefficients $x_1, x_2, \ldots, x_n$ in (2) are called the **coordinates** of the vector $\mathbf{v}$ with respect to the basis B, and the n-tuple or column vector

$$\mathbf{v}_B = \begin{bmatrix} x_1 \\ x_2 \\ \vdots \\ x_n \end{bmatrix} = (x_1, x_2, \ldots, x_n) \tag{3}$$

is called the **coordinate vector** of $\mathbf{v}$ with respect to the basis B.

Note that the order in which the basis vectors in B are written must be preserved, because a change in this order would affect the order in which the coordinates of $\mathbf{v}$ should be written. We therefore speak of coordinates and coordinate vectors with respect to an *ordered* basis. The coordinates in (1) of a vector $\mathbf{v} = (x_1, x_2, \ldots, x_n)$ in $\mathbf{R}^n$ may be called its **standard coordinates** to distinguish them from the coordinates of $\mathbf{v}$ with respect to some other basis for $\mathbf{R}^n$.

EXAMPLE 1 The vectors

$$\mathbf{v}_1 = (1, 1, -2), \qquad \mathbf{v}_2 = (3, 1, 3), \qquad \mathbf{v}_3 = (2, 3, 4)$$

form a basis B for $\mathbf{R}^3$. Find the coordinate vector $\mathbf{v}_B$ of the vector $\mathbf{v} = (5, 10, 5)$ with respect to the basis B.

Solution The vector equation

$$\mathbf{v} = x_1\mathbf{v}_1 + x_2\mathbf{v}_2 + x_3\mathbf{v}_3$$

—that is,

$$(5, 10, 5) = x_1(1, 1, -2) + x_2(3, 1, 3) + x_3(2, 3, 4)$$

—yields the linear system

$$\begin{aligned} x_1 + 3x_2 + 2x_3 &= 5 \\ x_1 + x_2 + 3x_3 &= 10 \\ -2x_1 + 3x_2 + 4x_3 &= 5. \end{aligned}$$

This system has the unique solution $x_1 = 2$, $x_2 = -1$, $x_3 = 3$. Thus the coordinate vector of $\mathbf{v} = (5, 10, 5)$ with respect to the basis B is

$$\mathbf{v}_B = \begin{bmatrix} 2 \\ -1 \\ 3 \end{bmatrix}.$$

Suppose now that $B' = \{\mathbf{v}'_1, \mathbf{v}'_2, \ldots, \mathbf{v}'_n\}$ is a new basis for the same n-dimensional vector space V considered previously. If we express the vector $\mathbf{v}$ in (2) as a linear combination

$$\mathbf{v} = x'_1\mathbf{v}'_1 + x'_2\mathbf{v}'_2 + \cdots + x'_n\mathbf{v}'_n \tag{4}$$

of the new basis vectors, then we get the new coordinate vector

$$\mathbf{v}_{B'} = \begin{bmatrix} x'_1 \\ x'_2 \\ \vdots \\ x'_n \end{bmatrix} = (x'_1, x'_2, \ldots, x'_n) \tag{5}$$

of the same vector $\mathbf{v}$ with respect to the new basis B'. The **change of basis problem** is the question of how the old coordinate vector $\mathbf{v}_B$ and the new coordinate vector $\mathbf{v}_{B'}$ of the vector $\mathbf{v}$ are related.

Let us explore this question in the case $n = 3$. First we express each of the new basis vectors in terms of the old basis vectors:

$$\begin{aligned} \mathbf{v}'_1 &= p_{11}\mathbf{v}_1 + p_{21}\mathbf{v}_2 + p_{31}\mathbf{v}_3 \\ \mathbf{v}'_2 &= p_{12}\mathbf{v}_1 + p_{22}\mathbf{v}_2 + p_{32}\mathbf{v}_3 \\ \mathbf{v}'_3 &= p_{13}\mathbf{v}_1 + p_{23}\mathbf{v}_2 + p_{33}\mathbf{v}_3. \end{aligned} \tag{6}$$

Then

$$\begin{aligned} \mathbf{v} &= x'_1\mathbf{v}'_1 + x'_2\mathbf{v}'_2 + x'_3\mathbf{v}'_3 \\ &= x'_1(p_{11}\mathbf{v}_1 + p_{21}\mathbf{v}_2 + p_{31}\mathbf{v}_3) \\ &\quad + x'_2(p_{12}\mathbf{v}_1 + p_{22}\mathbf{v}_2 + p_{32}\mathbf{v}_3) \\ &\quad\quad + x'_3(p_{13}\mathbf{v}_1 + p_{23}\mathbf{v}_2 + p_{33}\mathbf{v}_3), \end{aligned}$$

and thus

$$\begin{aligned} \mathbf{v} &= (p_{11}x'_1 + p_{12}x'_2 + p_{13}x'_3)\mathbf{v}_1 \\ &\quad + (p_{21}x'_1 + p_{22}x'_2 + p_{23}x'_3)\mathbf{v}_2 \\ &\quad\quad + (p_{31}x'_1 + p_{32}x'_2 + p_{33}x'_3)\mathbf{v}_3. \end{aligned} \tag{7}$$

Finally, comparing (2) and (7), we see that

$$\begin{bmatrix} x_1 \\ x_2 \\ x_3 \end{bmatrix} = \begin{bmatrix} p_{11} & p_{12} & p_{13} \\ p_{21} & p_{22} & p_{23} \\ p_{31} & p_{32} & p_{33} \end{bmatrix} \begin{bmatrix} x'_1 \\ x'_2 \\ x'_3 \end{bmatrix}.$$

Thus the relation between the old and new coordinate vectors of $\mathbf{v}$ is given by

$$\mathbf{v}_B = P\mathbf{v}_{B'}, \tag{8}$$

where $P = [p_{ij}]$ is the matrix of coefficients in (6). By generalizing this computation to the n-dimensional case, the following theorem can be proved.

Theorem 1: *Change of Basis for Coordinates*

Let $B = \{\mathbf{v}_1\ \mathbf{v}_2, \ldots, \mathbf{v}_n\}$ and $B' = \{\mathbf{v}'_1, \mathbf{v}'_2, \ldots, \mathbf{v}'_n\}$ be two bases for the vector space V. Then there exists an $n \times n$ matrix P such that the coordinate vectors $\mathbf{v}_B$ and $\mathbf{v}_{B'}$ of a vector $\mathbf{v}$ with respect to the bases B and B', respectively, are related by the equation

$$\mathbf{v}_B = P\mathbf{v}_{B'}. \tag{8}$$

The jth column vector of P is the coordinate vector $(\mathbf{v}'_j)_B$ of the jth new basis vector $\mathbf{v}'_j$ with respect to the old basis B. That is,

$$P = [(\mathbf{v}'_1)_B \quad (\mathbf{v}'_2)_B \quad \cdots \quad (\mathbf{v}'_n)_B]. \tag{9}$$

In the common case $V = \mathbf{R}^n$ there is, fortunately, no need to remember the specific description of the **transition matrix** P that is given in Theorem 1. In this case there is a more convenient and direct way to change coordinates from the basis $B = \{\mathbf{v}_1, \mathbf{v}_2, \ldots, \mathbf{v}_n\}$ to the basis $B' = \{\mathbf{v}'_1, \mathbf{v}'_2, \ldots, \mathbf{v}'_n\}$. Because all the basis vectors are column vectors, we can use them to construct the nonsingular $n \times n$ matrices

$$M_B = [\mathbf{v}_1 \quad \mathbf{v}_2 \quad \cdots \quad \mathbf{v}_n] \quad \text{and} \quad M_{B'} = [\mathbf{v}'_1 \quad \mathbf{v}'_2 \quad \cdots \quad \mathbf{v}'_n]. \tag{10}$$

Thus the matrix M_B of an ordered basis B for $\mathbf{R}^n$ has the vectors in B as its column vectors.

Now let us express a given vector $\mathbf{v}$ in terms of each basis. The equation

$$\begin{aligned} \mathbf{v} &= x_1\mathbf{v}_1 + x_2\mathbf{v}_2 + \cdots + x_n\mathbf{v}_n \\ &= x'_1\mathbf{v}'_1 + x'_2\mathbf{v}'_2 + \cdots + x'_n\mathbf{v}'_n \end{aligned} \tag{11}$$

then takes the vector form

$$[\mathbf{v}_1 \quad \mathbf{v}_2 \quad \cdots \quad \mathbf{v}_n]\begin{bmatrix} x_1 \\ x_2 \\ \vdots \\ x_n \end{bmatrix} = [\mathbf{v}'_1 \quad \mathbf{v}'_2 \quad \cdots \quad \mathbf{v}'_n]\begin{bmatrix} x'_1 \\ x'_2 \\ \vdots \\ x'_n \end{bmatrix}$$

—that is, simply

$$M_B\mathbf{v}_B = M_{B'}\mathbf{v}_{B'}. \tag{12}$$

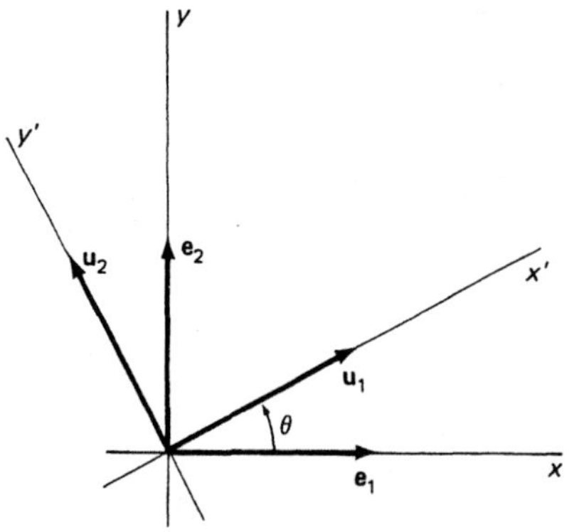

7.9 Rotated coordinate axes in the plane.

This is the key equation for change of coordinates in $\mathbf{R}^n$. For instance, in agreement with Equation (8), it follows that $\mathbf{v}_B = P\mathbf{v}_{B'}$ with $P = M_B^{-1}M_{B'}$. If as a standard practice we always begin with Equations (11) and (12) when we want to change coordinates in $\mathbf{R}^n$, then we can use Equation (12) directly to express either coordinate vector $\mathbf{v}_B$ or $\mathbf{v}_{B'}$ in terms of the other, and we need not remember in advance which transition matrix goes which way.

EXAMPLE 2 **(Rotation of Axes)** Suppose that the $x'y'$-axes in $\mathbf{R}^2$ are obtained by rotating the xy-axes counterclockwise through the angle θ (see Figure 7.9). If $\mathbf{e}_1$ and $\mathbf{e}_2$ are the standard unit basis vectors and $\mathbf{u}_1$ and $\mathbf{u}_2$ are the unit vectors along the rotated axes, then the old coordinates (x, y) of a point and its coordinates (x', y') in the rotated coordinate system satisfy

$$x\mathbf{e}_1 + y\mathbf{e}_2 = x'\mathbf{u}_1 + y'\mathbf{u}_2,$$

the form that Equation (11) takes here. Now

$$\mathbf{u}_1 = (\cos\theta, \sin\theta) \quad \text{and} \quad \mathbf{u}_2 = (-\sin\theta, \cos\theta)$$

as in Example 7 of Section 7.1, so Equation (12) takes the form

$$\begin{bmatrix} 1 & 0 \\ 0 & 1 \end{bmatrix}\begin{bmatrix} x \\ y \end{bmatrix} = \begin{bmatrix} \cos\theta & -\sin\theta \\ \sin\theta & \cos\theta \end{bmatrix}\begin{bmatrix} x' \\ y' \end{bmatrix}.$$

Hence the old coordinates of a point are given in terms of its rotated coordinates by the equations

$$x = x'\cos\theta - y'\sin\theta, \qquad y = x'\sin\theta + y'\cos\theta. \tag{13}$$

For instance, consider the curve $2xy = 1$ shown in Figure 7.10. To write its equation in the $x'y'$-system obtained by rotating through an angle of $\theta = 45°$—so that $\cos\theta = \sin\theta = 1/\sqrt{2}$—we simply substitute

$$x = \frac{x' - y'}{\sqrt{2}} \quad \text{and} \quad y = \frac{x' + y'}{\sqrt{2}}$$

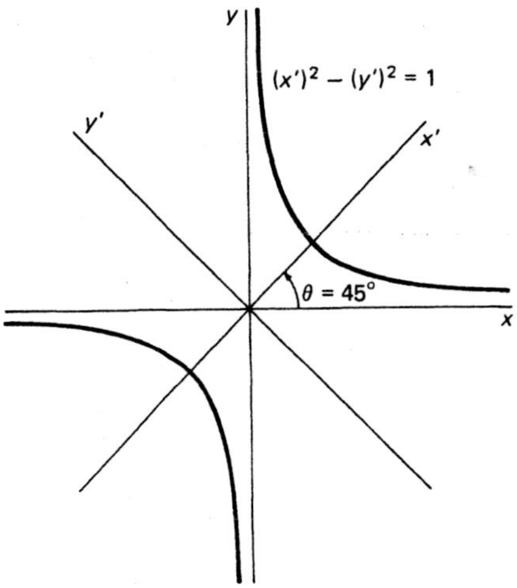

7.10 The graph of $2xy = 1$ is a hyperbola.

(using Equation (13)) and get

$$2 \cdot \frac{x' - y'}{\sqrt{2}} \cdot \frac{x' + y'}{\sqrt{2}} = 1;$$

that is,

$$(x')^2 - (y')^2 = 1.$$

This is the equation of the *rectangular hyperbola* in the rotated coordinate system, and its form is familiar to those who have studied conic sections in analytic geometry. In Section 8.1 we discuss the question of how to choose the angle θ of rotation to transform an equation in a desired manner.

MATRICES OF LINEAR TRANSFORMATIONS

In Section 7.1 we saw that any linear transformation $T:\mathbf{R}^n \to \mathbf{R}^m$ can be expressed in the form $T(\mathbf{v}) = A\mathbf{v}$ where A is an $m \times n$ matrix. To see how this result might be generalized, let us consider a linear transformation $T: V \to W$ from a 3-dimensional vector space V with basis $B = \{\mathbf{v}_1, \mathbf{v}_2, \mathbf{v}_3\}$ to a 3-dimensional vector space W with basis $C = \{\mathbf{w}_1, \mathbf{w}_2, \mathbf{w}_3\}$. We would like to see how T can be expressed in terms of coordinate vectors of elements of V and W.

We begin by expressing the images of the basis vectors in B in terms of those in C:

$$T(\mathbf{v}_j) = a_{1j}\mathbf{w}_1 + a_{2j}\mathbf{w}_2 + a_{3j}\mathbf{w}_3 \tag{14}$$

for $j = 1, 2, 3$. If

$$\mathbf{v} = x_1\mathbf{v}_1 + x_2\mathbf{v}_2 + x_3\mathbf{v}_3 \tag{15}$$

is a vector in V, then

$$\begin{aligned} T(\mathbf{v}) &= x_1 T(\mathbf{v}_1) + x_2 T(\mathbf{v}_2) + x_3 T(\mathbf{v}_3) \\ &= x_1(a_{11}\mathbf{w}_1 + a_{21}\mathbf{w}_2 + a_{31}\mathbf{w}_3) \\ &\quad + x_2(a_{12}\mathbf{w}_1 + a_{22}\mathbf{w}_2 + a_{32}\mathbf{w}_3) \\ &\quad\quad + x_3(a_{13}\mathbf{w}_1 + a_{23}\mathbf{w}_2 + a_{33}\mathbf{w}_3) \\ &= (a_{11}x_1 + a_{12}x_2 + a_{13}x_3)\mathbf{w}_1 \\ &\quad + (a_{21}x_1 + a_{22}x_2 + a_{23}x_3)\mathbf{w}_2 \\ &\quad\quad + (a_{31}x_1 + a_{32}x_2 + a_{33}x_3)\mathbf{w}_3, \end{aligned}$$

and so

$$T(\mathbf{v}) = y_1\mathbf{w}_1 + y_2\mathbf{w}_2 + y_3\mathbf{w}_3, \tag{16}$$

where

$$\begin{bmatrix} y_1 \\ y_2 \\ y_3 \end{bmatrix} = \begin{bmatrix} a_{11} & a_{12} & a_{13} \\ a_{21} & a_{22} & a_{23} \\ a_{31} & a_{32} & a_{33} \end{bmatrix} \begin{bmatrix} x_1 \\ x_2 \\ x_3 \end{bmatrix}.$$

Thus the coordinate vectors

$$\mathbf{x} = \mathbf{v}_B \quad \text{and} \quad \mathbf{y} = T(\mathbf{v})_C \tag{17}$$

of the vector $\mathbf{v}$ and its image $T(\mathbf{v})$ are related by

$$\mathbf{y} = A\mathbf{x}, \tag{18}$$

where the matrix A is defined in Equation (14). This computation is the typical case $n = m = 3$ of the proof of the following generalization of Theorem 2 in Section 7.1.

Theorem 2: *The Matrix of a Linear Transformation*
Let $T: V \to W$ be a linear transformation between finite-dimensional vector spaces. Let $B = \{\mathbf{v}_1, \mathbf{v}_2, \ldots, \mathbf{v}_n\}$ and $C = \{\mathbf{w}_1, \mathbf{w}_2, \ldots, \mathbf{w}_m\}$ be bases for V and W, respectively. Then there exists an $m \times n$ matrix A such that the coordinate vectors $\mathbf{x} = \mathbf{v}_B$ and $\mathbf{y} = T(\mathbf{v})_C$ of a vector $\mathbf{v}$ in V and its image $T(\mathbf{v})$ in W are related by

$$\mathbf{y} = A\mathbf{x}. \tag{18}$$

The jth column vector of A is the coordinate vector $T(\mathbf{v}_j)_C$ of the image under T of the jth basis vector $\mathbf{v}_j$. That is,

$$A = [T(\mathbf{v}_1)_C \quad T(\mathbf{v}_2)_C \quad \cdots \quad T(\mathbf{v}_n)_C]. \tag{19}$$

The matrix A defined in (19) is the **matrix of the linear transformation** $T: V \to W$ with respect to the bases B for V and C for W. Theorem 2 says that in terms of coordinate vectors, the linear transformation $T: V \to W$ acts exactly like a linear transformation between Euclidean spaces—multiplication by the matrix A transforms the *coordinate vector* $\mathbf{x}$ of an element of V into the *coordinate vector* $\mathbf{y} = A\mathbf{x}$ of its image in W.

EXAMPLE 3 Consider the polynomial spaces $\mathcal{P}_3$ and $\mathcal{P}_2$, with bases $B = \{1, x, x^2, x^3\}$ and $C = \{1, x, x^2\}$, respectively. The operation of differentiation yields the linear transformation $D: \mathcal{P}_3 \to \mathcal{P}_2$ defined by

$$D(c_0 + c_1x + c_2x^2 + c_3x^3) = c_1 + 2c_2x + 3c_3x^2.$$

Thus $D(1) = 0$, $D(x) = 1$, $D(x^2) = 2x$, and $D(x^3) = 3x^2$. Hence (19) tells us that the matrix of D with respect to the bases B and C is

$$A = \begin{bmatrix} 0 & 1 & 0 & 0 \\ 0 & 0 & 2 & 0 \\ 0 & 0 & 0 & 3 \end{bmatrix}.$$

The coordinate vector of the polynomial $c_0 + c_1x + c_2x^2 + c_3x^3$ with respect to B is $\mathbf{x} = (c_0, c_1, c_2, c_3)$, and as a check we compute the coordinate vector

$$\mathbf{y} = A\mathbf{x} = \begin{bmatrix} 0 & 1 & 0 & 0 \\ 0 & 0 & 2 & 0 \\ 0 & 0 & 0 & 3 \end{bmatrix} \begin{bmatrix} c_0 \\ c_1 \\ c_2 \\ c_3 \end{bmatrix} = \begin{bmatrix} c_1 \\ 2c_2 \\ 3c_3 \end{bmatrix}$$

of its image $c_1 + 2c_2x + 3c_3x^2$ under the transformation D.

LINEAR OPERATORS AND SIMILAR MATRICES

A linear transformation $T: V \to V$ of the vector space V into itself is called a **linear operator** on V. Assuming that V is finite-dimensional, we can use a single basis $B = \{\mathbf{v}_1, \mathbf{v}_2, \ldots, \mathbf{v}_n\}$ for V to describe both a typical vector $\mathbf{v}$ and its image $T(\mathbf{v})$. If

$$\mathbf{x} = \mathbf{v}_B \quad \text{and} \quad \mathbf{y} = T(\mathbf{v})_B \tag{20}$$

are the indicated coordinate vectors with respect to B, then

$$\mathbf{y} = A\mathbf{x}, \tag{21}$$

where A is the $n \times n$ matrix that is provided by Theorem 2 (with $B = C$). In this situation we call A the **matrix of the linear operator** T with respect to the basis B.

In certain applications it is important to know how the matrix of the linear operator $T: V \to V$ changes when the basis B for V is changed. If

$$\mathbf{x}' = \mathbf{v}_{B'} \quad \text{and} \quad \mathbf{y}' = T(\mathbf{v})_{B'} \tag{22}$$

are coordinate vectors with respect to a second basis B' for V, then Theorem 1 provides the transition matrix P such that

$$\mathbf{x} = P\mathbf{x}' \quad \text{and} \quad \mathbf{y} = P\mathbf{y}'. \tag{23}$$

Then substitution of (23) in (21) yields

$$P\mathbf{y}' = AP\mathbf{x}'.$$

Because P is invertible (Problem 32), it follows that

$$\mathbf{y}' = P^{-1}AP\mathbf{x}'. \tag{24}$$

Equation (24) implies that the matrix of T with respect to the new basis B' for V is

$$A' = P^{-1}AP. \tag{25}$$

Recalling from Section 6.2 the definition of similarity, we see that Equation (25) implies that the new matrix A' of T is similar to the old matrix A of T. The following theorem summarizes the results of this paragraph.

> ***Theorem 3:*** *Similar Matrices of Linear Operators*
> Let $T: V \to V$ be a linear operator on the finite-dimensional vector space V and let B and B' be two bases for V. If A is the matrix of T with respect to B, then the matrix of T with respect to B' is given by
>
> $$A' = P^{-1}AP, \tag{25}$$
>
> where P is the transition matrix such that coordinate vectors $\mathbf{x}$ and $\mathbf{x}'$ relative to B and B' are related through the equation $\mathbf{x} = P\mathbf{x}'$.

Sometimes a linear operator is given algebraically, but we need to describe its "action" geometrically (as in the case of the plane transformations discussed in Section 7.1). One way to investigate a linear operator T is to seek a new basis, relative to which the matrix of T is as simple as possible. Equation (25) enables us to compute the new matrix of T with respect to any proposed new basis.

We will see in Section 8.1 that the case in which $V = \mathbf{R}^n$, and the standard matrix of T is *symmetric*, is of special interest. By the **standard matrix** of the linear operator $T: \mathbf{R}^n \to \mathbf{R}^n$ is meant its matrix A with respect to the standard basis $B = \{\mathbf{e}_1, \mathbf{e}_2, \ldots, \mathbf{e}_n\}$ for $\mathbf{R}^n$. If the matrix A is symmetric, then we know from Theorems 3 and 4 in Section 6.4 that it has n mutually orthogonal eigenvectors $\mathbf{v}_1, \mathbf{v}_2, \ldots, \mathbf{v}_n$. These eigenvectors form a new orthogonal basis $B' = \{\mathbf{v}_1, \mathbf{v}_2, \ldots, \mathbf{v}_n\}$ for $\mathbf{R}^n$, and we can use B' to describe T geometrically.

If $\mathbf{x} = \mathbf{v}$ is a standard coordinate vector and $\mathbf{x}' = \mathbf{v}_{B'}$ is the coordinate vector of $\mathbf{v}$ with respect to B', then it follows from Equation (12), with $M_B = I$ and $M_{B'} = P$, that

$$\mathbf{x} = P\mathbf{x}' \quad \text{with} \quad P = [\mathbf{v}_1 \quad \mathbf{v}_2 \quad \cdots \quad \mathbf{v}_n]. \tag{26}$$

Thus the transition matrix P is the eigenvector matrix for which we know (by Equation (6) in Section 6.2) that

$$A' = P^{-1}AP = \begin{bmatrix} \lambda_1 & 0 & \cdots & 0 \\ 0 & \lambda_2 & \cdots & 0 \\ \vdots & \vdots & \ddots & \vdots \\ 0 & 0 & \cdots & \lambda_n \end{bmatrix}, \tag{27}$$

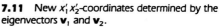

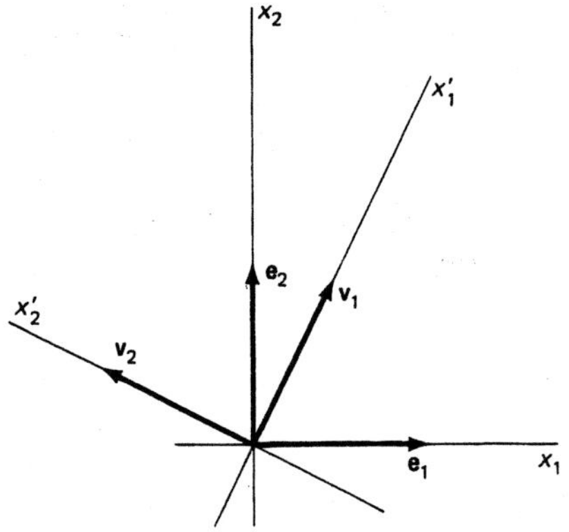

7.11 New $x_1'x_2'$-coordinates determined by the eigenvectors $\mathbf{v}_1$ and $\mathbf{v}_2$.

where λ_i is the eigenvalue corresponding to the eigenvector $\mathbf{v}_i$. Thus *if the standard matrix A of $T:\mathbf{R}^n \to \mathbf{R}^n$ is* ***symmetric****, then there exists a new orthogonal basis B' for $\mathbf{R}^n$ such that the matrix of T relative to B' is a* ***diagonal*** *matrix A'.*

The orthogonal basis $B' = \{\mathbf{v}_1, \mathbf{v}_2, \ldots, \mathbf{v}_n\}$ determines an orthogonal $x_1'x_2'\ldots x_n'$-coordinate system in $\mathbf{R}^n$ (as indicated in Figure 7.11 with $n = 2$). The fact that $T:\mathbf{R}^n \to \mathbf{R}^n$ has diagonal matrix A' with respect to B' means that T can be described in terms of a sequence of expansions or compressions in the new coordinate directions, possibly also including some reflections through the new coordinate planes. Because of the diagonal form of A' in (27), the image under T of the point with coordinate vector $\mathbf{x}' = (x_1', x_2', \ldots, x_n')$ is the point with coordinate vector

$$\mathbf{y}' = A\mathbf{x}' = (\lambda_1 x_1', \lambda_2 x_2', \ldots, \lambda_n x_n'). \tag{28}$$

Thus if $\lambda_i > 0$, then the operator T involves an expansion or compression in the x_i'-direction with factor $|\lambda_i|$. But if $\lambda_i < 0$, this expansion or compression is followed by a reflection through the coordinate plane orthogonal to the x_i'-axis.

EXAMPLE 4 Let $T:\mathbf{R}^2 \to \mathbf{R}^2$ be the linear operator defined (in standard coordinates) by $T(\mathbf{x}) = A\mathbf{x}$, where

$$A = \begin{bmatrix} 14 & 2 \\ 2 & 11 \end{bmatrix}.$$

The characteristic equation of A is

$$\begin{aligned} |A - \lambda I| &= (14 - \lambda)(11 - \lambda) - 4 \\ &= \lambda^2 - 25\lambda + 150 = (\lambda - 10)(\lambda - 15) = 0, \end{aligned}$$

so the eigenvalues of A are $\lambda_1 = 15$ and $\lambda_2 = 10$. We find readily that $\mathbf{v}_1 = (2, 1)$ is an eigenvector associated with $\lambda_1 = 15$ and that $\mathbf{v}_2 = (-1, 2)$ is an eigenvector associated with $\lambda_2 = 10$. Figure 7.12 shows the corresponding $x_1'x_2'$-coordinate system. The operator T is the composition of two expansions—one by a factor of 15 in the x_1'-direction and the other by a factor of 10 in the x_2'-direction.

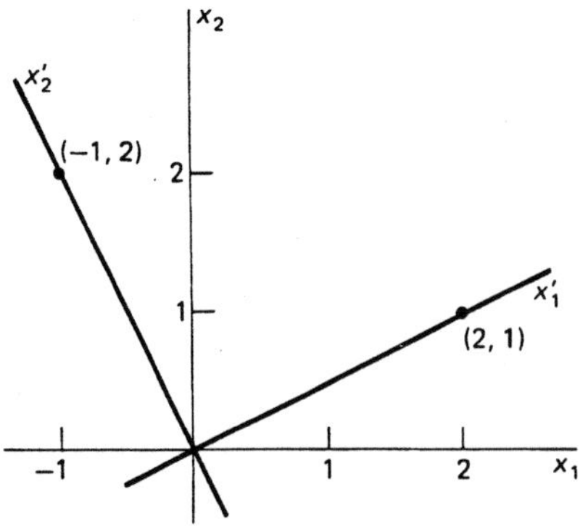

7.12 The coordinate system of Example 4.

In Problems 1–6, two linearly independent vectors $\mathbf{v}_1$ and $\mathbf{v}_2$ in $\mathbf{R}^2$ are given. Find the coordinate vector $\mathbf{v}_B$ of the vector $\mathbf{v}$ with respect to the basis $B = \{\mathbf{v}_1, \mathbf{v}_2\}$.

1. $\mathbf{v}_1 = (2, 1)$, $\mathbf{v}_2 = (-1, 1)$; $\mathbf{v} = (0, 3)$

2. $\mathbf{v}_1 = (1, 1)$, $\mathbf{v}_2 = (-1, 2)$; $\mathbf{v} = (-3, 0)$

3. $\mathbf{v}_1 = (1, 3)$, $\mathbf{v}_2 = (0, 1)$; $\mathbf{v} = (5, 10)$

4. $\mathbf{v}_1 = (2, 4)$, $\mathbf{v}_2 = (-1, 3)$; $\mathbf{v} = (10, 10)$

5. $\mathbf{v}_1 = (3, 4)$, $\mathbf{v}_2 = (2, 3)$; $\mathbf{v} = (1, 1)$

6. $\mathbf{v}_1 = (3, 1)$, $\mathbf{v}_2 = (1, 3)$; $\mathbf{v} = (8, 8)$

Problems 7 and 8 are the same as the first six, except that the basis $B = \{\mathbf{v}_1, \mathbf{v}_2, \mathbf{v}_3\}$ and the vector $\mathbf{v}$ in $\mathbf{R}^3$ are given. Find $\mathbf{v}_B$.

7. $\mathbf{v}_1 = (1, 2, 1)$, $\mathbf{v}_2 = (3, 2, -2)$, $\mathbf{v}_3 = (4, 7, 3)$; $\mathbf{v} = (3, 4, 5)$

8. $\mathbf{v}_1 = (1, 1, 2)$, $\mathbf{v}_2 = (4, 3, 5)$, $\mathbf{v}_3 = (5, 2, 2)$; $\mathbf{v} = (6, 7, 8)$

In Problems 9–12, two linearly independent vectors $\mathbf{u}_1$ and $\mathbf{u}_2$ in $\mathbf{R}^2$ are given. Express the standard coordinates (x, y) of a point in $\mathbf{R}^2$ in terms of its coordinates (x', y') with respect to the basis $B = \{\mathbf{u}_1, \mathbf{u}_2\}$.

9. $\mathbf{u}_1 = (3, 1)$, $\mathbf{u}_2 = (1, 4)$

10. $\mathbf{u}_1 = (1, 2)$, $\mathbf{u}_2 = (-3, 4)$

11. $\mathbf{u}_1 = (-1, 2)$, $\mathbf{u}_2 = (-3, -2)$

12. $\mathbf{u}_1 = (2, -5)$, $\mathbf{u}_2 = (5, 2)$

In Problems 13–16, two bases $B = \{\mathbf{u}_1, \mathbf{u}_2\}$ and $C = \{\mathbf{v}_1, \mathbf{v}_2\}$ for $\mathbf{R}^2$ are given. Express the coordinates (x_1, x_2) of a point with respect to the basis B in terms of its coordinates (y_1, y_2) with respect to the basis C.

13. $\mathbf{u}_1 = (2, -1)$, $\mathbf{u}_2 = (-1, 1)$; $\mathbf{v}_1 = (1, 0)$, $\mathbf{v}_2 = (0, 1)$

14. $\mathbf{u}_1 = (2, 3)$, $\mathbf{u}_2 = (1, 2)$; $\mathbf{v}_1 = (2, 0)$, $\mathbf{v}_2 = (0, 3)$

15. $\mathbf{u}_1 = (1, 1)$, $\mathbf{u}_2 = (-1, 1)$; $\mathbf{v}_1 = (2, 4)$, $\mathbf{v}_2 = (-4, 2)$

16. $\mathbf{u}_1 = (1, 2)$, $\mathbf{u}_2 = (-2, 1)$; $\mathbf{v}_1 = (5, 5)$, $\mathbf{v}_2 = (-5, 5)$

In Problems 17 and 18, two bases $B = \{\mathbf{u}_1, \mathbf{u}_2, \mathbf{u}_3\}$ and $C = \{\mathbf{v}_1, \mathbf{v}_2, \mathbf{v}_3\}$ for $\mathbf{R}^3$ are given. Express the coordinates (x_1, x_2, x_3) of a point with respect to the basis B in terms of its coordinates (y_1, y_2, y_3) with respect to the basis C.

17. $\mathbf{u}_1 = (1, 0, 0)$, $\mathbf{u}_2 = (0, 1, 0)$, $\mathbf{u}_3 = (0, 0, 1)$; $\mathbf{v}_1 = (1, 3, 2)$, $\mathbf{v}_2 = (2, -1, 3)$, $\mathbf{v}_3 = (4, 3, 2)$

18. $\mathbf{u}_1 = (1, 1, 1)$, $\mathbf{u}_2 = (3, 4, -2)$, $\mathbf{u}_3 = (4, 4, 3)$; $\mathbf{v}_1 = (0, 2, 1)$, $\mathbf{v}_2 = (4, 0, 5)$, $\mathbf{v}_3 = (6, 7, 0)$

In Problems 19–26, a symmetric matrix A is given. Use the method of Example 4 to describe geometrically the action of the linear operator T on $\mathbf{R}^2$ (or $\mathbf{R}^3$) that is defined in standard coordinates by $T(\mathbf{x}) = A\mathbf{x}$.

19. $\begin{bmatrix} 4 & 1 \\ 1 & 4 \end{bmatrix}$

20. $\begin{bmatrix} 5 & 2 \\ 2 & 5 \end{bmatrix}$

21. $\begin{bmatrix} 9 & -2 \\ -2 & 6 \end{bmatrix}$

22. $\begin{bmatrix} 13 & -4 \\ -4 & 7 \end{bmatrix}$

23. $\begin{bmatrix} 4 & 1 & 4 \\ 1 & 7 & 1 \\ 4 & 1 & 4 \end{bmatrix}$

24. $\begin{bmatrix} 1 & 2 & 2 \\ 2 & 7 & 1 \\ 2 & 1 & 7 \end{bmatrix}$

25. $\begin{bmatrix} 4 & 1 & 1 \\ 1 & 4 & 1 \\ 1 & 1 & 4 \end{bmatrix}$

26. $\begin{bmatrix} 5 & 1 & 3 \\ 1 & 7 & 1 \\ 3 & 1 & 5 \end{bmatrix}$

In Problems 27 and 28, a linear operator T on $\mathbf{R}^2$ is defined and a basis $B = \{\mathbf{v}_1, \mathbf{v}_2\}$ for $\mathbf{R}^2$ is given. Use Theorem 2 to find the matrix A of T with respect to the basis B.

27. $T(x_1, x_2) = (x_1 + x_2, x_1 - x_2)$; $\mathbf{v}_1 = (2, -1)$, $\mathbf{v}_2 = (-1, 1)$

28. $T(x_1, x_2) = (2x_1 + x_2, x_1 + 2x_2)$; $\mathbf{v}_1 = (2, 3)$, $\mathbf{v}_2 = (1, 2)$

29. Let V be an n-dimensional vector space; let the linear operator $T: V \to V$ be defined by $T(\mathbf{v}) = k\mathbf{v}$ where k is a constant. Show that the matrix of T with respect to an arbitrary basis for V is a diagonal matrix.

30. In each part of this problem the three given functions form a basis B for a subspace V of the space of all real-valued functions on $\mathbf{R}$. Find the matrix A of the differentiation operator $D: V \to V$ with respect to the basis B.
(a) 1, e^x, and xe^x
(b) e^x, xe^x, and x^2e^x

31. In Example 3 we saw that the matrix of the differentiation transformation $D: \mathcal{P}_3 \to \mathcal{P}_2$ with respect to the bases $B = \{1, x, x^2, x^3\}$ and $C = \{1, x, x^2\}$ is

$$A_D = \begin{bmatrix} 0 & 1 & 0 & 0 \\ 0 & 0 & 2 & 0 \\ 0 & 0 & 0 & 3 \end{bmatrix}$$

Now consider the integration operator $J: \mathcal{P}_2 \to \mathcal{P}_3$ defined by

$$J(c_0 + c_1x + c_2x^2) = c_0x + \tfrac{1}{2}c_1x^2 + \tfrac{1}{3}c_2x^3.$$

Find the matrix A_J of J with respect to the bases C and B. Then show that A_DA_J is the 3×3 identity matrix, consistent with the fact that the derivative of the integral of a quadratic polynomial is the same polynomial. Should A_JA_D be an identity matrix? Is it?

32. Let B and B' be two bases for the n-dimensional vector space V. By Theorem 1 there exist $n \times n$ matrices P and Q such that $\mathbf{v}_B = P\mathbf{v}_{B'}$ and $\mathbf{v}_{B'} = Q\mathbf{v}_B$ for every vector $\mathbf{v}$ in V. Prove that P is invertible and that $P^{-1} = Q$.

*7.4

Isometries, Rotations, and Computer Graphics

A linear operator $T: \mathbf{R}^n \to \mathbf{R}^n$ has especially interesting and useful geometric properties if its standard matrix is orthogonal. Recall from Section 6.4 that the $n \times n$ matrix A is *orthogonal* provided that $A^TA = I$. It follows that A is invertible with $A^{-1} = A^T$, and from Theorem 2 of the same section, A is orthogonal if and only if both its column vectors and its row vectors are orthonormal.

Suppose that $T: \mathbf{R}^n \to \mathbf{R}^n$ is defined by $T(\mathbf{x}) = A\mathbf{x}$ with A an orthogonal matrix. We want to show first that the linear transformation T **preserves dot products**, meaning that

$$T(\mathbf{x}) \cdot T(\mathbf{y}) = \mathbf{x} \cdot \mathbf{y} \tag{1}$$

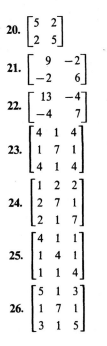

for any two vectors $\mathbf{x}$ and $\mathbf{y}$ in $\mathbf{R}^n$. This is so because $A^TA = I$ and $\mathbf{x}\cdot\mathbf{y} = \mathbf{x}^T\mathbf{y}$, so

$$\begin{aligned} T(\mathbf{x})\cdot T(\mathbf{y}) &= A\mathbf{x}\cdot A\mathbf{y} = (A\mathbf{x})^T A\mathbf{y} \\ &= \mathbf{x}^T A^T A\mathbf{y} = \mathbf{x}^T I\mathbf{y} \\ &= \mathbf{x}^T\mathbf{y} = \mathbf{x}\cdot\mathbf{y}. \end{aligned}$$

The fact that T preserves dot products implies in turn that T **preserves distances,**

$$|T(\mathbf{x}) - T(\mathbf{y})| = |\mathbf{x} - \mathbf{y}|, \tag{2}$$

because it follows from (1) that

$$\begin{aligned} |T(\mathbf{x}) - T(\mathbf{y})|^2 &= |T(\mathbf{x} - \mathbf{y})|^2 \\ &= \{T(\mathbf{x} - \mathbf{y})\}\cdot\{T(\mathbf{x} - \mathbf{y})\} \\ &= (\mathbf{x} - \mathbf{y})\cdot(\mathbf{x} - \mathbf{y}) = |\mathbf{x} - \mathbf{y}|^2. \end{aligned}$$

Thus the distance $|T(\mathbf{x}) - T(\mathbf{y})|$ between $T(\mathbf{x})$ and $T(\mathbf{y})$ is equal to that between $\mathbf{x}$ and $\mathbf{y}$.

A function $T: \mathbf{R}^n \to \mathbf{R}^n$ is called an **isometry** of $\mathbf{R}^n$ provided that it preserves distances—Equation (2) holds for all $\mathbf{x}$ and $\mathbf{y}$ in $\mathbf{R}^n$. Our discussion to this point shows that a linear transformation is an isometry if its standard matrix is orthogonal, and a proof of the converse is outlined in Problem 3.

> ***Theorem 1:*** *Isometries and Orthogonal Matrices*
>
> The linear transformation $T: \mathbf{R}^n \to \mathbf{R}^n$ defined by $T(\mathbf{x}) = A\mathbf{x}$ is an isometry if and only if its matrix A is orthogonal.

Problem 1 shows that every linear isometry of $\mathbf{R}^n$ preserves dot products. Because the angle θ between two vectors $\mathbf{x}$ and $\mathbf{y}$ in $\mathbf{R}^n$ is defined in terms of dot products,

$$\cos\theta = \frac{\mathbf{x}\cdot\mathbf{y}}{|\mathbf{x}||\mathbf{y}|}, \tag{3}$$

it follows that *every linear isometry of* $\mathbf{R}^n$ *preserves angles as well as distances.* Thus a linear isometry has the properties that one associates with the phrase **rigid motion.**

Note that not every isometry of $\mathbf{R}^n$ is linear. For instance, the translation defined by $T(\mathbf{x}) = \mathbf{x} + \mathbf{b}$ (with $\mathbf{b}$ fixed) preserves distances but is not linear. It can be proved that every isometry T of $\mathbf{R}^n$ is of the form

$$T(\mathbf{x}) = A\mathbf{x} + \mathbf{b}, \tag{4}$$

where A is an orthogonal matrix and $\mathbf{b}$ is a vector. Thus every isometry is a composition of a linear isometry and a translation. We confine our attention to the linear case with $\mathbf{b} = \mathbf{0}$ in (4), and we are particularly interested in the nature of linear isometries of $\mathbf{R}^2$ and of $\mathbf{R}^3$.

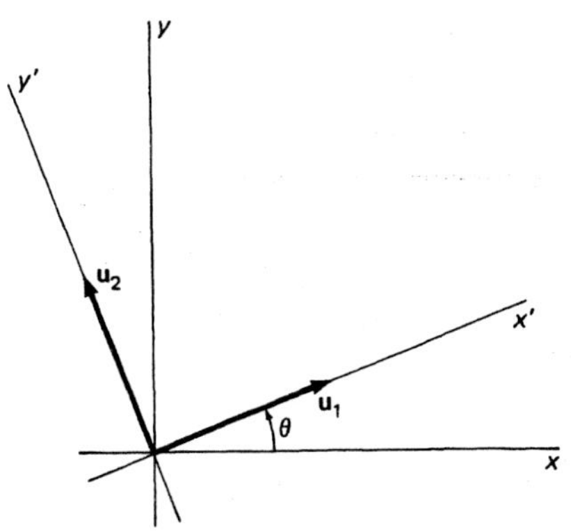

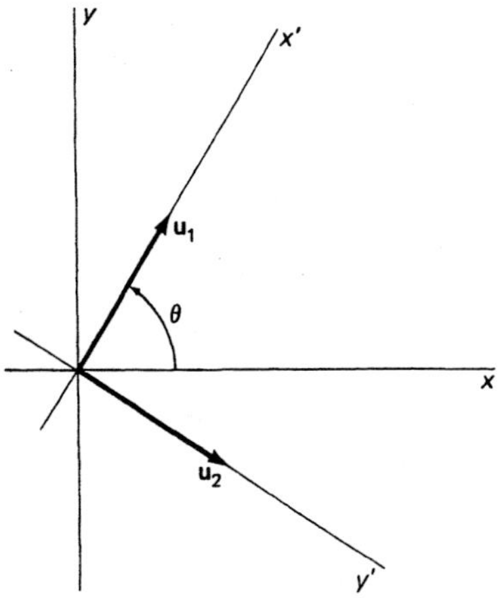

7.13 The new coordinate system is right-handed. **7.14** The new coordinate system is left-handed.

ISOMETRIES OF THE PLANE

Let $T: \mathbf{R}^2 \to \mathbf{R}^2$ be a linear isometry. Then the images of the standard unit basis vectors in $\mathbf{R}^2$ are the two orthogonal unit vectors $\mathbf{u}_1 = T(\mathbf{e}_1)$ and $\mathbf{u}_2 = T(\mathbf{e}_2)$, and Theorem 2 in Section 7.1 tells us that the matrix of T is $A = [\mathbf{u}_1 \quad \mathbf{u}_2]$. Because $\mathbf{u}_1$ and $\mathbf{u}_2$ are orthonormal, $\mathbf{u}_1$ must be carried to $\mathbf{u}_2$ by either a counterclockwise or a clockwise rotation of 90°. Figures 7.13 and 7.14 illustrate the two possibilities.

Let θ denote the counterclockwise angle from $\mathbf{e}_1$ to $\mathbf{u}_1$ (so $0 \le \theta < 2\pi$). Then the new x'-axis is determined by $\mathbf{u}_1$, and the question is this: Which of the two directions perpendicular to $\mathbf{u}_1$ is the positive direction on the new y'-axis determined by $\mathbf{u}_2$?

In the situation illustrated by Figure 7.13 we call the $x'y'$-system a *right-handed coordinate system.* It is apparent that

$$\mathbf{u}_1 = (\cos\theta, \sin\theta) \quad \text{and} \quad \mathbf{u}_2 = (-\sin\theta, \cos\theta),$$

so the matrix $A = [\mathbf{u}_1 \quad \mathbf{u}_2]$ of the isometry T is the matrix

$$R(\theta) = \begin{bmatrix} \cos\theta & -\sin\theta \\ \sin\theta & \cos\theta \end{bmatrix} \tag{5}$$

of a *counterclockwise* rotation of the plane through the angle θ.

In Figure 7.14 the $x'y'$-system is a *left-handed coordinate system.* Now it is apparent that

$$\mathbf{u}_1 = (\cos\theta, \sin\theta) \quad \text{and} \quad \mathbf{u}_2 = (\sin\theta, -\cos\theta),$$

so the matrix of T is

$$\begin{aligned} A &= \begin{bmatrix} \cos\theta & \sin\theta \\ \sin\theta & -\cos\theta \end{bmatrix} \\ &= \begin{bmatrix} \cos\theta & -\sin\theta \\ \sin\theta & \cos\theta \end{bmatrix} \begin{bmatrix} 1 & 0 \\ 0 & -1 \end{bmatrix}. \end{aligned}$$

Thus we have shown that the matrix of T is

$$A = R(\theta)\begin{bmatrix} 1 & 0 \\ 0 & -1 \end{bmatrix}. \tag{6}$$

The second factor on the right in (6) is the matrix of a reflection through the x-axis, so we have shown in this case that the isometry T is the result of a reflection in the x-axis followed by a counterclockwise rotation through some angle θ.

Having shown that the matrix of a linear isometry $T: \mathbf{R}^2 \to \mathbf{R}^2$ is either of the form in (5) or of that in (6), we have established the following characterization of linear isometries of the plane.

> ***Theorem 2:*** *Linear Isometries of* $\mathbf{R}^2$
> Every linear isometry $T: \mathbf{R}^2 \to \mathbf{R}^2$ is either
>
> **1.** A counterclockwise rotation about the origin through some angle θ with $0 \le \theta < 2\pi$, or
>
> **2.** A reflection through the x-axis followed by a counterclockwise rotation about the origin.

If $\theta = 0$ in (2), then we have simply a reflection. In Problem 8 we ask you to deduce from Theorem 2 that every linear isometry of $\mathbf{R}^2$ is the result of either one or two reflections in lines through the origin.

ISOMETRIES OF $\mathbf{R}^3$

Now we want to investigate the possibility of decomposing a linear isometry $T: \mathbf{R}^3 \to \mathbf{R}^3$ into reflections and rotations. In space we may reflect in any plane through the origin. For instance, the matrix

$$\begin{bmatrix} 1 & 0 & 0 \\ 0 & 1 & 0 \\ 0 & 0 & -1 \end{bmatrix}$$

is the matrix of the reflection in the xy-plane, for which $T(x, y, z) = (x, y, -z)$.

Similarly, we may rotate $\mathbf{R}^3$ about any line through the origin, in which case this line is called the **axis** of the rotation. For instance, the matrix

$$R_z(\theta) = \begin{bmatrix} \cos\theta & -\sin\theta & 0 \\ \sin\theta & \cos\theta & 0 \\ 0 & 0 & 1 \end{bmatrix} \tag{7}$$

is the matrix of a rotation about the z-axis through the angle θ (from the x-axis toward the y-axis). To see that this is so, note that

$$R_z(\theta)\begin{bmatrix} x \\ y \\ z \end{bmatrix} = \begin{bmatrix} x\cos\theta - y\sin\theta \\ x\sin\theta + y\cos\theta \\ z \end{bmatrix},$$

so each horizontal plane at height z is simply rotated through the same angle θ. Similarly, the matrix

$$R_x(\theta) = \begin{bmatrix} 1 & 0 & 0 \\ 0 & \cos\theta & -\sin\theta \\ 0 & \sin\theta & \cos\theta \end{bmatrix} \tag{8}$$

describes a rotation through the angle θ about the x-axis (from the y-axis toward the z-axis), whereas the matrix

$$R_y(\theta) = \begin{bmatrix} \cos\theta & 0 & -\sin\theta \\ 0 & 1 & 0 \\ \sin\theta & 0 & \cos\theta \end{bmatrix} \tag{9}$$

describes a rotation through the angle θ about the y-axis (from the x-axis toward the z-axis).

EXAMPLE 1 If T is the result of a rotation of 45° about the x-axis followed by a rotation of 45° about the y-axis, then the matrix of T is

$$R_y(45°)R_x(45°) = \begin{bmatrix} \frac{1}{\sqrt{2}} & 0 & \frac{-1}{\sqrt{2}} \\ 0 & 1 & 0 \\ \frac{1}{\sqrt{2}} & 0 & \frac{1}{\sqrt{2}} \end{bmatrix}\begin{bmatrix} 1 & 0 & 0 \\ 0 & \frac{1}{\sqrt{2}} & \frac{-1}{\sqrt{2}} \\ 0 & \frac{1}{\sqrt{2}} & \frac{1}{\sqrt{2}} \end{bmatrix}$$

$$= \begin{bmatrix} \frac{1}{\sqrt{2}} & \frac{-1}{2} & \frac{-1}{2} \\ 0 & \frac{1}{\sqrt{2}} & \frac{-1}{\sqrt{2}} \\ \frac{1}{\sqrt{2}} & \frac{1}{2} & \frac{1}{2} \end{bmatrix}.$$

But if the same two rotations are carried out in the reverse order, the corresponding matrix is

$$R_x(45°)R_y(45°) = \begin{bmatrix} 1 & 0 & 0 \\ 0 & \frac{1}{\sqrt{2}} & \frac{-1}{\sqrt{2}} \\ 0 & \frac{1}{\sqrt{2}} & \frac{1}{\sqrt{2}} \end{bmatrix} \begin{bmatrix} \frac{1}{\sqrt{2}} & 0 & \frac{-1}{\sqrt{2}} \\ 0 & 1 & 0 \\ \frac{1}{\sqrt{2}} & 0 & \frac{1}{\sqrt{2}} \end{bmatrix}$$

$$= \begin{bmatrix} \frac{1}{\sqrt{2}} & 0 & \frac{-1}{\sqrt{2}} \\ \frac{-1}{2} & \frac{1}{\sqrt{2}} & \frac{-1}{2} \\ \frac{1}{2} & \frac{1}{\sqrt{2}} & \frac{1}{2} \end{bmatrix}.$$

Note that $R_x(45°)R_y(45°) \neq R_y(45°)R_x(45°)$. In general, two rotations of $\mathbf{R}^3$ commute if and only if they have the same axis.

Now we want to analyze an arbitrary linear isometry $T: \mathbf{R}^3 \to \mathbf{R}^3$ defined by $T(\mathbf{x}) = A\mathbf{x}$. The characteristic polynomial

$$p(\lambda) = |A - \lambda I| = -\lambda^3 + c_2\lambda^2 + c_1\lambda + c_0 \tag{10}$$

of the 3×3 matrix A is of degree 3 and must therefore have a real root. (For those who are familiar with the intermediate value theorem, this is so because $p(\lambda) \to \infty$ as $\lambda \to -\infty$, whereas $p(\lambda) \to -\infty$ as $\lambda \to +\infty$. Thus the polynomial $p(\lambda)$ attains both positive and negative values. It has the intermediate value property because it is continuous, and therefore must attain the value zero somewhere.)

Therefore the matrix A has at least one real eigenvalue λ_1. If $\mathbf{v}_1$ is an associated eigenvector, then the vectors $\mathbf{v}_1$ and $T(\mathbf{v}_1) = A\mathbf{v}_1 = \lambda_1\mathbf{v}_1$ must have the same length, $|\mathbf{v}_1| = |\lambda_1\mathbf{v}_1| = |\lambda_1||\mathbf{v}_1|$, so it follows that $\lambda_1 = 1$ or $\lambda_1 = -1$.

Let $\mathbf{v}_1$ be a *unit* eigenvector associated with λ_1 and let W be the plane through the origin in $\mathbf{R}^3$ that is orthogonal to $\mathbf{v}_1$. Then let $\mathbf{v}_2$ and $\mathbf{v}_3$ be orthonormal vectors in W such that the orthonormal triple $\mathbf{v}_1$, $\mathbf{v}_2$, $\mathbf{v}_3$ determines a right-handed $x'y'z'$-coordinate system, as indicated in Figure 7.15. By Theorem 3 in Section 7.3, the matrix of the linear transformation T in this new coordinate system is

$$A' = P^{-1}AP = P^TAP \tag{11}$$

where $P = [\mathbf{v}_1 \quad \mathbf{v}_2 \quad \mathbf{v}_3]$. Because the isometry T preserves angles, the vectors $T(\mathbf{v}_2) = A\mathbf{v}_2$ and $T(\mathbf{v}_3) = A\mathbf{v}_3$ are orthogonal to $\mathbf{v}_1$, and so T carries the subspace W

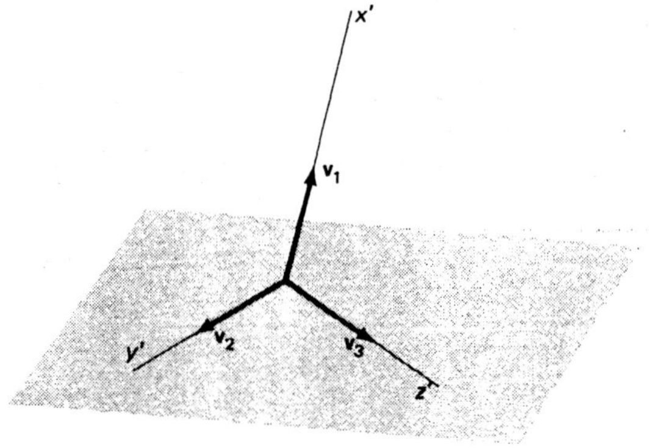

7.15 The new coordinate system.

to itself. It therefore follows from (11) that

$$A' = \begin{bmatrix} \mathbf{v}_1^T \\ \mathbf{v}_2^T \\ \mathbf{v}_3^T \end{bmatrix} [A\mathbf{v}_1 \quad A\mathbf{v}_2 \quad A\mathbf{v}_3];$$

$$A' = \left[\begin{array}{c|cc} \lambda_1 & 0 & 0 \\ \hline 0 & \multicolumn{2}{c}{\multirow{2}{*}{B'}} \\ 0 & & \end{array}\right], \tag{12}$$

since $\mathbf{v}_1^T A \mathbf{v}_1 = \lambda_1 \mathbf{v}_1^T \mathbf{v}_1 = \lambda_1$.

Now the fact that A is orthogonal implies first that A' is orthogonal (Problem 13), and then that the 2×2 matrix B' in (12) is orthogonal (Problem 14). Hence Theorem 1 implies that B' is the matrix of an isometry of the plane W (regarded as a copy of $\mathbf{R}^2$ with basis $\mathbf{v}_2$, $\mathbf{v}_3$), and then Theorem 2 implies that either

$$B' = \begin{bmatrix} \cos\theta & -\sin\theta \\ \sin\theta & \cos\theta \end{bmatrix} \quad \text{or} \quad B' = \begin{bmatrix} \cos\theta & \sin\theta \\ \sin\theta & -\cos\theta \end{bmatrix}. \tag{13}$$

Therefore there are four cases to consider, depending on whether $\lambda_1 = +1$ or $\lambda_1 = -1$ and on which of the two forms in (13) B' has.

CASE 1: If

$$A' = \begin{bmatrix} 1 & 0 & 0 \\ 0 & \cos\theta & -\sin\theta \\ 0 & \sin\theta & \cos\theta \end{bmatrix}$$

then, looking at the matrix in (8), we see that the transformation T is a rotation about the x'-axis through an angle θ.

CASE 2: If

$$A' = \begin{bmatrix} -1 & 0 & 0 \\ 0 & \cos\theta & -\sin\theta \\ 0 & \sin\theta & \cos\theta \end{bmatrix}$$

$$= \begin{bmatrix} 1 & 0 & 0 \\ 0 & \cos\theta & -\sin\theta \\ 0 & \sin\theta & \cos\theta \end{bmatrix} \begin{bmatrix} -1 & 0 & 0 \\ 0 & 1 & 0 \\ 0 & 0 & 1 \end{bmatrix}$$

then T consists of a reflection in the $y'z'$-plane followed by a rotation about the x'-axis.

CASES 3 AND 4: If

$$A' = \begin{bmatrix} \pm 1 & 0 & 0 \\ 0 & \cos\theta & \sin\theta \\ 0 & \sin\theta & -\cos\theta \end{bmatrix} \tag{14}$$

then the matrix A' is *symmetric*. In Problem 15 we ask you to show in this event that the remaining eigenvalues of A (taken in the proper order) are $\lambda_2 = 1$ and $\lambda_3 = -1$. Therefore it follows—see the discussion of Equation (27) in Section 7.3—that the new coordinate system can be chosen so that

$$A' = \begin{bmatrix} \pm 1 & 0 & 0 \\ 0 & 1 & 0 \\ 0 & 0 & -1 \end{bmatrix}. \tag{15}$$

If $\lambda_1 = +1$ here, then the transformation T is a reflection in the $x'y'$-plane, whereas if $\lambda_1 = -1$ it is a rotation of 180° about the y'-axis, because

$$\begin{bmatrix} \cos 180^\circ & 0 & -\sin 180^\circ \\ 0 & 1 & 0 \\ \sin 180^\circ & 0 & \cos 180^\circ \end{bmatrix} = \begin{bmatrix} -1 & 0 & 0 \\ 0 & 1 & 0 \\ 0 & 0 & -1 \end{bmatrix}.$$

This analysis of the four possibilities in (12) completes the proof of the following theorem.

Theorem 3: *Linear Isometries of* $\mathbf{R}^3$
Every linear isometry $T: \mathbf{R}^3 \to \mathbf{R}^3$ is either

1. A rotation about some line through the origin, or
2. A reflection in a plane through the origin followed by a rotation about the line through the origin orthogonal to this plane.

In case (1) of the theorem we naturally call T a **rotation** of $\mathbf{R}^3$. In case (2) T is called a **rotary reflection**; the reflection and the rotation obviously can be carried out in either order. Of course $\theta = 0$ in (1) yields the identity transformation of $\mathbf{R}^3$. In summary, Theorem 3 means that *every linear isometry T of $\mathbf{R}^3$ is either a rotation or a rotary reflection.* Looking at the four cases in the proof, we see that T is a rotation if $|A| = 1$ and a rotary reflection if $|A| = -1$.

For a tangible application of Theorem 3, consider a solid spherical ball whose center is at the origin. Then Theorem 3 implies that any rigid motion (in $\mathbf{R}^3$) of this ball that leaves the origin fixed is a rotation about some line through the origin. Therefore this rigid motion leaves fixed the two points in which the axis of rotation intersects the spherical surface of the ball. For instance, envision a spherical globe that rests on a stand, but which can be picked up for closer examination. If this globe is passed around the room as several people examine it, and the last person returns it to its stand, then some two opposite points on the globe wind up precisely where they started!

COMPUTER GRAPHICS

We consider now the problem of representing pictorially, on a computer screen, a body in space determined by n points $P_1, P_2, \ldots, P_n$ called its **vertices**, together with line segments called **edges** joining specified pairs of its vertices. Let (x_i, y_i, z_i) denote the coordinates of the ith vertex P_i. We will take the xy-plane to be the plane of the computer screen, with the positive z-axis pointing out in space toward the viewer, as indicated in Figure 7.16.

The most simple-minded scheme for representing the body on the computer screen involves an *orthogonal projection* into the xy-plane. To project each point $P_i(x_i, y_i, z_i)$ into the xy-plane, we simply ignore its third coordinate. Thus we plot the points $(x_1, y_1), (x_2, y_2), \ldots, (x_n, y_n)$ and then join each appropriate pair of these points with a line segment to represent the edges of the body. The result is a two-dimensional *line drawing* of the body. Unfortunately, such a line drawing will not normally represent the body well—imagine what happens when a cube is projected orthogonally into a plane parallel to one of its faces. Thus we need to be able to change either the plane of projection or the orientation of the body before projection.

It is simplest to rotate the body in space and then project its vertices in the direction parallel to the z-axis, thus orthogonally into the xy-plane of the computer

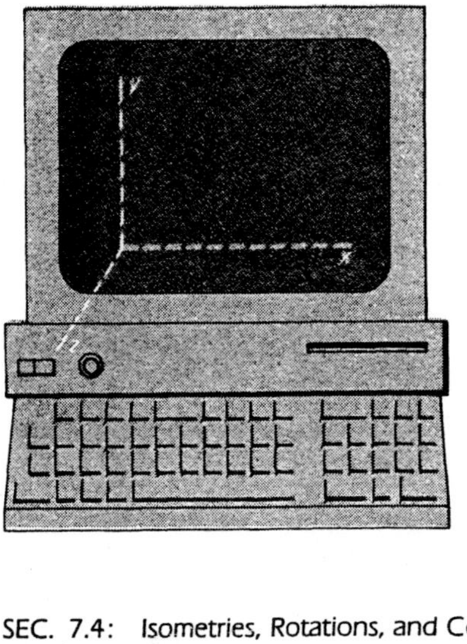

7.16 The computer screen and the xyz-coordinate system.

screen. In order to calculate the images of the vertices under a rotation, we introduce the **coordinate matrix**

$$P = \begin{bmatrix} x_1 & x_2 & \cdots & x_n \\ y_1 & y_2 & \cdots & y_n \\ z_1 & z_2 & \cdots & z_n \end{bmatrix} \tag{16}$$

of the body. Thus P is the $3 \times n$ matrix whose jth column vector consists of the coordinates of the jth vertex P_j of the body.

If the orthogonal 3×3 matrix A is the matrix of the rotation $T: \mathbf{R}^3 \to \mathbf{R}^3$, then the vertices of the rotated body are given by the columns of the product matrix

$$P' = AP = \begin{bmatrix} x'_1 & x'_2 & \cdots & x'_n \\ y'_1 & y'_2 & \cdots & y'_n \\ z'_1 & z'_2 & \cdots & z'_n \end{bmatrix}. \tag{17}$$

The projection (into the xy-plane of the coordinate screen) of the rotated body then has vertices $(x'_1, y'_1), (x'_2, y'_2), \ldots, (x'_n, y'_n)$ that we obtain by deleting the z-coordinates in the columns of the matrix in (17).

EXAMPLE 2 The triangle shown in Figure 7.17 has coordinate matrix

$$P = \begin{bmatrix} 5 & 0 & 0 \\ 0 & 5 & 0 \\ 0 & 0 & 5 \end{bmatrix}.$$

Let us rotate or "spin" this triangle about the y-axis through the angle $\theta \approx 36.87°$ such that $\cos\theta = \frac{4}{5}$ and $\sin\theta = \frac{3}{5}$. Consulting (9) for the matrix of a rotation about the y-axis, we find that the coordinate matrix of the rotated triangle is

$$P' = \begin{bmatrix} \frac{4}{5} & 0 & -\frac{3}{5} \\ 0 & 1 & 0 \\ \frac{3}{5} & 0 & \frac{4}{5} \end{bmatrix} \begin{bmatrix} 5 & 0 & 0 \\ 0 & 5 & 0 \\ 0 & 0 & 5 \end{bmatrix}$$

$$= \begin{bmatrix} 4 & 0 & -3 \\ 0 & 5 & 0 \\ 3 & 0 & 4 \end{bmatrix}.$$

Figure 7.18 shows the projection of this rotated triangle.

Now let us instead rotate or "tip" the original triangle of Figure 7.17 about the x-axis through the same angle $\theta \approx 36.87°$. Consulting (8) for the matrix of a rotation about the x-axis, we find that the coordinate matrix of the tipped triangle is

$$P'' = \begin{bmatrix} 1 & 0 & 0 \\ 0 & \frac{4}{5} & -\frac{3}{5} \\ 0 & \frac{3}{5} & \frac{4}{5} \end{bmatrix} \begin{bmatrix} 5 & 0 & 0 \\ 0 & 5 & 0 \\ 0 & 0 & 5 \end{bmatrix}$$

$$= \begin{bmatrix} 5 & 0 & 0 \\ 0 & 4 & -3 \\ 0 & 3 & 4 \end{bmatrix}.$$

Figure 7.19 shows the projection of this tipped triangle.

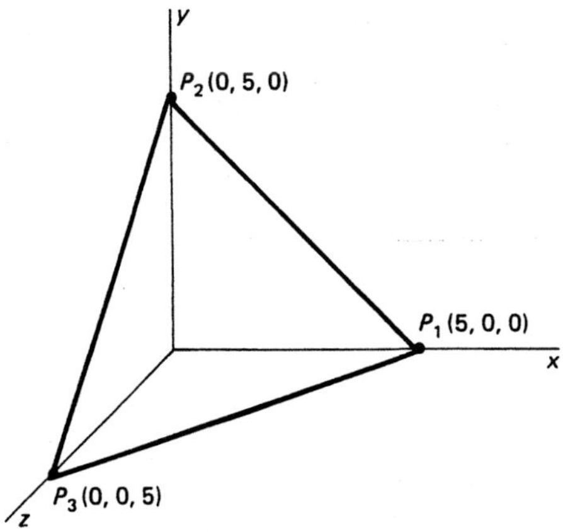

7.17 The triangle of Example 2.

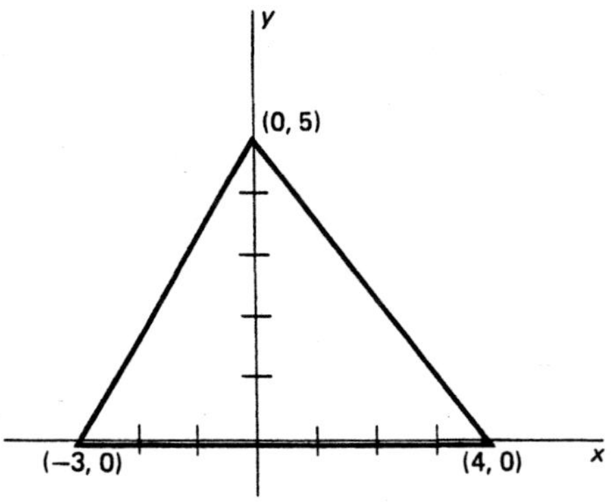

7.18 Projection of the spun triangle.

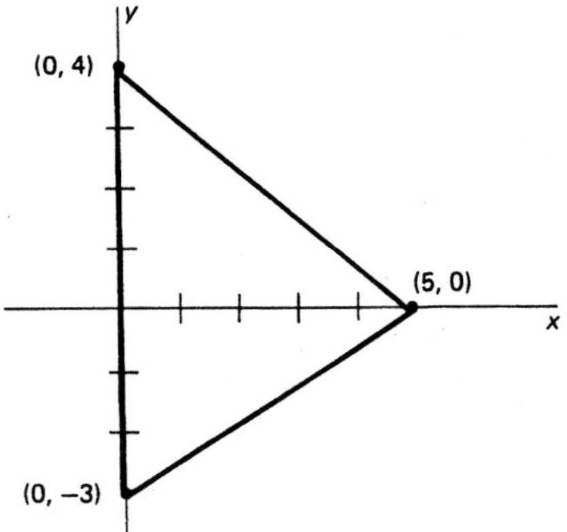

7.19 Projection of the tipped triangle.

```
100 REM--Program POLYHEDR
110 REM--Draws polyhedron whose vertices and
120 REM--edges are specified in data statements
130 REM
140 REM--Initialization:
150 REM
160      SCREEN 1  :  CLS  :  KEY OFF
170      WINDOW (-4,-4) - (4,4)
175      DIM A(3,3) : PI = 3.141593 : DEFINT I,J,K,M,N
180 REM--Vertex data:
190      DATA 6,-2,0,1,-2,2,0,-2,0,-1,2,0,1,0,2,0,2,0,-1
200 REM--Edge data:
210      DATA 9,1,2,1,3,2,3,1,4,2,5,3,6,4,5,5,6,4,6
220 REM--Read vertices:
230      READ N   'Number of vertices
240      DIM X(N), Y(N), Z(N)
250      FOR J = 1 TO N
260          READ X(J), Y(J), Z(J)
270      NEXT J
280 REM
290 REM--Spin:
300      INPUT "SPIN ANGLE (deg)"; SPIN
310      SPIN = SPIN*PI/180
320      A(1,1) = COS(SPIN) : A(1,2) = 0 : A(1,3) = -SIN(SPIN)
330      A(2,1) =     0     : A(2,2) = 1 : A(2,3) =     0
340      A(3,1) = SIN(SPIN) : A(3,2) = 0 : A(3,3) =  COS(SPIN)
350      GOSUB 600              'Multiply by spin matrix
360 REM
390 REM--Tip:
400      INPUT "TIP  ANGLE (deg)"; TIP
410      TIP = TIP*PI/180
420      A(1,1) = 1  :  A(1,2) =    0    : A(1,3) =    0
430      A(2,1) = 0  :  A(2,2) = COS(TIP): A(2,3) = -SIN(TIP)
440      A(3,1) = 0  :  A(3,2) = SIN(TIP): A(3,3) =  COS(TIP)
450      GOSUB 600      'Multiply by tip matrix
460 REM
500 REM--Plot edges:
510      READ M   'Number of edges
520      FOR K = 1 TO M
530          READ I, J   'Vertices of next edge
540          LINE (X(I),Y(I)) - (X(J),Y(J))
550      NEXT K
560      GOTO 560
570 REM
590 REM--Matrix multiplication:
600      FOR J = 1 TO N
610          X = X(J)  :  Y  =  Y(J)  : Z  =  Z(J)
620          X(J) = A(1,1)*X + A(1,2)*Y + A(1,3)*Z
630          Y(J) = A(2,1)*X + A(2,2)*Y + A(2,3)*Z
640          Z(J) = A(3,1)*X + A(3,2)*Y + A(3,3)*Z
650      NEXT J
660      RETURN
700      END
```

7.20 Listing of Program POLYHEDR.

A common practice in computer graphics is to combine

- a **spin**—a rotation about the y-axis, and
- a **tip**—a rotation about the x-axis,

followed by an orthogonal projection into the xy-plane, to produce an acceptable representation of a given body. Figure 7.20 shows a listing of an IBM-PC BASIC program written for this purpose.

The first entry in data line 190 is the number of vertices (six in this case) of the body we want to picture. Each succeeding *triple* of entries specifies one of these vertices. Thus our body has the vertices

$$P_1(-2, 0, 1), \quad P_2(-2, 2, 0), \quad P_3(-2, 0, -1), \quad P_4(2, 0, 1),$$
$$P_5(0, 2, 0), \quad \text{and} \quad P_6(2, 0, -1).$$

The first entry in data line 210 is the number of edges (nine in this case) that the body has. Each succeeding *pair* of entries specifies the vertices of one of these edges. Thus our body has edges

$$P_1P_2, \quad P_1P_3, \quad P_2P_3, \quad P_1P_4, \quad P_2P_5, \quad P_3P_6,$$
$$P_4P_5, \quad P_5P_6, \quad \text{and} \quad P_4P_6.$$

Figure 7.21 shows an artist's standard sketch of this body—it is a (truncated) prism.

Lines 230–270 read the coordinates of the vertices into three arrays X(J), Y(J), and Z(J) corresponding to the row vectors of the coordinate matrix P. Lines 300–350 first call for the desired angle of SPIN to be input, next set up the "spin matrix," and then go to the subroutine in lines 600–650 to multiply P by this spin matrix. Lines 400–450 first call for us to input the desired TIP angle and then set up the "tip matrix" and multiply by it. Figures 7.22–7.26 show several views of the prism produced by this program. The front, side, and top views were produced first to test the execution of the program. Figures 7.25 and 7.26 are representative views that involve both spinning about the y-axis and tipping about the x-axis.

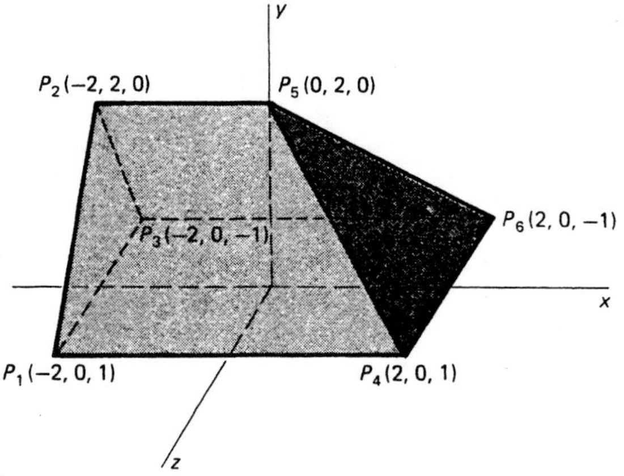

7.21 Artist's sketch of the prism.

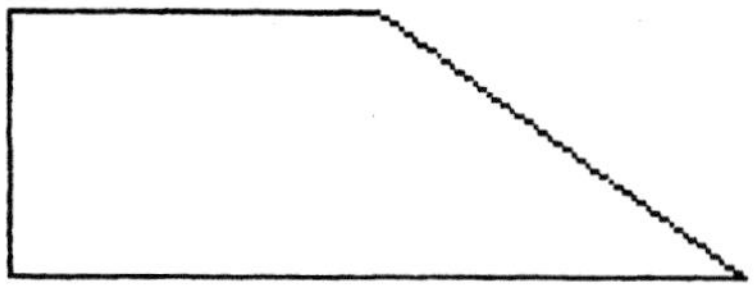

7.22 Front view of the prism (spin 0°, tip 0°).

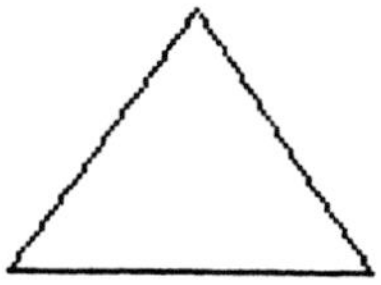

7.23 Side view of the prism (spin 90°, tip 0°).

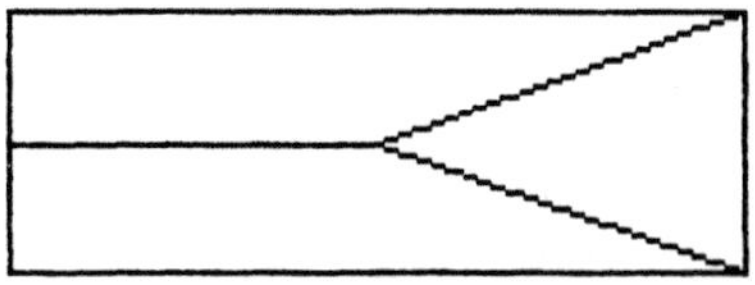

7.24 Top view of the prism (spin 0°, tip 90°).

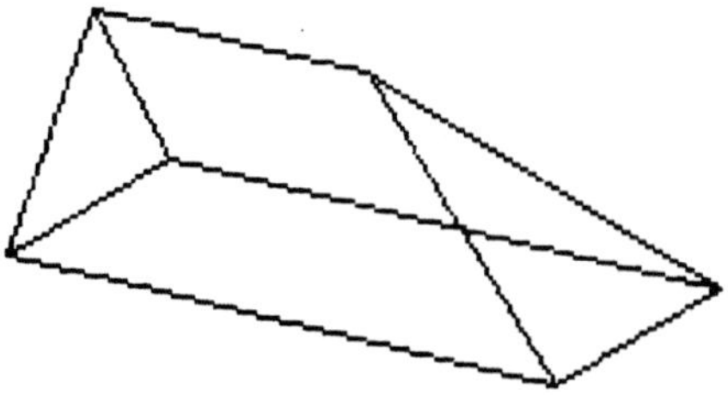

7.25 A three-dimensional projection of the prism (spin 30°, tip 30°).

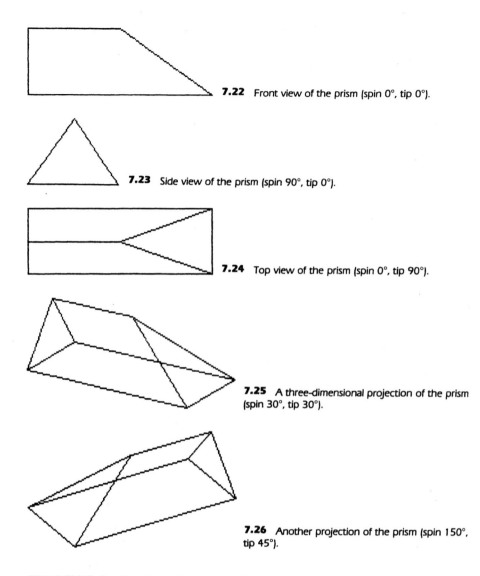

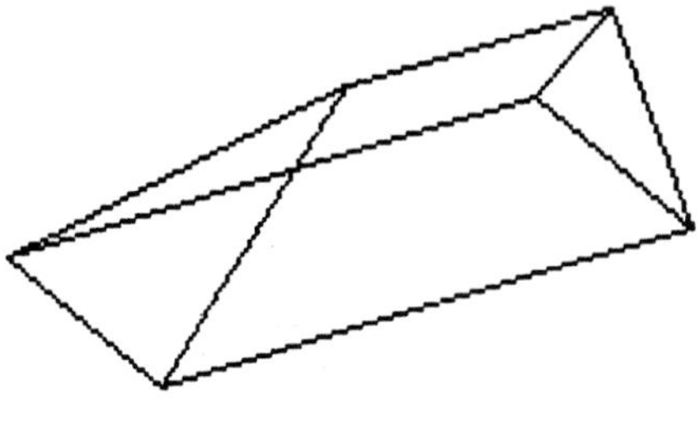

7.26 Another projection of the prism (spin 150°, tip 45°).

EXAMPLE 3 The view of the prism shown in Figure 7.25 involves a rotation of 30° about the y-axis followed by a rotation of 30° about the x-axis. Theorem 3 implies that the composition $T:\mathbf{R}^3 \to \mathbf{R}^3$ of these two rotations is a single rotation through *some angle* about *some axis* through the origin in $\mathbf{R}^3$. Though it involves considerable numerical computation, let us determine this axis and angle of rotation. Because $\cos 30° = \frac{1}{2}\sqrt{3}$ and $\sin 30° = \frac{1}{2}$, the matrix of T is

$$A = \begin{bmatrix} 1 & 0 & 0 \\ 0 & \frac{1}{2}\sqrt{3} & -\frac{1}{2} \\ 0 & \frac{1}{2} & \frac{1}{2}\sqrt{3} \end{bmatrix} \begin{bmatrix} \frac{1}{2}\sqrt{3} & 0 & -\frac{1}{2} \\ 0 & 1 & 0 \\ \frac{1}{2} & 0 & \frac{1}{2}\sqrt{3} \end{bmatrix} = \begin{bmatrix} \frac{1}{2}\sqrt{3} & 0 & -\frac{1}{2} \\ -\frac{1}{4} & \frac{1}{2}\sqrt{3} & -\frac{1}{4}\sqrt{3} \\ \frac{1}{4}\sqrt{3} & \frac{1}{2} & \frac{3}{4} \end{bmatrix}.$$

From the proof of Theorem 3 we know that $\lambda = 1$ is an eigenvalue of A. To find a corresponding eigenvector, we compute the reduced echelon form

$$E = \begin{bmatrix} 1 & 0 & 3.73205 \\ 0 & 1 & -3.73205 \\ 0 & 0 & 0 \end{bmatrix}$$

of $A - I$. (The exact value of the approximation 3.73205 that appears in these computations is $2 + \sqrt{3}$.) It follows that $\mathbf{v} = (3.73205, -3.73205, -1)$ is an eigenvector of A associated with the eigenvalue $\lambda = 1$. This vector $\mathbf{v}$ determines the axis of rotation for T.

To find the angle of rotation, we begin with the vector $\mathbf{u} = (1, 1, 0)$ orthogonal to $\mathbf{v}$ and calculate

$$\mathbf{w} = T(\mathbf{u}) = A\mathbf{u} = (0.86603, 0.61603, 0.93301).$$

Then $\mathbf{u}$ and $\mathbf{w}$ lie in the plane orthogonal to the axis of rotation, and it turns out that $\mathbf{u} \times \mathbf{w} = \frac{1}{4}\mathbf{v}$, so $(\mathbf{u}, \mathbf{w}, \mathbf{v})$ is a right-handed triple of vectors. Finally the angle θ of rotation between $\mathbf{u}$ and $\mathbf{w} = T(\mathbf{u})$ is given by

$$\cos\theta = \frac{\mathbf{u} \cdot \mathbf{w}}{|\mathbf{u}|\,|\mathbf{w}|} \approx 0.74103,$$

so $\theta \approx 42.18°$. Thus T is a rotation through this angle about the line through the origin determined by the vector $\mathbf{v} = (3.73205, -3.73205, -1)$, and the direction of rotation is the direction in which the curled fingers of the right hand point when the thumb points in the direction of $\mathbf{v}$.

7.4 PROBLEMS

1. Suppose that the linear transformation

$$T : \mathbf{R}^n \to \mathbf{R}^n$$

preserves distances. Show that it also preserves dot products. *Suggestion*: Expand $|\mathbf{u} + \mathbf{v}|^2 = (\mathbf{u} + \mathbf{v}) \cdot (\mathbf{u} + \mathbf{v})$.

2. Suppose that A is an $n \times n$ matrix and $\mathbf{u}$ and $\mathbf{v}$ are vectors in $\mathbf{R}^n$. Show that $\mathbf{u} \cdot A\mathbf{v} = (A^T\mathbf{u}) \cdot \mathbf{v}$.

3. Let the linear transformation $T : \mathbf{R}^n \to \mathbf{R}^n$ defined by $T(\mathbf{x}) = A\mathbf{x}$ be an isometry. Show as follows that the matrix A is orthogonal.
(a) Deduce from Problems 1 and 2 that $(A^TA\mathbf{x}) \cdot \mathbf{y} = \mathbf{x} \cdot \mathbf{y}$ for every pair of vectors $\mathbf{x}$ and $\mathbf{y}$ in $\mathbf{R}^n$.
(b) Conclude from the result of part (a) that $A^TA = I$.

4. If $F : \mathbf{R}^2 \to \mathbf{R}^2$ is the reflection in the line $x_1 = 1$, express F in the form $F(\mathbf{x}) = A\mathbf{x} + \mathbf{b}$. *Suggestion*: First translate the line $x_1 = 1$ to the y-axis by the translation $\mathbf{x} \to \mathbf{x} - \mathbf{e}_1$, then reflect in the y-axis, then translate the y-axis back to the line $x_1 = 1$.

5. If $F : \mathbf{R}^2 \to \mathbf{R}^2$ is the reflection in the line $x_1 - x_2 = 2$, express F in the form $F(\mathbf{x}) = A\mathbf{x} + \mathbf{b}$. *Suggestion*: Note that the given line passes through the point $(1, -1)$, and translate it to the line $x_1 = x_2$ and back.

6. If $F : \mathbf{R}^2 \to \mathbf{R}^2$ is the counterclockwise rotation through an angle of 90° about the point (2, 3), express F in the form $F(\mathbf{x}) = A\mathbf{x} + \mathbf{b}$. *Suggestion*: Translate the point (2, 3) to the origin, then rotate through 90°, then translate back.

7. Suppose that $F:\mathbf{R}^2 \to \mathbf{R}^2$ is the counterclockwise rotation through the angle θ about the point (5, 5), where $\theta \approx 36.87°$ is the angle with $\cos\theta = \frac{4}{5}$ and $\sin\theta = \frac{3}{5}$. Express F in the form $F(\mathbf{x}) = A\mathbf{x} + \mathbf{b}$.

8. Deduce from Theorem 2 in this section and from Problem 34 in Section 7.1 that every linear isometry of $\mathbf{R}^2$ either is a reflection or is the composition of two reflections.

9. In accordance with Theorem 3, express the *inversion* $T:\mathbf{R}^3 \to \mathbf{R}^3$ defined by $T(\mathbf{x}) = -\mathbf{x}$ as the composition of a rotation and a reflection through a plane orthogonal to the axis of rotation.

10. Let the orthogonal matrix A be the matrix of a rotation of $\mathbf{R}^3$ about a line through the origin. Let $F:\mathbf{R}^3 \to \mathbf{R}^3$ be the rotation through the same angle about a parallel line through the point $\mathbf{a}$. Show that F can be expressed in the form $F(\mathbf{x}) = A\mathbf{x} + \mathbf{b}$, and find $\mathbf{b}$.

11. Let $T:\mathbf{R}^3 \to \mathbf{R}^3$ be a right-handed 90° rotation with axis the line $y = x$ in the xy-plane (this line is determined by the vector $\mathbf{v} = (1, 1, 0)$). Find the matrix A of T. *Suggestion*: First rotate about the z-axis by $-45°$ to carry the line $y = x$ to the x-axis, then rotate by 45° about the x-axis, and finally rotate the x-axis back to the line $y = x$.

12. Let $T:\mathbf{R}^3 \to \mathbf{R}^3$ be a right-handed 45° rotation about the line L through the origin determined by the vector $\mathbf{v} = (1, 1, 1)$. Find the matrix A of T. *Suggestion*: First rotate about the z-axis to move L into the xz-plane, then rotate about the y-axis to move it to the x-axis.

13. Show that the matrix A' in Equation (12) is orthogonal.

14. Show that the 2×2 matrix B' in Equation (12) is orthogonal.

15. Show that the eigenvalues of the matrix A' in Equation (14) are $\lambda_1 = \pm 1$, $\lambda_2 = 1$, and $\lambda_3 = -1$.

16. Let $P_1P_2P_3$ be the triangle of Example 2 (shown in Figure 7.17) and let $\theta \approx 36.87°$ be the angle such that $\cos\theta = \frac{4}{5}$. Determine the image $Q_1Q_2Q_3$ of this triangle under a spin of θ about the y-axis, then a tip of θ about the x-axis, and then an orthogonal projection into the xy-plane.

17. Consider the rectangle in the xy-plane with vertices $P_1(0, 0, 0)$, $P_2(25, 0, 0)$, $P_3(25, 50, 0)$, and $P_4(0, 50, 0)$. Determine the image $Q_1Q_2Q_3Q_4$ of this rectangle in the xy-plane under the sequence of transformations described in Problem 16.

18. Consider the pyramid with vertices $P_1(-1, 0, 0)$, $P_2(0, 0, 2)$, $P_3(1, 0, 0)$, and $P_4(0, 2, 0)$. Determine the images of these four vertices under a spin of 45° about the y-axis, followed by a tip of 30° about the x-axis, and then an orthogonal projection into the xy-plane.

In Problems 19 and 20, determine (as in Example 3) the axis and angle of rotation corresponding to the given spin and tip.

19. First a spin of 90°, then a tip of 90°.

20. First a spin of 150°, then a tip of 45°.

CHAPTER REVIEW QUESTIONS

1. What is meant by a linear transformation T from $\mathbf{R}^n$ to $\mathbf{R}^m$?

2. Give several examples of transformations from $\mathbf{R}^2$ to $\mathbf{R}^2$ that are not linear.

3. Let A be an $m \times n$ matrix and $\mathbf{b}$ be an m-vector, and let $T:\mathbf{R}^n \to \mathbf{R}^m$ be defined by $T(\mathbf{x}) = A\mathbf{x} + \mathbf{b}$. Under what conditions on A and $\mathbf{b}$ is the transformation T linear?

4. Suppose that $T:\mathbf{R}^n \to \mathbf{R}^m$ is linear. Tell how to find an $m \times n$ matrix A such that $T(\mathbf{x}) = A\mathbf{x}$. Is there only one such matrix A? What is the jth column vector of A?

5. Use the answer to the final part of Question 4 to find the matrix of the linear transformation $T:\mathbf{R}^2 \to \mathbf{R}^2$ if T is a reflection in the line $y = -x$ followed by a 90° counterclockwise rotation. What is the geometric effect of the transformation T?

6. Explain briefly why every linear transformation $T:\mathbf{R}^2 \to \mathbf{R}^2$ with nonsingular matrix A is a finite composition of reflections, expansions, compressions, and shears.

7. Let V and W be vector spaces. Can there exist two different linear transformations from V to W that have the same values on a set of basis vectors for V? Why or why not?

8. Given two n-dimensional vector spaces V and W with bases $\{\mathbf{v}_1, \mathbf{v}_2, \ldots, \mathbf{v}_n\}$ and $\{\mathbf{w}_1, \mathbf{w}_2, \ldots, \mathbf{w}_n\}$, respectively, define explicitly an isomorphism from V to W.

9. Can a linear transformation $T: \mathbf{R}^n \to \mathbf{R}^n$ be a mapping *onto* $\mathbf{R}^n$ without being an isomorphism?

10. Let T be a linear transformation from $\mathbf{R}^7$ onto a 3-dimensional subspace of $\mathbf{R}^5$. What is the dimension of the kernel of T?

11. If the linear transformation $T: \mathbf{R}^7 \to \mathbf{R}^3$ has a 4-dimensional kernel, what can you conclude about the range of T?

12. Can a linear transformation $T: \mathbf{R}^5 \to \mathbf{R}^3$ have a zero kernel? Can a linear transformation $T: \mathbf{R}^3 \to \mathbf{R}^5$ be an onto mapping? Why or why not?

13. What is meant by the coordinate vector $\mathbf{x}$ of an element $\mathbf{v}$ of a vector space V with respect to the basis $B = \{\mathbf{v}_1, \mathbf{v}_2, \ldots, \mathbf{v}_n\}$?

14. Let $\mathbf{x}$ and $\mathbf{y}$ be the coordinate vectors of the same point of $\mathbf{R}^n$ with respect to the two bases

$$B = \{\mathbf{u}_1, \mathbf{u}_2, \ldots, \mathbf{u}_n\} \quad \text{and} \quad C = \{\mathbf{v}_1, \mathbf{v}_2, \ldots, \mathbf{v}_n\}.$$

Write a simple equation that can be solved for either of the vectors $\mathbf{x}$ and $\mathbf{y}$ in terms of the other.

15. Let B and C be bases for the finite-dimensional vector spaces V and W, respectively. What is meant by the matrix A of a linear transformation $T: V \to W$ with respect to these two bases? What is the jth column vector of A?

16. Let V be a vector space with basis $B = \{\mathbf{u}_1, \mathbf{u}_2, \ldots, \mathbf{u}_n\}$ and let T be a linear operator on V. Explain what is meant by the matrix A of T with respect to the basis B, and the sense in which the transformation T is described by the equation $\mathbf{y} = A\mathbf{x}$.

17. Let A_1 and A_2 be the matrices of the linear operator $T: V \to V$ with respect to two different bases for V. Explain why it follows that the matrices A_1 and A_2 have the same determinant and the same eigenvalues. Precisely what is the relationship between A_1 and A_2?

8

Further Applications

8.1

Conic Sections and Quadratic Forms

In this section we apply our knowledge of linear algebra to the geometrical problem of determining the graph in the xy-plane of an equation of the form

$$ax^2 + 2bxy + cy^2 + dx + ey + f = 0, \tag{1}$$

where the coefficients $a, b, \ldots, f$ are real constants with a, b, and c not all zero. Such an equation is called a **second degree equation in x and y**.

The reason we write $2b$ rather than b for the coefficient of the xy-term in (1) is that the nature of the graph is determined largely by the **associated quadratic form**

$$ax^2 + 2bxy + cy^2 = [x \quad y]\begin{bmatrix} a & b \\ b & c \end{bmatrix}\begin{bmatrix} x \\ y \end{bmatrix} \tag{2}$$

in x and y that corresponds to the symmetric 2×2 matrix

$$A = \begin{bmatrix} a & b \\ b & c \end{bmatrix}. \tag{3}$$

In general, the **quadratic form** q in the variables $x_1, x_2, \ldots, x_n$ that corresponds to the *symmetric* $n \times n$ matrix A is the function $q: \mathbf{R}^n \to \mathbf{R}$ defined by

$$q(\mathbf{x}) = \mathbf{x}^T A\mathbf{x}, \tag{4}$$

where $\mathbf{x}$ denotes the (column) vector with entries $x_1, x_2, \ldots, x_n$. In this section we are concerned with the case $n = 2$ that appears in (2), with $\mathbf{x} = (x, y) = [x \quad y]^T$.

The key to the analysis of the second degree equation in (1) is the fact that the symmetric matrix A in (3) is orthogonally diagonalizable (by Theorem 4 in Section 6.4). Using this fact we will show that, apart from a few degenerate cases, the graph of every second degree equation in x and y is a conic section. The phrase **conic sections** is derived from the fact that these are the curves in which a plane intersects a cone. The cone used is a right circular cone with two *nappes* extending infinitely far in both directions, as in Figure 8.1. There are three types of conic sections, as illustrated in Figure 8.2. If the cutting plane is parallel to some generator of the cone, then the curve

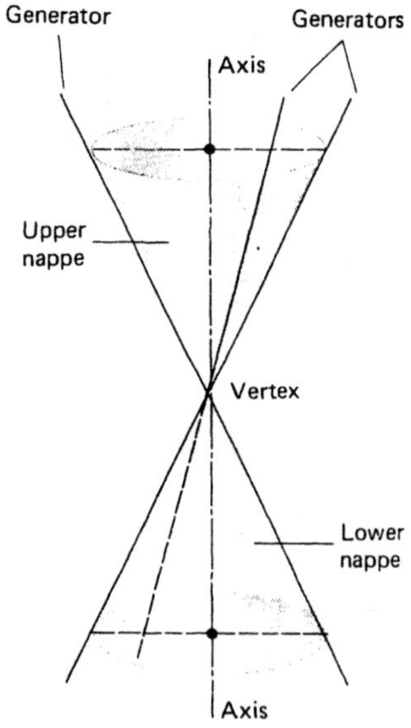

8.1 A cone of two nappes.

of intersection is a **parabola**. Otherwise it is either a single closed curve—an **ellipse**—or a **hyperbola** with two branches.

It turns out that if an appropriate *xy*-coordinate system is set up in the intersecting plane of Figure 8.2, then the equations of the three types of conic sections take the following forms:

$$\text{Parabola:} \quad y^2 = kx \quad \text{or} \quad x^2 = ky; \tag{5}$$

$$\text{Ellipse:} \quad \frac{x^2}{a^2} + \frac{y^2}{b^2} = 1; \tag{6}$$

$$\text{Hyperbola:} \quad \frac{x^2}{a^2} - \frac{y^2}{b^2} = 1 \quad \text{or} \quad \frac{y^2}{a^2} - \frac{x^2}{b^2} = 1. \tag{7}$$

[Derivations of these equations may be found in Section 14-6 of Edwards and Penney, *Calculus and Analytic Geometry*, 2nd ed., (Englewood Cliffs, N.J.: Prentice Hall, 1986).] Conic sections with these equations are illustrated in Figures 8.3–8.5. A conic

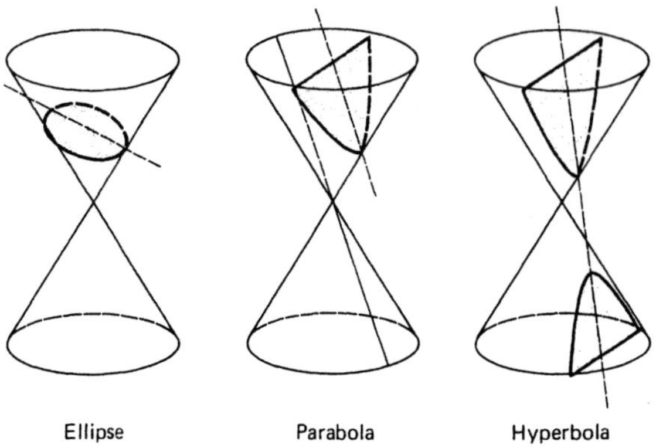

8.2 The conic sections.

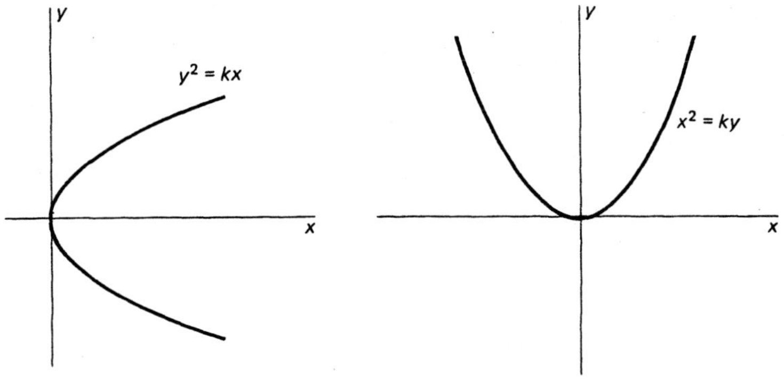

8.3 Parabolas with $k > 0$. If $k < 0$, then they open in the opposite directions.

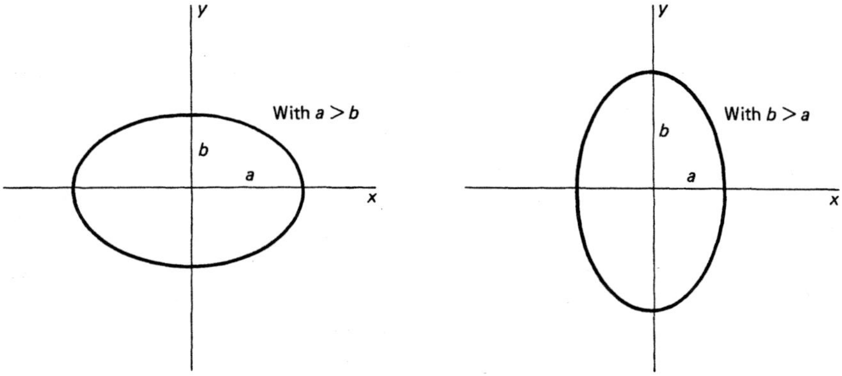

8.4 Ellipses $x^2/a^2 + y^2/b^2 = 1$ with $a > b > 0$ and with $b > a > 0$. If $a = b > 0$ the graph is a circle.

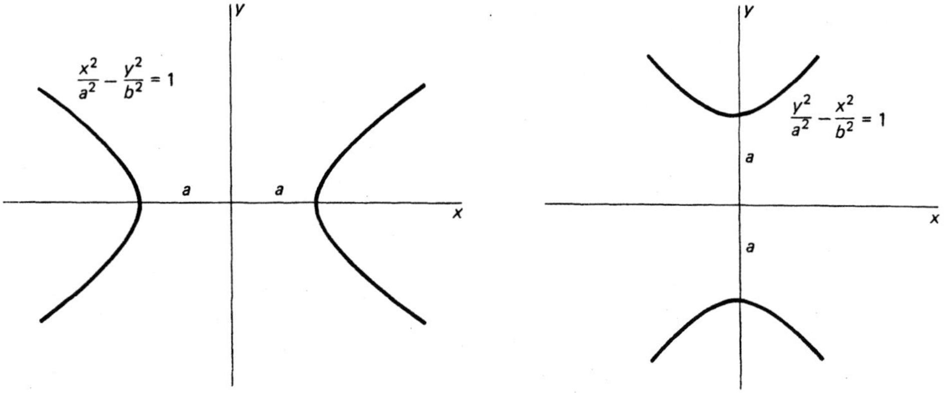

8.5 Hyperbolas with the equations in (7).

section is said to be in **standard position** relative to the coordinate axes if its equation takes one of the forms listed in Equations (5)–(7).

EXAMPLE 1 The equation $4x^2 + 9y^2 - 36 = 0$ can be written in the form

$$\frac{x^2}{9} + \frac{y^2}{4} = 1,$$

so its graph is an ellipse with $a = 3$ and $b = 2$. Note the significance of a and b: The ellipse has x-intercepts $(a, 0)$ and $(-a, 0)$, and y-intercepts $(0, b)$ and $(0, -b)$. It is also clear (replace x with $-x$ or y with $-y$) that the graph is symmetric about the y-axis as well as about the x-axis.

The equation $9x^2 - 4y^2 + 36 = 0$ can be written in the form

$$\frac{y^2}{9} - \frac{x^2}{4} = 1,$$

so its graph is a hyperbola whose two branches intersect the y-axis in the points $(0, -3)$ and $(0, 3)$. Its graph, too, is symmetric about each coordinate axis.

Finally, the equation $y^2 + 4x = 0$ can be written in the form

$$y^2 = -4x,$$

and hence its graph is a parabola that opens along the negative x-axis. The parabola has lone intercept $(0, 0)$ and is symmetric about the x-axis (replacement of y with $-y$ leaves the equation unchanged) though not about the y-axis.

In addition to a parabola, ellipse, or hyperbola, the graph of a second degree equation in x and y can be a line, a pair of lines, a single point, or the empty set. These special cases, illustrated in the following example, are referred to as **degenerate conics**.

EXAMPLE 2 The graph of the equation $x^2 = 0$ is the y-axis. The graph of the equation $y^2 - 1 = 0$ consists of the two parallel lines $y = +1$ and $y = -1$. The graph of the equation $x^2 - y^2 = 0$ consists of the intersecting lines $y = x$ and $y = -x$. The graph of the equation $x^2 + y^2 = 0$ consists of the single point $(0, 0)$. And the graph of the equation $x^2 + y^2 + 1 = 0$ is the empty set.

Note that none of the equations in (5)–(7) contains both an x^2-term and an x-term, nor does any contain both a y^2-term and a y-term. The presence of either of these pairs in a second degree equation signals that the graph is a conic section that has been translated from its standard position. If no xy-term is present, then such pairs of terms can be removed from the equation—for the purpose of identifying its graph—by a process of *completing the square* and *translation of coordinates.*

EXAMPLE 3 To identify the graph of the second degree equation

$$3x^2 - 2y^2 - 18x + 8y + 13 = 0, \tag{8}$$

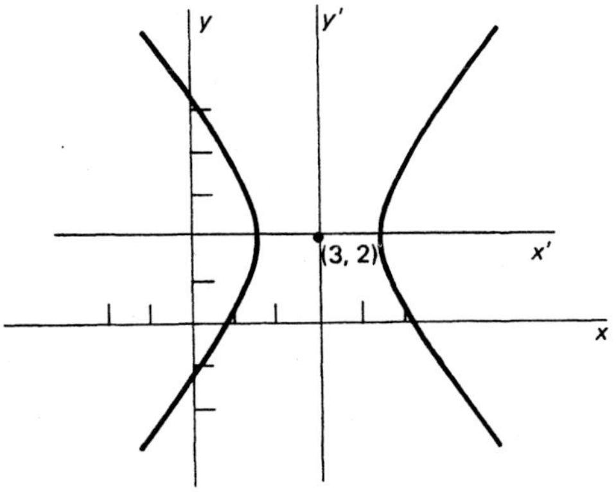

8.6 The translated hyperbola of Example 3.

we collect the x-terms and the y-terms and complete the square in each variable:

$$(3x^2 - 18x) - (2y^2 - 8y) + 13 = 0;$$
$$3(x^2 - 6x \qquad) - 2(y^2 - 4y \qquad) = -13;$$
$$3(x^2 - 6x + 9) - 2(y^2 - 4y + 4) = -13 + 27 - 8;$$
$$3(x - 3)^2 - 2(y - 2)^2 = 6.$$

We now make the substitution

$$x' = x - 3, \qquad y' = y - 2,$$

which corresponds to the choice of a new translated $x'y'$-coordinate system whose origin is at the old point $x = 3$, $y = 2$. The result is the equation

$$3(x')^2 - 2(y')^2 = 6;$$

that is,

$$\frac{(x')^2}{2} - \frac{(y')^2}{3} = 1.$$

This final equation has the form of the first equation in (7), with $a = \sqrt{2}$ and $b = \sqrt{3}$. Thus the graph of Equation (8) is a translated hyperbola and is in standard position in the $x'y'$-system, as shown in Figure 8.6.

An xy-term in a second degree equation is called a **cross-product term**. The presence of a cross-product term indicates that the graph is a conic section (possibly degenerate) that has been rotated out of standard position (and possibly translated as well). Our strategy for identifying the graph of a second degree equation containing a cross-product term is first to rotate the coordinate system by an orthogonal transformation in such a way that the cross-product term vanishes. Then, if necessary, we translate coordinates as in Example 3 to obtain a coordinate system in which the graph is a conic section in standard position, as in Figure 8.7.

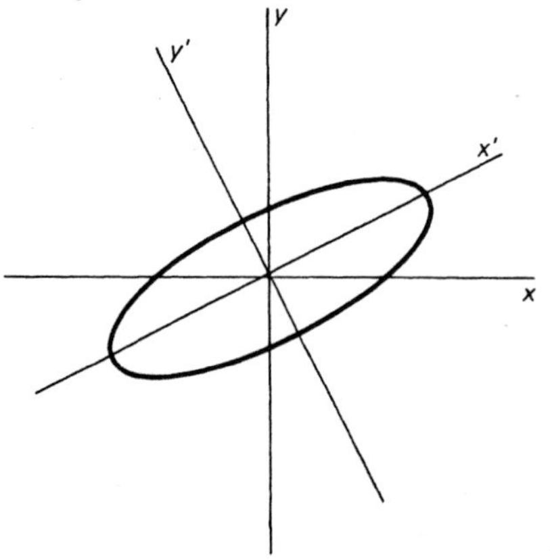

8.7 The ellipse is in standard position in the rotated $x'y'$-system.

To determine how to choose the appropriate rotation to eliminate a given cross-product term, we write the general second degree equation in the form

$$[x \quad y]\begin{bmatrix} a & b \\ b & c \end{bmatrix}\begin{bmatrix} x \\ y \end{bmatrix} + [d \quad e]\begin{bmatrix} x \\ y \end{bmatrix} + f = 0;$$

that is,

$$\mathbf{x}^T A\mathbf{x} + B\mathbf{x} + f = 0, \tag{9}$$

where

$$\mathbf{x} = \begin{bmatrix} x \\ y \end{bmatrix}, \qquad A = \begin{bmatrix} a & b \\ b & c \end{bmatrix}, \quad \text{and} \quad B = [d \quad e].$$

The associated quadratic form $q(\mathbf{x}) = \mathbf{x}^T A\mathbf{x}$ then contains the cross-product term (if $b \neq 0$).

We know by Theorem 4 in Section 6.4 that the symmetric matrix A is orthogonally diagonalizable. In particular, if $\mathbf{v}_1$ and $\mathbf{v}_2$ are orthonormal eigenvectors of A corresponding to the eigenvalues λ_1 and λ_2 and $P = [\mathbf{v}_1 \quad \mathbf{v}_2]$, then

$$P^T AP = \begin{bmatrix} \lambda_1 & 0 \\ 0 & \lambda_2 \end{bmatrix}. \tag{10}$$

We may interchange the eigenvectors $\mathbf{v}_1$ and $\mathbf{v}_2$, if necessary, to ensure that det $P = 1$. Then it follows from Theorem 2 in Section 7.4 that P is the matrix of a rotation of $\mathbf{R}^2$. The rotated x'- and y'-axes are determined by the unit eigenvectors $\mathbf{v}_1$ and $\mathbf{v}_2$, respectively, and the transition between the old xy-coordinates and the new $x'y'$-coordinates is given by

$$\mathbf{x} = P\mathbf{x}'; \quad \text{that is,} \quad \begin{bmatrix} x \\ y \end{bmatrix} = P\begin{bmatrix} x' \\ y' \end{bmatrix}. \tag{11}$$

Hence the quadratic form q is described in the new coordinates by

$$\begin{aligned} q(\mathbf{x}') = \mathbf{x}^T A \mathbf{x} &= (P\mathbf{x}')^T A (P\mathbf{x}') \\ &= \mathbf{x}'^T (P^T A P)\mathbf{x}' \\ &= [x' \quad y'] \begin{bmatrix} \lambda_1 & 0 \\ 0 & \lambda_2 \end{bmatrix} \begin{bmatrix} x' \\ y' \end{bmatrix} \\ &= \lambda_1 (x')^2 + \lambda_2 (y')^2. \end{aligned}$$

This proves the following theorem.

Theorem 1: *Principal Axes for a Quadratic Form*
Let $q(\mathbf{x}) = \mathbf{x}^T A \mathbf{x}$ be a quadratic form with symmetric 2×2 matrix A. Then there exists a rotation of $\mathbf{R}^2$ such that in the rotated $x'y'$-coordinate system, the quadratic form q is given by

$$q(\mathbf{x}') = \lambda_1 (x')^2 + \lambda_2 (y')^2, \tag{12}$$

where λ_1 and λ_2 are the eigenvalues of A. This rotation corresponds to the substitution $\mathbf{x} = P\mathbf{x}'$, where P orthogonally diagonalizes A and $\det P = 1$.

If P is as in Theorem 1 and we substitute $\mathbf{x} = P\mathbf{x}'$ in the second degree equation in (9),

$$\mathbf{x}^T A \mathbf{x} + B\mathbf{x} + f = 0,$$

the result is

$$\mathbf{x}'^T (P^T A P)\mathbf{x}' + BP\mathbf{x}' + f = 0;$$

that is,

$$\lambda_1 (x')^2 + \lambda_2 (y')^2 + d'x' + e'y' + f = 0, \tag{13}$$

where

$$BP = [d \quad e][\mathbf{v}_1 \quad \mathbf{v}_2] = [d' \quad e']. \tag{14}$$

Note that the constant term in the equation is not changed by this change of coordinates.

If the eigenvalues λ_1 and λ_2 are both nonzero, then the x'- and y'-terms in (13) can be eliminated by a translation. The result (apart from degenerate cases) is the equation of an ellipse or a hyperbola, depending on whether or not λ_1 and λ_2 have the same sign. If exactly one of these eigenvalues is zero, then the graph (if nondegenerate) is a parabola. Some of the special cases of the next theorem are treated in the problems.

> ***Theorem 2:*** *Graphs of Second Degree Equations*
> The graph of any second degree equation in x and y is—in an appropriately rotated and translated coordinate system—one of the following:
>
> **(i)** A nondegenerate ellipse, hyperbola, or parabola.
> **(ii)** Two intersecting lines (a degenerate hyperbola).
> **(iii)** Two parallel lines (a degenerate parabola).
> **(iv)** A single line (a degenerate parabola).
> **(v)** A single point (a degenerate ellipse).
> **(vi)** The empty set (an imaginary ellipse).

Examples 4 and 5 illustrate the way in which we may identify the graph of a given second degree equation in x and y.

EXAMPLE 4 Identify the graph of the equation

$$16x^2 + 24xy + 9y^2 + 15x - 20y = 0. \tag{15}$$

Solution The matrix form of Equation (15) is

$$\mathbf{x}^T A\mathbf{x} + B\mathbf{x} = 0, \tag{16}$$

where

$$A = \begin{bmatrix} 16 & 12 \\ 12 & 9 \end{bmatrix} \quad \text{and} \quad B = [15 \quad -20].$$

The characteristic equation of A is

$$\begin{aligned} |A - \lambda I| &= (16 - \lambda)(9 - \lambda) - 144 \\ &= \lambda^2 - 25\lambda = \lambda(\lambda - 25) = 0, \end{aligned}$$

so the eigenvalues of A are $\lambda_1 = 25$ and $\lambda_2 = 0$.

The eigenvectors corresponding to $\lambda_1 = 25$ are the nontrivial solutions of the system

$$\begin{bmatrix} -9 & 12 \\ 12 & -16 \end{bmatrix} \begin{bmatrix} x \\ y \end{bmatrix} = \begin{bmatrix} 0 \\ 0 \end{bmatrix}.$$

It follows readily that (4, 3) is an eigenvector associated with $\lambda_1 = 25$, so

$$\mathbf{v}_1 = \tfrac{1}{5}\begin{bmatrix} 4 \\ 3 \end{bmatrix}$$

is a *unit* eigenvector associated with λ_1. Similarly, the eigenvalue $\lambda_2 = 0$ leads to the system

$$\begin{bmatrix} 16 & 12 \\ 12 & 9 \end{bmatrix} \begin{bmatrix} x \\ y \end{bmatrix} = \begin{bmatrix} 0 \\ 0 \end{bmatrix}$$

with nontrivial solution $(-3, 4)$, so

$$\mathbf{v}_2 = \frac{1}{5}\begin{bmatrix} -3 \\ 4 \end{bmatrix}$$

is a unit eigenvector associated with $\lambda_2 = 0$.

The eigenvectors $\mathbf{v}_1$ and $\mathbf{v}_2$ yield the orthogonal diagonalizing matrix

$$P = \frac{1}{5}\begin{bmatrix} 4 & -3 \\ 3 & 4 \end{bmatrix}$$

such that $|P| = 1$ and

$$P^T A P = \begin{bmatrix} 25 & 0 \\ 0 & 0 \end{bmatrix}.$$

In the rotated coordinate system with x'- and y'-axes determined by the orthonormal eigenvectors $\mathbf{v}_1$ and $\mathbf{v}_2$, respectively, the quadratic form $\mathbf{x}^T A\mathbf{x}$ in (16) reduces to

$$[x' \quad y']\begin{bmatrix} 25 & 0 \\ 0 & 0 \end{bmatrix}\begin{bmatrix} x' \\ y' \end{bmatrix} = 25(x')^2.$$

And we see from (14) that the x'- and y'-terms in the transformed equation are given by

$$\begin{aligned} BP\mathbf{x}' &= [15 \quad -20](\tfrac{1}{5})\begin{bmatrix} 4 & -3 \\ 3 & 4 \end{bmatrix}\begin{bmatrix} x' \\ y' \end{bmatrix} \\ &= [0 \quad -25]\begin{bmatrix} x' \\ y' \end{bmatrix} = -25y'. \end{aligned}$$

Thus the substitution $\mathbf{x} = P\mathbf{x}'$ in (16) yields the equation

$$25(x')^2 - 25y' = 0; \quad \text{that is,} \quad y' = (x')^2$$

in terms of the rotated coordinates. We therefore see that the graph of Equation (15) is the rotated parabola shown in Figure 8.8. The $x'y'$-axes are obtained from the xy-axes by a counterclockwise rotation through the angle

$$\theta = \tan^{-1}\tfrac{3}{4} \approx 36.87°.$$

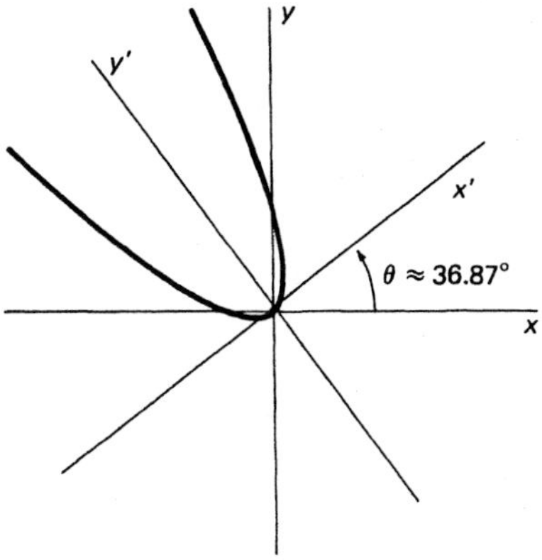

8.8 The rotated parabola of Example 4.

EXAMPLE 5 Identify the graph of the equation

$$34x^2 - 24xy + 41y^2 - 40x - 30y - 25 = 0. \tag{17}$$

Solution The matrix form of (17) is

$$\mathbf{x}^T A\mathbf{x} + B\mathbf{x} - 25 = 0 \tag{18}$$

where

$$A = \begin{bmatrix} 34 & -12 \\ -12 & 41 \end{bmatrix} \quad \text{and} \quad B = [-40 \quad -30].$$

The characteristic equation of A is

$$\begin{aligned} |A - \lambda I| &= (34 - \lambda)(41 - \lambda) - 144 \\ &= \lambda^2 - 75\lambda + 1250 \\ &= (\lambda - 25)(\lambda - 50) = 0, \end{aligned}$$

so the eigenvalues of A are $\lambda_1 = 25$ and $\lambda_2 = 50$.

Proceeding as in Example 4, we find the unit eigenvectors

$$\mathbf{v}_1 = \tfrac{1}{5}\begin{bmatrix} 4 \\ 3 \end{bmatrix} \quad \text{and} \quad \mathbf{v}_2 = \tfrac{1}{5}\begin{bmatrix} -3 \\ 4 \end{bmatrix}$$

associated with the eigenvalues $\lambda_1 = 25$ and $\lambda_2 = 50$, respectively. We therefore have here the same orthogonal diagonalizing matrix

$$P = \tfrac{1}{5}\begin{bmatrix} 4 & -3 \\ 3 & 4 \end{bmatrix}$$

as in Example 4, as well as the same rotated $x'y'$-coordinate system. In terms of x' and y' the quadratic form $\mathbf{x}^T A\mathbf{x}$ in (18) consequently reduces to

$$[x' \quad y']\begin{bmatrix} 25 & 0 \\ 0 & 50 \end{bmatrix}\begin{bmatrix} x' \\ y' \end{bmatrix} = 25(x')^2 + 50(y')^2.$$

To find the x'- and y'-terms in the transformed equation, we calculate

$$\begin{aligned} BP\mathbf{x}' &= [-40 \quad -30](\tfrac{1}{5})\begin{bmatrix} 4 & -3 \\ 3 & 4 \end{bmatrix}\begin{bmatrix} x' \\ y' \end{bmatrix} \\ &= [-50 \quad 0]\begin{bmatrix} x' \\ y' \end{bmatrix} = -50x'. \end{aligned}$$

Thus the substitution $\mathbf{x} = P\mathbf{x}'$ in (18) yields the equation

$$25(x')^2 + 50(y')^2 - 50x' - 25 = 0. \tag{19}$$

To identify the graph of this transformed equation, we complete the square:

$$\begin{aligned} 25[(x')^2 - 2x' + 1] + 50(y')^2 &= 25 + 25 = 50; \\ 25(x' - 1)^2 + 50(y')^2 &= 50. \end{aligned}$$

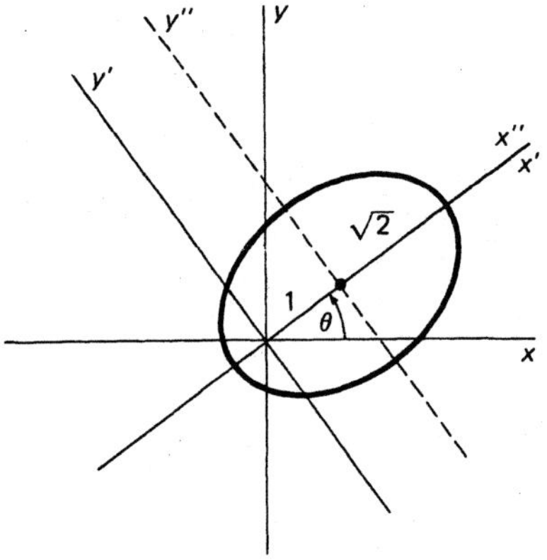

8.9 The rotated and translated ellipse of Example 5.

Hence we see finally that the graph of Equation (17) is the ellipse

$$\frac{(x'')^2}{2} + \frac{(y'')^2}{1} = 1 \tag{20}$$

in the $x''y''$-system of Figure 8.9 that is obtained from the rotated $x'y'$-system by a translation of 1 unit in the x'-direction.

8.1 PROBLEMS

In Problems 1–6, the graph of the given equation is a translated conic section, possibly degenerate. Identify it as one of the types listed in Theorem 2, give its equation in the appropriate $x'y'$-coordinate system, and give the origin (in terms of xy-coordinates) of the new coordinate system.

1. $2x^2 + y^2 - 8x - 6y + 13 = 0$

2. $x^2 + 3y^2 + 6x + 12y + 18 = 0$

3. $9x^2 - 16y^2 - 18x - 32y - 151 = 0$

4. $y^2 - 4x - 4y - 8 = 0$

5. $2x^2 + 3y^2 - 8x - 18y + 35 = 0$

6. $4x^2 - y^2 - 8x - 4y = 0$

In Problems 7–20, the graph of the given equation is a rotated conic section (possibly degenerate). Identify it; give the counterclockwise angle θ of rotation that yields a rotated $x'y'$-system in which the graph is in standard position, and give the transformed equation in $x'y'$-coordinates.

7. $3x^2 + 2xy + 3y^2 = 1$

8. $x^2 + 6xy + y^2 = 1$

9. $4x^2 + 4xy + y^2 = 20$

10. $9x^2 + 4xy + 6y^2 = 40$

11. $4x^2 + 6xy - 4y^2 = 5$

12. $19x^2 + 6xy + 11y^2 = 40$

13. $22x^2 + 12xy + 17y^2 = 26$

14. $9x^2 + 12xy + 4y^2 = 13$

15. $52x^2 + 72xy + 73y^2 = 100$

16. $9x^2 + 24xy + 16y^2 = 0$

17. $33x^2 + 8xy + 18y^2 = 68$

18. $40x^2 + 36xy + 25y^2 = 52$

19. $119x^2 + 240xy - 119y^2 = 0$

20. $313x^2 + 120xy + 194y^2 = 0$

In Problems 21–26, identify the graph of the given equation by carrying out first a rotation and then a translation. Give the angle of rotation, the translated center of coordinates in the rotated coordinate system, and the final transformed equation.

21. $73x^2 - 72xy + 52y^2 - 30x - 40y - 75 = 0$

22. $41x^2 - 24xy + 34y^2 + 20x - 140y + 125 = 0$

23. $23x^2 - 72xy + 2y^2 + 140x + 20y - 75 = 0$

24. $9x^2 + 24xy + 16y^2 - 170x - 60y + 245 = 0$

25. $161x^2 + 480xy - 161y^2 - 510x - 272y = 0$

26. $144x^2 - 120xy + 25y^2 - 65x - 156y - 169 = 0$

Problems 27–29 deal with special cases of the proof of Theorem 2. Consider the second degree equation

$$ax^2 + cy^2 + dx + ey + f = 0$$

that contains no xy-term.

27. Suppose that a and c are nonzero and have the same sign. Show that the graph is either an ellipse, a single point, or the empty set.

28. Suppose that a and c are nonzero and have different signs. Show that the graph is either a hyperbola or two intersecting lines.

29. Suppose that $a \neq 0$ and $c = 0$. Then show that the graph is
(a) A parabola if $e \neq 0$;
(b) Two parallel lines if $e = 0$ and a and $f \neq 0$ have opposite signs;
(c) The empty set if $e = 0$ and a and $f \neq 0$ have the same sign;
(d) A single line if $e = f = 0$.

30. Suppose that the graph of the second degree equation

$$ax^2 + 2bxy + cy^2 + dx + ey + f = 0$$

is a nondegenerate conic section. Use the results in Problems 27–29 to show that this conic section is
(a) An ellipse if $ac - b^2 > 0$;
(b) A hyperbola if $ac - b^2 < 0$;
(c) A parabola if $ac - b^2 = 0$.
The invariant $ac - b^2$ is called the **discriminant** of the quadratic form $ax^2 + 2bxy + cy^2$.

31. In Example 4 of Section 2.5 we encountered the equation

$$2929x^2 - 3456xy + 1921y^2 - 9000x - 12000y - 15625 = 0.$$

Use the methods of this section to verify that its graph is the ellipse shown in Figure 2.9 there.

8.2 Quadratic Forms and Extreme Values

In Theorem 1 of Section 8.1 we saw that if

$$q(\mathbf{x}) = ax^2 + 2bxy + cy^2 \tag{1}$$

is a quadratic form in two variables, then there exists a rotation of $\mathbf{R}^2$ such that in the rotated $x'y'$-coordinate system the quadratic form is given by

$$q(\mathbf{x}') = \lambda_1(x')^2 + \lambda_2(y')^2, \tag{2}$$

where λ_1 and λ_2 are the eigenvalues of the matrix

$$A = \begin{bmatrix} a & b \\ b & c \end{bmatrix} \tag{3}$$

of the quadratic form q. The transformation from (1) to (2) is effected by the substitution $\mathbf{x} = P\mathbf{x}'$, where P is the orthogonal matrix with $\det P = 1$ that diagonalizes A:

$$P^TAP = D = \begin{bmatrix} \lambda_1 & 0 \\ 0 & \lambda_2 \end{bmatrix}. \tag{4}$$

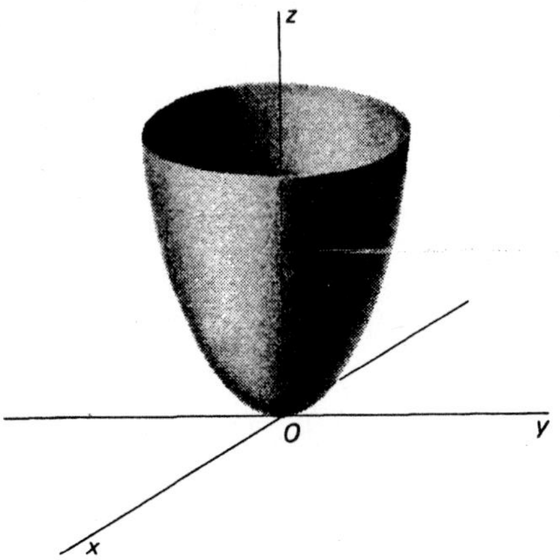

8.10 The elliptic paraboloid $z = x^2 + y^2$ opens upward.

The "reduction" of a quadratic form q to a sum of squares as in (2) is called a **diagonalization** of the quadratic form. By diagonalizing the quadratic form $q(\mathbf{x}) = ax^2 + 2bxy + cy^2$, we can determine what the graph in $\mathbf{R}^3$ of the equation

$$z = ax^2 + 2bxy + cy^2 \tag{5}$$

looks like. The reason is that the graph of the resulting equation

$$z = \lambda_1(x')^2 + \lambda_2(y')^2 \tag{6}$$

in the rotated $x'y'z$-coordinate system is readily discerned. If λ_1 and λ_2 are *both positive*, then the graph of Equation (6) is a *paraboloid* opening upward and resembling the graph shown in Figure 8.10. If λ_1 and λ_2 are *both negative*, then it is a paraboloid opening downward as in Figure 8.11. In either case the paraboloid is called an **elliptic paraboloid** because each nondegenerate cross section in a horizontal plane is an ellipse.

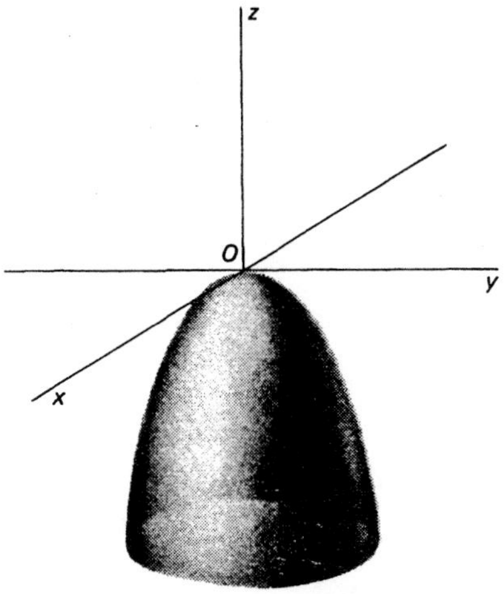

8.11 The elliptic paraboloid $z = -x^2 - y^2$ opens downward.

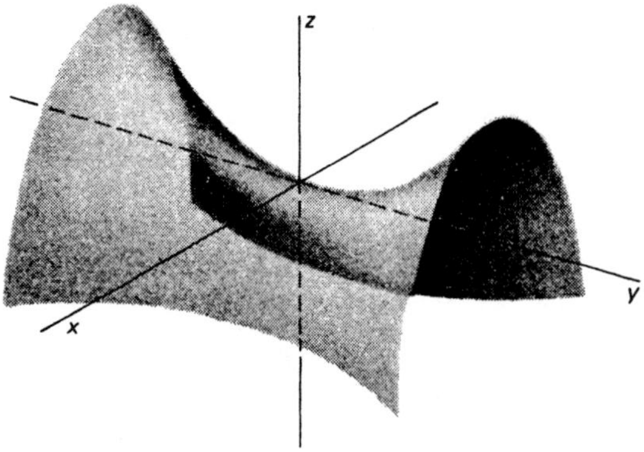

8.12 The hyperbolic paraboloid $z = y^2 - x^2$.

If the eigenvalues λ_1 and λ_2 are both nonzero but have *different signs*, then the graph of Equation (6) (in the rotated coordinate system) is a **hyperbolic paraboloid,** resembling the saddle-shaped surface shown in Figure 8.12. If exactly one of these eigenvalues is zero, then the graph is a **parabolic cylinder;** the one shown in Figure 8.13 is the case in which $\lambda_1 = 1$ and $\lambda_2 = 0$.

EXAMPLE 1 Investigate the graph of the equation

$$z = 34x^2 - 24xy + 41y^2. \tag{7}$$

Solution In Example 5 of Section 8.1 we saw that the associated symmetric matrix

$$A = \begin{bmatrix} 34 & -12 \\ -12 & 41 \end{bmatrix}$$

has eigenvalues $\lambda_1 = 25$ and $\lambda_2 = 50$ corresponding to the unit eigenvectors

$$\mathbf{v}_1 = \tfrac{1}{5}\begin{bmatrix} 4 \\ 3 \end{bmatrix} \quad \text{and} \quad \mathbf{v}_2 = \tfrac{1}{5}\begin{bmatrix} -3 \\ 4 \end{bmatrix}.$$

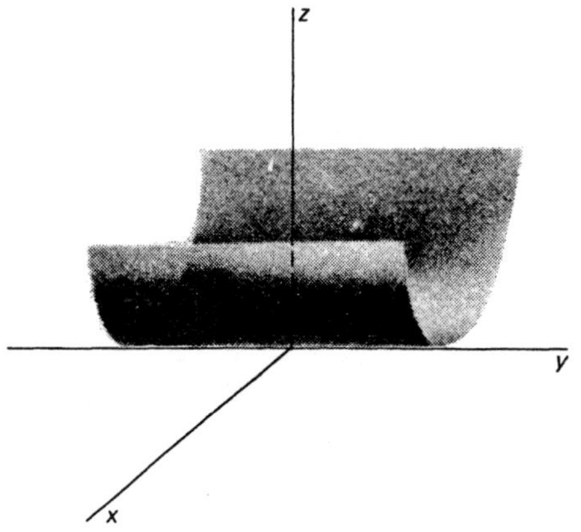

8.13 The parabolic cyclinder $z = x^2$.

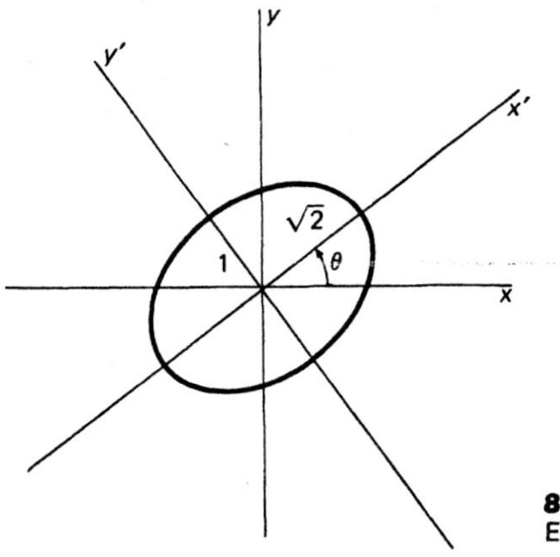

8.14 An elliptical cross section of the paraboloid of Example 1.

Consequently the substitution $\mathbf{x} = P\mathbf{x}'$, with $\mathbf{P} = [\mathbf{v}_1 \quad \mathbf{v}_2]$, transforms Equation (7) into the equation

$$z = 25(x')^2 + 50(y')^2. \tag{8}$$

This is the equation of an elliptic paraboloid in the rotated $x'y'z$-coordinate system. The x'- and y'-axes are determined by the eigenvectors $\mathbf{v}_1$ and $\mathbf{v}_2$ and hence are obtained from the x- and y-axes by a counterclockwise rotation through the angle $\theta = \tan^{-1}(\frac{3}{4}) \approx 36.87°$. To examine a typical cross section of the paraboloid of Equation (8), let us consider the one in the horizontal plane $z = 50$. Substitution of $z = 50$ in (8) yields the equation

$$50 = 25(x')^2 + 50(y')^2;$$

that is,

$$\frac{(x')^2}{2} + \frac{(y')^2}{1} = 1.$$

Thus this cross section is an ellipse with semiaxes $\sqrt{2}$ and 1, as indicated in Figure 8.14. Each horizontal cross section in a plane $z = k > 0$ is an ellipse "similar" to the one shown in Figure 8.14. Finally, the graph of the equation in (7) can be described as the result of rotating the elliptic paraboloid $z = 25x^2 + 50y^2$ through the indicated angle θ about the z-axis.

Figures 8.10–8.12 suggest a useful way of classifying quadratic forms with regard to the shapes of their graphs. Note that apart from the point at the origin, the elliptic paraboloid in Figure 8.10 lies entirely above the xy-plane $z = 0$, whereas the paraboloid in Figure 8.11 lies entirely below the xy-plane. By contrast, the hyperbolic paraboloid shown in Figure 8.12 contains points above the xy-plane as well as points below the xy-plane. The three quadratic forms

$$x^2 + y^2, \quad -x^2 - y^2, \quad \text{and} \quad -x^2 + y^2,$$

whose graphs are shown in Figures 8.10–8.12, illustrate (with $n = 2$) the three cases in the following definition.

> ***Definition:*** *Definite and Indefinite Quadratic Forms*
> Let A be a symmetric $n \times n$ matrix. Then the quadratic form $q(\mathbf{x}) = \mathbf{x}^T A\mathbf{x}$ is
>
> 1. **Positive definite** if $q(\mathbf{x}) > 0$ for all $\mathbf{x} \neq \mathbf{0}$;
> 2. **Negative definite** if $q(\mathbf{x}) < 0$ for all $\mathbf{x} \neq \mathbf{0}$;
> 3. **Indefinite** if the value of $q(\mathbf{x})$ is positive for some points $\mathbf{x}$ but negative for others.

EXAMPLE 2 The quadratic form $q_1(x, y) = 3x^2 + 4y^2$ is positive definite because $3x^2 + 4y^2 > 0$ unless $x = y = 0$. Similarly, the quadratic form $q_2(x, y) = -3x^2 - 4y^2$ is negative definite. The quadratic form $q_3(x, y) = 3x^2 - 4y^2$ is indefinite because $q_3(1, 0) = 3$, whereas $q_3(0, 1) = -4$, so $q_3(x, y)$ attains both positive and negative values. Note that the quadratic form $q_4(x, y) = 3x^2$ is neither positive definite nor negative definite nor indefinite. (Why?) Thus the three mutually exclusive classes of quadratic forms listed in the definition are *not* all-inclusive.

As Example 2 illustrates, the nature of the quadratic form $q(\mathbf{x}) = \mathbf{x}^T A\mathbf{x}$ is evident if the matrix A is a diagonal matrix. Otherwise, because A is symmetric we know from Theorem 4 in Section 6.4 that there is an orthogonal matrix P such that

$$P^T AP = D \tag{9}$$

where D is a diagonal matrix whose diagonal elements are the eigenvalues $\lambda_1, \lambda_2, \ldots, \lambda_n$ of A. Indeed, P is the $n \times n$ matrix whose column vectors are unit eigenvectors $\mathbf{v}_1, \mathbf{v}_2, \ldots, \mathbf{v}_n$ associated (in order) with these eigenvalues.

Our strategy then is to express the quadratic form q in terms of coordinates with respect to the basis $\{\mathbf{v}_1, \mathbf{v}_2, \ldots, \mathbf{v}_n\}$ for $\mathbf{R}^n$. The substitution $\mathbf{x} = P\mathbf{x}'$ relating standard coordinates $\mathbf{x} = (x_1, x_2, \ldots, x_n)$ and new coordinates $\mathbf{x}' = (x'_1, x'_2, \ldots, x'_n)$—as in Theorem 1 of Section 7.3—yields

$$\begin{aligned} q(\mathbf{x}') = \mathbf{x}^T A\mathbf{x} &= (P\mathbf{x}')^T A(P\mathbf{x}') \\ &= \mathbf{x}'^T(P^T AP)\mathbf{x}' = \mathbf{x}'^T D\mathbf{x}'; \end{aligned}$$

thus

$$q(\mathbf{x}') = \lambda_1(x'_1)^2 + \lambda_2(x'_2)^2 + \cdots + \lambda_n(x'_n)^2. \tag{10}$$

This establishes the following n-dimensional version of Theorem 1 in Section 8.1.

Theorem 1: *Principal Axes for a Quadratic Form*

Let $q(\mathbf{x}) = \mathbf{x}^T A\mathbf{x}$ be a quadratic form with symmetric $n \times n$ matrix A, and let P be an orthogonal matrix that diagonalizes A. Then the substitution $\mathbf{x} = P\mathbf{x}'$ yields the expression

$$q(\mathbf{x}') = \lambda_1(x'_1)^2 + \lambda_2(x'_2)^2 + \cdots + \lambda_n(x'_n)^2 \tag{10}$$

for the quadratic form q in terms of the $\mathbf{x}'$-coordinates and the eigenvalues λ_1, $\lambda_2, \ldots, \lambda_n$ of A.

If the eigenvalues $\lambda_1, \lambda_2, \ldots, \lambda_n$ of the symmetric matrix A are known, then the nature of the quadratic form $q(\mathbf{x}) = \mathbf{x}^T A\mathbf{x}$ can be determined by a glance at its diagonalization in (10). If these eigenvalues are all positive, then it is clear from (10) that $q(\mathbf{x}') > 0$ unless $\mathbf{x}' = \mathbf{0}$. Similarly, $q(\mathbf{x}') < 0$ for $\mathbf{x} \neq \mathbf{0}$ if the eigenvalues are all negative. But if A has both a positive eigenvalue λ_i and a negative eigenvalue λ_j, with associated eigenvectors $\mathbf{v}_i$ and $\mathbf{v}_j$, then (10) gives $q(\mathbf{v}_i) = \lambda_i > 0$ and $q(\mathbf{v}_j) = \lambda_j < 0$, so $q(\mathbf{x})$ has both positive and negative values. This yields the following result.

Theorem 2: *Eigenvalues and Quadratic Forms*

Let $q(\mathbf{x}) = \mathbf{x}^T A\mathbf{x}$ be a quadratic form with symmetric $n \times n$ matrix A. Then q is

1. Positive definite if the eigenvalues of A are all positive;
2. Negative definite if the eigenvalues of A are all negative;
3. Indefinite if A has both positive and negative eigenvalues.

Thus if the quadratic form $q(\mathbf{x}) = \mathbf{x}^T A\mathbf{x}$ is either positive or negative definite or indefinite, we can determine *which* it is by finding the eigenvalues of A. We need not find the corresponding eigenvectors nor actually carry out the change of coordinates $\mathbf{x} = P\mathbf{x}'$. Note, however, that Theorem 2 does not cover the case in which A has at least one zero eigenvalue and all the nonzero eigenvalues have the same sign. The quadratic form q is said to be **positive semidefinite** if each eigenvalue of A satisfies $\lambda_i \geq 0$ and **negative semidefinite** if each satisfies $\lambda_i \leq 0$. It follows from (10) that if q is positive semidefinite, then $q(\mathbf{x}) \geq 0$ for all $\mathbf{x}$, whereas $q(\mathbf{x}) \leq 0$ for all $\mathbf{x}$ if q is negative semidefinite.

EXAMPLE 3 The quadratic form

$$q(x, y, z,) = 2x^2 + 5y^2 + 2z^2 + 2xz$$

has matrix

$$A = \begin{bmatrix} 2 & 0 & 1 \\ 0 & 5 & 0 \\ 1 & 0 & 2 \end{bmatrix}.$$

The characteristic equation of A is

$$\begin{aligned}|A - \lambda I| &= (5 - \lambda)[(2 - \lambda)^2 - 1] \\ &= (5 - \lambda)(3 - \lambda)(1 - \lambda) = 0.\end{aligned}$$

Hence the eigenvalues $\lambda_1 = 5$, $\lambda_2 = 3$, and $\lambda_3 = 1$ of A are all positive, so part (1) of Theorem 2 implies that the quadratic form q is positive definite.

EXAMPLE 4 The quadratic form

$$q(x, y, z) = 6xy + 8yz$$

has matrix

$$A = \begin{bmatrix} 0 & 3 & 0 \\ 3 & 0 & 4 \\ 0 & 4 & 0 \end{bmatrix}$$

with characteristic equation

$$\begin{aligned}|A - \lambda I| &= (-\lambda)(\lambda^2 - 16) - (3)(-3\lambda) \\ &= (-\lambda)(\lambda^2 - 25) = 0.\end{aligned}$$

Thus A has eigenvalues $\lambda_1 = 5$, $\lambda_2 = 0$, and $\lambda_3 = -5$, so it follows from part (3) of Theorem 2 that the quadratic form q is indefinite.

The quadratic form $q(\mathbf{x}) = \mathbf{x}^T A\mathbf{x}$ is called **nondegenerate** provided that $|A| \neq 0$. It follows from Equation (9) that

$$|A| = |PDP^{-1}| = |D| = \lambda_1\lambda_2 \cdots \lambda_n, \tag{11}$$

so the determinant of A is equal to the product of its eigenvalues. Therefore *the quadratic form $q(\mathbf{x}) = \mathbf{x}^T A\mathbf{x}$ is nondegenerate if and only if the eigenvalues of A are all nonzero.* Our next theorem provides a quick way to classify a nondegenerate quadratic form in two variables without even calculating the eigenvalues of its matrix.

Theorem 3: *Quadratic Forms in Two Variables*

Let $q(x, y) = ax^2 + 2bxy + cy^2$ be a nondegenerate quadratic form in x and y, so that $\Delta = ac - b^2 \neq 0$. Then the quadratic form q is

1. Positive definite if $\Delta > 0$ and $a > 0$;
2. Negative definite if $\Delta > 0$ and $a < 0$;
3. Indefinite if $\Delta < 0$.

PROOF The quadratic form q has matrix

$$A = \begin{bmatrix} a & b \\ b & c \end{bmatrix}$$

with determinant $\Delta = ac - b^2$. If $\Delta > 0$, then Equation (11) yields $\lambda_1\lambda_2 = \Delta > 0$, so the eigenvalues λ_1 and λ_2 of A have the same sign. But then

$$ac = \Delta + b^2 = \lambda_1\lambda_2 + b^2 > 0,$$

so a and c also have the same sign. Moreover,

$$\lambda_1 + \lambda_2 = \text{trace}(A) = a + c$$

by Problem 33 in Section 6.1, so λ_1 and λ_2 have the same sign as a and c. Hence if $a > 0$, then λ_1 and λ_2 are both positive, so q is positive definite by part (1) of Theorem 2. On the other hand, if $a < 0$, then λ_1 and λ_2 are both negative, so q is negative definite.

If $\Delta < 0$ then the fact that $\lambda_1\lambda_2 = \Delta < 0$ means that λ_1 and λ_2 have different signs, so part (3) of Theorem 2 implies that q is indefinite. ■

EXAMPLE 5 The quadratic form $q_1(x, y) = 3x^2 + 4xy + 2y^2$ is positive definite because $\Delta = (3)(2) - (2)^2 = 2 > 0$ and $a = 3 > 0$. The quadratic form $q_2(x, y) = 3x^2 + 6xy + 2y^2$ is indefinite because $\Delta = (3)(2) - (3)^2 = -3 < 0$.

Theorem 3 has a useful n-dimensional generalization. Given a quadratic form $q(\mathbf{x}) = \mathbf{x}^T A\mathbf{x}$ with symmetric $n \times n$ matrix $A = [a_{ij}]$, we denote by Δ_k the determinant of the upper left-hand $k \times k$ submatrix of A; that is,

$$\Delta_k = \begin{vmatrix} a_{11} & a_{12} & \cdots & a_{1k} \\ a_{21} & a_{22} & \cdots & a_{2k} \\ \vdots & \vdots & \ddots & \vdots \\ a_{k1} & a_{k2} & \cdots & a_{kk} \end{vmatrix}. \tag{12}$$

Thus

$$\Delta_1 = a_{11}, \qquad \Delta_2 = \begin{vmatrix} a_{11} & a_{12} \\ a_{21} & a_{22} \end{vmatrix},$$

$$\Delta_3 = \begin{vmatrix} a_{11} & a_{12} & a_{13} \\ a_{21} & a_{22} & a_{23} \\ a_{31} & a_{32} & a_{33} \end{vmatrix}, \ldots, \Delta_n = |A|.$$

An accessible though somewhat lengthy proof of the following theorem can be found on pages 149–151 of *Advanced Calculus of Several Variables* by C. H. Edwards, Jr. (New York: Academic Press, 1973). Problems 41–43 deal with portions of the proof in the case $n = 3$.

> ***Theorem 4:** Determinant Classification of Quadratic Forms*
>
> Let $q(\mathbf{x}) = \mathbf{x}^T A\mathbf{x}$ be a nondegenerate quadratic form with symmetric $n \times n$ matrix A. Then q is
>
> **1.** Positive definite if and only if $\Delta_k > 0$ for each $k = 1, 2, \ldots, n$;
>
> **2.** Negative definite if and only if $(-1)^k\Delta_k > 0$ for each $k = 1, 2, \ldots, n$;
>
> **3.** Indefinite if neither of the previous two conditions is satisfied.

Note that the condition $(-1)^k\Delta_k > 0$ in part (2) says simply that the determinants $\Delta_1, \Delta_2, \ldots, \Delta_n$ alternate in sign: $\Delta_1 < 0, \Delta_2 > 0, \Delta_3 < 0, \Delta_4 > 0$, and so forth. The theorem says nothing about a degenerate quadratic form for which $|A| = 0$.

EXAMPLE 6 If

$$A = \begin{bmatrix} -3 & 1 & 2 \\ 1 & -2 & 1 \\ 2 & 1 & -5 \end{bmatrix}.$$

then computation gives $\Delta_1 = -3$, $\Delta_2 = 5$, and $\Delta_3 = -10$. Hence part (2) of Theorem 4 implies that the quadratic form

$$q(x, y, z) = -3x^2 - 2y^2 - 5z^2 + 2xy + 4xz + 2yz$$

is negative definite.

EXAMPLE 7 If

$$A = \begin{bmatrix} 3 & 2 & 1 \\ 2 & 2 & 3 \\ 1 & 3 & 2 \end{bmatrix},$$

then computation gives $\Delta_1 = 3$, $\Delta_2 = 2$, and $\Delta_3 = -13$. Thus the determinants Δ_1, Δ_2, Δ_3 are neither all positive nor alternating in sign, so part (3) of Theorem 4 implies that the quadratic form

$$q(x, y, z) = 3x^2 + 2y^2 + 2z^2 + 4xy + 2xz + 6yz$$

is indefinite.

*MAXIMA, MINIMA, AND SADDLE POINTS

Let $f:\mathbf{R}^n \to \mathbf{R}$ be a differentiable real-valued function on $\mathbf{R}^n$. In calculus one learns that in order for $f(\mathbf{a})$ to be either a local minimum value or a local maximum value of f, it is

* The remainder of this section is for those readers who are familiar with partial derivatives.

necessary for $\mathbf{x} = \mathbf{a}$ to be a **critical point** where the first-order partial derivatives of f all vanish:

$$\left.\frac{\partial f}{\partial x_1}\right|_{(\mathbf{a})} = \left.\frac{\partial f}{\partial x_2}\right|_{(\mathbf{a})} = \cdots = \left.\frac{\partial f}{\partial x_n}\right|_{(\mathbf{a})} = 0. \tag{13}$$

In order to state a *sufficient condition* for $f(\mathbf{a})$ to be either a local minimum or a local maximum value, we must consider the second-order partial derivatives of f at the critical point $\mathbf{x} = \mathbf{a}$. The **Hessian matrix** of f at $\mathbf{x} = \mathbf{a}$ is the symmetric $n \times n$ matrix

$$H = Hf(\mathbf{a}) = \left[\left.\frac{\partial^2 f}{\partial x_i \partial x_j}\right|_{(\mathbf{a})}\right] \tag{14}$$

of second order partial derivatives of f at $\mathbf{x} = \mathbf{a}$. For instance, if $n = 2$, then

$$H = \begin{bmatrix} \dfrac{\partial^2 f}{\partial x^2} & \dfrac{\partial^2 f}{\partial x \partial y} \\[2ex] \dfrac{\partial^2 f}{\partial y \partial x} & \dfrac{\partial^2 f}{\partial y^2} \end{bmatrix}. \tag{15}$$

The **quadratic form** of the function f at the point $\mathbf{x} = \mathbf{a}$ is the quadratic form

$$q(\mathbf{x}) = \mathbf{x}^T H \mathbf{x} \tag{16}$$

where H is the Hessian matrix defined in (14). For a proof of the following theorem, see pages 138–139 of Edwards, *Advanced Calculus of Several Variables.*

Theorem 5: *Maxima, Minima, and Saddle Points*

Suppose that the function $f: \mathbf{R}^n \to \mathbf{R}$ has continuous third order partial derivatives at the critical point $\mathbf{x} = \mathbf{a}$, and let $q(\mathbf{x}) = \mathbf{x}^T H \mathbf{x}$ be the quadratic form of f at that point. Then $f(\mathbf{a})$ is a

1. Local minimum value if q is positive definite;
2. Local maximum value if q is negative definite;
3. Neither a local minimum nor a local maximum value if q is indefinite, so $\mathbf{x} = \mathbf{a}$ is in this case a *saddle point* of f.

Theorem 5 can be applied by using Theorem 4 to classify the quadratic form $q(\mathbf{x}) = \mathbf{x}^T H \mathbf{x}$ of f at the critical point $\mathbf{x} = \mathbf{a}$. For instance, if $n = 2$ we let

$$\Delta_1 = \frac{\partial^2 f}{\partial x^2} \quad \text{and} \quad \Delta_2 = \frac{\partial^2 f}{\partial x^2}\frac{\partial^2 f}{\partial y^2} - \left(\frac{\partial^2 f}{\partial x \partial y}\right)^2, \tag{17}$$

where these second order partial derivatives stemming from (15) are evaluated at the critical point $\mathbf{x} = \mathbf{a}$. Then it follows from Theorems 4 and 5 that $f(\mathbf{a})$ is a

1. Local minimum value if $\Delta_1 > 0$ and $\Delta_2 > 0$;
2. Local maximum value if $\Delta_1 < 0$ and $\Delta_2 > 0$;
3. Neither a local minimum nor a local maximum value if $\Delta_2 < 0$.

These results constitute the *second derivative test* for functions of two variables.

EXAMPLE 8 If

$$f(x, y) = 4y - 3x^2 - 2y^2 + 4xy,$$

then

$$\frac{\partial f}{\partial x} = -6x + 4y \quad \text{and} \quad \frac{\partial f}{\partial y} = 4 + 4x - 4y.$$

After equating each of these derivatives to zero we readily solve for $x = 2$, $y = 3$. Thus $\mathbf{a} = (2, 3)$ is the only critical point of f. The second order partial derivatives of f are

$$\frac{\partial^2 f}{\partial x^2} = -6, \qquad \frac{\partial^2 f}{\partial y^2} = -4, \quad \text{and} \quad \frac{\partial^2 f}{\partial x \partial y} = \frac{\partial^2 f}{\partial y \partial x} = 4,$$

so the Hessian matrix of f at $\mathbf{a} = (2, 3)$ is

$$H = \begin{bmatrix} -6 & 4 \\ 4 & -4 \end{bmatrix}.$$

Then $\Delta_1 = -6 < 0$ and $\Delta_2 = 8 > 0$, so it follows that $f(2, 3) = 6$ is a local maximum value of f.

EXAMPLE 9 If

$$f(x, y, z) = 2x^2 + 2y^2 + 2z^2 + 2xz + 3y^2 \cos x,$$

then

$$\frac{\partial f}{\partial x} = 4x + 2z - 3y^2 \sin x,$$

$$\frac{\partial f}{\partial y} = 4y + 6y \cos x, \qquad \text{and}$$

$$\frac{\partial f}{\partial z} = 4z + 2x.$$

Hence $\mathbf{a} = (0, 0, 0)$ is a critical point of f. When we calculate the second order partial derivatives of f, we find that the Hessian matrix of f at $\mathbf{a} = (0, 0, 0)$ is

$$H = \begin{bmatrix} 4 & 0 & 2 \\ 0 & 10 & 0 \\ 2 & 0 & 4 \end{bmatrix}.$$

It therefore follows from Example 3 that the quadratic form $q(\mathbf{x}) = \mathbf{x}^T H \mathbf{x}$ is positive definite, so Theorem 5 implies that $f(0, 0, 0) = 0$ is local minimum value of f.

8.2 PROBLEMS

In Problems 1–10, a quadratic form $q(\mathbf{x}) = \mathbf{x}^T A \mathbf{x}$ is given. Find the eigenvalues of A in order to determine whether q is positive definite, negative definite, or indefinite.

1. $q(x, y) = 4xy$

2. $q(x, y) = 3x^2 + 2xy + 3y^2$

3. $q(x, y) = 5x^2 + 2xy + 5y^2$

4. $q(x, y) = 3x^2 + 8xy - 3y^2$

5. $q(x, y) = 9x^2 + 4xy + 6y^2$

6. $q(x, y) = 7x^2 + 12xy - 2y^2$

7. $q(x, y, z) = 3x^2 + 4y^2 + 3z^2 + 2xz$

8. $q(x, y, z) = x^2 + y^2 + 2z^2 + 6xy$

9. $q(x, y, z) = x^2 + 4y^2 + z^2 + 2xy + 8xz + 2yz$

10. $q(x, y, z) = 5x^2 + 7y^2 + 5z^2 + 2xy + 6xz + 2yz$

11–20. Apply Theorem 4 to solve Problems 1–10.

In Problems 21–24, a 4×4 matrix A is given. Classify the quadratic form $q(\mathbf{x}) = \mathbf{x}^T A \mathbf{x}$.

21. $\begin{bmatrix} 2 & 0 & 0 & 1 \\ 0 & 4 & 3 & 0 \\ 0 & 3 & 4 & 0 \\ 1 & 0 & 0 & 2 \end{bmatrix}$

22. $\begin{bmatrix} 2 & 0 & 1 & 0 \\ 0 & 3 & 0 & 1 \\ 1 & 0 & 2 & 0 \\ 0 & 1 & 0 & 5 \end{bmatrix}$

23. $\begin{bmatrix} 1 & 2 & 2 & 2 \\ 2 & 1 & 2 & 2 \\ 2 & 2 & 1 & 2 \\ 2 & 2 & 2 & 1 \end{bmatrix}$

24. $\begin{bmatrix} 4 & 1 & 1 & 4 \\ 1 & 4 & 1 & 4 \\ 1 & 1 & 4 & 4 \\ 4 & 4 & 4 & 1 \end{bmatrix}$

In Problems 25–30, describe geometrically the graph of the given equation.

25. $z = 3x^2 + 2xy + 3y^2$

26. $z = x^2 + 6xy + y^2$

27. $z = 4x^2 + 6xy - 4y^2$

28. $z = 9x^2 + 4xy + 6y^2$

29. $z = 33x^2 + 8xy + 18y^2$

30. $z = 40x^2 + 36xy + 25y^2$

Find and classify the critical points of the functions given in Problems 31–40.

31. $f(x, y) = 2x^2 + y^2 + 4x - 4y + 5$

32. $f(x, y) = 10 + 12x - 12y - 3x^2 - 2y^2$

33. $f(x, y) = 2x^2 - 3y^2 + 2x - 3y + 7$

34. $f(x, y) = xy + 3x - 2y + 4$

35. $f(x, y) = 2x^2 + 2xy + y^2 + 4x - 2y + 1$

36. $f(x, y) = x^2 + 4xy + 2y^2 + 4x - 8y + 3$

37. $f(x, y) = x^3 + y^3 + 3xy + 3$

38. $f(x, y) = x^2 - 2xy + y^3 - y$

39. $f(x, y) = 6x - x^3 - y^3$

40. $f(x, y) = 3xy - x^3 - y^3$

Problems 41–43 deal with parts of the proof of Theorem 4 in dimension $n = 3$. Let $q(x, y, z) = \mathbf{x}^T A \mathbf{x}$ be a quadratic form with symmetric 3×3 matrix $A = [a_{ij}]$.

41. If the principal subdeterminants Δ_1, Δ_2, and Δ_3 are all positive, prove that q is positive definite, as follows: If the eigenvalues $\lambda_1, \lambda_2, \lambda_3$ of A are not all positive (as we wish to prove), then exactly two of them, say λ_1 and λ_2, are negative. (Why?) If $\mathbf{v}_1$ and $\mathbf{v}_2$ are associated eigenvectors, show that $q(\mathbf{x}) < 0$ for all $\mathbf{x} \neq \mathbf{0}$ in the subspace V spanned by $\mathbf{v}_1$ and $\mathbf{v}_2$. But by the case $n = 2$ of the theorem, $q(x, y, 0) > 0$ unless $x = y = 0$. Why is this a contradiction?

42. If $\Delta_1 < 0$, $\Delta_2 > 0$, and $\Delta_3 < 0$, prove that q is negative definite, as follows. If $q^*(\mathbf{x}) = -q(\mathbf{x})$, then q is negative definite if and only if q^* is positive definite. Apply the result of Problem 41 to show that q^* is positive definite.

43. Deduce part (c) of Theorem 4 from parts (a) and (b).

8.3
Diagonalization and Differential Equations

Many science and engineering problems lead to the mathematical problem of solving a linear system of first order differential equations of the form

$$\begin{aligned} x_1' &= a_{11}x_1 + a_{12}x_2 + \cdots + a_{1n}x_n \\ x_2' &= a_{21}x_1 + a_{22}x_2 + \cdots + a_{2n}x_n \\ &\vdots \\ x_n' &= a_{n1}x_1 + a_{n2}x_2 + \cdots + a_{nn}x_n. \end{aligned} \tag{1}$$

The primes on the left denote derivatives with respect to the independent variable t, so

$$x_i' = x_i'(t) = \frac{dx_i}{dt},$$

and each coefficient a_{ij} on the right is *constant.*

By a **solution** of the system of equations in (1) is meant an n-tuple $(x_1(t), x_2(t), \ldots, x_n(t))$ of differentiable functions that satisfy these equations for all t in some interval on the t-axis. Thus we regard (1) as a system of n equations (with given coefficients) in the n unknown *functions* $x_1, x_2, \ldots, x_n$. A standard theorem in the theory of differential equations states that, given any n-vector $\mathbf{b} = (b_1, b_2, \ldots, b_n)$, then there exists a unique solution of (1) on the whole real line that satisfies the **initial conditions**

$$x_1(0) = b_1, x_2(0) = b_2, \ldots, x_n(0) = b_n. \tag{2}$$

In this section we describe the use of linear algebra to solve the system in (1) in the important special case in which the coefficient matrix $A = [a_{ij}]$ is *diagonalizable.* If we write

$$\mathbf{x} = \begin{bmatrix} x_1 \\ x_2 \\ \vdots \\ x_n \end{bmatrix} = (x_1, x_2, \ldots, x_n)$$

and agree to differentiate an n-tuple or vector of functions elementwise,

$$\frac{d\mathbf{x}}{dt} = \mathbf{x}'(t) = (x_1'(t), x_2'(t), \ldots, x_n'(t)),$$

then (1) takes the form

$$\frac{d\mathbf{x}}{dt} = A\mathbf{x}. \tag{3}$$

Given an n-vector $\mathbf{b}$, we would like to solve the **initial value problem**

$$\frac{d\mathbf{x}}{dt} = A\mathbf{x}, \qquad \mathbf{x}(0) = \mathbf{b}. \tag{4}$$

Let us begin with the case $n = 1$, in which we have the single (scalar) equation

$$\frac{dx}{dt} = ax. \tag{5}$$

Recall that the derivative of the exponential function

$$x(t) = ce^{at} \qquad (c \text{ an "arbitrary constant"}) \tag{6}$$

is

$$\frac{dx}{dt} = c(ae^{at}) = ax.$$

Consequently $x = ce^{at}$ is called the **general solution** of Equation (5). To get the **particular solution** that satisfies both (5) *and* the initial condition $x(0) = b$, we need only take c equal to the initial value b, obtaining $x(t) = be^{at}$, for then $x(0) = be^0 = b$. For instance, the general solution of the equation $x' = 3x$ is $x = ce^{3t}$, and the (particular) solution of the initial value problem

$$\frac{dx}{dt} = 3x, \qquad x(0) = 7$$

is $x(t) = 7e^{3t}$.

The simplest n-dimensional generalization of Equation (5) is the system $\mathbf{x}' = A\mathbf{x}$ in which A is a *diagonal* matrix,

$$A = D = \begin{bmatrix} k_1 & 0 & 0 & 0 & \cdots & 0 \\ 0 & k_2 & 0 & 0 & \cdots & 0 \\ 0 & 0 & k_3 & 0 & \cdots & 0 \\ 0 & 0 & 0 & k_4 & \cdots & 0 \\ \vdots & \vdots & \vdots & \vdots & \ddots & \vdots \\ 0 & 0 & 0 & 0 & \cdots & k_n \end{bmatrix}. \tag{7}$$

In this case $\mathbf{x}' = A\mathbf{x}$ is simply the system

$$\begin{aligned} x_1' &= k_1 x_1 \\ x_2' &= k_2 x_2 \\ &\vdots \\ x_n' &= k_n x_n \end{aligned} \tag{8}$$

of n scalar equations that are independent, or "uncoupled": The ith equation $x_i' = k_i x_i$ involves only the ith entry in $\mathbf{x}$ and is of the form in (5), so its general solution is of the form $x_i = c_i e^{k_i t}$. Thus we find quickly (and easily) that the **general solution** of the "diagonal system" in (8) is given by

$$\mathbf{x}(t) = (c_1 e^{k_1 t}, c_2 e^{k_2 t}, \ldots, c_n e^{k_n t}), \tag{9}$$

where $c_1, c_2, \ldots, c_n$ are arbitrary constants.

EXAMPLE 1 Find the solution of the system

$$\begin{aligned} x_1' &= 7x_1 \\ x_2' &= -3x_2 \\ x_3' &= 5x_3 \end{aligned} \tag{10}$$

that satisfies the initial conditions $x_1(0) = 6$, $x_2(0) = 4$, $x_3(0) = -8$.

Solution From (9) we see immediately that the general solution of (10) is

$$\mathbf{x}(t) = (c_1 e^{7t}, c_2 e^{-3t}, c_3 e^{5t}).$$

Because we require $\mathbf{x}(0) = (6, 4, -8)$, we choose $c_1 = 6$, $c_2 = 4$, and $c_3 = -8$. Hence the desired particular solution is given by

$$\mathbf{x}(t) = (6e^{7t}, 4e^{-3t}, -8e^{5t});$$

alternatively, by

$$x_1(t) = 6e^{7t}, \qquad x_2(t) = 4e^{-3t}, \qquad x_3(t) = -8e^{5t}.$$

Our strategy for solving a more general system $\mathbf{x}' = A\mathbf{x}$ is to attempt to make a substitution for $\mathbf{x}$ that transforms this system into a new system whose coefficient matrix is a *diagonal* matrix. The new diagonal system can then be solved easily as in (9), and we finally should be able to "reverse" the substitution process and use the solution of the transformed system to find a solution of the original system.

We now describe how this approach can be carried through provided that the original coefficient matrix A is *diagonalizable.* By Theorem 1 in Section 6.2 we know that this is so if and only if the $n \times n$ matrix A has n linearly independent eigenvectors $\mathbf{v}_1, \mathbf{v}_2, \ldots, \mathbf{v}_n$. If $\lambda_1, \lambda_2, \ldots, \lambda_n$ are the corresponding eigenvalues (not necessarily distinct) and

$$P = [\mathbf{v}_1 \quad \mathbf{v}_2 \quad \cdots \quad \mathbf{v}_n]$$

is the invertible $n \times n$ matrix with the eigenvectors as its column vectors, then

$$A = PDP^{-1} \tag{11}$$

where

$$D = \begin{bmatrix} \lambda_1 & 0 & 0 & \cdots & 0 \\ 0 & \lambda_2 & 0 & \cdots & 0 \\ 0 & 0 & \lambda_3 & \cdots & 0 \\ \vdots & \vdots & \vdots & \ddots & \vdots \\ 0 & 0 & 0 & \cdots & \lambda_n \end{bmatrix}.$$

Given $\mathbf{b}$ we know that the system $\mathbf{x}' = A\mathbf{x}$ has a solution satisfying the initial condition $\mathbf{x}(0) = \mathbf{b}$; our problem is to find this solution $\mathbf{x}(t) = (x_1(t), x_2(t), \ldots, x_n(t))$.

We actually are going to find first the n-tuple $\mathbf{y}(t) = (y_1(t), y_2(t), \ldots, y_n(t))$ of functions defined by

$$\mathbf{y} = P^{-1}\mathbf{x}. \tag{12}$$

We do this by substituting

$$\mathbf{x} = P\mathbf{y} \tag{13}$$

in $\mathbf{x}' = A\mathbf{x}$. Because the elements of P are constants it is easy to verify that $\mathbf{x}' = P\mathbf{y}'$. Therefore substitution of $\mathbf{x} = P\mathbf{y}$ in $\mathbf{x}' = A\mathbf{x}$ yields

$$P\mathbf{y}' = A(P\mathbf{y});$$

$$P\mathbf{y}' = (PDP^{-1})P\mathbf{y};$$

$$P\mathbf{y}' = PD\mathbf{y}.$$

Then multiplication on the left by P^{-1} gives the transformed system

$$\mathbf{y}' = D\mathbf{y}. \tag{14}$$

But the new system in (14) has the simple diagonal form in (8), except with $y_1, y_2, \ldots, y_n$ in place of $x_1, x_2, \ldots, x_n$ and with the eigenvalues $\lambda_1, \lambda_2, \ldots, \lambda_n$ in place of $k_1, k_2, \ldots, k_n$. Hence the general solution of (14) is given as in (9) by

$$\mathbf{y}(t) = (c_1 e^{\lambda_1 t}, c_2 e^{\lambda_2 t}, \ldots, c_n e^{\lambda_n t}). \tag{15}$$

Now that we know what $\mathbf{y}$ is, Equation (13) tells us that a solution $\mathbf{x}$ of the original system $\mathbf{x}' = A\mathbf{x}$ is given by $\mathbf{x} = P\mathbf{y}$; that is,

$$\begin{bmatrix} x_1 \\ x_2 \\ \vdots \\ x_n \end{bmatrix} = [\mathbf{v}_1 \quad \mathbf{v}_2 \quad \cdots \quad \mathbf{v}_n] \begin{bmatrix} c_1 e^{\lambda_1 t} \\ c_2 e^{\lambda_2 t} \\ \vdots \\ c_n e^{\lambda_n t} \end{bmatrix}.$$

Consequently

$$\mathbf{x}(t) = c_1 \mathbf{v}_1 e^{\lambda_1 t} + c_2 \mathbf{v}_2 e^{\lambda_2 t} + \cdots + c_n \mathbf{v}_n e^{\lambda_n t}. \tag{16}$$

For any choice of the arbitrary constants $\mathbf{c} = (c_1, c_2, \ldots, c_n)$ in (15), Equation (16) determines a corresponding solution of $\mathbf{x}' = A\mathbf{x}$. Substitution of $t = 0$ in (16) yields

$$\mathbf{x}(0) = c_1\mathbf{v}_1 + c_2\mathbf{v}_2 + \cdots + c_n\mathbf{v}_n = P\mathbf{c}.$$

So in order to satisfy the initial condition $\mathbf{x}(0) = \mathbf{b}$, we need only take

$$\mathbf{c} = P^{-1}\mathbf{b}, \tag{17}$$

though in practice it may be simpler to solve the system $P\mathbf{c} = \mathbf{b}$ for $\mathbf{c}$. Because every solution of the system $\mathbf{x}' = A\mathbf{x}$ can thus be expressed in the form in (16), we call (16) the **general solution** of the system. Our derivation of (16) and (17) constitutes a proof of the following theorem.

Theorem: *The System* $\mathbf{x}' = A\mathbf{x}$

Let the $n \times n$ matrix A be diagonalizable, with linearly independent eigenvectors $\mathbf{v}_1, \mathbf{v}_2, \ldots, \mathbf{v}_n$ and corresponding eigenvalues $\lambda_1, \lambda_2, \ldots, \lambda_n$. Then the solution of the initial value problem

$$\frac{d\mathbf{x}}{dt} = A\mathbf{x}, \qquad \mathbf{x}(0) = \mathbf{b}$$

is given by

$$\mathbf{x}(t) = c_1\mathbf{v}_1e^{\lambda_1 t} + c_2\mathbf{v}_2e^{\lambda_2 t} + \cdots + c_n\mathbf{v}_ne^{\lambda_n t} \tag{16}$$

with the coefficients given by

$$\mathbf{c} = (c_1, c_2, \ldots, c_n) = P^{-1}\mathbf{b}. \tag{17}$$

If the $n \times n$ matrix A is not diagonalizable, then the solution of the system $\mathbf{x}' = A\mathbf{x}$ requires more advanced techniques that will not be discussed here. Fortunately the diagonalizable case is the one that is most common in applications.

EXAMPLE 2 Find the solution of the system

$$\begin{aligned} x_1' &= 5x_1 - 6x_2 \\ x_2' &= 2x_1 - 2x_2 \end{aligned} \tag{18}$$

that satisfies the initial conditions $x_1(0) = 1$, $x_2(0) = -1$.

Solution In Example 1 of Section 6.1 we found that the coefficient matrix

$$A = \begin{bmatrix} 5 & -6 \\ 2 & -2 \end{bmatrix}$$

in (18) has eigenvalues $\lambda_1 = 2$ and $\lambda_2 = 1$ with associated eigenvectors $\mathbf{v}_1 = (2, 1)$ and $\mathbf{v}_2 = (3, 2)$, respectively. Then the formula in (16) gives the general solution

$$\mathbf{x}(t) = c_1\mathbf{v}_1e^{\lambda_1 t} + c_2\mathbf{v}_2e^{\lambda_2 t};$$

that is,

$$\begin{bmatrix} x_1 \\ x_2 \end{bmatrix} = c_1\begin{bmatrix} 2 \\ 1 \end{bmatrix}e^{2t} + c_2\begin{bmatrix} 3 \\ 2 \end{bmatrix}e^{t}.$$

Hence the general solution of the system in (18) is given by

$$\begin{aligned} x_1(t) &= 2c_1e^{2t} + 3c_2e^{t} \\ x_2(t) &= c_1e^{2t} + 2c_2e^{t}. \end{aligned} \tag{19}$$

When we substitute $t = 0$, the initial conditions $x_1(0) = 1$ and $x_2(0) = -1$ yield the equations

$$\begin{aligned} 2c_1 + 3c_2 &= 1 \\ c_1 + 2c_2 &= -1 \end{aligned}$$

that we readily solve for $c_1 = 5, c_2 = -3$. Using these values for the constants in (19), we get the desired particular solution

$$\begin{aligned} x_1(t) &= 10e^{2t} - 9e^t \\ x_2(t) &= 5e^{2t} - 6e^t. \end{aligned}$$

EXAMPLE 3 Find the general solution of the system

$$\begin{aligned} x_1' &= 4x_1 - 2x_2 + x_3 \\ x_2' &= 2x_1 \qquad + x_3 \\ x_3' &= 2x_1 - 2x_2 + 3x_3. \end{aligned} \tag{20}$$

Solution In Example 7 of Section 6.1 we found that the coefficient matrix

$$A = \begin{bmatrix} 4 & -2 & 1 \\ 2 & 0 & 1 \\ 2 & -2 & 3 \end{bmatrix}$$

in (20) has linearly independent eigenvectors $\mathbf{v}_1 = (1, 1, 1)$, $\mathbf{v}_2 = (1, 1, 0)$, and $\mathbf{v}_3 = (-1, 0, 2)$ associated with the eigenvalues $\lambda_1 = 3$, $\lambda_2 = 2$, and $\lambda_3 = 2$, respectively (so $\lambda = 2$ is a repeated eigenvalue corresponding to the eigenvectors $\mathbf{v}_2$ and $\mathbf{v}_3$). Hence the formula in (16) yields the general solution

$$\mathbf{x}(t) = c_1\mathbf{v}_1 e^{\lambda_1 t} + c_2\mathbf{v}_2 e^{\lambda_2 t} + c_3\mathbf{v}_3 e^{\lambda_3 t};$$

that is,

$$\begin{bmatrix} x_1 \\ x_2 \\ x_3 \end{bmatrix} = c_1 \begin{bmatrix} 1 \\ 1 \\ 1 \end{bmatrix} e^{3t} + c_2 \begin{bmatrix} 1 \\ 1 \\ 0 \end{bmatrix} e^{2t} + c_3 \begin{bmatrix} -1 \\ 0 \\ 2 \end{bmatrix} e^{2t}.$$

Thus the general solution of the system in (2) is given by

$$\begin{aligned} x_1(t) &= c_1e^{3t} + c_2e^{2t} - c_3e^{2t} \\ x_2(t) &= c_1e^{3t} + c_2e^{2t} \\ x_3(t) &= c_1e^{3t} \qquad\quad + 2c_3e^{2t}. \end{aligned}$$

An nth order (homogeneous) linear differential equation with constant coefficients is one of the form

$$x^{(n)} + a_{n-1}x^{(n-1)} + \cdots + a_2x'' + a_1x' + a_0x = 0 \tag{21}$$

where $x(t)$ is the unknown function; primes and the superscripts $(n), (n-1), \ldots$ denote differentiation with respect to the independent variable t. Such an equation can be transformed into an equivalent nth order system of the form $\mathbf{x}' = A\mathbf{x}$ by means of the substitutions

$$x_1 = x,\ x_2 = x', \ldots, x_n = x^{(n-1)}. \tag{22}$$

For instance, in the case of the second order equation

$$x'' + px' + qx = 0 \tag{23}$$

where p and q are constants, the substitutions $x_1 = x$, $x_2 = x'$ yield

$$x_1' = x' = x_2$$

and

$$x_2' = x'' = -px' - qx = -qx_1 - px_2;$$

that is,

$$\begin{bmatrix} x_1' \\ x_2' \end{bmatrix} = \begin{bmatrix} 0 & 1 \\ -q & -p \end{bmatrix} \begin{bmatrix} x_1 \\ x_2 \end{bmatrix}. \tag{24}$$

Similarly, in the case of the third order equation

$$x^{(3)} + px'' + qx' + rx = 0 \tag{25}$$

with constant coefficients, the substitutions $x_1 = x$, $x_2 = x'$, $x_3 = x''$ yield

$$\begin{aligned} x_1' &= x' = x_2, \\ x_2' &= x'' = x_3, \\ x_3' &= x^{(3)} = -px'' - qx' - rx \\ &= -rx_1 - qx_2 - px_3; \end{aligned}$$

that is,

$$\begin{bmatrix} x_1' \\ x_2' \\ x_3' \end{bmatrix} = \begin{bmatrix} 0 & 1 & 0 \\ 0 & 0 & 1 \\ -r & -q & -p \end{bmatrix} \begin{bmatrix} x_1 \\ x_2 \\ x_3 \end{bmatrix}. \tag{26}$$

If the general solution $\mathbf{x} = (x_1, x_2, x_3)$ of this system can be found, then $x = x_1$ provides what is called the **general solution** of the original equation in (25).

EXAMPLE 4 Find the general solution of the third order differential equation

$$x^{(3)} - 2x'' - 5x' + 6x = 0. \tag{27}$$

Solution With $p = -2$, $q = -5$, and $r = 6$, the coefficient matrix in (26) is

$$A = \begin{bmatrix} 0 & 1 & 0 \\ 0 & 0 & 1 \\ -6 & 5 & 2 \end{bmatrix}.$$

The characteristic equation of A is

$$\begin{aligned} |A - \lambda I| &= \begin{vmatrix} -\lambda & 1 & 0 \\ 0 & -\lambda & 1 \\ -6 & 5 & 2 - \lambda \end{vmatrix} \\ &= -(\lambda^3 - 2\lambda^2 - 5\lambda + 6) = 0. \end{aligned}$$

If we first spot the root $\lambda_1 = 1$, and then divide $\lambda - 1$ into $\lambda^3 - 2\lambda^2 - 5\lambda + 6$, we readily find the factorization

$$\lambda^3 - 2\lambda^2 - 5\lambda + 6 = (\lambda - 1)(\lambda + 2)(\lambda - 3) = 0.$$

Hence the matrix A has eigenvalues $\lambda_1 = 1$, $\lambda_2 = -2$, and $\lambda_3 = 3$.

To find the associated eigenvectors we need to solve the system

$$\begin{bmatrix} -\lambda & 1 & 0 \\ 0 & -\lambda & 1 \\ -6 & 5 & 2-\lambda \end{bmatrix} \begin{bmatrix} u \\ v \\ w \end{bmatrix} = \begin{bmatrix} 0 \\ 0 \\ 0 \end{bmatrix}$$

for each eigenvalue λ. But the first two equations here yield

$$v = \lambda u \quad \text{and} \quad w = \lambda v = \lambda^2 u.$$

Hence the eigenvector associated with λ is $(1, \lambda, \lambda^2)$. Consequently the eigenvectors associated with $\lambda_1 = 1$, $\lambda_2 = -2$, and $\lambda_3 = 3$ are $\mathbf{v}_1 = (1, 1, 1)$, $\mathbf{v}_2 = (1, -2, 4)$, and $\mathbf{v}_3 = (1, 3, 9)$, respectively.

These three eigenvectors of A are linearly independent, so the formula in (16) yields the general solution

$$\mathbf{x} = c_1\mathbf{v}_1 e^{\lambda_1 t} + c_2\mathbf{v}_2 e^{\lambda_2 t} + c_3\mathbf{v}_3 e^{\lambda_3 t};$$

that is,

$$\begin{bmatrix} x_1 \\ x_2 \\ x_3 \end{bmatrix} = c_1 \begin{bmatrix} 1 \\ 1 \\ 1 \end{bmatrix} e^{t} + c_2 \begin{bmatrix} 1 \\ -2 \\ 4 \end{bmatrix} e^{-2t} + c_3 \begin{bmatrix} 1 \\ 3 \\ 9 \end{bmatrix} e^{3t},$$

of the system $\mathbf{x}' = A\mathbf{x}$. The general solution $x = x_1$ of the original third order equation in (27) is then

$$x(t) = c_1 e^{t} + c_2 e^{-2t} + c_3 e^{3t}.$$

8.3 PROBLEMS

Find general solutions of the linear systems of differential equations given in Problems 1–20.

1. $x_1' = 5x_1 - 4x_2,$
$x_2' = 2x_1 - x_2$

2. $x_1' = 6x_1 - 6x_2,$
$x_2' = 4x_1 - 4x_2$

3. $x_1' = 5x_1 - 3x_2,$
$x_2' = 2x_1$

4. $x_1' = 5x_1 - 4x_2,$
$x_2' = 3x_1 - 2x_2$

5. $x_1' = 9x_1 - 8x_2,$
$x_2' = 6x_1 - 5x_2$

6. $x_1' = 10x_1 - 6x_2,$
$x_2' = 12x_1 - 7x_2$

7. $x_1' = 6x_1 - 10x_2,$
$x_2' = 2x_1 - 3x_2$

8. $x_1' = 11x_1 - 15x_2,$
$x_2' = 6x_1 - 8x_2$

9. $x_1' = 3x_1 + x_2,$
$x_2' = x_1 + 3x_2$

10. $x_1' = 4x_1 + 2x_2,$
$x_2' = 2x_1 + 4x_2$

11. $x_1' = 9x_1 + 2x_2,$
$x_2' = 2x_1 + 6x_2$

12. $x_1' = 13x_1 + 4x_2,$
$x_2' = 4x_1 + 7x_2$

13. $x_1' = 4x_1 + x_2 + 4x_3,$
$x_2' = x_1 + 7x_2 + x_3,$
$x_3' = 4x_1 + x_2 + 4x_3$

14. $x_1' = x_1 + 2x_2 + 2x_3,$
$x_2' = 2x_1 + 7x_2 + x_3,$
$x_3' = 2x_1 + x_2 + 7x_3$

15. $x_1' = 4x_1 + x_2 + x_3,$
$x_2' = x_1 + 4x_2 + x_3,$
$x_3' = x_1 + x_2 + 4x_3$

16. $x_1' = 5x_1 + x_2 + 3x_3,$
$x_2' = x_1 + 7x_2 + x_3,$
$x_3' = 3x_1 + x_2 + 5x_3$

17. $x_1' = 5x_1 - 6x_3,$
$x_2' = 2x_1 - x_2 - 2x_3,$
$x_3' = 4x_1 - 2x_2 - 4x_3$

18. $x_1' = 3x_1 + 2x_2 + 2x_3,$
$x_2' = -5x_1 - 4x_2 - 2x_3,$
$x_3' = 5x_1 + 5x_2 + 3x_3$

19. $x_1' = 3x_1 + x_2 + x_3,$
$x_2' = -5x_1 - 3x_2 - x_3,$
$x_3' = 5x_1 + 5x_2 + 3x_3$

20. $x_1' = 2x_1 + 3x_2 + 3x_3,$
$x_2' = -x_2 - 3x_3,$
$x_3' = 2x_3$

In Problems 21–28, use the method of Example 4 to find the general solution of the given differential equation.

21. $x'' - 3x' + 2x = 0$

22. $x'' - 2x' - 3x = 0$

23. $x'' - 25x = 0$

24. $x'' + 8x' + 15x = 0$

25. $x^{(3)} - 9x' = 0$

26. $x^{(3)} + 3x'' + 2x' = 0$

27. $x^{(3)} - 2x'' - x' + 2x = 0$

28. $x^{(3)} - x'' - 4x' + 4x = 0$

29. Show that the characteristic equation of the matrix

$$A = \begin{bmatrix} 0 & 1 \\ -q & -p \end{bmatrix}$$

is $\lambda^2 + p\lambda + q = 0$. If the roots λ_1 and λ_2 are real and distinct, show that the associated eigenvectors are $\mathbf{v}_1 = (1, \lambda_1)$ and $\mathbf{v}_2 = (1, \lambda_2)$. Conclude in this case that the general solution of the differential equation

$$x'' + px' + qx = 0$$

is $x(t) = c_1e^{\lambda_1 t} + c_2e^{\lambda_2 t}$.

30. Show that the characteristic equation of the matrix

$$A = \begin{bmatrix} 0 & 1 & 0 \\ 0 & 0 & 1 \\ -r & -q & -p \end{bmatrix}$$

is $\lambda^3 + p\lambda^2 + q\lambda + r = 0$. If the roots λ_1, λ_2, and λ_3 are real and distinct, show that each λ_i corresponds to the eigenvector $\mathbf{v}_i = (1, \lambda_i, \lambda_i^2)$. Conclude in this case that the general solution of the differential equation

$$x^{(3)} + px'' + qx' + rx = 0$$

is $x(t) = c_1e^{\lambda_1 t} + c_2e^{\lambda_2 t} + c_3e^{\lambda_3 t}$.

31. This problem deals with the nth order differential equation

$$x^{(n)} + a_{n-1}x^{(n-1)} + \cdots + a_1x' + a_0x = 0. \quad (21)$$

(a) Show that the substitution

$$x_1 = x, \quad x_2 = x', \ldots, x_n = x^{(n-1)} \quad (22)$$

yields the system $\mathbf{x}' = A\mathbf{x}$ with $n \times n$ coefficient matrix

$$A = \begin{bmatrix} 0 & 1 & 0 & \cdots & 0 \\ 0 & 0 & 1 & \cdots & 0 \\ \vdots & \vdots & \vdots & \ddots & \vdots \\ 0 & 0 & 0 & \cdots & 1 \\ -a_0 & -a_1 & -a_2 & \cdots & -a_{n-1} \end{bmatrix}.$$

(b) Expand $|A - \lambda I|$ along the first column to show by induction on n that the characteristic equation of A is

$$\lambda^n + a_{n-1}\lambda^{n-1} + \cdots + a_1\lambda + a_0 = 0.$$

(c) If the characteristic equation of part (b) has n distinct real roots $\lambda_1, \lambda_2, \ldots, \lambda_n$, show that each λ_i corresponds to the eigenvector

$$\mathbf{v}_i = (1, \lambda_i, \lambda_i^2, \ldots, \lambda_i^{n-1}).$$

Conclude in this case that the general solution of the differential equation in (21) is

$$x(t) = c_1e^{\lambda_1 t} + c_2e^{\lambda_2 t} + \cdots + c_ne^{\lambda_n t}.$$

9

Numerical Methods

9.1

Roundoff Errors, Pivoting, and Conditioning

Essentially all this book has dealt either explicitly or implicitly with the problem of solving a linear system

$$A\mathbf{x} = \mathbf{b}. \tag{1}$$

The second central problem of elementary linear algebra is the eigenvalue-eigenvector problem

$$A\mathbf{v} = \lambda\mathbf{v}, \tag{2}$$

but methods for solving this problem frequently involve the problem in (1) as well.

In order to present the basic theory and applications with maximal clarity and minimal distraction, we generally have kept the arithmetic as simple as possible. Our typical example has looked like

$$\begin{aligned} x + 2y + z &= 4 \\ 3x + 8y + 7z &= 20 \\ 2x + 7y + 9z &= 23 \end{aligned} \tag{3}$$

rather than like

$$\begin{aligned} (62.46312)x - (13.83165)y + (43.61778)z &= 55.43117 \\ (31.22778)x + (73.16050)y - (16.20055)z &= 91.33181 \\ (5.11017)x - (32.77253)y - (40.00172)z &= 15.60235. \end{aligned} \tag{4}$$

Unfortunately, a linear system encountered in a practical application may well look more like (4) than (3)—the coefficients that nature provides are seldom small whole numbers.

Moreover, implied in the contrast between (3) and (4) is a difference much more fundamental than the question of how much tedious arithmetic is required. In (3) the values of the coefficients are given precisely, and we can use Gaussian elimination to find the *exact solution* of the system. In (4) it is reasonable to assume that the coefficients in the "actual system" have been *rounded* to five decimal places. Therefore we can hope to find only an *approximate solution* of the original system.

In many practical situations it is inevitable that we can only approximate the actual solution and not find it exactly. For instance, suppose that some natural process is governed by the linear system $A\mathbf{x} = \mathbf{b}$, but that we do not know in advance the entries in A and $\mathbf{b}$. We must find the values of these entries empirically, perhaps by observing the process or by conducting an experiment, and because of inevitable errors in measurement we can expect only to find these values approximately, not exactly. Hence we begin with an approximation A^* to A and an approximation $\mathbf{b}^*$ to $\mathbf{b}$, and thus we solve the *approximate system*

$$A^*\mathbf{x}^* = \mathbf{b}^* \tag{5}$$

instead of the actual system $A\mathbf{x} = \mathbf{b}$. Even if we can find the exact solution $\mathbf{x}^*$ of the approximate system, the difference between $\mathbf{x}^*$ and the exact solution $\mathbf{x}$ of the actual system is an error built into this situation from the beginning.

In addition—and frequently even more critical—there may be numerical errors that appear in the process of computation. If we are solving a system like the one in (4) but with 100 or even 1000 unknowns and equations instead of three, we will be using a computer rather than working by hand. But although the computer makes the solution of such large systems feasible, it also contributes some numerical difficulties of its own. Most computers store and work internally with numbers in the form of floating point decimals. (Actually, floating point octal (base 8) or hexadecimal (base 16) numbers are ordinarily used, but we will not worry about the distinction between these representations of numbers and their decimal representations.) A **floating point decimal** is a number of the form

$$x = \pm 0.d_1 d_2 \cdots d_k \times 10^p, \tag{6}$$

where each d_i is a single digit, $d_1 \neq 0$, and p is an integer. The number k of digits to the right of the decimal point is the number of **significant digits** the computer uses in its internal computations. For instance, the IBM Personal Computer employs seven (decimal) digits in its single-precision mode of operation and 16 digits in its double-precision mode.

To illustrate the way a computer handles floating point decimals, let us envision a simple computer that retains only three significant digits. That is, it stores all numbers as *three-digit floating point decimals.* If the number

$$x = 67437$$

is obtained by this computer as an input or as the result of a computation, it first rewrites the number as 0.67437×10^5 and then rounds it to three significant digits. Hence the rounded value

$$x' = 0.674 \times 10^5$$

is stored in place of the actual value x. This rounding introduces the **roundoff error** (actual value minus rounded value)

$$x - x' = 0.00037 \times 10^5 = 37.$$

Real number x	Three-digit floating point number x'	Roundoff error $x - x'$	Relative error $(x - x')/x$
67437	0.674×10^5	37	5.5×10^{-4}
0.007424	0.742×10^{-2}	4×10^{-6}	5.4×10^{-4}
56.48	0.565×10^2	-0.02	-3.5×10^{-4}
3.73	0.373×10^1	0	0
286.7	0.287×10^3	-0.3	-1.0×10^{-3}

9.1 Some real numbers and three-digit floating point decimals.

A better measure of the possible effect of this error is provided by the ratio of the roundoff error to the actual value—the **relative error**

$$\frac{x - x'}{x} = \frac{37}{67437} \approx 5.5 \times 10^{-4}.$$

The table in Figure 9.1 shows several real numbers, the corresponding three-digit floating point numbers stored by our simple computer, and the resulting roundoff errors and relative errors.

EXAMPLE 1 Now let us see how our 3-significant-digit computer multiplies the two real numbers

$$x = 67437 \quad \text{and} \quad y = 0.007424,$$

which have the actual product

$$z = xy = 500.652288.$$

The computer calculates

$$\begin{aligned} x'y' &= (0.674 \times 10^5)(0.742 \times 10^{-2}) \\ &= 0.500108 \times 10^3 \end{aligned}$$

and then rounds the result to

$$z' = 0.500 \times 10^3.$$

Thus the computer replaces the actual product 500.652288 with the approximate product 500, making a roundoff error of 0.652288 and a relative error of 1.3×10^{-3}. Looking at the first two lines of the table in Figure 9.1, we see that the relative error in the product is over twice the relative error in either factor.

GAUSSIAN ELIMINATION WITH PIVOTING

Example 1 suggests one way in which roundoff error can accumulate as repeated arithmetical operations with fixed-digit floating point numbers are carried out. In a lengthy numerical computation involving hundreds or thousands of additions and multiplications, the cumulative roundoff error can be so large as to "swamp" the numbers being computed, so that the final results of the computation are worse than useless—they may be misleading and meaningless. This danger is critical when solving a linear system by Gaussian elimination—operation counts like those in Section 2.3 show that the solution of an $n \times n$ system involves approximately $\frac{1}{3}n^3$ multiplications, so the solution of a system of 100 equations in 100 unknowns will involve about a third of a million multiplications.

Moreover, it unfortunately turns out that the process of Gaussian elimination is peculiarly susceptible to the *magnification* of roundoff error, even when only a modest number of calculations is involved. To show how that can happen, let us consider the system

$$\begin{aligned} (0.001)x + y &= 1 \\ x - y &= 0 \end{aligned} \tag{7}$$

whose actual solution is

$$x = y = \frac{1}{1.001} \approx 0.999. \tag{8}$$

In the following two examples we examine two attempts to solve the system in (7) by Gaussian elimination, using the 3-significant-digit computer previously discussed.

EXAMPLE 2 To eliminate x we add -1000 times the first equation in (7) to the second equation. The result is

$$-1001y = -1000.$$

But the computer rounds 1001 to 0.100×10^3, and thereby rewrites this equation as

$$(-0.100 \times 10^3)y = -0.100 \times 10^3$$

and hence gets $y = 1$. The first equation in (7) then yields $x = 0$. The computer's result of $x = 0$, $y = 1$ is terrible—not even close to the actual solution $x = y \approx 0.999$ in (8).

EXAMPLE 3 Now let us begin by interchanging the two equations in (7), rewriting the system as

$$\begin{aligned} x - y &= 0 \\ (0.001)x + y &= 1. \end{aligned} \tag{9}$$

Now we eliminate x by adding -0.001 times the first equation to the second. The result is the equation

$$(1.001)y = 1,$$

which the computer rounds to

$$(0.100 \times 10^1)y = 0.100 \times 10^1.$$

Thus it gets $y = 1$ as before. But now back substitution in the first equation in (9) yields $x = y = 1$, an acceptable approximation to the actual solution $x = y \approx 0.999$.

Examples 2 and 3 show that, with finite-digit floating point arithmetic, equally plausible applications of the method of Gaussian elimination can yield quite different results. In Example 2 we performed the operation

$$\begin{bmatrix} 0.001 & 1 \\ 1 & -1 \end{bmatrix} \xrightarrow{(-1000)R_1 + R_2} \begin{bmatrix} 0.001 & 1 \\ 0 & -1001 \end{bmatrix} \tag{10}$$

on the coefficient matrix in (7) and, after rounding to three significant digits, got a terrible result. In Example 3 we performed the operation

$$\begin{bmatrix} 1 & -1 \\ 0.001 & 1 \end{bmatrix} \xrightarrow{(-0.001)R_1 + R_2} \begin{bmatrix} 1 & -1 \\ 0 & 1.001 \end{bmatrix} \tag{11}$$

on the coefficient matrix in (9); this time we got an acceptable result.

What explains the difference? A possible answer is suggested by the **pivot entries** that are highlighted in color in (10) and (11). In (10) a pivot entry near zero leads to the use of a large multiplier (namely, -1000) in "clearing out" the first column. But in (11) a pivot entry whose magnitude is large (compared to the other entry in the first column) leads to the use of a multiplier close to zero (-0.001 in this case). In finite-digit floating point arithmetic, small pivot elements and the resulting large multipliers will magnify roundoff errors, and therefore should be avoided whenever possible.

The method of **Gaussian elimination with pivoting** is designed to minimize the accumulation of roundoff errors in solving linear systems. The main idea of pivoting is to choose at each stage the pivot of greatest magnitude possible. To begin to reduce a given matrix A to row-echelon form by Gaussian elimination *with pivoting*, the entry in the first column with the largest absolute value is first identified and then placed in the upper left (1, 1) pivot position by interchanging appropriate rows of A. After dividing the first row by this element to get a 1 in the (1, 1) position, this 1 is used to clear out the remaining entries in the first column of A. At each subsequent stage the same thing is done to clear out the first column of the submatrix that, at this stage, remains to be "reduced," using the largest available pivot entry.

We illustrate the method of Gaussian elimination with pivoting by applying it to reduce to row-echelon form the augmented coefficient matrix

$$A = \begin{bmatrix} 1 & 2 & 1 & 4 \\ 3 & 8 & 7 & 20 \\ 2 & 7 & 9 & 23 \end{bmatrix} \tag{12}$$

of the system in (3) at the beginning of this section. The largest entry in the first column of $A = [a_{ij}]$ is $a_{21} = 3$, so we begin by interchanging rows 1 and 2 to place this entry in the (1, 1) pivot position for Column 1:

$$A \xrightarrow{\text{SWAP}(R_1, R_2)} \begin{bmatrix} 3 & 8 & 7 & 20 \\ 1 & 2 & 1 & 4 \\ 2 & 7 & 9 & 23 \end{bmatrix}$$

$$\xrightarrow{(1/3)R_1} \begin{bmatrix} 1 & \frac{8}{3} & \frac{7}{3} & \frac{20}{3} \\ 1 & 2 & 1 & 4 \\ 2 & 7 & 9 & 23 \end{bmatrix}$$

$$\xrightarrow[(-2)R_1 + R_3]{(-1)R_1 + R_2} \begin{bmatrix} 1 & \frac{8}{3} & \frac{7}{3} & \frac{20}{3} \\ 0 & -\frac{2}{3} & -\frac{4}{3} & -\frac{8}{3} \\ 0 & \frac{5}{3} & \frac{13}{3} & \frac{29}{3} \end{bmatrix}.$$

The largest of the remaining entries to be dealt with in Column 2 is the entry $\frac{5}{3}$ in the (3, 2) position, so our next step is to interchange Rows 2 and 3 in order to use this element as the pivot entry for Column 2:

$$\xrightarrow{\text{SWAP}(R_2, R_3)} \begin{bmatrix} 1 & \frac{8}{3} & \frac{7}{3} & \frac{20}{3} \\ 0 & \frac{5}{3} & \frac{13}{3} & \frac{29}{3} \\ 0 & -\frac{2}{3} & -\frac{4}{3} & -\frac{8}{3} \end{bmatrix}$$

$$\xrightarrow{(3/5)R_2} \begin{bmatrix} 1 & \frac{8}{3} & \frac{7}{3} & \frac{20}{3} \\ 0 & 1 & \frac{13}{5} & \frac{29}{5} \\ 0 & -\frac{2}{3} & -\frac{4}{3} & -\frac{8}{3} \end{bmatrix}$$

$$\xrightarrow{(2/3)R_2 + R_3} \begin{bmatrix} 1 & \frac{8}{3} & \frac{7}{3} & \frac{20}{3} \\ 0 & 1 & \frac{13}{5} & \frac{29}{5} \\ 0 & 0 & \frac{2}{5} & \frac{6}{5} \end{bmatrix}$$

$$\xrightarrow{(5/2)R_3} \begin{bmatrix} 1 & \frac{8}{3} & \frac{7}{3} & \frac{20}{3} \\ 0 & 1 & \frac{13}{5} & \frac{29}{5} \\ 0 & 0 & 1 & 3 \end{bmatrix}$$

Back substitution finally yields

$$z = 3, \qquad y = \frac{29}{5} - \frac{13}{5}(3) = -2, \qquad \text{and}$$

$$x = \frac{20}{3} - \frac{8}{3}(-2) - \frac{7}{3}(3) = 5$$

for the solution of the system in (3).

Because no rounding was involved in these computations, we got the exact solution of the system. See Problems 21 and 22 for examples illustrating the increased accuracy that Gaussian elimination with pivoting sometimes yields, as compared with Gaussian elimination without pivoting.

ILL-CONDITIONED SYSTEMS

Examples 2 and 3 illustrate the fact that Gaussian elimination has a propensity to magnify errors in the solution of a linear system $A\mathbf{x} = \mathbf{b}$. Either small errors in the original entries of A and $\mathbf{b}$ or small roundoff errors in intermediate computational steps can lead to large errors in the results. For this reason all carefully designed computer programs for Gaussian elimination employ pivoting (and perhaps other techniques as well) to attempt to control the accumulation of such errors.

There do exist, however, linear systems that are so extraordinarily sensitive to tiny errors as to defeat even the most careful strategies. We illustrate this phenomenon by means of several 2×2 systems each having the coefficient matrix

$$A = \begin{bmatrix} 1 & 1 \\ 1 & 1.001 \end{bmatrix}. \tag{13}$$

The system

$$\begin{aligned} x + \qquad y &= 2 \\ x + (1.001)y &= 2 \end{aligned} \tag{14}$$

has the exact solution $x = 2$, $y = 0$. The system

$$\begin{aligned} x + \qquad y &= 2 \\ x + (1.001)y &= 2.001 \end{aligned} \tag{15}$$

has the exact solution $x = 1$, $y = 1$. The system

$$\begin{aligned} x + \qquad y &= 2 \\ x + (1.001)y &= 2.002 \end{aligned} \tag{16}$$

has the exact solution $x = 0$, $y = 2$.

The systems in (14), (15), and (16) show that if one has a system $A\mathbf{x} = \mathbf{b}$ with the coefficient matrix A in (13) but the constant vector $\mathbf{b}$ is known to only three significant digits, then practically nothing about the solution vector $\mathbf{x}$ can be deduced! Very small changes in $\mathbf{b}$—on the order of roundoff errors—result in very significant changes in the solution. The general question that these examples raise is this: If the constant vector $\mathbf{b}$ in the system $A\mathbf{x} = \mathbf{b}$ is changed by $\Delta\mathbf{b}$, what can be said about the resulting change $\Delta\mathbf{x}$ in the solution vector $\mathbf{x}$? Observe that if

$$A\mathbf{x} = \mathbf{b} \quad \text{and} \quad A(\mathbf{x} + \Delta\mathbf{x}) = \mathbf{b} + \Delta\mathbf{b}, \tag{17}$$

then subtraction of the first equation in (17) from the second yields

$$A\Delta\mathbf{x} = \Delta\mathbf{b}, \tag{18}$$

so

$$\Delta\mathbf{x} = A^{-1}\Delta\mathbf{b}. \tag{19}$$

The heart of the matter is therefore the question as to how much the length of a vector is magnified when it is multiplied by a given matrix. This question is easiest to answer when the $n \times n$ matrix A is symmetric and all its eigenvalues are nonzero. In this case let the eigenvalues $\lambda_1, \lambda_2, \ldots, \lambda_n$ be ordered so that

$$0 < |\lambda_1| \le |\lambda_2| \le \cdots \le |\lambda_n|. \tag{20}$$

Let $\mathbf{v}_1, \mathbf{v}_2, \ldots, \mathbf{v}_n$ be the associated eigenvectors of A. Because

$$|A\mathbf{v}_i| = |\lambda_i \mathbf{v}_i| = |\lambda_i||\mathbf{v}_i|$$

for each i, $1 \le i \le n$, it follows from (20) that

$$|\lambda_1||\mathbf{v}_i| \le |A\mathbf{v}_i| \le |\lambda_n||\mathbf{v}_i| \tag{21}$$

for each eigenvector $\mathbf{v}_i$ of A. Because every vector $\mathbf{x}$ in $\mathbf{R}^n$ can be expressed as a linear combination of the mutually orthogonal eigenvectors $\mathbf{v}_1, \mathbf{v}_2, \ldots, \mathbf{v}_n$, it follows readily (see Problem 27) from the inequalities in (21) that the same inequalities hold for all $\mathbf{x}$:

$$|\lambda_1||\mathbf{x}| \le |A\mathbf{x}| \le |\lambda_n||\mathbf{x}|. \tag{22}$$

That is, *when the vector* $\mathbf{x}$ *is multiplied by the matrix* A*, its length* $\mathbf{x}$ *is amplified at least by the factor* $|\lambda_1|$ *and at most by the factor* $|\lambda_n|$.

We are now prepared to answer the question of how much the solution vector $\mathbf{x}$ of the system $A\mathbf{x} = \mathbf{b}$ is "perturbed" when the constant vector $\mathbf{b}$ is perturbed by $\Delta\mathbf{b}$.

Theorem: *The Relative Changes in* **b** *and* **x**

Let A be a nonsingular symmetric $n \times n$ matrix with its eigenvalues so arranged that

$$0 < |\lambda_1| \le |\lambda_2| \le \cdots \le |\lambda_n|,$$

and consider the linear system $A\mathbf{x} = \mathbf{b}$ with $\mathbf{b} \ne \mathbf{0}$. If $\mathbf{b}$ is replaced by $\mathbf{b} + \Delta\mathbf{b}$, then the relative change $|\Delta\mathbf{b}|/|\mathbf{b}|$ in $\mathbf{b}$ and the relative change $|\Delta\mathbf{x}|/|\mathbf{x}|$ in the solution vector $\mathbf{x}$ are related as follows:

$$\frac{|\Delta\mathbf{x}|}{|\mathbf{x}|} \le \frac{|\lambda_n|}{|\lambda_1|} \cdot \frac{|\Delta\mathbf{b}|}{|\mathbf{b}|}. \tag{23}$$

Thus if an error $\Delta\mathbf{b}$ is made in the value of $\mathbf{b}$, then the product on the right in Equation (23) provides an upper bound on the resulting relative error in the solution.

Proof Because $A\mathbf{x} = \mathbf{b}$, the second inequality in (22) yields

$$|\mathbf{b}| \le |\lambda_n||\mathbf{x}|.$$

Because $A\Delta\mathbf{x} = \Delta\mathbf{b}$ as in (18), the first inequality in Equation (22) yields

$$|\lambda_1||\Delta\mathbf{x}| \le |\Delta\mathbf{b}|.$$

Then multiplication of these last two inequalities gives

$$|\lambda_1||\Delta\mathbf{x}||\mathbf{b}| \le |\lambda_n||\mathbf{x}||\Delta\mathbf{b}|,$$

and, finally, division by $|\lambda_1||\mathbf{b}||\mathbf{x}|$ gives the desired inequality in (23). ■

Note that the matrix A enters in (23) only in the form of the ratio $|\lambda_n|/|\lambda_1|$ of the magnitudes of its (numerically) largest and smallest eigenvalues. The number

$$c(A) = \frac{|\lambda_n|}{|\lambda_1|} \tag{24}$$

is called the **condition number** of the nonsingular symmetric matrix A having numerically largest and smallest eigenvalues λ_n and λ_1. In terms of $c(A)$, the inequality in (23) takes the form

$$\frac{|\Delta\mathbf{x}|}{|\mathbf{x}|} \leq c(A) \cdot \frac{|\Delta\mathbf{b}|}{|\mathbf{b}|}. \tag{25}$$

If the condition number $c(A)$ is small, then (25) implies that a small relative error in $\mathbf{b}$ can result only in a small relative error in the solution $\mathbf{x}$. But if $c(A)$ is very large, then even a small relative error in $\mathbf{b}$ can result in a large relative error in the solution $\mathbf{x}$.

The system $A\mathbf{x} = \mathbf{b}$ is said to be **ill-conditioned** if small errors in the entries of either A or $\mathbf{b}$ can result in large errors in the solution; otherwise the system is said to be **well-conditioned**. Thus a well-conditioned system is one whose solution is "stable" with respect to small perturbations in A and $\mathbf{b}$. We do not attempt to say how small is "small;" these are generally descriptive rather than mathematically precise terms.

The inequality in (25) implies that if the condition number $c(A)$ is small, then the system $A\mathbf{x} = \mathbf{b}$ is well-conditioned (at least with regard to perturbations in $\mathbf{b}$). And if $c(A)$ is large then the system $A\mathbf{x} = \mathbf{b}$ is ill-conditioned for at least some values of $\mathbf{b}$.

EXAMPLE 4 The solutions of the systems in (14), (15), and (16) show that the system $A\mathbf{x} = \mathbf{b}$ with $\mathbf{b} = (2, 2)$ and

$$A = \begin{bmatrix} 1 & 1 \\ 1 & 1.001 \end{bmatrix} \tag{13}$$

is ill-conditioned. Let us see whether the condition number $c(A)$ explains this observation. The characteristic equation

$$|A - \lambda I| = \lambda^2 - (2.001)\lambda + 0.001 = 0$$

yields the eigenvalues $\lambda_1 \approx 0.0005$ and $\lambda_2 \approx 2.0005$ of A. Hence the condition number of A is

$$c(A) = \frac{|\lambda_2|}{|\lambda_1|} \approx \frac{2.0005}{0.0005} \approx 4000.$$

Thus $c(A)$ is large, and this is why the system $A\mathbf{x} = \mathbf{b}$ is ill-conditioned.

Remark Prior to our discussion of condition numbers, one might have conjectured that the matrix A in (13) is "bad" because its determinant is so small: $\det A = 0.001$. But the size of the determinant has nothing to do with conditioning. To see why, note that each of the equations in (14), (15), and (16) can be multiplied by 1000, and the same anomalous results are obtained, but $\det(1000A) = 10^6 \det A = 1000$. Yet when

A is multiplied by 1000, each of its eigenvalues is also multiplied by 1000, so the condition number $|\lambda_2/\lambda_1|$ is unchanged.

EXAMPLE 5 The coefficient matrix

$$A = \begin{bmatrix} 0.001 & 1 \\ 1 & -1 \end{bmatrix}$$

in (7) has eigenvalues $\lambda_1 \approx 0.619$ and $\lambda_2 \approx -1.618$, so its condition number is $c(A) \approx 1.618/0.619 \approx 2.61$. This is a relatively small condition number, so any linear system with coefficient matrix A is well-conditioned. This is why in Example 3 we were able to avoid roundoff error problem by means of pivoting.

When a linear system is ill-conditioned, there is little that can be done to avoid the possibility of large errors when the system is solved numerically, because small roundoff errors during the process of solution can have the same effect as small changes in the constant vector **b**. When an ill-conditioned system is encountered in an applied problem—as revealed by a large condition number—the usual approach is to attempt to reformulate the problem (perhaps by rescaling or dimensioning various variables) in order to avoid ill-conditioning.

We have defined the condition number $c(A)$ only for a nonsingular symmetric matrix A. For a definition of $c(A)$ that applies in the case of an arbitrary matrix A and yields the same inequality as in (25) for an arbitrary system $A\mathbf{x} = \mathbf{b}$, see Section 7.2 of Gilbert Strang, *Linear Algebra and Its Applications*, 2nd ed. (New York: Academic Press, 1980).

9.1 PROBLEMS

In Problems 1–8, use Gaussian elimination with pivoting to find the exact solution of the given linear system.

1. $\begin{aligned} x + 3y &= 9 \\ 2x + y &= 8 \end{aligned}$

2. $\begin{aligned} x - y &= 8 \\ 3x + 2y &= 9 \end{aligned}$

3. $\begin{aligned} 2x + 3y &= 1 \\ 3x + 5y &= 3 \end{aligned}$

4. $\begin{aligned} 5x - 6y &= 1 \\ 6x - 5y &= 10 \end{aligned}$

5. $\begin{aligned} x + 5y + z &= 2 \\ 2x + y - 2z &= 1 \\ x + 7y + 2z &= 3 \end{aligned}$

6. $\begin{aligned} x + 3y + 2z &= 2 \\ 2x + 7y + 7z &= -1 \\ 2x + 5y + 2z &= 7 \end{aligned}$

7. $\begin{aligned} 2x + 7y + 3z &= 11 \\ x + 3y + 2z &= 2 \\ 3x + 7y + 9z &= -12 \end{aligned}$

8. $\begin{aligned} 2x + 7y + z &= 28 \\ 3x + 5y - z &= 13 \\ x + 7y + 2z &= 32 \end{aligned}$

9–16. Repeat Problems 1–8, respectively, but find the approximate solution obtained by Gaussian elimination with pivoting when all calculations are rounded to three significant figures.

Find the eigenvalues and the condition number $c(A)$ of each matrix A given in Problems 17–20.

17. $\begin{bmatrix} 3 & 1 \\ 1 & 0.3333 \end{bmatrix}$

18. $\begin{bmatrix} 400 & 200 \\ 200 & 101 \end{bmatrix}$

19. $\begin{bmatrix} 2 & 1 \\ 1 & 0.5001 \end{bmatrix}$

20. $\begin{bmatrix} 100 & 100 \\ 100 & 100.01 \end{bmatrix}$

21. Consider the system

$$(0.0001)x + y = 1$$
$$x + y = 2.$$

(a) Find the exact solution.
(b) Solve by Gaussian elimination *without* pivoting, rounding all calculations to three significant digits.
(c) Solve by Gaussian elimination *with* pivoting, rounding all calculations to three significant digits.

22. Repeat the instructions of Problem 21 with the system

$$\begin{aligned} (0.00045)x + (0.0002)y - (0.0002)z &= 0.0005 \\ 3x + \quad 2y + \quad 4z &= 0 \\ 6x - \quad 3y - \quad 8z &= 5. \end{aligned}$$

23. Verify that the matrix A of Problem 19 is ill-conditioned by finding the exact solution of the system $A\mathbf{x} = \mathbf{b}$ with $\mathbf{b} = (2, 1)$ and again with $\mathbf{b} = (2, 1.0002)$.

24. Verify that the matrix A of Problem 17 is ill-conditioned by finding the exact solution of the system $A\mathbf{x} = \mathbf{b}$ with $\mathbf{b} = (30, 10)$ and again with $\mathbf{b} = (30, 10.001)$.

Problems 23 and 24 illustrate the instability of a linear system $A\mathbf{x} = \mathbf{b}$ with respect to perturbations in the constant vector $\mathbf{b}$. The following two problems illustrate instability with respect to perturbations in the coefficient matrix A.

25. Compare the exact solution of the system

$$(1.018)x + y = 20$$
$$x + y = \ 2$$

with the exact solution of the system

$$(1.02)x + y = 20$$
$$x + y = \ 2$$

obtained by rounding the coefficients to three significant digits.

26. Compare the exact solution of the system

$$(2.036)x - y = 10$$
$$(2.024)x - y = \ 4$$

with the exact solution of the system

$$(2.04)x - y = 10$$
$$(2.02)x - y = \ 4$$

obtained by rounding the coefficients to three significant digits.

27. Let A be a symmetric $n \times n$ matrix with its n eigenvalues so arranged that

$$|\lambda_1| \leq |\lambda_2| \leq \cdots \leq |\lambda_n|.$$

Then prove that

$$|\lambda_1||\mathbf{x}| \leq |A\mathbf{x}| \leq |\lambda_n||\mathbf{x}|$$

for every vector $\mathbf{x}$ in $\mathbf{R}^n$. *Suggestion*: Write

$$\mathbf{x} = c_1\mathbf{v}_1 + c_2\mathbf{v}_2 + \cdots + c_n\mathbf{v}_n$$

where $\mathbf{v}_1, \mathbf{v}_2, \ldots, \mathbf{v}_n$ are orthonormal eigenvectors of A, and note that

$$|\mathbf{x}| = (c_1^2 + c_2^2 + \cdots + c_n^2)^{1/2}.$$

28. The Hilbert matrices introduced in the problems for Section 5.5 are notoriously ill-conditioned. Consider the system

$$\begin{aligned} x_1 + \tfrac{1}{2}x_2 + \tfrac{1}{3}x_3 &= \tfrac{11}{6} = 1.83333\ldots \\ \tfrac{1}{2}x_1 + \tfrac{1}{3}x_2 + \tfrac{1}{4}x_3 &= \tfrac{13}{12} = 1.08333\ldots \qquad (26) \\ \tfrac{1}{3}x_1 + \tfrac{1}{4}x_2 + \tfrac{1}{5}x_3 &= \tfrac{47}{60} = 0.78333\ldots \end{aligned}$$

that has exact solution $\mathbf{x} = (1, 1, 1)$ and whose coefficient matrix is the 3×3 Hilbert matrix

$$A = \begin{bmatrix} 1 & \frac{1}{2} & \frac{1}{3} \\ \frac{1}{2} & \frac{1}{3} & \frac{1}{4} \\ \frac{1}{3} & \frac{1}{4} & \frac{1}{5} \end{bmatrix}.$$

Let $\mathbf{b} = (1.8, 1.1, 0.8)$ be the constant vector obtained by rounding to one decimal place in (26). Show by Gaussian elimination that the perturbed system $A\mathbf{x} = \mathbf{b}$ has exact solution $\mathbf{x} = (0.6, 2.4, 0)$. (This example is essentially the one given by Steven H. Weintraub on page 324 of the April 1986 issue of the *American Mathematical Monthly*.)

29. Now consider the system

$$
\begin{aligned}
x_1 + \tfrac{1}{2}x_2 + \tfrac{1}{3}x_3 + \tfrac{1}{4}x_4 &= \tfrac{25}{12} = 2.08333\ldots \\
\tfrac{1}{2}x_1 + \tfrac{1}{3}x_2 + \tfrac{1}{4}x_3 + \tfrac{1}{5}x_4 &= \tfrac{77}{60} = 1.28333\ldots \\
\tfrac{1}{3}x_1 + \tfrac{1}{4}x_2 + \tfrac{1}{5}x_3 + \tfrac{1}{6}x_4 &= \tfrac{57}{60} = 0.95000\ldots \\
\tfrac{1}{4}x_1 + \tfrac{1}{5}x_2 + \tfrac{1}{6}x_3 + \tfrac{1}{7}x_4 &= \tfrac{319}{420} = 0.75952\ldots
\end{aligned}
\tag{27}
$$

with exact solution $\mathbf{x} = (1, 1, 1, 1)$. Its coefficient matrix is the 4×4 Hilbert matrix

$$
A = \begin{bmatrix} 1 & \frac{1}{2} & \frac{1}{3} & \frac{1}{4} \\ \frac{1}{2} & \frac{1}{3} & \frac{1}{4} & \frac{1}{5} \\ \frac{1}{3} & \frac{1}{4} & \frac{1}{5} & \frac{1}{6} \\ \frac{1}{4} & \frac{1}{5} & \frac{1}{6} & \frac{1}{7} \end{bmatrix}
$$

that has inverse matrix

$$
A^{-1} = \begin{bmatrix} 16 & -120 & 240 & -140 \\ -120 & 1200 & -2700 & 1680 \\ 240 & -2700 & 6480 & -4200 \\ -140 & 1680 & -4200 & 2800 \end{bmatrix}.
$$

Suppose that $\mathbf{b} = (2.08, 1.28, 0.95, 0.76)$ is the constant vector obtained by rounding to two decimal places in (27). Use A^{-1} to solve the perturbed system $A\mathbf{x} = \mathbf{b}$ for its exact solution $\mathbf{x} = (1.28, -1.8, 7.2, -2.8)$.

9.2 Iterative Methods of Solution

Gaussian elimination is a direct and straightforward method for solving a linear system

$$
A\mathbf{x} = \mathbf{b}
$$

of n equations in n unknowns. Aside from the possibility of roundoff error, it gives the *exact solution* in a predetermined finite number of steps. If the number n is not too large, Gaussian elimination therefore is ordinarily the most effective method of solution of such a system.

There are, however, important applied problems involving hundreds or even thousands of equations and unknowns, for which Gaussian elimination would take far too long even if a powerful computer were used. Fortunately, the coefficient matrix A in such problems is usually of a very special type—though it is large, most of its entries are zero. An example is the matrix

$$
A = \begin{bmatrix} 2 & -1 & 0 & \cdots & 0 & 0 \\ -1 & 2 & -1 & \cdots & 0 & 0 \\ 0 & -1 & 2 & \cdots & 0 & 0 \\ \vdots & \vdots & \vdots & \ddots & \vdots & \vdots \\ 0 & 0 & 0 & \cdots & 2 & -1 \\ 0 & 0 & 0 & \cdots & -1 & 2 \end{bmatrix} \tag{1}
$$

in which each entry on the main diagonal is a 2, each entry on the two adjacent diagonals is a -1, and each remaining entry is zero. A matrix whose entries are mostly zeros is called a **sparse matrix**.

For large systems with sparse coefficient matrices, as well as for certain systems of moderate size, there are indirect methods of solution that provide a useful alternative to Gaussian elimination. Their only drawback is in producing *approximate* rather than exact solutions. Typically, one begins with an initial guess $\mathbf{x}^{(0)}$ for the solution vector and then generates a sequence $\mathbf{x}^{(1)}, \mathbf{x}^{(2)}, \mathbf{x}^{(3)}, \ldots$ of successively better *approximations* to the actual (exact) solution of $A\mathbf{x} = \mathbf{b}$. Each approximation $\mathbf{x}^{(k)}$ is used in calculating the next improved approximation $\mathbf{x}^{(k+1)}$, and the process can be terminated whenever $\mathbf{x}^{(k)}$ and $\mathbf{x}^{(k+1)}$ agree to the desired accuracy.

To describe such a procedure explicitly, let us begin with an $n \times n$ nonsingular system $A\mathbf{x} = \mathbf{b}$ such that each diagonal element a_{ii} of $A = [a_{ij}]$ is nonzero. Then we can solve the first equation for x_1 in terms of $x_2, x_3, \ldots, x_n$, the second equation for x_2 in terms of $x_1, x_3, x_4, \ldots, x_n$, and so on. Thus we solve the ith equation for x_i in terms of the other variables. In this way we rewrite the equations of the system $A\mathbf{x} = \mathbf{b}$ in the form

$$\begin{aligned} x_1 &= \frac{1}{a_{11}}(b_1 - a_{12}x_2 - a_{13}x_3 - \cdots - a_{1n}x_n) \\ x_2 &= \frac{1}{a_{22}}(b_2 - a_{21}x_1 - a_{23}x_3 - \cdots - a_{2n}x_n) \\ &\vdots \\ x_n &= \frac{1}{a_{nn}}(b_n - a_{n1}x_1 - a_{n2}x_2 - \cdots - a_{n,n-1}x_{n-1}). \end{aligned} \tag{2}$$

Observe that the system in (2) is of the form

$$\mathbf{x} = T\mathbf{x} + \mathbf{c} \tag{3}$$

where T and $\mathbf{c}$ are determined by the original A and $\mathbf{b}$. Now let $\mathbf{x}^{(0)}$ be an initial guess at the solution; we can choose $\mathbf{x}^{(0)} = \mathbf{0}$ if we have no better information. Then we can substitute $\mathbf{x}^{(0)}$ on the right in (3) and call the result $\mathbf{x}^{(1)}$:

$$\mathbf{x}^{(1)} = T\mathbf{x}^{(0)} + \mathbf{c}.$$

Likewise, we can substitute $\mathbf{x}^{(1)}$ on the right in (3) and call the result $\mathbf{x}^{(2)}$;

$$\mathbf{x}^{(2)} = T\mathbf{x}^{(1)} + \mathbf{c}.$$

Continuing in this fashion, once the kth approximation $\mathbf{x}^{(k)}$ has been found, we define the $(k + 1)$st approximation $\mathbf{x}^{(k+1)}$ to be

$$\mathbf{x}^{(k+1)} = T\mathbf{x}^{(k)} + \mathbf{c}. \tag{4}$$

Thus we plow each approximation back into the right-hand side in (4) to compute the next approximation. This is an *iterative* process—the words *iteration* and *iterative* are derived from the Latin verb *iterare*, "to plow again."

The iterative process described in (4) is called the **Jacobi iteration**. We may hope (though it is not always so) that the sequence $\mathbf{x}^{(1)}, \mathbf{x}^{(2)}, \ldots, \mathbf{x}^{(k)}, \ldots$ thereby produced is a sequence of better and better approximations converging to the actual solution of the original system $A\mathbf{x} = \mathbf{b}$.

EXAMPLE 1 Consider the system

$$\begin{aligned} 10x_1 + 2x_2 + x_3 &= 25 \\ 3x_1 + 20x_2 - x_3 &= 23 \\ x_1 - 3x_2 + 10x_3 &= 29. \end{aligned} \tag{5}$$

To rewrite it in the form in (2), we solve the three equations for x_1, x_2, and x_3, respectively:

$$\begin{aligned} x_1 &= 2.50 - (0.20)x_2 - (0.10)x_3 \\ x_2 &= 1.15 - (0.15)x_1 + (0.05)x_3 \\ x_3 &= 2.90 - (0.10)x_1 + (0.30)x_2. \end{aligned} \tag{6}$$

We begin the Jacobi iteration with the initial guess $\mathbf{x}^{(0)} = \mathbf{0}$. Substitution of $x_1 = x_2 = x_3 = 0$ on the right in (6) yields the first approximation

$$x_1 = 2.5, \qquad x_2 = 1.15, \qquad x_3 = 2.9,$$

so $\mathbf{x}^{(1)} = (2.5, 1.15, 2.9)$. Then substitution of these values on the right in (6) yields

$$\begin{aligned} x_1 &= 2.50 - (0.20)(1.15) - (0.10)(2.90) = 1.98 \\ x_2 &= 1.15 - (0.15)(2.50) + (0.05)(2.90) = 0.92 \\ x_3 &= 2.90 - (0.10)(2.50) + (0.30)(1.15) = 2.995, \end{aligned}$$

so our second approximation is $\mathbf{x}^{(2)} = (1.98, 0.92, 2.995)$. Obviously we can continue in this way so long as patience permits. The table in Figure 9.2 shows the results of the first nine iterations (with each value rounded to four decimal places). It appears that the approximations are converging to $x_1 = 2$, $x_2 = 1$, and $x_3 = 3$. By substitution, we readily verify that this is indeed the exact solution of the original system in (5).

Any serious application of the Jacobi iteration is carried out with a computer. Figure 9.3 lists the IBM-PC BASIC program that we used to compute the Jacobi approximations shown in Figure 9.2. Observe that the original augmented coefficient matrix $[A \quad \mathbf{b}]$ of the system in (5) appears in lines 300–320. The elements of A are stored in an array A(I, J) by the FOR-NEXT loop of lines 340–390, and the matrix T is

Iteration k	x_1	x_2	x_3
1	2.5000	1.1500	2.9000
2	1.9800	0.9200	2.9950
3	2.0165	1.0027	2.9780
4	2.0016	0.9964	2.9992
5	2.0008	0.9997	2.9988
6	2.0002	0.9998	2.9998
7	2.0001	1.0000	2.9999
8	2.0000	1.0000	3.0000
9	2.0000	1.0000	3.0000

9.2 The Jacobi approximations of Example 1.

```
100 REM--Program JACOBI
110 REM--Implements the Jacobi iteration method
120 REM--to approximate the solution of the
130 REM--system  Ax = b  whose augmented coefficient
140 REM--matrix is listed in lines 300-320.
150 REM
200 REM--Initialization:
210 REM
220       N = 3   'Number of equations and unknowns
230       DIM A(N,N), T(N,N), B(N), X(N), Y(N)
300       DATA   10,  2,  1, 25 : 'Enter augmented
310       DATA    3, 20, -1, 23 : 'coefficient
320       DATA    1, -3, 10, 29 : 'matrix here
340       FOR I = 1 TO N
350           FOR J = 1 TO N
360               READ A(I,J)
370           NEXT J
380           READ B(I) : B(I) = B(I)/A(I,I)
385           X(I) = 0
390       NEXT I
400       FOR I = 1 TO N
410           FOR J = 1 TO N
420               IF I = J THEN T(I,J) = 0
                     ELSE T(I,J) = -A(I,J)/A(I,I)
430           NEXT J
440       NEXT I
450 REM
500 REM--Jacobi iteration:
510 REM
520       K = 0    'Count 10 iterations at a time
530       WHILE K < 10
540          FOR I = 1 TO N
550              Y = B(I)
560              FOR J = 1 TO N
570                  Y = Y + T(I,J)*X(J)
580              NEXT J
590              Y(I) = Y : PRINT Y(I),
600          NEXT I
601          FOR I = 1 TO N
602              X(I) = Y(I)
603          NEXT I
610          PRINT
620          K = K + 1
630       WEND        'Endwhile
640 REM
650       INPUT "Want another 10 iterations"; Y$
660       IF Y$ = "Y" OR Y$ = "y" THEN GOTO 500
670 REM
680       END
```

9.3 Listing of Program JACOBI.

set up in the FOR-NEXT loop of lines 400–440. The actual Jacobi iteration is carried out by the FOR-NEXT loop in lines 540–600, where the new approximation Y(I) is calculated from the previous approximation X(I). Finally, in lines 601–603 the new approximation becomes the old approximation X(I) in preparation for the next iteration.

In the Jacobi iteration method, the entries $x_1, x_2, \ldots, x_n$ of $\mathbf{x}^{(k)}$ are *all* computed during the kth iteration and then *simultaneously* substituted on the right-hand side in (2) during the $(k+1)$st iteration. For this reason the Jacobi method is sometimes called the **method of simultaneous corrections.**

An alternative approach that often is more convenient is to use each new value immediately—as soon as it is available. Thus the new x_1 is given in terms of the old $x_2, x_3, \ldots, x_n$ by the first equation in (2), just as in the Jacobi method. But then the new x_2 is given in terms of the *new* x_1 and the old $x_3, x_4, \ldots, x_n$ by the second equation in (2). The new x_3 is given in terms of the *new* x_1 and x_2 and the old $x_4, \ldots, x_n$, and so on. This method of approximating the solution of $A\mathbf{x} = \mathbf{b}$ is called the **Gauss-Seidel iteration,** or the **method of successive corrections.**

EXAMPLE 2 To carry out the Gauss-Seidel iteration with the 3×3 system of Example 1, we use the same equations

$$\begin{aligned} x_1 &= 2.50 - (0.20)x_2 - (0.10)x_3 \\ x_2 &= 1.15 - (0.15)x_1 + (0.05)x_3 \\ x_3 &= 2.90 - (0.10)x_1 + (0.30)x_2, \end{aligned} \tag{6}$$

but successively rather than simultaneously. Substitution of $x_1 = x_2 = x_3 = 0$ on the right in the first equation then gives $x_1 = 2.5$. Then substitution of $x_1 = 2.5$ and $x_2 = x_3 = 0$ on the right in the second equation gives

$$x_2 = 1.15 - (0.15)(2.5) + (0.05)(0) = 0.775.$$

We complete the first iteration by substituting $x_1 = 2.5$, $x_2 = 0.775$, and $x_3 = 0$ on the right in the third equation to get

$$x_3 = 2.9 - (0.1)(2.5) + (0.3)(0.775) = 2.8825.$$

Thus the result of the first iteration is $\mathbf{x}^{(1)} = (2.5, 0.775, 2.8825)$.

Iteration k	x_1	x_2	x_3
1	2.5000	0.7750	2.8825
2	2.0568	0.9856	2.9900
3	2.0039	0.9989	2.9993
4	2.0003	0.9999	2.9999
5	2.0000	1.0000	3.0000
6	2.0000	1.0000	3.0000

9.4 The Gauss-Seidel approximations of Example 2.

The computations for the second Gauss-Seidel iteration are

$$x_1 = 2.5 - (0.2)(0.775) - (0.1)(2.8825) = 2.05675$$

$$x_2 = 1.15 - (0.15)(2.05675) + (0.05)(2.8825) \approx 0.98561$$

$$x_3 = 2.9 - (0.1)(2.05675) + (0.3)(0.98561) \approx 2.99001.$$

The results for the first six Gauss-Seidel iterations are shown in the table in Figure 9.4 (with each value rounded to four decimal places).

Figure 9.5 shows the Gauss-Seidel subroutine that was substituted for the Jacobi subroutine in lines 500–640 of the BASIC program listed in Figure 9.3 in order to perform the computations whose results are shown in Figure 9.4. Note that the Gauss-Seidel code is slightly simpler than the Jacobi code. The reason is that the new values simply replace the old values as each is computed, so the old and new values need not be stored separately.

It is worth observing that in order to reach the correct four-decimal-place approximation to the actual solution of the system in (5), the Jacobi method of Example 1 required eight iterations, whereas the Gauss-Seidel method of Example 2 required only five iterations. This observation is in accord with the natural conjecture that because the Gauss-Seidel method makes use of each improved value immediately (rather than waiting until the end of the current iteration), a smaller number of Gauss-Seidel iterations than Jacobi iterations should be needed for the same degree of accuracy. Indeed, it is a common rule of thumb that the Jacobi method requires roughly twice as many iterations as does the Gauss-Seidel method. But there exist examples in which the Jacobi method produces a sequence of approximate solutions that converge to the actual solution, whereas the sequence of Gauss-Seidel "approximations" does not even converge. (In all fairness, there are also systems in which the Gauss-Seidel method succeeds while the Jacobi method fails. Thus you had best arm yourself with *both* weapons.)

```
500 REM--Gauss-Seidel iteration:
510 REM
520        K = 0     'Count 10 iterations at a time
530        WHILE K < 10
540           FOR I = 1 TO N
550              Y = B(I)
560              FOR J = 1 TO N
570                 Y = Y + T(I,J)*X(J)
580              NEXT J
590              X(I) = Y : PRINT X(I),
600           NEXT I
610           PRINT
620           K = K + 1
630        WEND        'Endwhile
640 REM
```

9.5 Subroutine for Gauss-Seidel iteration.

A frequently satisfied condition under which both methods are known to produce sequences of approximations converging to the actual solution of $A\mathbf{x} = \mathbf{b}$ is this: that the coefficient matrix $A = [a_{ij}]$ be **strictly diagonally dominant**. This means that the absolute value of each diagonal entry a_{ij} of A is larger than the sum of the absolute values of the other elements in the same row of A. That is,

$$\begin{aligned}
|a_{11}| &> |a_{12}| + |a_{13}| + \cdots + |a_{1n}| \\
|a_{22}| &> |a_{21}| + |a_{23}| + \cdots + |a_{2n}| \\
&\ \vdots \\
|a_{nn}| &> |a_{n1}| + |a_{n2}| + \cdots + |a_{n,n-1}|.
\end{aligned}$$

For instance, the coefficient matrix

$$A = \begin{bmatrix} 10 & 2 & 1 \\ 3 & 20 & -1 \\ 1 & -3 & 10 \end{bmatrix}$$

of the system in (5) is strictly diagonally dominant because $10 > 2 + 1$, $20 > 3 + 1$, and $10 > 1 + 3$. As the following example indicates, a system whose coefficient matrix is not strictly diagonally dominant can sometimes be transformed into one whose coefficient matrix *is* strictly diagonally dominant—by the simple expedient of reordering the equations in the system.

EXAMPLE 3 No row of the matrix

$$A = \begin{bmatrix} 3 & -2 & 20 \\ 10 & 6 & -5 \\ 4 & 30 & -7 \end{bmatrix}$$

satisfies the definition of strict diagonal dominance. But if we first interchange the first and second rows and then interchange the second and third rows, we get the matrix

$$\begin{bmatrix} 10 & 6 & -5 \\ 4 & 30 & -7 \\ 3 & -2 & 20 \end{bmatrix},$$

which *is* strictly diagonally dominant.

SPARSE SYSTEMS

Here we discuss a pair of applications that involve linear systems having sparse coefficient matrices for which the iterative methods of this section are well suited. These applications illustrate also the idea of *discretization*—approximating a continuous mathematical model involving differential equations with a discrete mathematical model involving finite difference equations.

We consider first the end-point value problem

$$\frac{d^2y}{dx^2} + f(x) = 0, \qquad y(0) = y(1) = 0. \tag{7}$$

From a mathematical viewpoint, we seek a solution on the interval [0, 1] of the simple differential equation $y'' + f(x) = 0$ that satisfies the end-point conditions $y(0) = 0$ and $y(1) = 0$. From a physical viewpoint, Equation (7) may be regarded as a mathematical model of a thin heated rod lying on the x-axis along the interval $0 \leq x \leq 1$. In appropriate physical units, $y(x)$ is the steady-state temperature of the rod at the point x, and the function $-f(x)$ gives the rate at which heat is being generated within (or supplied to) the rod at the point x. The two end-point conditions signify that each end of the rod is held at temperature zero.

The crucial step in our discussion is the replacement of the differential equation in (7) with a system of finite difference equations. Given a point x in [0, 1] and a small number $h > 0$, note that the average rates of change of $y(x)$ on the intervals $[x, x + h]$ and $[x - h, x]$ are given by the quotients

$$\frac{y(x+h) - y(x)}{h} \quad \text{and} \quad \frac{y(x) - y(x-h)}{h},$$

respectively. Consequently the second derivative $y''(x)$ is approximated by

$$\frac{1}{h}\left\{\frac{y(x+h) - y(x)}{h} - \frac{y(x) - y(x-h)}{h}\right\} = \frac{y(x+h) - 2y(x) + y(x-h)}{h^2}. \tag{8}$$

Now let the interval [0, 1] be subdivided into $n + 1$ equal subintervals of length $h = 1/(n + 1)$ by means of the points

$$0 = x_0 < x_1 < x_2 < \cdots < x_n < x_{n+1} = 1,$$

where $x_i = ih$ for each $i = 0, 1, 2, \ldots, n + 1$. If we write y_i for $y(x_i)$, then, with $x = x_i$, the expression in (8) yields the approximation

$$y''(x_i) \approx \frac{y_{i+1} - 2y_i + y_{i-1}}{h^2}. \tag{9}$$

When we write the differential equation $y''(x) + f(x) = 0$ at each of the points $x_1, x_2, \ldots, x_n$ and replace the second derivative $y''(x_i)$ with the approximation in (9), we get the equations

$$\frac{y_{i+1} - 2y_i + y_{i-1}}{h^2} + f(x_i) = 0;$$

that is,

$$-y_{i+1} + 2y_i - y_{i-1} = h^2 f(x_i) \tag{10}$$

for $i = 1, 2, \ldots, n$, and the end-point conditions yield $y_0 = y_{n+1} = 0$. This is the desired discrete linear system. In matrix notation it is

$$A\mathbf{y} = \mathbf{b}, \tag{11}$$

where A is the "tridiagonal" matrix in (1),

$$\mathbf{y} = (y_1, y_2, \ldots, y_n),$$

and

$$\mathbf{b} = h^2(f(x_1), f(x_2), \ldots, f(x_n)).$$

If $n = 9$, for instance, then A is the 9×9 matrix

$$A = \begin{bmatrix} 2 & -1 & 0 & 0 & 0 & 0 & 0 & 0 & 0 \\ -1 & 2 & -1 & 0 & 0 & 0 & 0 & 0 & 0 \\ 0 & -1 & 2 & -1 & 0 & 0 & 0 & 0 & 0 \\ 0 & 0 & -1 & 2 & -1 & 0 & 0 & 0 & 0 \\ 0 & 0 & 0 & -1 & 2 & -1 & 0 & 0 & 0 \\ 0 & 0 & 0 & 0 & -1 & 2 & -1 & 0 & 0 \\ 0 & 0 & 0 & 0 & 0 & -1 & 2 & -1 & 0 \\ 0 & 0 & 0 & 0 & 0 & 0 & -1 & 2 & -1 \\ 0 & 0 & 0 & 0 & 0 & 0 & 0 & -1 & 2 \end{bmatrix}.$$

Observe how sparse A is—only 25 of its 81 entries are nonzero. If $n = 100$, then only 298 of 10,000 entries—that is, about 3%—are nonzero. Consequently the Jacobi and Gauss-Seidel programs listed in Figures 9.3 and 9.5 can be redesigned to require far less computer memory—an important factor if n is quite large. Although the matrix A is not *quite* strictly diagonally dominant, both methods produce sequences of approximations that converge (albeit rather slowly) to the actual solution.

Figure 9.6 shows a simple program that was written to implement the Gauss-Seidel method for the system in (11) in the case $n = 9$. We chose $f(x) = 12x$ so that the

```
100 REM--Program TRIDIAG
110 REM--Finite differences solution of the diff
120 REM--equation  y" + f(x) = 0.
130 REM
200 REM--Initialization:
210 REM
220       DEF FNF(X) = 12*X : DEFINT I
230       DEF FNG(X) = 2*X - 2*X*X*X
240       N = 9:  'N + 1 = no of subintervals
250       H = 1/(N + 1)
260       DIM Y(N)
270       FOR I = 1 TO N : Y(I) = 0
290       NEXT I
295 REM
300 REM--Successive corrections:
305 REM
310       Y(1) = (H*H*FNF(H) + Y(2))/2
320       FOR I = 2 TO N - 1
330           X = I*H
340           Y(I)=(H*H*FNF(X) + Y(I-1) + Y(I+1))/2
350           IF I/2 = I\2 THEN PRINT X, Y(I), FNG(X)
360       NEXT I
370       Y(N) = (H*H*FNF(N*H) + Y(N-1))/2
380 REM
400       GOTO 300  'For another iteration
410 REM--Press Ctrl/Break to stop execution
500       END
```

9.6 Listing of Program TRIDIAG.

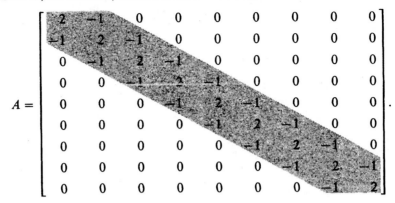

x_i	20th Iteration	40th Iteration	60th Iteration	80th Iteration	Actual Solution
0.0	0.000	0.000	0.000	0.000	0.000
0.1	0.156	0.192	0.197	0.198	0.198
0.2	0.307	0.374	0.383	0.384	0.384
0.3	0.446	0.533	0.544	0.546	0.546
0.4	0.560	0.657	0.670	0.672	0.672
0.5	0.638	0.735	0.748	0.750	0.750
0.6	0.667	0.754	0.766	0.768	0.768
0.7	0.632	0.703	0.713	0.714	0.714
0.8	0.519	0.568	0.575	0.576	0.576
0.9	0.314	0.338	0.341	0.342	0.342
1.0	0.000	0.000	0.000	0.000	0.000

9.7 Finite difference approximations to the solution of $y'' + 12x = 0$, $y(0) = y(1) = 0$.

actual solution $g(x) = 2x - 2x^3$ (whose second derivative is $-12x$) would be available for comparison with the approximate solutions. Program TRIDIAG was used to produce the data that are shown (rounded to three decimal places) in the table in Figure 9.7.

Next we discuss the problem of approximating the steady-state temperature $u(x, y)$ in a thin plate with insulated faces and shaped like the unit square shown in Figure 9.8. The four edges of the square plate are held at the temperatures indicated in the figure, and $u(x, y)$ is the "equilibrium" temperature at the point (x, y) reached after a long period of time. The standard continuous model for this physical situation is the partial differential equation

$$\frac{\partial^2 u}{\partial x^2} + \frac{\partial^2 u}{\partial y^2} = 0 \tag{12}$$

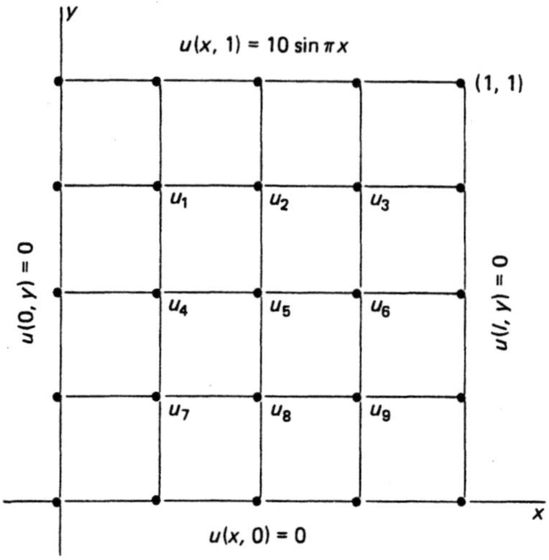

9.8 Grid points for approximating the temperature $u(x, y)$ in the unit square.

together with the boundary conditions

$$u(0, y) = u(x, 0) = u(1, y) = 0, \qquad u(x, 1) = 10 \sin \pi x. \tag{13}$$

Instead of discussing directly the partial differential equation above, we will base our mathematical model on the **average value property** that any solution $u(x, y)$ of Equation (12) is known to enjoy: If P is an interior point of the plate and C is a circle within the plate centered at P, then the temperature at P is the *average* value of the temperature on the circle C.

To set up our discrete mathematical model we employ the 25 **grid points** indicated in Figure 9.8. Sixteen of these are *boundary* grid points and nine are *interior* grid points. A discrete version of the average value property is the statement that *the temperature at each interior point is the average of the temperatures at the four neighboring grid points.* When we apply this condition at each of the nine interior grid points indicated in Figure 9.8, we get the nine equations

$$\begin{aligned}
u_1 &= \frac{1}{4}\left(u_2 + u_4 + 10 \sin \frac{\pi}{4}\right) \\
u_2 &= \frac{1}{4}\left(u_1 + u_3 + u_5 + 10 \sin \frac{\pi}{2}\right) \\
u_3 &= \frac{1}{4}\left(u_2 + u_6 + 10 \sin \frac{3\pi}{4}\right) \\
u_4 &= \frac{1}{4}(u_1 + u_5 + u_7) \\
u_5 &= \frac{1}{4}(u_2 + u_4 + u_6 + u_8) \\
u_6 &= \frac{1}{4}(u_3 + u_5 + u_9) \\
u_7 &= \frac{1}{4}(u_4 + u_8) \\
u_8 &= \frac{1}{4}(u_5 + u_7 + u_9) \\
u_9 &= \frac{1}{4}(u_6 + u_8),
\end{aligned} \tag{14}$$

using the given boundary conditions to determine the temperature at each boundary grid point.

The linear system of equations in (14) can be written in the matrix form

$$A\mathbf{u} = \mathbf{f}, \tag{15}$$

where $\mathbf{u} = (u_1, u_2, \ldots, u_9)$, $\mathbf{f} = (10/\sqrt{2}, 10, 10/\sqrt{2}, 0, 0, \ldots, 0)$, and the coefficient matrix is

$$A = \begin{bmatrix} 4 & -1 & 0 & -1 & 0 & 0 & 0 & 0 & 0 \\ -1 & 4 & -1 & 0 & -1 & 0 & 0 & 0 & 0 \\ 0 & -1 & 4 & 0 & 0 & -1 & 0 & 0 & 0 \\ -1 & 0 & 0 & 4 & -1 & 0 & -1 & 0 & 0 \\ 0 & -1 & 0 & -1 & 4 & -1 & 0 & -1 & 0 \\ 0 & 0 & -1 & 0 & -1 & 4 & 0 & 0 & -1 \\ 0 & 0 & 0 & -1 & 0 & 0 & 4 & -1 & 0 \\ 0 & 0 & 0 & 0 & -1 & 0 & -1 & 4 & -1 \\ 0 & 0 & 0 & 0 & 0 & -1 & 0 & -1 & 4 \end{bmatrix}. \tag{16}$$

This is a **band matrix** whose nonzero entries are confined to the indicated bands located near the main diagonal. In (16) these bands contain 37 of the 81 entries of A. But if we were using a 10×10 (rather than a 3×3) array of interior grid points, then A would be a 100×100 matrix, and these nonzero bands would contain fewer than 5% of its 10,000 entries.

Figure 9.9 shows a program written to implement the Gauss-Seidel method for the linear system in (15). Note that lines 410–490 correspond to the equations in (14). In addition to carrying out the successive corrections, the program also tabulates the values at the interior grid points of the exact solution

$$T(x, y) = \frac{10 \sin \pi x \sinh \pi y}{\sinh \pi} \tag{17}$$

of the boundary value problem given in (12) and (13). The table in Figure 9.10 shows some data produced by this program (rounded to two decimal places). The convergence is rapid, and the accuracy is reasonable for such a crude grid of discrete points to approximate the square. All iterations after the tenth agreed to the indicated accuracy.

A DISCRETE SYSTEM

Discrete systems can be modeled even more precisely than continuous systems if they are not overly complicated. Suppose you enter a casino with \$100 and play roulette; your strategy is to bet \$50 on red or black at each turn of the wheel and to continue until you have won \$500 or until you have lost all your money. It would be wise to know two facts before you begin. First, what is the probability that you lose all your money before winning \$500? Second, what is the expected length of this procedure —what is the average number of bets you will make before the game ends one way or the other?

Let us suppose that all transactions are carried out using \$50 chips, so that at the beginning of each play you have n chips where $0 \leq n \leq 10$. Here is the key idea: Let x_n be the probability that you eventually win your goal of 10 chips *given you have exactly*

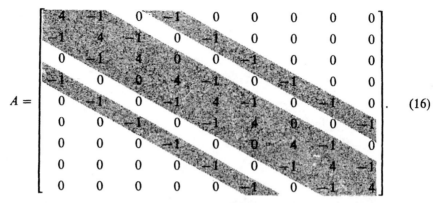

```
100 REM--Program BANDMAT
110 REM--Finite difference approximation to
120 REM--steady state temperature in unit square.
130 REM
200 REM--Initialization:
210 REM
220       PI = 3.141593
230       DEF FNSINH(X) = (EXP(X) - EXP(-X))/2
240       DEF FNT(X,Y) = 10*SIN(PI*X)*FNSINH(PI*Y)/FNSINH(PI)
250       DIM F(3), U(9), W(9)
260       F(1) = 10*SIN(PI/4) : F(2) = 10 : F(3) = F(1)
270       FOR I = 1 TO 9
275           U(I) = 0
280       NEXT I
290       FOR I = 1 TO 3
300           W(I)   = FNT(I/4,3/4)
310           W(I+3) = FNT(I/4,1/2)
320           W(I+6) = FNT(I/4,1/4)
330       NEXT I
340 REM
400 REM--Successive corrections:
405 REM
410       U(1) = (U(2) + U(4) + F(1))/4
420       U(2) = (U(1) + U(3) + U(5) + F(2))/4
430       U(3) = (U(2) + U(6) + F(3))/4
440       U(4) = (U(1) + U(5) + U(7))/4
450       U(5) = (U(2) + U(4) + U(6) + U(8))/4
460       U(6) = (U(3) + U(5) + U(9))/4
470       U(7) = (U(4) + U(8))/4
480       U(8) = (U(5) + U(7) + U(9))/4
490       U(9) = (U(6) + U(8))/4
500       FOR I = 1 TO 9
510           PRINT I, U(I), W(I)
520       NEXT I : PRINT
550 REM
600       GOTO 400    'For another iteration
610 REM--Press Ctrl/Break to stop execution
650       END
```

9.9 Listing of Program BANDMAT.

	3rd Iteration	6th Iteration	9th Iteration	10th Iteration	Actual Solution
u_1	2.99	3.28	3.31	3.32	3.20
u_2	4.36	4.65	4.69	4.69	4.53
u_3	3.15	3.30	3.32	3.32	3.20
u_4	1.19	1.47	1.50	1.51	1.41
u_5	1.81	2.09	2.13	2.13	1.99
u_6	1.35	1.49	1.51	1.51	1.41
u_7	0.43	0.56	0.58	0.58	0.53
u_8	0.67	0.81	0.82	0.82	0.75
u_9	0.50	0.57	0.58	0.58	0.53

9.10 The approximate and actual temperatures at interior grid points of the square plate.

n chips. Note that $x_0 = 0$ and that $x_{10} = 1$. Moreover, if p is the probability that you win on a given play of the game, then

$$x_n = px_{n+1} + (1 - p)x_{n-1}.$$

The reason is that on a given play of the game, only two things can happen: You win one chip with probability p or lose one with probability $1 - p$. In the former case you then have probability x_{n+1} of winning all 10; in the latter case you then have probability x_{n-1} of winning all 10. These events are exhaustive and mutually exclusive, and so your probability of winning all 10 is the sum of px_{n+1} and $(1 - p)x_{n-1}$. Thus we obtain the following equations relating the numbers x_0, $x_1, \ldots, x_{10}$:

$$\begin{aligned} x_0 &= 0, \\ x_n &= px_{n+1} + (1 - p)x_{n-1}, \qquad 1 \le n \le 9, \\ x_{10} &= 1. \end{aligned}$$

It is very easy to write a program to implement the Gauss-Seidel iteration for the solution of these equations. We omit all details other than the conclusions:

- If you are lucky enough to find a roulette wheel for which $p = 0.5$ exactly, then $x_2 = 0.2$, in agreement with intuition.
- If you find a roulette wheel with a 37th slot marked 0, then $p = \frac{18}{37}$ and $x_2 \approx 0.159236$.
- If you find a roulette wheel with both a 0 and a 00, then $p = \frac{18}{38}$ and $x_2 \approx 0.125574$.

It is clear why U.S. casinos favor the third sort of roulette wheel.

Now we turn our attention to the expected number of plays or rounds in a game. Again, the secret is to find the right sort of *conditional* function: Let y_n be the expected number of plays remaining when you have exactly n chips. Then $y_0 = 0$, $y_{10} = 0$, and

$$y_n = 1 + py_{n+1} + (1 - p)y_{n-1}.$$

The difference between this case and the previous one is the presence of the extra term 1, for it takes one round to move from n chips to $n + 1$ or $n - 1$, as the case may be. Here are the results:

$$\begin{aligned} &\text{If} \quad p = 2, \quad \text{then} \quad y_2 = 17 \quad \text{(exactly)}. \\ &\text{If} \quad p = \tfrac{18}{37}, \quad \text{then} \quad y_2 \approx 15.0828. \\ &\text{If} \quad p = \tfrac{18}{38}, \quad \text{then} \quad y_2 \approx 14.1410. \end{aligned}$$

You may draw your own conclusions. We conclude with a warning, though not one about gambling: For these sorts of equations, the Gauss-Seidel iteration is quite slow to converge if the number of equations is very large. It would require a very fast computer to obtain reasonable accuracy if (say) you began with \$100, made \$50 bets, and asked the probability of eventually winning a million dollars. (With $p = 0.5$ it is exactly 0.0001; with $p = \frac{18}{37}$ it is less than 1 chance in 5×10^{470}.)

9.2 PROBLEMS

In Problems 1–10, use the Jacobi iteration method to approximate the solution of each given system. Carry out at least four iterations; compare your results with the exact solutions.

1. $10x_1 + x_2 = 21$
$x_1 + 10x_2 = 12$

2. $10x_1 - 2x_2 = 26$
$x_1 - 10x_2 = 32$

3. $20x_1 - 3x_2 = 54$
$x_1 + 30x_2 = 63$

4. $5x_1 + 2x_2 = 26$
$3x_1 + 10x_2 = 42$

5. $7x_1 - 2x_2 = 30$
$3x_1 + 11x_2 = 1$

6. $13x_1 + 3x_2 = 17$
$2x_1 - 7x_2 = 25$

7. $10x_1 + x_2 + x_3 = 33$
$x_1 + 10x_2 + x_3 = 15$
$x_1 + x_2 + 10x_3 = 24$

8. $10x_1 + x_2 - 2x_3 = 13$
$x_1 + 10x_2 + 3x_3 = 1$
$2x_1 - x_2 + 10x_3 = 35$

9. $10x_1 - x_2 + x_3 = 20$
$2x_1 + 20x_2 - x_3 = 23$
$3x_1 - 2x_2 + 20x_3 = 24$

10. $30x_1 + 2x_2 - 3x_3 = 61$
$x_1 + 20x_2 - 3x_3 = 39$
$2x_1 - 5x_2 + 40x_3 = 34$

11–20. Repeat Problems 1–10, respectively, except use the Gauss-Seidel iteration method.

21. Consider the system

$$x_1 - 100x_2 = 101$$

$$100x_1 + x_2 = 99$$

in which the coefficient matrix is not diagonally dominant.
(a) Show that the approximations produced by Jacobi iteration diverge.
(b) Interchange the two equations, then try Jacobi iteration again.

22. In order to apply the iteration methods of this section to the $n \times n$ system $A\mathbf{x} = \mathbf{b}$, it is necessary that each diagonal element a_{ii} of A be nonzero. If this condition is not satisfied, explain why it is always possible to interchange equations (or unknowns, or both) in such a way to obtain an equivalent system with all diagonal elements nonzero.

23. In this problem we outline the derivation of a sufficient condition for convergence of the Jacobi iteration method. Given a nonsingular $n \times n$ system $A\mathbf{x} = \mathbf{b}$ with actual solution $\mathbf{x}^*$, write it in the Jacobi form

$$\mathbf{x} = T\mathbf{x} + \mathbf{c}$$

of Equation (3) in this section. Suppose that the matrix T is diagonalizable with real eigenvalues $\lambda_1, \lambda_2, \ldots, \lambda_n$ each having absolute value less than 1. Show under this condition that the sequence $\mathbf{x}^{(0)}, \mathbf{x}^{(1)}, \mathbf{x}^{(2)}, \ldots$ of Jacobi approximations converges to $\mathbf{x}^*$.
(a) Let $\mathbf{r}^{(k)} = \mathbf{x}^{(k)} - \mathbf{x}^*$ be the error after the kth iteration. Subtract the equations $\mathbf{x}^* = T\mathbf{x}^* + \mathbf{c}$ and $\mathbf{x}^{(k+1)} = T\mathbf{x}^{(k)} + \mathbf{c}$ to show that

$$\mathbf{r}^{(k)} = T^k\mathbf{r}^{(0)}.$$

(b) Now use the fact that $T = PDP^{-1}$, where D is the diagonal matrix with diagonal elements $\lambda_1, \lambda_2, \ldots, \lambda_n$, to show that $\mathbf{r}^{(k)}$ approaches zero as k increases without bound.

24. Explain how to alter the program TRIDIAG to solve the problem

$$\frac{d^2y}{dx^2} = 20x^3, \qquad y(0) = y(2) = 0.$$

25. Consider the end-point value problem

$$\frac{d^2y}{dx^2} + y = 0, \qquad y(0) = 0, \qquad y\left(\frac{\pi}{2}\right) = 1,$$

which has the exact solution $y(x) = \sin x$. Let $y_0, y_1, y_2, \ldots, y_{n+1}$ denote the values of $y(x)$ at the successive points that subdivide $[0, \pi/2]$ into $n + 1$ equal subintervals (so $y_0 = 0$ and $y_{n+1} = 1$). Explain why the equations

$$y_i = \tfrac{1}{2}(y_{i-1} + h^2 y_i + y_{i+1})$$

for $i = 1, 2, \ldots, n$ constitute a discrete model for the end-point value problem. Then explain how to alter the program TRIDIAG in order to approximate the solution of this $n \times n$ linear system.

26. Consider the steady-state temperature $u(x, y)$ in the square plate of Figure 9.11, with boundary conditions

$$u(0, y) = u(x, 0) = u(x, 3) = 0, \qquad u(3, y) = 1.$$

Thus the temperature is held at 1 on the right edge and at zero on the other three edges. Set up the 4×4 system $A\mathbf{u} = \mathbf{f}$ as in (15) for the temperatures u_1, u_2, u_3, u_4 at the indicated interior grid points. Identify the matrix A and the vector $\mathbf{f}$.

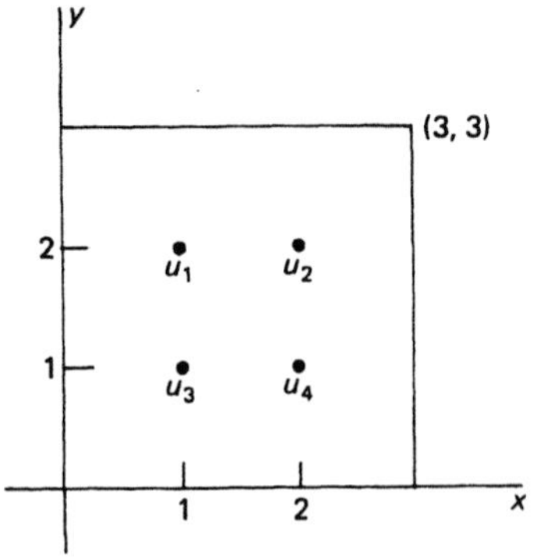

9.11 The square plate of Problem 26.

27. Consider the steady-state temperature $u(x, y)$ in the triangular plate of Figure 9.12, with boundary conditions $u = 0$ on the edges $x = 0$ and $y = 0$ and $u = 1$ on the edge $x + y = 5$. Set up the 6×6 system $A\mathbf{u} = \mathbf{f}$ as in (15) for the temperatures $u_1, u_2, \ldots, u_6$ at the indicated interior grid points. Identify the matrix A and the vector $\mathbf{f}$.

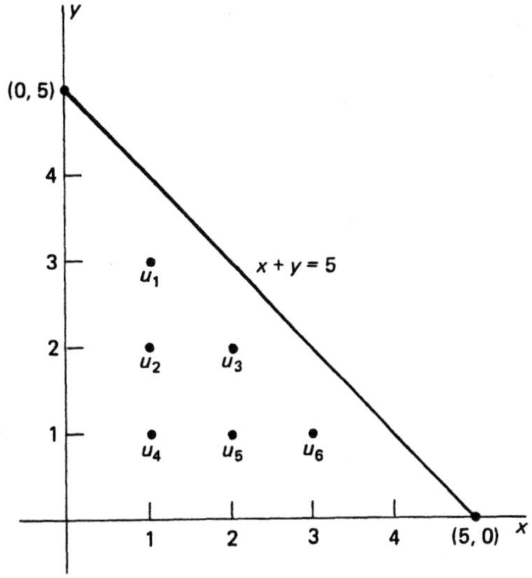

9.12 The triangular plate of Problem 27.

28. A spider is placed on one vertex of a cube of unit edge length. The spider crawls along the edges of the cube. When she reaches a vertex, she picks one of the three edges that meet there at random, each with probability $\frac{1}{3}$, and continues her journey. Show that the probability that she eventually reaches the vertex opposite her starting point is 1. What is the expected length of her journey from the initial vertex to the one opposite it?

29. Repeat Problem 28 for a spider on a regular dodecahedron of edge 1. *Note*: The surface of a dodecahedron consists of twelve regular pentagons; three edges meet at each vertex.

30. Peter and Paul match coins. (Each flips a fair coin; if both are heads or both are tails, Peter wins one coin from Paul. If the coins show one head and one tail, Paul wins one coin from Peter.) Peter begins with 10 coins and Paul begins with 5. What is the probability that Peter wins all the coins? (The game is over when one player has won all the coins.) What is the expected length of the game?

31. Solve Problem 30 if the game is modified as follows: If both coins are heads, Peter wins one from Paul; otherwise Paul wins one from Peter.

32. Repeat Problem 28 for a spider on the edges of an octahedron (the regular solid with eight equilateral triangles as faces and four edges meeting at each vertex).

33. A marker is placed on the x-axis at the point $x = 0$. From then on, every second it moves one unit to the left or one to the right, at random, with equal probability $\frac{1}{2}$ for each direction. Let x_n be the probability that the counter eventually reaches the position $x = 1000$ given it is at position $x = n$.
(a) Write the equations that relate the various values of x_n in compact notation.
(b) Prove that the solution of these equations is unique.
(c) Show by direct substitution that $x_n = A + Bn$ is a solution (A and B are constants).
(d) Evaluate B and then A, to find the value of x_0, the probability that the counter eventually reaches the position $x = 1000$.

(e) Solve this problem if 1000 is replaced by an arbitrary integer M.

34. If you play red or black at roulette, win with probability $p = \frac{18}{37}$, begin with \$100, and always bet \$50, what is the probability that you eventually win \$10,000? Solve this problem as follows.

(a) Let x_n be the probability that you eventually win 200 \$50 chips given you have n such chips. Write the difference equation that expresses x_n in terms of x_{n+1} and x_{n-1}.

(b) Prove that the solution of these equations is unique.

(c) Show by direct substitution that

$$x_n = A + B\left(\frac{19}{18}\right)^n$$

is a solution.

(d) Use the conditions $x_0 = 0$ and $x_{200} = 1$ to find the constants A and B.

(e) Evaluate x_2 to answer the original question.

9.3

Appendix: Automated Gaussian Elimination

Although there are special situations that call for the indirect iterative methods of Section 9.2, the heart of computational linear algebra is the direct method of Gaussian elimination that we first discussed in Section 1.2. In this final section we present two IBM-PC BASIC programs for carrying out the process of Gaussian elimination on a computer. Program ROWOPS partially automates the process for the purpose of practicing the use of elementary row operations to reduce a given matrix to echelon form. Program ECHELON fully automates the process for the purpose of finding as quickly as possible the reduced echelon form of a given matrix.

Figure 9.13 shows a listing of Program ROWOPS. When this program is executed, you are first asked (in the subroutines beginning at lines 500 and 800) to input and (if necessary) edit the $m \times n$ matrix A that you wish to reduce to echelon form. You are then presented with the following menu.

```
Select (by number) one of the following choices:
    1—Add k times row p to row q
    2—Interchange rows p and q
    3—Multiply row p by k
    4—Divide row p by k
    5—Display inverse matrix of A
    6—Calculate determinant of A
    7—Quit or start over
Your choice?
```

Choices 1 through 4 lead (via line 340) to the subroutines starting at lines 1100–1400, respectively. Each of these subroutines first asks you with which row(s) you wish to work and then carries out the desired operation. The result is displayed (almost instantaneously) by the display subroutine starting at line 700. You are then presented again with the menu of choices to indicate what you want to do next. Figures 9.14 and 9.15 show some typical output of Program ROWOPS.

If you input initially a *square* $n \times n$ matrix A, then an $n \times n$ identity matrix C is set up by the subroutine starting at line 600. In this case each row operation that is

```
100 'Program ROWOPS
110 '
120 'For practice in using elementary row operations
130 'to reduce a matrix to echelon form.
140 '
150  DIM A(10,10), C(10,10)   :'Up to 10x10 matrices
160  DEFINT I,J,M,N,P,Q,X
180 '
200  GOSUB 500       :'Input the mxn matrix A
210  GOSUB 600       :'Set up the identity matrix
220  GOSUB 800       :'Edit the matrix A
230 '
250 'Carry out row operations:
260 '
270  CLS
300  GOSUB 700       :'Display the matrix A
310  GOSUB 900       :'To choose desired operation
320 '                 (Integer X specifies choice made)
330  IF X = 7 THEN GOTO 400     :'To quit or start over
340  ON X GOSUB 1100, 1200, 1300, 1400, 1500, 1600
350 '            (To carry out the desired operation)
360  GOTO 300           :'To choose another operation
370 '
400  INPUT "Want to input another matrix (Y/N)"; Y$
410  IF Y$ = "Y" OR Y$ = "y" THEN GOTO 200
420  STOP
430 '
500 'Subroutine to input matrix A:
505 '
509  PRINT
510  INPUT "Number m of rows of matrix A"; M
515  INPUT "Number n of columns of matrix A"; N
516  PRINT
520  FOR I = 1 TO M
525      FOR J = 1 TO N
530          PRINT "A(";I;",";J;") = ";
540          INPUT A(I,J)
550      NEXT J
560  NEXT I
570  D = 1      :'Initialize determinant
580  RETURN
590 '
600 'Subroutine to set up identity matrix:
610 '
620  FOR I = 1 TO M
630      FOR J = 1 TO N
640          IF I = J THEN C(I,J) = 1
                      ELSE C(I,J) = 0
650      NEXT J
660  NEXT I
670  RETURN
680 '
700 'Subroutine to display the matrix A:
705 '
```

9.13 Listing of Program ROWOPS.

```
706  PRINT
710  PRINT "The current matrix A is
715  PRINT
730  FOR I = 1 TO M
740      FOR J = 1 TO N
750          PRINT A(I,J),
760      NEXT J : PRINT
770  NEXT I
780  PRINT
790  RETURN
795 '
800 'Subroutine to edit the matrix A:
805 '
810  CLS
820  GOSUB 700    :'To display the matrix A
830  INPUT "Want to change an entry (Y/N)"; Y$
840  IF Y$ = "N" OR Y$ = "n" THEN RETURN
850  PRINT "Enter the row I and the column J
855  PRINT "of the element you want to change:"
860  PRINT
870  INPUT "I,J"; I,J
880  INPUT "New value of this entry"; A(I,J)
890  GOTO 800      :'For any other changes
895 '
900 'Subroutine to choose desired operation:
910 '
920  PRINT "Select (by no.) one of the following choices:"
930  PRINT
940  PRINT "      1 -- Add k times Row p to Row q
950  PRINT "      2 -- Interchange Rows p and q
960  PRINT "      3 -- Multiply Row p by k
970  PRINT "      4 -- Divide Row p by k
980  PRINT "      5 -- Display inverse matrix of A
990  PRINT "      6 -- Calculate determinant of A
1000 PRINT "      7 -- Quit or start over
1010 PRINT
1020 INPUT "Your choice"; X
1025 PRINT
1030 RETURN
1040 '
1100 'Subroutine to add multiple of one row to another:
1105 '
1110  PRINT "Specify  k,p,q  to add k times Row p to Row q:"
1120  PRINT
1130  INPUT "k,p,q"; K,P,Q
1140  FOR J = 1 TO N
1150      A(Q,J) = A(Q,J) + K*A(P,J)
1160      C(Q,J) = C(Q,J) + K*C(P,J)
1170  NEXT J
1180  RETURN
1190 '
1200 'Subroutine to interchange rows:
1205 '
1210  PRINT "Specify  p,q  to interchange Rows p and q:
```

9.13 (continued)

```
1215  PRINT
1220  INPUT "p,q"; P,Q
1230  FOR J = 1 TO N
1240      SWAP A(P,J), A(Q,J)
1250      SWAP C(P,J), C(Q,J)
1260  NEXT J
1265  D = -D
1270  RETURN
1280 '
1300 'Subroutine to multiply a row by a constant:
1305 '
1310  PRINT "Specify  k,p  for k times Row p:
1320  PRINT
1330  INPUT "k,p"; K,P
1340  FOR J = 1 TO N
1350      A(P,J) = K*A(P,J)
1360      C(P,J) = K*C(P,J)
1370  NEXT J
1375  D = D/K
1380  RETURN
1390 '
1400 'Subroutine to divide a row by a constant:
1405 '
1410  PRINT "Specify  k,p  to divide Row p by k:
1420  PRINT
1430  INPUT "k,p"; K,P
1440  FOR J = 1 TO N
1450      A(P,J) = A(P,J)/K
1460      C(P,J) = C(P,J)/K
1470  NEXT J
1475  D = K*D
1480  RETURN
1490 '
1500 'Subroutine to display the inverse matrix:
1505 '
1510  IF M<>N THEN PRINT
      "There is no inverse matrix because m and n not equal.":
      RETURN
1520  PRINT "If you have now reduced the original matrix A"
1525  PRINT "to the identity matrix, then A inverse is"
1530  PRINT
1540  FOR I = 1 TO N
1545      FOR J = 1 TO N
1550          PRINT C(I,J),
1560      NEXT J  :  PRINT
1570  NEXT I
1580  PRINT
1590  RETURN
1595 '
1600 'Subroutine to calculate determinant:
1605 '
1610  IF M<>N THEN PRINT
      "There is no determinant because m and n not equal.":
      RETURN
```

9.13 (continued)

```
1620  FOR I = 1 TO N
1630      D = D*A(I,I)
1640  NEXT I
1650  PRINT "If you have now reduced the original matrix A"
1655  PRINT "to a triangular matrix, then"
1660  PRINT
1670  PRINT "      det A = "; D
1675  PRINT
1680  RETURN
1690 '
1700  END
```

9.13 (end)

```
The current matrix A is

 1             2             3
 4             5             6

Select (by no.) one of the following choices:

     1 -- Add k times Row p to Row q
     2 -- Interchange Rows p and q
     3 -- Multiply Row p by k
     4 -- Divide Row p by k
     5 -- Display inverse matrix of A
     6 -- Calculate determinant of A
     7 -- Quit or start over

Your choice? 2

Specify  p,q  to interchange Rows p and q:

p,q? 1,2

The current matrix A is

 4             5             6
 1             2             3

Select (by no.) one of the following choices:

     1 -- Add k times Row p to Row q
     2 -- Interchange Rows p and q
     3 -- Multiply Row p by k
     4 -- Divide Row p by k
     5 -- Display inverse matrix of A
     6 -- Calculate determinant of A
     7 -- Quit or start over

Your choice?
```

9.14 Output of Program ROWOPS.

```
The current matrix A is

 1             2             3
 3             7             11
 0             2             4

Select (by no.) one of the following choices:

     1 -- Add k times Row p to Row q
     2 -- Interchange Rows p and q
     3 -- Multiply Row p by k
     4 -- Divide Row p by k
     5 -- Display inverse matrix of A
     6 -- Calculate determinant of A
     7 -- Quit or start over

Your choice? 1

Specify  k,p,q  to add k times Row p to Row q:

k,p,q? -3,1,2

The current matrix A is

 1             2             3
 0             1             2
 0             2             4

Select (by no.) one of the following choices:

     1 -- Add k times Row p to Row q
     2 -- Interchange Rows p and q
     3 -- Multiply Row p by k
     4 -- Divide Row p by k
     5 -- Display inverse matrix of A
     6 -- Calculate determinant of A
     7 -- Quit or start over

Your choice?
```

9.15 (end)

performed on A is also silently and simultaneously performed on C. Once you have reduced the original matrix A to upper triangular form, you can (by choice 6) find the determinant of A. And when you have reduced A to the $n \times n$ identity matrix, you can (by choice 5) find the inverse matrix A^{-1}. At any time you can (by choice 7) quit or start over with a new matrix A.

Figure 9.16 shows a listing of Program ECHELON. When this program is executed and an $m \times n$ matrix A is input, the *reduced* echelon form of A is computed and displayed. If $m = n$, then det A is computed. And if det $A \neq 0$, then the inverse matrix A^{-1} is computed and displayed. Figures 9.17 and 9.18 show some typical output of Program ECHELON.

```
100 'Program ECHELON
110 '
120 'Computes the reduced echelon form of the input
130 'matrix A, as well as the determinant of a square
140 'matrix and the inverse matrix if A is nonsingular.
150 '
170  DIM A(10,10), C(10,10)   :'Up to 10x10 matrices
180  DEFINT F,I,J,K,M,N,P,Q
185  DEFDBL A,C,D,L
190 '
200  GOSUB 600       :'Input the mxn matrix A
210  GOSUB 700       :'Set up the identity matrix
220  GOSUB 900       :'Edit the matrix A
230 '
240 '
250 'Main reduction loop:
255 '
260  P = 1  :  Q = 1     :'Start at upper left
270  IF M = N THEN F = 1 ELSE F = 0
275 '    (Flag F = 1 means to calculate inverse)
280  WHILE P <= M  AND  Q <= N
285    '
290    CMAX = 0   :   K = P   :'Pick the largest
300    FOR I = P TO M          :'pivot in Column q
305        X = ABS(A(I,Q))
310        IF X > CMAX THEN CMAX = X  :  K = I
320    NEXT I
330    IF CMAX < .00001 THEN F = 0  :  D = 0  :
       Q = Q + 1   :  GOTO 500
335    '
340    FOR J = 1 TO N  :'Interchange Rows k and p
350        SWAP A(P,J), A(K,J)
360        IF F = 1 THEN SWAP C(P,J), C(K,J)
370    NEXT J
380    IF K > P THEN D = -D
385    L = A(P,Q)
390    '
395    FOR J = 1 TO N   :'Make pivot value equal 1
400        A(P,J) = A(P,J)/L
410        IF F = 1 THEN C(P,J) = C(P,J)/L
420    NEXT J
430    D = D*L
435    '
440    FOR I = 1 TO M  :'Kill rest of Column q
445        L = A(I,Q)
450        FOR J = 1 TO N
460            IF I <> P THEN
                   A(I,J) = A(I,J) - L*A(P,J)
470            IF F = 1 AND I <> P THEN
                   C(I,J) = C(I,J) - L*C(P,J)
480        NEXT J
485    NEXT I
490    P = P + 1  :  Q = Q + 1  :'On to next pivot
500  WEND           :'End loop!
```

9.16 Listing of Program ECHELON.

```
510 '
515  PRINT "The reduced echelon form of A is"
520  PRINT
525  GOSUB 800     :'Display subroutine
530 '
535  IF M = N THEN
     PRINT USING "det A = ###.####";D : PRINT
540  IF F = 0 THEN GOTO 999    :'To stop
545  FOR I = 1 TO N  :  FOR J = 1 TO N
550      A(I,J) = C(I,J)
555  NEXT J  :  NEXT I
560 '
565  PRINT "The inverse of the matrix A is
570  PRINT
575  GOSUB 800     :'Display subroutine
580  GOTO 999      :'To stop
590 '
600 'Subroutine to input matrix A:
605 '
609  PRINT
610  INPUT "Number m of rows of matrix A"; M
615  INPUT "Number n of columns of matrix A"; N
616  PRINT
620  FOR I = 1 TO M
625      FOR J = 1 TO N
630          PRINT "A(";I;",";J;") = ";
640          INPUT A(I,J)
650      NEXT J
660  NEXT I
670  D = 1      :'Initialize determinant
680  RETURN
690 '
700 'Subroutine to set up identity matrix:
710 '
720  FOR I = 1 TO M
730      FOR J = 1 TO N
740          IF I = J THEN C(I,J) = 1
                      ELSE C(I,J) = 0
750      NEXT J
760  NEXT I
770  RETURN
780 '
800 'Subroutine to display the matrix A:
810 '
820  PRINT
830  FOR I = 1 TO M
840      FOR J = 1 TO N
850          PRINT USING "###.####     ";A(I,J),
860      NEXT J : PRINT
870  NEXT I
880  PRINT
890  RETURN
895 '
900 'Subroutine to edit the matrix A:
```

9.16 (continued)

```
905 '
910  CLS
915  PRINT "The matrix A is"  :  PRINT
920  GOSUB 800     :'To display the matrix A
930  INPUT "Want to change an entry (Y/N)"; Y$
940  IF Y$ = "N" OR Y$ = "n" THEN PRINT : RETURN
950  PRINT "Enter the row I and the column J
955  PRINT "of the element you want to change:"
960  PRINT
970  INPUT "I,J"; I,J
980  INPUT "New value of this entry"; A(I,J)
990  GOTO 900       :'For any other changes
995 '
999  END
```

9.16 (end)

The work of reducing A to the desired form is carried out by the WHILE-WEND loop in lines 280–500. Starting with $p = 1$ and $q = 1$ at the upper left-hand corner of matrix A, suppose that we have reached the element a_{pq} in the pth row and qth column; that is, only the lower right $(p - 1) \times (q - 1)$ submatrix of A remains to be reduced to echelon form. Then the FOR-NEXT loop in lines 300–320 finds the largest element a_{kq} (with $k \geq p$) in the qth column. The FOR-NEXT loop in lines 340–370 interchanges the kth and pth rows in order to use the largest possible pivot. The FOR-NEXT loop in lines 395–420 divides the pth row by a constant to put a 1 in the pqth pivot position. Finally, the loop in lines 440–485 uses this pivot element to clear out the rest of the qth column (so that $a_{iq} = 0$ if $i \neq p$). Then p and q are incremented in line 490, and the reduction process terminates when either $p > m$ or $q > n$.

```
The matrix A is


  3.0000        4.0000
  5.0000        7.0000

Want to change an entry (Y/N)? N

The reduced echelon form of A is


  1.0000        0.0000
  0.0000        1.0000

det A =   1.0000

The inverse of the matrix A is


  7.0000       -4.0000
 -5.0000        3.0000

Ok
```

9.17 Output of Program ECHELON.

```
The matrix A is

  2.0000        3.0000        7.0000        1.0000
  1.0000       -2.0000       -7.0000        4.0000
  1.0000        7.0000       20.0000       -5.0000

Want to change an entry (Y/N)? N

The reduced echelon form of A is

  1.0000        0.0000       -1.0000        2.0000
  0.0000        1.0000        3.0000       -1.0000
  0.0000        0.0000        0.0000        0.0000

Ok
```

9.18 Output of Program ECHELON.

```
The matrix A is

237.000   38.000  116.000   42.000  104.000   29.000   51.000
290.000   45.000  142.000   51.000  132.000   32.000   65.000
112.000   18.000   55.000   20.000   49.000   14.000   24.000
253.000   40.000  124.000   45.000  112.000   30.000   55.000
106.000   17.000   52.000   19.000   47.000   13.000   23.000
257.000   41.000  126.000   46.000   14.000   31.000   56.000
224.000   36.000  110.000   40.000  100.000   28.000   49.000

The reduced echelon form of A is

  1.000    0.000    0.000    0.000    0.000    0.000    0.000
  0.000    1.000    0.000    0.000    0.000    0.000    0.000
  0.000    0.000    1.000    0.000    0.000    0.000    0.000
  0.000    0.000    0.000    1.000    0.000    0.000    0.000
  0.000    0.000    0.000    0.000    1.000    0.000    0.000
  0.000    0.000    0.000    0.000    0.000    1.000    0.000
  0.000    0.000    0.000    0.000    0.000    0.000    1.000

det A =   1.0000

The inverse of the matrix A is

  1.000   -1.000   -6.000    3.000    0.000   -1.000    1.000
  1.000    2.000    8.000   -8.000    2.000    3.000   -3.000
 -2.000    2.000   13.000   -5.000   -1.000    1.000   -2.000
 -1.000   -1.000   -4.000    2.000    2.000    1.000    0.000
 -0.000    0.000   -2.000    1.000    7.000   -3.000   -0.000
  0.000   -1.000   -4.000    3.000   -2.000   -1.000    2.000
  0.000   -0.000    2.000   -2.000  -14.000    6.000    1.000
```

9.19 Output for the 7 × 7 matrix *A*.

In order to test the numerical accuracy of Program ECHELON, we input the 7×7 matrix

$$A = \begin{bmatrix} 237 & 38 & 116 & 42 & 104 & 29 & 51 \\ 290 & 45 & 142 & 51 & 132 & 32 & 65 \\ 112 & 18 & 55 & 20 & 49 & 14 & 24 \\ 253 & 40 & 124 & 45 & 112 & 30 & 55 \\ 106 & 17 & 52 & 19 & 47 & 13 & 23 \\ 257 & 41 & 126 & 46 & 114 & 31 & 56 \\ 224 & 36 & 110 & 40 & 100 & 28 & 49 \end{bmatrix}.$$

The determinant of A is exactly $\det A = 1$, and the inverse of A is exactly

$$A^{-1} = \begin{bmatrix} 1 & -1 & -6 & 3 & 0 & -1 & 1 \\ 1 & 2 & 8 & -8 & 2 & 3 & -3 \\ -2 & 2 & 13 & -5 & -1 & 1 & -2 \\ -1 & -1 & -4 & 2 & 2 & 1 & 0 \\ 0 & 0 & -2 & 1 & 7 & -3 & 0 \\ 0 & -1 & -4 & 3 & -2 & -1 & 2 \\ 0 & 0 & 2 & -2 & -14 & 6 & 1 \end{bmatrix}.$$

Figure 9.19 shows the actual program output for the 7×7 matrix A, produced in about 17 seconds of running time.

Answers to Odd-Numbered Problems

SECTION 1.1 (page 9)

1. $x = 3, y = 2$ **3.** $x = -4, y = 3$ **5.** Inconsistent—no solution
7. $x = 4t - 10, y = t$ (infinitely many solutions) **9.** $x = 4, y = -1, z = 3$ **11.** $x = 1, y = 3, z = -4$
13. $x = y = z = 0$ **15.** Inconsistent—no solution **17.** Inconsistent—no solution
19. $x = 3t + 8, y = 2t + 3, z = t$ **21.** $x = -2t + 3, y = 3t + 2, z = t$
23. *Suggestion*: The two lines both pass through the origin.
25. (a) No solution (b) A unique solution (c) No solution (d) No solution (e) A unique solution (f) Infinitely many solutions

SECTION 1.2 (page 21)

1. $x_1 = 1, x_2 = 0, x_3 = 2$ **3.** $x_1 = 11t + 13, x_2 = 5t + 2, x_3 = t$
5. $x_1 = 4t + 13, x_2 = t + 6, x_3 = 3t + 5, x_4 = t$ **7.** $x_1 = -8s + 19t + 3, x_2 = 2s - 7t + 7, x_3 = s, x_4 = t$
9. $x_1 = 1, x_2 = 3, x_3 = -5, x_4 = 6$ **11.** $x_1 = 3, x_2 = -2, x_3 = 4$
13. $x_1 = 3t + 4, x_2 = -2t + 3, x_3 = t$ **15.** Inconsistent—no solution
17. $x_1 = -2t + 3, x_2 = t - 4, x_3 = -3t + 5, x_4 = t$
19. $x_1 = -s - t + 3, x_2 = 2s - 3t + 5, x_3 = s, x_4 = t$ **21.** $x_1 = 2, x_2 = 1, x_3 = 3, x_4 = 4$
23. (a) None (b) $k \neq 2$ (c) $k = 2$ **25.** (a) $k \neq 4$ (b) $k = 4$ (c) None
27. (a) None (b) $k \neq 11$ (c) $k = 11$

SECTION 1.3 (page 29)

1. $\begin{bmatrix} 1 & 0 \\ 0 & 1 \end{bmatrix}$ **3.** $\begin{bmatrix} 1 & 0 & -2 \\ 0 & 1 & 3 \end{bmatrix}$ **5.** $\begin{bmatrix} 1 & 0 & -5 \\ 0 & 1 & -3 \end{bmatrix}$ **7.** $\begin{bmatrix} 1 & 0 & 5 \\ 0 & 1 & -1 \\ 0 & 0 & 0 \end{bmatrix}$ **9.** $\begin{bmatrix} 1 & 0 & 2 \\ 0 & 1 & 4 \\ 0 & 0 & 0 \end{bmatrix}$

11. $\begin{bmatrix} 1 & 3 & 0 \\ 0 & 0 & 1 \\ 0 & 0 & 0 \end{bmatrix}$ **13.** $\begin{bmatrix} 1 & 0 & 0 & 3 \\ 0 & 1 & 0 & -2 \\ 0 & 0 & 1 & 2 \end{bmatrix}$ **15.** $\begin{bmatrix} 1 & 0 & -1 & 2 \\ 0 & 1 & 3 & -1 \\ 0 & 0 & 0 & 0 \end{bmatrix}$

17. $\begin{bmatrix} 1 & 0 & 0 & 2 & -3 \\ 0 & 1 & 0 & -1 & 4 \\ 0 & 0 & 1 & -2 & -5 \end{bmatrix}$ **19.** $\begin{bmatrix} 1 & 0 & 2 & 1 & 3 \\ 0 & 1 & -2 & -3 & 1 \\ 0 & 0 & 0 & 0 & 0 \end{bmatrix}$

21. $x_1 = 3, x_2 = -2, x_3 = 4$ **23.** $x_1 = 3t + 4, x_2 = -2t + 3, x_3 = t$ **25.** No solution

27. $x_1 = -2t + 3, x_2 = t - 4, x_3 = -3t + 5, x_4 = t$

29. $x_1 = -s - t + 3, x_2 = 2s - 3t + 5, x_3 = s, x_4 = t$

31. The sequence $(\frac{1}{4})R_2, (-2)R_2 + R_1, (\frac{1}{6})R_3, (-\frac{1}{2})R_3 + R_1, (-\frac{5}{4})R_3 + R_2$ of row operations transforms the first matrix in Equation (1) to I_3.

33. $\begin{bmatrix} 1 & 0 \\ 0 & 1 \end{bmatrix}$ $\begin{bmatrix} 1 & * \\ 0 & 1 \end{bmatrix}$ $\begin{bmatrix} 0 & 1 \\ 0 & 0 \end{bmatrix}$ $\begin{bmatrix} 0 & 0 \\ 0 & 0 \end{bmatrix}$

SECTION 1.4 (page 41)

1. $\begin{bmatrix} 5 & -15 \\ 18 & 5 \end{bmatrix}$ **3.** $\begin{bmatrix} -26 & 20 \\ 12 & -6 \\ 22 & 18 \end{bmatrix}$ **5.** $AB = \begin{bmatrix} -9 & 1 \\ -10 & 12 \end{bmatrix}, BA = \begin{bmatrix} -2 & 8 \\ 11 & 5 \end{bmatrix}$

7. $AB = [26], BA = \begin{bmatrix} 3 & 6 & 9 \\ 4 & 8 & 12 \\ 5 & 10 & 15 \end{bmatrix}$ **9.** $BA = \begin{bmatrix} 4 \\ 7 \\ -22 \end{bmatrix}$ **11.** $AB = [11 \quad 1 \quad 5 \quad 3]$

13. $AB = \begin{bmatrix} 3 & 16 \\ -14 & -1 \end{bmatrix}, BC = \begin{bmatrix} 10 & 17 \\ 2 & 0 \end{bmatrix},$ and $(AB)C = \begin{bmatrix} 32 & 51 \\ -2 & -17 \end{bmatrix} = A(BC)$

15. $AB = \begin{bmatrix} 3 & -3 & 6 \\ 2 & -2 & 4 \end{bmatrix}, BC = [4 \quad 5]$, and $(AB)C = \begin{bmatrix} 12 & 15 \\ 8 & 10 \end{bmatrix} = A(BC)$

17. $\begin{bmatrix} 1 & 0 & -5 & 4 \\ 0 & 1 & 2 & -7 \end{bmatrix} \begin{bmatrix} x_1 \\ x_2 \\ x_3 \\ x_4 \end{bmatrix} = \begin{bmatrix} 0 \\ 0 \end{bmatrix}$ and $\mathbf{x} = s(5, -2, 1, 0) + t(-4, 7, 0, 1)$

19. $\begin{bmatrix} 1 & 0 & 0 & 3 & -1 \\ 0 & 1 & 0 & -2 & 6 \\ 0 & 0 & 1 & 1 & -8 \end{bmatrix} \begin{bmatrix} x_1 \\ x_2 \\ x_3 \\ x_4 \\ x_5 \end{bmatrix} = \begin{bmatrix} 0 \\ 0 \\ 0 \end{bmatrix}$ and $\mathbf{x} = s(-3, 2, -1, 1, 0) + t(1, -6, 8, 0, 1)$

21. $\mathbf{x} = s(1, -2, 1, 0, 0) + t(-2, 3, 0, 1, 0) + u(-7, -4, 0, 0, 1)$

23. $B = \begin{bmatrix} 2 & -1 \\ -3 & 2 \end{bmatrix}$ **25.** $B = \begin{bmatrix} 3 & -7 \\ -2 & 5 \end{bmatrix}$

29. $A^2 = \begin{bmatrix} a^2 + bc & ab + bd \\ ac + dc & bc + d^2 \end{bmatrix}, A^2 + (ad - bc)I = \begin{bmatrix} a^2 + ad & ab + bd \\ ac + dc & d^2 + ad \end{bmatrix} = \begin{bmatrix} a(a + d) & b(a + d) \\ c(a + d) & d(a + d) \end{bmatrix} = (a + d)A$

31. (a) $(A + B)(A - B) = \begin{bmatrix} -25 & -34 \\ -71 & -34 \end{bmatrix} \neq \begin{bmatrix} -8 & -45 \\ -44 & -51 \end{bmatrix} = A^2 - B^2$

33. $\begin{bmatrix} 1 & 0 \\ 0 & 1 \end{bmatrix}$ $\begin{bmatrix} -1 & 0 \\ 0 & -1 \end{bmatrix}$ $\begin{bmatrix} +1 & 0 \\ 0 & -1 \end{bmatrix}$ $\begin{bmatrix} -1 & 0 \\ 0 & +1 \end{bmatrix}$ **35.** $\begin{bmatrix} 2 & -1 \\ 2 & -1 \end{bmatrix}$ **37.** $\begin{bmatrix} 0 & 1 \\ -1 & 0 \end{bmatrix}$

39. $A(c_1\mathbf{x}_1 + c_2\mathbf{x}_2) = c_1A\mathbf{x}_1 + c_2A\mathbf{x}_2 = c_1 \cdot \mathbf{0} + c_2 \cdot \mathbf{0} = \mathbf{0}$ **43.** $A^2 = \begin{bmatrix} 6 & -3 & -3 \\ -3 & 6 & -3 \\ -3 & -3 & 6 \end{bmatrix} = 3A$

SECTION 1.5 (page 56)

1. $A^{-1} = \begin{bmatrix} 3 & -2 \\ -4 & 3 \end{bmatrix}$, $\mathbf{x} = \begin{bmatrix} 3 \\ -2 \end{bmatrix}$ **3.** $A^{-1} = \begin{bmatrix} 6 & -7 \\ -5 & 6 \end{bmatrix}$, $\mathbf{x} = \begin{bmatrix} 33 \\ -28 \end{bmatrix}$

5. $A^{-1} = \begin{bmatrix} 2.0 & -1.0 \\ -2.5 & 1.5 \end{bmatrix}$, $\mathbf{x} = \begin{bmatrix} 4.0 \\ -3.5 \end{bmatrix}$ **7.** $A^{-1} = \begin{bmatrix} 1.75 & -2.25 \\ -1.25 & 1.75 \end{bmatrix}$, $\mathbf{x} = \begin{bmatrix} 0.75 \\ -0.25 \end{bmatrix}$ **9.** $\begin{bmatrix} 5 & -6 \\ -4 & 5 \end{bmatrix}$

11. $\begin{bmatrix} -5 & -2 & 5 \\ 2 & 1 & -2 \\ -4 & -3 & 5 \end{bmatrix}$ **13.** $\begin{bmatrix} -13 & 42 & -5 \\ 3 & -9 & 1 \\ 2 & -7 & 1 \end{bmatrix}$ **15.** $\begin{bmatrix} -22 & 2 & 7 \\ -27 & 3 & 8 \\ 10 & -1 & -3 \end{bmatrix}$ **17.** $\frac{1}{4}\begin{bmatrix} -2 & -6 & -3 \\ -2 & -2 & -1 \\ -2 & -2 & 1 \end{bmatrix}$

19. $\frac{1}{6}\begin{bmatrix} -21 & 11 & 8 \\ 9 & -5 & -2 \\ -3 & 3 & 0 \end{bmatrix}$ **21.** $\begin{bmatrix} 0 & 1 & 0 & 0 \\ -2 & 0 & 1 & 0 \\ 1 & 0 & 0 & 0 \\ 0 & -3 & 0 & 1 \end{bmatrix}$ **23.** $X = \begin{bmatrix} 7 & 18 & -35 \\ -9 & -23 & 45 \end{bmatrix}$

25. $X = \begin{bmatrix} 7 & -14 & 15 \\ -1 & 3 & -2 \\ -2 & 2 & -4 \end{bmatrix}$ **27.** $X = \begin{bmatrix} 17 & -20 & 24 & -13 \\ 1 & -1 & 1 & -1 \\ -5 & 6 & -7 & 4 \end{bmatrix}$

SECTION 1.6 (page 62)

1. $y = -2 + 3x$ **3.** $y = 3 - 2x^2$ **5.** $y = 5 - 3x + x^2$ **7.** $y = \frac{4}{3}x + x^2 - \frac{4}{3}x^3$
9. $y = x^3 + 2x^2 + 3x + 4$ **11.** $x^2 + y^2 - 6x - 4x - 12 = 0$; center (3, 2), radius 5
13. $x^2 + y^2 + 4x + 4y - 5 = 0$; center $(-2, -2)$, radius $\sqrt{13}$
15. $2x^2 + xy + y^2 = 10$ (coefficients approximate) **17.** $y = 3 + 2/x$

SECTION 1.7 (page 66)

1. $A^n \to \begin{bmatrix} 0.5 & 0.5 \\ 0.5 & 0.5 \end{bmatrix}, \begin{bmatrix} C \\ S \end{bmatrix} \to \begin{bmatrix} 500 \\ 500 \end{bmatrix}$ **3.** $A^n \to \begin{bmatrix} 0.375 & 0.375 \\ 0.625 & 0.625 \end{bmatrix}, \begin{bmatrix} C \\ S \end{bmatrix} \to \begin{bmatrix} 375 \\ 625 \end{bmatrix}$

5. $A^n \to \begin{bmatrix} \frac{1}{3} & \frac{1}{3} \\ \frac{2}{3} & \frac{2}{3} \end{bmatrix}, \begin{bmatrix} C \\ S \end{bmatrix} \to \begin{bmatrix} 333 \\ 667 \end{bmatrix}$ **7.** $A^n \to \begin{bmatrix} 0 & 0 \\ 0 & 0 \end{bmatrix}, \begin{bmatrix} F \\ R \end{bmatrix} \to \begin{bmatrix} 0 \\ 0 \end{bmatrix}$

9. $A^n \to \begin{bmatrix} -1.0 & 2.5 \\ -0.8 & 2.0 \end{bmatrix}, \begin{bmatrix} F \\ R \end{bmatrix} \to \begin{bmatrix} 50 \\ 40 \end{bmatrix}$

SECTION 1.8 (page 70)

1. 50, 31, 13, 47, 31, 23, 8, 29 **3.** 29, 84, 96, 93, 15, 51, 58, 59 **5.** 99, 99, 89, 170, 71, 68, 66, 123
7. V I O L I N **9.** E L E M E N T A R Y
11. C O N A N D O Y L E

SECTION 2.1 (page 78)

1. 0 **3.** 100 **5.** -100 **7.** $x^2 + x$ **9.** $(x - y)^2$ **11.** $x = 10$, $y = -7$ **13.** 2, -4 **15.** 6, -3

17. 2, -3 **19.** $\frac{1}{17}$, $-\frac{13}{17}$ **27.** $x = \begin{vmatrix} u & 8 \\ v & 5 \end{vmatrix} = 5u - 8v$, $y = \begin{vmatrix} 5 & u \\ 3 & v \end{vmatrix} = 5v - 3u$

29. $(2 - \lambda)x - 3y = 0$, $3 - (2 - \lambda)y = 0$. So $x = \begin{vmatrix} 0 & -3 \\ 0 & \lambda - 2 \end{vmatrix} = 0$ and $y = \begin{vmatrix} 2 - \lambda & 0 \\ 3 & 0 \end{vmatrix} = 0$

SECTION 2.2 (page 88)

1. 0 (Property 3) **3.** -1 (Properties 2 and 6) **5.** 24 (Property 6) **7.** 3 **9.** 8 **11.** 5 **13.** 60
15. -210 **17.** 120 **19.** 0 **21.** 30 **23.** 40 **25.** Multiply the second row by abc ($abc \neq 0$).
27. Expand the left-hand side along the first column.
29. Expand the left-hand side along the third column.

SECTION 2.3 (page 98)

1. 10 **3.** -22 **5.** -6 **7.** 56 **9.** 78 **11.** -74 **13.** 8 **15.** 39 **17.** -30 **19.** 114
21. $|C| = 36|B^{-1}| = 36/|B| = 36/9|A| = \frac{4}{2} = 2$ **25.** $0 = |\mathrm{O}| = |\mathrm{A}^n| = |\mathrm{A}|^n$
27. $|A| = |P^{-1}BP| = |P^{-1}||B||P| = (1/|P|)|B||P| = |B|$
31. If $AB = I$, then $1 = |AB| = |A||B|$, so $|A| \neq 0$ and $|B| \neq 0$. So A^{-1} exists. Thus $A^{-1}(AB) = A^{-1}I$, and therefore $B = A^{-1}$. Interchange the symbols A and B for a proof in the case $BA = I$.

SECTION 2.4 (page 106)

1. $(x_1, x_2, x_3) = (-0.6, -1, 0.8)$ **3.** $\frac{23}{73}, -\frac{53}{73}, -\frac{32}{73}$ **5.** 2, 3, 0 **7.** $-\frac{8}{7}, -\frac{10}{7}, \frac{1}{7}$ **9.** $\frac{9}{37}, -\frac{7}{37}, -\frac{8}{37}$

11. $\frac{1}{10}\begin{bmatrix} 2 & 4 & 2 \\ -5 & 0 & -10 \\ -6 & -2 & -6 \end{bmatrix}$ **13.** $-\frac{1}{73}\begin{bmatrix} 11 & 2 & -4 \\ -19 & -30 & -13 \\ -28 & -25 & -23 \end{bmatrix}$ **15.** $\frac{1}{35}\begin{bmatrix} -15 & 25 & -26 \\ 10 & -5 & 8 \\ 15 & -25 & 19 \end{bmatrix}$

17. $\frac{1}{29}\begin{bmatrix} 11 & -14 & -15 \\ -17 & 19 & 10 \\ 18 & -15 & -14 \end{bmatrix}$ **19.** $\frac{1}{37}\begin{bmatrix} -21 & -1 & -13 \\ 4 & 9 & 6 \\ -6 & 5 & -9 \end{bmatrix}$

SECTION 2.5 (page 113)

1. $\begin{vmatrix} x & y & 1 \\ 1 & 1 & 1 \\ 3 & 7 & 1 \end{vmatrix} = 0$: $-6x + 2y + 4 = 0$, so $y = 3x - 2$ **3.** $y = -2x^2 + 3$ **5.** $y = x^2 - 3x + 5$
7. $(x - 3)^2 + (y - 2)^2 = 25$ **9.** $(x + 2)^2 + (y + 2)^2 = 13$ **13.** $4x^2 - 7xy + 4y^2 = 100$
15. $400x^2 - 481xy + 225y^2 = 3600$

SECTION 3.1 (page 128)

1. $|\mathbf{a}| = \sqrt{5}$, $|-2\mathbf{b}| = 2\sqrt{13}$, $|\mathbf{a} - \mathbf{b}| = 4\sqrt{2}$, $\mathbf{a} + \mathbf{b} = (-2, 0)$, and $3\mathbf{a} - 2\mathbf{b} = (9, -10)$
3. $2\sqrt{2}$, 10, $\sqrt{5}$, $(-5, -6)$, $(0, 2)$ **5.** $\sqrt{10}$, $2\sqrt{29}$, $\sqrt{65}$, $3\mathbf{i} - 2\mathbf{j}$, $-\mathbf{i} + 19\mathbf{j}$
7. 4, 14, $\sqrt{65}$, $4\mathbf{i} - 7\mathbf{j}$, $12\mathbf{i} + 14\mathbf{j}$ **9.** $\mathbf{u} = (-\frac{3}{5}, -\frac{4}{5})$, $\mathbf{v} = -\mathbf{u}$ **11.** $\mathbf{u} = (\frac{8}{17}, \frac{15}{17})$, $\mathbf{v} = -\mathbf{u}$
13. $(0, -4)$ **15.** $(8, -14)$
17. $-3\mathbf{u} + 2\mathbf{v} = \mathbf{0}$. If you prefer, $\mathbf{v} = \frac{3}{2}\mathbf{u}$ or $\mathbf{u} = \frac{2}{3}\mathbf{v}$. Any way you cut it, $\mathbf{u}$ and $\mathbf{v}$ are linearly dependent.
19. If $a\mathbf{u} + b\mathbf{v} = \mathbf{0}$, then

$$\begin{bmatrix} 2 & 2 \\ 2 & -2 \end{bmatrix}\begin{bmatrix} a \\ b \end{bmatrix} = \begin{bmatrix} 0 \\ 0 \end{bmatrix}.$$

The determinant of the matrix is nonzero, so this matrix equation has a unique solution. $(a, b) = (0, 0)$ is one solution and therefore is the only solution. Thus $\mathbf{u}$ and $\mathbf{v}$ are linearly independent.
21. $\mathbf{w} = 3\mathbf{u} + 2\mathbf{v}$ **23.** $\mathbf{w} = \mathbf{u} - 2\mathbf{v}$ **25.** $\mathbf{w} = 2\mathbf{u} - 3\mathbf{v}$
27. (a) Write $\mathbf{u} = (u_1, u_2)$ and $\mathbf{v} = (v_1, v_2)$. Then

$$\begin{aligned} \mathbf{u} + \mathbf{v} &= (u_1 + v_1, u_2 + v_2) \\ &= (v_1 + u_1, v_2 + u_2) = \mathbf{v} + \mathbf{u}. \end{aligned}$$

Part (b) is similar.

SECTION 3.2 (page 139)

1. $\sqrt{51}$, (5, 8, −11), (2, 23, 0) **3.** $3\sqrt{21}$, $9\mathbf{i} - 3\mathbf{j} + 3\mathbf{k}$, $-14\mathbf{i} - 21\mathbf{j} + 43\mathbf{k}$

5. $\begin{vmatrix} 3 & 5 & 8 \\ -1 & 4 & 3 \\ 2 & -6 & -4 \end{vmatrix} = 0$; linearly dependent **7.** Determinant: $-5 \neq 0$; linearly independent

9. Echelon form: $\begin{bmatrix} 1 & -2 & 1 \\ 0 & 1 & -2 \\ 0 & 0 & 0 \end{bmatrix} \begin{bmatrix} a \\ b \\ c \end{bmatrix} = \begin{bmatrix} 0 \\ 0 \\ 0 \end{bmatrix}$.

Thus $c = 1$, $b = 2c = 2$, $a = 2b - c = 3$, and $3\mathbf{u} + 2\mathbf{v} + \mathbf{w} = \mathbf{0}$.

11. $-11\mathbf{u} - 4\mathbf{v} + \mathbf{w} = \mathbf{0}$ **13.** Echelon form: $\begin{bmatrix} 1 & -7 & -1 \\ 0 & 1 & -9 \\ 0 & 0 & 1 \end{bmatrix} \begin{bmatrix} a \\ b \\ c \end{bmatrix} = \begin{bmatrix} 0 \\ 0 \\ 0 \end{bmatrix}$.

Thus $a = b = c = 0$, and the vectors are therefore linearly independent.

15. Echelon form: $\begin{bmatrix} 1 & 3 & 1 \\ 0 & 1 & 1 \\ 0 & 0 & 1 \end{bmatrix} \begin{bmatrix} a \\ b \\ c \end{bmatrix} = \begin{bmatrix} 2 \\ 2 \\ 3 \end{bmatrix}$.

Hence $a = 2$, $b = -1$, and $c = 3$, so $\mathbf{t} = 2\mathbf{u} - \mathbf{v} + 3\mathbf{w}$.
17. $\mathbf{t} = 2\mathbf{u} + 6\mathbf{v} + \mathbf{w}$ **19.** $(0, u, v) + (0, y, z) = (0, u + y, v + z)$; $c(0, y, z) = (0, cy, cz)$
23. (2, 1, 3) + (4, 1, 5) = (6, 2, 8) **25.** (−1)(2, 2, 1) = (−2, −2, −1) but $-1 \neq 0$
27. If $\mathbf{u}$ is in V, then $0\mathbf{u}$ is in V, but $0\mathbf{u} = \mathbf{0}$.

SECTION 3.3 (page 150)

1. $\theta \approx 1.41075$ (about 80.83°) **3.** $\theta \approx \pi/2$ (exactly 90°)
5. $\angle A \approx 1.37278$ (about 78.65°); $\angle B \approx 1.12202$ (about 64.29°); $\angle C \approx 0.64679$ (about 37.058°)
7. The angle is exactly $\pi/3$ (60°) **9.** $\mathbf{v} = \frac{8}{3}\mathbf{a} + \frac{4}{3}\mathbf{b} - \mathbf{c}$ **11.** $\mathbf{v} = \frac{1}{3}\mathbf{a} + \frac{5}{11}\mathbf{b} - \frac{1}{33}\mathbf{c}$
13. $\mathbf{b}_{\parallel} = (2, 2, 2)$; $\mathbf{b}_{\perp} = (0, 1, -1)$ **15.** $\mathbf{b}_{\parallel} = (4, 2, 2)$; $\mathbf{b}_{\perp} = (1, -1, -1)$ **17.** $\mathbf{p} = (\frac{3}{2}, 3, \frac{3}{2})$
19. $\mathbf{p} = (4, \frac{7}{2}, \frac{9}{2})$ **21.** $\mathbf{c} = \mathbf{a} \times \mathbf{b} = (5, -5, -5)$ **23.** $\mathbf{c} = (2, -4, 2)$
25. If $\mathbf{b}_1 \cdot \mathbf{a} = 0$ and $\mathbf{b}_2 \cdot \mathbf{a} = 0$, then $(\mathbf{b}_1 + \mathbf{b}_2) \cdot \mathbf{a} = \mathbf{b}_1 \cdot \mathbf{a} + \mathbf{b}_2 \cdot \mathbf{a} = 0 + 0 = 0$, and so on.
29. $\mathbf{w} \cdot (r\mathbf{a} + s\mathbf{b}) = r(\mathbf{w} \cdot \mathbf{a}) + s(\mathbf{w} \cdot \mathbf{b}) = 0 + 0 = 0$.

SECTION 3.4 (page 160)

1. $x = t$, $y = 2t$, $z = 3t$ **3.** $x = 4 + 2t$, $y = 13$, $z = -3 - 3t$ **5.** $x = 3 + 3t$, $y = 5 - 13t$, $z = 7 + 3t$
7. $x = 2 + 2t$, $y = -3 - t$, $z = 4 + 3t$ **9.** $2x + 2y - z = 30$ **11.** $x - 3y + 2z = 14$
13. $3x + 4y - z = 0$ **15.** $2x - y - z = 0$ **17.** The lines meet at the point (2, −1, 3).
19. $s + t = 2$, $2s + 2t = 0$, $2s + 2t = -2$; the equations are clearly inconsistent, so the lines do not meet.
21. $x = 2 - 2t$, $y = -1 - t$, $z = 3t$ **23.** $x = \frac{1}{2}(10 - t)$, $y = -\frac{1}{2}(10 - 5t)$, $z = t$ **25.** $3x + 2y + z = 6$
27. The lines meet at the point (1, −1, 2). The equation of the plane is $x - y + z = 4$.
29. (7, −5, 13) **31.** (a) 4 (b) 2

SECTION 4.1 (page 170)

1. $(x_1, x_2, 0) + (y_1, y_2, 0) = (x_1 + y_1, x_2 + y_2, 0)$; $c(x_1, x_2, 0) = (cx_1, cx_2, 0)$. Yes, it *is* a subspace.
3. No (Conditions (i) and (ii) are both violated.) **5.** Yes **7.** No: (1, −1) + (2, 2) = (3, 1), not in W.
9. No (Conditions (i) and (ii) are both violated.) **11.** Yes
13. No: (1, 1, 1, 0) + (1, 1, 0, 1) = (2, 2, 1, 1), not in W **15.** (−1, 0, 1, 0) and (4, 2, 0, −1)
17. (1, −3, 1, 0) and (−2, 1, 0, 1) **19.** (1, 2, −1, 0) **21.** (−3, 2, −4, 1)

23. W is nonempty; choose $\mathbf{u}$ in W. Then $0\mathbf{u} = \mathbf{0}$ must be in W.
31. If $\mathbf{w}$ and $\mathbf{x}$ are in $U + V$, then $\mathbf{w} = \mathbf{u}_1 + \mathbf{v}_1$ and $\mathbf{x} = \mathbf{u}_2 + \mathbf{v}_2$, where $\mathbf{u}_1$ and $\mathbf{u}_2$ are in U and $\mathbf{v}_1$ and $\mathbf{v}_2$ are in V. So

$$\begin{aligned} \mathbf{w} + \mathbf{x} &= (\mathbf{u}_1 + \mathbf{v}_1) + (\mathbf{u}_2 + \mathbf{v}_2) \\ &= (\mathbf{u}_1 + \mathbf{u}_2) + (\mathbf{v}_1 + \mathbf{v}_2), \end{aligned}$$

which is the sum of an element of U and an element of V and thus is an element of $U + V$. So $U + V$ satisfies condition (i) of Theorem 1; the verification of condition (ii) is even easier.

SECTION 4.2 (page 179)

1. $\mathbf{v}_2 = \frac{3}{2}\mathbf{v}_1$: linearly dependent **3.** Linearly dependent (see Example 6) **5.** Linearly independent
7. $\mathbf{v}_1 \neq \alpha\mathbf{v}_2 + \beta\mathbf{v}_3$—check second components, and so on—linearly independent **9.** $\mathbf{w} = 2\mathbf{v}_1 - 3\mathbf{v}_2$
11. $\mathbf{w} = \mathbf{v}_1 - 2\mathbf{v}_2$ **13.** No solution **15.** $\mathbf{w} = 3\mathbf{v}_1 - 2\mathbf{v}_2 + 4\mathbf{v}_3$ **17.** Linearly independent
19. Linearly independent **21.** $\mathbf{v}_1 - 2\mathbf{v}_2 - \mathbf{v}_3 = \mathbf{0}$ **23.** Linearly independent
25. $\mathbf{0} = a\mathbf{u}_1 + b\mathbf{u}_2 + c\mathbf{u}_3 = a\mathbf{v}_1 + b\mathbf{v}_1 + 2b\mathbf{v}_2 + c\mathbf{v}_1 + 2c\mathbf{v}_2 + 3c\mathbf{v}_3 = (a + b + c)\mathbf{v}_1 + (2b + 2c)\mathbf{v}_2 + 3c\mathbf{v}_3$:

$$\begin{aligned} a + b + c &= 0 \\ 2b + 2c &= 0 \\ 3c &= 0. \end{aligned}$$

$c = b = a = 0$; linearly independent
27. Let $\mathbf{v}_1 = \mathbf{0}$. Then $1\mathbf{v}_1 + 0\mathbf{v}_2 + 0\mathbf{v}_3 + \cdots + 0\mathbf{v}_n = \mathbf{0}$. **29.** This is the contrapositive of Problem 28.
31. Note that Span(T) is a subspace; apply Problem 30.

SECTION 4.3 (page 187)

1. $\begin{vmatrix} 4 & 5 \\ 7 & 6 \end{vmatrix} = -11 \neq 0$: Yes **3.** No (and no computation is needed).
5. No (and no computation is needed). **7.** Yes **9.** $(-5, 0, 1)$, $(2, 1, 0)$ **11.** $(-3, 1, 1)$
13. $(3, 0, 1, 0)$, $(0, 4, 0, 1)$ **15.** $(11, 7, 1)$ **17.** $(-11, -3, 1, 0)$, $(-11, -5, 0, 1)$
19. $(3, -2, 1, 0)$, $(-4, -3, 0, 1)$ **21.** $(-1, -1, 1, 0)$, $(-5, -3, 0, 1)$ **23.** $(2, -3, 1, 0)$
25. $(-2, 1, 0, 0, 0)$, $(2, 0, 1, 1, 0)$, $(-3, 0, -4, 0, 1)$

SECTION 4.4 (page 196)

1. Row(A) has basis $(1, 0, 11)$, $(0, 1, -4)$; Col(A) has basis $(1, 1, 2)$, $(2, 5, 2)$.
3. $(1, 0, 1, 5)$, $(0, 1, 1, 3)$; Col(A) has basis columns 1 and 2 of A.
5. $(1, 0, -2, 0)$, $(0, 1, 3, 0)$, $(0, 0, 0, 1)$; columns 1, 2, and 4 of A.
7. $(1, 0, -3, 4)$, $(0, 1, 2, 3)$; columns 1 and 2 of A.
9. $(1, 0, 0, 3)$, $(0, 1, 0, -2)$, $(0, 0, 1, 4)$; columns 1, 2, and 3 of A.
11. $(1, 0, 2, 1, 0)$, $(0, 1, 1, 2, 0)$, $(0, 0, 0, 0, 1)$; columns 1, 2, and 5 of A.
13. $\{\mathbf{v}_1, \mathbf{v}_2\}$ **15.** $\{\mathbf{v}_1, \mathbf{v}_2, \mathbf{v}_4\}$ **17.** $\{\mathbf{v}_1, \mathbf{v}_2, \mathbf{e}_2\}$
19. $\{\mathbf{v}_1, \mathbf{v}_2, \mathbf{e}_2, \mathbf{e}_3\}$ **21.** The first two. **23.** The first, second, and fourth. **25.** See Theorem 3.

SECTION 4.5 (page 206)

1. Yes **3.** No: $I_3 + (-I_3)$ is singular. **5.** Yes **7.** No: $2f(1) \neq 1$. **9.** No: $0 \cdot 1 \cdot x^3 = 0$.
11. Yes **13.** Yes **15.** Yes **17.** No: $-\cos 2x - \sin^2 x + \cos^2 x = 0$.
19. $A = 3$, $B = -2$. **21.** $A = 2$, $B = -2$, $C = 0$ **23.** $y(x) = 3e^x - 2e^{2x}$ **25.** $y(x) = 4\cos 2x + 3\sin 2x$
27. (a) If $ae^x + be^{-x} = 0$ then $ae^{2x} + b = 0$, which is impossible unless $a = 0$, and it follows that $b = 0$. So e^x and e^{-x} are linearly independent. They span the solution space by Theorem 2, so these two functions form a basis for the solution space.

29. (a) $W(0) = -6 \neq 0$, so $W(x)$ is never zero. (b) $y(x) = 2e^x - 3e^{-x} + e^{2x}$.
31. (b) A basis is

$$\begin{gathered}\{1, 0, 0, 0, 0, \ldots\}, \\ \{0, 1, 0, 0, 0, \ldots\}, \\ \{0, 0, 1, 0, 0, \ldots\}, \\ \vdots\end{gathered}$$

33. (c) *Suggestion*: $\dfrac{1}{z} = \dfrac{1}{a + bi} = \dfrac{a - bi}{a^2 + b^2}$.

SECTION 5.1 (page 219)

1. Yes **3.** Yes **5.** $7 + 7 = 14$ **7.** $25 + 19 = 44$ **9.** 45° and 45°
11. 41.08° and 48.92° (both are approximations) **13.** $\{(2, 1, 0), (-3, 0, 1)\}$
15. $\{(2, 1, 0, 0), (3, 0, 1, 0), (-5, 0, 0, 1)\}$ **17.** $\{(7, -3, 1, 0), (-19, 5, 0, 1)\}$
19. $\{(-13, 4, 1, 0, 0), (4, -3, 0, 1, 0), (-11, 4, 0, 0, 1)\}$ **21.** $\{(-1, -1, 1, 0, 0), (0, -1, 0, -1, 1)\}$
25. If $i \neq j$ then $|\mathbf{e}_i - \mathbf{e}_j| = \sqrt{2}$.
27. If $\mathbf{v}$ is in V and $\mathbf{v}$ is in $V^\perp$, then $\mathbf{v}$ is orthogonal to $\mathbf{v}$, so $\mathbf{v} \cdot \mathbf{v} = 0$. Therefore $|\mathbf{v}|^2 = 0$, so $|\mathbf{v}| = 0$, and so $\mathbf{v} = \mathbf{0}$.

SECTION 5.2 (page 228)

1. (5, 5, 5) **3.** (4, 0, 4, 4) **5.** $(2, -2, 2, 4, -6)$ **7.** $\mathbf{x} = (12/7, 8/7)$; $\mathbf{p} = (20/7, 4/7, 16/7)$
9. $\mathbf{x} = (11/4, 13/12)$; $\mathbf{p} = (23/6, 5/3, 43/6)$ **11.** $\mathbf{x} = (2, 1)$; $\mathbf{p} = (3, 1, 5, 4)$
13. $\mathbf{x} = (\frac{7}{4}, \frac{3}{2}, \frac{3}{4})$; $\mathbf{p} = (\frac{1}{4}, \frac{11}{4}, \frac{1}{4}, \frac{3}{4})$
15. $\mathbf{x} = (4, -1, 2)$; $\mathbf{p} = (5, -5, 0, 0)$ **17.** $\mathbf{x} = (20, 24)$; $\mathbf{p} = (12, 20, 24)$
19. $\mathbf{x} = (-1, 0, 1)$; $\mathbf{p} = (2, -1, 0, 1)$ **21.** $\mathbf{x} = (-5, 1)$; $\mathbf{p} = (-2, 6, -5, 1)$ **29.** $\mathbf{p} = (7, 6, 5, 6)$

SECTION 5.3 (page 237)

1. $y = \frac{1}{3}(2 + 3x)$ **3.** $y = \frac{1}{3}(11 + 6x)$ **5.** $y = \frac{1}{10}(18 + 23x)$ **7.** $y = 3 + 2x$ **9.** $y = \frac{1}{7}(-32 + 23x)$
11. $y = \frac{1}{3}(15 - 7x^2)$ **13.** $y = \frac{1}{8}(-3 + 11x^2)$ **15.** $y = 2 + 3x + x^2$ **17.** $y = \frac{1}{6}(-11 + 18x + 17x^2)$
19. $y = \frac{1}{10}(21 + x + 15x^2)$ **21.** $z = \frac{1}{9}(19 + 10x - 4y)$ **23.** $z = \frac{7}{10}(5 + x - y)$
25. $y = (0.4729)e^{(1.5270)x}$ **27.** $y = (2.990)x^{0.4006}$ **29.** Approximately $121\frac{2}{3}$ thousand cases
31. Approximately \$3686

SECTION 5.4 (page 244)

1. (3, 2) and $(-2, 3)$ **3.** (3, 1, 2) and $(-11, 1, 16)$; $\mathbf{p} = (5, 2, 5)$
5. (2, 2, 2, 1) and $(-11, 2, 2, 14)$; $\mathbf{p} = (9, 12, 12, 9)$ **7.** (1, 1, 0), $(-1, 2, 0)$, and $(-1, 1, 1)$
9. (2, 1, 1), $(-4, 7, 1)$, and $(-1, -1, 3)$
11. (1, 1, 0, 1), $(1, -2, 3, 1)$, and $(-4, 3, 3, 1)$; $\mathbf{p} = (5, -2, 5, 4)$
13. (2, 1, 0, 0), $(3, -6, 5, 0)$, and $(1, -2, -3, 7)$; $\mathbf{p} = (1, -2, -3, 7)$
15. (2, 1, 1, 0), $(4, -1, -7, 6)$, and $(7, -23, 9, 2)$ **17.** (2, 1, 1, 1), $(0, 1, 0, -1)$, and $(-6, 11, -10, 11)$
19. (1, 0, 1, 1, 0), $(-1, 3, -1, 2, 3)$, and $(7, 3, -1, -6, 3)$
21. (1, 0, 0, 1, 0), $(-1, 4, 0, 1, 2)$, and $(1, -4, 33, -1, 9)$

SECTION 5.5 (page 255)

1. If $\mathbf{u} = (x, y)$ then $\langle \mathbf{u}, \mathbf{u} \rangle = 2x^2 + 3y^2 \geq 0$, and clearly $\langle \mathbf{u}, \mathbf{u} \rangle = 0$ if and only if $\mathbf{u} = \mathbf{0}$.
3. $\langle \mathbf{u}, \mathbf{u} \rangle = 2(x - y)^2 + y^2$ **5.** $\langle \mathbf{u}, \mathbf{u} \rangle = (2x + 3y)^2 + 2y^2$ **7.** $\mathbf{u}_1 = (1, 0)$, $\mathbf{u}_2 = (1, 1)$

9. $\mathbf{u}_1 = (1, 0)$, $\mathbf{u}_2 = (-3, 2)$ **11.** $\langle \mathbf{u}, \mathbf{u} \rangle = (x + y)^2 + (x + z)^2 + y^2$
13. $\mathbf{u}_1 = (1, 0, 0)$, $\mathbf{u}_2 = (-1, 2, 0)$, $\mathbf{u}_3 = (-2, 1, 3)$
15. It is clear that properties (i) and (iii) hold, and (ii) is a routine verification. Also

$$\langle p, p \rangle = \{p(0)\}^2 + \{p(1)\}^2 + \{p(2)\}^2 \geq 0$$

for all p; if $\langle p, p \rangle = 0$ then $p(0) = p(1) = p(2) = 0$, and it follows that $p(x)$ is identically zero.
17. $\alpha = b/a$ and $\beta = c - (b^2/a)$, and the desired result now follows.

SECTION 6.1 (page 269)

1. $\lambda_1 = 3$, $\mathbf{v}_1 = (2, 1)$; $\lambda_2 = 2$, $\mathbf{v}_2 = (1, 1)$ **3.** $\lambda_1 = 5$, $\mathbf{v}_1 = (2, 1)$; $\lambda_2 = 2$, $\mathbf{v}_2 = (1, 1)$
5. $\lambda_1 = 4$, $\mathbf{v}_1 = (3, 2)$; $\lambda_2 = 1$, $\mathbf{v}_2 = (1, 1)$ **7.** $\lambda_1 = 4$, $\mathbf{v}_1 = (4, 3)$; $\lambda_2 = 2$, $\mathbf{v}_2 = (1, 1)$
9. $\lambda_1 = 4$, $\mathbf{v}_1 = (5, 2)$; $\lambda_2 = 3$, $\mathbf{v}_2 = (2, 1)$ **11.** $\lambda_1 = 5$, $\mathbf{v}_1 = (5, 7)$; $\lambda_2 = 4$, $\mathbf{v}_2 = (2, 3)$
13. $\lambda_1 = 1$, $\mathbf{v}_1 = (0, 1, -3)$; $\lambda_2 = 2$, $\mathbf{v}_2 = (1, 0, 2)$; $\lambda_3 = 0$, $\mathbf{v}_3 = (0, 1, -2)$
15. $\lambda_1 = 1$, $\mathbf{v}_1 = (2, 1, 1)$; $\lambda_2 = 2$, $\mathbf{v}_2 = (1, 0, 2)$; $\lambda_3 = 0$, $\mathbf{v}_3 = (1, 1, 0)$
17. $\lambda_1 = 1$, $\mathbf{v}_1 = (1, 0, 1)$; $\lambda_2 = 2$, $\mathbf{v}_2 = (-1, 1, 2)$; $\lambda_3 = 3$, $\mathbf{v}_3 = (1, 0, 0)$
19. $\lambda_1 = 1$, $\mathbf{v}_1 = (1, 0, 1)$; $\lambda_2 = 1$, $\mathbf{v}_2 = (-1, 1, 2)$; $\lambda_3 = 3$, $\mathbf{v}_3 = (1, 0, 0)$
21. $\lambda_1 = 2$, $\mathbf{v}_1 = (1, 1, 1)$; $\lambda_2 = 2$, $\mathbf{v}_2 = (-1, 0, 2)$; $\lambda_3 = 1$, $\mathbf{v}_3 = (1, 1, 0)$
23. $\lambda_1 = 1$, $\mathbf{v}_1 = (1, 0, 0, 0)$; $\lambda_2 = 2$, $\mathbf{v}_2 = (2, 1, 0, 0)$; $\lambda_3 = 3$, $\mathbf{v}_3 = (3, 2, 1, 0)$; $\lambda_4 = 4$, $\mathbf{v}_4 = (4, 3, 2, 1)$
25. $\lambda_1 = 1$, $\mathbf{v}_1 = (1, 0, 0, 0)$; $\lambda_2 = 1$, $\mathbf{v}_2 = (1, 1, 0, 0)$; $\lambda_3 = 2$, $\mathbf{v}_3 = (1, 1, 1, 0)$; $\lambda_4 = 2$, $\mathbf{v}_4 = (1, 1, 1, 1)$
34. $\lambda_1 = 3$, $\mathbf{v}_1 = (3, 2, 1)$; $\lambda_2 = 4$, $\mathbf{v}_2 = (5, 7, 7)$; $\lambda_3 = 5$, $\mathbf{v}_3 = (-1, 1, 2)$
35. $\lambda_1 = 2$, $\mathbf{v}_1 = (3, 4, 0, 3)$; $\lambda_2 = -2$, $\mathbf{v}_2 = (1, 0, 1, 2)$; $\lambda_3 = 3$, $\mathbf{v}_3 = (3, 1, 2, 4)$; $\lambda_4 = 5$, $\mathbf{v}_4 = (1, 1, 0, 1)$

SECTION 6.2 (page 278)

1. $P = \begin{bmatrix} 2 & 1 \\ 1 & 1 \end{bmatrix}$, $D = \begin{bmatrix} 3 & 0 \\ 0 & 1 \end{bmatrix}$ **3.** $P = \begin{bmatrix} 3 & 1 \\ 2 & 1 \end{bmatrix}$, $D = \begin{bmatrix} 3 & 0 \\ 0 & 2 \end{bmatrix}$ **5.** $P = \begin{bmatrix} 4 & 1 \\ 3 & 1 \end{bmatrix}$, $D = \begin{bmatrix} 3 & 0 \\ 0 & 1 \end{bmatrix}$

7. $P = \begin{bmatrix} 5 & 2 \\ 2 & 1 \end{bmatrix}$, $D = \begin{bmatrix} 2 & 0 \\ 0 & 1 \end{bmatrix}$ **13.** $P = \begin{bmatrix} 0 & 3 & 1 \\ 0 & 1 & 0 \\ 1 & 2 & 0 \end{bmatrix}$, $D = \begin{bmatrix} 2 & 0 & 0 \\ 0 & 2 & 0 \\ 0 & 0 & 1 \end{bmatrix}$

15. $P = \begin{bmatrix} 1 & -1 & 1 \\ 1 & 0 & 1 \\ 1 & 2 & 0 \end{bmatrix}$, $D = \begin{bmatrix} 1 & 0 & 0 \\ 0 & 1 & 0 \\ 0 & 0 & 0 \end{bmatrix}$

17. $P = \begin{bmatrix} 1 & -1 & 1 \\ 1 & 0 & 1 \\ 1 & 2 & 0 \end{bmatrix}$, $D = \begin{bmatrix} 2 & 0 & 0 \\ 0 & 1 & 0 \\ 0 & 0 & -1 \end{bmatrix}$

19. $P = \begin{bmatrix} 1 & -1 & 1 \\ 1 & 0 & 1 \\ 1 & 2 & 0 \end{bmatrix}$, $D = \begin{bmatrix} 1 & 0 & 0 \\ 0 & 3 & 0 \\ 0 & 0 & 2 \end{bmatrix}$

21. $\lambda = 1$: $\mathbf{v}_1 = (1, 1, 0)$ and $\mathbf{v}_2 = (0, 0, 1)$—not diagonalizable.
23. $\lambda_1 = 1$: $\mathbf{v}_1 = (1, 1, 1)$; $\lambda_2 = 2$: $\mathbf{v}_2 = (1, 1, 0)$—not diagonalizable.

25. $P = \begin{bmatrix} 1 & 1 & 1 & 1 \\ 0 & 1 & 1 & 1 \\ 0 & 0 & 1 & 1 \\ 0 & 0 & 0 & 1 \end{bmatrix}$, $D = \begin{bmatrix} 1 & 0 & 0 & 0 \\ 0 & 1 & 0 & 0 \\ 0 & 0 & -1 & 0 \\ 0 & 0 & 0 & -1 \end{bmatrix}$

27. $\lambda_1 = 1$: $\mathbf{v}_1 = (1, 0, 0, 0)$; $\lambda_2 = 2$: $\mathbf{v}_2 = (1, 1, 1, 1)$—not diagonalizable.

SECTION 6.3 (page 288)

1. $\begin{bmatrix} 63 & -62 \\ 31 & -30 \end{bmatrix}$ **3.** $\begin{bmatrix} 96 & -96 \\ 64 & -64 \end{bmatrix}$ **5.** $\begin{bmatrix} 125 & -124 \\ 93 & -92 \end{bmatrix}$ **7.** $\begin{bmatrix} 1 & 93 & 0 \\ 0 & 32 & 0 \\ 0 & 0 & 32 \end{bmatrix}$ **9.** $\begin{bmatrix} 1 & -92 & 31 \\ 0 & 32 & 0 \\ 0 & 0 & 32 \end{bmatrix}$

11. $\begin{bmatrix} 1 & 0 & 0 \\ 6 & -5 & -2 \\ -15 & 15 & 6 \end{bmatrix}$ **13.** $\begin{bmatrix} 3 & -3 & 1 \\ 2 & -2 & 1 \\ 0 & 0 & 1 \end{bmatrix}$ **15.** 50% city, 50% suburbs

17. 37.5% city, 62.5% suburbs **19.** $\frac{1}{3}$ city, $\frac{2}{3}$ suburbs **21.** $\lambda_1 = 1$, $\mathbf{v}_1 = (5, 4)$; $\lambda_2 = 0.8$, $\mathbf{v}_2 = (5, 2)$
23. $\lambda_1 = 1.05$, $\mathbf{v}_1 = (10, 9)$; $\lambda_2 = 0.75$, $\mathbf{v}_2 = (10, 3)$. For large values of n,

$$A^n \approx \tfrac{1}{60}(1.05)^n \begin{bmatrix} -30 & 100 \\ -27 & 90 \end{bmatrix}.$$

SECTION 6.4 (page 297)

1. $\lambda_1 = 4$, $\mathbf{v}_1 = (1, 1)$; $\lambda_2 = 2$, $\mathbf{v}_2 = (1, -1)$ **3.** $\lambda_1 = 10$, $\mathbf{v}_1 = (2, 1)$; $\lambda_2 = 5$, $\mathbf{v}_2 = (-1, 2)$
5. $\lambda_1 = 4$, $\mathbf{v}_1 = (1, 1, 0)$; $\lambda_2 = 2$, $\mathbf{v}_2 = (0, 0, 1)$; $\lambda_3 = -2$, $\mathbf{v}_3 = (1, -1, 0)$
7. $\lambda_1 = 6$ (multiplicity 2), $\mathbf{v}_1 = (1, 1, 1)$, $\mathbf{v}_2 = (1, -2, 1)$; $\lambda_3 = 0$, $\mathbf{v}_3 = (1, 0, -1)$
9. $\lambda_1 = 6$, $\mathbf{v}_1 = (1, 0, 1)$; $\lambda_2 = 3$, $\mathbf{v}_2 = (1, 1, -1)$; $\lambda_3 = 0$, $\mathbf{v}_3 = (-1, 2, 1)$
11. $\lambda_1 = 9$, $\mathbf{v}_1 = (1, 1, 1)$; $\lambda_2 = 6$, $\mathbf{v}_2 = (1, -2, 1)$; $\lambda_3 = 0$, $\mathbf{v}_3 = (1, 0, -1)$
13. $\lambda_1 = 6$, $\mathbf{v}_1 = (1, 1, 1)$; $\lambda_2 = 3$ (multiplicity 2), $\mathbf{v}_2 = (1, -2, 1)$, $\mathbf{v}_3 = (1, 0, -1)$
15. $\lambda_1 = 2$ (multiplicity 3), $\mathbf{v}_1 = (1, 0, 1, 0)$, $\mathbf{v}_2 = (1, 0, -1, 0)$ $\mathbf{v}_3 = (0, 1, 0, 1)$;
$\lambda_2 = 0$, $\mathbf{v}_4 = (0, -1, 0, 1)$
17. $\lambda_1 = 2$ (multiplicity 2), $\mathbf{v}_1 = (1, 0, 1, 0)$, $\mathbf{v}_2 = (0, 1, 0, 1)$; $\lambda_2 = 0$ (multiplicity 2),
$\mathbf{v}_3 = (1, 0, -1, 0)$, $\mathbf{v}_4 = (0, -1, 0, 1)$
19. $\lambda_1 = 3$ (multiplicity 2), $\mathbf{v}_1 = (1, -1, 0, 0, 0)$, $\mathbf{v}_2 = (0, 0, 1, 0, -1)$; $\lambda_2 = 5$ (multiplicity 3),
$\mathbf{v}_3 = (1, 1, 0, 0, 0)$, $\mathbf{v}_4 = (0, 0, 1, 0, 1)$, $\mathbf{v}_5 = (0, 0, 0, 1, 0)$
20. $\lambda_1 = 2$: dimension 1; $\lambda_2 = 4$: dimension 2; $\lambda_3 = 6$: dimension 3.

SECTION 7.1 (page 315)

1. $A = \begin{bmatrix} 1 & 1 \\ 1 & -1 \end{bmatrix}$ **3.** Not linear: $2T(0, 1) = (4, 6) \neq (4, 3) = T(0, 2)$. **5.** Not linear **7.** $A = \begin{bmatrix} 1 & -3 \\ 3 & -1 \\ 2 & 5 \end{bmatrix}$

9. $A = \begin{bmatrix} 2 & -3 & 4 \\ 3 & -5 & -7 \end{bmatrix}$ **11.** $T(x, y) = (3x + 4y, 2x + 3y)$ **13.** $T(x, y) = (x + 4y, 2x + 5y, 3x + 6y)$

15. $T(x, y, z) = (x + 3y, 2x + 5z, 4y + 6z)$ **17.** $A = \begin{bmatrix} 2 & 0 \\ 0 & -1 \end{bmatrix}$ **19.** $A = \begin{bmatrix} 1 & 0 \\ 0 & -1 \end{bmatrix}$ **21.** $\begin{bmatrix} 0 & 3 \\ 2 & 0 \end{bmatrix}$

23. $A = \begin{bmatrix} 2 & 0 \\ 0 & 1 \end{bmatrix}\begin{bmatrix} 1 & 0 \\ 0 & 3 \end{bmatrix}$ has the effect of an expansion by 3 in the y-direction followed by an expansion by 2 in the x-direction (or vice versa—the order is not important in this rare instance).

25. $A = \begin{bmatrix} 0 & 1 \\ 1 & 0 \end{bmatrix}\begin{bmatrix} 3 & 0 \\ 0 & 1 \end{bmatrix}\begin{bmatrix} 1 & 0 \\ 0 & 2 \end{bmatrix}$ has the effect of an expansion by 2 in the y-direction, followed by an expansion by 3 in the x-direction, followed by a reflection in the line $y = x$.

27. $A = \begin{bmatrix} 1 & 0 \\ 1 & 1 \end{bmatrix}\begin{bmatrix} 1 & 1 \\ 0 & 1 \end{bmatrix}$ has the effect of a positive unit shear in the x-direction followed by a positive unit shear in the y-direction.

29. $A = \begin{bmatrix} 1 & 0 \\ 2 & 1 \end{bmatrix}\begin{bmatrix} 1 & 0 \\ 0 & 3 \end{bmatrix}\begin{bmatrix} 1 & 2 \\ 0 & 1 \end{bmatrix}$ has the effect of a shear of +2 in the x-direction, followed by an expansion of +3 in the y-direction, followed by a shear of +2 in the y-direction.

31. $\begin{bmatrix} -1 & 0 \\ 0 & 1 \end{bmatrix}\begin{bmatrix} 1 & 0 \\ 0 & -1 \end{bmatrix} = \begin{bmatrix} -1 & 0 \\ 0 & -1 \end{bmatrix} = \begin{bmatrix} \cos\pi & -\sin\pi \\ \sin\pi & \cos\pi \end{bmatrix}$, thus has the effect of a rotation of 180°.

33. You should compute the product $\begin{bmatrix} \cos\theta & -\sin\theta \\ \sin\theta & \cos\theta \end{bmatrix}\begin{bmatrix} 1 & 0 \\ 0 & -1 \end{bmatrix}\begin{bmatrix} \cos\theta & \sin\theta \\ -\sin\theta & \cos\theta \end{bmatrix}$.

SECTION 7.2 (page 323)

1. $T(0, 0) \neq \mathbf{0}$ **3.** $T(-x, -y) \neq -T(x, y)$ **5.** $\begin{bmatrix} -1 & 1 \\ -3 & 2 \end{bmatrix}$ **7.** $\begin{bmatrix} 0 & -1 \\ 2 & 3 \end{bmatrix}$ **9.** $\begin{bmatrix} 26 & -11 \\ 8 & -3 \end{bmatrix}$

11. $\begin{bmatrix} -5 & 9 \\ -8 & 13 \\ 18 & -29 \end{bmatrix}$ **13.** 2; 0 **15.** 1; 2 **17.** 2; 0 **19.** 3; 0 **21.** 2; 2 **23.** 3; 1

25. Range: $3x - 2y = 0$. Kernel: $x + 2y = 0$.

SECTION 7.3 (page 334)

1. (1, 2) **3.** (5, −5) **5.** (1, −1) **7.** (−57, −4, 18) **9.** $x = 3x' + y'$, $y = x' + 4y'$
11. $x = -x' - 3y'$, $y = 2x' - 2y'$ **13.** $x_1 = y_1 + y_2$, $x_2 = y_1 + 2y_2$
15. $x_1 = 3y_1 - y_2$, $x_2 = y_1 + 3y_2$
17. $x_1 = y_1 + 2y_2 + 4y_3$, $x_2 = 3y_1 - y_2 + 3y_3$, $x_3 = 2y_1 + 3y_2 + 2y_3$
19. Eigenvectors: (1, 1) and (1, −1); corresponding eigenvalues: 5 and 3
21. Eigenvectors: (2, −1) and (1, 2); corresponding eigenvalues: 10 and 5
23. Eigenvectors: (1, 1, 1), (1, −2, 1), and (1, 0, −1); corresponding eigenvalues: 9, 6, and 0
25. Eigenvectors: (1, 1, 1), (1, −2, 1), and (1, 0, −1); corresponding eigenvalues: 6, 3, and 3
27. $\begin{bmatrix} 4 & -2 \\ 7 & -4 \end{bmatrix}$

SECTION 7.4 (page 349)

11. $A = \begin{bmatrix} (2+\sqrt{2})/4 & (2-\sqrt{2})/4 & \frac{1}{2} \\ (2-\sqrt{2})/4 & (2+\sqrt{2})/4 & -\frac{1}{2} \\ -\frac{1}{2} & \frac{1}{2} & \frac{1}{2}\sqrt{2} \end{bmatrix}$ **17.** $Q_1(0, 0)$, $Q_2(20, -9)$, $Q_3(20, 31)$, $Q_4(0, 40)$

19. A right-handed rotation of 120° about the axis determined by the vector $\mathbf{v} = (1, -1, -1)$.

SECTION 8.1 (page 363)

1. $2(x')^2 + (y')^2 = 4$: ellipse; origin (2, 3) **3.** $9(x')^2 - 16(y')^2 = 144$: hyperbola; origin (1, −1)
5. The single point (2, 3) **7.** $4(x')^2 + 2(y')^2 = 1$: ellipse; 45°
9. The two parallel lines (a "degenerate parabola") $(x')^2 = 4$; $\tan^{-1}(\frac{1}{2}) \approx 26.57°$
11. $(x')^2 - (y')^2 = 1$: hyperbola; $\tan^{-1}(\frac{1}{3}) \approx 18.43°$ **13.** $2(x')^2 + (y')^2 = 2$: ellipse; $\tan^{-1}(\frac{2}{3}) \approx 33.69°$
15. $4(x')^2 + (y')^2 = 4$: ellipse; $\tan^{-1}(\frac{4}{3}) \approx 53.13°$ **17.** $2(x')^2 + (y')^2 = 4$: ellipse; $\tan^{-1}(\frac{1}{4}) \approx 14.04°$
19. The two perpendicular lines $y' = x'$ and $y' = -x'$ (a "degenerate hyperbola"); $\tan^{-1}(\frac{5}{12}) \approx 22.67°$
21. $(x' - 1)^2 + 4(y')^2 = 4$: ellipse; $\tan^{-1}(\frac{4}{3}) \approx 53.13°$
23. $2(y' - 1)^2 - (x' - 2)^2 = 1$: hyperbola; $\tan^{-1}(\frac{4}{3}) \approx 53.13°$
25. $(x' - 1)^2 - (y')^2 = 1$: hyperbola; $\tan^{-1}(\frac{8}{15}) \approx 28.07°$

SECTION 8.2 (page 375)

1., **11.** 2 and -2: indefinite **3.**, **13.** 6 and 4: positive definite **5.**, **15.** 10 and 5: positive definite
7., **17.** 4, 4, and 2: positive definite **9.**, **19.** 6, 3, and -3: indefinite
21. $\Delta_4 = 21$, $\Delta_3 = 14$: positive definite **23.** $\Delta_4 = -7$, $\Delta_3 = 5$: indefinite
25. Elliptic paraboloid, opening upward, low point at (0, 0, 0); $z = 4(x')^2 + 2(y')^2$; $\theta = 45°$
27. Hyperbolic paraboloid, saddle point at the origin; $z = 5(x')^2 - 5(y')^2$; $\theta = \tan^{-1}(\frac{1}{3}) \approx 18.43°$
29. Elliptic paraboloid, opening upward, low point at (0, 0, 0); $z = 34(x')^2 + 17(y')^2$;
$\theta = \tan^{-1}(\frac{1}{4}) \approx 14.04°$
31. Global minimum -1 at $(-1, 2)$ **33.** Saddle point at $(-\frac{1}{2}, -\frac{1}{2}, \frac{29}{4})$
35. Global minimum -9 at $(-3, 4)$
37. Saddle point at (0, 0, 3), local maximum 4 at $(-1, -1)$ **39.** No extrema

SECTION 8.3 (page 383)

1. $\lambda_1 = 3, \lambda_2 = 1$; $\mathbf{v}_1 = (2, 1), \mathbf{v}_2 = (1, 1)$; $x_1 = 2c_1e^{3t} + c_2e^t, x_2 = c_1e^{3t} + c_2e^t$
3. $\lambda_1 = 3, \lambda_2 = 2$; $\mathbf{v}_1 = (3, 2), \mathbf{v}_2 = (1, 1)$; $x_1 = 3c_1e^{3t} + c_2e^{2t}, x_2 = 2c_1e^{3t} + c_2e^{2t}$
5. $\lambda_1 = 3, \lambda_2 = 1$; $\mathbf{v}_1 = (4, 3), \mathbf{v}_2 = (1, 1)$; $x_1 = 4c_1e^{3t} + c_2e^t, x_2 = 3c_1e^{3t} + c_2e^t$
7. $\lambda_1 = 2, \lambda_2 = 1$; $\mathbf{v}_1 = (5, 2), \mathbf{v}_2 = (2, 1)$; $x_1 = 5c_1e^{2t} + 2c_2e^t, x_2 = 2c_1e^{2t} + c_2e^t$
9. $\lambda_1 = 4, \lambda_2 = 2$; $\mathbf{v}_1 = (1, 1), \mathbf{v}_2 = (1, -1)$; $x_1 = c_1e^{4t} + c_2e^{2t}, x_2 = c_1e^{4t} - c_2e^{2t}$
11. $\lambda_1 = 10, \lambda_2 = 5$; $\mathbf{v}_1 = (2, 1), \mathbf{v}_2 = (1, -2)$; $x_1 = 2c_1e^{10t} + c_2e^{5t}, x_2 = c_1e^{10t} - 2c_2e^{5t}$
13. $\lambda_1 = 9, \lambda_2 = 6, \lambda_3 = 0$; $\mathbf{v}_1 = (1, 1, 1), \mathbf{v}_2 = (1, -2, 1), \mathbf{v}_3 = (1, 0, -1)$; $x_1 = c_1e^{9t} + c_2e^{6t} + c_3$,
$x_2 = c_1e^{9t} - 2c_2e^{6t}, x_3 = c_1e^{9t} + c_2e^{6t} - c_3$
15. $\lambda_1 = 6, \lambda_2 = \lambda_3 = 3$; $\mathbf{v}_1 = (1, 1, 1), \mathbf{v}_2 = (1, 0, -1), \mathbf{v}_3 = (1, -1, 0)$. (Actually one may choose $\mathbf{v}_2$ and $\mathbf{v}_3$ to be any two linearly independent vectors (x, y, z) satisfying $x + y + z = 0$.) The solution to this problem may be written in the form

$$x_1(t) = c_1e^{6t} - (c_2 + c_3)e^{3t},$$
$$x_2(t) = c_1e^{6t} + c_3e^{3t},$$
$$x_3(t) = c_1e^{6t} + c_2e^{3t}.$$

17. $x_1(t) = 6c_1 + 3c_2e^t + 2c_3e^{-t}, x_2(t) = 2c_1 + c_2e^t + c_3e^{-t}, x_3(t) = 5c_1 + 2c_2e^t + 2c_3e^{-t}$
19. $x_1(t) = c_1e^{2t} + c_3e^{3t}, x_2(t) = -c_1e^{2t} + c_2e^{-2t} - c_3e^{3t}, x_3(t) = -c_2e^{-2t} + c_3e^{3t}$
21. $x(t) = c_1e^{2t} + c_2e^t$ **23.** $x(t) = c_1e^{5t} + c_2e^{-5t}$ **25.** $x(t) = c_1e^{3t} + c_2e^{-3t} + c_3$
27. $x(t) = c_1e^{2t} + c_2e^t + c_3e^{-t}$

SECTION 9.1 (page 395)

1. $x = 3, y = 2$ **3.** $x = -4, y = 3$ **5.** $x = 4, y = -1, z = 3$ **7.** $x = 1, y = 3, z = -4$
9. $x = 3.00, y = 2.00$ **11.** $x = -3.91, y = 2.94$ **13.** $x = 3.94, y = -0.975, z = 2.95$
15. $x = 0.62, y = 3.08, z = -3.94$ **17.** $\lambda_1 \approx -0.00003, \lambda_2 \approx 3.33333, c(A) \approx 111{,}111$
19. $\lambda_1 \approx 0.00008, \lambda_2 \approx 2.50002, c(A) \approx 31{,}250$
21. (a) $x = 1.00010001\ldots, y = -0.99989998\ldots$ (b) $x = 0, y = 1$ (without pivoting)
(c) $x = 1, y = 1$ (with pivoting)
23. $x = 1, y = 0$ with $\mathbf{b} = (2, 1)$; $x = 0$, $y = 2$ with $\mathbf{b} = (2, 1.0002)$
25. The solution before rounding is $x = 1000, y = -998$. The solution after rounding is $x = 900$, $y = -898$.

SECTION 9.2 (page 411)

(The exact solution is given for the first five problems.)
1. $x_1 = 2, x_2 = 1$ **3.** $x_1 = 3, x_2 = 2$ **5.** $x_1 = 4, x_2 = -1$ **7.** $x_1 = 3, x_2 = 1, x_3 = 2$

9. $x_1 = 2, x_2 = 1, x_3 = 1$
21. (a) The iteration is not convergent. (b) The iterates rapidly converge to $x_1 = 1, x_2 = -1$

27. $$\begin{bmatrix} 4 & -1 & 0 & 0 & 0 & 0 \\ -1 & 4 & -1 & -1 & 0 & 0 \\ 0 & -1 & 4 & 0 & -1 & 0 \\ 0 & -1 & 0 & 4 & -1 & 0 \\ 0 & 0 & -1 & -1 & 4 & -1 \\ 0 & 0 & 0 & 0 & -1 & 4 \end{bmatrix} \begin{bmatrix} u_1 \\ u_2 \\ u_3 \\ u_4 \\ u_5 \\ u_6 \end{bmatrix} = \begin{bmatrix} 1 \\ 0 \\ 1 \\ 0 \\ 0 \\ 1 \end{bmatrix}.$$ 29. 35

31. Approximately 0.0041082 (the exact probability is 244/59,393); approximately 19.87675 (the exact expected length is 1,180,540/59,393).
33. (a) $x_n = \frac{1}{2}x_{n+1} + \frac{1}{2}x_{n-1}$ if $n < 1000$; $x_{1000} = 1$ (d) $0 \le x_n \le 1$, so $B = 0$; thus $A = 1$
(e) $x_n = 1$ for all $n \le 1000$

Index

A

B

C

D

E

F

G

H

I

J

K

L

M

N

O

P

Q

R

S

T

U

V

W

X

Y

Z